SARAH SCHENIRER
AND THE BAIS YAAKOV MOVEMENT

THE LITTMAN LIBRARY OF
JEWISH CIVILIZATION

Life Patron
COLETTE LITTMAN

Dedicated to the memory of
LOUIS THOMAS SIDNEY LITTMAN
who founded the Littman Library for the love of God
and as an act of charity in memory of his father
JOSEPH AARON LITTMAN
and to the memory of
ROBERT JOSEPH LITTMAN
who continued what his father Louis had begun
יהא זכרם ברוך

'Get wisdom, get understanding:
Forsake her not and she shall preserve thee'
PROV. 4:5

The Littman Library of Jewish Civilization is a registered UK charity
Registered charity no. 1000784

SARAH SCHENIRER
AND THE
BAIS YAAKOV MOVEMENT

A Revolution in the Name of Tradition

NAOMI SEIDMAN

London
The Littman Library of Jewish Civilization
in association with Liverpool University Press

The Littman Library of Jewish Civilization
Registered office: 14th floor, 33 Cavendish Square, London WIG OPW

in association with Liverpool University Press
4 Cambridge Street, Liverpool L69 7ZU, UK
www.liverpooluniversitypress.co.uk/littman

Managing Editor: Connie Webber

Distributed in North America by
Oxford University Press Inc., 198 Madison Avenue
New York, NY 10016, USA

First published 2019
First published in paperback 2023

Catalogue records for this book are available from
the British Library and the Library of Congress

ISBN 978–1–837643–90–5

Publishing co-ordinator: Janet Moth
Copy-editing: Ezra Margulies and Connie Webber
Proof-reading: Norm Guthartz
Index: Pierke Bosschieter
Design and typesetting by Pete Russell, Faringdon, Oxon.

Printed and bound by CPI Group (UK) Ltd., Croydon, CR0 4YY

Acknowledgements

AMONG the pleasures of choosing (or, as it sometimes feels, being chosen by) a topic is the social worlds that open up before the researcher seeking guidance, sources, scholarly conversation, and honest response. In this regard, Sarah Schenirer and Bais Yaakov were particularly generative, connecting me with a diverse and extraordinarily generous group of people who had taken an interest in the topic and were willing to accompany me along this journey. I benefited from the research of and scholarly conversation with a number of brilliant women who are passionately interested in Bais Yaakov: Shani Bechhofer, Leslie Ginsparg Klein, Irena Klepfisz, Agniezska Oleszak, Stacy Rigler, Jackie Rosensweig, Talia Weisberg, and Deborah Weissman. My work could not have proceeded without the help of knowledgeable, patient, and competent librarians and archivists: Zachary Baker at Stanford University; Maureen Callahan at the Sophia Smith Collection of Women's History at Smith College; Dominik Cobanoglu at the Jewish Museum Vienna; Tracey Felder at the Leo Baeck Institute; Zachary Loeb, Melanie Meyers, Ilya Slavutskiy, and Vital Zajka at YIVO, and other helpful and warm staff in the Lillian Goldman Reading Room at the Center for Jewish History; Catherine Madsen at the Yiddish Book Center; Misha Mitsel at the Joint Distribution Committee Archives; Daphna Itzkovich and Zvi Oren at the Ghetto Fighters Museum and Photo Archive; and Marion Weston at the NYU Bobst Library, who helped me access the Shoah Visual History archive. Menachem Butler, Ruchama Fund, Lonna Gordon, Jolanta Mickute, Hannah Rose, Chaim Sznicer, Jeffrey Shandler, and Moe Z. led me to sources I needed. Shimon Szimonowitz helped identify rabbinic citations in Sarah Schenirer's work. Kalman Sporn shared not only two family photos (reproduced here), research on his grandmother Yachat Sofer (who attended the 1929 Neshei Agudath Israel conference), but also his friendship and enthusiasm for Bais Yaakov. His brother Shimon Sporn, a gifted genealogist, helped identify important figures in Bais Yaakov history. Joel Rosenberg shared his mother's 1935 report card with me, and gave me permission to reproduce it. Friends and colleagues such as Natalia Aleksiun, Deena Aranoff, Christopher Barthel, David Biale, Frieda Birnbaum, Isaac Bleaman, Daniel Boyarin, Jonathan Boyarin, Glenn Dynner, Ayala Fader, Rena Fischer, Ilan Fuchs, Tobias Grill, Marion Kaplan, Sam Kassow, John Kloppenborg,

Chana Kronfeld, Rachel Manekin, Alan Mintz (of blessed memory), Anita Norich, Shana Penn, Jeffrey Shandler, Isaac Schonfeld, Anna Shternshis, and Dina Stein shared their thoughts on my research with me, responded to my work in public forums, or read drafts of this book. I thank Eliyana Adler and Antony Polonsky for permission to republish, in revised form, the article that appeared in Polin, Volume 30: *Education in East European Jewish Society*, also published by the Littman Library.

In the last few weeks of work on this manuscript, Dariusz Dekiert, Joanna Lisek, and Marcin Wodziński graciously permitted me to read and cite Sarah Schenirer's Polish diary before its 2018 publication. Daniel Goldschmidt researched the relevant copyright laws. Sarah Schenirer's living descendants, Michal Schenirer Avni and Osnot Schenirer Bekhor (Israel), and Michael Goodman (Florida) and Glenn Goodman (New York), generously provided permission to translate their great-aunt's writings, genealogical information on their ancestry, and family photos.

I benefited from sharing parts of this research at various programmes, institutions, groups, and (in the case of Chulent) roving parties: Beth Tzedec synagogue in Toronto, the Center for Jewish History Working Group on Gender, Chulent, Columbia University, Cornell University, the Graduate Theological Union, the Jewish Theological Union, the Jewish Orthodox Feminist Alliance, the New York Working Group on Jewish Orthodoxies at Fordham University, the Polin Museum, the Netivot Shalom Rosh Hodesh group, Tikkun Leil Shavuot at the Berkeley JCC, the University of Toronto, and YIVO. Just as we were reviewing proofs, Kathryn Hellerstein invited me to speak at the University of Pennsylvania; at that talk, Basya Schechter and Jessi Roemer sang us through the 1931 Bais Yaakov songbook. I thank all who invited me to, hosted, and provided me with honest responses at these events. A final credit, too, to the OTD Facebook groups, and particularly to the smart and funny Bais Yaakov graduates among them, for their enthusiasm and support.

In 2012 I spent the summer reading through the *Bais Yaakov Journal* as the Workmen's Circle / Dr Emanuel Patt Visiting Professor at YIVO. In 2015 the Hadassah-Brandeis Institute awarded me the Helen Hammer Translation Award to fund my work translating Sarah Schenirer's Yiddish writings. Deborah Olins took a personal interest in this project, giving me a copy of Laura Schor's book, *The Best School in Jerusalem: Annie Landau's School for Girls, 1900–1960*, which served as a model for what I hoped to accomplish. I am enormously grateful to YIVO and HBI for their support and confidence in me.

Ula Madej-Krupitski was a research assistant extraordinaire, locating material I never imagined existed, translating Polish sources into English, and answering dozens of questions I had about Jewish culture in interwar Poland. Chris Moreland and Talia Rogers also graciously helped me organize my material.

At the Littman Library I was lucky to work with Connie Webber, who invited me to write this book, Janet Moth, and Ezra Margulies, who read my work with extraordinary attention and respect, and saved me from countless mistakes. The ones that undoubtedly remain are of course my own. I am grateful to Pete Russell for his elegant and sympathetic design, and especially for coping with my massive picture captions, and to Pierke Bosschieter for indexing.

My husband and son, John and Ezra Hillel Schott, shared my enthusiasm for this project and kept life going when I was otherwise occupied. My deepest love, always.

My mother, Sara Abraham Seidman, has been sharing her memories of Bais Yaakov in Europe since before my own first day at Bais Yaakov. I hope I have inherited at least a little of her talent for telling a story.

My father, Hillel Seidman, of blessed memory, passed away before I thought to ask him about his experiences with the movement. Nevertheless, he left behind evidence about what it meant to him, and always took evident pride in having married a Bais Yaakov teacher and raised three Bais Yaakov girls. Among the names inscribed on his gravestone are close family members murdered in the Holocaust, including his two sisters, 'Sarah and Rechil, teachers in Bais Yaakov'. It is to these two young women, aunts whom I never met, that I dedicate this book.

Contents

APPENDICES

List of Illustrations

Sarah Schenirer's application for a Polish identity card

Last name: *Schenirer*

First name: *Sara*

Date of birth: *3 July 1883*

Place of birth: *Kraków*

Father's name: *Zalel*

Mother's name: *Roza*

Mother's maiden name: *Lack*

Profession: *private teacher*

Address: *Katarzyny Street no. 1, apartment no. 7*

Height: *medium*

Face: *oval*

Hair: *brown*

Eyes: *brown*

Birthmarks: –

Identity of this person is confirmed by:

Passport number 3798/29 border control

Document issued in: *Kraków*

Handwritten signature of the person applying for ID

ID no: *3887. SA931001*   Mailed: *1 September 1933*

National Archives Kraków; call number STGKR 990, p. 675

675

Do uzyskania dowodu osobistego.

Nazwisko: Schenirer

Imię: Sara

Data urodzenia: 3.VII.1883

Miejsce urodzenia: Kraków

Imię ojca: Zalel

„ matki: Roza

z domu: Lack

Zawód: nauczycielka pryw.

Miejsce zamieszkania w Krakowie:

ul. Katarzyny Nr. d. 1 m. 7

Wzrost: średni

Twarz: owalna

Włosy: szatyne

Oczy: piwne

Znaki szczególne: —

Tożsamość osoby potwierdza:

dow. os. pasp. 3798/29 Nar. Grodz.
(imię i nazwisko, wiek, zawód, mieszkanie)

legitymując się Kraków
(nazwa dokumentu legitymacyjnego)

Podpis świadka:

Podpis własnoręczny osoby, otrzymującej dowód: Sara Schenirer

Wydano dowód osobisty Nr. 3887. dnia 1. IX. 1933

SA-930001

Podpis urzędnika:

Dowód osobisty — wydanie. — Druk M. U. ewid. ludn.

Note on Transliteration

THE transliteration of Hebrew in this book reflects consideration of the type of book it is, in terms of its content, purpose, and readership. The system adopted therefore reflects a broad approach to transcription, rather than the narrower approaches found in the *Encyclopaedia Judaica* or other systems developed for text-based or linguistic studies. The aim has been to reflect the pronunciation prescribed for modern Hebrew, rather than the spelling or Hebrew word structure, and to do so using conventions that are generally familiar to the English-speaking reader.

In accordance with this approach, no attempt is made to indicate the distinctions between *alef* and *ayin*, *tet* and *taf*, *kaf* and *kuf*, *sin* and *samekh*, since these are not relevant to pronunciation; likewise, the *dagesh* is not indicated except where it affects pronunciation. Following the principle of using conventions familiar to the majority of readers, however, transcriptions that are well established have been retained even when they are not fully consistent with the transliteration system adopted. On similar grounds, the *tsadi* is rendered by 'tz' in such familiar words as barmitzvah. Likewise, the distinction between *ḥet* and *khaf* has been retained, using *ḥ* for the former and *kh* for the latter; the associated forms are generally familiar to readers, even if the distinction is not actually borne out in pronunciation, and for the same reason the final *heh* is indicated too. As in Hebrew, no capital letters are used, except that an initial capital has been retained in transliterating titles of published works (for example, *Shulḥan arukh*).

Since no distinction is made between *alef* and *ayin*, they are indicated by an apostrophe only in intervocalic positions where a failure to do so could lead an English-speaking reader to pronounce the vowel-cluster as a diphthong—as, for example, in *ha'ir*—or otherwise mispronounce the word. An apostrophe is also used, for the same reason, to disambiguate the pronunciation of other English vowel clusters, as for example in *mizbe'aḥ*.

The *sheva na* is indicated by an *e*—*perikat ol, reshut*—except, again, when established convention dictates otherwise.

The *yod* is represented by *i* when it occurs as a vowel (*bereshit*), by *y* when it occurs as a consonant (*yesodot*), and by *yi* when it occurs as both (*yisra'el*).

Names have generally been left in their familiar forms, even when this is inconsistent with the overall system.

Introduction

IT SEEMS IMPORTANT to acknowledge at the outset the unusual circumstances of my involvement with my subject-matter: I attended Bais Yaakov of Boro Park for elementary school; a Bais Yaakov high school in Brooklyn and then one in Queens; Michlalah Jerusalem College for Women (a slightly more 'modern' seminary or institute of higher learning for young women); and, finally, another Bais Yaakov seminary in Brooklyn. All these schools, arguably including Michlalah, are more or less direct descendants of the school system that Sarah Schenirer founded in interwar Poland. The one in Boro Park, along with its high school counterpart two blocks away, were actually among the first Bais Yaakov schools to be established in the United States. Nevertheless, this book is no natural outgrowth of my personal history: shortly after my last stint in the seminary in Brooklyn, I left the Orthodox world, and—at least in my academic research—have rarely looked back. Rather, it is the product of an unplanned encounter that took place, entirely appropriately, in Kraków, the city in which Sarah Schenirer resided nearly her entire life.

In the summer of 2010 I brought a group of students from the Graduate Theological Union in Berkeley, where I was teaching, on a study trip to Poland. We launched our trip with a week at the Jewish Culture Festival in Kraków. As anyone who has attended the festival knows, it is among the most interesting and vibrant Jewish cultural phenomena in the world today, and there was more than enough going on to occupy my time and thoughts. But what stayed with me from that week was the memory of a group of four or five young women I ran into in the courtyard of the famous Remuh Synagogue[1] in the Kazimierz quarter of Kraków. It was clear to me the instant I set eyes on them that they were Bais Yaakov girls:[2] the cut of their long skirts, their hairstyles and blouses, their gait

[1] Remuh is the Polish-language version of the Hebrew acronym 'Rema' used in referring to Rabbi Moses Isserles (1525 or 1530–1572), the Kraków rabbi who was known as 'the Maimonides of Polish Jewry' for his leadership and his halakhic expertise: in adapting Rabbi Joseph Karo's *Shulḥan arukh* for use by Polish Jewry he established the regulations that informed Polish Jewish life and are the basis of the Ashkenazi religious sytem to this day. His synagogue and the neighbouring cemetery in which his gravestone still stands are in the centre of what used to be the Jewish quarter of Kraków, Kazimierz.

[2] The term 'Bais Yaakov girl' reflects current usage (even for high-school students or those

and posture, their voices, even their faces. In that same moment of recognition, it also occurred to me that they must have been travelling back to New York or another Orthodox centre in North America after having spent a post-high-school year at a seminary in Israel, in exactly the way I had travelled with two schoolmates after my year at Michlalah. But there was also something different about them. My friends and I stayed with Orthodox family connections everywhere we went in Europe; later, I joked that I hadn't so much been to Europe as to Boro Park in Zurich, Boro Park in Paris, and then Boro Park in London. These girls were on a rather different itinerary. I was acutely aware, as I always am when I see Orthodox Jews in airports or other public spaces, that I registered to them as a stranger, an outsider to their world. Even though strangers speak with unusual freedom and intimacy at the festival, there was a kind of invisible protective shield around this group that repelled easy conversation. Nevertheless, I summoned my nerve and asked them if they were in town for the festival. One of the girls answered that they were there to visit the grave of a woman named Sarah Schenirer. 'Oh, right! The founder of Bais Yaakov!' I said, to their evident surprise.

Thinking about the encounter later in my hotel room, it occurred to me that these girls were not American Jewish 'tourists' in Kraków, but rather, that they were on a pilgrimage. They were on a younger and female variation of a phenomenon that has grown in the last decade or two, the hasidic pilgrimages to the gravesites or ruined synagogues of past hasidic leaders. These pilgrimages, as well as the journeys of descendants of Polish Jews to the places in which their ancestors lived, are by now well-known phenomena. But if the young women I had met were part of a larger pattern of visits to Sarah Schenirer's grave (as I soon found out they were), they were taking part in yet another kind of trip to Poland, one probably invisible to people who lacked my ingrained ability to spot a Bais Yaakov girl a mile off. These were Orthodox young women travelling to pay homage to a woman related to them not through blood or hasidic affiliation, but rather through the symbolic connections forged within an educational movement for girls. Among the other cultural practices of Bais Yaakov, the behavioural markers that made its students so recognizable, a new practice seemed to have arisen since the time I had belonged to this group. It was a variation on the European journeys young women of my own generation had taken, and an echo of or even return to the very origins of the movement.

attending seminaries). In what follows I will use this term to reflect the collocation; otherwise I will use 'young women' for older adolescents.

Mulling over the encounter, something else occurred to me. I had been in Kraków for three or four days without remembering that Bais Yaakov was founded in the city, or learning that Sarah Schenirer was buried here, or that (as I later found out) the building that housed the Bais Yaakov teachers' seminary—the crown jewel of the system—was still standing. But perhaps this wasn't so surprising. While of course her name was engraved in my memory, as it is for every Bais Yaakov girl past or present, the Kraków connection had not stuck, because I had the vague impression that she had lived in a small town, not in the large city that Kraków clearly was and had long been. This impression no doubt came from the Bais Yaakov anthem that narrated her story, and whose mournful tune I loved as a child. As the first lines of the song already signal, the story of Sarah Schenirer as it is told and retold to generations of Bais Yaakov students constitutes a powerful myth of origin:[3]

In a little town in Poland not so many years ago
  Sat a seamstress very sad
Sewing clothes for the body
  While the soul remained unclad.

Bais Yaakov started there in Poland
  In a tiny little store,
But with Sarah as its leader
  Its success began to soar.

Sarah, mother of Bais Yaakov
  Is today with us no more,
But her spirit will continue
  To live on forevermore.[4]

In reflecting that the 'little town' in which this sad seamstress had sat was actually the bustling metropolis of Kraków, the notion took hold that there was more to the story of Sarah Schenirer than I had understood from the legends about a simple seamstress who founded a movement. The seeds for this book were thus sown that Friday afternoon in 2010 in the Kazimierz quarter of Kraków, a few blocks away from where Sarah Schenirer's religious revolution began, and at the very site—the courtyard of the sixteenth-century synagogue of Rabbi Moses

[3] I am using 'myth' not in the sense of falsehood, but rather in the sense of a story that is retold because it encapsulates the ideals and ideology of the culture in which it circulates.

[4] 'Sarah Schenirer, Mother of Bais Yaakov' was composed by Rochel (Lieberman) Blau, a Bais Yaakov principal and teacher, and a graduate of one of the first Bais Yaakov schools in America. See Lichtenstein, *Seamstress of Souls*, 5.

Isserles—to which she herself had led seminary students on pilgrimages. My research thus follows in the footsteps of the girls I met then as well as in the footsteps of the groups of Bais Yaakov girls in the movement's earliest years, returning to the Polish origins of a school system I experienced only many decades after its founding, and in a very different geographical and cultural context.

This book is not an attempt to provide an exhaustive or a comprehensive history of the establishment of the movement. It is, rather, an exploration of the phenomenon of Bais Yaakov, guided by a set of questions that already presented themselves in inchoate form at that encounter in 2010. What was it that I had instantly seen in the group of young women? What is a Bais Yaakov girl, as a historical phenomenon, as a 'new kind of woman'?[5] Was there anything that connected the city of Kraków today with Kraków in the interwar period? How were the first Jewish girls who attended the institution Sarah Schenirer had founded related to the group of girls I had run into that afternoon? Who was Sarah Schenirer, and how had she helped create this new type of young Jewish woman, who in turn remembered (and misremembered) her?

I was drawn to these reflections in part because I had encountered a group of Bais Yaakov girls away from their more usual environment, the classroom or a Brooklyn street. In leaving Bais Yaakov behind, I had somehow managed to forget that the image of a pious, obedient, and sheltered Orthodox Jewish girl was highly stereotypical. Leslie Ginsparg Klein has convincingly deconstructed that stereotype, demonstrating the creative energies and youthful enthusiasm that continue to shape the Bais Yaakov experience.[6] My own parents had diligently arranged for me to attend school in Jerusalem at 16 (after I graduated early from high school), and then provided the addresses of friends and relatives in Europe for the adventure that followed. These travels had in fact begun earlier—in tenth grade I was part of a group of Bais Yaakov girls who travelled by bus from New York to Baltimore as delegates to the annual Bais Yaakov Convention. Among the impressions that remain of that experience was the excitement of recognizing the continental reach of Bais Yaakov. We sang songs about *aḥdus* (unity) at the top of our lungs, danced for hours, heard speeches, saw performances, and swapped stories with those fascinating and exotic creatures—'out-of-town' Bais Yaakov girls. Along with the insularity of Bais Yaakov and the stringencies of 'Torah-true' Judaism, I was also given ample opportunities to travel, perform,

[5] Isaac Breuer described the Bais Yaakov student as 'a new kind of woman in the East' in *25 Jahre Aguda* (Frankfurt, 1937), 17, 19, cited in Oleszak, 'The Beit Ya'akov School in Kraków', 290.

[6] See Ginsparg Klein, '"No Candy Store"'.

and sing, supported by networks of connections and deep roots in a fervently remembered shared past. All of these elements were part of the culture of Orthodox Jewish girlhood that shaped me, and that I recognized in those young women in Kraków.

As I aim to show in this volume, the young Bais Yaakov women of the interwar years were accorded even more extraordinary freedoms, travelling (as my mother did) to attend seminaries at a younger age than their later American counterparts, and sent off to found schools on their own, away from their families. This was not an incidental part of the system, which, far from imprisoning young girls in a conservative environment, granted them liberties in a community that, before the rise of Bais Yaakov, had been more inclined to restrict young women's movements to protect them from the alien currents of the day.

Some have argued that Bais Yaakov became increasingly conservative in its post-Holocaust rebirth. But the revolutionary character of the movement has always been inseparable from its conservative and traditional elements. Conversely, this revolutionary aspect has never been entirely forgotten, even if some of the charismatic boldness that characterized its beginnings has since given way to what Max Weber calls the 'routinization' of charisma, or has faded from memory. The notion of Bais Yaakov as a revolution is remembered less in the mournful anthem about Sarah Schenirer the seamstress than in a story that circulated in the Bais Yaakov of my day (and earlier). When she would walk around the towns of Poland in her tireless efforts to found Bais Yaakov schools, Jewish boys would throw stones at her. She would bend down, pick up the stones, and say to her assailants, 'From these stones will I build my schools.'[7] At first this story puzzled me. Who were these boys? Why would anyone object to such a saintly mission, such a clearly legitimate and holy project? Only gradually did I come to understand that Bais Yaakov had been controversial among Orthodox Jews at the outset (and of course, was also denigrated by many Zionists and secularists). Even after it had become a fait accompli, discussions about its legitimacy continued, and continue to the present day. The woman we spoke of as pious and modest was seen by some in the Orthodox community as a dangerous innovator, and had thus faced opposition (stones), which she turned into support (schools).

[7] This story is recounted, among other places, in a children's book about Schenirer: E. G. Friedenson, *Mama's Will* (Yid.), 13. Shoshana Bechhofer notes that the story increasingly came to be told without reference to 'any reason for the opposition', putting in the background the 'mostly unspoken question about the legitimacy of the Bais Yaakov movement'; Bechhofer, 'Ongoing Constitution of Identity', 104.

She was a brave and determined pioneer who stood up to elements within her own community, and may even be seen as having saved Orthodoxy by making a place in it for girls and women.

That this story was a little cryptic in its presentation is no surprise: while the Bais Yaakov discourse grants full honours to Sarah Schenirer, it strives to do so while also normalizing her mission within the world of Orthodox values. It is by now almost unthinkable that such a valuable institution might have been subject to religious criticism. Bais Yaakov teachers thus aim to tell the story of the origins of the school system without undue reference to her opponents within the Orthodox community or to the leaders who failed to see the necessity of her mission before she—a 'simple' woman—did. While Bais Yaakov regularly frames her as a pioneer and innovator, the notion of her as a radical or rebel is more foreign to the culture of the school (though, as we shall see, her diary stands as evidence that she saw herself as something of a rebel, at least in her girlhood). For all the obliqueness with which this aspect of her story is told, her spirit and courage come through, and it is this strand of Bais Yaakov discourse, which champions a woman's independence and initiative, that connects the stories about Sarah Schenirer with the American, European, and Israeli adolescents who travel, often unchaperoned, to the memorial erected at her presumed gravesite.[8]

It is precisely the interplay and tensions in the Bais Yaakov movement between tradition and innovation, radicalism and piety, that interest me. This tension manifests itself not only in the question of the character of Bais Yaakov, as a new phenomenon devoted to Jewish tradition and continuity, but also in the role of its founder. While Bais Yaakov girls are regularly reminded of the heroic and visionary role of Sarah Schenirer in founding the movement, her legacy is still challenged by a few of its historians and Agudah enthusiasts, who sometimes insist that its astonishing success should be attributed not to her pioneering efforts, but rather to the adoption of her fledgling system by the political organization of world Orthodoxy, Agudath Israel. Some have simply told the story by sole recourse to the (male) rabbinic establishment and the various 'great men' who

[8] Schenirer was not buried in the New Jewish Cemetery ('new', that is, in relation to the old cemetery adjacent to the Rema Synagogue, though it dates from 1800) in the centre of Kazimierz, but rather in the even newer cemetery consecrated in 1932 in the outlying district of Podgórze; her grave was destroyed along with nearly all the others in the cemetery with the construction in 1942 of the Płaszów concentration camp. The reconstructed monument to Schenirer that now stands in the cemetery was erected at the initiative of Bais Yaakov alumnae in 2003. See the Epilogue for a description of this commemoration project.

served Bais Yaakov as school administrators, political advocates, halakhic authorities, fundraisers, and editors.[9]

My intention in this book is not to settle the question of who deserves credit for the success of Bais Yaakov, but rather to register the tensions within a discourse that records the charisma of a legendary founding figure as it traces the movement's institutional development. My aim is to capture something of the complexity of Bais Yaakov as a revolution in the name of tradition, led by a solitary, pious woman alongside the rabbis, editors, activists, and leaders who granted Bais Yaakov its religious legitimacy, funded its efforts, publicized its writings, and professionalized its methods. In this regard, my task is not only to record 'the truth' about the development of Bais Yaakov, although I am certainly aiming to do that, but also to explore the discourse that arose around the movement, which is sometimes particularly telling when it is *not* entirely 'true'. One example: Sarah Schenirer's role in the founding of Orthodox girls' education in Poland is generally overstated, since Bais Yaakov was not the first attempt to provide a traditional but up-to-date Jewish education for Orthodox girls. The Havatselet school system, founded in 1916 in Warsaw and extending elsewhere in Poland in the interwar period, pre-empted Bais Yaakov in that respect. The Yavneh schools, a non-partisan educational system for Orthodox girls as well as boys, arose in Lithuania during this same period (not to be confused with the Yavneh schools in Poland, which were organized under that name by the religious Zionist Mizrahi movement in 1927).[10] Nevertheless, Bais Yaakov emerged

[9] Bechhofer relates a conversation with a Bais Yaakov principal she does not name who told her that 'if [she] knew the history, [she] would understand that the "true story" of the origins of Bais Yaakov was that it was all due to the efforts of several men rather than to the woman, Sarah Schenirer' (Bechhofer, 'Ongoing Constitution of Identity', 12). As I discuss in Chapter 3, this alternative 'myth of origin' has roots in interwar Bais Yaakov; see E. G. Friedenson, 'Agudath Israel and "Bais Yaakov"' (Yid.), which tells the story of Bais Yaakov without mentioning Schenirer. Deborah Weissman cites an article by Rabbi Y. M. Abramowitz in a 1972 Agudah publication that asserts that 'The foundation of the "Bais Ya'akov" movement for girl's [*sic*] education is without a doubt an original Agudah creation' (Weissman, 'Bais Ya'akov: A Women's Educational Movement', 56). Ari Bach, in the 1954 inaugural issue of the American *Beth Jacob Monthly*, describes how the 'greatest of our people could not remain passive' in the face of the crisis of girls' defections, and 'the solution presented by the G'dolei Yisroel [the great Torah sages] showed results' (Bach, 'Why Beth Jacob?', 14–15). These represent a few of the histories of Bais Yaakov that do not mention Schenirer.

[10] For more on the the Yavneh school system in Lithuania, see Etzion, 'Yavneh Schools in Lithuania' (Heb.). For more on the Yavneh schools in Poland, see Kazdan, *The History of Jewish School Systems* (Yid.), 505–19. Kazdan lists three Yavneh *gymnasia* with 830 children; 142 boys'

apparently without knowledge of those institutions being established elsewhere in Poland and Lithuania, and saw its efforts as pioneering, if not revolutionary. The movement can hardly be understood without recognizing how central to its identity was its own sense of being 'first'. This achievement, along with the fact that it was the only one of these three systems with a female founding figure (even if she was soon helped by the male Orthodox establishment), is embedded in Bais Yaakov's identity, and I would argue was critical to its success both in the interwar years and today, when Bais Yaakov constitutes an international movement.

My sense of Sarah Schenirer as both historically and symbolically important to the Bais Yaakov movement explains why her own writings are included in the second half of this volume. I offer a translation into English of her collected Yiddish writings as they appeared in a 1933 volume published by the movement. I was surprised to discover, when I began this research project, that this volume, which had appeared two years before her death in 1935 and was reissued by her students in Brooklyn in 1955, had never been translated into English. Both editions are out of print and remain hard to locate (although a PDF of the 1955 edition may be downloaded from the National Yiddish Book Center website). This state of affairs persists despite the fact that, in her introduction to the 1955 volume, Vichna Kaplan, one of Sarah Schenirer's most distinguished students and a long-time leader of Bais Yaakov in North America, encouraged her students not merely to read the words of her teacher, but also to 'learn them and reread them continually'. It is curious that a movement that so reveres its founder, that gathers in huge assemblies to remember her on the ten-year anniversaries of her death (most recently for the eightieth *yahrzeit* in March 2015, which brought thousands of Bais Yaakov girls to the Barclays Center in Brooklyn), and that also keeps the memory of Vichna Kaplan alive, nevertheless fails to provide Sarah Schenirer's admirers and 'students' with either her original Yiddish writings or, for the great majority who cannot read Yiddish, an English translation of them.[11] It is true that brief excerpts and summaries of her memoir circulate

schools with 9,385 children; ten girls' schools with 303 children; and fifteen 'courses' (perhaps vocational programmes) with 1,059 students. Yavneh was thus much smaller than Bais Yaakov, particularly when only its girls' schools are counted. It is possible that the presence of a famous girls' school system limited the growth of the Polish Yavneh schools in the area of girls' education.

[11] A Hebrew translation of the writings and other Bais Yaakov material, entitled *Em beyisra'el* ('A Jewish Mother'—literally, 'A Mother in Israel'), appeared in 1955 and was reissued in 1975 and 1984.

widely in various languages, but many illuminating details are lost in these publications which—as is always the case with collective memory—adapt the story of the founding of the movement for contemporary purposes.[12] She was a prolific writer, contributing to nearly every issue of the *Bais Yaakov Journal*. She also kept a journal and wrote plays, a textbook on the Jewish religion, a series of articles about the Torah portion of the week, speeches, fundraising solicitations, and many letters. Her writings are paramount for anyone seeking to understand the development and motivations of the movement. They are crucial, as well, for analysing how Bais Yaakov legitimated itself within Orthodoxy, how a revolution in girls' education found textual grounding within a tradition that seemed to lack the resources or motivation to support such a venture. Finally, they make fascinating reading, lending telling detail and psychological depth to a figure who is generally reduced to the flatter dimensions of hagiography.

At various stages in the process of writing this book, I vacillated between providing a translation of Sarah Schenirer's writings preceded by an academic introduction, and a history of the movement with just a selection from those writings as an appendix. I ended up producing a hybrid of these two projects, translating her *Collected Writings* in its entirety (including the sections added to the 1955 edition) and composing what turned out to be a book-length study of Sarah Schenirer and the Bais Yaakov movement. Both projects, it seemed to me, were important, since we still lack not only a translation of her writings but also (with the exception of a number of excellent dissertations, from which I have benefited enormously) an academic introduction to the movement she founded.[13] I also became curious about her diary, which she mentions and even quotes from in a number of articles, and which an advertisement announced would be included in the *Collected Writings*. While the promised excerpts from Sarah Schenirer's diary were not included in the published collection, a few pages of the diary were published in Hebrew translation in 1955, and another few appeared in Polish in 2014. A complete translation of the 1955 publication appears in Appendix A, supplemented with additional entries that were only published in 2014.[14] As my work on

[12] For a description of and argument against the ways in which contemporary Bais Yaakov revises history by imposing more stringent standards of modesty on photographs of the early movement, see Ginsparg Klein, 'The Troubling Trend of Photoshopping History'. On this general trend of Orthodox censorship of its own history, see M. B. Shapiro, *Changing the Immutable*.

[13] The dissertations include: Atkin, 'The Beth Jacob Movement in Poland'; Bechhofer, 'Ongoing Constitution of Identity'; Ginsparg, 'Defining Bais Yaakov'; Rigler, 'Girls' Education in Inter-Bellum Poland'; and Weissman, 'Bais Ya'akov: A Women's Educational Movement'.

[14] See Sarah Schenirer, 'From the Diary' (Heb.), and 'Sarah Schenirer: Diary (excerpts)'.

this book was nearing completion, I also received permission to read and cite short passages from the complete diary, which will be published in both Polish and English translation.[15]

This book largely follows a historical route, beginning with the circumstances of Kraków Orthodoxy at the beginning of the twentieth century that constitute the background of the emergence of the movement. Chapter 2 explores the first few years of Sarah Schenirer's enterprise, a story we have access to almost solely through her own writings and the legends that surround Bais Yaakov's origins. Nevertheless, these legends and memories are crucial to our understanding of the movement, its development in later years, and indeed up to our own day. The third chapter analyses the crucial transition of the movement from these charismatic beginnings to the institutionalization of Bais Yaakov, focusing particularly on the year 1925, which marked the shift from a movement still under the sway of its founder to one dominated by its Central Offices (there were four!) and the larger organizational framework of Agudath Israel, the political organization of Orthodox Jews. This shift was accompanied by a burst of literary creativity centred around the *Bais Yaakov Journal*. Chapter 4 explores this literature, arguing that it constituted a new discourse that spoke to and for Orthodox girls and women. Bais Yaakov forged a rhetoric which celebrated (rather than merely defending) girls' Torah study and religious activism, uncovering traditional resources that could be mobilized for these new purposes. Chapter 5 turns back to history and sociology, probing the character of Bais Yaakov as a 'revolution in the name of tradition' by exploring the parallels and resonances of the movement with such Orthodox phenomena as German neo-Orthodoxy, hasidism, and the yeshiva, as well as with other revolutionary elements of its immediate context, including socialism, Zionism, feminism, and Yiddishism. While Bais Yaakov presented itself as combatting the secular ideologies of the interwar period, it also adopted some features of these 'isms' in shaping its own distinctive and novel character. The fifth chapter ends with a reading of the relationship—sociological, symbolic, discursive—between Bais Yaakov and the traditional Jewish family. An epilogue briefly follows the history of this discourse and the phenomenology of the movement during the Holocaust and after, when Bais Yaakov grew from a European movement to an international system with two major centres in Israel and North America. There are many areas of the history of Bais Yaakov that remain to be explored. This book is an initial venture into a rich and still insufficiently known topic, and I hope that it will be followed by other works that

[15] Schenirer, *Sara Shenirer: Pisma Autobiograficzne*.

investigate areas not covered in this book, correct any mistakes I may have made, mobilize archival material I did not see or discuss, and provide other perspectives than the ones advanced here.

A note on transliteration. There are many methods of transliterating Hebrew and Yiddish, and authors are generally advised to be consistent in their approach. But there are particular issues for writers about Bais Yaakov that complicate this excellent advice. Bais Yaakov, and the other organizations to which I often refer in these pages, such as Agudath Israel and Bnos Agudath Israel, have all been spelled in a bewildering variety of forms by different writers (Beth Jacob, Bet Ya'akov, Beys Yankev; Agudat Yisra'el, Agudas Israel; Bnot, Benot, Bnoys, etc.). This book follows the most common English spellings of each of these names. In addition, I often shorten Agudath Israel to 'the Agudah', also in line with general usage. In the case of the spelling of Bais Yaakov and Bnos, I have also taken into consideration the fact that the very names of these movements are evidence of their unique character. With the exception of Bais Yaakov schools in Israel, which even in the pre-state period used the modern Israeli Sephardi pronunciation, Bais Yaakov had an unusual approach to Hebrew: teachers and students, especially in the seminaries, often combined the Ashkenazi pronunciation—Bais rather than Beit—with a 'correct' and 'academic' approach that distinguished their Hebrew from that of their fathers and brothers. Bais Yaakov girls generally said, and in the United States still say, 'Yaakov' instead of 'Yankev' or 'Yakiv', 'Torah' instead of 'Toyre', 'Bnos' instead of 'Bnoys', and so on. This pronunciation avoids the Yiddish nasalization of the *ayin* and the rendering of the vowel 'o' as either 'oy' or 'e'. Bais Yaakov girls are systematically trained in Hebrew grammar, while boys in yeshiva often are not. This 'academic' approach to the language, possibly combined with the pervasive influence of German neo-Orthodox teachers and leaders in the movement, led to the creation of a gendered idiolect that might be called 'Bais Yaakov Hebrew'. The pronunciation of its own name is thus a marker of the distinctiveness of the movement, and I have tried to preserve it in transliteration. I also kept the ubiquitous collocation 'Bais Yaakov girl', occasionally specifying whether I am referring to girls or young women. In all other respects the transliteration of Hebrew and Yiddish follows the publisher's house style (see p. xiv). The material in brackets is my own addition to Sarah Schenirer's text; for the most part, I have limited these interpolations to providing the sources of her citations, and to converting Hebrew dates into the Gregorian calendar. The references to rabbinic literature in these interpolations are not meant to suggest that she was quoting these sources directly; as she indicates, she read many Yiddish texts that compiled and translated earlier sources, and many of the phrases she quotes from rabbinic literature are attested in numerous versions and variations.

A final note: I have described my route to this research topic as a circuitous and unexpected one. It opened new vistas and invited renewed thinking on a subject that I mistakenly assumed I already knew. In this way, my research brought me back to some of the more submerged experiences of my own early life and helped me reconsider who I am now. Without the skills I acquired in my Bais Yaakov education, and which remain a part of what I bring to this topic, I could hardly have taken on this project, or any of the other research projects of my academic career. These skills are not merely textual and linguistic, as writing this book helped me realize. I was educated within a movement that prized girls' intellectual achievements, encouraged academic enquiry, and (at least to some extent) rewarded female independence and initiative, and for that I am deeply grateful.

One of the truisms about scholarship is that it is always, inevitably, also autobiography. This was true in a very specific way for me in writing this book. Among the many discoveries I made while exploring the interwar history of the movement was the fact that my late father, Hillel Seidman, was among the first academic researchers of the movement. He dedicated two books to the topic: the first, published in 1936, was a biography of Sarah Schenirer, in which his admiration for the 'revolution' she had accomplished was on full display (if that was not evident enough from his marrying a Bais Yaakov seminary graduate and teacher, sending his three daughters to Bais Yaakov schools, and working on behalf of the movement both before and after the Holocaust).[16] The second, published a year later, surveyed the legal challenges faced by Bais Yaakov and the other schools under the jurisdiction of the Agudath Israel in conforming to shifting government regulations.[17] Among the regular pleasures of the two summers I spent in the YIVO reading room scrolling through microfiche issues of the *Bais Yaakov Journal* was encountering my father's name, and once even his photograph, among the other regular contributors to the periodical. His many contributions

[16] In *Bais Yaakov Journal*, 124, which appeared shortly after Schenirer's death in 1935, the Central Organization of Bais Yaakov in Kraków called for a biography of her to be written. While my father's work is not identified as this biography, it appeared the following year.

[17] My father, according to the introduction to his 1937 book, was also involved in lobbying government officials and preparing legal briefs in support of Bais Yaakov, in his capacity as political secretary of the Agudah party in the Polish parliament.

to the journal included a poem in Polish (at the age of 14!), an opinion piece arguing that Bais Yaakov teachers should be trained to teach Jewish religion in public schools, and an article in the special 1938 Polish supplement on antisemitism. Recognizing my father as a young man in the literature of Bais Yaakov helped me see that the movement had dramatic effects on the men as well as the women who participated in it.

Nor was it only my father I encountered in this project. In the final months of work on this book I spent many lively and informative hours interviewing my mother, Sara Seidman (née Abraham), about her experiences at the Bais Yaakov seminary founded in 1935 in Czernowitz (then in Bukovina, now in western Ukraine) just before the outbreak of the Second World War, as well as her activities as a Bais Yaakov teacher. My mother taught in three Bais Yaakov schools during and after the war: the first was in her home town in Torda, Romania, which she founded on her own as a teenager immediately after leaving Czernowitz on the outbreak of war; the second was in the displaced persons camp of Föhrenwald (where she first met my father); and the third was among the refugee population in Paris.[18] My mother opened the world of interwar, wartime, and post-war Bais Yaakov for me in a way that printed words could never achieve, and provided more than a few important details I had not found in written sources. Sarah Schenirer's hope had always been to 'return the hearts of daughters to their mothers and mothers to their daughters'. In some way that I hope she would not entirely disapprove of, she thus helped strengthen the bond between this particular mother and her daughter.

[18] For a description of my mother's experiences at the Czernowitz seminary and afterwards, see Frieman, 'Facing Adversity'.

PART ONE

A HISTORY OF A REVOLUTION

CHAPTER ONE

'In a Place Where There Are No Men' Before Bais Yaakov

'In a place where there are no men, try to be a man' [*Avot* 2: 6]; that is to say, in a place where men do not want to or cannot arise, a woman will arise and demonstrate what a pure soul can accomplish, and she will take the place of the powerful and determined 'man'.

BAILA BAKST[1]

WHILE KRAKÓW is the birthplace of the Bais Yaakov movement, it was actually conceived, as it were, in Vienna, where Sarah Schenirer had fled with a flood of refugees after the outbreak of the First World War brought the Russian army into Galicia. The idea of founding a school for Orthodox girls came to her, she relates in her memoir, as she was listening to a particularly inspiring sermon by Rabbi Moses David Flesch on the sabbath of Hanukah, in late 1914, in his synagogue in Vienna:

Riveted to my seat, I listened with great fascination to the fiery, spirited words of the rabbi.

In his sermon, the rabbi depicted the greatness and sublimity of the historical figure of Judith, and through her, he eloquently and passionately called upon Jewish women and daughters to act according to the model of this one-time Jewish heroine.[2] . . .

Even as I was caught up in the spiritual description of the character of Judith, it

[1] Bakst, 'In a Place Where There Are No Men' (Heb.), 95. According to Yaffa Gora, Schenirer herself related 'this quasi-midrashic statement' about her endeavours in public lectures; see Y. Gora, 'The Early Days of the Bais Yaakov Movement' (Heb.), 168. The story also appears in Benisch, *Carry Me in Your Heart*, 27.

[2] Judith is a character in the eponymous apocryphal book, which appears in the Septuagint but not in the Masoretic Hebrew text canonical for Jews. She is, however, known to Jewish tradition through midrashic retellings of her story, which associate her deeds with Hanukah. Judith is a pious, courageous, and beautiful widow, who kills the general Holofernes and takes his head back to her fellow Jews, who are—to her mind—insufficiently trusting of God to deliver them from foreign conquest. While she is subsequently courted by many suitors, Judith remains unmarried.

occurred to me: ah, if only all those women and girls in Kraków were here now to learn who we are and where we come from.[3]

'At that moment', Sarah Schenirer continues, 'was born a variety of schemes, great grandiose aims.'

The Viennese origins of Bais Yaakov are no mere happenstance. The canonical story of the founding of the movement insists that the inspiration did not and could not have come to her in Kraków, where Orthodox rabbis did not address their female congregants from the pulpit and—more to the point—where Jewish girls' education was treated with utter neglect. Thus although she secured a blessing for her project from the influential Belzer Rebbe, Rabbi Yissachar Dov Rokeach, after she returned to Kraków, she took the initial steps of this journey entirely on her own. Pearl Benisch describes how Sarah Schenirer's efforts were propelled by the 'distressing spectacle' of 'organized youth who were following all those powerfully influential "isms"'. Benisch continues:

> In order to spare the boys, our rabbis, the giants of the Torah, put up a great fight to repel the foreign currents that were flooding Poland. Nobody, however, cared about the Jewish girls. They believed that girls should be educated at home by their mothers. In agony, Sarah confronted our leaders' indifference to the tragic situation of the girls, who were left prey to these alien ideas.[4]

Sarah Schenirer's founding of a girls' school system was thus a pioneering venture into unexplored territory, in which the initiative of a single woman solved a problem that no one else around her recognized, cared about, or could resolve.

There is one detail in her memoir, however, that complicates this picture. After returning to Kraków from Vienna, she consulted her brother about how to realize her dream. He cautioned her against the project, asking 'What's the point of getting mixed up with party politics?' From her brother's perspective, her grand ideas threatened to draw her not into virgin territory, but rather into a fractious political arena. Extrapolating from her brother's words, it was not the case that no one in Kraków had so far considered using religious education to combat the defection of Jewish girls. Rather, this strategy, however obvious and even laudable it might be, was impracticable given the political realities of Orthodox life.

Rachel Manekin has conducted extensive research on the political landscape of Kraków Orthodoxy alluded to in this advice, enabling us to fill in some missing

[3] All references to Schenirer's writings for which I have not provided a source appear in English translation in the second part of this volume.

[4] Benisch, *Carry Me in Your Heart*, 25. In fact, according to her autobiography, Schenirer returned to Kraków while the war still raged.

details in the story of Bais Yaakov's origins. It is not simply a matter of how a 'simple seamstress' came up with a solution that the rabbinic leadership of her day had failed to envisage.[5] The more appropriate question is, how did she succeed in a cultural environment that stymied others with more status, power, money, and social capital? How did a woman manage to navigate the polarized political and religious forces at work around her? What role did the inspiration she found in Vienna play in this Polish context? And—to anticipate the answers to these questions—how might her marginal status in the Orthodox world have helped rather than hindered her project?

As Manekin shows, the problem of the defection of girls from Orthodoxy was vividly apparent in early twentieth-century Jewish Kraków. The crisis had deep roots, beginning with the 1869 Compulsory Education Law issued by the Habsburg empire requiring all children in Austro-Hungary between the ages of 6 and 14 to attend public school. Orthodox parents were often reluctant to send their sons to these schools, since it would prevent them from studying Torah. Hence, some preferred to pay a fine rather than comply.[6] Aaron Marcus, a German Jewish intellectual who moved to Kraków after embracing hasidism, advocated that parents deliberately send their daughters there instead; since space in the new public schools was limited, such a strategy would allow them to circumvent compulsory education for their sons.[7] In the decades that followed, some Orthodox parents, even in hasidic circles, began to send their daughters to convent schools, which were seen as both more conservative and more fashionable than public schools.

The secular education of Orthodox girls may have 'protected' their brothers from exposure to public schools, but it had its consequences. As Manekin puts it, the result of such education was the 'blossoming of a generation of Jewish young women from Orthodox homes who were fervent "Poles" in their language, their intellectual lives, and their appearance'.[8] Zevi Scharfstein observed that marriages that resulted from mismatches between yeshiva-educated young men and Polonized Orthodox young women were doomed from the start, for 'against her will she is married to a man whom she mocks in her heart'.[9] Many girls resisted entering into such unions, defying their parents and leaving heads of

[5] The designation of Schenirer as 'a simple seamstress' (or dressmaker) appears frequently in the literature. For one example, see Grunfeld-Rosenbaum, 'Sara Schenierer', 412; and see J. Friedenson, 'The Bais Yaakov Girls' Schools' (Heb.), 62, 63.

[6] See Manekin, '"Something Entirely New"' (Heb.), 67–8.

[7] Ibid. 70.

[8] Ibid. 68.

[9] Scharfstein, 'On Our Brothers' Lives in Galicia' (Heb.), 11–12, quoted in Manekin, '"Something Entirely New"' (Heb.), 69–70.

yeshivas and hasidic leaders bemoaning the lack of suitable mates for their students. The Gerer Rebbe reportedly lamented that he had two thousand young male followers who had little hope of finding a good match.[10]

Evidence of young girls leaving the Orthodox world surfaced in the widely publicized 'Araten case', which concerned Michalina Araten, a hasidic girl from Kraków who fled her parents' house in 1900 with the intention of converting and marrying her gentile lover. Articles discussing the case in the Orthodox press spoke of an 'epidemic' of such defections and conversions, and the issue was debated in a wide range of publications in the first decade of the twentieth century.[11] If the problem of girls' defection from Orthodoxy was plain to see, so were the causes of this crisis. Marcus, who had advised Kraków's parents to fill the public schools with their daughters, now recommended that the girls either be withdrawn from secular schools as soon as the legal requirement of seven grades was fulfilled, or kept from attending such schools altogether, paying a fine if necessary. Other leaders in the community took similar stances, suggesting that parents find ways to limit their daughters' secular instruction and insisting that a basic education sufficed for nearly any occupation to which an Orthodox girl might aspire. While most of these writers focused on the damage wrought by secular education, some blamed the crisis on Orthodox fathers who failed to provide their daughters with Jewish instruction. Sons were at least partially inoculated against the lures of modernity by the Torah study that occupied their time and kept them under adult supervision. Girls, however, were heedlessly exposed to sophisticated secular ideas without any similar exposure to their own tradition.[12]

In short, Sarah Schenirer was far from being the first to recognize that providing girls with a systematic and uplifting religious education could stem the tide of defection and apostasy. In a 1900 response to the Araten case, the Orthodox Zionist Simon Lazar proposed the establishment of girls' schools in Galicia as a way of addressing the dangers that modernity held for Jewish women.[13] His pro-

[10] This anecdote appears in Sorasky, *The History of Torah Education* (Heb.), 428, and elsewhere. A related anecdote that circulated after the war is that Rabbi Meir Shapiro, founder and head of the Yeshivat Hakhmei Lublin, told the Bais Yaakov teacher and director of the Czernowitz teachers' seminary Esther Hamburger (later Gross): 'If not for your work in educating Jewish daughters, I would have to close my yeshiva in Lublin.' See Chevroni, 'The Unacknowledged Heritage'.

[11] Manekin writes that at least 400 young Jewish women, not all of them Orthodox, converted to Christianity in Kraków in the last years of the nineteenth and first years of the twentieth century. See '"Something Entirely New"' (Heb.), 76.

[12] Ibid. 72–3.

[13] Writing in *Hamagid*, no. 9 (1900), quoted in Manekin, 'Orthodox Jewry', 190.

posal was rejected by some in the more conservative Orthodox press, no doubt in part because it was coming from outside their own circles. One writer responded to Lazar's proposal by insisting that it was untrue that girls received no Jewish education, since they were raised in homes in which religious knowledge and values were transmitted from parents to children. While such home education was clearly permitted, organized systems for educating Jewish girls were not:

> But the study of Torah, by which is undoubtedly meant the Torah of Moses and the books of the Prophets, is more harmful than helpful, since, as the rabbis say, 'Anyone who teaches his daughter Torah, it is as if he is teaching her *tiflut* [licentiousness, trivialities]' [BT *Sot.* 20*a*].[14]
>
> [Lazar] knows this but smiles and speaks of the difference between rabbinic times and our more educated times. But I hold fast to the principle that the holy Sages foresaw what would happen in later eras.[15]

This writer rejected Lazar's proposal on the familiar grounds that rabbinic literature warned against—or even forbade—teaching Torah to daughters, a prohibition that new conditions could not reverse. Other strictly Orthodox writers were more inclined to consider the admittedly radical option of formal education for girls. In 1902, the Kraków Orthodox newspaper *Maḥzikei hadat* published a number of articles in which writers put forth proposals for an organized approach to girls' education. One representative article recommended teaching girls 'the sacred scripture, Hebrew, and Jewish history' to counteract the secular education

[14] On the meaning of *tiflut*, see the quotation from Ilan Fuchs later in this chapter. The halakhic issue of women's Torah study is a complex one with a long history. It begins not with Rabbi Eliezer's dictum but rather with the biblical commandment to 'teach these words to your children'—literally 'sons', but the male plural can also be understood as meaning 'children', in which the inclusion of daughters is ambiguous. BT *Kid.* 29*b* debates this question, concluding that Torah should be taught 'to your sons and not your daughters'. The *Shulḥan arukh* in *Yoreh de'ah*, 246: 6 further specifies that Rabbi Eliezer's opinion refers only to the Oral Law. While it would be preferable for a father not to teach his daughter the Written Torah, 'if he does teach her the Written Torah it is not comparable to *tiflut*'. Despite the fact that Rabbi Eliezer's dictum contradicts that of Ben Azzai, who permits the same practice, and makes sense primarily in the context of the specific discussion around *Sotah*, his dictum, often quoted in isolation from this context and without reference to the more lenient opinion of Ben Azzai, has become the most influential rabbinic opinion in both halakhic and sociological discourse around the issue of women's Torah study. For a fuller discussion, see Biale, *Women and Jewish Law*, 29–41. Translations from rabbinic sources are my own, except where otherwise indicated.

[15] 'The Tongue Expresses Great Things' (Heb.), *Maḥazikei hadat*, 13 (1900), quoted in Manekin, '"Something Entirely New"' (Heb.), 74.

that was leading Orthodox young women into prostitution or 'seduction' by strangers.[16]

The most public and official discussion of this issue came up during a rabbinical congress that met in Kraków in 1903. The assembly was initiated by the Ashkenazi rabbi of Cairo, Aaron Mendel Hakohen (1866–1927), with the aim of establishing a worldwide organization of Orthodox rabbis to help communities face the pressing problems they shared. Rabbi Mendel chose Kraków for the meeting for its distinguished religious history, and as a relatively tolerant context for Jewish political initiative.[17] What he failed to consider was the threat such international collaboration might pose to a community that prided itself on the stringency of its religious life and was defensive of its local stature and authority. The congress ran into general indifference and open opposition before it had even begun, with many Galician rabbis choosing not to attend. The leadership of Kraków Orthodoxy was dogged by the fear that communities with looser standards—Sephardi or German Jewish—would drag down those east European Jews who maintained stricter levels of halakhic observance. The rabbi of Kraków, Hayim Leibush Horowitz, attended only reluctantly, explaining his hesitation in his opening remarks by insisting that a rabbinical conference was unnecessary, since 'there is nothing to innovate or correct in Judaism'. Moreover, Horowitz asserted, 'it is impossible to create a general rabbinic association because each group has its own customs'. Despite this inauspicious beginning, the conference found some willing participants even among the Polish rabbinate. During the deliberations, Menahem Mendel Hayim Landau, the rabbi of Nowy Dwór, a town near Warsaw, brought up an issue that had been receiving press attention in recent years and which spanned the Jewish world at large, that of Jewish prostitutes and traffickers who were part of the international white slave trade. Indirectly acknowledging the traditional taboo on direct sexual speech, Landau began by apologizing for 'having to spread the disgusting skirt before everyone's eyes, and to reveal our shame in this terrible matter'.[18] As Manekin relates, the rabbis present had asked Landau 'not to speak about this painful subject, so as not

[16] *Kol maḥazikei hadat*, no. 7 (1902), quoted in Manekin, 'Orthodox Jewry', 189.

[17] For more on this conference, see the report by Landau entitled *Mekits nirdamim* (Who Awakens Those Who Sleep); Manekin, 'Orthodox Jewry', 183–7, 190; and Bacon, 'The Rabbinical Conference in Krakow (1903)', 207. Bacon notes that there are 'three very different and often contradictory accounts [of the conference] by three central participants: Rabbi Aharon Mendl of Cairo, Eliyahu Akiva Rabinowich of Poltova, and Rabbi Menachem Mendl Landau of Nowy Dwór' (ibid. 212–13 n.).

[18] See Landau, *Mekits nirdamim*, 52.

to desecrate Israel's name in public'.[19] Forgoing open allusion to the problem, Landau turned to the solution, pleading that the assembled rabbis agree that for the Orthodox girl whose 'heart is already far from her people and we cannot hope that the generation that is born from her will be raised in the Jewish spirit', the only solution was to educate her in 'the knowledge of Torah'.

Landau readily acknowledged the halakhic obstacles to such a project: 'It is true that the Talmud forbids teaching Torah to girls, since "Anyone who teaches his daughter Torah, is teaching her *tiflut*."' He nevertheless argued that Rabbi Eliezer's prohibition referred to 'earlier times, when "there was no wisdom in a woman except [weaving] with a spindle" [BT *Yoma* 66*b*], and they were secluded inside their homes and knew nothing of the outside world'. Since girls were no longer shielded from the wider world, but rather were exposed to every other kind of text, 'why should the study of Torah be worse than other subjects?'[20] In other words, girls were certainly acquiring an education in 'licentiousness' at their secular schools and from the novels they read in their leisure time; given that reality, did it really make sense to keep them from studying Torah out of fear that it might lead them to licentiousness?

Although Rabbi Landau did not dwell on this, in its talmudic context the dictum, attributed to Rabbi Eliezer in BT *Sotah* 20*a*, is a response to Ben Azzai's recommendation that women be taught Torah 'so that if she drinks [and does not die immediately] she will know that some merit has delayed [her punishment]'. Whether this means that Torah learning will earn women merit (which will protect them from the effects of the waters), or that it will enable them to understand the reasons in cases where the waters do not give the correct result, Eliezer's response seems to imply that men should not aid women in their sexual transgressions by giving them either the merit that allows them to withstand the trial of the bitter waters or the knowledge of why the test might fail; if a woman is ignorant of the fine print of the *sotah* ritual, she will not imagine she can get away with adultery. Taken out of this specific, complicated context, the logic of Rabbi Eliezer's connection between adultery and female Torah study is difficult to discern—and more than a little disturbing in a world in which the Torah excites only praise. The later Gemara, which comments on the Mishnah, revises

[19] The fear of speaking openly about Jewish involvement in prostitution was not limited to Orthodox rabbis. Many in the Jewish world were caught between denouncing the white slave trade and avoiding the discussion of subjects that might increase antisemitism. On this issue, see Bristow, *Prostitution and Prejudice*, 234–6.

[20] See Landau, *Mekits nirdamim*, 54–5; see also Manekin, 'Orthodox Jewry', 191.

Rabbi Eliezer's words, 'Anyone who teaches his daughter Torah, is teaching her *tiflut*', asking: 'Can it enter your mind [that by teaching her Torah he is actually teaching her] *tiflut*! Rather say, [it is considered] *as though* he had taught her *tiflut*' (BT *Sot.* 21*a*). As Rachel Biale puts it, 'The Talmud thus "hastens to defend the holiness of the Torah" from the imputation that it could become *tiflut* under any conditions.'[21]

In response to Rabbi Landau's recommendation, Meir Rapoport, a prominent member of the Kraków Jewish community, proposed 'the establishment in every city of Talmud Torahs [supplementary afternoon schools] for girls, where they could learn prayers, blessings, and the laws pertaining to Jewish homes'. But this proposal, Rabbi Landau relates in his account of the congress, was opposed by those in attendance who were determined to reject any innovation at all. As the Orthodox journalist Eliyahu Akiva Rabinowich proclaimed: 'Even this custom they wish to bring to Israel—Talmud Torahs for women! God forbid! Such a thing will never be!'[22] The proposal to educate girls, Manekin points out, was novel, but just as novel was the fact that rabbis were meeting in a group to discuss the broader educational landscape, in a culture where rabbis tended to devote themselves more narrowly to their own cadre of students or followers.[23] This very novelty militated against the success of the congress. According to Gershon Bacon, 'Aharon Mendl himself had opened the door to scepticism and opposition to the conference with his published statements and proposed agenda, which called for the standardization and updating of traditional customs and employed "red-flag" phrases such as "the spirit of the times"'.[24] Wariness of new ideas and initiatives, combined with the dispiriting worry that proclamations by the congress might well be ignored, made it difficult to take action.

On educational as on other matters, the rabbinical congress accomplished nothing, and Rabbi Mendel returned to Cairo 'in sorrow and dismay, [his] world darkened'.[25] As Manekin summarizes the episode,

> The failure of the rabbinical congress in Kraków symbolized the victory of Galician Orthodoxy. Rabbi Horowitz, who was elected to his position because of his moderation and his broad education, was unable to withstand the pressures that were placed upon him, and thus a genuine confrontation with the problems of the hour was prevented.[26]

[21] Biale, *Women and Jewish Law*, 34.

[22] See Landau, *Mekits nirdamin*, 56–7; Manekin, 'Orthodox Jewry', 192.

[23] Manekin, email communication (10 July 2016).

[24] Bacon, 'The Rabbinical Conference in Krakow (1903)', 207.

[25] Aaron Mendel Hakohen, *Keneset hagedolah* (Alexandria, 1904), ii. 48, quoted in Manekin, 'Orthodox Jewry', 187.

[26] Manekin, 'Orthodox Jewry', 187.

While the rabbinical congress recognized Orthodox girls' education as the major strategy for dealing with the crisis of Orthodox young women, it also made it clear that anyone who suggested implementing such an innovation risked being seen as willing to go against what was understood to be a clear rabbinic prohibition, and more generally as capitulating to modernity rather than valiantly resisting it.[27] A 1904 group called Agudath Yeshurun, led by the highly respected Rabbi Sholom Mordechai Schwadron (known as 'the Maharsham'), issued a public call in the Orthodox newspaper *Hamitspeh* expressing its hope that 'a solution might be sought and also found to revive Torah and all those principles related to religion, and also in regard to the question of education, to raise our sons and our daughters to Torah and the ways of the land [*derekh erets*]'.[28] The last phrase apparently referred to the German neo-Orthodox slogan that signalled a commitment to combining tradition and modernity, Torah and secular studies. In eastern Europe, this moderate approach was regarded with suspicion among the stricter Orthodox and hasidic mainstream, and after the proclamation by Agudath Yeshurun was attacked as heresy in the Orthodox press, the group retracted its recommendations. As Manekin remarks, the fact that the earliest and loudest voices that called for change came from moderates like Lazar and German-born writers like Marcus rendered change that much more difficult to effect in strictly Orthodox circles.[29]

[27] Manekin also discusses the proposals of two rabbis who founded a group in 1904 called Agudat Yeshurun to actively work to improve both girls' and boys' Jewish education, which met with similar opposition and failure. See '"Something Entirely New"' (Heb.), 79–80. Similar problems cropped up for male Jewish education, and these demonstrate some of the difficulties in finding solutions. Issues included whether the community should work to exempt students from taking exams on the sabbath, an effort that might have the effect of actually encouraging some families to allow their sons and daughters to attend public school. A *gymnasium* that opened with the intention of training young Orthodox men in both Jewish and secular studies in order 'to save them from attending Polish *gymnasia*' was condemned by the Sanzer hasidim and compelled to shut its doors after three months. As the director of this school saw it, he was rescuing Polish Jewish youth from a worse fate, while his opponents in the Orthodox leadership were abandoning the Jewish masses for fear that, by opening 'modern' Orthodox institutions, they would provide avenues for hasidic boys to attend such schools, granting legitimacy to options that had hitherto been condemned. Similar considerations made it difficult for the community to lobby for Jewish students in public schools to be exempt from writing on the sabbath. See Manekin, 'Orthodox Jewry', 186–91.

[28] 'Agudat Yeshurun', *Hamitspeh*, 10 (16 May 1904), quoted in Manekin, '"Something Entirely New"' (Heb.), 79 n. 26. Manekin adds that the Maharsham may have had a personal stake in this issue, given that his granddaughter Dvortshe had refused to marry a hasid.

[29] Manekin, email communication (10 July 2016).

Lazar and Marcus were not alone in calling for change. The various Jewish organizations formed to combat the international white slave trade also urged rabbis to respond to the crisis.[30] Activists in the anti-white slavery movement debated whether prostitution was voluntary, forced, or a matter of fraud and 'seduction', and blamed the problem on a variety of factors, from the frivolity and materialism of girls to, more sympathetically, the pauperization of Jewish eastern Europe and the migrations that broke up families. At least a few of the activists also took aim at Orthodox society as contributing to the conditions that drove some women to prostitution. Bertha Pappenheim, who co-founded the Jüdische Frauenbund with Sidonie Werner and travelled frequently to Galicia beginning in 1903, was particularly persistent in pointing the finger at traditional Jewish society. In a 1907 speech to the Jüdische Frauenbund, Pappenheim claimed that

> there are an immense number of young Jewish women—mostly in Russia and Galicia—who fall into prostitution even while they are still living with their very religious parents. This too can be explained; these girls know that their only value is sexual. Their individuality, their desires and curiosity are only rarely treated as valid . . . this is why the most strictly Orthodox communities in the east have contributed the largest share of human merchandise to the traffic in girls and women.[31]

For Pappenheim, an Orthodox feminist, the struggle against the traffic in Jewish women was accompanied by a sharp critique of the 'centuries-long suppression of Jewish women' in traditional Judaism, and, in particular, of its neglect of girls' education.[32] She was not shy about making these views clear: in 1912 she met the

[30] In London, the Jewish Association for the Protection of Girls and Women was founded in 1885 to provide services for poor girls and women among the immigrants coming from the east; a similar organization, the Jüdische Frauenbund (Jewish Women's League), was founded in Germany in 1904. These organizations met unaccompanied girls and women at ports and train stations, fed and housed poor immigrants, and found ways to expose traffickers and brothels. On the over-representation of Jews in the trade, see Jewish Association for the Protection of Girls and Women, *Official Report*, which counted 19 of 182 known traffickers in Germany who were Jewish, 65 of 101 in Austria, 80 of 93 in South America (these were identified as Russian or Polish Jews), 38 of 39 in Galicia, 104 of 124 in Russia, 68 of 105 in Hungary, and 34 of 127 in France. On Bertha Pappenheim as founder of the Jüdische Frauenbund, see Loentz, *Let Me Continue to Speak the Truth*.

[31] Pappenheim, 'Zur Sittlichkeitsfrage', 22. I have seen no evidence for Pappenheim's claim that most victims of sex trafficking came from very religious homes; of the many cases of prostitution discussed in Edward Bristow's *Prostitution and Prejudice*, only one clearly involved a hasidic girl, who, in a widely publicized 1909 case, temporarily fell into the hands of sex traffickers in the course of running away from her home in Nowy Targ to Kraków, where she intended to convert. See Bristow, *Prostitution and Prejudice*, 218–19.

[32] Pappenheim, 'Zur Sittlichkeitsfrage', 22.

Aleksanderer Rebbe, delivering 'a vivid lecture' on the problem of prostitution in Galicia (the rebbe, she notes, piously turned his back to her as she spoke, but responded with interest and concern).[33] The effects of these interventions, Pappenheim conceded, were minimal. In the press, at rabbinic and other conferences, and even in hasidic courts, the problem of girls' defection from Orthodoxy (whether to become secular, to convert, or to become prostitutes) was a topic of persistent concern, with the solution of religious education proposed from many different quarters. Nevertheless, the Orthodox community in Galicia was too politically splintered to effectively organize, and too wary of outsiders to accept their recommendations or help.

But German solutions for east European problems were too promising to be permanently ruled out. Another attempt to forge ties among the different Orthodox communities was made at the historic founding conference in Katowice, Silesia (27–29 May 1912), of what would become, after the First World War, the Agudath Israel, the political organization of world Orthodoxy. The conference, initiated by Jacob Rosenheim and other neo-Orthodox German Jewish activists, managed to attract the interest of some very influential east European leaders, most importantly the Gerer Rebbe, Abraham Mordecai Alter, leader of the largest hasidic group in interwar Poland, numbering around a quarter of a million.[34] Once again, the problem of girls' defections was raised: after opening speeches, the general discussion began, in fact, with Abraham Schnur, the rabbi of Tarnów, proposing that 'the question of educating boys and girls is crucial for Galicia; this work must proceed under our control'. Schnur cited Exodus 19: 3, *ko tomar leveit ya'akov* ('so shall you say to the House of Jacob'), as evidence that it was appropriate to teach Torah to women, who represent the Jewish 'house'.[35] Aaron Marcus, who had been advocating for girls' education for over a decade

[33] This meeting is described in a letter dated 6 May 1912, in the 'Letters from Abroad' section of Pappenheim, *Bertha Pappenheim: Leben und Schriften*, 59–60. Aleksander (Aleksandrów) hasidism constituted the second-largest hasidic group in Poland, after Gerer (Góra Kalwaria) hasidism, with perhaps 100,000 members. The Grand Rabbi of Aleksander in 1912 was Shmuel Tsvi Dancyger (1840–1923).

[34] Katowice lies on the border between central and eastern Europe, and thus was an appropriate location for the congress. On the Katowice gathering, see the official report: *Agudas Jisroel*. For a summary, see Bacon, *The Politics of Tradition*, 34–6. The Gerer Rebbe did not attend the gathering, but he sent a written message and two of his closest followers as emissaries.

[35] *Agudas Jisroel*, 72. Bible translations are based on the 1985 JPS version, with capitalization adapted to the publisher's style. Departures of substance from the original are individually noted below.

at this point, also spoke in a voice breaking with emotion about the urgency of the problem, calling the situation in Poland a 'burning disgrace, a desecration of God's name of the worst sort . . . when not one of our rabbis lifts a finger to lead our daughters away from the baptismal font'.[36] Despite the hopes raised by the new ties between German and east European Orthodoxy, the political organization did not get off the ground until after the First World War. For the problem of Jewish girls' education, this meant that, once again, nothing was done.

For those hesitant to make changes to the traditional system of educating girls (or to be seen as advocating such changes), the safer response to the problem of defection from Orthodoxy was to tighten restrictions on young women. In 1909, after two sisters, great-granddaughters of the Sanzer Rebbe, abandoned the Orthodox world, the Gerer hasidim of Kraków adopted new regulations forbidding girls from attending school beyond the seventh grade, speaking Polish on the sabbath, attending the theatre, or learning Hebrew.[37] Among the Hungarian followers of the Hatam Sofer (Rabbi Moses Schreiber), the founder of militant Orthodoxy, rabbis exhorted the community not only to restrict girls' secular education but also to find ways to keep them within the confines of their homes. In a 1924 book on the subject of raising daughters, Rabbi Benjamin Berger of Beled, Hungary, denied the halakhic permissibility of organized Jewish education for girls, recommending instead that parents should spend sabbaths studying Yiddish ethical literature with their daughters, since such practices would also ensure that 'the daughter will then be at home and not wandering around the streets or other outdoor places with no purpose, which can only lead to trouble'.[38] But as the continuing crisis attested, it was increasingly difficult to address the problem of girls' attraction to modern ideologies and pastimes solely through tighter restrictions. Even the ostensibly Orthodox tutors brought into the house to teach and inspire daughters, as a speaker at the 1903 congress lamented, were themselves often 'tainted' by the currents of modernity they were hired to combat.

In brief, educational solutions to the evident crisis in the Orthodox world were publicly discussed in Kraków Orthodox circles for at least fifteen years before Sarah Schenirer opened her first school. Even the halakhic and rhetorical bases that could (and eventually did) permit such schools were already evident and established. There are a number of possible approaches to the question of

[36] *Agudas Jisroel*, 97.

[37] *Hamitspeh*, nos. 37, 38 (1909), quoted in Manekin, 'Orthodox Jewry', 192 n. 82.

[38] Berger, *On the Education of Girls* (Heb.), 51.

whether Jewish law permits Torah study for women, but Rabbi Landau laid out the one that would become canonical in Bais Yaakov discourse: given the defection of girls from Orthodoxy in Galicia, the necessity of teaching girls 'Torah, and the commandments and Jewish history and religion' was 'extremely urgent in our time, a matter of "It is time to act for the Lord" [Ps. 119: 126].' Rabbi Landau's abbreviated citation of the verse in Psalms, 'It is time to act for the Lord, for they have violated your teachings', mobilizes a familiar midrashic reading that views the verse as warrant for overturning even a clear halakhic directive when a situation urgently demands extreme measures.[39]

To Rabbi Landau's opinion we can add the far more influential comments by Rabbi Israel Meir Hakohen (Kagan), better known as the Hafets Hayim after his popular book of that title and the most respected Torah sage of his generation. The Hafets Hayim discussed women's exemption from Torah study in various early writings, never giving a hint of encouragement to women who might choose to study Torah despite this exemption. In one aside, he objected to women deciding Jewish law on their own behalf, for instance in matters relating to *nidah* (conduct during menstruation), insisting that 'a woman who needs to ask a question of Jewish law in such matters should consult only a learned teacher and not another woman, and she must never, for Heaven's sake, dare to render a halakhic judgment on her own'.[40] In 1911, however, the Hafets Hayim published what was to be the first of a series of writings encouraging Torah study for women, albeit within the long-established limits of the Written rather than Oral Torah (or rabbinic literature). In a marginal comment on Rabbi Eliezer's dictum, he wrote:

It seems that this was specifically in previous times, when parental transmission was very strong and people behaved just as their ancestors did, as it says, 'Ask your father and he shall tell you', so we could say that one should not teach a daughter Torah but instead rely on direct transmission from parent. But now, because of our many sins, this transmission from parents to children is much weaker, and it sometimes happens that there are no parents at all. And especially for those girls who have become accustomed to studying the writings and language of the nations, it is a great commandment to teach

[39] The *mishnah* in *Ber.* 54*a* reads *hefeiru*, not in the past tense ('they have violated') but as an imperative ('violate!'). The Talmud applies this principle in four separate instances. Whether such a principle remains valid after the rabbinic period and who might be authorized to decide its applicability are matters of some dispute, not surprisingly, given the sweeping power of the principle.

[40] Israel Meir Hakohen Kagan, *Nidḥei yisra'el*, 41*b*, in *Kitvei haḥafets ḥayim*, ii. 159 and iii. 17, quoted in Brown, 'On the Value of Torah Study' (Heb.), 111.

them the Pentateuch and the Prophets and the ethics of the Sages, such as the *Pirkei avot* [Ethics of the Fathers] and the book *Menorat hama'or* [The Candelabrum of Light], in order to implant our holy faith in them. And if we fail to do this, they may abandon the way of God completely and transgress the fundamentals of our religion, God forbid.[41]

In 1918 the Hafets Hayim wrote again on this topic, reaffirming that Torah study for women was 'a great commandment of the day' and proposing a similar curriculum that included the Torah and ethical literature. Once again, he specified that, within the corpus of rabbinic literature, women should be limited to the study of the *Pirkei avot*, an ethical rather than halakhic (legal) tractate of the Mishnah.[42]

At the beginning of the twentieth century, east European Orthodoxy was establishing the permissibility of organized Torah study for women, within generally understood limits.[43] But Jews in German lands had long recognized not only the permissibility but also the value of such study. In 1853 the leader of German neo-Orthodoxy, Rabbi Samson Raphael Hirsch, established the *Realschule*, with an initial enrolment of fifty-five boys and twenty-nine girls. A philosophically sophisticated and textually rigorous Jewish education for both sexes was the cornerstone of his plan for rescuing Orthodoxy from the depredations of the Reform movement, at a time when the Jewish family or synagogue life could no longer be counted on to perform such a function. Instruction was co-educational in the three elementary-school grades of the *Realschule* and segregated in the nine grades of the secondary school that was established a decade later. By the

[41] Israel Meir Hakohen Kagan, *Likutei halakhot: sotah* 21 (New York, 1959), quoted in Brown, 'On the Value of Torah Study' (Heb.), 112–14. Brown reflects on the feminist, radical, and even 'Reform' character of this comment, which seems to recommend changing Jewish law because of societal transformations; Brown ultimately rejects such an interpretation as far from the Hafets Hayim's mentality, and argues that the openness to women's Torah study was in keeping with his inclination to broaden Torah study among all Jews, learned and unlearned alike.

[42] Cited in Ellinson, *Women and the Commandments* (Heb.), 159–60. It is worth noting that the Hafets Hayim was not advocating an organized girls' school system in these comments, and there is no evidence that he was aware of Schenirer's fledgling efforts in 1918. Although Bais Yaakov quoted the 1918 opinion in various publications, it was not until 1933, months before his death, that the Hafets Hayim responded to an Agudah request to provide an endorsement of Bais Yaakov in the face of continuing opposition in the Orthodox community. This endorsement appears in many Bais Yaakov publications, including the 1955 reissue of Sarah Schenirer's *Collected Writings*. For the circumstances of the 1933 request, see Benisch, *Carry Me in Your Heart*, 116.

[43] In addition to organized education, it was well known that many individual Jewish women also received a traditional education from fathers or teachers, or on their own. On these individual women who were learned in Torah, see Zolty, *'And All Your Children'*, 246–61.

start of the twentieth century, 600 students were studying in the boys' and girls' secondary schools. Hirsch legitimated such formal Torah study for girls less by halakhic argumentation (though he was certainly familiar with the literature on the topic) than by recourse to a domesticating (and bourgeois) rhetoric, arguing that 'No less [than sons] should Israel's daughters learn the content of the Written Torah and the laws which they are required to perform in their lifetime as daughter and young woman, as mother and housewife.'[44] Acknowledging the traditional limits of the religious curriculum for girls and women, Hirsch specified that 'women should not pursue specialized Torah study or theoretical knowledge of the Law, which are primarily the function of men'. He nevertheless insisted that basic Torah study 'should indeed form part of the mental and spiritual training not only of our sons, but of our daughters as well'.[45]

While ingrained suspicion of German Jewish neo-Orthodoxy undoubtedly militated against the rapid adoption of Hirsch's model in eastern Europe, historical precedents for Jewish education for Orthodox girls outside the home existed in the east as well. We know that girls sometimes attended mixed-sex *ḥeders* (one-room traditional schools), although generally for shorter periods and at younger ages than boys. There were also *ḥeders* that served only female pupils: Abraham Greenbaum cites an 1894 survey of elementary school education in the Russian empire that reports over 10,000 girls studying in *ḥeders*, and another survey from 1912 that showed that an average of 7 per cent of the pupils in Russian *ḥeders* were female.[46] In the 1920s, Alter Kacyzne took a photograph captioned 'A *ḥeder* for girls, Łaskarzew, Poland'.[47] Shaul Stampfer has reminded us that the absence of formal schools did not necessarily mean that girls and women were ignorant of Jewish narratives, values, or texts: 'The conventional image of the extremely low level of women's education in traditional Jewish society can be accepted only if one adopts a narrow definition of education, which limits it to schooling and assumes that a religious text written in Hebrew is significant, whereas one written in Yiddish is not.'[48] Whether in girls' *ḥeders*, with private tutors, which supplemented public or convent schools, or through education provided in the home,

[44] Hirsch, *Horeb*, 371. Samson Raphael Hirsch (1808–88) was a German rabbi known as the founder of German Jewish neo-Orthodoxy, who formulated the philosophy of *torah im derekh erets* (Torah with 'the way of the land'), a principled approach to combining Torah with some aspects of modernity.

[45] Hirsch, *Hirsch Siddur*, 122.

[46] Greenbaum, 'Traditional Education of East European Jewish Women', 4.

[47] See Zalkin, 'Heder', in the online edition of the *YIVO Encyclopedia* (the photograph does not appear in the print edition); <http://www.yivoencyclopedia.org/article.aspx/Heder> (accessed 13 July 2016).

[48] Stampfer, *Families, Rabbis, and Education*, 187.

girls generally did receive at least a rudimentary Jewish education, and occasionally considerably more—Sarah Schenirer herself is proof of what a motivated autodidact could achieve. Moreover, there were girls' schools that were established in response to the same crisis discussed at the 1903 Kraków congress: Greenbaum cites Russian Jewish activists disturbed by reports of girls' conversions in Galicia, who proposed that 'qualified women . . . organize high-level girls' *ḥeders* in order to stem this trend'.[49] Such initiatives were more likely to come from Zionist or religious Zionist circles: the Yehudiah school system emerged from what was, in the 1890s, a girls' *ḥeder* in Vilna; the Zionist feminist Puah Rakovsky was hired to direct a school by that name in Warsaw in 1893, to which she added a girls' *gymnasium* (college-preparatory secondary or high school). Students at Yehudiah, which had a religious Zionist orientation, received a rigorous education not only in Hebrew but also in Bible, Jewish history, and other Jewish subjects.[50] As Eliyana Adler shows, Yehudiah used much the same rhetoric as Sarah Schenirer did in justifying its programme, describing the need for a 'meaningful Jewish education' in place of the 'dry lessons in religion available in public schools'.[51]

But such efforts were also seen in more strictly Orthodox circles. A Jewish girls' *gymnasium* called Havatselet opened in Warsaw in 1916, initiated by two German neo-Orthodox rabbis with doctoral degrees—*doktor rabbiners* as they were known—Dr Emanuel Carlebach and Dr Pinchas Kohn, with the support of a number of strictly Orthodox rabbis, including the Gerer Rebbe. Havatselet eventually grew to include satellite schools in Warsaw, Kalisz, and other cities, and in the 1920s often collaborated with the larger Bais Yaakov movement. Gutta Sternbuch describes the high school, which she attended in the early 1930s, as 'a very religious school attended by girls from the entire Ger Chasidic dynasty. . . Girls from less religious homes also attended, but all of the families were *shomer Shabbos* [sabbath-observant].'[52] In Lithuania, a group of young men from both Mizrahi and anti-Zionist circles calling themselves the Tse'irei Israel (Youth of Israel), displaced by the war from their homes and yeshivas, took it upon themselves to acquire a broad general education, and then undertook to do the same for both boys and girls within a traditional Jewish, but worldly, framework. Rabbi Joseph Leib Bloch from the Telshe yeshiva was thinking along parallel lines, and

49 Greenbaum, 'Traditional Education of East European Jewish Women', 5.

50 For more on Yehudiah, see Kazdan, *The History of Jewish School Systems* (Yid.), 412.

51 Adler, *In Her Hands*, 149.

52 For a description of the school, see Sternbuch and Kranzler, *Gutta*, 17–32.

he and the group joined forces to found the non-partisan Yavneh school system, with the first of the girls' schools opening in Telz in 1921.[53] Sarah Schenirer's initiative, described so often as pioneering and unique, was thus part of a larger surge of activity around Orthodox girls' education during and immediately after the First World War. These efforts were spurred by the crisis of defection and the presence of German Jewish rabbis with doctoral degrees who aimed to bridge the divide between the new educational ordinances propagated by the German Occupational Government and the traditional Orthodox educational system by helping modernize Jewish education.

In Kraków, however, despite the urgency of the crisis, the obviousness of the educational strategies to combat it, the availability of halakhic pathways that could legitimate these strategies, and historical precedents as well as contemporary models for girls' Jewish education, nothing was done to establish a girls' school system until Sarah Schenirer took her first steps. The presence of diverse hasidic groups and the long religious history of the city may have militated against a solution there. The non-partisan character of the Tse'irei Israel bears witness to the more moderate religious profile of Lithuanian Orthodoxy. The more stringently religious and politically fractious Kraków context presented particular challenges: Torah study is not only a basic religious value for Jewish men, it is also intricately connected, within traditional Orthodoxy, to masculinity itself in its ideal form. Women's Torah study, particularly *lishmah* (for its own sake), or on a high level, or of rabbinic literature and Jewish law, was thus viscerally felt to be wrong and unnatural, in addition to its being halakhically problematic. As Daniel Boyarin writes,

> Torah study (particularly of the Talmud) was the very sign of Jewish masculinity, the quintessential performance of rabbinic Jewish maleness. In other words, precisely the stylized repetitions that produced gender differentiation (and thus cultural as well as sexual reproduction) within classical Jewish praxis were the repetitive performances of the House of Study, including the homosocial bonding . . . The House of Study was thus the rabbinic Jewish equivalent of the locker room, barracks, or warship; compare the historically similar taboos against the presence of women in those environments.[54]

Boyarin is referring here to the rabbinic culture of late antiquity, but his notion of Torah study as intricately linked with male practice in a setting that *required* the

[53] Etzion, 'Yavneh Schools in Lithuania' (Heb.), 351–70.

[54] Boyarin, *Unheroic Conduct*, 143–4. In a footnote (p. 144 n. 54), Boyarin clarifies that he believes that 'there is no essential difficulty with women coming in contact with Torah, but a structural necessity to restrict Torah study "officially" to men'.

exclusion of women (rather than simply excluding them by happenstance) certainly holds as least as true for nineteenth- and twentieth-century east European Orthodoxy, which saw impressive new types of yeshivas that were even further removed from ordinary mixed-sex environments than their precursors.[55] Sarah Schenirer thus had to face not only the political obstacles to reaching consensus faced by all activists in the Orthodox community, but also the cultural obstacles that stood in the way of a woman who threatened the exclusive bond between men and the Torah in such an 'unnatural' and 'corrupt' fashion.

Given these difficulties, how did a woman succeed where a large number of men had failed? Manekin suggests that the First World War, during which many were driven to abandon religious observance, accounts for changing rabbinic views on girls' education: 'The weakness and feelings of powerlessness of the spiritual leadership in the face of the harsh devastation dulled the controversies and weakened the opposition' to cultural efforts like Sarah Schenirer's.[56] The founding of the Polish state in 1918 also played a part in softening resistance to organized girls' education. According to Agnieszka Oleszak, the reason Bais Yaakov was enthusiastically embraced by the Kraków branch of Agudath Israel that formed in 1919, despite the fact that in 1903 the Kraków rabbinical congress had cut off discussion of the issue of girls' education, was that in the new state of Poland political conditions had changed for Orthodox Jews. Oleszak mentions the 1918 granting of female suffrage, the Agudah's involvement in Polish politics and the necessity of recruiting Orthodox voters, and 'the compulsory law of education introduced in February 1919'.[57] This recent scholarship is an important corrective to the sketchier histories that described Bais Yaakov's origins by reference solely to Sarah Schenirer. Of what significance is it, given this larger context, that 'an ordinary woman' established the girls' school in Kraków that became Bais Yaakov?

In retrospect, it could hardly have been otherwise. Iris Parush has described what she calls the 'benefit of marginality' that accrued to Jewish women in eastern Europe:

With nineteenth-century European Jewish society undergoing processes of seculariza-

[55] See Stampfer, *Families, Rabbis, and Education*, 224–6.

[56] Manekin, '"Something Entirely New"' (Heb.), 84.

[57] Oleszak, 'The Beit Ya'akov School in Kraków', 281. Support for Oleszak's argument that the Agudath Israel's adoption of Bais Yaakov was partly motivated by electoral concerns may be found in the many political advertisements in the *Bais Yaakov Journal* urging readers to vote for Agudah.

tion and modernization, the exclusion of women from Torah study and from the public religious sphere, and the redirection of them to 'inferior' forms of study and reading, turned out to be a source of advantage and of empowerment . . . Hence, women had opportunities for reading diverse texts for pleasure, freely and intimately, at a time when men were forced to struggle for a chance to read in this way, and took great risks to realize them.

Parush concludes, 'The supposedly inferior space allotted to women in both practical life and the life of culture and religion, a space meant to perpetuate their marginality, revealed itself as not merely a confining enclosure but also as room for productive maneuvering.'[58] Outside of rabbinic scrutiny, and freed from the commandment to devote every waking moment to Torah study, young women read what they pleased, a freedom that led them to secularize at a more dramatic rate than men. This 'benefit' is clearly in the background of the emergence of Bais Yaakov, a context in which the marginality of girls and women to organized religious life provided optimal conditions for women to become agents of assimilation. But marginality held some benefits for a woman inclined towards strengthening tradition, too. From this perspective, Sarah Schenirer's gender was not a handicap in achieving her goals, but rather an asset. In Kraków, divisions among the various hasidic courts and different communities, according to Manekin, led to 'incessant power struggles that made it difficult to accept decisions related to the whole community', and quickly turned halakhic problems into political ones, 'with rabbis worried about voicing opinions in ways that would arouse the wrath of stricter rivals'.[59] While Sarah Schenirer's brother was a regular at the Belzer court, hasidic affiliations were clearly held more lightly by women than men (and certainly by an unmarried woman, who lacked a husband to solidify her connection with the rebbe).[60] She found support among one of the most famously stringent of the hasidic leaders, but Bais Yaakov did not become a Belzer school, and Belz initially kept its distance from the project that had commenced with the approbation of Yissachar Dov Rokeach. While Bais Yaakov acquired the legitimacy it needed when she secured his blessing, it could avoid any identification with Belz that might limit its reach or entangle it in inter-hasidic rivalries. While men taking a stance on girls' education inevitably aligned themselves with a particular religious ideology, it was difficult to pin Sarah Schenirer down on a religious spectrum governed by male affiliations. Such an

[58] Parush, *Reading Jewish Women*, 63, 67, 70.

[59] Manekin, '"Something Entirely New"' (Heb.), 76.

[60] On this point, see Wodziński, 'Women and Hasidism', 405.

ecumenical position, transcending the fragmentation and sectarian politics of Orthodoxy, it could be argued, was available *only* to a woman.[61] The fact that the movement brought together girls from such diverse backgrounds, 'floating above' the divisions of the Orthodox world, eventually became a feature in which Bais Yaakov took much pride.[62]

Marginality held yet another benefit: Sarah Schenirer acquired the blessing of the Belzer Rebbe and the support of others in the Orthodox community without entering into the halakhic argumentation that had so vexed the 1903 rabbinical congress. It was female participation in halakhic (and particularly talmudic) argument that aroused the strongest reproach, by the Hafets Hayim and others. Avoiding halakhic argument might have been one reason for the vague phrasing of the note seeking Rokeach's blessing. Written, according to Sarah Schenirer's memoir, by her brother, the note stated only that 'she wants to lead Jewish girls along the Jewish path', thus avoiding any mention of women's Torah study (and maximizing the flexibility of the blessing she received). It is striking, in fact, that while Sarah Schenirer spoke over decades in many different forums on the issue of women's Torah study, she wrote about Bais Yaakov without once, to my knowledge, citing the *tana* Rabbi Eliezer. By contrast, the various rabbis who discussed the issue in 1903 and afterwards, including those whose writings appeared in Bais Yaakov publications, rarely failed to mention the talmudic sage's prohibition, even if they found ways to limit its application. Her failure to cite Rabbi Eliezer or other rabbinic sources on the topic would *only* have been possible for a woman. In avoiding these texts, she also avoided the unseemly spectacle of a woman quoting halakhic discussions in the Mishnah or Talmud, areas deemed beyond the purview of women by those who took the view (as Bais Yaakov does) that Rabbi Eliezer's prohibition refers to the Oral Law, or rabbinic literature. There can be no doubt that she knew these sources, even if she had not read them on a page of Talmud. She was remarkably well versed in classical Jewish literature (which, according to her memoir, she read in Yiddish translation). Moreover, Rabbi Eliezer's dictum and similar texts appeared in press stories and circulated in everyday discourse whenever the topic of girls' education came up. But even if she was familiar with this opinion, as a woman she did not *have* to

[61] As Rabbi Abraham Joseph Wolf put it, 'Bais Yaakov managed to contribute to the continuity of Polish hasidism and the Lithuanian yeshiva movement' (Wolf, 'Did Sarah Schenirer Innovate?' (Heb.), 40).

[62] For testimony about the rich diversity of the Bais Yaakov seminary cohort, see Y. Gora, 'The Early Days of the Bais Yaakov Movement' (Heb.), 166–7.

mention it, and, if she so wished, she could carry on along her way as if Rabbi Eliezer had never uttered it. In this way, her gender allowed her a kind of alibi, a strategic or principled ignorance of a rabbinic discourse that could only be damaging to her cause. Her writings assume with profound and unswerving conviction that studying Torah is a supreme value for women as for all other Jews (she also believed that study must be accompanied by deed). This attitude may have been shared by some men, but even men who felt its force were compelled, as she was not, to wrestle with Rabbi Eliezer's long shadow.

Her gender may have had yet another paradoxical benefit: it allowed her to bow to the rabbinic prohibition against teaching women Torah even while attempting to do precisely that. Rabbi Eliezer's famous dictum referred to a father teaching his daughter Torah. By contrast, female-initiated Torah study *is* permitted, and even considered to have some degree of value by such respected authorities as Maimonides.[63] Given that this project was initiated by a woman, Bais Yaakov could be understood as 'voluntary' female Torah study, albeit in collective and organized form.[64] This was not only a halakhic issue: if women were to take on the task for themselves—an idea that must have seemed inconceivable to rabbis faced with the evidence of female disaffection with Orthodoxy—no man need risk his reputation by teaching girls Torah, or recommending that they be taught Torah; nor need any man take time away from his own obligation to study Torah for the lesser responsibility of teaching girls. Even the rabbinic opinion that women who study Torah receive a lesser reward might be taken as evidence that their Torah study is purer, since it is done for its own sake rather than for reward![65]

Sarah Schenirer was not able to avoid halakhic argument completely. In the years that followed the founding of Bais Yaakov, she was often required to defend

[63] *Mishneh torah*, Laws of Talmud Torah 1: 13.

[64] That men need not concern themselves with women's voluntary Torah study came to the fore in a letter written in the 1980s by the American halakhist Rabbi Moshe Feinstein (through his grandson and secretary Rabbi Mordechai Tendler) to Rabbi Meir Fund, in which Feinstein responded to a question about a women's Mishnah study group, saying that 'men do not need to concern themselves with what women do'. Feinstein asked how the biblical Deborah reached her position as judge. 'Obviously'—he answered his own rhetorical question—she was self-taught, and 'that is not one of the great sins against which one must protest'. Cited in Fuchs, *Jewish Women's Torah Study*, 114.

[65] While I have no direct evidence that this perspective was explicitly voiced in the interwar period, it was expressed in an Internet forum on Orthodox women's Torah study recorded and analysed in Bechhofer, 'Ongoing Constitution of Identity', 243–4.

the movement against those who challenged its legitimacy on halakhic grounds, for instance in the public meetings that served as a first step to the establishment of a Bais Yaakov in a small town. As Dr Leo Deutschländer said in a memorial speech after her death (and shortly before his own), she was sometimes required to use 'the tactics of a man', by which he meant not only that she held her own in public debates with hasidic fathers, but also that she did so by quoting rabbinic sources and halakhic discussions: 'How many times did she have to show a talmudic passage to true Jewish men, hasidic fathers, or Orthodox bureaucrats, reminding them of a *midrash*, citing a great sage', in order to persuade them of the legitimacy of her mission?[66] While she did not cite such texts to defend girls' Torah study in her writings, there are a few passages in her *Collected Writings* that show her approach to halakhah more generally. In the 1929 article celebrating the founding of a women's Agudah organization (which became Neshei Agudath Israel, often referred to simply as 'Neshei') at the World Congress of Agudath Israel, she defended the new organization against those who considered women's political visibility to be immodest by citing the dictum 'now is the time' (*et la'asot*), the shorthand phrase for the principle mentioned above, also known as *hora'at sha'ah*, a phrase that loosely translates as 'the exigencies of the time', which permits recourse to otherwise forbidden practices when circumstances demand. She also appealed to this principle, as she relates in her memoir, to alleviate her pangs of conscience when observing that male supporters were slighting their own obligation to study Torah in order to help in her work. But while she was clearly familiar with the principle of *hora'at sha'ah* (and perhaps took it as her unspoken warrant for the Bais Yaakov mission), she only used it very sparingly, avoiding it entirely in her discussion of the central aim and practice of Bais Yaakov. In this way, she forged a powerful rhetoric about the value of Torah study for all Jews that was untouched by rabbinic scepticism about women's learning, halakhic regret about the necessity for abandoning traditional approaches to the question of girls' education, and the appearance of having overthrown a rabbinic prohibition—even on the grounds of urgency.

Evidence that Sarah Schenirer's avoidance of halakhic argumentation was a principled stance rather than a sign of ignorance or lack of intellectual sophistication is perhaps clearest in her 1929 article describing the founding of the international organization of Agudah women, in which she touched on the topic of the *agunah*.[67] The problem had reached crisis point during the First World War and its

[66] Deutschländer, 'Sarah Schenirer and Bais Yaakov' (Yid.), 6.

[67] The *agunah* is a Jewish woman who is 'chained' to an absent husband, either because he

aftermath, when war casualties, displacement, and migration combined to create a surge of *agunot*. Jewish social agencies were founded to help care for women and children impoverished by the lack of a male provider, but some in the Jewish world also called upon rabbis to set these 'chained' women free, to enable them to remarry, through halakhic means. Among the women's organizations that spoke out on this issue in the 1920s were the Frauenbund, the Zionist women's organization WIZO, and the Polish Yiddish Froyen Asotsiyatsia (Polish Jewish Women's Association), led by Puah Rakovsky. In addressing the issue of the *agunah*, Sarah Schenirer did not appeal to the principle of *hora'at sha'ah* to argue for rabbinic action on this matter, although she used the principle to legitimate the public gathering of Agudah women (which presumably fell under much less clear rules about women's public visibility and political organization). She insisted that the Orthodox inability to resolve the issue of a woman 'chained' to an absent husband had nothing to do with Orthodox indifference to her plight, since 'no one takes the pain of the *agunah* more seriously than we do'. The situation rather represented an acknowledgement of what Jewish law made clear, and which no rabbi could reverse. However pained Orthodox women might be by the situation of the *agunah*, 'we also know that the Torah and Jewish law are supreme. And that is why we religious women, in just the same way as religious men, submit to the Torah and Jewish law, which always works for our benefit and happiness.' While other groups might challenge the rabbis in the name of women's rights, such groups did not and could never represent the Orthodox woman, who stood alongside the Orthodox man in stalwart defence of the Torah.

As an article in the *Bais Yaakov Journal* noted, 1929 was an active year for Jewish women's organizations. Aside from the Bnos conference in Łódź, and the Vienna Women's Conference that was part of the second World Congress of Agudath Israel (11–17 September), Hamburg hosted the World Congress of Jewish Women on 4–6 June, and the Women's International Zionist Organization (WIZO) met in Zurich from 23 to 26 July. The *agunah* issue was an important topic of concern for all the women's organizations that sponsored these conferences, along with the related problems of child abandonment, poverty, and prostitution.[68] Bertha

refuses to grant her a divorce or because he has disappeared, and she therefore cannot remarry. Because there is no prohibition in the Torah against a man having two wives, only a woman can be an *agunah*. The suffering of *agunot* prompted some religious authorities to seek halakhic solutions to the problem, particularly during the First World War. Treatises on the topic include Yosef Engel's *Sefer otserot yosef* (Vienna, 1921).

[68] See A.L., 'Łódź, Hamburg, Warsaw' (Yid.), 1.

Pappenheim, the Frauenbund leader, petitioned rabbis to modernize marriage, divorce, and inheritance laws for the sake of the approximately 20,000 *agunot* in eastern Europe who 'were living in misery, in danger of being lured or tricked into fake marriages and eventual prostitution'.[69] At the 1927 International Conference for the Protection of Jewish Girls and Women in London (which Dr Deutschländer attended on behalf of the Agudah), Pappenheim spoke bitterly and forcefully about the failure of the rabbinate to address this issue:

> We have at this meeting several rabbis from Eastern Europe, and I had hoped that they would listen to us, and do something to improve the difficult position of so many Jewish women. It is not only a question of *'agunoh'*, but also of facilitating divorce. I had hoped that a Sanhedrin of Rabbis would come together, and that they would introduce the needful ritual reforms, and re-organize Jewish ceremonial dealing with this matter. That is what I had hoped, but I have been told that we must not expect it, for the Rabbis do not have the power or the authority to introduce the changes asked for. In that case we must continue to flounder within this *'golus'* [exile], but it is a *'golus'* within a *'golus'*.[70]

As other writings make even clearer, Pappenheim was not persuaded that the rabbis were truly powerless to address the problem of the *agunah*; she was particularly offended that rabbis seemed willing to reform Jewish law to make business dealings easier, while claiming that the same could not be done to ease the way for women.[71]

[69] Kaplan, 'Bertha Pappenheim', 157. For these activities, Kaplan cites *Blätter des jüdischen Frauenbunds* (July 1936), 21. On Pappenheim's work on behalf of Bais Yaakov and her visit to the school shortly before her death, see Pappenheim, 'Kleine Reise-Notiz', 1–2, and the account of her meeting in Frankfurt with Agudah leaders in January 1936 described in H. K., 'Beth-Jacob-Schul-Werk', 27. See also Rosenheim, 'New Tasks for Bais Yaakov and Bnos' (Yid.), 38.

[70] Jewish Association for the Protection of Girls and Women, *Official Report*, 50. The German neo-Orthodox Rabbi Meyer Hildesheimer, who spoke after Pappenheim, protested that many rabbis indeed sympathized with the plight of the *agunah*, but were restrained by the limits of what could be done within Jewish law. Dr Deutschländer, who spoke later in the conference, pointed to his presence as evidence that Orthodox Jews cared very deeply about the *agunah* and other women's issues, and recommended educating girls as a solution to the involvement of Jewish women in sex trafficking. Despite these responses, the Frauenbund did not give up the notion of convening a rabbinical conference to deal with marriage reform, sending a petition demanding such a conference to the same 1929 World Congress of the Agudah at which the women's branch was founded. A report on the congress attests that the topic was discussed, the inviolable sacredness of Jewish marriage bond affirmed, and a resolution on the *agunah* problem postponed to another meeting. See 'After the Second World Congress', 2–3, for an account by a participant.

[71] See Kaplan, *The Jewish Feminist Movement in Poland*, 117. The problem perceived by Pappenheim and other activists was double: it was too difficult for women to obtain a divorce, thus trapping *agunot* in a cycle of poverty. But it was also too easy to enter into a Jewish marriage, since

While it may have been Pappenheim whom Sarah Schenirer had in mind when she excoriated those who 'put forth various resolutions that stand in absolute contradiction to the ideals and aspirations of religious women', there were also Polish women who fought on behalf of *agunot*. One of these was Puah Rakovsky's friend and collaborator Leah (Levin-Epstein) Proshansky, who wrote on the subject for the Warsaw-based monthly *Froyen Shtim*, the periodical of the Yiddishe Froyen Asotsiatsiya.[72] The inaugural issue of the journal called attention to the problem of *agunot*, referring particularly to men who had left their families to emigrate. Proshansky's article on the subject later that same year excoriated such husbands for leaving their flesh and blood to suffer hunger and poverty but reserved its harshest criticism for the rabbinic leadership that treated the problem with indifference. While rabbis were quick to criticize women for succumbing to immodest fashion trends, they were silent in the face of the greater evil of abandonment, the circumstance that led some women to take up prostitution to feed their families. Proshansky was clearly an educated woman, versed in the classical Hebrew sources and the intricacies of Jewish law; the article is sprinkled with biblical references and learned rabbinic citations, sometimes in Aramaic, which were explained in footnotes for less educated readers. Like Rakovsky, Proshansky may have been raised in an Orthodox home where she received a strong Jewish education. Alternatively, by 1925 there were already institutions, including Yehudiah and some Tarbut schools in which Talmud was taught, where a girl could acquire an impressive set of Jewish textual skills, including in rabbinic literature.

In her essay, Proshansky directly takes on the notion that the Polish rabbinate sympathized with abandoned women but was unable to help them in a circumstance so clearly hedged by Jewish law (her stance might be paraphrased by a

Jewish law stipulated that a marriage could be contracted by a man bestowing a ring on a woman in the presence of two witnesses; no rabbi need be present. Sex traffickers took advantage of this to seduce women into prostitution, and reformers looked for ways to make it harder to enter Jewish marriage. On these marriages, see Bristow, *Prostitution and Prejudice*, 103–6.

[72] *Froyen Shtim*, edited by Rakovsky, began to appear in 1925—not long after the *Bais Yaakov Journal*. According to Hyman, the YFA was initiated by 'Rokhl Stein, who became its chairperson, Leah Proshansky, and Puah Rakovsky, who had called for the establishment of such an organization in her 1918 pamphlet, *Di yidishe froy*. In contrast to the Bundist YAF (Yidisher Arbeter Froy), which came into being in 1925, the YFA was middle-class in its membership, independent of all political parties though not apolitical, and Zionist in its orientation . . . YFA's goals included organizing women to secure economic and political rights as well as equal opportunities for education, and providing assistance to the vast number of needy among Polish Jewry.' See Hyman, 'Yiddishe Froyen Asotsiatsiya'.

well-known quote ascribed to a later American Orthodox feminist, Blu Greenberg: 'Where there was rabbinic will, there was a halakhic way.'[73] In Proshansky's words, rabbinic literature is full of halakhic accommodations to urgent circumstances. She mentions as an example *heter iska*, the rabbinic ruling rendering it permissible to lend money with interest despite a biblical prohibition; it was just such flexibility in regard to business matters that Pappenheim noted. For men saddled with mentally ill wives, rabbis found a way (known as the *heter me'ah rabanim*, the permission of a hundred rabbis) to allow the husband to divorce his wife without her consent. The general principle of *piku'aḥ nefesh doḥeh shabat*, which states that in a life-and-death situation even the sabbath may be desecrated, should also apply to these women, whose situation is one of equally extreme need. Finally, Proshansky writes, the principle of *et la'asot* might also prod rabbis—if they deigned to concern themselves with women's issues—to find a solution that would allow such women to remarry.[74] Proshansky's article makes clear that there were feminists in Sarah Schenirer's immediate context who were thoroughly comfortable with halakhic argumentation, and had no problem criticizing rabbis and the Orthodox leadership. It is no surprise, then, that at the very first moments of the establishment of an organization that could represent Orthodox women, Sarah Schenirer felt the need to defend Orthodoxy against the charge that it disregarded these issues and to insist that other organizations not claim to speak on behalf of all Jewish women. While Pappenheim and Proshansky used their Jewish cultural capital to advocate ways to free the *agunah*, Sarah Schenirer refrained from citing Jewish sources in a way that could be understood as criticizing rabbis.

Her avoidance of halakhic discourse in this and other situations was undeniably sincere, but it also worked to further her project. Unlike Proshansky and her virtuoso talmudic performance, she did not infringe on the rabbis' exclusive ownership of talmudic expertise. Her reluctance to enter this discussion should not only be read as modest self-exclusion; it also freed her to operate in a different realm. The question of women's Torah study, after all, was intricately connected to one of the most disturbing sections of rabbinic literature: the ordeal undergone by the woman suspected of adultery to determine her innocence or guilt. The passage in BT *Sotah* 20*a* that ends with Rabbi Eliezer's words begins with a graphic and grotesque description of the effects of the bitter waters on a guilty woman: 'She had scarcely finished drinking when her face turned green, her eyes

[73] Greenberg, *On Women and Judaism*, 44.

[74] Proshansky, 'On Abandoned Women' (Yid.), 12–13.

protruded and her veins swelled, and it was proclaimed: "Remove her lest the Temple court be defiled!"' The rabbis of Sarah Schenirer's more immediate environment also regularly brought up the sexual transgressions of contemporary Jewish women, although they did so in service of forging permission to permit girls to study Torah. The question of women's Torah study was thus embedded for both the rabbis of late antiquity and their twentieth-century successors in a discourse that associated women with *tiflut*. Ilan Fuchs describes the meaning of this term:

> A single word with an elusive etymology, *tiflut* becomes extraordinarily elastic, expanding at will to encompass a variety of female types. It may vibrate with seduction and promiscuity, accuse of innate cognitive limitations, occasionally both at the same time. Intuitively faithful, yet an intellectual lightweight unable to master complex analysis and logic, a woman may still be a potential adulteress should she learn 'cunning' from Torah . . . The image of woman as faithful Jew engaging sacred texts occurs historically only in narratives of exceptional women or in lists of the female luminaries of Jewish history, emerging only in recent decades as an ideal for women as a class.[75]

But as Rabbi Landau noted at the 1903 conference, the pressing issue of girls' defection from Orthodoxy demanded more than a rabbinic warrant to educate Jewish girls. What was required was also a discourse that could attract these girls, a literature that would 'arouse in their hearts love of the Torah and tradition' and help combat their absorption in romantic novels. As Rabbi Landau clearly saw, the Polish rabbinate lacked the ability to speak to women.[76] A woman who could avoid citing Rabbi Eliezer and his peers (and who understood the allure of modern literature) had greater hopes of inspiring the younger generation than a man who had been trained to consider the problem only through a halakhic lens.

Sarah Schenirer may also have found success where others did not because her new idea was clothed, as it were, in traditional garb. By all accounts, her traditional appearance and her unimpeachable piety reassured those who worried about the novelty of women's Torah study. Even the neo-Orthodox influence, which she was always careful to credit, did not come embodied, in her case, in the modern garb of the German rabbis with doctoral degrees who made strides with educational reforms in both Warsaw and Lithuania, much less in the overtly feminist discourse of such activists as Bertha Pappenheim, despite the overlap in their lives and work.[77] Nor to my knowledge did she ever mention, in her excoria-

[75] Fuchs, *Jewish Women's Torah Study*, 227–8.

[76] Landau, *Mekits nirdamim*, 56.

[77] Boyarin calls Schenirer Pappenheim's 'younger counterpart and eventual associate', suggesting that the sermon Schenirer heard from Rabbi Flesch may have been a result of Pappen-

tions of the evils of modernity, the international white slave trade, although the central offices of the Bais Yaakov movement in Vienna and London often spoke of the schools as part of the struggle to protect young women from the sex traffic.[78] German neo-Orthodoxy was introduced to Kraków through a Polish woman, and already imbued with Sarah Schenirer's traditionalism. Such an attire must have inspired confidence in the eyes of the first men who were moved to support her project. The solution, when it came, was not imposed from without, or decided from above, but rather grew from native soil, from the world of Orthodox women themselves. As Rachel Manekin writes: 'After seventeen years in which the issue [of girls' education] remained atop the public agenda, during which time everyone was anticipating that change would come from the rabbinic leadership, Schenirer undertook the work from below, at the grass-roots level.'[79]

Manekin actually finds it hard to believe Sarah Schenirer's account of the 1914 epiphany in Vienna, given that she was already 31 years old by that winter and had lived for nearly her entire life in a city where girls' education was a subject of near-obsessive public discussion. Stronger evidence that the idea of leading Orthodox girls back to Torah came to her before 1914 can be found in the extracts from her Polish diary as presented in translation in the present volume, which demonstrate that she formed a hope—if not a plan—of bringing Jewish girls back to Orthodoxy as early as 1908. In a 1910 diary entry described as 'the last day

heim's feminist activism, and noting that 'Bertha Pappenheim's last public activity was to take a trip to Cracow for a meeting of the Board of Trustees of the Bais Yaakov movement' (*Unheroic Conduct*, 336).

[78] See, for instance, the quote from Rebekah Kohut in Deutschländer, *The History of the Beth Jacob Girls Schools*, 5: 'Bajs Jakob will destroy the menace of moral destruction which is facing hundreds of daughters of poverty-strucken [*sic*] Eastern European Jewry, all of which was discussed in London in 1928, at an international conference [on white slavery].' Kohut may be referring to the second Jewish International Conference on White Slavery, which was held in London on 22–24 June 1927 (not 1928), which Deutschländer attended as an Agudah representative, and at which he made important connections with Bertha Pappenheim and other feminists. The stationery of the Bais Yaakov Central Office in Vienna in the early 1930s bore the masthead 'The Girls' Association "Bais Yaakov", for the Education, Cultivation, and Protection of Jewish Girls'. As is clear from the wide network of supporters of Bais Yaakov (which included Eleanor Roosevelt, for instance), Jewish and women's organizations who were otherwise uninterested in Orthodox initiatives considered Bais Yaakov an important means of defence against the traffic in Polish Jewish girls and women. Even the President of Poland, Ignacy Mościcki, praised Bais Yaakov during a visit to the Rabka summer colony in 1929 by saying that it 'saves our maidenhood from moral and religious dangers and from political radicalism'. See Atkin, *The Beth Jacob Movement in Poland*, 119.

[79] Manekin, '"Something Entirely New"' (Heb.), 80.

before my wedding', she laments the bitter fate that will keep her from acting on her long-cherished dream:

When I think about that, I just can't stop crying. But maybe I should be brave enough to say: 'No! I don't want to!' Only you, you my diary, allow me to express it all, even as you keep silent, stubbornly silent. And my ideal, somewhere in my soul, is only to work for my sisters! Oh, if I could only persuade them one day what it means to be a true Jewish woman, who doesn't do things just because of her mother or because she's afraid of her father, but only out of true love for the Creator himself, who has elevated us above all of the nations and sanctified us with his commandments. Ah! If I could manage to do that, I would be so happy, a hundred times happier than any millionaire. Have I lost my mind? Now, in this era of progress, I dream about something like that.

The diary is evidence that she had conceived a plan to work with Orthodox girls by 1908, in Kraków rather than in Vienna. But it also describes this dream as an inexpressible and impossible one, shared only with an anthropomorphized diary that serves as sole companion not only against a hostile world, but also against traditional parents who fail to understand her. While Bais Yaakov literature often portrays her as the perfect daughter of a respectable and distinguished traditional family, she seems to have also felt disconnected from and misunderstood by her parents, although she did not consider defecting from Orthodoxy, but rather concealed a sense of religious mission that contradicted her parents' expectations. Nor did she consider it necessary (until her brother suggested it) to find support for her plan among the rabbis of her time, despite Manekin's suggestion that 'everyone was anticipating that change would come from the rabbinic leadership'. Far from hoping to find male supporters for her project (although eventually she did), she feared that marriage would spell the end of her dream. In this she was right: results were achieved only when she, a solitary woman working outside both the network of Orthodox leadership and the institution of Orthodox marriage, set to work teaching Jewish girls Torah.

If she did not get the idea of leading Jewish girls back to Torah observance from Rabbi Flesch's inspiring sermon, how can we understand its role in her account of Bais Yaakov's origins? What did she hear on that sabbath morning in late 1914, and what did it come to mean to her and to the founding narrative of Bais Yaakov? She claimed not to remember the details of Flesch's sermon, but she knew that it involved the biblical figure of Judith, a brave widow who saves her brethren from the general Holofernes and, though courted by many following this heroic deed, remains unmarried.[80]

[80] On Judith, see n. 2 above. Joseph Friedenson, in an essay on Bais Yaakov, recounts the story of

Sarah Schenirer was not a widow but a divorcee that Hanukah (her 1910 marriage to Shmuel Nussbaum was over by 1913), and her diary entry attests to her belief that only an unattached woman might have the freedom to devote herself to the work she hoped to accomplish. Rabbi Flesch's sermon did not give her the idea of teaching girls Torah; there is no hint that he mentioned girls' education, and we know that she had been thinking about this issue for years. But he supplied a rabbinic warrant and model, simultaneously modern and traditional, for heroic female initiative in the face of male paralysis, praising a Jewish woman who zealously defended the tradition of her people in the absence of men. In praising Judith, Flesch was bestowing rabbinic approbation on both the biblical heroine and the female worshippers in his synagogue. The address to the women of the congregation that Sarah Schenirer heard demarcated a potential path between the world of Orthodox Jewish men and that of girls and women, one that did not require rabbinical approval (though clearly she needed that as well), but rather finding a man who encouraged women to act on their own. That this path led through Vienna was no coincidence: Bais Yaakov drew from German neo-Orthodoxy in many ways, and it made sense for her to give credit for inspiring the movement to the rabbi who introduced her, after that first sermon, to the thought of Samson Raphael Hirsch in the evening lectures she regularly attended. But it is also significant that she did not consider Hirsch's Frankfurt *Realschule* a viable model for Bais Yaakov, which needed to conform to the stricter gender segregation of Polish Orthodoxy.[81] The lesson she learned on that sabbath morning was not that German neo-Orthodoxy could provide Polish Jews with a model of girls' religious education, but rather that a pious and determined Polish woman could find her own way to do what others had previously failed to do.

She makes it clear in her memoir that even as she was inspired by the content of Rabbi Flesch's sermon, she was also taken aback by its form. Her Polish

Rabbi Flesch's sermon but substitutes the rabbinic tale of Hannah and her seven sons for that of Judith, although Schenirer does not mention Hannah in her account of the sermon. This may reflect, perhaps unconsciously, the tendency of later Bais Yaakov discourse to domesticate Schenirer and the schools' students by substituting, in this case, a selfless mother for a childless (as far as we know) widow who decapitates a foreign general. It is also true that Hannah's story is better known than Judith's. See 'The Bais Yaakov Girls' Schools' (Heb.), 63.

[81] According to Grunfeld, when she attended the *Realschule* (1908–18), 'The school was housed in two large buildings connected on every floor by a hall. Dr Lange went from the boys' building to the girls' side through the halls. Both buildings held ten classes of approximately thirty pupils each' (Rubin (ed.), *Daughters of Destiny*, 121).

upbringing had failed to prepare her for a modern-style sermon by a Viennese *Rabbiner* (as she calls Rabbi Flesch),[82] especially one which so directly addressed female congregants. Jewish women warranted the attention of the Polish Orthodox rabbinate primarily when their behaviour was brazen enough to attract notice. Halakhic discourse around their education was rarely separable from rabbinic anxieties (anchored in talmudic discourse) over women's sexuality. But the story of Judith presented a woman who was better—less fearful, more trusting in God, and certainly less light-headed—than the men around her, and who earned their respect and admiration (after initial opposition). As Shoshana Bechhofer writes, 'Judith had to take on a male role (warrior) to save the Jewish nation. This allusion was not lost upon Sarah Schenirer; this is the moment when she decided to emulate Judith's heroism and started to plan a girls' school.'[83]

Lavish praise of Jewish women, past and present, became a staple of Bais Yaakov literature, not only in the stories of 'Great Jewish Women' of the past that filled the pages of the *Bais Yaakov Journal* but, more strikingly, in the admiring impressions visiting Agudah leaders recorded of the seminary girls. As we have seen, in revising Rabbi Eliezer's dictum, the Gemara '"hastens to defend the holiness of the Torah" from the imputation that it could become *tiflut* under any conditions'.[84] But the German neo-Orthodox discourse developed by Hirsch and his followers was interested in chivalry not only with regard to the Torah, but also towards women, in accordance with the dictates of the polite bourgeois discourse of the period. East European rabbis were less practised in this chivalry, but, given the new phenomenon of Bais Yaakov, they caught on quickly, and praise for women is on full display in the literature of the movement. Joseph Friedenson, a historian of Bais Yaakov, an Agudah journalist, and son of the editor of the *Bais Yaakov Journal*, cites an account of girls learning Torah in the

[82] Schenirer uses the German term for rabbi here, indicating her awareness that he was a 'modern', neo-Orthodox rabbi in the German sense, rather than the sort of rabbi whom she would have been accustomed to in Poland. In fact, Rabbi Moses David Flesch was born and educated in Pressburg (now Bratislava), Czechoslovakia, in the militant Orthodox community that arose around the Hatam Sofer, before he moved to Frankfurt to study with Rabbi Salomon Breuer (who was also a student in Pressburg), and finally to Vienna to become rabbi of the Stumpergasse synagogue.

[83] Bechhofer, 'Ongoing Constitution of Identity', 65. Bechhofer reads the ideological pressures that have transformed the memory of Schenirer in contemporary Bais Yaakov, but does not discuss the striking fact that, in a significant number of retellings, the figure of Judith is replaced with either the Maccabees, in which male warriors save the Jewish people, or the story of Hannah and her seven sons, in which a mother sacrifices her sons for the sake of the Torah rather than beheading a foreign general.

[84] Biale, *Women and Jewish Law*, 34.

summer colony of Rabka as 'reminiscent of a yeshiva, where students learn Torah for its own sake'. Among a group of 200 Bais Yaakov teachers assembled in the colony, 'the thirst to learn and absorb what was learned was primary among them, and everything else was of no importance. They bemoaned every moment lost, and implored their teachers to keep teaching.'[85] Such descriptions cast Bais Yaakov students in terms that are more commonly used to refer to men—*torah lishmah* (for its own sake), or refraining from *bitul torah*, time-wasting activities that detract from Torah study. These qualities of unceasing devotion to Torah study are the highest praise available in rabbinic idiom, and Bais Yaakov eventually earned this reputation from Torah-educated men. But it was Rabbi Flesch's sermon that opened the way for an Orthodox literature that competed to praise Jewish women, as well as the more particular development of the religious admiration of Orthodox men for young women, precisely in the arena previously reserved for male accomplishment.

Rabbi Flesch's sermon, along with the lectures that Sarah Schenirer attended in the following months, might also be seen as the first instance of what would become standard Bais Yaakov practice, especially in the seminaries and summer programme, of lectures and classes taught by men. Among the many distinguished lecturers that the Vienna-based Agudah organization Keren Hatorah provided for the summer colonies were Jacob Rosenheim, president of the world Agudah; New York rabbi Leo Jung; and the Yiddish linguistics professor and Orthodox activist Dr Shlomo Birnbaum. Rabbi Flesch was the first of these to demonstrate the potential influence men could exert on young Polish Jewish women, whose experiences with rabbis and hasidic leaders were closer to that of Sarah Schenirer, who had to travel at her own expense to deliver a note, through her brother, to the Belzer Rebbe.

Evidence that she saw herself as a woman who stepped in, like Judith, to fill a male vacuum may be gleaned from an anecdote that appears in various forms in Bais Yaakov literature and is cited in the epigraph to this chapter. In Pearl Benisch's account:

> On one occasion [Schenirer] mentioned to a few older students the passage in *Pirkei Avos* (Ethics of the Fathers), *Be-makom sha-ein anashim, histadel lihiyos ish*—'in a place where there are no men, try to be a man'. 'There are times, there are communities', she said, 'where there are no men to care. Then you must stand up and be the "man" who takes responsibility into his own hands', she added apologetically. Yes, she became a Torah

[85] J. Friedenson, 'The Bais Yaakov Girls' Schools' (Heb.), 74.

giant who revolutionized the Jewish world with the novel idea of Torah education for girls.[86]

Leo Deutschländer, in the speech quoted above, similarly said that 'at times, when defending the Bais Yaakov movement she had founded and nurtured, she was required to use the tactics of a man to fend off the opposition of parents and activists who were too short-sighted to see the bold vision of Bais Yaakov'.[87] In the narrow sense, Deutschländer meant that she was forced to make a halakhic argument for the permissibility of her project, but his words could also refer to her leadership more generally. Benisch's translation of the maxim from *Pirkei avot* actually introduces an element of gendered language to the text, whereas the original Hebrew phrase could be read as: 'try to be a human being [*or* leader] even where others have lost their sense of humanity [*or* failed to lead]'. In its application to Sarah Schenirer's 'masculine' initiative, it might be rendered as, 'where there is no man, [even a woman should] try to be a man'. With this radical, midrash-like reading of *Pirkei avot*, Sarah Schenirer establishes a principle whereby a woman might—and should—step into a role left vacant by all male candidates, even if she does so regretfully or 'apologetically'. The 'Torah giants' of her day were not indifferent to the tragic situation of the girls, but rather—we might infer from Rabbi Landau's record of the 1903 rabbinical congress—deeply ashamed of their impotence in the face of public scandals that opened the hasidic and Orthodox worlds to mockery and demonstrated how powerless they were over girls and women. We can take Rabbi Landau at his word when he speaks of the 'fire that consumes my bones and the open wounds on my heart' when thinking of such shameful defections.[88] Nevertheless, the religious culture in which these rabbis operated and their fear of not being heeded prevented them from responding effectively to this crisis. From Sarah Schenirer's perspective, their inability to act may well have added up to the same thing, the neglect of the problem of girls' Jewish education. The rabbinic retreat left the field open for an enterprising woman who acted where they could not.

There were other Orthodox educational initiatives for girls that emerged in this period, including Havatselet in Warsaw and the Yavneh school system in Lithuania. Both these systems were aided by rabbis from the German neo-Orthodox tradition, who arrived in the wake of the German occupying army to help the Orthodox communities in the east respond to the challenges of

[86] Benisch, *Carry Me in Your Heart*, 27. Benisch cites *Pirkei avot* 2: 5.

[87] Deutschländer, 'Sarah Schenirer and Bais Yaakov' (Yid.), 6.

[88] Landau, *Mekits nirdamim*, 52.

modernity. Havatselet began as a modern and professional form of religious education for girls, supported by the know-how of Rabbi Dr Pinchas Cohen and Rabbi Dr Joseph Carlebach. The group of young men that initiated the Yavneh school system also took it upon themselves to get western-trained support in their aim of educating themselves in worldly knowledge, including from Leo Deutschländer, later a supporter of Bais Yaakov. In the case of Bais Yaakov, this assistance from the west happened somewhat differently. Rather than central European male activists and leaders coming east to spread their message, a Polish woman went west, was inspired by the teachings of a follower of the Hirschian school, and brought these teachings home, taking them on as her own. Bais Yaakov too would soon require and accept professional assistance, and quickly enough become embedded in the hierarchical and male-dominated world of the international organization of Orthodox Jewry, the Agudah. By 1925, this process—the subject of the third chapter of this book—was well under way. So too would it welcome the support of more progressive Orthodox feminists like Pappenheim, who spent a week at the Kraków seminary in the autumn of 1935, giving her professional opinion on how to improve the system.[89] But none of these organizations or collaborators were present at the outset, and Sarah Schenirer proceeded without institutional support or collaboration. For all the difficulties of this enterprise in its first few years, its grass-roots beginnings remained a source of symbolic power long after the institutionalization of Bais Yaakov, providing the channels that could connect girls with local traditions and securing this attachment with that rarest of creatures—a 'Torah giant' who was also a woman.

[89] On Bertha Pappenheim's report on this trip see n. 69 above.

CHAPTER TWO

'A New Thing that Our Ancestors Never Imagined'
Beginnings (1917–1924)

We do not count ourselves among those who cherish novelty; for us, 'a new thing that our ancestors never imagined' is a flaw.

RABBI ABRAHAM JOSEPH WOLF[1]

AT ITS HEIGHT in the interwar period, Bais Yaakov generated an abundance of reports, periodicals, and other literature. But for a description of the earliest days of the movement, nearly all that exists comes from the writings of Sarah Schenirer. The stories she told were circulated, amplified, censored, and imbued with the character of legend or tale, becoming a myth of origins that emerged from these beginnings and that in turn kept these memories alive. The mythical character of the accounts of Bais Yaakov's origins has been often noted. Joanna Lisek remarks that she was already a legend in her own time, and compares the stories that circulated in eastern Europe about this 'simple seamstress' who achieved greatness with the legends told of early hasidic leaders.[2] Even those who knew her well and worked with her personally could hardly refrain from speaking in such terms. In a 1953 essay, Judith Grunfeld-Rosenbaum introduces her account of the first years of Bais Yaakov by saying, 'Now we have come to the part of the story that sounds rather like an old-fashioned fairy tale, when the dressmaker turns overnight into a teacher and the workshop into a schoolroom, and the customers, instead of sending in their orders, send their children to be pupils of this school.'[3] Miriam Dansky, in a biography of Grunfeld-Rosenbaum, is similarly self-conscious about retelling 'the famous central story' about Sarah Schenirer's efforts, describing it as 'the equivalent of a secular "rags to riches" story—a spiritual success story. The early difficult beginnings, the struggles, and then at long last the universal recognition, the overflowing blessing of

[1] Wolf, 'Did Sarah Schenirer Innovate?' (Heb.), 37.
[2] Lisek, 'Orthodox Yiddishism', 130.
[3] Grunfeld-Rosenbaum, 'Sara Schenierer', 414.

[Schenirer's] labor.'[4] In a much earlier reflection on the mythical origins of Bais Yaakov, Elimelech Steyer suggests that the movement's success depended on the fairy-tale quality of its foundational myth, which was a prime source of the attraction of Bais Yaakov in a cultural arena comprising legends and dreams:

> I remember those days as if in a dream. Galicia, just after the end of the First World War . . . Young women moved about the streets of their *shtetls* like sleepwalkers. Girls with dreamy eyes and long braids, their hearts split within them. They were torn between secular culture and literature and the dreams and legends of secular nationalism.
>
> It was an era of legend.
>
> And then Sarah Schenirer appeared in the *shtetl* squares. And she, too, was a legend.
>
> Only by means of a legend was it possible to fight against legends.[5]

In analysing the literary and mythical character of the legend, Steyer delicately hints at the rivalry between mainstream Orthodoxy and its prime competitor for the devotion of Orthodox youth, Zionism, which similarly mobilized the power of legends or dreams in a slogan attributed to Theodor Herzl: 'If you will it, it is no dream.' To counter the dreams spun by the secular ideologues of Jewish nationalism required an equally powerful legend, one that could appeal to the dreamers and sleepwalkers of the Jewish street. The prose of rabbinic decisions and conference resolutions traced in the previous chapter was an important part of the landscape from which Bais Yaakov emerged, and this rabbinic rhetoric would soon penetrate deep into the growing movement. But the appeal of the movement also depended in some hard-to-measure degree, and certainly among dreamy young girls, on the allure of its central story, the legend of the seamstress who began a school with twenty-five young pupils, and ended up founding a movement that revived Orthodox Judaism at a moment of grave peril.

Despite the near-sacred status of Sarah Schenirer's memoir and other autobiographical writings, retellings of the myth of Bais Yaakov's origins regularly omit some details of her account. As with the two parallel biblical descriptions of the creation of the first woman in Genesis, the movement seems to have not one, but two beginnings. According to her memoir, her dream of bringing Orthodox girls back to Torah did not entail founding a school but rather reaching out to adolescents through lectures, a youth movement, and a library. By November 1916, she reports, she had established an Orthodox Girls' Union, delivered 'beautiful' public lectures to young audiences, and was assembling a library for which she 'shipped the reading material from Frankfurt—the works of Samson Raphael

[4] Dansky, *Rebbetzin Grunfeld*, 78, 83.

[5] Eliezer Steyer, 'We Were as Dreamers' (Heb.), 60.

Hirsch, Marcus Lehmann, and others of that sort'.[6] While she succeeded in inspiring young women in many ways, they nevertheless remained unmoved when she turned to the importance of Jewish observance; her words on this topic prompted 'ironic smiles on many of their faces', prompting her to write:

> The truth is that I wasn't entirely happy with my newly founded Orthodox Girls' Union. The activities of the Union were impressive enough, and the members listened to my lectures with enthusiasm and took an interest in the ideas I expressed . . .
>
> Yes, the girls were inspired by a beautiful talk, charmed by an exalted thought, moved by a poetic passage in the Bible. But despite that, they still couldn't submit to the commandments of Jewish law and fulfil the Torah. And no wonder: most of the members were already young women, and it wasn't easy to persuade them to take on a new, truly Jewish life, with its customs and traditions.

Given the limits of what could be accomplished with young women, she came to the conclusion that 'One had to begin with children . . . I would have to start schools for young girls.'

Educating Jewish girls, as we have seen, was not a new idea. Previous discussions of ways that the Orthodox community could combat the defection of its young women had all revolved around the establishing of organized schools for girls. Sarah Schenirer soon enough followed this very path, and her successes stand as evidence for its logic and efficacy. Why, then, did she not follow that route in the first place? Neo-Orthodoxy in central Europe had long before set up a youth movement (called Ezra) and a college student union for Orthodox young men and women; Agudath Israel would soon start providing the same cultural options for its youth, to compete with the clubs, libraries, and lectures offered by secularist movements of various stripes. But no such activities were available in Kraków, and it was this gap that she initially attempted to fill. And while she took her brother's suggestion to seek a blessing from a leading rabbi to found a school, she sought no such imprimatur for these prior activities.

Of course, within ten years, Bais Yaakov was indeed to accomplish all that she had dreamed of, and with full rabbinic endorsement. The Bnos Agudath Israel movement, officially inaugurated by Eliezer Gershon Friedenson in 1926 as a merger of existing informal groups, aimed to inspire adolescent women of

[6] On Hirsch, see Ch. 1 n. 44 above. Marcus Lehmann (1831–90) was a German neo-Orthodox rabbi and prolific writer of short stories, most of them first published in the weekly newspaper *Der Israelit*, which he founded in 1860 and which served the German-speaking Orthodox community through to the 1930s. The works of Hirsch and Lehmann, in German or Yiddish translation, were a mainstay of the Bais Yaakov organization and its publications, which otherwise lacked modern reading material.

roughly the same age as those she had failed to persuade with her 'exalted' talks. In this sense, the Orthodox Girls' Union was a (premature, in retrospect) forerunner to Bnos. The Bais Yaakov Teachers' Seminary in Kraków had both a library and a reading room, and Bnos provided similar facilities in dozens of small towns.[7] Sarah Schenirer herself continued to lecture on behalf of the Bais Yaakov idea, and Bais Yaakov girls in schools, seminaries, and summer colonies had ample opportunities—so unfamiliar to her when she first heard Rabbi Flesch address his female congregants—to hear from distinguished rabbis and charismatic leaders. These later efforts built on the educational foundation that Bais Yaakov had laid, and Orthodox observance was at the heart of these enterprises, as she had hoped a decade earlier.

Her initial failure with older girls may nevertheless be integral for understanding the relationship between the movement and its founder. Within Bais Yaakov literature, she is ubiquitously cast as a 'mother' to 'her thousands of daughters'. She does occasionally refer to Bais Yaakov pupils as 'my children', but these references are relatively rare. She far more frequently addresses the teachers, seminarians, and Bnos participants as her 'sisters' (or 'spiritual sisters'). Her diary is testimony to her hope of bringing young women 'back to Torah' as an act of 'sisterhood'. Thus, in the autumn of 1910, aged 27, she wondered, 'When will I be able to act on behalf of my sisters?' She expressed a double concern: on the one hand, she aimed to inspire young women to lead Orthodox lives, as did the rabbis and journalists who were concerned about female defections. But, unlike the rabbis, she also dreamed of constructing a social context in which she herself could be at home, where her 'old-fashioned' religious sensibilities and commitments would not be mocked but celebrated and shared in a youthful environment. In a diary entry dated late 1910, she speaks of going to 'a lecture at the folk university . . . by Potocki on recent Polish literature', adding that 'Even though the talk was good . . . I felt odd, not in my element.' In the same entry, she acknowledges that she knows she shouldn't be attending these lectures and meetings, but asks, 'what can I do . . . where can I go? There aren't any organizations for Jewish girls.' Correcting herself, she says that she means that there aren't any organizations for women who observe the sabbath, as she does.

While Bais Yaakov hagiographies paint a portrait of a woman motivated

[7] The Bais Yaakov memorial volume *Remember* lists a number of such libraries, two with more than a thousand books. In the case of the town of Zduńska Wola, Bnos managed to fund a library with 'well-chosen books' by staging plays put on by Bnos members, which drew large audiences from all around the town. See Szaranski, *Remember*, 40.

solely by her concern for her students, unblemished piety, and obedience to rabbinic dictate, her writings are less shy about acknowledging her intellectual ambitions, her attraction to the cultural offerings on display in Kraków, her pride in her own quick wit, her loneliness and sensitivities, and even her rebellious streak: 'Once my teacher caught me unprepared for a class in nature, and she responded to the situation with these words: "The best students in the class are Freilich, Probstein, Rubinstein, and Schenirer, but of all the students, Schenirer is also the best at slacking off—and that is really quite an accomplishment . . ." So there you have it, both the best and the laziest . . . two opposites!'

Unlike the more numerous rebels who defected from Orthodoxy, her intellectual gifts and non-conformity coexisted with a deep religiosity, a feature shared by very few of her peers. Her memoir and diary entries are punctuated by references to the ways in which this quality isolated her from those around her from an early age. She relates that by the time she was 6 years old she had a nickname in school, 'Little Miss Hasid' [*husidke*]', a nickname that stuck with her for many years. Writing about her own adolescence, she describes the consequences of her willingness to rebuke Jewish girls acting in an un-Jewish fashion: 'Sometimes I would reproach a Jewish girl, and she would just laugh and respond that I was a Little Miss Hasid.' Describing a trip she took to a resort in 1908 with a group of friends and family, she recounts that although 'the time passed pleasantly' something bothered her: 'Many people there allowed themselves to eat questionable food, which might have mixed meat and milk, and when I didn't eat with them, they mocked me, laughing and calling me "Little Miss Hasid".' A diary entry from 1910 (when she was 27) that records her dream that she might live to see Jewish girls 'studying the essential teachings of Judaism in the same way that they study the frivolous poetry of the gentiles' also testifies to her fear of being ridiculed for her religiosity: 'But have I lost my mind? How people would mock me then! They would point at me and say: "Look at Little Miss Hasid, that backward, pathetic woman."'

This mockery did not subside with the founding of Bais Yaakov. The literature of the movement attests to the ways in which she was ridiculed by secularists on her travels, in the popular press, and even in Orthodox circles.[8] The movement

[8] See the story 'Ridicule or Encouragement' (Heb.), in Rottenberg (ed.), *A Mother in Israel* (Heb.), ii. 33, which describes the mockery with which Schenirer and a group of teachers travelling with her were treated by 'activists in a rival women's organization'. For mockery in the press, see the article 'The Sensational Press about Bais Yaakov' (Yid.), according to which Schenirer had come in for particular mockery in papers like *Ekspres* and *Heyntike nayes*, in which outrageous lies

was also fodder for the press: A 1927 article in the Warsaw daily *Moment* describes the disciplinary proceedings taken against girls in the shtetl of Przeworsk who broke the rules against socializing with boys with a headline that parodies a well-known Bais Yaakov slogan: 'Bais Yaakov, come let us walk [*Bais ya'akov lekhu venelkha*, Isa. 2: 5] to trial.' While the slogan ends 'by the light of the Lord', this journalist substituted 'to trial', using exaggeration and ironic biblical citation ('Bais Yaakov girls caught in the act!!!', 'Should our sister be treated like a whore?', Gen. 34: 31) to maximize the story's comic effect.[9] Word of the movement even reached New York through a 'Letter from Warsaw' in the *Forward* that described the Bais Yaakov seminary in Kraków as 'a "college" where girls learn to salt meat and bless candles', as if the combination of serious education, traditional observance, and young girls was intrinsically ludicrous; the correspondent also ridiculed the forty-eight members of the Bais Yaakov committee in the town of Żyrardów for holding elections at which seven presidents and forty-one vice presidents were chosen.[10] This mockery was deplored even by some outside Bais Yaakov circles: the activist and writer Hillel Zeitlin wrote that despite the great achievements of the school, it was 'laughed at from all quarters, if not actively suppressed'.[11] In short, the disdain and mockery that Sarah Schenirer encountered as a child was part of how the world greeted the movement she led as an adult.

It would be wrong, then, to subsume the Bais Yaakov project entirely within the rabbinic discourse of Orthodox Kraków, which saw the schools as a solution for the problem of the defection of young women, fortuitously led by a pious older woman who could do real and symbolic work on behalf of the movement. Sarah Schenirer's writings make it clear that Bais Yaakov also created a space where a woman like herself could finally be accepted, in a way she had dreamed of during her childhood and adolescence. Unlike the youth groups she occasionally attended in earlier years, Bais Yaakov allowed her to live out her enthusiasm both for hiking up mountains and for exalted prayer at their peak, for Orthodox

were circulated about the Bais Yaakov schools and, 'in particular, our highly respected leader, Sarah Schenirer'. After Schenirer's death, E. G. Friedenson wrote that 'I have a letter before me describing how coldly she [Schenirer] was received in Warsaw and Łódź. What could some old-fashioned Jewess contribute to the discussion of girls' education?' ('Sarah Schenirer and the Pioneering Spirit' (Yid.), 1).

[9] Itsik, 'Bais Yaakov, Come Let Us Walk to Trial' (Yid.), 4.

[10] Kuper, 'Letter from Warsaw' (Yid.), 2.

[11] Zeitlin was a founder of and regular columnist for *Moment*, where Bais Yaakov was often mocked. Zeitlin, 'Bais Yaakov, on the First Conference' (Yid.), 3.

observance and for inspiring and enlightening public lectures, for the excitement of youth organizations and for the spiritual satisfaction of reviving tradition. With her Bais Yaakov and Bnos 'sisters', even as the age gap separating them widened and even if some in the wider world continued to laugh at her efforts, she was constructing the world she had longed for in her own youth.

The ideological writings that legitimated Bais Yaakov regularly made clear that the most exalted role that a woman could fill was that of wife and mother, bracketing or diminishing the importance of adolescence and young womanhood, the dangerous and liminal period that separates the girl living under her parents' roof from the woman who lives under her husband's. By contrast, the Kraków culture of youth movements and self-education in which she ambivalently participated celebrated and mobilized the energies and freedom of this life-stage, one made available in the modernizing world through delayed marriage and other socio-economic developments.[12] Sarah Schenirer lived the life of an economically self-sufficient, unmarried, well-travelled, nature-loving, and intellectually curious young woman for far longer than previous generations would have countenanced, remaining unmarried until the age of 28, and then reluctantly entering into a marriage that would last only briefly. A diary entry from September 1913 alludes to her divorce: 'Four weeks after this great misfortune, I knew that without a few days of rest I wouldn't be able to go on living, so I said to myself: "To the mountains my dear brother, freedom awaits you there."'[13] Quoting a well-known Polish poem by Wincenty Pol, she signals her anticipation of the pleasures and healing effect of travelling, especially in nature. The lines that follow describe such adventures as a six-hour cart ride and eleven-hour hike with evident pride, recognizing them as the means by which she recovered her sense of self after a painful crisis while reconnecting with her devotion to God and awe at his creation.

Living as a single woman gave her the freedom she needed to transmit her love of travelling and nature to Bais Yaakov nearly from the start. While the movement is often seen as the path that led Jewish girls and women back to their Orthodox families, it just as frequently took them out of their family homes, not only to the forests of Poland but also to its 'streets' and 'marketplaces', as Rabbi

[12] Stampfer has shown that the age of marriage rose in all sectors of east European Jewish society in the nineteenth century, including among the Orthodox. See Stampfer, *Families, Rabbis, and Education*, 23–4.

[13] Schenirer and Samuel Nussbaum were divorced on 10 June 1913. For the quote, see Appendix A, n. 11, below.

Tuvye Yehudah Gutentag said in a speech on the occasion of her first *yahrzeit*:

> Before Sarah Schenirer, any Jewish daughter with *ḥaredi* [ultra-Orthodox] parents was forbidden to take a step away from her home, to participate in life and spend time with girls her own age, out of fear that the plague of heresy would ambush her, and at a time of plague, the Talmud says, 'remain indoors'. Any step beyond the walls of her father's house leads the daughter along a road from which she will not return, from which none return. Any peek into a book, any enjoyment with her friends, poses a mortal danger. But when Sarah Schenirer came along and created a purely *ḥaredi* environment, produced a *ḥaredi* literature for girls, and raised the flag of the Jewish girl on high—the Jewish girl shook off the humiliation of her exile among secular people, shook off the alien culture and her sense of inferiority vis-à-vis the non-Jew, and so it became possible for her to walk proudly on the streets of life, to emerge from her parents' home and go out to the marketplace, without being cut off from her spiritual base, without fear that this world would lead her straight to hell.[14]

Miriam Feldman, describing her experiences in Bnos, remembers travelling to the mountains 'in the back of the wagon . . . The bumpety-bump of the rickety wheels on the rocky dirt road was music to our ears.' The main lesson learned in Bnos, she writes, was that *frum* [Orthodox] girls can have fun within the realm of Torah, and that we did not need the irreligious youth groups.[15] If Bais Yaakov restored the traditional Jewish home, it did so initially by rescuing girls from their confinement within its walls and providing new avenues for their mobility and freedom. Given Sarah Schenirer's passion for travel, it is no surprise that she made a point of offering graduating seminary students a copy of *tefilat haderekh* (a short prayer recited at the beginning of every journey). As Leo Deutschländer put it in his memorial speech at the seminary, her thinking on the subject was straightforward: 'Seminarians become teachers, which means that they will travel, so let them say the prayer for the road!'[16]

That she cherished her own freedom is evident from her memoir and diary. An entry for 14 October 1910, shortly after her engagement, suggests that she believed that a direct relation with the Creator was most easily sustained outside the family or home. Despite her use of the word 'sister', Bais Yaakov literature nevertheless insisted, and continues to insist, on seeing her as a 'mother', reinscribing her in the traditional family setting and obscuring the ways in which she resisted, evaded, and reshaped normative roles for Orthodox women. Pearl Benisch is only echoing a much more general trend when she calls her 'Mother

14 Tavyomi (Gutentag), 'The Wisdom of Women' (Heb.), 24.

15 Rubin (ed.), *Daughters of Destiny*, 21.

16 Deutschländer, 'Sarah Schenirer and Bais Yaakov' (Yid.), 10.

Figure 2.1 Bnos Agudath Israel colony in Rajcza, 1931. Rajcza is a village in Lower Silesia near Rabka that became a popular tourist destination and ski resort in the interwar years. Most of the hotels and boarding houses were owned and run by Jewish families

Courtesy of the Photograph Archives of the Joint Distribution Committee Photograph Archive, 12569

Schenirer', although the designation is usually appended to her first rather than her last name. While 'Mother Sarah' recalls the biblical Sarah (traditionally known as *sarah imenu*, 'our mother Sarah'), Benisch reaches further back to link her with Eve, the primordial Mother of all humankind: 'Unfortunately and tragically, Sarah Schenirer was denied her own biological children. However, she was granted the *zechus* [merit] to be a mother not to one, ten, or twenty children, but to scores, hundreds, thousands, generation after generation of Jewish children. She was like Chavah, the first woman, a mother of *kol chai*, every living being.'[17]

Even her close collaborator Judith Grunfeld-Rosenbaum, who served as principal of the Kraków seminary while she was director, speaks in similar fashion, stressing her own youth in comparison with Sarah Schenirer's age. Describing her arrival at the summer colony of Robów (in a hamlet near Nowy Targ) in 1925 (when she was 23 and Sarah Schenirer was 42), Rosenbaum compares their respective relationships with the students: 'When I came, I brought a bit of youthful action along. Although Sarah Schenirer was not old, she was not young in her ways. She was the pure soul behind all our actions, but I was the young friend, the confidante. I was able to relate to them and they to me.'[18] Her dream of creating a world of Orthodox 'sisters' may have been realized, and she was certainly revered in this movement, but these remarks demonstrated that, as in her younger years, she found herself excluded from the youthful fellowship that owed so much to her.

Perhaps it is not entirely surprising that when the much younger Friedenson (born in 1899) brought together a number of existing informal groups to establish the Bnos youth movement in March 1926, Sarah Schenirer did not attend the founding conference in Łódź (she sent her warm wishes in a letter). In an essay written for the first anniversary of that conference and addressed, as so often, to her 'sisters', she describes the power of youth in general, and of a youth movement in particular: 'Youth means: joy, courage in life, optimism, and a powerful belief in eternal ideals!' Yet in spite of these words of praise and her evident enthusiasm about this new organization, she still harboured mixed feelings about it:

For a whole year I have stood at the side without daring to openly congratulate the newly formed movement of Bnos Agudath Israel. I was like someone who has finally arrived at a long-awaited goal and feels such powerful emotions that they cannot bring themselves to cross the threshold for a long, long time. I couldn't believe my eyes, even considering

[17] Benisch, *Carry Me in Your Heart*, 39.

[18] Rubin (ed.), *Daughters of Destiny*, 129.

how many people showed up to the large public meeting in Łódź a year ago [in 1926]. I said to myself, this cannot be real!

Although she does not say so, her disappointment ten years earlier with the Orthodox Girls' Union may have contributed to the 'powerful emotions' that kept her from initially participating in this new initiative. Bnos, which brought into the Bais Yaakov movement hundreds of adolescent girls with whom she was not personally acquainted, and whose dedication to the cause could not always be counted on (as evidenced, for instance, by the ongoing and often fruitless attempts at imposing the Yiddish-only rule, collecting membership dues, or enforcing modesty in dress), may have raised the spectre, for a woman now ten years older than she had been when she first established an Orthodox youth organization, of exposing herself to new disappointments, or even to youthful disrespect.

Her initial attempt to create an Orthodox youth movement rather than a school system sheds light on other aspects of her vision as well. Jacquelyn Rosensweig has recently argued that Bais Yaakov should be seen as not one, but rather two movements: she began with a class full of very young pupils, and Bais Yaakov followed this model in a network of afternoon schools that served the population of school-age girls.[19] With the movement's astonishing growth and the absence of young women knowledgeable enough in Torah to teach in and staff these additional schools, the need to train a cohort of teachers quickly became obvious. The first of these teachers, according to Sarah Schenirer's account, were 'two of my most industrious students', who were 'barely 13'. By 1923, a kind of informal teachers' college was being run from her own two-room tenement apartment. Once the word spread, Orthodox activists and parents in small towns throughout Poland began to look for teachers, and the seminary was transformed, under Leo Deutschländer's leadership, into a more professional institution run out of an eight-room apartment, supplemented by a teacher-training course (*Fortbildungskurs*) held every summer between 1925 and 1930. These efforts culminated in a professional teachers' seminary that moved into its own Kraków building in 1931. It was the graduates of these teacher-training programmes, and what eventually became a network of seminaries in Kraków, Vienna, and Czernowitz, Bukovina (there was also a smaller teacher-

[19] In a personal email (31 Dec. 2015). Bertha Pappenheim also sees the movement as having 'a double purpose': to train teachers through a deep Jewish education 'and at the same time to influence younger girls in the schools'; see H. K., 'Beth-Jacob-Schul-Werk', 27.

training programme in Bratislava, Czechoslovakia), who went on to teach in the burgeoning Bais Yaakov school system.[20]

But it is possible to tell this familiar story in a different way. Rather than young women being trained to staff the network of small-town afternoon schools (or full-day schools in larger cities), perhaps the supplemental schools existed to support the creation of an elite cadre of knowledgeable young women, particularly in the three teachers' seminaries. The urge to create and shape an elite institution explains why, when Yehudah Leib Orlean took over the directorship of the teachers' seminary in Kraków in 1933, he deliberately reduced the student body from 150 to 120 and raised both the entrance requirements and curricular standards.[21] This had the effect of expanding the geographical reach of the student body from its primary home in Poland and, in the early 1930s, Lithuania to, after 1935, elsewhere in eastern and central Europe as well as the United States, Canada, Switzerland, Belgium, and France.[22] The heart of the system, from this perspective, was not the network of supplemental small-town schools, where instruction was uneven, teacher turnover high, enrolment fluctuating and uncertain, and the schools themselves subject to sudden closure. Rather, it was the cadre of seminary-trained teachers, the young women who travelled to small towns to promote Bais Yaakov and disseminate what they had learned, and who, in the famous summer colonies, impressed visiting activists and rabbis with their commitment to Torah study. It was with reference to these young women that Isaac Breuer commented that Bais Yaakov had created 'a new kind of woman in the East'.[23]

An anecdote shared by Grunfeld-Rosenbaum captures the novelty and power of this youthful piety, describing the impression made on a girl named Golda in the small town of Będzin (Yid., Bendin) by an emissary from the Kraków seminary:

> At the movie-hall, a young girl stood before the audience. She was dark-haired, vivacious and pretty, with laughing dark eyes. And she was clever and sure of herself. She stood up and spoke to the audience with confidence about Torah life and Torah values. As she

[20] Not all teachers were graduates of the seminaries, as 'Esther' and the memoir of Gutta Sternbuch demonstrate. 'Esther' founded and taught at a Bais Yaakov school without any professional certification (Shandler (ed.), *Awakening Lives*, 335). Sternbuch went to the Kraków seminary, but she began teaching before she entered. See Sternbuch and Kranzler, *Gutta*, 28–30.

[21] See J. Friedenson, 'The Bais Yaakov Girls' Schools' (Heb.), 72. At the opening of the new seminary building in 1931, the school had only eighty students.

[22] Ibid. 74.

[23] See Introduction, n. 5, above.

spoke Golda felt a heaviness falling away from her heart. Here were all the values which she had been taught from childhood—but had hitherto only paid lip-service to—embodied in the person of this young attractive girl.[24]

Such young women constituted the raison d'être of the movement, its most committed activists and most visible standard bearers. By contrast, the schools for younger girls provided, in Hillel Seidman's words, 'an important place of work and source of income for hundreds of teachers' in a difficult economic environment.[25] Sarah Schenirer's revolution not only expanded the educational options for Orthodox girls, it also created a cohort of educated, mobile, committed, and independent Orthodox young women, giving them unprecedented opportunities to combine religious commitment and socio-economic freedom. These seminarians and young faculty at the Kraków seminary were her closest associates, her travelling companions on her many trips around Poland, and the ones who welcomed her on her return from every journey.

Sarah Schenirer's account of her great programme to save Jewish girls through inspiring lectures, a library, and a youth movement thus sheds light on some of the ways that Bais Yaakov culture developed. Her descriptions of the beginnings of Bais Yaakov (as it was named by the 1919 Agudah committee in Kraków that undertook its support) also provide insight into how she viewed the school she founded after these other projects had failed. Recounting a conversation with the father of a prospective student, a man who would go on to become one of her first supporters, she writes: 'A hasidic man comes to enrol his daughter and asks me: "What are you actually setting out to accomplish here?" I answer that I won't just be teaching them to pray, because that they could learn without me. My main intention is to arouse their desire to be Jewish.'[26] She denies that what she is doing is merely a continuation of the old traditional way of educating girls, of teaching them enough simple Hebrew to allow them to read from a prayer-book. Such a denial may have been necessary because her school did indeed resemble a traditional *ḥeder* in many respects, including its threadbare appearance, the fact that it had only one teacher, and an educational programme that taught basic Jewish textual skills. As Stampfer puts it, 'The *ḥeder* was a private one-teacher school. Studies were conducted in the home of the teacher and he was paid directly by the parents.'[27] One of the few contemporaneous journalistic

[24] Dansky, *Rebbetzin Grunfeld*, 125.
[25] Seidman, *Renesans Religijny*, 24.
[26] From other references, we can identify this man as Motl Luksenberg, a Gerer hasid who became an important supporter of the system.
[27] Stampfer, *Families, Rabbis, and Education*, 149.

mentions of the school also describes its curriculum: prayers (*davenen*), religion, writing in Yiddish, Jewish history, stories conveying the Orthodox way of life, handiwork or embroidery, and sewing by machine.[28] The curriculum, including the handiwork and sewing, is familiar from other sources we have that describe girls' *ḥeder* education.[29] The Bible, not to mention the rabbinic commentaries that would be taught in the seminary, are conspicuously missing; the school combined a basic traditional course of study (with the possible exception of 'religion' as a separate unit) with practical instruction, a dimension of Bais Yaakov that was to persist in the interwar years.[30]

The nineteenth-century *ḥeder* typically served younger children from the age of 3 (once they were toilet-trained) to around 10 (when they advanced to a Talmud *ḥeder*); but generally girls did not attend for as long as this. As memoirs attest, Sarah Schenirer kept at least some of her students by her side until they reached their teens, long enough for them to acquire enough education to serve, first, as her assistants, and then as teachers in the schools that arose in Kraków and, subsequently, in the neighbouring towns. In this way, she supplemented the norms of the *ḥeder* with apprenticeship practices (and among her earliest teachers was indeed a young helper in her workshop). In 1923 she formed a fledgling seminary in her apartment to train young teachers to serve in these schools. Leo Deutschländer, in town to attend the meeting of the World Agudath Israel (16–20 September 1924), describes climbing the narrow stone steps of a tenement building on 1 Katarzyna Street, the halls of which swarmed with young children. The teachers' seminary consisted of a two-room apartment, with a small kitchen separated from the larger rooms by a curtain. 'Here, in Sara Schenirer's own room, twenty-five girls sit by the table and study; some are seated on boxes in the middle of the room as there is no more space at the table.' In this 'ascetically furnished room', teacher and students shared their 'frugal meals'.[31] As was the

[28] *Der yid* (17 July 1919), 14, cited in Oleszak, 'The Beit Ya'akov School in Kraków', 278.

[29] See, for instance, Hinde Bergner, who attended a mixed *ḥeder* in Redim (Radymno, in Galicia) in the 1870s, in which 'The rebbetsin taught the girls how to sew. She would also tell us many stories about Jewish holy men, Hasidic rebbes, and the great scholars.' See Bergner, *On Long Winter Nights*, 82.

[30] Among the many interviews conducted with survivors by the Spielberg Shoah Foundation, about sixty women mention having studied in a Bais Yaakov school, generally in a small town. When asked what they learned, the most common response was 'to pray'. See e.g. Regina Guttman, Interview 51175, segment 26, Visual History Archive, USC Shoah Foundation, 2000, and Bella Nadler, Interview 16785, segment 6, Visual History Archive, USC Shoah Foundation, 1996 (accessed 12 May 2017).

[31] Dansky, *Rebbetzin Grunfeld*, 97–8.

practice in the traditional *ḥeder*, which also combined household and educational functions and was led by a private individual who lacked formal training or community certification, Sarah Schenirer opened a private school in her own overcrowded living quarters, serving as teacher despite a lack of training or higher education. For all these similarities to the traditional *ḥeder* that characterized both the seminary and the supplemental schools for younger girls, she nevertheless insisted to the hasidic father that she intended something new, a vision she explained through the difference between teaching girls the mechanics of Jewish prayer and inspiring in them 'the desire to be Jewish'. For her, the poverty, bareness, and overcrowding of her school did not signify 'backwardness' or a regression to traditional educational models displaced by more modern facilities and methods, but rather the asceticism of youthful idealism and the exaltation of revolution. Her school was not mired in the accidental poverty of so many similar institutions, but rather was grounded in a principled asceticism that signalled fierce religious commitment. In this way, despite or rather through the primitive conditions of the early schools, she simultaneously signalled her affiliations with Orthodox tradition and the pioneering social currents of her urban environment.

As she relates, teaching the meaning rather than merely the form of blessings and prayers had immediate and powerful effects:

> I start by telling them what it means to make a blessing. I explain that every person must make a blessing when they're about to eat God's gift, otherwise they are considered to be stealing. The next morning a mother comes in to tell me with the greatest happiness that her 6-year-old daughter noticed her 5-year-old brother drinking water without making a blessing. She shrieked at him: 'Thief! When you drink God's water you have to make a blessing!'

This anecdote describes how she explained the practice of blessing before eating or drinking to her young charges as a recognition that all things are God's creations. But the divine–human economy, as it were, does not exhaust the meaning of Jewish blessings, which may also involve social actors, in this case the teacher, the parent, the young pupil, and her younger brother. The pupil learns her lesson well, prompting her mother to report back to the teacher and, by praising her daughter, also praise (or bless, and thus repay) the woman who taught her. For the 6-year-old daughter who rebukes her brother, the Jewish knowledge she has absorbed translates into social capital and authority over a less knowledgeable or committed sibling. The evident pride—mixed, no doubt, with humour—with which the mother of these children relates the story to Sarah Schenirer, and the pride that impels the latter to repeat this story, is sufficiently explained by the sense of accomplishment both women feel in seeing a lesson well learned (even if the further lesson of how to respectfully convey religious teachings remains beyond the young Bais Yaakov pupil's grasp). But there is also the faintest hint of a different sort of pride, one in the new ability of older sisters to correct their younger brothers, and more generally, in the potential of religious knowledge to reorganize gender patterns within a community in which religious authority was traditionally reserved for brothers, fathers, rabbis, and other men. Years later, Joseph Friedenson would strike this note again, describing how graduates of the Kraków seminary under Orlean's directorship accumulated such great stores of Jewish knowledge 'that they would put their fathers and brothers to shame'.[32]

The traditional discourse around girls' religious education as it was discussed in the Orthodox press, in rabbinical congresses, and in halakhic responsa invariably placed men in the position of those who know Torah, who may choose to teach it to their daughters or withhold such teachings from them, and who set the limits for which subjects and sources women may study. The rabbinic warning that 'whoever teaches his daughter Torah [it is as if he] teaches her *tiflut*' implicitly acknowledges that Torah study may confer on women a degree of (sexual?) power over men, by enabling them to evade male control. In the official rhetoric of Bais Yaakov, girls' Torah study leads only to greater piety and more complete obedience to rabbinic authority and Jewish observance. Sarah Schenirer's account of this early incident, remembered for fifteen years and retold in an anniversary essay on the movement, is evidence that girls' religious study could also be wielded within a social field of power. In her memory, this effect was in fact nearly instantaneous, emerging within days of her initial experiment.

Sarah Schenirer's shifting relations with men are also part of the story of Bais Yaakov's origins. Alongside a Mrs Halberstam, a granddaughter of the founder of the Sanz hasidic dynasty (which had recently experienced the scandalous and humiliating defection of another Sanzer granddaughter, Anna Kluger),[33] she found an early supporter in

[32] J. Friedenson, 'The Bais Yaakov Girls' Schools' (Heb.), 73.

[33] Anna Kluger, great-granddaughter of the founder of the Sanzer hasidic dynasty, ran away from home in 1909 with her younger sister to pursue her education after leaving the hasidic groom her family had chosen for her. The two young women sued their parents for support, which created a sensation and was widely reported in the press. Kluger eventually earned a doctorate in Polish history. For more, see Manekin, '"Something Entirely New"' (Heb.), 82–3.

Mr M. Luksenberg [Motl Luksenberg, the hasidic father mentioned above] who as soon as he became aware of the mission of the school threw himself heart and soul into the project. It makes me very uncomfortable that he gives us a few hours of his regular time for learning Torah each day, but I comfort myself with the thought that girls' education is so important and burning a problem that it certainly constitutes an instance of 'It is time to act for the Lord, so one may violate the Torah.'[34]

The phrase from Psalms with which she comforts herself about the necessity of taking time away from Luksenberg's Torah study is of course the same one that had been used at least since the 1903 rabbinical congress to legitimate Torah study for girls. She uses it not for that purpose, but to legitimate (in her own mind) taking time away from male Torah study to support the Torah study of girls and women. As in the anecdote about the pupil and her younger brother, what begins as a narrow religious principle turns out to register powerfully within the social order where it is brought to bear. According to her autobiography, she had come into contact with rabbinic figures on at least two different occasions. The first, in Vienna, began with the novel experience for her of being addressed and (indirectly, as a woman) praised by a rabbi, teacher, and follower of Samson Raphael Hirsch. The second, in Marienbad, involved a journey to receive the blessing of a hasidic rebbe through the medium of a note passed through her brother. She created a new culture of girls and women in the Bais Yaakov movement, but she also inaugurated a new form of relationship between east European Orthodox men and women. In a community in which the latter were objects rather than subjects of Jewish legal discourse, in which rabbis refrained from addressing women directly and even (according to Benisch) 'were indifferent to their plight', she met a hasidic father who was willing not only to have a religiously meaningful conversation with her about how to teach Judaism, but also to sign on to the project, work on her behalf and, one is tempted to say, serve as her helpmeet. While the east European traditional ideal was for an *eshet ḥayil* (a 'woman of valour') to devote her time to earning money that could enable her husband and sons to devote themselves to learning Torah, her relationship with Luksenberg reversed this traditional arrangement, with she herself providing the halakhic justification for this reversal. In this passage, a woman, armed with the proper

[34] This verse appears in the 1985 JPS translation as 'It is a time to act for the Lord, for they have violated your teaching', but I have translated it to conform more closely to the midrashic sense in which it is used here (and more generally throughout Bais Yaakov writings), as meaning that the Torah may be violated in an emergency for the sake of an important value. See also Ch. 1 n. 39 above.

knowledge of Torah, considers the halakhic exceptions to the rule that men devote themselves to Torah study, while it is a man who devotes his material energies to further Torah study among girls.

Bais Yaakov would soon find many more such men. Beginning with the 1923 Agudah creation of the Keren Hatorah foundation to support Orthodox educational institutions, including Bais Yaakov, the top ranks of the organization were filled by male Agudah leaders and activists: Leo Deutschländer, director of Keren Hatorah and the World Centre for Bais Yaakov in Vienna and founder of the Vienna Teachers' Seminary; Eliezer Gershon Friedenson, editor of the *Bais Yaakov Journal* and founder of the Bnos youth movement; Rabbi J. M. Bidermann and Aleksander Zysha Friedman, directors of the Horev educational arm of Agudah, which had its offices in Warsaw and managed Bais Yaakov's organizational and juridical status; Yehudah Leib Orlean, and many others. In subsequent years, this male leadership would prompt some observers to give credit for Bais Yaakov to these rabbis, leaders, and activists rather than to Sarah Schenirer, whose efforts would be depicted as having provided only a meagre start.[35] Her own retelling of the beginnings of Bais Yaakov, however, implies a different reading of this history: in remembering Mr Luksenberg, she makes clear that she viewed him as her helper, and suggests more generally that the role of men in the movement might be similarly framed.

By November 1917, she relates, the project of establishing a school for young girls had already been accomplished, adding that 'one more thing gives me joy: I'm not alone'. Her joy in finding supporters is certainly reflective of her sense of mission, her recognition that her work could hardly succeed without the enthusiasm of parents and the embrace of the community at large. But it is also a deeply personal conclusion to a memoir that begins as a story of isolation and alienation, relating how her religious devotion had condemned her to derision and mockery. From its earliest weeks, her school served as a balm for a long-festering personal wound, even as it marked the beginnings of a culture in which the worship of God, the study of Torah, and the nourishing of human friendships and collaborations—even between unrelated Orthodox men and women—could find simultaneous expression.

[35] See Introduction, n. 9, above.

CHAPTER THREE

'Building Bais Yaakov'
Institution and Charisma

The wisest of women builds her house
(Prov. 14: 1)

When the daughters of Zelophehad heard that the land was to be apportioned among the tribes—but only to males, not to females—they gathered together to take counsel, saying: the mercies of flesh and blood are not like the mercies of God. Human beings are more merciful to males than to females. But he who spoke and brought the world into being is different—his mercies are for males and females equally. His mercies are for all!

(*Sifrei* Num. 133)

BY THE TIME Sarah Schenirer died in 1935 at the age of 51, the movement she had started in 1917 to provide Orthodox girls with a rigorous Jewish education was already well established, with perhaps 225 schools and 36,000 students throughout Poland and beyond. Together with the boys' schools that functioned alongside Bais Yaakov under the aegis of Agudath Israel, it constituted the largest Jewish private school network in interwar Poland.[1] The great majority of its pupils were enrolled in small supplementary schools, generally with only one teacher, that they attended before or after their public-school day.[2] Beginning in 1929, Bais Yaakov established full-day schools in the larger cities, with a programme of secular studies that conformed to state regulations in addition to Jewish studies.[3] By the 1930s, large cities like Warsaw and Łódź had a number of

[1] This Agudah network of girls' and boys' schools, organized under a single umbrella in 1929, was called Horev. Other school systems included the Cysho Yiddishist school system; the Tarbut Zionist Hebrew school system; the Shulkult Zionist Yiddish-Hebrew schools; and Religious Zionist (Mizrahi) schools, under the name Yavneh or Tahkemoni. See Appendix D below for the distribution of Bais Yaakov schools in 1935.

[2] An undated document from the Vilna office of the Agudah's educational organization, Horev, entitled 'By-Laws of the Beth Jacob Schools', dictated that such schools were to run for seven years (in accordance with the seven grades of education required by Polish law), for two hours a day, five times a week. Students entered at 6 or 7, and graduated at 13 or 14. See 'By-Laws of the Beth Jacob Schools', 1.

[3] See Eisenstein, *Jewish Schools in Poland*, 96. Miriam Eisenstein describes the secular

Figure 3.1 A group of Bais Yaakov women sewing lace curtains in Rymanów (date not known). The woman on the right is the donor's mother, Sara Ginsburg Keller

United States Holocaust Memorial Museum, courtesy of Itta Keller Ben Haiem

Bais Yaakov schools serving different age groups and neighbourhoods. While handiwork and dressmaking were included from the very first years, the movement later expanded and professionalized its curriculum, establishing a vocational high school and vocational post-high school in Warsaw and Łódź respectively; the latter, renamed Ohel Sarah after Sarah Schenirer's death, served around 300 students at its height.[4] These schools combined Jewish subjects with courses in dressmaking, tailoring, secretarial skills, bookkeeping, business, child care, hygiene, and nursing. (The Łódź school also hosted a two-year *hakhsharah* training programme for Bnos members preparing to emigrate to the Land of Israel; the first graduates arrived in Tel Aviv in 1934, setting up an urban kibbutz that served as a centre for both Bais Yaakov and Bnos.) Vocational training was not an in-cidental part of Bais Yaakov's curriculum. Deborah Weissman describes the socio-economic challenges that faced interwar Polish Orthodoxy, including rapid urban growth 'that outstripped economic development', the 1919 Sunday Rest Law that put Orthodox businesses at a disadvantage, and diminishing government financial support for Jewish schools. She argues that 'the rapid, successful spread of the Bais Yaakov idea may have been due less to the ideological power of the movement or the charisma of its leaders than to the socioeconomic necessity of vocational training for Polish Jewish girls, supported by the Jewish community'.[5]

At least some of the young women turning to Bais Yaakov for vocational training were interested in the difficult and underpaid work of teaching, and the movement also had three teachers' seminaries. The 'crown jewel' of the system was in Kraków; it had begun in 1923 in Sarah Schenirer's two-room apartment

programme as including Polish history, mathematics and science, and literature and culture, taught for a minimum of ten to twelve hours per week; new state demands after 1932 required the addition of classes in drawing, music, and physical education (ibid. 78–9). According to Kazdan, the language of instruction in the secular subjects in these Bais Yaakov schools was Polish. On these full-day schools, see Kazdan, *The History of Jewish School Systems* (Yid.), 487–9.

[4] On the variety of schools, see Kazdan, *The History of Jewish School Systems* (Yid.), 487–99, and J. Friedenson, 'The Bais Yaakov Girls' Schools' (Heb.), 69–72. The Bais Yaakov vocational high school in Warsaw, which was founded in 1929, was directed by Abraham Mordechai Rogovy, the editor of the Agudah daily *Yidishe Tageblat*. The postgraduate vocational school in Łódź opened in 1934, was directed by Eliezer Gershon Friedenson, editor of the *Bais Yaakov Journal*, and was renamed Ohel Sarah after Schenirer's death. A strong impetus towards vocational training was provided by new regulations in the 1930s requiring owners of businesses to have training in accounting and business or hire workers with certificates in those fields.

[5] Weissman, 'Bais Ya'akov: A Historical Model', 145.

in 1 Katarzyna Street, moved into an eight-room apartment in 30 Augustiańska Street in 1924 or 1925, and established itself in a permanent home, a new five-story building at 10 Stanisława Street, in 1931 (it was the only one of the three seminaries to have its own building). A smaller teachers' seminary that served central European Bais Yaakov schools opened in Vienna in 1930 under the directorship of Leo Deutschländer.[6] A third opened in 1935 in Czernowitz, under the leadership of Esther Hamburger Gross, a German-trained educator who had taught in the Kraków seminary and led teacher-training courses in Bratislava.[7] As the location of these seminaries suggests, by the mid-1930s, Bais Yaakov had expanded its reach far beyond its Polish birthplace, with schools throughout Europe as well as in the United States and the Land of Israel.[8]

The transition from a movement inaugurated and led by an individual to an educational organization with an international reach began in 1919, when members of the local chapter of Agudath Israel in Kraków undertook at their inaugural meeting to support Sarah Schenirer and her fledgling school system by taking on responsibility for all the financial aspects of the school. Her original class of twenty-five had grown, between 1917 and 1919, to 280 pupils. By 1921 there were, according to Joseph Friedenson, three Bais Yaakovs—as the Kraków committee had named the schools—and the system had outgrown Kraków, with schools in the nearby small cities of Tarnów and Ostrowiec (an additional four schools were established in 1922 and the seminary in Sarah Schenirer's apartment opened in 1923). A more fateful development came in August 1923, when the Agudath Israel met in Vienna for its long-delayed first World Congress, with 600 delegates from across the Orthodox world in attendance. It was this congress that voted to establish Keren Hatorah, the foundation that supported Orthodox education, and to include Bais Yaakov, which numbered about sixty schools by that year,

[6] Deutschländer writes that the seminary in Vienna attracted students from Czechoslovakia, Hungary, Romania, Finland, Denmark, Italy, Holland, Germany, and Switzerland (Deutschländer, *Tätigkeitsbericht*, 3).

[7] For more on these different categories of school, see J. Friedenson, 'The Bais Yaakov Girls' Schools' (Heb.), 69–71. Deutschländer reports on the appointment of Hamburger in *Tätigkeitsbericht*, 5. According to Sorasky, the seminary in Czernowicz was initiated by Rabbi Baruch Hager of Seret-Vizhnitz (1895–1963) and Rabbi Yosef Naftali Stern of Pressburg (1888–1971); see Sorasky, *The History of Torah Education* (Heb.), 434.

[8] According to a 1935 internal report, Bais Yaakov included 225 schools with 27,119 pupils in Poland; 18 schools with 1,569 pupils in Czechoslovakia; 18 schools with 1,292 pupils in Romania; 16 schools with 2,000 girls in Lithuania; and 11 schools with 950 pupils in Austria. See J. Friedenson, 'The Bais Yaakov Girls' Schools' (Heb.), 71.

under its aegis. The following year, when the Keren Hatorah leadership met in Kraków, its director, Leo Deutschländer, was able to see the seminary at first hand and began to involve himself more fully in the movement.

Along with the 1923 decision by the Agudah to include Bais Yaakov in the activities of Keren Hatorah and the 1924 visit by Deutschländer to Kraków, a crucial third factor in the growth of Bais Yaakov was the decision by another young Agudah activist, Eliezer Gershon Friedenson, to support the movement, even before the world congress at which that support became official. Speaking about the early 1920s, Friedenson writes:

> In those days I would travel around towns and cities organizing Agudah groups, which the secularists and ideological rivals did not appreciate. They would greet my lectures with a hail of questions and challenges. I knew how to fight back against these rivals, until one of them sent me into stunned silence. My opponent asked: 'Where are your girls? They're in our clubs!' This question tormented me for many days, until I came to Kraków. A friend brought me to Sarah Schenirer's school, and there I found the answer. This was a field it was forbidden to neglect . . . And so I decided to devote myself to serving Sarah Schenirer, which is how the *Bais Yaakov Journal* was born.[9]

Within a few months of his 1923 meeting with Sarah Schenirer, Friedenson had put out the first ten-page issue of the periodical from his Łódź office, seeking to publicize the existence of an Orthodox girls' educational system. The *Bais Yaakov Journal* appeared twice more in the next six months, and although publication was occasionally halted because of financial difficulties, for most of its sixteen-year run, it appeared monthly and sometimes more frequently than that. From 1924 to 1929, the journal had a Polish supplement, *Wschód* ('East'); in 1929, when Bais Yaakov committed itself to promoting Yiddish, it dropped the Polish supplement (though it made an exception for a special issue on antisemitism in 1938). By the third issue, in spring 1924, the journal also included a supplement for younger children (which later became a separate publication) called *Kindergarten*. A sister publication, the *Bais Yaakov Ruf* ('Call'), based in Kovno (Kaunas) and aimed at the Lithuanian branch of the movement, began to appear in 1935. (Some of the larger schools, including the Kraków seminary and Ohel Sarah, had their own student newspapers). When the *Bais Yaakov Journal* ceased publication with the outbreak of the Second World War, it was the longest-running Yiddish publication aimed at Jewish girls and women in Poland. After many difficulties, by the late 1930s it was earning enough of a profit for Friedenson to expand his

[9] Cited in J. Friedenson, 'The Movement from Its Beginnings' (Heb.), 126.

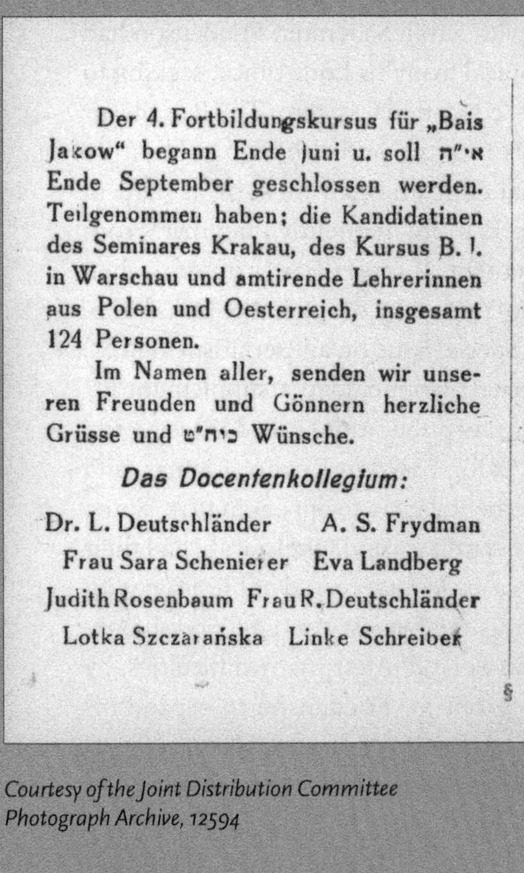

Der 4. Fortbildungskursus für „Bais Jakow" begann Ende Juni u. soll א"י"ה Ende September geschlossen werden. Teilgenommen haben; die Kandidatinen des Seminares Krakau, des Kursus B. J. in Warschau und amtirende Lehrerinnen aus Polen und Oesterreich, insgesamt 124 Personen.

Im Namen aller, senden wir unseren Freunden und Gönnern herzliche Grüsse und כו"ח"ט Wünsche.

Das Docentenkollegium:

Dr. L. Deutschländer A. S. Frydman
Frau Sara Schenierer Eva Landberg
Judith Rosenbaum Frau R. Deutschländer
Lotka Szczarańska Linke Schreiber

Courtesy of the Joint Distribution Committee Photograph Archive, 12594

Figure 3.2 A postcard sent from the Bais Yaakov holiday home in Rabka, the Tatra mountains, 1928. The writing on the front of the building reads 'Bais Yaakov Holiday Home, Rabka (the High Tatra mountains), 1928'. The back of the postcard has a printed message in German that reads, 'The fourth teacher-training course of Bais Yaakov began at the end of June and will conclude, God willing, at the end of September. Participants include teachers-in-training from the Kraków seminary, the teacher training course in Warsaw, and more advanced teachers from Poland and Austria, totalling 124 people. In the name of all these participants, we send our friends and supporters warm greetings and best wishes on the upcoming Jewish holidays.' The card is signed by 'The teaching faculty: Dr L. Deutschländer, A.S. Frydman, Frau Sara Schenierer, Eva Landberg, Judith Rosenbaum, Frau R. Deutschländer, Lotka Szczarańska, Linke Schreiber'.

publishing house, which since 1928 had furnished Bais Yaakov with school books and literature of interest to Orthodox girls and women.[10]

Bais Yaakov was not limited to this educational network. In 1926, the enterprising Friedenson brought together six existing groups to found Bnos Agudath Israel, the Agudah youth movement for older girls and young women that served graduates of the Bais Yaakov supplemental schools (pupils generally graduated at 13 or 14). Bnos shared many other ties with Bais Yaakov. For instance, teachers in small-town Bais Yaakov schools were generally expected to organize chapters of Bnos and serve as Bnos leaders.[11] As with Tse'irei Agudath Israel, the Agudah youth movement for young men founded in 1919, Bnos provided lectures, public programmes, libraries, reading rooms, clubs, co-operatives of various sorts, an employment bureau, and other opportunities for socializing, study, philanthropy, and activism for Orthodox adolescents.[12] It also founded and ran an organization for younger girls, called Batya. A 1935 article by an anonymous member captured the experience of Bnos: 'What does Bnos give a girl? It's hard to say. Ask a boy what he gets from a *shtibl* [small hasidic prayer house], will he know what to say? Maybe he'll say—what is a home? Bnos is a home for our youth. All our working girls. All day she is surrounded with unpleasant people who smirk ironically at how religious she is. Maybe she hides how she feels or becomes bitter, but at Bnos she can be herself.'[13] While the male youth movement, Tse'irei Agudah, was often embroiled in the 'political cauldron' that was Agudah in the interwar period, according to Gershon Bacon, Bnos limited itself to cultural activities and supporting Bais Yaakov.[14]

This list of organizations and accomplishments, impressive as it is, still fails to capture the character of Bais Yaakov as what Deborah Weissman has called 'a total institution', which organized the lives of Orthodox girls and young women and provided them with a new kind of 'home' away from home. As Weissman writes, 'the movement developed a complete system of slogans, mottoes, symbols, special holidays and celebrations, literature, songs, leadership roles, and other organizational techniques'.[15] These activities were not limited to the school

[10] The first publication of Friedenson's press was Schenirer's two-volume *Yahadus*, a textbook for teaching the Jewish religion.

[11] By 1937 there were nearly 300 Bnos groups serving over 14,132 members. See Bacon, *The Politics of Tradition*, 172.

[12] For more on Tse'irei Agudath Israel, see ibid. 118–41.

[13] 'What Is Bnos?' (Yid.), 12.

[14] Bacon, *The Politics of Tradition*, 172. Bnos members did, however, fight for their equal share of Agudah's allotment of immigration certificates to Palestine, as I discuss in the next chapter.

[15] Weissman, 'Bais Ya'akov: A Historical Model', 146.

day, but spilled over to weekends and the sabbath. Summer was an opportunity to leave the cities and towns behind, and study Torah or hike under the trees and open skies. Bais Yaakov not only sponsored its famous teacher-training courses then, it also offered summer colonies and camps. Bnos, too, sponsored leadership training programmes and other camps each summer. Many observers noted that Sarah Schenirer and her co-workers invented an entirely new subculture within Orthodox modernity, as well as a new model of Jewish girlhood, the Bais Yaakov student, whose knowledge of and passion for Torah reinvigorated Orthodoxy as a whole at a moment of grave danger to Orthodox continuity.

Bais Yaakov has frequently been called a revolution in Jewish education.[16] I would like to propose that Bais Yaakov was a particular kind of revolution: a charismatic social movement that followed the trajectory that Max Weber claims is inevitable for such movements if they are not to fail, from charisma to institutionalization and routinization. A charismatic movement is led by a venerated individual who operates outside the social hierarchies of his time (Weber assumes that such a leader will be male), attracting devoted followers and passionate adherents by his extraordinary qualities, 'by virtue of which he is set apart from ordinary men and treated as endowed with supernatural, superhuman, or at least specifically exceptional powers or qualities . . . and on the basis of them the individual concerned is treated as a leader'.[17] Such leaders rise not by climbing the usual institutional ladder of training and promotion, but from outside social structures and hierarchies, attracting followers whose dedication similarly supplants traditional norms or challenges more established forms of authority. As Weber writes:

> Charismatic authority is thus specifically outside the realm of everyday routine and the profane sphere. In this respect, it is sharply opposed to rational, and particularly bureaucratic, authority . . . Pure charisma is specifically foreign to economic considerations. Whenever it appears, it constitutes a 'call' in the most emphatic sense of the word, a 'mission' or a 'spiritual duty'. In the pure type, it disdains and repudiates economic exploitation of the gifts of grace as a source of income, though, to be sure, this often remains more an ideal than a fact.[18]

Charismatic movements, according to Weber, typically include some form of charismatic education, in which young people are removed from their homes and immersed in a more encompassing social framework where they can dedicate themselves to their mission more completely.

[16] See Seidman, *Renesans Religijny*, 32; J. Friedenson, 'The Bais Yaakov Girls' Schools' (Heb.), 61.

[17] Weber, *On Charisma*, 48.

[18] Ibid. 51–2.

The memoir literature on Bais Yaakov attests to Sarah Schenirer's charisma among her followers, describing the devotion with which she was treated by seminary girls who crowded to the window to catch sight of her when she returned from her travels, and the ecstasy with which they danced with or around her at graduation campfires in the summer colonies. This charisma continued and perhaps even grew after her death, when her students were sustained by her memory in times of danger.[19] Indeed, Chaim Kazdan, in his history of the Jewish school systems in interwar Poland, goes so far as to call the Bais Yaakov movement a 'cult of Sarah Schenirer', citing the fervent memories, poems, hymns, and stories recorded about her.[20] Her position outside the usual frameworks within which Orthodox leaders are recognized and promoted, far from being an obstacle to her achievements, is in Weber's scheme an inextricable part of her charisma. For those embedded within these traditional frameworks, however, the eccentric workings of charisma had a different effect. Leo Deutschländer describes how shocked he was at first sight of the two-room apartment in which in 1923 she established a boarding school for future Bais Yaakov teachers, none older than 16:

An old tenement building on a dirty street. Wretched and dilapidated. On the stairs we pass unsavoury characters. In this building a two-room apartment has been rented out —for the Bais Yaakov boarding school. This is where 50 future Bais Yaakov teachers live! We open the door, step inside. First we go through a tiny kitchen, where food for 50 people is prepared. Through a curtain are the other two large, primitive rooms, which serve as the dining room, the dormitory, the work and leisure room, wardrobe and washroom for all. A horror overtakes us: This is how future teachers live? Crowded, with two to a bed . . . What about basic hygiene?[21]

[19] In speaking of Schenirer's forbidding publication of her photograph, Pearl Benisch writes that students rather 'carried the image of our revered teacher in our hearts and minds. In the most tragic times when we were thrown into pits, interned in ghettos, confined to concentration camps . . . when we were ready to give up, Frau Schenirer's image stood before us. Her lively dark eyes penetrated us with her uncommon love and encouragement . . . In those trying times, the picture of Frau Schenirer helped them endure the trials' (Benisch, *Carry Me in Your Hearts*, 225–6). A story that circulated after the Holocaust ascribes supernatural powers to her. When Nazi guards ordered a Jewish boy to destroy her tombstone with sledgehammers, one sledgehammer after another broke without the tombstone being harmed. When a guard tried to destroy the tombstone himself, the same thing happened, until the guard 'turned white as a sheet, dropped the sledgehammer, and ran away'. The tombstone was ultimately destroyed, but only later. See Leibowitz with Gliksman, *Rebbetzin Vichna Kaplan*, 58.

[20] Kazdan, *The History of Jewish School Systems* (Yid.), 480. Grunfeld also uses the word 'cult' to describe the devotion of students to Schenirer. See Grunfeld-Rosenbaum, 'Sara Schenierer', 418.

[21] Deutschländer, *Bajs Jakob: Sein Wesen*, 23. Other reports describe the seminary as having

But the threadbare and overcrowded conditions of Bais Yaakov, in this early period, were also a sign, for those who could read it, of the spiritual purpose of its devotees, who scorned the comforts of middle-class Jewish life in exchange for the mission of spreading the Torah word. Deutschländer continues: 'I look at the girls. They seem young, fresh, perfectly content. I can see that at least some of them come from respectable homes, where they lack for nothing.'[22] One of the girls, asked how she coped with the difficult conditions, responded that there was a special magic in the apartment that made her forget its poverty: 'We have never felt luckier than we feel now, living together as a group. Oh! You must see for yourself how we spend our Friday evenings, around our sabbath table.'[23] Judith Grunfeld-Rosenbaum, describing the scene (which she did not see with her own eyes), emphasizes 'the heroic hours that were spent in study and happy privation' among the 'first willing disciples who lived with Sarah Schenirer in her two-room flat, sharing every hour of the day under her guidance for several months'.[24]

Such followers and disciples, with the energies of youth and willingness to experience 'happy privation' for the sake of a cause, may have been needed to build a network of schools essentially from scratch, with few other resources than human capital. Weber notes, however, that movements established by charismatic leaders are weakened by their idiosyncratic nature or lack of formal organization; charismatic individuals are often ill suited for organizing and institutionalizing the movements they found. The intense personal devotion that characterizes charismatic movements thus must cede, Weber writes, to a more 'stable community of disciples or a band of followers or a party organization', under an authority that has been 'either traditionalized or rationalized, or a combination of both'.[25] These more lasting forms of (post-) charismatic movements reassert the legitimacy of social hierarchies and reintegrate the movements into existing political, social, and economic frameworks, bringing order to the instability that is an inevitable feature of charisma.

I would argue not only that Bais Yaakov was a charismatic movement that was institutionalized about six or seven years after its founding, but also that it defined itself as just such a movement. Bais Yaakov recorded and treasured the memory of its founder and her marginal status within the Orthodox world, cher-

twenty or twenty-five rather than fifty students. See Grunfeld-Rosenbaum, 'Sara Schenierer', 414–15.

[22] Deutschländer, *Bajs Jakob: Sein Wesen*, 23.

[23] Ibid. 24.

[24] Grunfeld-Rosenbaum, 'Sara Schenierer', 414.

[25] Weber, *On Charisma*, 54.

ishing the privations of the early years and speaking with fondness and pride of Sarah Schenirer's promotion of young adolescents to serve as teachers in her movement. But the movement took equal pride in its institutionalization and rapid growth, reporting rapturously about the grand meeting hall in Łódź—the Philharmonic—where Bnos sometimes held conventions, and the Kraków seminary building, with its professional and 'hygienic' kitchens and dining rooms, dormitories, offices, library, reading room, lecture hall, roof garden, and 'modern ultra-violet ray equipment therapy which was used at various schools under the guidance of a school physician and trained nurses'.[26]

The two strands of the Bais Yaakov narrative, its charismatic origins and its rapid institutionalization, are entangled in particularly intricate ways. They are not only successive moments in the history of the movement, but also indicators of its dual character and the distinctive tensions at its height. I have described the move from the overcrowded apartment in 30 Augustiańska Street to the new seminary building as part of the trajectory of Bais Yaakov from charisma to (literally) institution. But the forces of charisma and institution, revolution and routine, centre and periphery, operated in tandem even after the institutionalization of the movement. An illustration of this appears in the widely circulated Bais Yaakov story about the ceremony to lay the cornerstone for the new seminary building in Kraków, held on 13 September 1927. The ceremony was attended by a host of Orthodox dignitaries, for whom a dais was erected on the site. Grunfeld-Rosenbaum describes the 'notables' sitting on the decorated dais, while 'Frau Schenirer, who stood with her disciples among the audience—shunning, as a pious woman of her type would do, glaring platform publicity—sent a prayer to G-d. It was in joyful anticipation of her dreams fulfilled, as well as in trembling fear, lest comforts and the luxury of normal standards might stifle the heroic efforts that had brought this movement into being.'[27] While the names of these 'notables' have disappeared from collective memory, the detail that remains in Bais Yaakov lore is the figure of Sarah Schenirer standing in the crowd rather than on the dais. This story, widely repeated in Bais Yaakov publications, has become a legend testifying to her modesty.[28]

But unlike many stories of the early Bais Yaakov years, we also have contemporary evidence for this scene, since the cornerstone-laying ceremony was

[26] The ultraviolet ray equipment was donated by a Berlin philanthropist named Jacob Michael. See Atkin, 'The Beth Jacob Movement in Poland', 161.

[27] Grunfeld-Rosenbaum, 'Sara Schenierer', 423.

[28] For an analysis of three of these stories, see Bechhofer, 'Ongoing Construction of Identity', 67–75.

Figure 3.3 A classroom in the Kraków seminary, 1930s

Courtesy of the Ghetto Fighters' House Museum Photo Archive, Israel

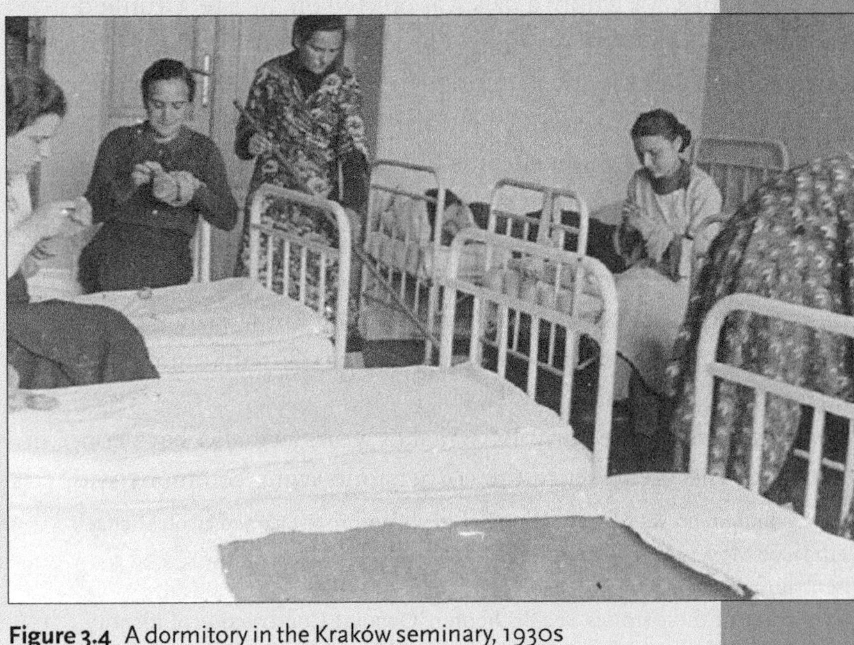

Figure 3.4 A dormitory in the Kraków seminary, 1930s

Courtesy of the Ghetto Fighters' House Museum Photo Archive, Israel

covered in the *Bais Yaakov Journal*. As the anonymous correspondent (probably Friedenson) reported, thousands of curious men, women, and children streamed from the surrounding streets to crowd the ceremony site, where they stood segregated by gender.[29] There was indeed a dais, as Grunfeld-Rosenbaum reported, on which sat a group of distinguished rabbis and Agudah leaders, as well as rows of seats before the dais for distinguished guests (the report does not specify whether a section of these seats was reserved for women). Crowd control was provided by members of the Tse'irei Agudath Israel for the men and Bnos for the women. There was also a heavy police presence, a press table to the left of the dais for the many local and international press correspondents from Jewish and non-Jewish newspapers, and a choir from the Old Synagogue singing the Polish national anthem and other songs. The cornerstone was designed by the artist Uriel Birnbaum (youngest son of Nathan Birnbaum), who was responsible for much of the artwork of Agudah publications. Rabbi Isaac Meir Levin, president of the Agudah in Poland and son-in-law of the Gerer Rebbe, delivered a moving keynote address that lasted for over an hour.[30] A few other Agudah leaders, including Deutschländer, briefly greeted the crowd. According to this report, 'Among the women were the Bais Yaakov teachers Miss Rosenbaum, Miss Landsberg, and Miss Szczarańska—with Frau Schenirer at their head—along with many distinguished female guests from the area.' It was Rosenbaum who provided, in 1953, the first version of the story that now circulates so widely.

While Grunfeld-Rosenbaum focused on Sarah Schenirer's presence at the event, the news article emphasized its 'grandiosity', the interest the ceremony aroused among the Orthodox public, and the respect paid to Kraków Orthodoxy by various non-Jewish members of the Polish parliament and other government officials. The article also emphasized the separation of men and women in the crowd, which was a regular feature of Orthodox reporting on large public events under the aegis of the Agudah, to ensure that readers who had not attended understood that the dictates of modesty had not been breached (public events were understood to be places of potential immodesty, and opponents of Orthodox political organization cited them among their objections). The report mentioned the speaker list, which did not include Sarah Schenirer, but did not note this absence, no doubt because this reflected standard Agudah practice. While

[29] 'The Grand Celebration' (Yid.), 2. As the report noted, the cornerstone was engraved with the *Bais Yaakov Journal*'s logo.

[30] Yitzhak Meir (known as Itshe-Meir) Levin would go on to become a member of the Polish Sejm (parliament) and later of the Israeli Knesset.

she occasionally spoke to mixed-sex audiences that included fathers and mothers in order to publicize the activities of Bais Yaakov throughout the small towns of Poland, the reports of larger rabbinical gatherings and Agudah conferences that I have read do not mention female speakers, except when these addressed exclusively female audiences. In short, it seems to me that her presence on, rather than absence from, the dais would have been cause for comment.

In contrast to this newspaper report, the story that circulated after the war, beginning with Grunfeld-Rosenbaum's 1953 account, took Sarah Schenirer's absence from the dais as testimony to her modesty—her unwillingness to participate in public spectacle or take credit for her achievements. But we have no evidence that she turned down an invitation to speak or even sit on the dais. In other words, it is at least as accurate to describe the Orthodox male establishment as setting limits on female public visibility as to suggest that it is the woman who 'shuns the spotlight'. Grunfeld-Rosenbaum's description might thus be read less as a token of an east European woman's modesty (for what choice did she have?) than as the indirect protest of a central European woman at Sarah Schenirer's enforced silence at an event that owed so much to her initiative. As collective memory, the story thus exemplifies a profound ambivalence in Bais Yaakov culture about the relationship between its female founder and the gender-segregated, male-dominated rabbinic culture that oversaw the movement she founded. As Shoshana Bechhofer argues in her reading of how Bais Yaakov formed its identity, it is significant that the occasion of the cornerstone-laying ceremony is not remembered as 'a moment of unmitigated joy . . . instead, it represents the tension between revolution and establishment'.[31] Unlike the contemporary *Bais Yaakov Journal* report, the story renders Sarah Schenirer's displacement from the dais as visible and notable; as Bechhofer puts it: 'The camera shot is a close-up of Schenirer, while the scene, populated by extras, is a blur.'[32] The centre and periphery of the scene are thus reversed. What was taken for granted or seen as peripheral by the journalist in 1927 is the centre of the story told by a woman teacher in 1953. While the long list of distinguished rabbis and leaders painstakingly recorded by the correspondent has faded, it is only Sarah Schenirer whose presence at the ceremony is remembered by Bais Yaakov.

The question of Sarah Schenirer's place at the cornerstone ceremony attests to the inevitable complexity of collective memory in a movement that has undergone institutionalization. For Bais Yaakov, this complexity has revolved around a number of issues. The first is the degree to which she can be credited with the

[31] Bechhofer, 'Ongoing Constitution of Identity', 72. [32] Ibid. 105.

movement's success. Her 'cult status', to use Kazdan's term, has been shadowed by a discourse that treats her contribution more evenly, or even with dismissiveness. The accounts of Bais Yaakov that slight or fail to mention her begin in 1925 and continue to our own day.[33] The second question is how to conceptualize the relationship between the Agudah and Bais Yaakov. Did Agudath Israel take over or merely support the movement? Include it under its activities or help Sarah Schenirer in her work? Did Deutschländer, as Judith Grunfeld-Rosenbaum puts it, 'rear the child he had found in its promising infancy' by making 'Beth Jacob a well-organized movement'?[34] Rather than attempting to decide these questions or choose among the alternatives, it might be more useful to read them as symptomatic of the status of Bais Yaakov as a movement that followed the path from charisma to institution.

The institutionalization of Bais Yaakov did not, of course, follow an unbroken line, nor did it take place with one turn of events or decisive vote. Among the relevant markers for this road that I have already mentioned are: the 1919 decision by the Kraków Agudah to support Sarah Schenirer's school; the 1923 world congress in Vienna that established Keren Hatorah and placed Bais Yaakov under its financial aegis; Leo Deutschländer's 1924 visit to her boarding school; and the 1931 move to the new seminary building. I would argue, however, that a less well-known event marked the most decisive turn towards institutionalization: the Bais Yaakov conference that was held in February 1925 at the Havatselet *gymnasium* in Warsaw. Hillel Seidman draws attention to this conference as a pivotal moment, 'a breakthrough in the history of Bais Yaakov. It provides an impetus to coordinate, standardize, and expand Bais Yaakov schools.'[35] As opposed to the enthusiasm that marks the stories of Bais Yaakov's origins, an aura of bureaucratic order and sombre authority pervades the *Bais Yaakov Journal* report, which is presented as a series of bullet points. The unnamed 'special correspondent' described the attendees as a sizeable number of delegates from the school committees that had been established in many small towns, along with a number of Bais Yaakov teachers and Agudah activists. The conference, which began with an opening address by Aharon Lewin, the rabbi of Sambor and an Agudah delegate in the Polish parliament, took up the problem of setting Bais Yaakov on more solid ground than it had so far known. It decided on twenty-two resolutions, divided into six cate-

[33] Oleszak provides citations for Agudah publications from the interwar period that do not mention Schenirer, or which slight her contribution. Deutschländer is among these writers; see Oleszak, 'The Beit Ya'akov School in Kraków', 282. See Introduction, n. 9, above.

[34] See Grunfeld-Rosenbaum, 'Sara Schenierer', 426.

[35] Seidman, *Renesans Religijny*, 18.

gories: type of school; curriculum; training of teachers; textbooks; organization; literature. The first set of resolutions, on the type of school Bais Yaakov intended to establish, made it clear that the organization embraced even more ambitious goals than Sarah Schenirer had initially set, resolving to build a network of day schools at which 'all subjects, Jewish studies and general studies, would be taught in a strong religious spirit' (as we have seen, such day schools were established only in a few larger towns).[36] Acknowledging that such schools were difficult to open, the second resolution listed afternoon schools as a temporary alternative. On both the curriculum and the problem of textbooks and Orthodox literature, which were discussed at length at the conference, the assembled delegates and teachers resolved to form committees that could work towards a solution. Resolution 6, on teacher training, was the only one to mention Sarah Schenirer (I have not found evidence of her presence). The resolution reads, in its entirety: 'The training of Bais Yaakov teachers must be divided into two tracks: the first for teachers in grades 1–4, and the second for teachers up to the seventh grade. New pedagogical forces [*pedagogishe kreftn*] to train teachers must be added to those of Frau Schenirer.'

Despite the first resolution to move ahead with Bais Yaakov along the path it charted, the ninth resolution retreated from the aim of continual expansion: 'It is resolved not to prematurely open new schools until there are properly trained teachers who can work in them.' For the first time, the mission of Bais Yaakov was to be constrained by the lack of qualified staff. Young people would no longer be assigned the status of teacher on the grounds that they seemed capable and mature, as Sarah Schenirer had done, according to school legend. The minutes do not spell out what difficulties had already arisen from sending unprepared teachers into the field, but speeches and reports from the conference confirm the tone of reproach and bureaucratic resolve. In his lecture on the state of Orthodox literature, Aleksander Zysha Friedman (known as Zysha), a Warsaw-based Agudath Israel leader, acknowledged 'what everyone knows, that we have no teaching materials, which is the biggest obstacle to the development of our movement. Our schools give the impression that the printing press has yet to be invented.' Friedman also reproved the *Bais Yaakov Journal* for failing at the job it had undertaken by appearing so irregularly. But the allusion to schools devoid of printed material seems to have been an indirect reference to Sarah Schenirer's handwritten 'lessons', some of them transcriptions of lectures she had heard

[36] All quotations in this paragraph are from 'The Resolutions of the First Bais Yaakov Conference' (Yid.), 74.

from Rabbi Flesch and others, her own handwritten, 'simple, primitive and old-fashioned' teaching manuals, which the students in the first years of the seminary were required to copy out by hand. One of these lessons, as Grunfeld-Rosenbaum transliterates and translates it, was a sort of play:

Teacher—Wus bist du? (What are you?)

Pupil—Yach bin a Yiddish kind. (I am a Jewish child.)

Teacher—Mit wus bist du a Yiddish kind? (What makes you a Jewish child?)

Pupil—Yach bin a Yiddish kind, weil ich hob die heilige Toira wus hot gegeben der heiliger Bescheffer die Himlen un die Erd. (I am a Jewish child, because I have the holy Torah, given by the Holy Creator) . . .

And so it goes on, for pages and pages.[37]

As a graduate of a German teachers' seminary recruited by Jacob Rosenheim to work in the Bais Yaakov summer teacher-training programme, Grunfeld-Rosenbaum was part of the solution to the problem of Sarah Schenirer's 'primitive' pedagogy. Along with her taught a few other university-educated German speakers, including Betty Rothschild and Rosalie Mannes.[38] Bais Yaakov, which after an explosive start, continued to grow steadily in the interwar period, took a small step backwards with the resolution 'not to open new schools until there were properly trained teachers to fill them'. The graph published in the 100th issue of the *Bais Yaakov Journal* (and translated and reproduced in Benisch's *Carry Me in Your Heart*) shows that between the years 1922/3 and 1923/4 the number of schools in the system tripled (from 7 to 22) and the number of pupils quadrupled (from 1,040 to 4,490); between 1923/4 and 1924/5, Bais Yaakov opened an additional 27 schools and welcomed 2,095 more pupils. But in the year after the 1925 Warsaw conference this pace slowed considerably, and only six schools were added, with an additional 755 pupils.[39] The summer of 1925, only a few months after the Warsaw conference resolved to put teacher training on a proper footing, saw the first teacher-training course (*Fortbildungskurs*), staffed by leaders of the German Agudah and German-trained teachers.

[37] Grunfeld-Rosenbaum, 'Sara Schenierer', 415–16. While this description is clearly meant to signal the primitive character of Schenirer's pedagogy, it may more generously be read as a script (admittedly an unsophisticated one) written to engage young pupils through performance. Schenirer wrote numerous plays for Bais Yaakov, and performances were a powerful recruitment tool for the movement.

[38] For more on these teachers, see J. Friedenson, 'The Movement from its Beginnings' (Heb.), 127.

[39] 'The Rise of the Bais Yaakov Movement' (Yid.), 183–4.

Even clearer evidence that the conference signalled a new era is supplied by the resolutions relating to organization. The first of these (Resolution 11) proposed that 'A Bais Yaakov central office should be set up in Warsaw to oversee the existence of the schools and their appropriate development.' Number 12 proposed that this central office should forge close contacts with the schools, issue precise reports on their activities, and lend appropriate help to them, while Number 13 resolved that it should establish an inspection committee to visit the schools. Number 14 resolved that it should establish an Orthodox women's speakers' bureau to send out speakers who could spread the word about Bais Yaakov. This is not to say that the movement's character entirely changed. Along with the decision to establish a variety of commissions and committees, the delegates also voted that existing Bais Yaakov schools should 'organize sabbath and holiday events, and sponsor evening celebrations on a regular basis'. Charisma, it seems, can also be routinized and legislated.

The language of 'precise instructions' (*genoyen onvayzungen*), 'properly trained teachers' (*geherik-oysgebildete lererins*), and 'proper development' (*geheriker entviklung*) captures this meeting's pivotal nature, marking the transition of leadership from Sarah Schenirer to the new central office. The headquarters therefore moved from Kraków to Warsaw, where it was directed by Aleksander Zysha Friedman, whose rare gift for organization and administration was widely acknowledged in Agudah circles.[40] It may not be surprising that, shortly after the 1925 conference, Friedenson published an essay in the *Bais Yaakov Journal* warning of the dangers of Bais Yaakov falling into chaos. Beginning with the question, 'How was this movement created?' Friedenson answers by giving the by now familiar description of the despair and paralysis of Orthodoxy in the face of the defection of its young women. He continues:

> So it was a true surprise for organized Orthodoxy when, at a certain time, [girls' education] became an established fact. It began as a little flicker, but grew and grew into a roaring flame. Bit by bit, of its own accord, very nearly by instinct, girls' schools were founded, women's organizations established, a periodical issued, and gradually literature produced. This was all created without any organizing hand, without any financial support, without pedagogical methods, and generally with no system or concept of organization. And when one is faced with such an established fact, one might take it as one's own accomplishment. And that wouldn't be entirely wrong—since the organizers, activists, and leaders of this movement were in fact active members of the Agudath Israel. But we can no longer escape the lack of system in the movement . . . Agudath

[40] On Aleksander Zysha Friedman, see Seidman, *Personalities I Knew* (Heb.), 77–89.

Israel has to understand that it must in general pay much closer attention to this movement . . . for if not, it might God forbid fall even further into chaos [*hefker*].[41]

Using a stream of passive constructions, Friedenson manages to tell the story of Bais Yaakov without once mentioning Sarah Schenirer's name. Perhaps he is actually being gracious to her, avoiding blaming her for the movement's poor state. Nevertheless, the effect of his article is to position Bais Yaakov as an ownerless object, begging to be picked up and brought to order.

Agnieszka Oleszak has shown that Friedenson was not alone in obscuring Sarah Schenirer's role during this delicate transition. Deutschländer was also sometimes inclined to minimize her role. While narrating the entrance of Keren Hatorah to the field, he fails entirely to mention her, writing: 'We can hardly speak of the existence of girls' education, as it was in very poor condition in almost all countries at the beginning of Keren Hatorah's existence . . . The situation changed radically when the Bait Ya'akov movement affiliated with Keren Hatorah.'[42] While Bais Yaakov existed and grew for six or seven years before Deutschländer's arrival on the scene, its story as a full-fledged educational system properly begins with Keren Hatorah.

The imposition of professional standards, as Oleszak argues, was regularly justified by reference to the unhygienic conditions and unprofessional teaching methods of Bais Yaakov in the years before the arrival of the German neo-Orthodox administrators.[43] In this way, the discourse around the movement, which sometimes described it as an 'endeavour to safeguard the moral and physical welfare of our womanhood', saw it as both a solution for and part of the problem of east European poverty and lack of discipline and professionalism. Given the critical terms in which Bais Yaakov was described in such reports, it was not so much an insult to Sarah Schenirer to refrain from mentioning her role as a form of chivalry.

As the Agudah soon found out, chaos and charisma are not so easily tamed. As the 1925 conference resolved, a central Bais Yaakov office was duly established in Warsaw a few months later, in conjunction with the Horev Educational Organization that operated in the Agudah offices in the city. But this Warsaw office represented only one of three central offices affiliated with Bais Yaakov in Poland. Bais Yaakov regularly described the offices connected to the teachers' seminary in Kraków as the 'Bais Yaakov Centre', issuing bulletins from this location

[41] E. G. Friedenson, 'Agudath Israel and "Bais Yaakov"' (Yid.), 127.

[42] Deutschländer, *Das Erziehungswerk der gesetztreuen Judenheit*, 12, cited in Oleszak, 'The Beit Ya'akov School in Kraków', 282.

[43] See Oleszak, 'The Beit Ya'akov School in Kraków', 287–8.

throughout the 1930s, even as, in Łódź, Friedenson established yet another 'central office' which issued the *Bais Yaakov Journal* and other movement literature. Joseph Friedenson suggests that there was a harmonious division of labour among these centres: Warsaw dealt with legal matters, Kraków with teacher training and the organization of the system (precisely what the 1925 resolution intended to transfer to Warsaw), and Łódź handled Bais Yaakov's publications, Bnos, and the Ohel Sarah network (the Horev office in Warsaw had its own publication operation, which also published Bais Yaakov literature).[44] And to these three centres we should add the Vienna office of Keren Hatorah, where Leo Deutschländer, like his enterprising counterparts in Łódź and Warsaw, far exceeded his official mandate or initial assignment.

As this multiplicity of centres might suggest, the routinization of Bais Yaakov was more aspiration than reality, affecting some areas of the movement while leaving others untouched. In a speech at a Bais Yaakov conference in 1933, the year he took over as director of the Kraków seminary and central office, Yehudah Leib Orlean acknowledged the disorganization that plagued the movement as he attempted to sternly combat it:

> Under no circumstances should people be operating without the consent of the central office. You should read the correspondence that piles up in our office about all the various individuals in the movement who have broken discipline. Not only that, some of them are proud of themselves, wanting us to publicize their transgressions so that others can follow in their path. We have to be firm with these people, even if they threaten to close down the school if we don't agree with them . . . We have to safeguard the purity of our principles, which derive from fifteen years of experience with two hundred schools as well as the opinion of the great Torah sages of Poland.[45]

Such reports reveal how difficult it was to control the network of supplementary schools in small towns, which were local initiatives funded by community support and tuition. Bais Yaakov teachers in these localities were often expected to fundraise on behalf of the school (and for their own salaries), while teaching and leading Bnos groups. Although the Bais Yaakov central offices in Kraków and Vilna sometimes raised official objections to this expectation, local school com-

[44] J. Friedenson, 'The Bais Yaakov Girls' Schools' (Heb.), 69.

[45] See Orlean, 'The Bais Yaakov Movement on Firm Foundations' (Yid.), 6. 'By-Laws of the Beth Jacob Schools', 1, sets out the responsibilities of school committees and teachers, making it clear that the committees (which were to have three to five members) were expected to find a hygienic, airy, and dry location for the school; to provide for the teacher's salary and board; and to collect tuition, 'so that the teacher will not have to concern herself with this'.

mittees penalized teachers for lack of public speaking ability or various other faults unrelated to teaching.[46] Schools even closed to avoid fulfilling their financial obligations. The repeated resolutions, conference after conference, that relationships be maintained between leadership and schools speak volumes about the difficulties of managing the system. In a 1934 speech, Orlean also described with remarkable frankness the challenges in persuading parents to respect the Bais Yaakov code of conduct on modesty, for instance. Not only did parents fail to send their daughters to school appropriately dressed, they also pressured local schools to lower standards because they objected to 'their daughters being trained to be "rebetzins" (rabbis' wives)'.[47] Parents enrolled and withdrew their daughters at will, compelling teachers to repeat material they had already covered; others failed to pay the tuition fees. Of course, there were occasions when the system worked as it was meant to. Yitzhok Shafran, who served on the school committee in Goworowo, relates proudly that, despite the poverty of the town, the school operated there without interruption from its founding until the war, had close relations not only with the seminary in Kraków (from which it drew all its teachers) but also with Sarah Schenirer, and produced graduates of the highest calibre.[48]

Under these conditions it was difficult to establish how many Bais Yaakov schools there were. While the graph of the movement printed in the *Bais Yaakov Journal* in 1933 shows a steadily rising line, it obscures the rapidity and frequency with which schools closed and reopened. As public reports of the movement showed, in 1933, thirty-five schools closed, while fourteen reopened later that year; another thirty-nine closed the next year, with twenty-seven reopening.[49] Teachers left to marry, or fell ill; others were let go for financial reasons or because they had lost the confidence of the local committee. Some schools were shut down by one or another of the central offices for failing to conform to Agudah ideology or Bais Yaakov standards; others were closed by the authorities. Still others shut down to avoid financial obligations, only to reopen a few months

[46] Orlean, 'The Bais Yaakov Movement on Firm Foundations' (Yid.), 6. In this same speech, Orlean advocated dividing the 200 schools into groups of five, with the most highly qualified teacher in the group inspecting the other schools in rotation over the course of the school year.

[47] Orlean continued: 'There is to be no compromise. Children must be taught when they are very young that no part of the body should be exposed.' From 'Curricular Problems in the Schools', *Bais Yaakov Journal*, 109 (1934), cited in Atkin, 'The Beth Jacob Movement in Poland', 61.

[48] Shafran, 'The Bais Yaakov School' (Yid.), 110.

[49] 'Beth Jacob Central Organization in 1933', *Bais Yaakov Journal*, 117 (1934), 16, cited in Atkin, 'The Beth Jacob Movement in Poland', 63.

later as a 'new school'.[50] Aside from the confusion created by schools opening and closing without notice, some also occasionally opened using the name of Bais Yaakov without bothering to establish a connection with the central offices. A 1928 announcement in the Orthodox weekly *Di yidishe shtime* declared that the central office in Kraków took no responsibility for Bais Yaakov schools that operated without permission to use the name, or that hired teachers who had not attended the Bais Yaakov seminary. In addition, teachers trained at the seminary who accepted positions in unauthorized schools 'would be stricken from our rolls'.[51] Nearly a decade later, conditions had apparently not improved: In a 1937 article in the *Bais Yaakov Journal* taking stock of the development of the school system, 'A.F.' (perhaps Aleksander Zysha Friedman) laments that along with the many towns that had no Bais Yaakov schools as yet, there were 'many others where the school operates on a local basis with no ties whatsoever with the central body'.[52] The opposite circumstance also sometimes complicated keeping track of the system. In the ultra-traditional region known to Jews as *Unterland* (present-day Slovakia, parts of Ukraine, and northern Transylvania), local rabbis accepted the need to open schools for girls, schools that would be staffed by graduates of the seminaries in Vienna and Kraków. Nevertheless, this acceptance was conditioned on two factors: the pupils would not study Bible or other traditional Jewish sources from the original texts, and the schools would not be called Bais Yaakov, a name that was 'tainted' in their eyes by its affiliation with the Agudah, a 'modern' political organization.[53] During the years of its rapid growth, then, the very borders of the system were sometimes hard to discern.

We are fortunate to possess a detailed description of what opening a Bais Yaakov school in a small town might entail, in an essay by 'Esther' (a pseudonym) submitted to the YIVO autobiography contest. Despite lacking teaching credentials or a seminary education, the 17-year-old 'Esther' received a letter offering her a teaching position in a small town that she had never visited and which she does not name. Arriving after an arduous journey ('I didn't even know where this little town was located') to the town and the house of the rabbi, 'I learned that

50 'A Look at Our School Life', *Bais Yaakov Journal*, 120 (1935), 2, cited and discussed in Atkin, 'The Beth Jacob Movement in Poland', 66.

51 'Communiqué from the Bais Yaakov Central Office' (Yid.), 4.

52 A.F., 'What Should Be Done?' *Bais Yaakov Journal*, jubilee edn. (May 1937), cited in Eisenstein, *Jewish Schools in Poland*, 87.

53 For more on the Bais Yaakov schools that operated 'in disguise' in this region, see Grill, *Der Westen im Osten*, 297.

the Beys Yaakov school had yet to be established. What they had written to me was purely imaginary. It turned out that nothing was ready.'[54] After forming a Bais Yaakov committee from among the fathers of the town and delivering a speech that drew and inspired a large crowd, 'Esther' went to work: 'All by myself, I assigned sixty children to classes, scheduled lessons, and even went along to rent space for the school. I had to write appeals, post announcements, give lectures. I had to accomplish all this and quietly, too, because the school was still unofficial. The men's committee did very little.'[55] The pupils, 'Esther' discovered, had 'never learned to read or write Yiddish'. But the real trouble began when the chairman of the school committee, at whose house she was boarding, intercepted a letter from a socialist friend of hers, a former Bnos 'sister'. Other challenges arose, first when 'the poorer children stopped coming to the school', and then when 'police began to show interest in the school, which still wasn't licensed because it hadn't met the state's financial requirements'.[56] Under these multiple pressures, the school closed, and 'Esther' was compelled to return home defeated.[57]

This particular case may provide insight into the movement as a whole. Given its astonishingly rapid growth, its reliance on local initiatives, the unclear borders between Bais Yaakov schools and others with a similar ideological orientation, and the underground character of some of its schools, it is not surprising that, as Joseph Friedenson remarked, data about the Bais Yaakov schools include contradictory tallies of pupils and schools.[58] Orlean worked to get the upper hand on the movement, and floated initiatives for supervising local schools. He instituted a complicated system comprising regular inspections; the selection of model schools that would guide the others in the vicinity, with a special ceremony at each model school 'in honour of its being selected'; exhibits by the children of such schools at the seminary in Kraków; and special scholarships to the seminary for their best graduates.[59] It is unclear to what extent any aspect of this plan

[54] Shandler (ed.), *Awakening Lives*, 335.

[55] Ibid. 336.

[56] Even more established schools and more experienced teachers could run into similar difficulties. Vichna Eisen (later Kaplan) describes her time teaching in Brisk (now Brest in Belarus), where the Brisker Rov, Yitzkhok Zev Soloveitchik, took it upon himself to make sure the teachers were paid. Nevertheless, she failed to receive the salary she had been promised and resigned in frustration. (She returned after her students sent her a telegram in the Brisker Rov's name ordering her to come back, though he had no knowledge of this.) See Leibowitz with Gliksman, *Rebbetzin Vichna Kaplan*, 100–1.

[57] Ibid. 337, 338.

[58] J. Friedenson, 'The Bais Yaakov Girls' Schools' (Heb.), 70.

[59] Orlean, 'The Bais Yaakov Movement on Firm Foundations' (Yid.), 6.

was ever carried out. Nevertheless, Bais Yaakov continued to grow in the 1930s, propelled not only by the power of its ideology, but also by the availability of young women looking to make a living, and the continuing need for this type of education. By the 1930s, Bais Yaakov was a complex system, with a leadership spread out among three Polish cities and one in Austria, and which operated under the authority of another, larger and even more complex organization, the Agudath Israel. Bais Yaakov conferences repeatedly attempted to bring the far-flung movement into curricular uniformity and institutional order, but such attempts were only partly successful.

Institutionalization took on a special character in Bais Yaakov, given the central role gender played in the movement. The transition I have been tracing was not only from charisma to (a very disorganized form of) organization, but also from a movement led by a Polish woman to a more complex network headed by male leaders, both German and Polish. The transition to male leadership was part of this institutionalization process. Teachers in the afternoon supplementary schools were virtually all female, and even the high schools and seminaries had a largely female teaching staff, but the various offices of Bais Yaakov and Horev were directed and staffed by men, and men lectured in the seminaries and summer colonies and served as honoured guests at examinations and graduations. The presence of men at these ceremonies and in the offices of Bais Yaakov was the very mark of its institutionalization, but it also constituted one of the revolutionary aspects of the system. Sarah Schenirer, who had grown up in a more strictly gender-segregated society in which rabbis did not ordinarily address women (many would also not look at a woman), much less praise their learning, recorded her gratified surprise at hearing a rabbi speak so directly and warmly to his female congregants. But Bais Yaakov was soon enough to witness many interactions not only with German neo-Orthodox leaders, for whom such interactions were no doubt easier, but also, more remarkably, between east European men and women. Everyone, it seems, wanted to see Bais Yaakov students in their element, learning Torah outdoors, passionately and with complete devotion. Among the lecturers at the summer colonies were Jacob Rosenheim, president of the World Agudah; Rabbi Dr Leo Jung, leader of American Orthodoxy; Dr Solomon Birnbaum, lecturer in Yiddish at Hamburg University and Orthodox activist; Aleksander Zysha Friedman, Yehudah Leib Orlean, and Eliezer Gershon Friedenson. Joseph Friedenson describes the atmosphere at the summer colonies as reminding us of 'a yeshiva, with students that are engaged in studying Torah *lishmah* [for its own sake]':

> The whole Torah, from 'In the beginning' [Gen. 1: 1] to 'before the eyes of all Israel' [Deut. 34: 12], is clear to them. The older girls also understand Rashi, as well as Maimonides and the Malbim. Some of them understand and draw sustenance from profound hasidic teachings. Their comprehension of problems in contemporary Jewish life is extraordinary, and some of them know entire books of the Prophets or Proverbs by heart. They have a fine understanding of the moral literature [*muser*] and nearly every one of them is a talented speaker, able to inspire crowds with 'words that kindle fire' [Ps. 29: 7].[60]

Bracketing for a moment these remarkable intellectual achievements, it is worth noting the male attention they attracted. While the practice of orally examining a yeshiva student is a familiar one, and Jewish memoirs record the less official exams administered by older men to prospective sons-in-law, public display and rabbinic notice of young women's dedication to Torah study and accomplishments are far rarer. Such distinguished visitors as Rosenheim and Deutschländer not only conveyed legitimacy on female Torah study (within limits), but also constructed new social practices and arenas where men could witness and praise female religious and intellectual accomplishments. The praise of students sometimes extended, as well, to the supplemental schools in small towns. In Goworowo, the town rabbi attended the year-end examinations along with the parents, and 'everyone was truly amazed at the beautiful responses the pupils gave, and their deep knowledge of the entire curriculum'. The adults were particularly impressed with the students in the higher grades, 'who could recite entire chapters of Isaiah by heart, and then interpret each verse as well as conveying the essence of the chapter as a whole'.[61] These novel arrangements had characterized the movement from the outset, as for instance when Mr Luksenberg assumed the role of Sarah Schenirer's helper in her first school. Women themselves were emboldened to make overtures: the Neshei Agudath Israel, shortly after its founding in 1929, hosted Rabbi Israel Meir Kagan, the famed

[60] Joseph Friedenson quotes an anonymous report from a visitor to the summer colony in Rabka in 1929 that first appeared in the *Bais Yaakov Journal*, 45 (1929), in 'The Bais Yaakov Girls' School in Poland' (Heb.), 74. The summer courses for training teachers operated from 1925 to 1930, initially for two months and later for three. In the first year, at Robów, 48 students attended. In 1926 and 1927, when the courses were held in Jordanów, 98 and 76 students, respectively, attended. In 1928, 1929, and 1930, in Rabka, between 125 and 240 students attended each year. See Atkin, 'The Beth Jacob Movement in Poland', 117–19. In 1931, Bais Yaakov transitioned from using the summer to train teachers to establishing leadership programmes for Bnos leaders and camps (often called Yehudis) for younger Bais Yaakov pupils.

[61] Shafran, 'The Bais Yaakov School', (Yid.), 110.

Hafets Hayim, in a lecture to an audience of women on family purity laws. At least some male Agudah leaders actively sought talented women as collaborators. When Eliezer Gershon Friedenson heard of a particularly gifted Bais Yaakov teacher in the town of Kurów, a Mrs Rachel Schildkraut, he recruited her to work in the Łódź offices of the *Bais Yaakov Journal*.[62] Bais Yaakov was thus radical in constructing strong ties among girls and women, bringing social forms traditionally associated with men to the world of women. But it was also radical in those arenas that brought men and women together, whether in the various offices of Bais Yaakov or in the summer colony in Rabka.

The novelty of Bais Yaakov as a site of interactions between men and women could hardly go unnoticed within Polish Orthodoxy, and was the subject of a number of halakhic responsa. The Boyaner Rebbe, Moshe Friedman of Kraków, ruled in 1924 that 'men can be present at the school registration and collect tuition monies, provided at least two of them are present, neither a bachelor'. Married men were also permitted to lecture in the schools. Rabbi Elchanan Wasserman went further, in ruling that men could be appointed to run a school and give lectures to groups of women.[63] Yehudah Leib Orlean was appointed director of the Kraków seminary only after an exchange of letters between the Agudah president Jacob Rosenheim and the Gerer Rebbe (of whom Orlean was a devoted follower) on the permissibility of a man filling the position.[64] Such decisions were made on the local as well as national level. Yitzhok Shafran describes how he was recruited to serve on the Goworowo Bais Yaakov Committee by the town rabbi, who invited him to a meeting in 1932 and proclaimed, 'Itshe! I want you to be the secretary and treasurer of the Bais Yaakov.' Shafran, astonished, answered, 'But I'm an unmarried man. It's not appropriate. People will talk.' One of the assembled men, 'a fiery Jew, burning with love of Israel and the fear of God', called out: 'Stupid fanaticism! Yiddishkeyt is drowning and you are being called on to rescue it!' Shafran continues, 'Naturally, I took the position and held it until the war broke out.'[65] While in 1903 the rabbinic world could not find warrant for permitting organized Torah study for girls, in the 1920s it paved the halakhic and cultural way for full male support for and participation in such a system.

Social rules and norms continued to police these new arrangements, and Agudah worked hard to make sure that public events did not result in a breach of

[62] See Szaranski (ed.), *Remember* (Heb.), 86.

[63] *Bais Yaakov Bulletin* (1924–5), 9, cited in Weissman, 'Bais Ya'akov: A Women's Educational Movement', 59.

[64] On the letter exchange, see Seidman, *Personalities I Knew* (Heb.), 198.

[65] Shafran, 'The Bais Yaakov School', (Yid.), 112–13.

the rules of gender segregation, maintaining a position against both women's suffrage and women holding public office. But the very phenomenon of an Orthodox girls' youth movement, however strictly it was policed, challenged the strict gender segregation of traditional Jewish society. Bais Yaakov plays, for instance, were only open to female audiences, but because they were often the most exciting event in a small town, they excited interest beyond the world of Orthodox girls. One columnist for the Warsaw daily *Haynt* claimed that stories about the sensation caused by Bais Yaakov plays were a perennial phenomenon:

> I knew in my heart that when the beloved holiday of Hanukkah came to an end, the 'Provincial Mirror' [column] would be inundated with stories and anecdotes regarding Bais Yaakov. What kind of stories? The Bais Yaakov schools have a well-established protocol that repeats itself every year, everywhere from Hoduciszki to Lututów. The formula is that Bais Yaakov girls put on a play—but only for women. The not-so-fair sex must not make an appearance in the hall. Many fights break out over this issue. This is exactly what just happened in Chmielnik. The Chmielnik Bais Yaakov was determined to show the sinners and freethinkers that one could be a pious Jewish girl and still take an interest in the arts. The schoolgirls thus put on a play on the sabbath of Hanukkah, 'Judith'. The young people in Chmielnik are theatre-crazy, and they were very excited. 'Even if it's Gerer theatre, it's still theatre!' They awaited this evening, as one awaits, pardon the comparison, the Messiah. The posters finally went up, with a small postscript in black on white, 'Entrance only for women!'[66]

The eager boys in Chmielnik, according to this report, decided to dress in women's clothing in order to sneak into the performance. But when they arrived at the movie theatre where the play was being performed, they were stopped by young Gerer hasidim assigned to guard the door and make sure that only women entered. After the young cross-dressers were expelled, the report describes the hasidic guards permitting themselves to watch the play, their eyes gleaming with 'holy sparks', sighing with wonder at the pleasures unfolding before them. A similar incident apparently scandalized the town of Błonie, where the rabbi had to be called in to expel hasidic youth who had dressed as women in their eagerness to see a production of 'The Binding of Isaac'; the play, the reporter wryly commented, featured a cast in which some girls were playing male characters, which meant that the cross-dressed boys in the audience were watching cross-dressed girls on stage.[67]

[66] 'Provincial Mirror' (Yid.), 4. Schenirer wrote a play called 'Judith' for Bais Yaakov performance, which appears in Rottenberg (ed.), *A Mother in Israel* (Heb.), iii. 32–65.

[67] 'A Hasidic Revolt in Błonie' (Yid.), 2.

However sensationalized these newspaper reports may be, there can be no doubt that the innovative cultural practices of Bais Yaakov excited the interest, if not the envy, of boys and young men. As with the secularizing reading practices Iris Parush charts, innovations could spread from the female to the male realm, despite the strict gender segregation of Orthodox society and the pressures placed on young men to devote all their time to Torah study. It is not surprising, then, that boys and young men in the Agudah were eager to try their hand at these new varieties of Orthodox theatre (of course, more amateur theatre in the form of the Purim *spiel* had long been part of traditional culture). One case is the adult-education club Khinukh, founded by a Warsaw chapter of the Tse'irei Agudath Israel that operated for a few years in the 1930s. According to the *Haynt*, Khinukh provided lectures and classes to young women as well as men at its club (although in separate groups). Despite this transgression of gender boundaries and the competition Khinukh posed to its other educational offerings, Agudah leaders in Warsaw initially looked the other way. Agudah intervened, however, when the club proposed to raise funds by staging a play, pronouncing that it would permit only a performance of *The Selling of Joseph* (presumably because it featured only male characters), that the play could be performed only to single-sex audiences, and that cast members would be either male or female, but not mix the sexes. Overlooking the long history of male cross-dressing in the Purim *spiel*, the Khinukh activists (mischievously?) argued that they could not possibly fulfil the last demand, since 'women wouldn't be able to throw Joseph into a pit and no man would be able to play the role of Potiphar's wife'. After trying and failing to control the production, the Agudah shut down the play shortly before the first performance.[68] As these episodes reveal, theatre, so attractive to young people of both sexes and so important a tool in the propagation of Orthodox youth culture, was a particularly difficult activity to control. Even if the rules of gender segregation were followed, theatre gave rise to new problems relating to what stories could be staged and who would play the characters. As the argument of the Khinukh leaders implied, even performances that did not blur the boundaries between men and women onstage or in the audience might end up

[68] 'A Great Uprising in the "Fortress" of the Agudah' (Yid.), 6. This rift was apparently behind the public renunciation of Agudah by Shmuel Nadler, among its most respected young writers. Nadler spoke at the Khinukh club the evening after the aborted opening, excoriating the Agudah for hypocrisy, passivity, and meddling in the activities of its youth. A week or so later, he renounced his Orthodoxy at a talk at the Warsaw Jewish Literary Union. For more on Nadler and this episode, see Eddy Portnoy, 'Politics and Poesy'.

Figure 3.5 Bais Yaakov girls in Buczacz in a play called *Joseph and His Brothers*. Esther Wagner (née Willig) can be seen in the second row, fifth from the right. In the afternoons (she was tutored in the mornings, because her parents did not want to expose her to the culture of public or Catholic schools), she first attended the Tarbut School and later Bais Yaakov, which her father helped establish

United States Holocaust Memorial Museum, courtesy of Esther Wagner

blurring these boundaries in their casting, by having girls play rabbis, or boys play seductive Egyptian women.

Bais Yaakov created opportunities for other forms of interaction between men and women (and potential indiscretion), despite the vigilance of the leadership and regulation of such interaction. The Yiddish press took pleasure in recounting stories of Bais Yaakov students and Agudah activists thrown together by a movement that in theory kept men and women apart. A 1934 report detailed the case of the founding of a Bais Yaakov school in Kazimierz Dolny, where the main Agudah activist, a married hasid who was barely 21, went to the seminary 'to handpick a teacher'. He came back with 'a young and pretty graduate', and took it upon himself to 'keep her from being bored while preventing her from socializing with young men'. In the eyes of the young activist, the columnist writes, this principle applied to other men, but not to himself (as seemed to be the case for the hasidic guards at the play in Chmielnik). The story ends with a resident of the town passing by the schoolhouse in the middle of the night and catching sight, through the window, of the Agudah leader and the Bais Yaakov teacher 'in a very un-Agudah-like pose'.[69]

If it is not entirely fictional, this scandalous story sheds light on some of the dangers that even a movement as religious as Bais Yaakov potentially faced in its efforts to expand. Bais Yaakov brought men and women together at every level—as parents of students, as members of school committees, and as colleagues and collaborators in schools, camps, and other programmes. The highest echelons of Bais Yaakov of course also included men and women. This was one arena where the leadership of the Agudah had to acknowledge public activity by women and allow for the working relations between the sexes that the movement often required.[70] While many of the encomiums to Sarah Schenirer after her passing are formulaic, others are by men who clearly knew her well, and who felt her death as a profound and personal loss (Leo Deutschländer's remarkable reflections on her are discussed in the next chapter). Seminary students also had opportunities to forge relationships with male teachers. Gutta Sternbuch, who studied in the Kraków seminary in the mid-1930s, describes Rabbi Orlean, who took over as director of the seminary in 1933 after working in a Bais Yaakov school in War-

[69] 'Curious News from across the Country' (Yid.), 3.

[70] Such connections could spill over from the work to the marital arena. Although I do not know how the Bais Yaakov teacher Tsila Neugroschel (later Rebbetzin Sorotzkin) met her first husband, Abraham Orlean, he was the brother of Yehudah Leib Orlean, Tsila's co-worker in the seminary.

saw, as a Gerer hasid, a 'young man, still in his thirties, with a pale face and a long black beard', 'a philosopher, a visionary, an innovator, a speaker—and a true friend'. She continues: 'He developed a personal relationship with each one of us. He was compassionate and caring, and he understood our young restless hearts. All the girls brought their personal struggles to him, and he helped each one individually.'[71]

As Sternbuch recalls, Orlean's introductory lecture to the incoming students describing their responsibility to educate 'young Jewish souls' ended with: 'Holy children, I envy you.' The power of these words, which 'affected [Gutta] profoundly', no doubt lay in part in the unexpected reversal of the hierarchies that normally separate adult teachers from adolescent students, a learned man from the young girls assembled in his classroom. The hierarchy long established by halakhic discourse, in which male Torah study, as obligatory rather than voluntary, was more valuable than that of women, gave way in this moment to the (rhetorical, whether stylized or sincerely felt) envy of a learned man of the crucial, sacred responsibilities of Bais Yaakov seminarians.

The institutionalization of Bais Yaakov throughout the 1920s, then, brought a charismatic movement led by a woman into the orbit of a male-dominated, more established organization. It normalized some of the eccentricity of the beginnings of Bais Yaakov, when 14-year-old apprentice girls in Sarah Schenirer's workshop were promoted to serve as teachers for the system or when, a little later, 15-year-old girls crowded into a two-room apartment to live and study with her.[72] But the more professional school system under the Agudah, which brought together a Gerer hasid and the 'restless' young women he claimed to envy, did not spell an end to the novelties of the movement.

If Bais Yaakov conforms to Weber's model in many regards, it also deviates from it in significant ways. Sarah Schenirer's charisma (if we grant the appropriateness of that term) upended social norms, as Weber would have predicted. Her taking on a public role was unprecedented for an Orthodox woman of her time and place. But this revolution, as conservatives in the movement always stressed, was for the sake of and in accordance with Jewish law and tradition. She

[71] Sternbuch and Kranzler, *Gutta*, 44. For more on Orlean, who managed to acquire a broad philosophical education (in addition to his Jewish knowledge) without ever having attended a secular school, see Seidman, *Personalities I Knew* (Heb.), 191–205. A photo of Orlean appears on the second page of the appendix of Seidman's volume.

[72] For a description of the promotion of a 14-year-old apprentice, see J. Friedenson, 'The Movement from its Beginnings' (Heb.), 135.

proceeded with her plan only after receiving a rabbinic imprimatur, and would certainly have desisted, according to Rabbi Abraham Joseph Wolf, the German-born director of the Bais Yaakov seminary in Benei Berak, if such permission had been denied. In an essay entitled 'Did Sarah Schenirer Innovate in Any Way?' Rabbi Wolf explains:

> The reason for the question is that we are no great lovers of innovation. 'Things that come from afar and our ancestors could not have imagined' is no great praise for us. We see how quickly the latest fashion becomes outmoded . . . But the Torah is in our eyes always new. The obligation of renewal, a principle that is embedded in nature, is directed entirely to our ancient Torah. But 'the new is forbidden by the Torah'.[73] So was the establishment of Bais Yaakov not something *new*? Were not the founders of Bais Yaakov cultural innovators? Many people mistakenly believe this.[74]

Rejecting the easy explanation that Sarah Schenirer changed only the external *form* while maintaining the traditional *content* of Jewish girls' education, Wolf insists that even external forms may not be tampered with. Nevertheless, she was not an innovator because she received the approval of 'rabbinic sages whose words are Torah'. Moreover, her work did not emerge from any criticism of traditional systems of educating girls, but rather from regretful necessity, an attitude marked by 'nostalgia and a hope of restoring the previous situation'. She 'fervently wished that Bais Yaakov could reach the level that previous generations had achieved through the mother's teaching alone'.[75]

Rabbi Wolf views Sarah Schenirer as an innovator in only the most superficial sense of the term, and in a more profound way portrays her as a follower of tradition. This assessment accords with the ubiquitous descriptions of her as a 'modest', 'simple', 'pious', and 'motherly' woman who shunned the spotlight, which help resolve the dissonance between Orthodox expectations of adult women and her visible and unusual role as an (unmarried) public speaker, prolific writer, and ardent cultural activist (whether innovator or not). But they also illuminate the ways in which piety and charisma, traditionalism and radicalism are uniquely combined in Sarah Schenirer and the movement she founded.

The distinctive character of this radical piety might be brought into sharper focus by comparing Bais Yaakov in interwar Poland with the Yavneh schools that

[73] Wolf quotes a dictum of the Hatam Sofer which midrashically rereads a mishnaic ruling forbidding the eating of new grain before bringing the barley offering (*Orl.* 3: 9); in the Hatam Sofer's wordplay, a slogan for Orthodox approaches to modernity, this *mishnah* applies to and forbids all forms of innovation. See my discussion at the beginning of Chapter 5 below.

[74] Wolf, 'Did Sarah Schenirer Innovate?' (Heb.), 37.

[75] Ibid. 39.

arose in Lithuania at roughly the same time and with many of the same goals. Unlike Havatselet, founded by two German neo-Orthodox activists who worked with local leaders to modernize Orthodox schools, both Yavneh and Bais Yaakov began as independent grass-roots movements. The Yavneh school system owed its existence to a group of about 300 yeshiva boys, both Zionists and non-Zionists, who began meeting weekly in 1915 in Vilna, where many had fled as refugees, to speak and hear lectures in Hebrew. By the end of the war, the group, which called itself Tse'irei Israel, had developed the broader goal of 'educating a new generation of worldly, knowledgeable, and God-fearing Jews'. At its first conference in autumn 1918 in Kovno, the group instituted a two-year teacher-training programme, preparing its members to establish the Yavneh school system. As Isaac Raphael Etzion writes:

> The participants in these courses were yeshiva boys, who decided—in response to 'the needs of the hour'—that it was necessary to mobilize as teachers of religious schools. Some were already ordained rabbis. The director of this [teacher-training] course was Dr Leo Deutschländer, though it was administered, on a day-to-day basis, by Rabbi Isaac Shmuelevitz. Dr Deutschländer taught psychology and pedagogy; Dr Joseph Carlebach taught geography of the Land of Israel; Rabbi Abraham Eliyahu Kaplan, Talmud and history; Rabbi Isaac Shmuelevitz taught Bible and Hebrew; Dr Halberstadt, natural history; Dr Schlesinger, physics and mathematics. Twenty-six young men graduated from this course with teaching certificates.[76]

Forty Yavneh schools were founded in 1920, the first year of the movement, according to the plan laid out at the inaugural conference: 'elementary schools for girls; high schools for boys; teacher-training institutes, and kindergartens'. Among the first schools to open, with the strong support of Rabbi Joseph Leib Bloch of the Telz (Lithuanian Telšiai) yeshiva, was an elementary school for girls in that town. Telz became a centre of the girls' school system, when a highly regarded girls' *gymnasium* and a teachers' seminary opened in 1927 and 1930 respectively (two other girls' *gymnasia* were founded in Ponevezh and Kovno). As in the Yavneh schools for boys, the language of instruction was Hebrew, and each school provided, along with its Jewish studies programme, a rigorous curriculum of secular studies, with a staff of Orthodox instructors, many with higher degrees. The girls' *gymnasium* in Telz, for instance, taught Lithuanian, Hebrew, Latin, German, French, philosophy, drawing, and music.[77] The system remained

[76] See Etzion, 'Yavneh Schools in Lithuania' (Heb.), 356.

[77] For more on the Telz girls' *gymnasium*, see <http://batkamaat.org/>, initiated by Isabelle Rozenbaumas to document the life at the school.

officially non-partisan in the 1920s, but the influence of the Agudah gained in the 1930s. According to Mordechai Zalkin, 'despite its political affiliation with the Lithuanian branch of the Agudath Israel, the pedagogical worldviews of Yavneh in Lithuania were much closer to that of the Mizrahi schools in Poland [also called Yavneh] than they were to the educational network of Agudath Israel in Poland, which operated under the direct influence of hasidic *rebbes*'.[78]

The parallels are clear. Bais Yaakov also emerged as a grass-roots initiative to meet 'the needs of the hour', and similarly undertook teacher training at an early stage, with the help of German neo-Orthodox leaders and teachers—the two programmes were even directed by the same man. The educational systems grew rapidly, and both came under the influence of the Agudah, Bais Yaakov more quickly and completely than Yavneh. Despite these similarities, there are also illuminating differences: it was a sign of the ideological and cultural liberalism of Yavneh that the system used the same name for boys' and girls' schools; in some small towns, Yavneh schools were even co-educational, an unthinkable option for a Bais Yaakov. And while Bais Yaakov embraced a form of Orthodox Yiddishism in 1929, Yavneh was always committed to Hebrew as the language of instruction. Bais Yaakov thus bore the marks of its more stringent, hasidic-influenced, Polish environment, while Yavneh (the school system based in Lithuania) was shaped by the more moderate Orthodoxy of the context in which it developed.

But while Bais Yaakov was more conservative than Yavneh, it was also in many respects more radical. It was founded not by a group of men but by a single woman, who took it upon herself to do what various men had been unable to accomplish in her hasidic community. And while Yavneh was more professional in first training teachers and then founding schools, Bais Yaakov took a wilder route. The stricter gender segregation of Bais Yaakov culture was certainly a reflection of the more stringent Orthodoxy within which it emerged, which could have the effect of alienating girls by putting a chasm between men and women, even as it protected youth from the dangers of mixing the sexes. In conforming to these stricter norms, Bais Yaakov took what might have been seen as a limitation on its activities as a source of strength, creating the kind of vibrant same-sex atmosphere that was harnessed in hasidic circles. It was thus more radical not despite, but *because* it emerged from a stricter type of Orthodoxy. Anxieties about the novelty of the movement may have been allayed by Sarah Schenirer's evident piety and her resemblance to a traditional mother that

[78] Zalkin, 'Let It Be Entirely Hebrew' (Heb.), 125.

was so often invoked in the movement's publications, but this piety could not entirely obscure that Bais Yaakov was, *pace* Wolf, an innovation. In all these ways, charisma and constraint, stringency and radicalism, were mutually enforcing mechanisms rather than conceptual opposites.

Scholars since Weber have suggested that charisma and institution might be more intricately intertwined than he assumed, complicating his notion that the two forms of social movements progress in clearly marked stages. Indeed, Sarah Schenirer's charisma, if the religious fervour and devotion she inspired in her students can be described as such, persisted long after the movement became institutionalized. The descriptions of the mass outcry at her funeral are evidence that they continued, and perhaps even increased, after her death. Her charisma, moreover, was not the only source of such energies in the movement. While she conforms to Weber's model of a single charismatic figure who founds a movement there were many other adored teachers and venerated leaders in Bais Yaakov. After 1925, she shared the role of female spokesperson and public face of the movement with Judith Grunfeld-Rosenbaum: while the 'motherly' Sarah Schenirer fired up crowds of Orthodox parents in the Polish hinterland and persuaded them to undertake the establishment of a Bais Yaakov in their towns, the 'elegant' Grunfeld-Rosenbaum travelled to capital cities like London and Amsterdam, had tea with wealthy (and often non-Orthodox) Jews, and persuaded them to write cheques to fund these schools.

Bais Yaakov thus relied upon many kinds of charismatic leaders, which included Sarah Schenirer, her staff, and the Agudah activists who participated in the movement, and extended to the seminary students themselves, whether they were impressing a small-town audience with their religious eloquence, studying Torah under the trees, or otherwise at work in the movement. As Judith Grunfeld-Rosenbaum puts it:

> A Beth Jacob school was a school but it was also an organization and a club, brightened by the constant power of love and romance, a hero worship and a discipline that was almost like the discipline of a secret cult. All these things wove an original pattern into the quiet regular routine of school life. The teachers were all young. They all lived away from their own homes, away from their parents, and were devoting themselves to one purpose alone, consumed by a fire which had been kindled by Sarah Schenirer.[79]

Bais Yaakov required 'discipline' and a 'quiet regular routine', but it also drew upon charisma ('hero worship'), freedom from social norms ('away from their parents'), and adventure ('like high adventurers or great artists', as Grunfeld-

[79] Grunfeld-Rosenbaum, 'Sara Schenierer', 418.

Rosenbaum terms the young teachers). Institutionalization routinizes charisma, but sometimes also embraces and magnifies it. However elaborate the bureaucracy that governed (or tried to govern) the system, however powerful the rabbinic and political oversight, however stringent the Jewish observances that Bais Yaakov students willingly or ambivalently accepted, the movement continued to provide the sorts of intoxicating freedom, intellectual power, and spiritual fervour that were experienced by the earlier participants.

Charisma and institution coexisted within Bais Yaakov, both as a system and in its individual components, long past the beginnings of institutionalization, as dialectical energies, secret doubles, or uncomfortable tensions. In her description of the cornerstone-laying ceremony quoted above, Grunfeld-Rosenbaum wrapped a sense of injustice in a discourse of feminine modesty by having Sarah Schenirer shun the spotlight rather than confront the gender segregation practices of Orthodox Polish Jewry. This was the context in which both women worked, and which they were largely powerless to change. Shoshana Bechhofer has suggested that the later circulation of Grunfeld-Rosenbaum's story 'represents the tension between revolution and establishment. It is here that Schenirer hands Bais Yaakov over to the established Jewish community so that it will become a system rather than a movement.'[80] We have no record of Sarah Schenirer's words or thoughts on that occasion, but she did speak at some length and with remarkable candour on a related occasion, the opening of the seminary building four years later, in the autumn of 1931.

In contrast with the laying of the cornerstone, this occasion seems not to have been marked by any elaborate ceremony. The *Bais Yaakov Journal* briefly reports that the seminary was opened both later than hoped and prematurely, while the building was still under construction, to accommodate the new students who had been admitted in anticipation of its completion (in fact, the facade was never finished). It was in these circumstances that Sarah Schenirer gave voice to her thoughts in a diary entry that was published in the *Bais Yaakov Journal* later that year. The article, entitled 'The Last Night on Augustiańska 30', appears on the page facing the description of the hurried opening of the unfinished building, and forms an informal counter-narrative to the more institutional version of this turn of events: 'The clock strikes two, my eyes are sticky with sleep, but a strange feeling has seized me that demands to be expressed, and transmitted to you, my darlings, through our dear *Bais Yaakov Journal*.' Noticing that the most recent diary entry was from the summer colony in Rabka in 1930, she chides herself for

[80] Bechhofer, 'Ongoing Constitution of Identity', 72.

letting a whole year pass by without writing, despite the momentous events she witnessed and her often expressed determination to write more regularly. 'So what actually is this energy that pursues me now, so late at night, to pick up this book, what is this magic that intoxicates me and commands me: Write! Write!' Acknowledging that the next day would bring a particularly significant development, she dismisses this simple answer, since what she feels is not exhilaration but something more complicated:

> Such an uncanny feeling knocks at my heart, precisely now, when we are about to realize our dreams. Fear and dread wash over me: will those beautiful walls not allow—God forbid—the penetration of an alien spirit? Will the girls who come here to spread our great ideal not have economic motives in mind, and so desecrate the great idea to which I have dedicated my whole life? . . . My teachers bear a great responsibility, and they must always remember that they are historical heroines and pioneers, and history will learn to value and boast of them in times to come.[81]

Her concern about the potential dangers posed to her movement by the move from 30 Augustiańska Street to 10 Stanisława Street, which is to say from an overcrowded apartment to a well-appointed and spacious five-story seminary building and professional path to employment during difficult times, certainly expresses her piety and the purity of her ideological mission (it also may be the source of Grunfeld-Rosenbaum's transcription of her prayer at the cornerstone-laying ceremony). This is no simple piety, however, but rather a shrewd acknowledgement of the ways in which better organization might threaten the pioneering spirit of Bais Yaakov. Memoirs of later years show that girls did indeed come to the seminary with 'economic motives in mind', or in any case without the evident enthusiasm of the first students. Gutta Sternbuch acknowledges that she entered the Kraków seminary in the autumn of 1935 only reluctantly, as an avowed 'sceptic', under pressure from her parents and while simultaneously pursuing a degree at Warsaw University: 'I didn't want any more of what I imagined would be uninteresting, outworn and old-fashioned studies' (she was soon to be won over by the brilliance of Yehudah Leib Orlean).[82] On the eve of the most visible move to institutionalization that Bais Yaakov was to make, it was Sarah Schenirer who provided a critique of the transition, expressing the concern that the growth and success of the movement might also prove its downfall.

But there may also have been something personal in her expression of fear and dread. Freud's famous essay on the uncanny (*unheimlich*) reminds the reader

81 Schenirer, 'The Last Night on Augustiańska 30' (Yid.), 4.

82 Sternbuch and Kranzler, *Gutta*, 44.

of the complexity of the German (and German-derived Yiddish) term, which combines an evocation of 'home' and 'hominess' (*heimlich*) with a negation that signifies 'unhousedness' and 'concealment'; the uncanny arises, among other occasions, in 'haunted houses' and sites in which present and past, life and death, presence and absence, the hidden and the unconcealed appear in disturbingly close proximity.[83] All of these associations (as well as the Yiddish *heymish*) may have been operating on that 'last night' before the move. She was moving from the apartment in Augustiańska Street, which Deutschländer described as 'having nine healthy and spacious rooms' on three floors, but which had become as crowded as the two-room apartment in 1 Katarzyna Street, which it had previously replaced. According to Chana Wiselewsky Garfinkle, who attended the seminary in 1929, Sarah Schenirer lived in the Augustiańska apartment along with her students. Echoing the description of the smaller apartment in Katarzyna Street, Garfinkle writes: 'The apartment we lived in was one of many in a tenement. Our accommodations were cramped because Sarah Schenirer wanted to have as many students as possible regardless of the lack of funds. There were no separate classrooms and bedrooms. During the day we would sit on crates and chairs to learn our lessons while at night we cleared the room and unfolded the beds to sleep on.' As in Katarzyna Street, she worked and slept alongside the girls, and in the long nights she stayed awake to write and study, took breaks to walk through the apartment 'untangling jumbles of bedclothes and picking up fallen blankets. Lovingly, she covered each girl as a mother does for her child.'[84]

While the seminary building had living space for teachers and a 'house master', Sarah Schenirer did not live there herself. By April 1931 she was married to Yitzhak Landau, of whom we know only that he was the grandson of Shlomo Rabinowicz, the first rebbe of the Radomsk hasidic dynasty. They apparently resided in the two-room Katarzyna Street apartment, which Sarah Schenirer still owned or rented.[85] During the last months of her illness, she moved into an apartment in 8 Kordeckiego Street 'in order to be closer to her students', resisting the pleas of her husband and relatives that she stay in bed in order to walk the short distance to 10 Stanisława Street on special occasions.[86] She was thus

[83] Freud, 'The Uncanny'. [84] Rubin (ed.), *Daughters of Destiny*, 176.

[85] According to city records, Sara Landau was residing at 1 Katarzyna in 1933; Landau listed herself as a private tutor, perhaps because she lacked a formal teaching certificate.

[86] For a description of these arrangements in the last weeks of Schenirer's life, see 'To Eternal Rest' (Yid.), 12–13.

'unhoused' by this 'dream' house, the modern facilities that offered sleeping quarters separated from eating, learning, and other functions. This 'last night' may mark not only the move to a building that had no space for her to live in, but also the more profound way her marriage cut her off, at least in the night-time hours, from the girls she saw as her 'own children'. There are many unanswered questions about her personal life, but in this uncanny meditation on houses and homelessness, she comes close to drawing the curtains on what remained concealed in her public life. Nor are these only personal issues: her role as a now marginalized figure in Bais Yaakov, spiritual leader and symbolic figurehead of a system in which organizational decisions had been delegated elsewhere, rendered her a ghost in her own house, an absent presence and haunting absence, at the moment in which the most visible institution of Bais Yaakov was about to open its doors.

CHAPTER FOUR

'So Shall You Say to the House of Jacob' Forging the Discourse of Bais Yaakov

> Rabbi Yose the Galilean was once walking on a road when he met Beruriah, whom he asked, 'Which road shall I take to go to the city of Lydda?' She replied, 'Foolish Galilean, did the Sages not say, "Do not talk overmuch with women" [*Avot* 1: 5]? You should have said "Which way Lydda?"'
>
> (BT *Eruv.* 53*b*)

CONFERENCE REPORTS are not usually counted among the great works of human drama, but Rabbi Menahem Mendel Hayim Landau's record of the 1903 Kraków rabbinical congress is an exception to the rule. He recalls the pain of the rabbi from Cairo who organized the international event with such high hopes, only to see his efforts dashed at every turn; the rage of the conference attendees at those who dared to bring up the problem of Orthodox women who had turned to prostitution; and the deep shame felt by Landau himself, and no doubt many others, at the impotence of the Orthodox rabbinate in the face of the challenges raised at the conference. A particularly poignant and illuminating moment came during a discussion of the causes of young women's defection from their Orthodox upbringing. Along with the absence of educational institutions that could cement their attachment to Torah, and of reliable teachers and tutors who could teach them without corrupting them in the process, one speaker raised a warning about the dangers posed by girls and women reading for pleasure. Their immersion in Polish novels, which were filled with immorality and love stories, rendered the Orthodox world unappealing to them: after encountering the heroes that populated these novels, they disdained the yeshiva boys chosen by their parents to be their husbands. Against this threat, Rabbi Pinhas Horowitz declared that 'it was incumbent on the rabbis to compose or persuade others to compose, under rabbinical supervision, books in non-Jewish languages for Jewish women, which would include tales of Torah giants and the history of the Jewish people, and which could inspire their hearts to love Torah and Israel'.[1] Another speaker, however, objected that it was exceedingly danger-

[1] Landau, *Mekits nirdamim*, 56.

ous to attempt to create an Orthodox literature, even if it could be accomplished, 'and we need to appoint a special committee of rabbis who have expertise in secular subjects, and who would be able to judge what was written' in such books. Rabbi Landau praised the men who had initiated the discussion of girls' reading material, but argued that the matter was too urgent to postpone. He added, with a touch of wry humour: 'But let us not waste our time. We must face the facts. The strictly Orthodox rabbis of our time, in our lands, lack the ability to write books in secular languages that would be compatible with both the spirit of Judaism and the spirit of the times. Nor would they know how to evaluate such books.'[2] Where the first two speakers recognized the perils of secular literature and saw the need for producing literary works under strict rabbinical supervision, Rabbi Landau's response demonstrates his broader perspective on the new realities of Orthodox life. In theory, rabbis were the leaders of their communities, establishing rules with regard to reading as well as all other details of life. In practice, however, the rabbinical imposition of rules depended on the consent of those who followed them. The old rabbinic discourse about whether teaching girls Torah was permissible was beside the point if girls and women were unwilling to follow the dictates of rabbis (and, moreover, failed to clamour for the right to study Torah). The task of the present age was, rather, to produce works that could successfully compete with the secular literature that had already captured so many hearts. Here, the rabbis were not legislators but suitors, seeking the favours of young women in an arena in which women held all the cards. And this task, Rabbi Landau regretfully informed the assembled rabbis, was beyond what their yeshivas had prepared them to accomplish.

Rabbi Landau not only saw the issue clearly, he was able to articulate a solution: 'Behold, there was in Germany a righteous man, devoted in all his deeds, wise in all forms of knowledge, and his name was Rabbi Samson Raphael Hirsch.'[3] As Rabbi Landau went on to explain, this Rabbi Hirsch had confronted much the same problem in Germany, and among his disciples were a few—Landau named Marcus Lehmann—who had already written lively and interesting Orthodox books for girls and women, which should immediately be translated into Polish. Landau also called for the translation of Hirsch's *Horeb*, which he suggested fathers could read with their daughters. Nine years before the 1912 founding conference of the Agudath Israel, symbolically held in the German-Polish border town of Katowice, which brought together the German-speaking followers of Hirsch with east European rabbis and leaders, Rabbi Landau dis-

[2] Ibid. [3] Ibid.

cerned the ways in which Hirschian Orthodoxy, which arose as a response to the challenges posed by the Haskalah and Reform movements, could come to the aid of its imperilled east European counterpart.

Long before Polish rabbis considered ways to reach Orthodox girls and women, Hirsch had clearly seen the necessity of addressing young people of both sexes. Alongside the philosophical brilliance of his 1837 magnum opus *Horeb* was the novelty of its title page, which announced that the book was directed to 'Israel's thinking young men and young women' (*fur Jissroëls denkende Junglinge und Jungfrauen*). His *Neunzehn Briefe über Judenthum*, which would become a staple of the Bais Yaakov curriculum, was similarly addressed to the younger generation. Whatever had impelled Hirsch to write to young women as well as young men, the need to forge a discourse that could attract women was at least as pressing in eastern Europe, though also more difficult to achieve. Hirschian neo-Orthodoxy included nearly parallel educational institutions for girls and boys and a youth movement (named Ezra) that served young people of both sexes. It was clear to at least some Agudah activists that Polish Orthodoxy would have to emulate its German counterpart. Writing in the *Bais Yaakov Journal* in 1924, A. Gefen called for the formation of a youth movement for Orthodox girls and young women along German lines:

> In Germany, our Orthodox brothers have already long recognized the necessity of such a movement. Striving to maintain the adherence of its daughters to Torah and Jewish tradition, they give her first of all a religious education in the school and then bolster that connection by creating a cohort, the women's groups created for her by Agudath Israel that are called Ezra. And [in Germany] it is impossible to tell the difference, in terms of Jewish knowledge, whether theoretical or practical, between sons and daughters, brothers and sisters. Unfortunately that is not the case among us.[4]

While Gefen suggests that Ezra served girls and boys in a 'separate but equal' manner, Judith Grunfeld-Rosenbaum puts it a little differently, viewing the movement as also forging ties among boys and girls, which helped the latter feel more closely attached to a tradition that fully included them: 'When the boys went to shul on Shabbos, we girls also went. This is why Sarah Schenirer needed educators from Germany. We had something to give to these girls.'[5] But the model provided by German neo-Orthodoxy was not always directly applicable. While Ezra allowed girls to sing in mixed groups (Rosenbaum claims that she was not

[4] Gefen, 'Organizing Orthodox Young Women' (Yid.), 57.

[5] See Rubin (ed.), *Daughters of Destiny*, 128–9. For more on Ezra and the 'Association of Orthodox University Students', see Dansky, *Rebbetzin Grunfeld*, 31–6.

even aware that some Jews forbade women from singing in the presence of unrelated men), such leniency was unimaginable in many sectors of Polish Orthodoxy.[6] Kraków's Orthodox leaders had to find ways to bridge the chasm between girls and boys, fathers and daughters, rabbis and young women, while maintaining the strict segregation between the sexes which characterized that community. And while Hirsch had philosophical training that he could harness for the purposes of addressing youth sceptical of what Judaism had to offer, east European Orthodox writers, as Rabbi Landau pointed out, generally lacked his ability to communicate religious values in modern terms, and also had little experience of addressing women.

Despite these obstacles, Bais Yaakov was able to forge an Orthodox discourse designed to attract young women, producing a long-running journal that featured a wide variety of articles of Jewish and general literary interest as well as other books and publications for a female readership. This enterprise began in 1923, even before the World Congress at which Agudath Israel founded Keren Hatorah, when the young Po'alei Agudah (Agudah Workers' Organization) activist and writer Eliezer Gershon Friedenson decided to support Bais Yaakov by publishing a periodical with that name. The first, ten-page issue of the *Bais Yaakov Journal* appeared in Łódź in the autumn of that year (Tishrei 5684). As it turned out, translations of novels by German neo-Orthodox writers were not needed to fill out the pages of the periodical, although the first issue included an article on the upcoming festival of Sukkot by Samson Raphael Hirsch, and a few of Lehmann's novels were serialized in later years. Nor were 'tales of Torah giants' featured in this first issue, although these too occasionally appeared in later issues. The adventures and romance that girls and women found in Polish novels and which rabbis at the 1903 congress had hoped to replace with pious tales about great rabbis and events in Jewish history nevertheless featured prominently in the new journal. But the excitement and romance, it turned out, were supplied not by virile heroes or bearded rabbis but by the girls and young women themselves, through the romantic adventure that was Bais Yaakov.

The first issue of the *Bais Yaakov Journal* set the basic template, serving as the movement's primary mouthpiece by spreading word of its sacred mission and its remarkable accomplishments. A secondary goal was to bolster support for the Agudah among girls and women; the paper later endorsed Agudah candidates

[6] There was a branch of Ezra in Warsaw, which included a women's group frequented by Bais Yaakov teachers, but Ezra was overtaken in Poland by Bnos and Tse'irei Agudath Israel, the separate youth movements of the Agudah.

for national elections and called on its readers to vote. The masthead proclaimed its basic aspiration: 'Bais Yaakov: Orthodox Journal, dedicated to spreading religious thought among Jewish women and girls, and resolving the question of girls' education in the spirit of Torah and tradition.' The journal proclaimed its affiliations with Agudath Israel, the Bais Yaakov movement, and Orthodoxy; its literary and linguistic aspirations to provide the 'best reading material' in 'modern Yiddish'; its resistance to 'shameful foreign influences'; and its commitment to 'rebuild . . . the Jewish home'.[7] The goals were traditional in supporting the rebirth of Orthodoxy, but the form was that of a manifesto, the very hallmark of new cultural and political movements, and one which focused on appealing to girls and young women. The *Bais Yaakov Journal* thereby simultaneously signalled its commitment to tradition and to modernity.

The journal made its appearance at the very beginning of the institutionalization of Sarah Schenirer's enterprise under Agudath Israel leadership. In doing so it served to unify the movement at a pivotal stage through the eminently modern means of the printed press. With this stroke, Bais Yaakov could claim an even wider reach than its energetic founder could have hoped to achieve, connecting far-flung local initiatives with each other and with the Kraków centre. Sarah Schenirer herself continued to travel widely, lobbying to found new schools and then attending openings, graduations, and other special events. Participants in the movement as it grew also had numerous opportunities to meet at national and regional conferences, and the 1925 Bais Yaakov conference formalized the requirement that Bais Yaakov teachers attend professionalization courses at least

[7] A letter from the editor, on the second page of this first issue, detailed these aims: 'With this we begin to publish the *Bais Yaakov Journal*, striving to enrich Orthodox literature and the Orthodox press, and to create a religious literature in modern Yiddish.' E. G. Friedenson appended a nine-point précis of his vision for the new publication, beginning with 'Bais Yaakov will serve as an organ for Jewish women and girls that is grounded in traditional Jewish principles' and 'Bais Yaakov will provide the best reading material for the Jewish woman, inspiring her and implanting in her the desire to be Jewish, true to the Torah and observant of God's commandments.' A fourth bullet-point announced that 'Bais Yaakov will stand watch over the process of finally fulfilling the resolutions of the second national conference of Agudath Israel in Poland, both in organizing Jewish women and girls under the historical-traditional name of Bais Yaakov and in spreading a network of Orthodox girls' schools in every city and town'; a fifth declared that 'Bais Yaakov will combat and free Jewish women from shameful foreign influences and nourish Torah ideals', and a sixth that 'Bais Yaakov will help rebuild and strengthen the grand Jewish fortress—the Jewish home.' Among the final points is that 'Bais Yaakov will awaken the Jewish woman's love and longing for the Holy Land, as it helps build up the Land of Israel in the spirit of Torah and tradition.' See E. G. Friedenson, 'Letter from the Editor'.

בית יעקב

ארטאדאקסישער חודש-זשורנאל.

Łódź, Sierpień 1924. | ROK I-SZY. | № 8 | ערשטער יאהרגאנג. | ב"ה, לאדז, מנחם אב, תרפ"ד.

הרה"צ ר' שמשון רפאל ד"ר הירש זצ"ל.

א היסטארישער טרויער.

אמר הקב"ה: אתם בביתם בבל' אחת של תנם—אני אקבע לכם בבל' לדורות.

האט געזאגט דער בביכול: איהר האט געוויינט איין מאל גהנם—וועל איך אייך פעסטזע- צען א לדורות'דיג געוויין.

* * *

ג-ט האט געשיקט זיינע נביאים צו זיין זינדיג פאלק, צום ישראל-פאלק, וואס האט זיך פערבלענדעט די אויגען, פערשטאפט זיך די אויערן, פערשטיינערט זיך דאס הארץ און עס מתרה געווען, פריהערויס געזאגט די צרות וואס וועלען אויף איהם קומען, — ס'האט פון דעם קיינער נישט געוואלט הערען. ביז, — עס איז אנגעקומען דער אנגעזאגטער „וביום פקדי ופקדתי", ס'האט אויפגעשיינט ג-ט'ס שטראף אבצאהלונגס-טאג — ס'האט זיך אויסגעגאסען זיין צארן אויף יהודה און ישראל, מנשה און אפרים און זיי פערוויסט.

גרויזאם און שוידערליך איז געווען ג-ט'ס משפט און פסק-דין אויף זיין בית המקדש און קדשי-הקדשים, אויף זיין ציון און ירושלים, אויף זיין פאלק און לאנד, אויף זיינע מלכים און כהנים, אויף זיינע שרים און זקנים; ג-ט'ס היכל איז ביז צום יסוד חרוב געווארען און זיין פאלק האט ער איבערגעגעבען דעם שונא'ס שווערד אין געמאנגענשאפט און — א שרעקליך מורא'דיגען הונגער-טויט...

* * *

ביי די טייכען אין בבל זענען מיר געזעסען און געוויינט; פון אונזערע אויגען האבען זיך שטראמענווייז געגאסען ביטער-זאלציגע טרעהרען.—

עס האבען אונז בעווייגט אונזערע עלטערן, וואס רוהען אין חברון און אונזער מוטער רחל אין בית-לחם; אפילו דער „עתיק-יומין" זעלבסט האט אויך געדופען צו טרויער-קלאג, און די גאנצע רוחניות'דיגע וועלט האט זיך געווייקט אין א ים פון טרעהרען און אבילות...

און פון דעמאלט אן טרויערט און וויינט ישראל אהן אויפהער.

ישראל בעוויינט דאס בית המקדש, קדשי הקדשים און ג-ט'ס נאמען, וואס ווערט פערשוואכט ביי די אומות העולם; ער בעקלאגט יעקב'ס הויז-געזונט און ג-ט'ס פאלק, וואס זענען געפאלען דורכ'ן שונא'ס שווערדען, זיינע אלטע און נייע שווערע פלאגען און שלאקען, צרות און גזירות, בזיונות און רדיפות, בלבולים און חרפות און — זיינע חטאים און עוונות...

* * *

ס'זענען שוין איבער זיבעט דעטאלט צוויי טויזענד יאהר און נאך זיצען מיר, ווי ביי די בבל-טייכען און וויינען אויף אונזערע חורבנות. דער מת ליגט נאך פאר אונזערע אויגען, די ערד וויל איהם נישט פערדעקען. מיר האבען נישט קיינעם, ווער ס'זאל אונז א טרייסט-ווארט כאטש בלויז זאגען... די חטאים-קלעפ טהון אונז נאך וועה, — נישטא צו זיי קיין רפואה! —

* * *

ווי פרוכטבאר זענען געווען אונזערע עלטערן'ס טרעהרען!—געפאלען זענען זיי אין א וויסטען אומגעזייטען מדבר, פונדעסטוועגען האבען זיי זיך געוואקסען און געצווייגט מיט אונצעהליגע פירות אזוי, ווי האבען דערגרייכט מיט זייערע צווייגען צו יעדע מדינה, מקום און ווינקעל, וואו די ווייבער'ס אור-אור-אייניקלעך געפינען זיך נאר; זיי האבען מיט זיך פערפולט די וועלט.

ווי מרים'ס „באר". וואס איז מיטגעגאנגען מיט ישראל'ן אינ'ם וויסטען מדבר, כדי איהם אנצושריקען שטענדיג, הן בעת'ן רוהען הן בעת'ן וואנדערען, אזוי געהט אויך אט דער טרעהרען-קוואל מיט איהם אין דעם אויסערגעוועהנליכען אונענדליכען גרויסען פעלקער-מדבר. — —

* * *

ווי לאנג מיר וועלען האבען אין זיך א נשמה, כל זמן ס'וועט נאך קלאפען א יודיש הארץ, כל זמן ס'וועט נאך טליען א יהדות-פינק, אפילו ווען ס'זאל

Figure 4.1 (a–g) ***Bais Yaakov Journal*** **over the years.**
Over the *Bais Yaakov Journal*'s sixteen-year lifespan there were changes in its design, its frequency of publication, the system of numbering the issues, and the way it was described in its masthead. The seven mastheads reproduced here represent some of the changes that were made over the years.

From the Library of the YIVO Institute for Jewish Research, New York

(a) No. 8, 1924, is subtitled 'Orthodox monthly'

בית יעקב

ארטאדאקסישער פאמיליען־זשורנאל

Łódź, kwiecień 1925 r. | Rok II-gi | № 16. | צווייטער יאהרגאנג | ב"ה, לאדז, ניסן, תרפ"ה.

הרב טובי' הורוויטץ

וואס פעהלט די יודישע טעכטער?

(b) No. 16, 1925, is subtitled 'Orthodox family journal'

פערטער יאהרגאנג Nr. 4 — פרייז 30 גר. — ערשיינט איינמאל אין חודש

בית יעקב לכו ונלכה באור ד׳ (ישעי׳)

פאמיליען-זשורנאל

אשה יראת ד׳ היא תתהלל (משלי)

בית יעקב

ארגאן פון „בנות אגודת ישראל" אין פוילען

ב״ה לאדז, שבט, תרפ״ז.

Łódź, Styczeń, 1927 r.

רעדאקטאר: א. ג. פרידענזאן. אדרעס פון רעד. און אדמ.: Łódź, Aleksandrowska 28.

דער פראגראם פון „בנות אגודת ישראל": פליכט-ערפילונג פון דער יודישער פרוי אין דער לעבונג פון די יודישע פראבלעמען אין גייסט פון תורה ומסורה.

אדרעס פון דער בא״י-צענטראלע: Sekretarjat B. A J., Łódź, skrz. pocz. 146.

לכבוד דעם יובילעאום פון בנות אגודת ישראל

לכבוד דעם ערשטען יאהר-טאג זינט דער גרינדונג פון „בנות אגודת ישראל", טרעטען מיר צו ארויסצוגעבען א גראנדיעזע פראכט-אויסגאבע פון אונזער זשורנאל.

במשך דער ערשטען יאהר זייט ס׳עקזיסטירט די בנות-בעוועגונג, איז פיל, פיל געטון געווארען. מ׳קאן מיט רעכט בעהויפטען, אז פערהעלטניסמעסיג, לויט די מיטלען און כוחות, וואס זענען געווען אינ׳ם רשות פון די וואס שטעהען ביי דער ארבייט, איז דאס וואס מיר האבען שוין איצט, נאר א דאנק די יענִיגע, וועלכע האבען די ערשטע פערשטאנען די פאהן צו דערהויבען און נישט געקארגט קיין מיה און ענערגיע לטובת אונזער היילִיגען אידעאל.

די יודישע וועלט בכלל און די ברייטע ארטאדאקסישע וועלט בפרט, ווייסט אבער גאר ווייניג, וועגען דעם אלעם. און אט האלטען מיר פאר אונזער היילִיגסטען פליכט, ארויסצוגעבען איין מאל א גרויסען רייכען נומער „בית יעקב", בכדי צו אינפארמירען דער ארטאדאקסישער עפענטליכקייט, וואס עס איז שוין ביז איצט בעזה״ש דערגרייכט געווארען און וואס עס קען נאך פילפאך מעהר דערגרייכט ווערען ביי דער געהעריגער מיטהילף און אונטערשטיצונג פון דער ארטאדאקסישער געזעלשאפט אין לאנד און אויסלאנד.

מיר רופען דעריבער אלע ארגאניזאציעס און שולען, אונז בייהילפיג צו זיין אין דער דאזיגער אונטערנעהמונג, וועלכע וועט אהן שום ספק ברענגען נוצען אונזער בעוועגונג און צוהעלפען אויסבויען דעם ריזיגען בנין, צו וועלכען דער פונדאמענט איז א דאנק די ביז-איצטיגע אנשטרענגונגען שוין געלונגען צו צעמענטירען און פערפעסטיגען.

בעזונדערס ערנסט איז אונזער רוף געווענדעט צו די שוין עקזיסטירענדע בנות-גרופען: איהר, וואס ווייסט ווי שווער און דארניג עס איז דער ענטוויקלונגס-וועג צו דער פערווירקליכונג פון אונזער גרויסער היסטארישער זאך. איהר דארפט אלעס אנווענדען, דאס עס זאל צושטאנד קומען די ערשיינונג פון אונזער גראנדיעזער אויסגאבע, צו אייער אייגענעם כבוד און צום רוהם פון גאנצען ערוואכטען ארטאדאקסישען יודענטום. יש קונה עולמו בשנה אחת — אין א איינציגען מאמענט קאן מען די גאנצע וועלט געווינען — יא! דאס איז יעצט דער מאמענט. אויב חלילה עס וועט אונז נישט געלינגען פאר דער גאנצער ארטאדאקסישער וועלט צו בעווייזען מיט פאקטען און ציפערן, וואס מיר האבען אין ערשטען יאהר וואסערע כוחות אוועקגעלעגט פאר אונזערע אידעאלען — דאן שטעהען מיר אונטער א מורא פון פערצווייפלונג צו קענען אונזער טעטיגקייט אויף להבא פערברייטערען און פערשטארקען.

א קלייניגקייט בעטען און פאדערען מיר פון אייך: יעדע שולע פון בנות-גרופע, זאל שאפען 25 אבאנענטען צו 1 זלאטי פאראויס פאר דעם פראכט-נומער לכבוד אונזער יובילעאום. צו אונזער יעצטיגען רוף מוזען זיך ערנסט צו הערען די אלע וואס ווילען זעהען די ארגאניזאציע „בנות אגודת ישראל" אלס א בליהענדע רויז אין ארטאדאקסישען גארטען און אלס א מעכטיגער פאקטאר אין דער תורה-אויפלעבונג פונ׳ם יודישען פאלק אין דער איצטיגער גייסטיג-קריטישער צייט. געדענקט! נאר דעמאלט וועט אונזער יובילעאום זיין ווירקליך א פייערליכער און גראנדיעזער ווען אין אלע יודישע הייזער וועט זיך געפינען דער פראכט-נומער פון אונזער זשורנאל און וועט קלאר מאכען, וואס מיר ווילען, צו וואס מיר שטרעבען און וואס מיר האבען געטון דאס ערשטע יאהר און וואס מיר פלאנען

(c) **No. 4, 1927** (fourth year of publication), has the supertitle 'Family journal' and the subtitle 'Organ of the Bnos Agudath Israel in Poland'. It also lists the price (30 groszy), the frequency of publication (monthly), and the editor (E. G. Friedenson), and is adorned with two insets citing slogans of the movement: 'Bais Yaakov, come let us walk in the light of the Lord' (from the book of Isaiah) and 'It is for her fear of the Lord that a woman is to be praised' (from the book of Proverbs).

לאנדעס-קאנפערענץ פון בנות-אגודת-ישראל אין פוילען,

בית יעקב

חודש זשורנאל

אָרגאַן פאַר די אינטערעסען פון בית-יעקב-שולען און אָרגאַניזאַציעס בנות-אגודת-ישראל אין פוילען

רעדאַקטאָר: א. ג. פרידענזאָן.

דער ציעל פון די בית-יעקב שולען:

דאָס פּראָגראַם פון בנות אגודת ישראל:

Łódź, P. K. O. 65.613

אכטונג דעלעגאַטינס און געסט!

Sekretarjat Łódź, skrz. poczt. 146

(d) No. 42, 1929 (sixth year of publication), is subtitled 'An organ serving the interests of the Bais Yaakov schools and the Bnos Agudath Israel Organization in Poland, E. G. Friedenson, editor'. Two ornamental insets describe the mission of these organizations: 'The aim of the Bais Yaakov schools is to educate Jewish girls in the spirit of the Jewish Torah and Israel's historical, eternal ideals', and ' The programme of the Bnos Agudath Israel is to fulfil the duties of the Jewish woman to resolve the problems of Jewish life in the spirit of Torah and tradition.' The annual subscription price is listed as 8 złoty, or 2 dollars for international subscribers.

דערשיינט יעדן צווייטן פרייטיק

בית יעקב

ליטעראַרישער ָנאַמיליען-זשורנאַל

יאַרגאַנג 9

אָרגאַן פאַר די אינטערעסן פון די בית-יעקב-שולן און אָרגאַניזאַציעס בנות-אגודת-ישראל אין פוילן

רעדאַקטאָר: א. ג. פרידנזאָן

נומער 79

ב"ה, לאָדזש-קראָקע-וואַרשע, — פרייטיק פ' ויצא י' כסלו תרצ"ב.

חברות!

פירט דורך מיט דער שטאַרקסטער אָנשטרענגונג אין יעדן אָרט די תרומת-חברה אַקציע!

וואָס מיין דערפאָלג די אַקציע וועט האָבן, אַלץ שטאַרקער און קרעפטיקער עס וועט ווערן אונדזער באַוועגונג!

דער ערשטער סימן פון זיין אָנגישלאָסן אין דער בנות-מחנה איז תרומת-חברה. די וואָס פאַרשפּרייטן תרומת-חברות, טוען א גרויסע אידעאַלע זאַך פאַר בנות-אגודת-ישראל און די אָרגאַניזאַציעס וואָס טוען דאָס נישט האָבן נישט קיין שום זכות אין דער באַוועגונג.

אפילו אין די ערטער וואו ס-עקזיסטירט נישט אפיציעל קיין בנות-גרופּע, ווערט דאַרט דורך אונדזערע סימפּאַטיקער געפירט די תרומת-חברה-אַקציע! ווען איר האָט נאָך נישט באַקומען די ביכלעך, אָדער די צאָל פון די צוגעשיקטע ביכלעך איז צו ווייניק שרייבט דערוועגן אין דער צענטראַלע:

Sekretarjat B. A. I. Łódź, skrz. poczt. 146.

ירידה!

מיר לעבן איבער א מוראדיקע ירידה. מיר דאַרפן זען ווידער עולה צו זיין. ווי אַזוי — דאָס איז דאָס פּראָגראַם פון די עולים.

ביז היינט האָט דער פאַרבונד פון עולים נישט פאַרמאָגט קיין בלאַט אויף יידיש. וואָס זאָל קענען צוקומען צו א ברייטערן עולם און איבערגעבן דעם רעיון און די שיטה. דאָס איז אַצינד מעגלעך געוואָרן דורכן באַשאַפן

פני דרך

עולים בלעטער

וואָס איז אַרויס פון דרוק היינטיקן חודש כסלו אין

פאַרלאַג „בית יעקב“ אין לאָדזש.

שטענדיקע מיטאַרבעטער: ד"ר שלמה בירנבוים, אליעזר שינדלער, שמואל אסטערזעצער. אין נומער א' געפינט זיך א גרויסער מאמר פון ד"ר נתן בירנבוים: רעליגיעזיטעט — מאָדערניזם — דאָס יונגע דור; משה צעכאַוואַל שרייבט א פייערדיק אויפגעשריי: איר לעבעדיקע קברים, אליעזר שינדלער גיט גידאַנקן וועגן „פני דרך“. ווייטער אינטערעסאַנטע זענען די הערות וואָס קומען אין יעדן נומער.

אַדרעס פון רעדאַקציע: PANY DEJRECH, Hamburg 13, Dillstr. 19.

אַדרעס פון אַדמיניסטראַציע: PANY DEJRECH Łódź, Kilińskiego 44, skrz. poczt. 146.

פּרייז פון א נומער 65 גר. מיט פּאָרטע. א פערטל יאָר 1.50. אין אויסלאַנד 7 סענט.

ביי 10 עקז. 20% ראַבאַט. געלט שיקן: P. K. O. 67.795

אָן געלט ווערט נישט געשיקט!

(e) **No. 79, 1931** (ninth year of publication), is described as a bi-weekly, 'appearing every other Friday'; the place of publication is now listed as Łódź–Kraków–Warsaw

לעצטער נומער פון צענטן יאָרגאַנג

בית יעקב

ליטעראַרישע שריפט פאַר שול און היים
דינט די ענינים פון בית־יעקב שולן און אָרגאַניזאַציעס בנות־אגודת־ישראל אין פוילן
רעדאַקטירט דורך א״ג פרידנזאָן

ב״ה, לאָדזש־קראָקע־וואַרשע.	נומער 107	צענטער יאָרגאַנג	אלול תרצ״ג

תוכן: נאָך די „בית־יעקב״ קאָנפערענצן — א״ג פרידנזאָן. שופר־קלאַנגען (ליד) — אליעזר שינדלער. אַ וואָרט צו דער דיעקוסיע — שרה שענירער. רעליגיע און ווירטשאַפט — ד״ר יוסף קאַרלעבאַך. אויף די זינד וואָס כ׳האָב געזינדיקט — העשיל קלעפּפיש. ס׳איז מיר צוגעפאַלן די נאַכט — אלימלך שטייער. איינע אַ נאַכט — שמואל נאַדלער. וועלן גייען אויף, וועלן גייען אונטער — שמואל פליסקין. במתון — ז. שאַכנאָוויטש. אויף דער שוועל פון עלפטן יאָר — *** באַריכטן פון בית־יעקב קאָנפערענצן און פגישות פון „בנות״. קאָרעספּאָנדענציעס און מודעות.

נאָך די בית־יעקב קאָנפערענצן

(f) **No. 107, 1933** (last issue of the tenth year of publication), is subtitled 'Literary journal for school and home dealing with matters concerning the Bais Yaakov schools and the Bnos Agudath Israel organizations in Poland'

גרייט אייך צום היסטארישן בנות־קאנגרעס!

בית־יעקב

ליטעראַרישע שריפט פאר שול און היים

דינט די ענינים פון בית־יעקב שולן און אָרגאַניזאַציעס בנות אגודת־ישראל אין פוילן

רעדאַקטירט דורך א.ג. פרידענזאָן

אַלע בנות־חברות

האָבן דעם

יובל־

ושעטאָן!

פערצנטער יאָרגאַנג	נומער 137	כ״ה תשרי תרצ״ז	לאָדזש־וואַרשע־קראָקע

תּוכן:

ד״ר בן־ציון פעסלער / מלכות ש־די
דוד אפטייקער / תפילת השבלים בעמק יזרעאל
הרב ב. ז. יאַקאָבזאָן / דאָס גליק פון תשובה
ד״ר העשיל קלעפפיש / די פרויען וואָס קומען צו אונדז
י. ל. ארלעאַן / אַרבעטן און גלייבן
ד״ר יצחק ברויער / וואָס הייסט אגודיזם
ז. שאַכנאָוויטש / דער וועג אהיים
ישראל עמיאָט / דער ווילנער גאון
אלימלך שטייער / בריוו פון תהום
אלטער שנור / גיקליבענע פערל
י. קרני / (שיר)
אסתר הייטנער / פאַרוואָס (דערציילונג)

פראָבלעמען פון נאָנטן בנות־קאָנגרעס:

בית־יעקב אַלס פאָלקס־שול / א שטאַרקע און פעסטע אָרגאַניזאַציע / נשי אגודת ישראל / בתיה־פאַרבאַנד / קולטור־אַרבעט / ליטעראַטור און פרעסע / ארץ־ישראל / יהדות און יידישקייט / סאָציאַלע ענינים און פילאַנטראָפּישע הילף.

א) ד״ר משה אשער **פאַרהייליגע קדושה**
פאָלערנדיקע אָפּהאַנדלונג איבערן צניעות און קדושה־לעבן פון דער יידישער יוגנט. נייער צוגאַנג צו דער באַהאַנדלונג פון סעקסועלע פראַגן שטרענג לויט דער תורה.
52 זייטן — — — פרייז 95 גראָשן.

ב) הלל זיידמאַן **Renesans Kobiety Żydowskiej**
גרעסערע גישיכטלעכע בראָשור וועגן דער בית־יעקב און בנות־באַוועגונג אין דער פוילישער שפּראַך. דער באַקאַנטער מחבר איז ערוב פאַרן חשיבות פון דער אויסגאַבע.
52 זייטן — — — פרייז 95 גראָשן.

ג) הרב בנימין זאב יאַקאָבזאָן
ד״ר שמואל דייטשלענדער
א ביאָגראַפישע אָפּהאַנדלונג איבערן לעבן און שאַפן פון ד״ר שמואל דייטשלענדער. די בראָשור איז גישריבן זייער האַרציק און מיר באַקומען א קלאָר בילד פון דעם לעבן און שאַפן פון דער גרויסער פערזענלעכקייט.
32 זייטן — — — פרייז 50 גראָשן.

ד) שרה שענירער **די מאַמיס צוואה**
זאַמל־בוך מיט מאמרים, בריוו, מעשיות און דערציילונגען פאַר קינדער און יוגנט.
120 זייטן — — — פרייז 1.25 גילדן.

ה) א״מ ראַזאָווי
דער מענטש און זיין לעבנס־וועג
(שמונה פרקים להרמב״ם — אין יידיש)
זייער א וויכטיקע בראָשור פאַר דער יוגנט. נעמט אַרום די וויכטיקסטע מוסר־פּראָבלעמען פון מענטשלעכן לעבן און קלערט אויף דעם תכלית פון מענטשנס זיין אין שאַפן.
32 עמודים — — — פרייז 95 גר.

ו) רבי יעקב ראָזנהיים
אגודת־ישראל אַלס אויפגאַבע און פאַרווירקלעכונג
אידעאָלאָגישע אָפּהאַנדלונג איבער אגודיזם. אידעאָלאָגיע, רעיון און ווירקלעכקייט
28 עמודים — — — פרייז 50 גר.

ז) אויך וועט איר באַקומען גישיטע קאָמפּלעטן 30 העפטן בית־יעקב־זשורנאַל, דערונטער יובליי־אויסגאַבעס
צום פרייז פון 6.70 גילדן.

אויף יעדן טשעק אויפשרייבן אויף וואָס דאָס געלט ווערט גישיקט!

ביי א גרעסערע צאָל בראָשורן ווערט גיגעבן ראַבאַט.

אַדרעס: Bajs Jakow, Łódź, Kilińskiego 44.
Konto Rozrachunkowe, Kartoteka 15.

(g) No. 137, 1936 (fourteenth year of publication), with the same subtitle as the previous image (no. 107), carries the announcement: 'Prepare for the historic Bnos Congress!'

one summer in three. But even when such resolutions were actually fulfilled, they still left many pupils and teachers in the supplementary schools with only tenuous connections to the rest of the movement. Two of the most detailed memoirs we have of Bais Yaakov teachers describe young women who took teaching positions, one at 16 and the other at 17, without having attended a seminary or teacher-training course.[8] As with the press in other modernizing societies, the *Bais Yaakov Journal* constructed an 'imagined community', in Benedict Anderson's terminology, connecting individuals who had never met within a network of affiliation.[9]

The *Bais Yaakov Journal* facilitated these connections in a number of ways. It regularly included reports from the urban centres and the outlying regions, detailing not only founding ceremonies and graduations, official pronouncements, and conference resolutions, but also more personal impressions. More generally, it served as a platform for women's writing: Sarah Schenirer contributed to nearly every issue, but the journal was always on the lookout for new talent. It periodically issued calls for submissions, hosting a conference in 1929 on the state of Orthodox literature, and later that same year sponsoring a contest for 'original Orthodox literature', with a first prize of 1,000 złoty (almost $200 at the time), and a smaller prize for the composition of a Bais Yaakov anthem.[10] In a 1932 article on the subject, Heshl Klepfish lamented the continuing dearth of women writers, and hypothesized that women were scared off by ingrained prejudices among editors; urging women to resist such prejudices, he called on them 'Take up your pen!'[11] The *Bais Yaakov Journal* published contributions by women in a range of genres, including poetry, short stories, memoirs, historical articles, and book reviews. Some writers of the first rank appeared in its pages (Miriam Ulinover, Rosa Jacobson, and Shmuel Nadler, for instance), but most were enthusiastic amateurs, as the journal itself frankly acknowledged in periodic assessments of the still 'undeveloped' state of Orthodox literature.

The pattern was set in this as in other regards in the first issue, which featured B. Aliza's poem, 'Awake!', which like many other literary works published in the pages of the *Bais Yaakov Journal* was dedicated to the movement:

[8] See Sternbuch and Kranzler, *Gutta*, 28–31, and Shandler (ed.), *Awakening Lives*, 335–7.

[9] On the uses of print journalism to establish 'imagined communities', see Anderson, *Imagined Communities*, 34–5.

[10] The contest was announced on the cover of the *Bais Yaakov Journal*, 45 (1929).

[11] H. Klepfish, 'Women, To the Pen!' (Yid.), 10.

Jewish daughter, Jacob's child, stand up! Awake!
Take courage and free yourself from slavery,
foreign powers! Oh! Too many have been sacrificed
On foreign altars. Enough shedding of your marrow, your blood!

. . . .

Jewish Deborah, Jacob's daughter! Awake with courage!
With Jewish heroism!
Just as on Mount Sinai you laid your wreath;
You showed wisdom and maturity, O House of Jacob!
Awake also today, Miriam. Youth of Jacob's household,
With majestic beauty—with the radiance of Sinai.[12]

The poem is perhaps less simple than might at first appear. Like much Bais Yaakov literature, Aliza's poem simultaneously mobilizes traditional religious imagery and novel realities. The double meaning of the term 'House of Jacob' that figures in the last stanza is a case in point: it refers to the historical Jewish people, the (female) descendants of Jacob whose experiences are recorded in the Bible as they are freed from slavery; but the poem also addresses the modern movement known as Bais Yaakov, which represents a new iteration of these ancient acts of freedom, dedication, heroism, and wisdom. The Jewish daughter 'freed from slavery', as any reader would recognize, is the modern Orthodox woman who has cast off the influence of 'foreign altars' (which is to say, of Paris fashion), but may actually be called Deborah or Miriam, biblical names of continuing currency.

The title and repeated invocations of the imperative 'Awake!' also have multiple connotations. The title evokes the traditional liturgy of redemption, as for instance, in the verse 'Awake! Awake! Your light has come!' that is part of the service on a Friday night that welcomes the sabbath, considered as a bride. In using these traditional tropes to celebrate the religious awakening of actual girls rather than metaphorical brides, and in the fact that the poem's author is, presumably, a woman (who hides behind a pseudonym), the poem also signals its novelty and modernity. Although this literary allusion was no doubt unintended, Aliza's piece also echoes a famous 1866 poem by the *maskil* Yehudah Leib Gordon, 'Awake, My People!' Both compositions advocate a synthesis between continuity and renewal. But whereas Gordon addresses traditional Jews who have yet to respond to the call of modernity, Aliza targets women who have fallen prey to the temptations of the age and forsaken their religious identity.

That the *Bais Yaakov Journal* also hoped to hear from its female readership is

[12] Aliza, 'Awake!' (Yid.).

evident from the periodic reader surveys, the column dedicated to discussing the challenges faced by Bnos chapters, and 'From Sister to Sister', the regular letters column that featured surprisingly frank exchanges (perhaps fictional) between young women sharing the difficulties they were facing. The first survey, carried out in 1924 when the journal had been out for only a year, was directed to older readers, especially activists and teachers, and attempted to solicit responses to the publication, asking such questions as: 'What do you think of the journal, and which articles particularly appeal to you?' and 'Who in your circles reads the journal—men or women, old or young?'[13] A second survey, conducted in 1931, was directed towards achieving a better understanding of the life experiences of younger readers, and specified that the responses could be mailed in anonymously or pseudonymously.[14] This survey asked whether girls were happy with the education they had received; whether they expected as adults to work or to be housewives; and whether they considered it wrong to associate with irreligious people. This last question reflected a long-standing, controversial issue in Bais Yaakov: its missionary character. Girls were urged to 'work with our estranged sisters, and . . . never rest until we gather them all under the banner of our Torah', even while the movement worried about how to shield its students from 'alien' influences. A 1921 school document listing 'Duties of Students' included the item 'Behaviour—politeness, not associating with children who will provide a negative influence.'[15] Articles in the *Bais Yaakov Journal* regularly referred to what was called 'the influence [*hashpo'e*] problem'. This was not just a theoretical issue: in the autobiographical essay she submitted to a YIVO competition, 'Esther' describes herself as caught between the double injunctions of avoiding excessive familiarity with secular Jews while also reaching out to them (she also seemed to object to the suspicion that she was vulnerable to 'entrapment'):

They talked about 'nets spread to entrap our souls'. Evidently, it wasn't enough that we hadn't become like 'those Jews', but we also had to continue to protect ourselves from them. I had my doubts . . . Was this the way to carry out what I was taught, or did I not understand the meaning of 'to study and to teach'? Wouldn't I accomplish a great deal more if I brought our ideals to these allegedly alien circles?'[16]

13 'Survey' (Yid.).

14 'Our First Survey' (Yid.). Perhaps the editorial staff of the journal had forgotten the 1924 survey, or more likely they considered this one to be of a different kind.

15 For a reproduction of the document that lists the duty of students to avoid friendships with 'bad children', see Rottenberg (ed.), *A Mother in Israel*, iv. 3.

16 Shandler (ed.), *Awakening Lives*, 330.

While 'Esther' reports that her Bnos group erred on the side of protecting its members, in the survey and other discussions it provided, the *Bais Yaakov Journal* took a more hands-off approach. The published responses to the survey indicated the willingness of the editors to let readers have their say, rather than closing off discussion by imposing Orthodox standards from above. On the thorny question of whether to avoid irreligious Jews, the editor began by noting that the question had elicited the greatest number of responses:

> And no wonder. Jewish life is tangled and torn, with different ideas and contradictory world-views pushing against each other even in a single family circle. The father a hasid, the mother a pious woman, one daughter belongs to Bnos and the second is a Zionist or Bundist or a member of some other irreligious movement, and what is one supposed to do in such a case? On one hand the bonds of family or long friendship, on the other a chasm between world-views . . . The holiest institution of Jewish life is the family, from which we acquire our sense of deepest friendship, community, and kinship . . . But on the other hand when we see a friend sinking into heresy, should we really risk staying in touch with her?[17]

The journal made no recommendations, merely complimenting the participants for their intelligence and sensitivity in facing these issues squarely.

Other questions asked readers whether they preferred to confide in a parent or friend; whether they enjoyed painting, drawing, music, or dance; and whether they were interested in becoming economically independent or housewives. The journal published a wide range of responses without editorial comment. To the question about hobbies, responses included both 'Jewish music' and 'going to concerts', an activity frowned upon in Bais Yaakov. Most of the readers whose answers were recorded reported that they preferred to talk with their friends rather than their parents, since 'Parents today don't understand' their children. On the question of whether the girls expected to work once they became adults, it published answers that might be called normative ('a woman's work is in the home') and as well as less normative ones: 'I am in favour of women's emancipation, so I believe that women should be economically independent. A woman must be concerned with her own destiny exactly as a man is.'[18]

In this survey and in many other ways, the *Bais Yaakov Journal* demonstrated its willingness to confront challenges to the Orthodox world-view with remarkable frankness, allowing sceptical and modern voices to be heard alongside more pious ones. Such tactics may have been learned from German neo-Orthodoxy: Hirsch's *Nineteen Letters* begins with a challenge from Benjamin to his old friend

[17] 'What Does Our Survey Teach Us?' (Yid.), 13.

[18] 'Answers to Our First Survey' (Yid.), 13.

Naftali, wondering how the latter can maintain his loyalty to a way of life in which, among other problems, 'the broad principles of universal morality are narrowed into anxious worry about insignificant trifles'.[19] The *Bais Yaakov Journal* went even further in some respects, allowing onto its pages the voices of (apparently) actual readers rather than fictional (or fictionalized) characters, refraining from always delivering the correct answer to their concerns (or delaying a response), and devoting itself to the particular worries and challenges faced by girls and young women.

The journal clearly took pride in what it saw as its own open-minded responsiveness to its constituents, reporting on 'An Evening of Debate' held in the Bais Yaakov seminary in which a 'heated discussion' took place among teachers and students about the journal's content. The article, signed by 'a student', commented, 'our secretary could hardly control the meeting'.[20] One of the 'From Sister to Sister' columns featured an exchange of letters between 'Hannah' and 'Sarah': the 17-year-old Hannah, who describes herself as very depressed and always feeling as if 'my head were about to explode', speaks of her fierce unwillingness to marry the boy her father has chosen for her, her desire to 'live for myself', to be 'free and independent', unlike her hasidic mother, who had married at 17 and given birth to her at 18. Sarah provides the expected answer to this girl's dilemma, but only in the next issue, allowing Hannah's predicament to hang unanswered in the meantime. She begins by expressing her understanding of Hannah's problems, and notes that she herself faced a similar situation by escaping to the big city, where life was exciting, until she recognized the emptiness and dangers of the pursuit of pleasure. The exchange ends with Sarah encouraging Hannah to avoid making any drastic moves, and extending an invitation to the younger woman to pay her a visit and see a harmonious Orthodox marriage.[21]

[19] Hirsch, *The Nineteen Letters*, 25.

[20] 'A Debate Evening' (Yid.), 4. Vichna Eisen (later Kaplan) and Judith Grunfeld-Rosenbaum were among the participants. Among the points of dispute were questions about whether the *Bais Yaakov Journal* should take a stance on various political controversies of the day, and about the role of agrarian colonization in the movement—this last issue was in response to Nathan Birnbaum's impassioned argument that Orthodox Jewry should revitalize itself through agricultural labour and more fervent forms of messianic expectation, an argument that was rejected by rabbis in the Agudah as inappropriate for Orthodox youth. Evenings of open debate were a regular feature of Bais Yaakov life. The Kraków seminary reserved Monday evenings for open discussions of school affairs; students took turns summarizing current events during meals; and sabbath meals involved Torah talks by students, which were critiqued by the student body afterwards. On these activities, see Atkin, 'The Beth Jacob Movement in Poland', 89.

[21] 'From Sister to Sister' ('Hannah') (Yid.), 13, and 'From Sister to Sister' ('Sarah') (Yid.), 14.

Openness had its limits, of course. The autobiography of 'Esther' includes a pointed reflection on the nature of self-government and open discussion in Bnos culture, beginning with the suggestion that the enthusiasm in Bnos for debate owed something to the principles of talmudic argumentation. Perhaps the new culture of democracy in Poland also played a part. Describing her return to Bnos after her disappointing experience founding a small-town Bais Yaakov chapter, she relates that the group 'was not happy with' her:

> First of all, I opposed what was being said there too frequently. We had a certain 'freedom' to speak out, but this wasn't what they had in mind. Rather, they envisioned the Talmudic argumentation of the good old days in the yeshivas, where even a certain number of questions regarding 'the outside world' were discussed. But all this was used as a means of showing that 'our way' was everlasting, that 'our way' was correct, that we were God's chosen people.[22]

'Esther' is no doubt right that the taste for passionate debate was constrained in Bais Yaakov (and Bnos) culture by unwritten rules about how far one could go. Nevertheless, these limits were not narrow: the journal included articles on such worldly topics as Gandhi, Tolstoy, Pascal, 'The Shylock Legend in the Middle Ages', and 'Dulcinea and the New Woman in Modern Literature', and published Yiddish translations of the mystical writings of the Bengali poet Rabindranath Tagore, participating along with the rest of Europe in a Tagore craze. Even Freud was not out of bounds, appearing in an article on the importance of child psychology in education.[23] The notion that its readers were expected to be at home in the wider world was propagated by such articles as 'Leah Halpern—The Young Artist', which detailed both the loyalty to Orthodoxy and the artistic accomplishments of a young ceramic artist in Amsterdam, whose bowls were valued at over $200. The writer, Meir Schwartzman, declared it a 'great mistake' to think that women could not be both observant Jews and prominent in various artistic fields: 'It is useful for the young women's movement in the east to familiarize itself with various women artists in the west, who play an important role in the best art circles even while being strongly traditional and religious.'[24] As the journal aimed to convey to its readers, religious observance need not be an obstacle to women's worldly accomplishments, allowing even for a lucrative career in the fine arts.[25]

[22] Shandler (ed.), *Awakening Lives*, 341.

[23] See K-K, 'Pedagogical Signposts' (Yid.), 81.

[24] Schwartzman, 'Leah Halpern: The Young Artist' (Yid.).

[25] One girl who followed her Bais Yaakov education with a career in the arts is Sara Grynberg from Goworowo, described by her brother as an intellectual with varied interests, who after completing seven grades of Polish public school, followed by a Bais Yaakov school that she graduated

While the *Bais Yaakov Journal* focused much of its energy on giving a voice to girls and young women, it also featured male writers (and a nearly entirely male editorial board).[26] But the very context of writing for a newspaper with a largely female readership lent this aspect of the journal a unique flavour. Male contributors, too, addressed the phenomenon of Bais Yaakov with something of the enthusiasm and passion that B. Aliza had shown in the inaugural issue, writing poems and songs to the movement, to the 'mother' who led it, and to the 'sisters' who were acting so heroically within it. The journal twice published an 'Anthem of the Bnos Agudath Israel', first in 1929 and then in 1931 (with the musical notation included—see Appendix E) by an Orthodox young man named Shmuel Nadler, who was for a time considered 'the court poet of Agudah', and who was one of the few writers in Orthodox publications who attracted critical interest in the wider Yiddish literary world. Nadler's anthem proclaims:

'Come to us, you distant sisters
You have wandered too long
Throw away your tired idols
Come back to the ancient home.'

A stirring rhyming refrain is repeated three times:

Fierce and mighty, great and bright
[*shtark un mekhtig, groys un lekhtig*]
Are our efforts, aims, and goal
to be faithful to the old-new
Torah, God, and Jewish folk![27]

from at 16, went to Pułtusk to apprentice herself in a photographic studio. She returned home the next year and set up a shop with her own equipment in the family backyard. According to her brother, 'She hung a blanket there, as background. She had a chair and her own retouching equipment. I remember when the photographs were lying in water, when they were taken to the darkroom in the vestibule of the house.' Icchok Grynberg, Interview, Warsaw, 2004, Centropa (http://www.centropa.org/).

[26] While photographs that appeared in the journal showed a group of men at work on the paper, *Remember* mentions that one particular talented married Bais Yaakov teacher, Rachel Schildkraut, was recruited to work on the paper by E. G. Friedenson, who met her on a visit to her town. See Szaranski, *Remember*, 86.

[27] Nadler, 'Hymn of the Bnos Agudas Israel' (Yid.), 6, 7. It is not clear whether Nadler's hymn to Bnos won the prize for a Bais Yaakov anthem announced in issue 45 of the journal. He may have meant 'strong Jewishness' rather literally: he also wrote 'Be Well and Strong', an article in the special issue on religious education of the *Bais Yaakov Journal*, 94/5 (1935), stressing the importance of physical education in the movement (cited in Atkin, 'The Beth Jacob Movement in Poland', 101). For more on Nadler's literary career, see Caplan, 'Shmuel Nadler's *Besht-Simfonye*'.

Nadler's composition shows that editors and publishers were interested in expanding the range of genres available for Orthodox literary production beyond its traditional limits.[28] His anthem is striking in other respects as well. He speaks in a collective female voice, ventriloquizing the young Orthodox women speaking to their 'sisters' even as he praises them for their power and strength of will. This reverses the more usual way language works to render the feminine invisible by marking the collective as masculine. The praise of women (though for their beauty rather than their power) is, of course, a ubiquitous topos of male lyrical poetry in the Western tradition, but such odes by young men to women were hardly a familiar feature of Orthodox writing before the *Bais Yaakov Journal* opened the floodgates. Along with Nadler's rapturous song, the journal published Dr Bentsion Pressler's 'Hymn to the Jewish Daughter', a free-verse ode to Jewish women that appeared in 1931, which begins 'You have the ripeness of the eastern sun | Your blood is as thick and juicy [*zaftig*] | As oranges', and ends, 'Therefore you are uniquely beautiful | O daughter, Jewish daughter!'[29] Not all these odes and songs were to exemplary women. Elimelech Steyer, a frequent contributor to the journal and one of the most prolific Orthodox writers in the interwar period, wrote 'A Letter to a Sister', a poem to a 'wandering sister filled with doubt, racked with pain'. The poet proclaims: 'Doubt is sin | Joy a commandment | And everywhere is God | And always only God!'[30]

Writings such as these went beyond the heterosexual romance that so obsessively shapes the European lyrical tradition but which was ruled out for Orthodox literature, and suggested new kinds of relationship between men and women. As Beatrice Lang Caplan writes, this literature took aesthetic values as secondary: 'In addition, certain subjects that one would expect to be of importance to the young readers and writers of this literature were effectively taboo: including relationships between the sexes, opposition to parents and teachers,

[28] In documenting the spread of journals and newspapers among the hasidic yeshivas in Poland from 1913 to 1937, Stampfer suggests that the *Bais Yaakov Journal* may have provided a model for this production; he notes that 'almost all of these journals were published after 1924, the year the *Beit ya'akov* (House of Jacob) journal published by the Orthodox Beit Ya'akov school movement first appeared. Many of the sisters of yeshiva students attended these schools and, while I know of no way of checking whether the fact that young women had a journal was an incentive for young men to call for journals, the timing is thought-provoking' (Stampfer, *Families, Rabbis, and Education*, 269). Stampfer does not note that the *Bais Yaakov Journal* published young men as well as women; hasidic yeshiva students, then, could have been inspired by the journal more directly, as contributors, and not only as the brothers of young female readers.

[29] Pressler, 'Hymn to the Jewish Daughter' (Yid.).

[30] Steyer, 'A Letter to a Sister' (Yid.).

and any critique of the traditional way of life.'[31] Despite these taboos, young men found ways to praise their 'sisters', the young women of Bais Yaakov, in pure religious language in which passion and female strength were nevertheless plain to see. It was yet another sign of a strong male identification with women in Agudah circles that at least two of the male writers for the journal took on matronymic pseudonyms—Ben-Rivkah and Avraham Tsvi Ben-Hadassah—and many others dedicated their poems and stories to mothers and grandmothers.[32]

Perhaps the most innovative and important aspect of the *Bais Yaakov Journal* was its construction of an Orthodox discourse around gender. As a movement that aimed to organize Orthodox girls and women within a larger environment in which 'the woman question' was ubiquitous and pressing, Bais Yaakov could hardly avoid taking a stance on the issue. One of the most frequent writers on the subject, Rabbi Tuvye Yehudah Gutentag, laid out the challenge directly in a 1927 article on 'Women in Judaism'. As he wrote, in previous generations 'the woman question' would have meant halakhic questions about Jewish family life. In the present generation, however, the question referred to equality of rights, and those who asked rabbis for their thoughts on this matter were generally not sincerely attempting to discern the Torah view:

> They come with complaints that at this historical moment, when most enlightened European nations are openly declaring and instituting women's emancipation, the rabbis and sages only diminish the status of women, treating them like second-class citizens, directly and indirectly limiting their right to vote in community elections, invalidating their testimony in court, and forbidding them from learning Torah.
>
> And many rabbis, who are not familiar with modern ways of thinking, are at a loss about how to respond to such challenges . . . Even if these issues have roots in secular

[31] Caplan, 'Shmuel Nadler's *Besht-Simfonye*', 602.

[32] In general, matronyms, or names that refer to mothers or other female ancestors, are far less common in European naming culture than patronyms, but Jewish surnames include quite a few matronyms (Sorkin, Rivkin, and even Freud, after Sigmund Freud's great-great-grandmother Freide); interestingly, a number of prominent secular male Yiddish writers of the same period also adopted matronymic pseudonyms, for instance Avraham Glanz *Leyeles* (son of Leah) and Isaac *Bashevis* Singer (son of Batsheva). There are of course circumstances in which matronymic appellations are used in traditional Jewish circles, as in praying for the recovery of a sick person. Women often took on pseudonyms as well, for instance Rokhl Bas Tovim (daughter of 'good' people, or respected members of the community), who adopted a variation on the pseudonym of a female writer of *tkhines* (supplicatory prayers) collections for women, Sarah Bas Tovim. Bronia Baum (1896–1946), a regular contributor to *Bais Yaakov Journal* and other Orthodox periodicals, used the pseudonym Bas Tovim and Bas Bela (daughter of Bella).

life, they still poke their branches into the Torah way of life. And in response to such questions we can only say: 'Answer the fool according to his folly' [Prov. 26: 5].[33]

Rabbi Gutentag (whose answers to these challenges the editors boldly postponed to a later issue) made it clear that even if attacks on the Orthodox treatment of women were arrogant 'folly', the Orthodox world was in no position to avoid responding to them, although traditional rabbis were poorly equipped for the job. Of course, the female readership of the *Bais Yaakov Journal*, some of whom no doubt struggled with similarly 'foolish' questions and who themselves were probably frequently required to defend their religious enthusiasm to irreligious friends or even family, was also eager for a meaningful defence of Orthodoxy on these sore points.

Gutentag was correct in implying that a yeshiva education was no great training for engaging in debates with modern proponents of women's rights. A discourse on women and Judaism is not entirely absent from the traditional sources: rabbinic literature includes halakhic discussions of women's roles, midrashic tales of Jewish women, and general remarks about women or gender differences. But these disparate and often contradictory sources appear in a wide range of texts, and so require selection and synthesis before they can serve as a unified and coherent discourse on gender. But a more profound problem is that, to put it mildly, rabbinic sources do not always translate well into modern language. The *Bais Yaakov Journal*, given its readership, could hardly ignore the potential effects of hearing Rabbi Eliezer's opinion on teaching women Torah, or such dictums as 'Let the words of the Torah be burned rather than entrusted to women' (JT *Sot.* 3: 4 16*a*). For all these reasons it had to construct a discourse on gender, rather than finding one at the ready on the rabbinic bookshelf.

As in so many other controversial areas, it was German neo-Orthodoxy that paved a path for Polish Orthodoxy to follow. Samson Raphael Hirsch's notion of the 'Mensch Yisroel', the fully rounded and spiritually committed human being comfortable in both a Torah environment and in the wider world, applied to both genders. In contrast to Orthodoxy in eastern Europe, German neo-Orthodoxy did not assume an intellectual chasm between the sexes. As Marc B. Shapiro puts it, 'In this [German] conception women's education came to be regarded as an intrinsically positive manifestation, not merely an unavoid-

[33] Tavyomi (Gutentag), 'Women in Judaism' (Yid.), 100. The article was reworked into Yiddish from a chapter of *Tal leyisra'el* (Piotrkow, 1926), a collection of sermons that Gutentag (later changed to Tavyomi) had recently published.

able measure taken to prevent religious breakdown, which was the attitude of so many east European supporters of the Beth Jacob movement.'[34] Alongside this conception of the inherent worth of educating women, Hirsch also developed a psychologically intricate conception of masculinity and femininity that borrowed from and reshaped influential modern notions of gender complementarity. The conception of men and women as inherently different but complementary, according to Ian Watt, arose as ideological support for new socio-economic divisions of labour that kept middle-class women in the house while viewing men as the natural providers for the family. This act of relegation was bolstered by the view of the woman as the more spiritual sex, the 'angel in the house' who brought her 'softer', more 'modest' nature to family life, while men went out into the world to earn a living.[35]

Paula Hyman has demonstrated that this ideology had enormous influence among nineteenth-century Jews moving into the European bourgeoisie, in both acculturating and more traditional circles. Jewish women, in this context, were expected to impart otherwise threatened religious and moral virtues to their children. The mother therefore represented 'a living example for the children, whom she has constantly under her eyes'.[36] While more liberal communities assigned responsibility for transmitting Jewish values solely to the mother, assuming that fathers were too absorbed in their economic roles to take on this burden, neo-Orthodox discourse could hardly release fathers from what was after all the long-standing centrality of men in the responsibility for the religious education of their children. German rabbis and leaders thus only partially adopted European gender ideologies, retaining the halakhic language of male versus female obligations but combining it with some of the bourgeois views of women as more spiritual than men (they also repudiated widespread notions of natural male dominance as signifying greater strength). In forging this discourse, Orthodox writers set out to discern the underlying philosophical logic and psychological coherence of why Jewish law assigned men and women different obligations and roles. And they did so with an eye to how this discourse would be perceived by modern youth sceptical of traditional observance. Hirsch therefore explained the halakhic principle of women's exemption from positive time-bound commandments by reference to the symbolic principles embedded in them. Since 'God's Torah takes it for granted that our women have more fervour and more faithful

[34] M. B. Shapiro, *Between the Yeshiva World and Modern Orthodoxy*, 210.

[35] Watt, *The Rise of the Novel*, 135–84.

[36] *Archives Israélites*, 13 (1852), 612, cited in Hyman, *Gender and Assimilation*, 28.

enthusiasm for their God-serving calling', while men are more subject to 'the temptations which occur in the course of business and professional life', men require the reminders constituted by these commandments more urgently than women.[37] While the rabbis in the Talmud did not seem to have worried much about whether their pronouncements would grate on women's ears, the German rabbis who attempted to restate their teachings were raised in a culture in which men were expected to treat women with bourgeois chivalry (or sentimentality). It was these conditions that shaped German neo-Orthodox thought in the nineteenth century, and some would also apply to Poland in the twentieth.

Hirsch wrote on a wide range of topics, but editors of the *Bais Yaakov Journal* were particularly interested in reprinting his writings on women. In one illustrative article on 'Women and Family according to the Talmud', Hirsch asserts that 'women have been granted by God greater spiritual capacities and gifts, which is why they reach maturity before males'.[38] Rather than viewing the different obligations incumbent on men and women as a consequence of the patriarchal character of Jewish culture, or deriving them (as is often done) from women's obligations to family and children, Hirsch recasts women's exemption as an acknowledgement of their more refined spirituality.

The bourgeois underpinnings of Hirsch's writings on gender are perhaps most visible in his commentary on a verse in Genesis 12, describing Abraham moving his tent east of Bethel. Hirsch notes the masculine form of the verb 'to move', and the feminine ending of *ohalah*, '*her* tent':

> For external matters the man, internal ones the woman; as leader, guiding star, to submit the whole household in every way to the Will of God, the man is in authority, in every other matter of managing and directing the home, the woman has precedence. Such is the principle of intimate happy Jewish life, the origin of which has its roots in Abraham's tent.[39]

The 'happy Jewish life' lived by Abraham and Sarah may have owed something to the socio-economic conditions of nineteenth-century Germany, which placed women in the domestic sphere and men in the public sphere while bringing both realms together in a harmonious rhetoric of marital balance and family unity. Hirsch's explanations of family purity similarly viewed these laws as evidence for the Torah's understanding of marital sexual attraction: the period of sexual sep-

[37] Hirsch, *Pentateuch*, commentary on Lev. 23: 43. Women's exemption from positive time-bound commandments comes from BT *Kid*. 29*a*.

[38] Hirsch, 'Women and Family', 7.

[39] Hirsch, *Pentateuch*, commentary on Gen. 12: 8.

aration keeps marital passion alive and deepens mutual love.[40] Rabbinic literature on menstruation provides many different views on the subject, including some that support the notion that the period of sexual separation deepens marital love (BT *Nid.* 31*b*). Of all the available explanations for this separation, it is this principle that is selected to represent 'the Torah view' for moderns, as it is the one least liable to offend women and best able to recommend observance on the 'modern' grounds of family harmony.[41]

For an east European culture newly facing the need to attract women to observance, the availability of this 'old-new' discourse was a godsend. Nevertheless, some aspects applied more easily than others. The nineteenth-century bourgeois conditions in the background of the writings of Hirsch and his followers came up against both the traditional east European ideal (never achieved by more than a small number) of the *eshet ḥayil*, the woman who works to support her husband and family while he learns Torah, and—more importantly—the immediate realities of east European impoverishment, which required women along with men to face 'the temptations which occur in the course of business'.[42] Bais Yaakov itself was deeply invested in providing young women with vocational skills, beyond their role as teachers in the school system. The *Bais Yaakov Journal* repeatedly called for the community to 'hire our religious sisters' and proposed an employment bureau to facilitate that goal. Sarah Schenirer's will recognized this reality, asserting that 'My dearest wish is to have authentic Jewish daughters. Let them also be seamstresses, dressmakers, bookkeepers, as long as they are true Jews.'[43] The idea of modesty, which in the west connected women to their

[40] 'Family purity' is the usual English rendering of the Hebrew term *taharat hamishpaḥah*, a euphemism that first arose in German neo-Orthodox circles to replace the more traditional term *hilkhot nidah*, 'the laws of menstruation'.

[41] Writing about later developments in this literature, Jonah Steinberg similarly understands this discourse as apologetic: 'the modern Orthodox literature concerning menstruation seeks to obscure the earlier themes of revulsion and avoidance, stressing companionship and intimacy even as it prescribes meticulous physical separation' ('From a "Pot of Filth"', 7). BT *Nidah 3b* states that 'Because a man may become overly familiar with his wife and thus be repelled by her, the Torah said that she should be a niddah for seven clean days (after her flow) so that she will be as pleasing to her husband as on the day of her marriage' (quoted in Steinberg, 'From a "Pot of Filth"', 18–19). In modern rewritings, this insight about male desire is expanded to refer to an eternal *mutual* honeymoon.

[42] Of course, there were bourgeois Orthodox families in Kraków, though many of these also found themselves in difficult straits during the Depression. On Jewish *embourgeoisement* in Kraków, see Manekin, 'Orthodox Jewry', 166.

[43] Quoted in Orlean, 'A Woman of Valour' (Heb.), 42.

domestic roles, in the east guided their (inevitable) entry into the worlds of business and commerce. The vocational programmes thus aimed to help young women find positions outside such perilous workplaces as factories, considered likely to encourage both sexual licentiousness and sabbath desecration. In this geographical and socio-economic context, Hirsch's placement of Jewish women in the 'tent' could be recovered only through metaphorical displacement. The Łódź-based vocational school Ohel Sarah recalled in its name not only Sarah Schenirer but also the matriarch Sarah, whose modesty Orthodox discourse stressed through the biblical phrase 'in the tent' (*hineh ba'ohel*, Gen. 18: 9), even while the school itself prepared young women to leave the 'tent' and enter the world of work.[44]

That addressing 'the woman question' would be a central task of the *Bais Yaakov Journal* was already evident in the first issue, which featured a long article with that title by Yehudah Leib Orlean. Orlean began (as Gutentag later did) by acknowledging the challenge that modern feminism represented to Orthodoxy and Jewish law, and laid out the argument that the Torah bases itself not on discrimination but on the wise recognition of the complementarity of the sexes. Orthodoxy thus suits women far better than the equality insisted on by feminists, which can only make mutual antagonists of men and women. Feminism, Orlean argues, mistakes the nature of happiness in its focus on the individual, while traditional Judaism correctly views family and community as more important than the individual. The notion that Orthodox women obey men, rather than the Torah, is simply wrong. As Orlean writes, a non-Jew walking into a Jewish home would be surprised to find 'a close and harmonious relationship between the sexes', which reflects the absolute deference of both husband and wife to the Torah. Orthodoxy, moreover, is more natural for a woman than heresy, given her inborn modesty and religious gifts.[45]

While Orlean rests his case on the harmony of the traditional Jewish home, the more immediate goal of the *Bais Yaakov Journal* was to draw girls and young women to the movement, and it went so far as to expect them to delay marriage in order to devote themselves to teaching.[46] The most distinctive practices of Bais Yaakov had little to do with gender complementarity, traditional family, or

[44] In Gen. 18, when the angels who visit Abraham ask him where Sarah is, he says 'there, in the tent'. The Talmud suggests that the Torah tells us that Sarah remained in the tent during the visit 'to inform you that the matriarch Sarah was modest' (BT *BM* 87*a*). The verse in Genesis became a code for referring to the modesty of women.

[45] Orlean, 'The Woman Question' (Yid.), 6.

[46] See Rubin (ed.), *Daughters of Destiny*, 178, and the Epilogue to Part I, below.

marital love. It is no surprise, then, that a second discourse about gender arose in the movement, one that spoke more directly to the experiences of participants, where the important relationships were among girls and young women, teachers and students united by their devotion to the Torah (a devotion traditionally assigned in Orthodox Jewish culture to the male sphere). Sarah Schenirer instituted an array of practices that had previously been limited to boys and men—reciting the afternoon and evening prayers, going to the graves of great rabbis, attending synagogue on Friday nights, spending sabbaths and holidays with members of the group rather than with family. In the seminary, students prayed together three times a day, a practice obligatory for men but neither required nor (for the afternoon and evening prayers) usually upheld by women. She also encouraged her students to pray in synagogue on Sabbath mornings, emphasizing 'the importance of *tefilah betsibur*—public prayer with a male quorum. To fulfil this commandment, she was prepared to sacrifice everything.'[47] Some services traditionally observed in synagogue, however, were celebrated by students in the seminary. For instance, while students generally went home or to relatives for the long Passover and Sukkot holidays, they spent Rosh Hashanah and Yom Kippur together, reciting the final prayer service of Yom Kippur not in the nearby synagogue where they had spent most of the day but in the seminary; the girls were so caught up in their singing and dancing that followed it that breaking the fast was sometimes long delayed. Judith Grunfeld-Rosenbaum describes how Sarah Schenirer introduced the observance of new holidays into the seminary, holidays whose observance had previously been limited to men. For instance, she transformed the kabbalistic practice of observing the eve of the New Moon as a fast day (called *yom kipur katan*) into a day of pilgrimage, in which she, 'followed by one hundred and twenty girls, would walk to the Rema's Shul in [Kazimierz] . . . Our tehillim [book of Psalms] in hand, we assembled around the tombstones.'[48] These practices depended neither on the special nature of women nor on marital harmony for their religious character. On the contrary, they assumed that the whole field of Jewish religious practice and culture was open to female

[47] Deutschländer, 'Sarah Schenirer and Bais Yaakov' (Yid.), 11, describes how, during her last illness, she would attempt to hear communal prayer through the wall of her apartment. The use of the word *mitsvah* to refer to a woman's voluntary communal prayer is striking here. There is much evidence that Bais Yaakov girls said the afternoon and evening prayers together as a group and attended synagogue services at times that were previously reserved for married women, or when women traditionally stayed at home (for instance, on Friday evenings). See the brief memoir by a young woman who came to the seminary to visit her friend—the first American at the seminary—in Rubin (ed.), *Daughters of Destiny*, 193, 211.

[48] Ibid. 133.

exploration and appropriation. Sarah Schenirer's article for the first issue of the *Bais Yaakov Journal*, which appeared on the page facing Orlean's, makes just that argument:

The Torah is binding on everyone, from the individual to the collective, whether one is a priest or an Israelite, a learned person or an ordinary Jew, a judge or a working man, a prophet or a villager. One must fulfil the commandments at home as in the field, in private or in the business world, in the Temple as in the street, in a store as in a workshop.[49]

This list of all those who are obligated to fulfil the commandments fails to mention gender, the primary category that distinguishes levels of Torah obligation. While Orlean insisted that gender represented a lens through which one could understand the Torah, Sarah Schenirer does not. She speaks in a more universal register, highlighting how it 'opens our eyes to see the divine power in nature'. Her piety thus establishes a direct relationship between God and human beings—all human beings. It is nature, the primordial divine creation, that opens the way for this relationship. Sarah Schenirer's diaries make it clear that she felt God's presence most powerfully in the Polish mountains and forests, an attitude with both European Romantic and hasidic roots.[50] Love of nature also shaped the social experience of Bais Yaakov, in which girls spent the summer months in rustic accommodation, praying and learning amidst the glories of nature, but outside the strictly segregated Orthodox urban sphere. Her approach privileged the religious power of nature—as the outdoors—over the 'natural' site of women's religiosity, the 'tent' or home. While she and Orlean were equally committed to Torah observance, it was the former's ostensibly simple ideas that opened the possibilities for female religious experience beyond the femininity and domesticity that the ostensibly more sophisticated German neo-Orthodox discourse reserved for women.

[49] Schenirer, 'The Goal of the Bais Yaakov Schools' (Yid.), 5.

[50] Schenirer's interest in Romanticism might be gleaned from a reference in her writings to a conference she attended in Vienna on the German proto-Romantic writer Johann Gottfried Herder. More normative rabbinic Judaism, in contrast to hasidism, has not always embraced this path to God—*Pirkei avot* (Ethics of the Fathers) quotes Rabbi Yaakov as saying: 'One who, while walking along the way and reviewing his studies, gets distracted and says, "How beautiful is that tree! How beautiful is that ploughed field!" Scripture regards him as if he has forfeited his soul' (3: 7). Such suspicion of nature worship is evident in descriptions of Bais Yaakov seminarians at Rabka, who were so engrossed in their Torah study that they paid no attention to their beautiful surroundings. But such a remark is foreign to Schenirer's own view, which saw no contradiction but rather harmony in the study of Torah amidst God's creation.

The young women devoting themselves to Torah study in the Polish woods were far indeed from the domestic sphere in which German neo-Orthodox discourse placed them. It may be no surprise that, when Jacob Rosenheim, the Frankfurt-based president of the world Agudah, visited the summer colony in Jordanów (the third of the teachers' training courses) in the late summer of 1927, he devoted his address to the students to the subject of the Torah's attitude toward the proper roles of men and women. Rosenheim cited the 'highly significant' verse, 'A woman must not put on man's apparel' (Deut. 22: 5), explaining that this verse was meant not only to restrict cross-dressing, but also to convey the importance of the 'boundaries between the life-mission and the activities of men and women'. Aside from the general ways that men and women were forbidden from impinging on each other's distinctive roles, the Torah also established gender differences within the spiritual realm, and more particularly within Torah study. He continued:

> Even as we speak, the Bais Yaakov movement is taking root among Polish Jewry. With it, new spiritual longings are being aroused in the feminine psyche. These are beginning to shape public life for Polish Jews, so it is crucial that we pay close attention to the boundaries set by the Torah between men and women.[51]

Rosenheim went on to spell out the lines drawn within Judaism between male and female spiritual realms, emphasizing that women needed to recognize and support the historical primacy of male Torah study even as they, too, were beginning to learn Torah.

But other voices also shaped the movement's discourse on women. A 1938 article in the *Bais Yaakov Journal* on 'Jewish Women and Torah Study' by Rabbi Abraham Schnur (who had spoken so powerfully on the topic at the 1912 Agudah conference in Katowice) begins by stressing that women have 'the same responsibility' to study Torah as men, with the exception of the Oral Torah. He then adds, more radically, that men are obligated to support women's Torah study. Schnur cites a responsum by the Boyaner Rebbe permitting such support, but reinforces the halakhic argument by offering a creative translation of Proverbs 31, the biblical text that praises 'the woman of valour'. For the woman who wishes to learn Torah, Schnur writes, *gart un mit festkayt ire lendn un shtarkt ire orems* ('gird her loins with steadfastness, and strengthen her arms'). While Proverbs envisions a woman who 'girds her loins with strength' to support her family (traditionally understood to be a woman who supports a husband who spends

[51] Rosenheim, 'At the Third Summer Course in Jordanów' (Ger.), 25–6.

his time studying Torah), Schnur chooses to read the verse as an imperative for men to strengthen these 'women of valour' so that they might learn Torah![52]

The discourse that simply assumed that Torah study was as exalted an enterprise for women as for men, girls as for boys, for all its apparent simplicity, was of course also constructed, like its German neo-Orthodox counterpart. Bais Yaakov was compelled to find language that was traditional in form but capacious enough to embrace the movement's novelties, beyond its oft-stated commitment to 'rebuilding the traditional Jewish home'. The argument for girls' education as a regrettably necessary response to a cultural crisis was important for establishing its halakhic legitimacy, but it could hardly serve as a rousing call to arms for girls and young women. For this, something else was required, and Sarah Schenirer was bold about providing it, describing her excitement about the 1929 establishment of the Neshei Agudath Israel not as a regrettable necessity, but rather as a long-delayed awakening:

> The Orthodox woman has awakened from her long, lethargic sleep and begun to organize . . . It has not been long since we first established the Bnos organization in Poland, and already from the dais of the World Congress the powerful voice of the religious Jewish woman rings out on the world stage. She is no longer isolated . . . In every corner of the world she has close and intimate sisters in spirit.

Nevertheless, she was also compelled to defend the legitimacy of such political visibility, and here she took the well-trodden route of 'It is time to act for the Lord':

> I know full well that many of our pious Jews will view this with suspicion. We hold sacred the ideal of women's modesty: 'She is in the tent' [*hineh baohel*] . . . No doubt a portion of the community will regard our congress with suspicion and fear and see it as a deviation—God forbid—from Israel of old. But these same pious Jews need to understand that this conference is a necessary response to the dangers that prey on our sisters from various secularist [*freye*] directions. *Et la'asot lahashem*, 'It is time to act for the Lord'—from this perspective must our public efforts be understood.

The tensions inherent to Sarah Schenirer's project appear in unusually close proximity here. She begins by celebrating the visibility and power of Jewish women, declaring an end to their long slumber and cultural isolation. But she also acknowledges that Jewish tradition (and her contemporary Orthodox critics) value Jewish women's modesty and invisibility, coded here in the Genesis passage in which Abraham informs the angels that Sarah is in her tent. It is only in response to these critics that she makes reference to the 'needs of the hour'.

[52] Schnur, 'Jewish Women and Torah Study' (Yid.).

In speaking of girls' formal Torah study, especially to girls, she largely refrained from apologetics, crafting a discourse that deemed such a project *inherently* valuable, and made no reference to those who felt otherwise. The very name of the movement, Bais Yaakov, established biblical warrant for women's Torah study by pointing to Exodus 19, the biblical account of the revelation at Sinai (which Judith Plaskow uses as painful evidence that 'At the central moment of Jewish history, women are invisible').[53] The verse in Exodus 19: 3, 'Thus shall you say to the House of Jacob and declare to the children of Israel', has long been taken to refer to a kind of double revelation—*first* to the women ('the House of Jacob') and *then* to the men ('the children of Israel').[54] This name was apparently given to Sarah Schenirer's school by the Kraków Agudah committee that pledged to support the movement in 1919. Legend has it, however, that it actually came from Sarah Schenirer herself, who explained it to a visiting Orthodox leader who lamented the dire state of her facilities: 'That doesn't matter. For as it clearly states [in Exod. 19: 3], *ko tomar leveit ya'akov*—the word *ko* ['thus'] adds up to 25 in *gematriya* [rabbinic letter numerology, in which the letters *kaf* and *heh* respectively equal 20 and 5]. With this number was said the first word to the Jewish woman, the House of Jacob.'[55] She alludes here to a ubiquitous trope in Bais Yaakov literature, which views the first word of the verse—*ko*, which adds up to 25—as a prophecy of the twenty-five students in the first Bais Yaakov class.[56] This intertextual play extends to the ritual realm: among the holidays of the movement was one with no historical precedent, the celebration of a special Bais Yaakov holiday on 3 Sivan (three days before the Mosaic revelation at Sinai, and thus the date of God's message to Moses to teach Torah to women). On this day, 'for hours and hours we danced, we daughters and our spiritual mother, singing without cease the words, *Ko tomar leveit ya'akov, ko tomar leveit ya'akov*'.[57] In this way the innovations of the movement are fused with Torah, embedding Bais Yaakov in the very moment of Sinaitic revelation.

53 Plaskow, *Standing Again at Sinai*, 25. Plaskow points out that the rabbis 'found a way to read women's presence into the text, for instance in reading Exod. 19: 3 as first addressing the women' (p. 27).

54 This reading is attested in the Mekhilta on Exod. 19: 3 and repeated by Rashi on that verse.

55 'Thus shall you say to the House of Jacob' (Heb.), in Rottenberg (ed.), *A Mother in Israel* (Heb.), ii. 27.

56 Different sources present different numbers for students in the first class. Benisch mentions seven, including as the first two Hindy and Devorah Birenbaum; see *Carry Me in Your Heart*, 35. Bacon, citing more official sources, has thirty in the first class; see *Politics of Tradition*, 168.

57 Y. Gora, 'The Early Days of the Bais Yaakov Movement' (Heb.), 173–4.

While Bais Yaakov created a rhetoric that could support its activities with powerful precedents, the question of locating the students in the tradition was a more vexed one; there was a range of attempts, none of which stood the test of time and achieved canonicity. In Sarah Schenirer's last letter to her students she based herself on Orlean's graduation speech and compared Bais Yaakov's pupils and staff to the priests who served in the Temple. Speaking to graduates of the summer teacher-training course, Orlean had exhorted the students, 'You are going out into the world to build Temples! Like the priests your hearts must be pure.' The analogy was sometimes, even more boldly, extended to Sarah Schenirer. Chava Greenfeld, remembering the solemn atmosphere in the seminary as the latter recited the Kiddush blessing God for sanctifying the sabbath, wrote that the students felt that they were in 'a sacred place, as if in a temple, and she was the high priest!'[58] The analogy Orlean and Greenfeld found for the new phenomenon of Bais Yaakov is a remarkable and somewhat exotic one, far from the realities of post-Temple Judaism. The priests were an all-male cadre, dedicated to religious life but separated from both learning and the family. In this way, the analogy suited the structure of Bais Yaakov, which also set up an elite corps apart from ordinary family life, in order to serve a higher collective goal. The priestly analogy is not entirely new: Chava Weissler has shown that comparing women lighting sabbath candles or 'sacrificing' challah (a portion of dough) with the service of the high priest was a popular theme in women's supplicatory prayers (*tkhines*).[59]

Orlean's analogy, like that of the *tkhines*, imagined an exalted ritual function for what might be seen as women's worldly activities—whether cooking or founding schools for girls. The analogy of priesthood provided him with another important connotation, its strong association with purity (it also helped him avoid saying that Bais Yaakov girls were like yeshiva students). Orlean continued his speech to the graduates: 'Before the high priest began his sacred service they would ask him, "Is there perhaps something alien [i.e. inimical to a holy endeavour] in your heart?" . . . You are going out into the wider world, and will be entrusted with the pure souls of children . . . How terrible will be your sin if your heart—God forbid—is not entirely pure.' Orlean transposes the language of *avodah zarah*, idol (literally, 'alien') worship, from the Temple context to his own, finding Jewish terms for a distinctively modern concern, the necessity to guard against secularity and other alien influences.

58 Greenfeld, 'The Day We Were Orphaned' (Heb.), 163.

59 See Weissler, *Voices of the Matriarchs*, 59–63.

Here and elsewhere, Orlean (or Sarah Schenirer) showed skill in mobilizing the biblical rhetoric of purity in the service of a traditionalist ideology, in which impurity was associated with alien influences. But it was also associated with the laws of family purity, the one arena in which biblical purity laws continued to operate after the destruction of the Temple (of course, according to rabbinic interpretation) and another topic well represented in Bais Yaakov literature. One particularly thorough treatment of the subject appears in a 1935 article by Ella Shmuelevitz in the *Bais Yaakov Ruf*, the journal of the Bais Yaakov movement in Lithuania. She begins by asking: 'What is family purity [*taharat hamishpaḥah*]? Many women, especially of the upper classes, will answer, "family purity is an ancient and obsolete custom that subjects Jewish women to a series of irrational commandments. It is extremely unhygienic—the filthy ritual bath exposes Jewish women to all kinds of disease".'[60] Shmuelevitz responds to this challenge by recourse not to Jewish law but rather to sociology: 'But the statistics show otherwise', she writes. 'Sexual diseases are rampant precisely in irreligious circles. This fact shows us clearly that family purity provides us with a kind of protection—not only for the body but also the soul.' Far from being unhygienic, Shmuelevitz writes, the ritual bath provides 'poor women with a rare opportunity to bathe'. Moreover, the laws of *nidah* are designed to enhance marital love: 'Sometimes husband and wife drift apart, and then decide to separate for a period in the name of family happiness, to reawaken in each other feelings of love. Those who observe family purity need no such expedients. Because of this, husband and wife are always interested in one another.' To those who say that such practices are unsuitable for enlightened women, Shmuelevitz adds: 'The Torah is for everyone, rich and poor. Family purity brings peace to the family, which leads to the well-being of the entire Jewish people.'[61]

Sarah Schenirer's essay on 'The Sacred Obligations of Jewish Women' also considers the question of menstrual laws, similarly imagining the laughter these 'micro-obligations' might provoke in 'today's ostensibly intelligent woman'. But while Shmuelevitz constructs an apology for family purity on the grounds of health, hygiene, and family harmony, Sarah Schenirer presents a defence of the scientific validity of these laws through the evidence put forward by a tannaitic sage with expertise in both *nidah* and astronomy. This equation of Jewish law and science, odd as it may seem, had roots in Hirsch's pedagogical philosophy, which brought together secular and Jewish subjects, Torah and natural science, viewing

[60] Shmuelevitz, 'Family Purity' (Yid.), 7. [61] Ibid. 7–8.

them as inextricably linked.[62] Nevertheless, it is striking that even with regard to this commandment, which so readily invites an apologetic discourse recommending observance as a route to conjugal harmony, she took another path, one which managed to discuss the laws of *nidah* without reference to the sexual and marital context in which they play out. She may have found such talk immodest, perhaps even unseemly for an unmarried woman. While she borrowed Orlean's analogy to praise the *purity* of Bais Yaakov students' religious commitment as teachers of the next generation, their 'purity' as wives and mothers awakened no parallel creativity.

That Bais Yaakov was led by a woman who was unmarried for most of the interwar period—and who played the role not of mother, daughter, or wife, but rather of leader, activist, and Torah giant—was something that those writers who preferred a bourgeois domestic discourse had to address. In a fascinating eulogy delivered in the seminary, Leo Deutschländer responded to the challenge posed to Orthodoxy not by modern feminists but rather—perhaps more powerfully—by a pious woman leader like Sarah Schenirer. Giving her credit for creating, ex nihilo, 'an enormous achievement, a network of schools, a powerful movement', Deutschländer acknowledged that this creation was not always done 'only with love, with tenderness, with a smile'. She 'demanded and protested, raged against those activists and leaders who were so indifferent to the burning question of girls' education'. Her commitment and fervour, Deutschländer continued, put her in a difficult position:

How many times, when arguing with Torah-true men, with hasidic fathers, with strict administrators, did she have to point to a *midrash* or cite a passage of Talmud in order to substantiate her principles, to build her school on healthy foundations? . . . More than once, in defence of the purity of her movement, was she compelled to resort to manly stratagems in order to properly respond to indifferent fathers or short-sighted adminis-

[62] See Rubin (ed.), *Daughters of Destiny*, 120, for a discussion of how science, math, and Jewish study were combined in Judith Grunfeld's Hirschian education in Frankfurt. Schenirer was not alone among Eastern European Orthodox Jews to combine science and Jewish law around issues of menstrual purity. On 22 December 1935, at the first national conference of Bnos and Bais Yaakov of Lithuania, Rabbi Avraham Dov-Ber Kahana Shapiro, the chief rabbi of Lithuania, spoke to the reportedly one thousand women in attendance about the health benefits of observing the laws of *nidah* (while emphasizing that such laws were obligatory whether such benefits might be found or not). The 124-page brochure expanding on those remarks that appeared in 1936 (in two editions) is remarkable for its abundant citations not only of Jewish law, but also of contemporary medical journals on a range of scientific issues. See Kahana-Shapiro, *Lecture on Family Purity* (Yid.).

trators. That was certainly enough to make her feel her proper self-worth, to arouse her to fight the so-called degradation of woman, her second-class status. For certainly, like other women, she felt the full force of her relegation to the women's section of the synagogue, to the outer quarters of the tent, the segregation between men and women, the honour granted to the man in the Jewish home.

How strong must have been her desire to visit a Jewish *ḥeder*, to spend time in a yeshiva, sit at a hasidic rebbe's table, participate in an important men's gathering. For those were certainly for her the brightest places, the most cherished ideals . . . With how much light, how much spirit, how much enthusiasm would she have passed these experiences on to her students! After all, were these men strangers or secular Jews? They were her own Jewish brothers, fervent Torah Jews. So why should she be kept from hearing them, seeing them, participating in their life for the good of her ideals? Why should she, the historical personality, the famous figure, be kept within such strict limits, so undervalued? Why should that be?[63]

Deutschländer's poignant question marks the end of a section, leaving the reader suspended, for a moment, in this remarkable state—a man imagining how an Orthodox woman might feel about her exclusion from the spiritual treasures she covets. The next brief sentence provides the only possible answer to this painful conundrum: 'This is what Judaism requires.' Deutschländer continues by describing the reasons for strict segregation between the sexes, acknowledging the special honour Jewish tradition bestows upon men, 'which is impossible for Europeans to understand'. He acknowledges that 'the Jewish male is obligated in more commandments, and so deserves more respect [but] this does not take one hair away from the importance of women. For what difference does it make who lays *tefilin*, who wears *tsitsit*, who sits in a sukkah, who learns Talmud? All Jews are one, truly one.' Returning to Sarah Schenirer, he concludes that this situation could not arouse protest 'in such a meritorious woman':

No, absolutely not! Not a shred of dissatisfaction, not a hint of anger, not a trace of frustration. But was it possible to detect in her a kind of resignation, a sort of submission? Oh well! What was there to be done about it? She was what she was, and there was no changing that. But no! Not a hint of resignation, no sign of complaint, not the faintest clue that she was dissatisfied with her lot. At peace with herself, happy to confront every setback, every restraint that was put on her, every limitation she faced. This, too, is Torah; this too is the will of God. 'Blessed [is the One] who made me according to his will.'[64]

Deutschländer's long-standing and close collaboration with Sarah Schenirer, and

[63] Deutschländer, 'Sarah Schenirer and Bais Yaakov' (Yid.), 10.

[64] Deutschländer quotes here the blessing recited by women at the point in the morning service where men bless God 'who has not made me a woman'.

the heightened emotion caused by the occasion, elicit a rather different set of reflections on the role of women in traditional Jewish life than most of those that appear in the *Bais Yaakov Journal* on the topic. The question here is not whether a Jewish wife might live in harmony with her husband, but rather how the relationship between Orthodox men and women might be experienced by a woman like Sarah Schenirer, who worked alongside men for the accomplishment of shared goals while nevertheless being excluded from taking part in some of their greatest spiritual pleasures. The (imagined) secular onlooker looking in with such disdain that is sometimes described in articles dealing with Orthodoxy and women in the *Bais Yaakov Journal* might be dismissed as foolish ('Answer the fool according to his folly', Rabbi Gutentag wrote), but the (also projected) feelings of a woman who treasured Jewish life and had done so much to save it, who knew her way around the Talmud and longed to taste the religious delights reserved for men, posed a more painful dilemma. But Deutschländer makes it clear (as Grunfeld-Rosenbaum does in her own reflections on the cornerstone-laying ceremony) that this protest does not derive from Sarah Schenirer's own complaints, or even her sense of 'resignation'.

After the Second World War, the bourgeois discourse developed in the interwar years along the lines laid out by Hirsch and his followers, which spoke of women's 'special gifts' and saw Bais Yaakov as a preparatory school for future wives and mothers, gained ascendancy, while the alternative discourse I have traced here receded to the margins. Nevertheless, the memory of Sarah Schenirer's life and the early years of Bais Yaakov hinted at it and supplied another model of Orthodox womanhood. In these stories, girls and women could be remembered and championed in a range of roles—as hikers as well as wives, Torah scholars as well as mothers, pilgrims as well as parents, and writers as well as readers.

The *Bais Yaakov Journal* already recognized the power of these stories even as they were unfolding. In 1923, in the inaugural issue, Friedenson expressed his desire to spread the word about Bais Yaakov and to provide 'the best reading material' for Orthodox girls and women. In the sixteen years of its existence, it achieved that and more: it created a laboratory for exploring the possibilities of Orthodox womanhood in the modern era, and a mirror for the participants in the Bais Yaakov movement to catch sight of themselves and the wonders they had wrought.

CHAPTER FIVE

'A New Kind of Woman'
Bais Yaakov as Traditionalist Revolution

> Last summer, in Kraków, I saw the type of Jewish girl graduating from these [Bais Yaakov] schools. It is a type utterly unheard of before, filled with a missionary zeal to spread Judaism among Jews, to uplift the level of individual and communal life. These young women will write their names in golden letters into the records of contemporary Israel.
>
> RABBI DR LEO JUNG, New York, 1933[1]

IN AN INFLUENTIAL essay, Jacob Katz proposes that Orthodoxy should be read as a modern phenomenon, despite its widespread understanding (both among Orthodox Jews and others) as a faithful continuation of traditional Jewish life. Acknowledging that Jews who never abandoned traditional observance were the majority in Germany until the mid-nineteenth century and in eastern Europe at least until the First World War, Katz nevertheless argues that 'it would be incorrect to view the behavior of modern adherents to tradition as simply reproducing what I call tradition-bound society'. As opposed to earlier generations of halakhically observant Jews, 'their loyalty to tradition was the result of a conscious decision, or was at the very least a stance assumed in defiance of a possible alternative suggested by the lifestyle of other Jews'. For these reasons, Katz suggests that modern adherence to tradition should be viewed as a distinct historical phenomenon that he calls 'traditionalism', which is a 'new form of Judaism' rather than a continuation of 'the old ways of thinking'.[2] Something of the paradox embedded in this understanding of Orthodoxy rises to the surface, for Katz, in the slogan coined by the Hatam Sofer: 'Anything new is forbidden according to the Torah' (*hadash asur min hatorah*, from Mishnah *Orl.* 3: 9); this slogan midrashically expands a mishnaic dictum forbidding the consumption of new grain to express a (new) form of resistance to all innovation, even with regard to customs rather than halakhah. Orthodoxy in this historical sense is a new

[1] In Deutschländer, *History of the Beth Jacob Schools*, 1.

[2] Katz, 'Orthodoxy in Historical Perspective', 2, 4.

phenomenon that, among its strictest proponents, stands in principled opposition to introducing anything new into the Jewish tradition.

The tension between tradition and innovation, continuity and change, is particularly evident in the activities of the Agudath Israel. Although the Agudah proclaimed as its slogan the desire 'to solve all the problems of our time in accordance with the spirit of the Torah and tradition', it was compelled to take up modern means in this holy struggle. As Gershon Bacon puts it, 'despite its stated goal of defending traditional Jewish society from the inroads of modernity, Agudat Israel itself demonstrated in no small measure the effects of the values, tools and vocabulary of modern culture and politics'.[3] Bacon sees the clearest evidence of the Agudah's 'accommodation with modernity in order to defend what it saw as traditional Judaism' in its educational activities, and in particular its adoption and support of Bais Yaakov.[4] Despite the movement's commitment to 'rebuild the traditional Jewish home', it remained in its basic aim and many of its details an innovation in traditional life, as its supporters generally acknowledged.[5] Joseph Friedenson, son of the Agudah activist, editor, and publisher Eliezer Gershon Friedenson, and himself an Orthodox journalist and historian of the movement, contrasts the novelty of Bais Yaakov with the more incremental modernization of religious education for boys:

> What was the difference between the educational institutions of Agudath Israel for boys and for girls? Those for boys were primarily nothing more than a continuation of the old traditional-religious schools, even if these were modernized in some way. This was entirely different for the educational institutions for girls, which were organized by the Agudah under the name Bais Yaakov. This was an entirely novel phenomenon, and even a complete reversal in the approach of strictly traditional parents to the problem of educating their daughters.[6]

Writing in 1936, Hillel Seidman called Bais Yaakov 'a revolution in the minds of thousands of Jewish women, and therefore families, too, a revolution in the relations of Jewish life in our time'.[7] To expand on this thought, the revolution that was Bais Yaakov was not limited to the direct participants in the movement, but also reshaped marriage practices, family structures, and the face of Orthodoxy at large.

[3] Bacon, *The Politics of Tradition*, 49.

[4] Ibid. 142 and 164.

[5] The one exception I am aware of is Rabbi A. Y. Wolf, founder of the Bais Yaakov in Benei Berak, whose essay 'Did Sarah Schenirer Innovate?' makes the case that, despite appearances, she did not. See my discussion in Chapter 3 above, and later in this chapter.

[6] J. Friedenson, 'The Bais Yaakov Girls' Schools' (Heb.), 61.

[7] Seidman, *Renesans Religijny*, 32.

In creating its distinctive culture, Bais Yaakov drew from a wide range of cultural models, some of them Jewish and others not, transforming them for its own purposes. As a women's movement searching for a place within a tradition that lacked precedent for women's Torah study and arenas for religious activism, it looked first of all for traditional structures that might be repurposed for use by women. But it also borrowed from secular movements and ideologies, defending itself against its rivals by appropriating their most attractive elements and reshaping them for religious purposes.

As I have been suggesting, the model that presented itself most immediately was German neo-Orthodoxy, which had faced a similar crisis in the previous century and had constructed a set of responses to the challenges of modernity that might be borrowed for Polish use. In drawing on German neo-Orthodox models, Bais Yaakov followed a larger Agudah pattern, though as a women's movement it was freer to draw from more liberal strands of German Orthodox culture. It also appropriated elements from within east European Orthodoxy, particularly from hasidism and the yeshiva world. Where borrowing from German models constituted a geographical or denominational shift—from west to east, more modern to more stringent Orthodoxy—in the case of the hasidic and yeshiva worlds Bais Yaakov rather performed a gender shift, taking religious and educational practices, ideals, and structures that had previously organized and inspired boys and men and retooling them for groups of girls and women.

Bais Yaakov also adapted a range of practices and structures from the larger intellectual and political culture of Polish Jewry. It arose alongside other ideologically affiliated youth movements, cultural organizations, and school systems, and formed one stripe in an educational tapestry that also included the Zionist Tarbut, the Labour Zionist Shul-Kult, and the Yiddishist Cysho school systems. Although these were staunch ideological rivals or even enemies, they developed along parallel tracks and inevitably displayed many similarities as they competed for the allegiance of students and parents in an ideologically unstable social field. Hillel Kieval's description of interwar Prague holds true as well for Poland: 'The very categories German, Czech, Jew; liberal, Communist, patriot; mystic, rationalist, Orthodox, and assimilationist . . . existed in a state of perpetual movement, seeming to appear only to collapse, regroup, and melt away.'[8] While Bais Yaakov and the Agudah were anti-Zionist, non-Yiddishist, non-socialist (although the Po'alei Agudath Israel was often suspected of socialist tendencies), and certainly not feminist, these ideological identities were clearest at the organizational

[8] Kieval, *Languages of Community*, 224.

centres of these movements, and tended to get rather murkier in the peripheries. Yitzhok Shafran writes, of the Bais Yaakov of Goworowo, that 'although everyone knew that the school was supported and administered by the Agudah, all segments of the town's population sent their children there, so the school took on a broad and nonpartisan character, with teachers concerned only with providing girls with a religious education'.[9] Secular and Orthodox Zionist ideologies held attractions for parents and pupils in Bais Yaakov, and perhaps also some teachers, and this manifested itself in a variety of ways. But sympathy for these ideological opponents was not the only reason Bais Yaakov mobilized tropes and structures that originated elsewhere. These were necessary tools to fight the secular world, and Bais Yaakov did not hesitate to Judaize or desecularize elements of these movements in its mission of bolstering Torah and tradition.

Along with its borrowing from a range of influences in its religious and secular environment, Bais Yaakov also attempted to root itself in tradition, and more particularly in the practices and structures of the traditional Orthodox home. In many cases, this was limited to the discursive rather than actual realm, since joining the movement often meant, for girls and young women, leaving their actual homes. Squaring this circle involved a metaphorical expansion and displacement of the language and practices of the family and the home. In order to rescue the traditional Jewish home (which had shown itself to be useless in combating the crises of modernity), Bais Yaakov had to reinvent it, replacing biological mothers with the 'Bais Yaakov mother', who commanded the love and respect of her 'daughters'. While this was the central metaphor that the movement mobilized, it also produced new forms of 'family', 'kinship', 'sisterhood', and 'home'. This expansion of kinship terminology beyond the nuclear family, according to Deborah Weissman, is a distinctive marker of modern social movements: socialists, communists, and Zionists all called fellow members 'friend' and 'comrade'. 'More germanely', writes Weissman, witness 'the use of "brother" and "sister" by, for instance, Pentecostal, women's liberation, and Black Power groups.'[10] As a traditionalist phenomenon with few traditional precedents, Bais Yaakov mobilized discursive tools such as those developed by other new social and political movements, selecting from a range of available options and creatively transforming them for its own purposes, which were ironically so distinct from theirs.

Bais Yaakov, for obvious reasons, did not always acknowledge its cultural and

[9] Shafran, 'The Bais Yaakov Schools' (Yid.), 110.

[10] Weissman, 'Bais Ya'akov: A Women's Educational Movement', 115.

ideological indebtedness to secular movements, but its cultural and ideological adherence to the teachings of Samson Raphael Hirsch is duly recorded. It is even given pride of place as the very origin of the movement, as Sarah Schenirer credits Rabbi Flesch's sermon for inspiring her to rekindle the religiosity of Polish Orthodox girls. This inspiration continued to guide the movement, both directly in the form of German-speaking, university-trained leaders and teachers such as Leo Deutschländer and Judith Grunfeld-Rosenbaum, and less directly, through literature. Admission requirements for prospective students at the Kraków seminary, for instance, included not only seven years of school, two letters of recommendation, and modesty in dress, but also possession of (in addition to the Pentateuch and a prayer book) Hirsch's *Nineteen Letters*.[11] In an article in the *Bais Yaakov Journal* in which she describes a trip to Frankfurt, Sarah Schenirer expresses with remarkable directness her own sense of what Bais Yaakov owed to Hirsch. Marvelling at the involvement of the girls in religious activities ('they go to synagogue') and the general liveliness of the Orthodox scene, she describes sitting alone in the salon of Hirsch's grandchildren, paging through a family album:

> The album was full of family memorabilia, but the last page was blank. I took my pen and wrote the following words: 'I know that it takes chutzpah for a stranger to insert themselves in someone else's family album, but when it comes to a spiritual mission, all the rules of polite society may be overthrown. With these lines, let it be known that there was someone who carried on the work of a brilliant person.'[12]

In this remarkable incident, Sarah Schenirer literally inscribes herself in the genealogy of the Hirsch family, claiming the Hirsch pedigree for her movement, and granting him the honour of parentage of so worthy a descendant, while insisting on the validity and primacy of spiritual kinship over the usual rules of both biological descent and polite society.

Bais Yaakov more generally could be described as following the spiritual and pedagogical influence of the neo-Orthodox slogan *torah im derekh erets* (Torah with secular/practical education), a programme that found initial expression in Hirsch's *Realschule* and was adopted (and adapted) by Bais Yaakov. Subjects such as Jewish ethics, law, history, Hebrew grammar, and Bible were taught as discreet courses; students were graded and examined regularly; physical education, critical thought, and creative expression were encouraged; and, at the seminary level, pedagogy, psychology, and other secular subjects were taught, including Sarah Schenirer's favourites: Polish and German literature. In Weissman's summary,

[11] *Bais Yaakov Journal*, 55, cited in Weissman, 'Bais Ya'akov: A Women's Educational Movement', 62.

[12] Schenirer, 'In Frankfurt am Main' (Yid.), 61.

the innovations introduced into Orthodox educational culture by Bais Yaakov included:

> formal curriculum, teacher training, improved textbooks, the daily schedule of classes and the ringing of bells to mark the change of classes, the external, modern appearance of the schools, the emphasis on hygiene, an emphasis on the kindergarten as a unit, the introduction of secular studies and, particularly, of vocational training, the introduction of physical education as a part of the curriculum, the use of modern facilities such as gymnasia and laboratories, the exposure to world literature and art, and, lastly, the conceptualization of 'Judaism' as a subject area.[13]

Ironically, perhaps, the modern educational methods borrowed from German neo-Orthodoxy may have been acceptable to the stricter east European society because Bais Yaakov combined them with a commitment to the traditional principle of sexual segregation. The modernity of Bais Yaakov, in this regard, may have been yet another example of 'the benefit of marginality' for women.[14] Sarah Schenirer could provide a modern Orthodox education to early twentieth-century Jewish girls because they were not obligated to study (only) Torah. As long as traditional sexual segregation was maintained and women refrained from the study of the Oral Torah, the shape, pace, curriculum, and so forth of girls' education was of little concern to rabbis. Thus Bais Yaakov could readily include secular studies in its curriculum while the yeshiva movement was fighting a mighty battle to deal with government regulations and other pressures to provide or increase instruction in secular subjects for boys. If women were under no obligation to devote themselves fully to Torah study, Bais Yaakov could provide some of what girls were receiving in the public schools or those of other ideological movements, and thus compete more vigorously in a market in which parents expected their daughters to have some worldly education.

It is true that some in more stringently Orthodox and hasidic circles continued to object to what was going on in the female sphere, cleverly denigrating Bais Yaakov by referring to it rather as 'Bais Esau' (the House of Esau, Jacob's evil twin). In Slovakia and northern Transylvania—the area referred to by Jews as 'Unterland'—the objection to Bais Yaakov rested at least in part on the ways that it adopted Hirschian ideals of *Torah and derekh erets*, the fully rounded *mensch yisroel* in whom Torah and secular learning were harmoniously combined. While

[13] Weissman, 'Bais Ya'akov: A Women's Educational Movement', 69. I would argue that vocational training was in fact a sign of continuity with traditional education for girls in east Europe, where handiwork was part of the curriculum, and apprenticeship and being a pupil could overlap.

[14] Parush, *Reading Jewish Women*, 62 ff.

B"H [Blessed be God]
Seven-Grade Girls' School Bais Yaakov in Rayshe
Under the administration of the Agudath Israel

Certificate

Student Halpern Yocheved	**Class** *Pre-first (?): First*
City Rayshe [Rzeszów]	
Born Rayshe, 12 July 1928	

School Year 1934–1935	**I.**	**II.**
Jewish practices	*Outstanding*	
Attitude towards work	*Outstanding*	
Attitude to surroundings	——	
Interest in studies	*Outstanding*	
Understanding of studies	——	
Mastery in the subjects of:		
Prayer	*Very good*	
Meaning of prayer:	——	
Pentateuch	——	
Judaism	*Good*	
History	——	
Grammar	——	
Yiddish	*Very good*	
Organization	*Very good*	
Absent hours	6	
Late hours	2	
Excused absences	6	
Signature of the parents		
	11 Nisan 5695 [14 April 1935]	
	Shvegult [?]	*D. Levin*
	Teacher	Administration

Figure 5.1 Bais Yaakov report card, 1935

This report card, showing the grades of Yocheved Halpern (unsigned by her parents), was issued by the Bais Yaakov in Rzeszów in 1935, and was brought to the United States along with the Halpern family in 1939. It is reproduced here by permission of her son Joel Rosenfeld, of Boro Park, Brooklyn. Rzeszów is a mid-sized city approximately 170 kilometres east of Kraków that had a Jewish population of around 14,000 in the interwar period. The Rzeszów Bais Yaakov was founded in 1927 with 120 students, and by 1935, with 287, constituted the largest Bais Yaakov outside Kraków, Warsaw, or Łódź. As a beginning student in the earliest grade of this afternoon school, Yocheved was just learning basic skills, leaving more advanced subjects such as Bible, grammar, and history for later grades.

ב"ה

7 קל. ארטאד טעכטער־שול „בית־יעקב"
אין ריישא

אונטער דער הנהלה פון „אגודת־ישראל"

צייגניש

תלמידה באלפערן רבקה פלאס IV/V

שטאט ריישא

געבוירן ריישא 1928 ...

שול־יאר תרצ"ג	I.	II.
יידישע ערציאונג	[illegible]	
באציאונג צו אנדערע	[illegible]	
באציאונג צו סביבה		
פאראינטערעסירונג מיט לימודים	[illegible]	
פארטשריט אין לימודים		
באהערשן דעם לימוד פון: תפלה	[illegible]	
פירוש התפלה		
חומש	—	
יהדות	[illegible]	
געשיכטע	—	
דקדוק	—	
יידיש	[illegible]	
ארדנונג	[illegible]	
פארפעלטע שעה'ן	6	
פארשפעטיקטע שעה'ן	2	
אנטשולדיקטע שעה'ן	6	
אונטערשריפט פון די עלטערן		

[illegible], תרצ"ג

[illegible] פארוואלטונג

[illegible] לערערין

this model, for Hirsch, worked equally for both sexes, the more strict sexual segregation in those ultra-traditional circles made this notion 'an unachievable fantasy'. It was men who embodied the principle of Torah, while women must be kept from direct access to its sources (translations of the Bible into Yiddish were permitted, in this view). While schools that were staffed by Bais Yaakov seminarians were founded in this region, they did not use the name Bais Yaakov, and resisted association with the larger movement.[15] In such cultural responses, it becomes clear that the resistance to the encroachment of 'Western' ideas was closely linked to fears of the encroachment of girls and women into previously male spheres. One of the major hasidic figures in the Unterland region, the Munkaczer Rebbe, Hayim Elazar Shapira (1868–1937), complained that 'in these houses of Esau that are near rooms of prayer, arguments and insults were heard through the walls, songs of young girls, *Lekha dodi*, heard during the silent prayer of hasidism, and who has heard of such a thing? Since when did our forefathers permit teaching holy songs and music to young girls?'[16] The force of the Munkaczer Rebbe's objection revolved around the threat Bais Yaakov represented to male piety: the reason it constituted a transgression was because the voices of the girls praying together the Friday evening service (and we know they loved to sing, loudly) could carry through walls and windows. But more generally, Bais Yaakov could find both a home in the Orthodox world and the freedom to shape its own culture because it was a girls' movement. Occasionally, the distinction between the looser standards that applied to girls and young women and the stricter ones that applied to the education of boys and men was openly expressed. In a 1927 article in the *Bais Yaakov Journal* on 'Schoolbooks for Bais Yaakov Schools', Rabbi Tuvye Yehudah Gutentag made clear his support for the radical ideal of providing Bais Yaakov with textbooks on an array of subjects—Bible, Hebrew, Judaism (written by Sarah Schenirer)—since such books 'help gradually introduce students to a subject' rather than immediately plunging them into a primary source. After detailing the wisdom of this method, Gutentag then made it clear that he was talking only about Bais Yaakov, since textbooks were 'not appropriate for a *ḥeder* [for boys], where time-honoured methods prevail'.[17]

[15] See Grill, *Der Westen im Osten*, 297–8.

[16] Rabbi Hayim Elazar Shapira of Munkacz's letter appeared in the *Jüdische Zeitung*, cited in Fuchs, *Jewish Women's Torah Study*, 36. Rabbi Shapira's mention of 'arguments' is intriguing: might he be objecting not to bad behaviour but to what sounded like talmudic argumentation, a prototypically male activity?

[17] Tavyomi (Gutentag), 'On Textbooks' (Yid.), 7. This issue was not thereby resolved. Writing

For all these reasons, Bais Yaakov schools did not produce female counterparts of their learned brothers, but a distinct institutional culture of learning practices limited to girls. While Agudah leaders worked politically and organizationally with German 'doctor rabbis', their own yeshivas were led and staffed by east European scholars and sages; Bais Yaakov, in contrast, had German-born educators and activists, both male and female, working at the highest levels.[18] In one sense, sexual segregation marked the limits of the Bais Yaakov revolution; in another, however, it was the movement's most powerful asset, allowing for freedoms unheard of in the world of male Orthodoxy, and harnessing the energies of same-sex community for women.[19] The denominational distinction between the stricter Orthodoxy of the Polish lands and the more modern neo-Orthodoxy that emerged in Germany, or the geographical distinction between central and east European Jewry, thus reappears demarcated by *gender* within the east European Orthodox culture, with girls inhabiting a more modern and central-European world than their male counterparts.

For all the readily acknowledged influence of German neo-Orthodoxy on Bais Yaakov, the movement also echoed some of the larger tensions that complicated the collaboration of eastern and western leaders and activists in the Agudah. German Orthodox leaders were credited with professionalism and political experience, but suspected of being halakhically lenient and less knowledgeable in rabbinic literature. The culture gap took on a different shape for women, however. Rabbi Jehiel Weinberg described Orthodox women in Frankfurt, centre of Hirsch's activities, as knowledgeable and committed Jews; by contrast, those in

in 1932, the Yiddishist Solomon Birnbaum asked why the Yiddish textbooks in use in Bais Yaakov schools (some of his own composition) could not also be used for boys: 'Must it be like that? Is there some crucial reason that boys should not learn to read and write correctly? Must it continue to be the case that among us, people will not really know even one language?' (Birnbaum, 'A Problem' (Yid.), 32).

[18] It is telling that in the framework of the ultra-Orthodox culture that emerged in Benei Berak in the 1950s under the influence of the Hazon Ish (Rabbi Abraham Karelitz, 1878–1953), a German-born rabbi like Abraham Joseph Wolf, despite the strictness of his Orthodoxy and acknowledged brilliance, would not have been considered an appropriate role model for a yeshiva, but was welcome as the director of a Bais Yaakov school. See Friedman, *The Haredi Woman* (Heb.), 10.

[19] Elements of German neo-Orthodoxy that served young men and women alike, for instance the youth movement Ezra, were borrowed, but reworked to cater only for women; thus, the Bnos Agudath Israel announced at its 1926 opening conference that it intended to forge connections with the Ezra's women's groups, while Tse'irei Agudath Israel, the youth movement for men founded by the Agudah in 1919, declared its allegiance only to the Agudah.

eastern Europe were ignorant (he praised Bais Yaakov for reversing this trend).[20] But Bais Yaakov did not merely seek to catch up with the most educated of central European women, but also to surpass them, by adding to Frankfurt Orthodoxy an element of its own: the hasidic enthusiasm that characterized Polish Jews and which could make an educated Jewish girl also a passionate, strictly observant, and fervently devout one. A 1929 article in the *Bais Yaakov Journal* reported on three women's conferences that had taken place in the previous few months. It compared the Bnos conference favourably not only with the WIZO (Women's International Zionist Organization) conference in Warsaw but also with a conference of Orthodox women in Hamburg, noting that 'despite the fact that the Hamburg conference also in principle subordinated itself to the dictates of Torah, that was only a sign of its aristocratic-conservative taste for the charms of tradition, and by no means and in no way the fiery, *heymish yiddishkeit* that breathed such life into the Bnos conference'.[21] Observers often described Bais Yaakov as combining the fervour of hasidism with the more enlightened orientation of western Jewries. As Sarah Schenirer proudly reported, the direction of influence was not one-sided, from west to east; 'the Jews in western lands place great hopes in eastern Jewry and particularly Bais Yaakov to develop the most powerful weapons in the war against assimilation and heresy'.[22] This was true more generally of Orthodoxy in the interwar period. While the secessionist community of Frankfurt initiated the efforts that culminated in the foundation of the Agudath Israel by recruiting east European rabbis and leaders into its movement, in the interwar period the much larger Polish Orthodoxy was increasingly setting the tone.

Hasidism was an important influence on Bais Yaakov, but the references to its hasidic character often misread the nature of this influence as a natural outgrowth of Sarah Schenirer's upbringing in a hasidic family and community. Marcin Wodziński has made a persuasive case that hasidic affiliation in the nineteenth and early twentieth century was solely available to men, pointing to 'the total absence of any evidence that women ever defined themselves, or were defined by others, as Hasidic'.[23] When such forms of identification did arise (as for instance in the 1930s in Habad-Lubavitch circles), this was owing to the influence of Bais Yaakov, rather than vice versa.[24] Sarah Schenirer's nickname *husidke*

[20] See M. B. Shapiro, *Between the Yeshiva World and Modern Orthodoxy*, 210.

[21] A.L., 'Łódź, Hamburg, Warsaw' (Yid.), 1.

[22] Schenirer, 'Important Guests' (Yid.), 16.

[23] Wodziński, 'Women and Hasidism', 405.

[24] See Loewenthal, 'Spiritual Experience', 440–1.

('Little Miss Hasid') does not contradict Wodziński's claim: it did not make her, or indicate her willingness to become, a member of a hasidic group, much less a follower of the Belzer Rebbe. The pejorative targeted her religious zealotry and, through the marker of the feminine diminutive, suggested that it was odd for a young girl to take on a hasidic identity. Nor did her self-description as the daughter and sister of Belzer hasidim translate into her considering herself a Belzer hasid (or *husidke*), or searching for a hasidic synagogue in Vienna, or viewing Bais Yaakov as a Belzer, or even a hasidic project. While she proceeded with her plans only after receiving the blessing of the Belzer Rebbe, her movement soon allied itself with the Agudah, which was dominated by Gerer hasidism. Belz maintained a strong opposition to both the Agudah and Bais Yaakov through the interwar period.[25]

Bais Yaakov did not affiliate with any single hasidic group during the interwar period. By contrast, it was pan-hasidic or ecumenical rather than parochial, avoiding involvement in the fractured, fractious Orthodox scene the best it could, and bringing together girls from a range of hasidic groups and beyond, from circles that did not ordinarily meet. Bais Yaakov was pan-hasidic in yet another way: hearkening back to the (imagined) period that preceded the modern era of fierce divisions, it attempted to recover and reimagine the hasidic movement in a purer and more revolutionary form.

Far from proving Sarah Schenirer's natural connection with the hasidic world, the important moment in which she acquired the blessing of Rabbi Yissachar Dov Rokeach demonstrates rather the limits of just how hasidic a woman could be. As Wodziński describes the experience of women supplicators at a hasidic court: 'even where women could come before the *tsadik*, as a rule they had to be accompanied by a man (usually their husband or father)'. A *kvitl* (note) making the request to the *tsadik* on a woman's behalf would be 'sent via her husband or father'.[26] Sarah Schenirer's memoir in fact attests that her brother wrote a *kvitl* on her behalf, asking for divine help because 'she wants to lead Jewish girls along the Jewish path'. She implicitly invites us to compare this relationship with the one

[25] This opposition is sometimes explained by the centrality of a rival hasidic group, Gur (Ger), in the Agudah. Bobov was also opposed to Bais Yaakov, as Judith Grunfeld-Rosenbaum notes, on the grounds that 'mixing girls from so many backgrounds' would cause some of them to abandon the strictures of their own customs. See Rubin (ed.), *Daughters of Destiny*, 135.

[26] Wodziński, 'Women and Hasidism', 414, 415. Wodziński notes that women sometimes supported and patronized hasidic courts without considering themselves followers of the *rebbe*. Schenirer's grandmother, who 'would spare no expense to serve the holy Sanzer Rebbe', did not thereby consider herself a Sanzer hasid, nor did Schenirer claim that affiliation.

she had with Rabbi Flesch in Vienna, but it is instructive to compare it, as well, with Jiří Langer's encounter with hasidism. Langer was a young man from an acculturated Prague family (and friend of Kafka) who became a fervent Belzer follower in the years before the First World War, learning, singing, and dancing with the hasidim and receiving personal spiritual instruction and advice from the rebbe. He describes the world of hasidic yeshiva students:

The boy's soul, suddenly taken by an inexplicable yearning for the rabbi, finds no peace at home. Not only in his nightly dreams, but also—and this is for the Hasidim a sign of grace—while awake the shining form of the rabbi appears before his eyes. Finally, he decides: He leaves a comfortable home—often against his father's will and his mother's tears—and travels to the city of the rabbi, in order to 'cleave' forever. As soon as he arrives and it is determined that he is serious, he is greeted with open arms by the 'Chevre' [social group]. Soon he finds himself in the middle of a circle of friends, who 'draw near' to him through various tendernesses and it doesn't take long to find an older student who has 'the same soul' to study with, which he accepts with great joy. How blessed he feels.[27]

Women had no place (as partners) in the intense friendship and closeness available to the young hasid in such a passionate fellowship, no doubt because these relationships were so erotic. Speaking of the Belzer court that Sarah Schenirer herself was to visit a few years later, Langer writes: 'The saint never looks on the face of a woman. If he must speak to women—as, when he receives a *kvitel* [from a woman]—he looks out of the window while he speaks.'[28]

Sarah Schenirer herself makes clear that she felt this exclusion keenly and personally. Hasidic practices not only kept women outside the rapturous religious experiences of the rebbe's court, they also made women's experience of Judaism that much poorer. As she lamented to Judith Grunfeld-Rosenbaum:

The trains which run to the little 'Shtetlach' (towns) where the Rebbes live are crowded. Thousands of Hassidim are on their way to them to spend the Yamim Noraim (Solemn Holy Days) with the Rebbe. Every day sees new crowds of old men and young men in the Hassidic garb, eager to secure a place in the train, eager to spend the holiest days in the year in the atmosphere of their Rebbe, to be able to extract from it as much holiness as possible . . . And we stay at home, the wives, the daughters with the little ones. We have an empty Yomtov.[29]

[27] Mordechai Georgo (Jiří) Langer, *Die Erotik der Kabbala* (Prague, 1923), 116, trans. by and cited in Halper, 'Coming Out of the Hasidic Closet', 206. Halper argues that Langer 'experienced (or reimagined his experience) in the Hasidic world as homoerotic', 207.

[28] Jiří Langer, *Nine Gates* (1961), 11, cited in Loewenthal, 'Spiritual Experience', 434.

[29] Grunfeld-Rosenbaum, 'Sara Schenierer', 410–11.

Sarah Schenirer's connection with hasidism was thus both fraught and indirect, and whatever hasidic enthusiasm she brought to Bais Yaakov must be understood as imagined rather than directly experienced and emerging from the painful experience of social and spiritual exclusion. Her efforts could not actually change the structure of the hasidic court to draw in the daughters and wives of hasidim, although, as Naftali Loewenthal has shown, the Bais Yaakov revolution did lead to an increased awareness in hasidic circles of the importance of outreach to women, as demonstrated by the organization of opportunities for female study of hasidic sources in Lubavitch, with the full support of Yosef Yitzkhok Schneerson, the sixth rebbe.[30] She borrowed from hasidic practices to produce a female counterpart to the hasidic world that did not overstep the strict separation of men and women. Rather than bringing men back home to the sabbath table or allowing women into the hasidic court, Bais Yaakov aimed to recreate a version of the intense, all-male environment of a hasidic court for young women. This was most obvious in the seminaries, where the girls not only studied together, but also spent sabbaths (and some holidays) singing, sharing meals, and praying. While these holidays would traditionally have been observed in the home or a sexually segregated synagogue, where women were not permitted to sing, Bais Yaakov enabled girls and women to recreate, within a female world, the religious experiences from which they had been excluded.[31]

Even more innovative was Sarah Schenirer's adoption of hasidic pilgrimage for female purposes. As is clear from her diary, she loved to travel, and her description of the hasidic pilgrimage to the rebbe's court dwells nearly as enviously on the rail journey, among the streams of hasidim all sharing the experience of heading to the same place, as on the time spent in the rebbe's presence. Individual pilgrimages to hasidic courts were not entirely unknown among Bais Yaakov teachers and students: Judith Grunfeld-Rosenbaum, after her first summer in the teacher-training course, visited the court of the Gerer Rebbe and shortly after that travelled with Sarah Schenirer to the court of Bobov, to enquire about the Bobover Rebbe's opposition to Bais Yaakov. Chava Weinberg Pincus, the first American student at the Kraków seminary, travelled to the Gerer court

[30] The society of Ahot Hatemimim, which focused on the study of Habad sources, was established in Riga in 1938. See Loewenthal, 'Spiritual Experience', 440–1.

[31] The question of whether women could sing in mixed-sex groups, obviously crucial for youth movements that included men and women, came up in connection with the French Orthodox youth group Yeshurun, which was attacked by some sectors of the Orthodox community for allowing girls to sing at its gatherings. On Rabbi Jehiel Weinberg's ruling that such singing was permissible, see M. B. Shapiro, *Between the Yeshiva World and Modern Orthodoxy*, 215–16.

with the German-educated teacher Esther Hamburger for Rosh Hashanah (it is no accident that these women, with the exception of Sarah Schenirer, were outsiders to the hasidic world; such outsiders, according to Wodziński, were often more welcome at the court than the daughters or wives of hasidim).[32] The more direct appropriation of hasidic pilgrimage practices in Bais Yaakov was not to hasidic courts but rather to the graves of deceased rabbis. In the *yom kipur katan* ritual that Sarah Schenirer initiated, after praying in Rabbi Moses Isserles's famed synagogue, she and her students would enter the adjacent cemetery to recite psalms at his grave and at the graves of the other great rabbis and sages.[33] Naftali Loewenthal sees 'a touch of inspiration' in her transformation of *yom kipur katan*, traditionally observed by fasting, into an occasion for pilgrimage and grave-visiting, thereby opening 'a path of spiritual encounter insulated from the grief of mourning'.[34] Perhaps the more revealing comparison is not the kabbalistic versus Bais Yaakov understanding of the new moon ritual, but rather male pilgrimage to hasidic courts versus female pilgrimage to rabbinic graves. If group travel to living rabbis was ruled out, deceased ones might be more open to visits by young women; in any case, they could hardly protest. And surely this should be accompanied by joy, not fasting. It is true that male hasidim also travelled in groups to gravesites, and that cemetery rituals and practices were particularly fertile ground for Ashkenazi women's spirituality. Sarah Schenirer innovated, however, in finding collective female expression for these practices, creating occasions for groups of young women to walk the streets of Kraków, hike the steep slopes of Polish mountains, and take trains together throughout the country.[35] While there is, in traditional Judaism, a religious framework for a collective of males (in forming a quorum for prayer, for example), she gave meaning to a female collective. This was an innovation she proved happy to display in public:

[32] For Judith Rosenbaum's travels to Góra Kalwaria, near Warsaw, and the trip she took with Schenirer to Bobov to face the opposition of the *rebbe* to Bais Yaakov, see Rubin (ed.), *Daughters of Destiny*, 133–5. For Chava Weinberg Pincus's travels, see *Daughters of Destiny*, 197–8. Wodziński comments that non-Jews, even women, were sometimes treated with more respect in hasidic courts than Jewish women, given that they could be of greater use to *rebbes* ('Women and Hasidism', 418).

[33] Rubin (ed.), *Daughters of Destiny*, 133.

[34] Loewenthal, 'Spiritual Experience', 435. I would add to Loewenthal's insight here that it is interesting that in the 1970s American Jewish feminists revived widespread celebration of Rosh Hodesh, the new moon, as a special festival for women; by contrast, Schenirer reshaped for female purposes a festival that had been associated with exclusively male groups of mystical adepts.

[35] On Schenirer leading nighttime hikes up steep mountains to arrive at the peak in time for morning prayers, see Rubin (ed.), *Daughters of Destiny*, 204.

in pilgrimage rituals that took large groups of young women down city streets, Bais Yaakov displayed women's religious devotion for all the world to see, shielding itself from criticism by the sincerity and enthusiasm of this devotion.

That Bais Yaakov was somehow hasidic was a common observation. Less frequently uttered was the corollary, that Sarah Schenirer functioned as a hasidic rebbe. A Polish Jewish periodical in Kraków reporting on her funeral noted that she 'was an active woman in the public sphere . . . well respected in the Agudah, and among the Agudah schools, venerated almost religiously'. The correspondent describes the funeral, in which 'crowds of thousands of Orthodox Jews accompanied this pious and learned woman to the place of her eternal rest', as evidence that she was honoured 'in a way that is usually reserved only for distinguished hasidic rebbes and great rabbis'.[36] But people within Bais Yaakov circles also apparently made this association, if less explicitly. The legends that arose around her, for instance, seem to mimic the content, form, and stylistic tropes of the hasidic tale. The children's biography of Sarah Schenirer published in 1936, and a supplementary volume to the Hebrew collection of her writings published in 1955, include dozens of such tales (many overlapping). Some of these are first-person accounts of interactions with her, but others are anonymous and undated, or take place in indistinct locations—in other words, they bear the hallmarks of legend rather than history. One such tale with a particularly hasidic flavour is entitled 'The children prevailed':

Sarah Schenirer once visited a large city. On the train platform, all the Bais Yaakov girls and their teacher awaited her. The joy of these students knew no bounds. Each one tried to get closer to the beloved mother. They pushed and shoved, the way hasidim crowd around the rebbe to greet him.

The teacher wanted Sarah Schenirer to reach the city in peace, so she hired a carriage to take her and Sarah into town. This angered the students, because they'd have to go back without the company of their beloved mother, whom they hoped to hear a saying or story from, as was her habit.

There were two particularly aggressive and stubborn girls among them, who jumped and hung onto the back of the carriage and wanted to travel that way to town. The teacher admonished them for their impoliteness and ordered them to let go of the carriage.

Sarah Schenirer heard this, and said: 'That's not the way to educate girls, by distancing them when they want to be close, bringing them low when they want to ascend. One has to go down to their level or raise them to yours. And since we can't raise them all to our level, we have to choose the second path and go down to them, and thus they'll be raised after all.'

[36] Obituary in *Nowy Dziennik*, 11.

Sarah Schenirer descended from the carriage, linked arms with the girls, and thus they walked together into the city.

The girls celebrated their victory.[37]

Sarah Schenirer not only possessed the charisma and (overly) devoted followers of a hasidic rebbe, she also understood how to bridge the hierarchical gap that separated exalted leader from devoted follower through her humility and good sense, in the manner of a beloved rebbe who seeks closeness (or, more theologically, cleaving, *devekut*) with his followers. The language of this tale more specifically evokes the mystical (as well as psychological) discourse of *yeridah letsorekh aliyah* ('descent for the sake of ascent'). The rebbe's special closeness to the life of the community, his involvement with their daily cares and anxieties, and his acceptance of their religious experiences at whatever level his followers might be, is explained by recourse to the notion that he 'is occasionally compelled to descend to a lower and even dangerous plane in order to rescue the scattered sparks of light', for 'every descent of the Zaddik means an elevation of divine light'. As with hasidic leaders like Rabbi Nahman of Bratslav, Sarah Schenirer's kabbalistic terminology 'hides an almost hyper-modern sensitiveness to problems'.[38] In the case of Bais Yaakov, this was the pressing crisis of a generation gap, which sometimes required adults to 'descend' to the level of children rather than demanding that the latter pay respect to their elders.

As a quasi-hasidic tale, the kabbalistic terminology cited in Sarah Schenirer's interaction with her followers is lent an extra twist of meaning by its appropriation by a female teacher and leader rather than a hasidic rebbe. She demonstrates both the hasidic trait of warm and 'modest' leadership in her ability to 'descend' to her young followers, and midrashic sophistication by finding such concrete embodiment for what is otherwise a metaphorical use of the terms higher and lower planes. But her modesty stands in some tension with the immodest implications of the story, the rather bold insinuation (whether by her or those who repeated or imagined her words) that a woman, too, might fill the cosmic, powerful, and authoritative role of a hasidic rebbe (and perhaps better for also being a 'mother').

Arguably, the most salient and obvious model for Bais Yaakov was the yeshiva. The movement comprised schools and other programmes in which Torah was studied in a rigorous and intensive fashion. It also shared some of the history of the development of the yeshiva movement, following in belated but accelerated

[37] See E. G. Friedenson (ed.), *Mama's Will*, 22–3; also 'The Girls Triumphed' (Heb.), in Rottenberg (ed.), *A Mother in Israel* (Heb.), ii. 29–30.

[38] Scholem, *Major Trends*, 346.

fashion its broad pattern of growth in the nineteenth and twentieth centuries, from small study-groups reliant on local community support to well-endowed institutions in major cities that attracted youth from across Europe and sometimes beyond. The teachers' seminaries (particularly the one in Kraków) were elite academies along the lines of the best-known Lithuanian yeshivas, recruiting ambitious adolescents from throughout the Jewish world. Like earlier generations of yeshiva boys, Bais Yaakov seminarians and graduates formed a cohort of travelling scholars, and relied on this network for local knowledge, professional introductions, and a hot meal and place to stay. That they were indeed scholars is emphasized by Grunfeld-Rosenbaum in her 1953 essay, which describes visits of distinguished lecturers to the summer colonies, once 'they had become used to the fact that there was a colony of girls who were themselves already young scholars and intelligent listeners'.[39]

Shaul Stampfer has argued that historians of the east European yeshiva take too little notice of its physical arrangements and housing for non-local students, and fail to consider the nineteenth-century transition from the practice of boarding students with local families to allowing them to live together first in rented apartments and then in prototype dormitories. Stampfer considers this last development of great consequence, since dormitories 'limited contact between students and the outside world of adults and increased the power of school authorities'. The rise of dormitories reflected the need to 'shape the character of a young student', Stampfer writes, by immersing him 'in the setting of a total institution that could block out external influences'.[40] Menachem Friedman similarly describes this isolation from the outside world as a feature of the yeshiva movement from the 1806 opening of the Volozhin yeshiva to our own day:

> The Volozhin-type yeshiva became an independent community by bringing together in one place a group of young men, unmarried for the most part and cut off from their families, in an all-encompassing setting where they live all day, every day, for nearly the whole year. This community is specifically established as a framework for the fulfilment of the ideal of learning (*talmud torah*), and this sets it apart from its surroundings. The yeshiva's purpose is seen not only to educate the student in depth, but to form them intellectually and spiritually. Almost by definition, this situation—all-day study in a collective life cut off from the everyday secular world—is marked by a special strictness, a search for 'completeness' (*shleymus*), or, in other words, a degree of religious tension characteristic of the monastery.[41]

[39] Grunfeld-Rosenbaum, 'Sara Schenierer', 425.

[40] Stampfer, *Families, Rabbis, and Education*, 214.

[41] Friedman, 'Haredim Confront the Modern City', 78.

Bais Yaakov mimicked features of the yeshiva in the different stages of its development. In the first years, Sarah Schenirer taught in the apartment in which she lived, a feature characteristic of a traditional *ḥeder.* The young teachers who went out to start schools, even into the 1930s, often boarded with families who were supporters of the movement. The notion of boarding and eating at the homes of local families, so familiar a feature of the yeshiva experience of traditional nineteenth-century life, thus finally became available (in changed form, since these were teachers rather than students) to young women in the twentieth. But it was in the seminaries that Bais Yaakov came closest to fashioning the 'total institution' described by Stampfer and Friedman for adolescent girls. These institutions limited their contact with both the outside world and their own families during the most dangerous years of young adulthood. In Gershon Bacon's description of the Kraków seminary, 'The atmosphere of this boarding school, with its twenty-four hour a day emphasis on piety, study and personal development, strongly resembled that of the *yeshiva*.'[42] And like the graduates of elite yeshivas, the seminarians formed a cadre of intellectuals and activists whose ties, ideally and often in reality, continued long after graduation.

The institution that Bais Yaakov most closely resembled was Yeshivat Hakhmei Lublin. Deborah Weissman writes that, 'in its modern appearance and mildly innovative character, [the yeshiva] represented to some extent a male counterpart to Bais Ya'akov's attempt at an accommodation with modernity'.[43] The decision to construct a prestigious yeshiva that could be the pride of the Orthodox world through its selectiveness, rigour, and modern facilities was taken at the 1923 World Congress of the Agudath Israel in Vienna, the meeting that also established the Keren Hatorah fund to take on the development both of Yeshivat Hakhmei Lublin and of Bais Yaakov.[44] Both projects required international coordination and fundraising, and were followed closely in the Agudah press. The cornerstone-laying ceremony for the yeshiva, covered in the new *Bais Yaakov Journal* (issue 5–6) and featuring the Torah luminaries of Poland speaking to huge crowds that included large delegations from the Bais Yaakov and the Havatselet schools, took place in 1924, three years before the Kraków seminary's very similar

[42] Bacon, *Politics of Tradition*, 170.

[43] Weissman, 'Bais Ya'akov: A Women's Educational Movement', 65.

[44] The selectivity of Bais Yaakov was a slightly different matter than that of the elite yeshiva, since Bais Yaakov had to do more than educate the brightest girls—it also had to meet the needs of an educational movement. In the 1930s, according to Rebbetzin Basya (Epstein) Bender, approximately two-thirds of her incoming class was let go after three months, having been deemed unsuitable as teachers. See Rubin (ed.), *Daughters of Destiny*, 179.

ceremony, and the yeshiva opened in 1930, a year before Bais Yaakov moved into the new seminary building. The buildings even bear (miraculously, both are still standing) a physical resemblance: they are five stories high, and both (according to the publicity material prepared for them) had separate dining rooms (for meat and dairy), grand lecture halls, and spacious dormitories.

But precisely because the similarities between Bais Yaakov and the yeshiva, and young women devoted to learning Torah and the ideal yeshiva boy, were so plain to see, the literature of the movement took pains to stress the differences between the two types of institution, securing the distinction of male Torah study even while praising girls.[45] Unlike the Yavneh schools in Lithuania, Bais Yaakov maintained a separate female organizational identity: it had no male counterparts, and unlike some more modern educational Orthodox institutions for girls that were founded later, its schools were generally not called yeshivas. The major difference was of course the exclusion of Talmud from the Bais Yaakov curriculum, an exclusion which extended not only to the text itself but also to the way it was studied in the yeshiva environment (partner study, full-day focus on one text, etc.). This distinction was not always entirely clear: while some seemed to consider the Oral Torah as comprising solely the Mishnah and Talmud (even here an exception was made for the homiletic *Ethics of the Fathers*, a mishnaic tractate that was a core text of the Bais Yaakov curriculum), others considered biblical commentaries, which often recounted talmudic sources, as also prohibited. 'Esther' relates her excitement when 'A woman named Sarah Schenirer' came to her town to found a school; when she asked her father whether she would be able to study Rashi's commentary on the Bible, her father responded, 'Girls don't study Rashi and Gemara.' The curriculum was certainly more basic in the supplemental schools, but the seminary did teach the Bible along with commentaries such as those of Rashi and of Samson Raphael Hirsch.[46] In such ways, the supposedly firm distinctions between the

[45] Naomi Cohen suggests that girls' education remained neglected in eastern Europe for longer than in Germany precisely because the east European yeshiva was so devoted to Torah 'for its own sake', an 'obvious[ly] impossible idea for girls', that it 'ruled out this framework as a potential model which might somehow be adapted for them'. By contrast, the ideal of the Mensch Yisroel, the well-rounded individual idealized by Hirsch and his followers, was open to mobilization for women as well as for men. See Cohen, 'Women and the Study of Talmud', 32.

[46] E. G. Friedenson, for instance, described the examinations of the seminarians at the teacher-training course in Rabka as covering 'the commentaries of the Torah, as well as the homiletics of the rabbis', in 'Pictures and Notes', *Bais Yaakov Journal*, 46 (1929), cited in Atkin, 'The Beth Jacob Movement in Poland', 118.

male and female curriculum were sometimes blurred, in a school environment in which female intellectual ambition was a driving force.

Bais Yaakov also worked to distinguish its practices from those of the yeshiva by tempering its devotion to women's Torah study with an insistence that its intellectual accomplishments were directed to practical religious ends—or, in the oft-quoted phrase, *lo hamidrash hu ha'ikar, ela hama'aseh* (*Avot* 1: 17), 'It is not the study that is important, but rather the deed.' In its original context and in many of its later applications, this phrase refers to general study (or speech) rather than women's Torah study specifically. But it could be mobilized for the purposes of qualifying the notion of women's Torah study for its own sake, a prototypically male practice. In her analysis of post-war Bais Yaakov, Shoshana Bechhofer calls attention to a certain verbal tic in the movement's discourse, the tendency to follow any description of its high level of intellectual engagement with an immediate insistence on the practical utility of this knowledge or its impact on one's character—a theme she calls 'Yes, but'.[47] While less frequent than later, this seemed to be characteristic of Bais Yaakov in the interwar years as well. The first conference of the school administrators, held in Łódź in 1930, stressed the importance of teaching the Hebrew language (no doubt with a view to competing with Tarbut schools, with their focus on modern Hebrew), while also proclaiming its greater commitment to 'the development of personality and character training'.[48] In a graduation speech at the seminary at the end of the first year in the new building, Meir Rapoport, the president of the Kraków Agudah (and the same man who spoke of founding schools for girls at the 1903 conference), praised the students for their vast store of knowledge, immediately adding that 'it is not the study that is important, but rather the deed', which in this case referred to the 'implanting of the spirit of Torah in young souls, the primary mission of the Bais Yaakov teacher'.[49] Writing in the post-war years about how the schools' learned and scholarly graduates 'put their fathers and brothers to shame with their great knowledge', Joseph Friedenson continues, 'But a great principle was always stressed by Rabbi Yehudah Leib Orlean, which is that "It is not the study that is important, but rather the deed."' The girls themselves saw their knowledge as unimportant and the fear of God as the important principle in their work and roles.[50] The insistence that Torah study, even in its pure form or

[47] Bechhofer, 'Ongoing Constitution of Identity', 116.

[48] *Bais Yaakov Journal*, 52 (1930), 19, cited in Atkin, 'The Beth Jacob Movement in Poland', 51.

[49] 'The Examinations in the Bais Yaakov Seminary' (Yid.), 13.

[50] J. Friedenson, 'The Bais Yaakov Girls' Schools' (Heb.), 73.

for its own sake, was always subsumed, for women, to other aims worked to resolve the tension that beset women's high-level intellectual engagement within an Orthodox value system. These other aims evolved in time. The intellectual achievements of the cadre of seminary graduates were recognized as important in the pre-war period because they secured their attachment to Orthodox observance and enabled their success as teachers in the movement. In the post-war period, in contrast, they were often tied more closely with the task of raising a Jewish family and supporting a husband who learnt Torah on a full-time basis.

If Bais Yaakov was almost but not quite a yeshiva system for girls, the role of its leader was also sometimes difficult to categorize, given the mismatch between her institutional function and traditional roles for Orthodox women. This category crisis was only partially resolved by the rhetorical recourse to her role as 'mother of thousands', which jibed with some elements of her work, but was difficult to reconcile with her function as chief ideologue of the movement and the author of its first textbook (*Yahadus*, 1928) and many other learned and popular discourses. The advertisement for Sarah Schenirer's forthcoming *Collected Writings* stressed the uniqueness of the book, described as a *leyn- un lernbukh* (book to read and study), for Jewish youth. 'For the first time in hundreds of years, [we have] a learned and important *sefer* (religious book) in Yiddish by a woman, and by Frau Schenirer, to boot, who is responsible for bringing thousands of Jewish daughters back to the wellspring of Jewish faith and Jewish knowledge.'[51] In the introduction to the 1933 collection of her work, signed by the 'Central Secretariat of the Bnos Agudas Yisroel in Poland', the book is described as 'a handbook for the Jewish daughter', which she 'should read and learn regularly over and over again'. Her writings 'are not just to read and review but also to learn—to learn daily'. According to its title and the introduction, *Collected Writings* is a *bukh* (secular book), while the advertisement calls it both a book and a *sefer* (religious book); moreover, it was to be 'learned' (as well as 'read'), a choice of verb that signals the practice of sacred text study. The incongruence between a woman-authored text and a prototypically male activity—a 'book' that should nevertheless be 'learned'—seems to push descriptions of Sarah Schenirer's work in conflicting directions. In her introduction to the second (1955) edition of *Collected Writings*, Vichna Kaplan describes the book as 'a will—a holy will from a mother which must be read with attention to every word'. But even more importantly, its instructions must be followed, since the book is 'like a *Shulḥan arukh*

[51] The advertisement appeared numerous times, with varying language, throughout 1932. I quote from the one entitled 'Bais Yaakov, Sign Up' (Yid.).

[the canonical sixteenth-century halakhic code] for every Jewish daughter'.[52] The various descriptions of the text as *sefer*, book, private family missive, handbook, and law code suggest the challenge posed by female religious textual production within a culture that lacked categories to account for such a phenomenon.

Bais Yaakov also took on other textual practices that had previously been associated with the yeshiva or synagogue. In the early 1930s, the movement raised funds for a Torah scroll for its largest Yehudis summer camp by selling certificates in schools and Bnos groups, with each certificate purchasing a single letter of the Torah. The movement followed the progress of the scribe closely, celebrating milestones with special ceremonies and offering lectures on scribal practice and law. The completion of the work was celebrated in the camp in Długosiodło (north-east of Warsaw) for three days beginning on Tu Be'av of 1933 (7 August), with representatives from Bais Yaakov schools from all over Poland participating in the formal completion of the scroll. This occasion, according to the report, 'was a source of joy for Bais Yaakov children and united them into one family, with its own *sefer* Torah'.[53] The project combined traditional Jewish activities and new phenomena in interesting ways: Although the purchase of letters to fund the writing of a Torah scroll is something women occasionally participate in as individuals, the collective funding of a Torah scroll for its own use by a national network of young girls is much more remarkable. And despite the language of the report, Torah scrolls ordinarily unite not families (although families sometimes commission them) but rather synagogues or study halls. Moreover, they are traditionally placed in the male section of a synagogue, where men read from and interact with the Torah, with women relegated to the role of spectators. In this regard, the acquisition, installation, veneration and (presumably) use of a Torah scroll by a girls' movement that saw itself as a family brought together traditional and modern practices in innovative ways.

Acknowledging the influence of German neo-Orthodoxy, the yeshiva, and hasidism was often a delicate matter, given that these crossed either denominational boundaries or gender lines. But it was far more difficult to acknowledge the

[52] The *Shulḥan arukh*, written by Joseph Karo in Safed and first published in 1565, is a widely consulted codification of Jewish law. Vichna Eisen Kaplan (1913–86) was a student of Sarah Schenirer who, together with her husband Rabbi Boruch Kaplan, opened the first Bais Yaakov high school in Williamsburg, Brooklyn, in 1938. She later opened the first Bais Yaakov teachers' seminary, which provided teachers for Bais Yaakov and other Jewish day schools in America and Israel.

[53] '"Yehudis" Summer Camp Acquires Its Own Torah Scroll' (Yid.), 15.

influence of secular ideologies and movements, which were fervently repudiated by Bais Yaakov and the Agudath Israel as anathema to everything they stood for. Nevertheless, the contemporary world of cosmopolitan Kraków, with its public lectures, youth movements, and political activism, was clearly a rich matrix of influences for Sarah Schenirer and Bais Yaakov. Her diary is evidence that, as a young woman, she was familiar with and attracted to the cosmopolitan culture of Kraków, with its public lectures on Polish literature and European philosophy, and its theatre, and youth clubs. She was explicit about her aim to construct religious variations of these innovations. While some Agudah leaders saw the use of modern means such as a political organization, youth movements, journalism, etc. as mere strategies to fight the corruptions of modernity, the founder of Bais Yaakov was more open about her own attraction to at least some of what modernity could offer.[54]

The closest and most direct competitors of Bais Yaakov and Bnos were the Zionist youth movements, especially the religious Zionist ones. Zionism was generally considered a greater threat to Orthodoxy than other secular movements since it used religious language and symbols and spoke to deep longings among religious youth. Zionists took full advantage of this shared language in order to recruit Orthodox followers. In a 1937 article reflecting on the atmosphere in small Polish towns, Elimelech Steyer describes how 'between the afternoon and evening prayers the stammering sexton would suddenly stand up, bang on the table, and announce: "Jews! The Land of Israel is a Jewish state!", and among us *beit midrash* [house of study] boys would appear Hebrew teachers with their spectacles, and invite us to join their club'.[55] The recruitment apparently worked in both directions: 'Esther' relates that, in her initial enthusiasm for the ideals of Bnos, 'I read books that gave me issues to debate with the Zionist girls, among whom we recruited.'[56]

As powerful as the ideological rivalry was, the two movements were also, often literally, neighbours in a shifting ideological landscape that included the Zionist religious party Mizrahi (which had its own complicated relationship with the Zionist mainstream), occasional political alliances between Zionist and religious parties, and an Orthodox population with a range of Zionist and anti-Zionist opinions. In Lithuania, where a more moderate form of Orthodoxy prevailed, in towns too small to sustain two Orthodox schools there were even initial forays to establish new institutions that would combine features of the

[54] See Bacon, *The Politics of Tradition*, 67–9.

[55] Steyer, 'Then, When They Appeared . . .' (Yid.), 12.

[56] Shandler (ed.), *Awakening Lives*, 324.

Mizrahi and Agudah systems. The plans fell prey to the evident ideological differences between the camps, but the attempt suggests that those ideological distinctions which activists and leaders held to be sacred mattered far less to parents.[57] Despite the official stance of the movement, Bais Yaakov students sometimes also belonged to Zionist organizations or participated in Zionist activities, despite the contradictions embedded in their choices.[58] In such a fluid ideological environment, Bais Yaakov publications were compelled to explain what distinguished the movement's avowed love of the Land of Israel, interest in developments in the new settlements, devotion to Hebrew, and preparation courses for young Bnos pioneers hoping to emigrate to Palestine, from those of the Mizrahi movement, or even secular Zionists.[59] The distinction was crucial: Zionism was a secular or even anti-religious movement, while Bais Yaakov was committed to the Land of Israel along traditional religious rather than secular-national principles. While arguing that Zionism sinned in tearing Jews away from their religion and creating strife within the Jewish community, Bais Yaakov wanted to ensure that its antagonism to Zionism did not stifle the love for the Land of Israel among young Orthodox Jews.

Bais Yaakov specifically sought to distinguish itself from the Zionist Tarbut school system, stressing that Orthodox parents should not consider it an appropriate substitute for a Bais Yaakov education. Tarbut schools were even more dangerous than others, since 'they study the Bible, and in some they even study Talmud for forty minutes a day, which allows them to stuff the minds of Jewish children with the most heretical ideas'.[60] A 1926 *Bais Yaakov Journal* article by 'Ben-Rivkah' compared classes in a Tarbut and Bais Yaakov school 'in one of the cities of Poland'. In the former, where Hebrew was spoken with the Sephardi pronunciation, the author witnesses a pupil reading aloud from a schoolbook: *hakelev nove'aḥ hav, hav, hav* ('the dog barks, *arf, arf, arf*), and reflects on the Zion-

[57] Zalkin, 'Let It Be Entirely Hebrew' (Heb.), 129.

[58] In her interview for the Visual History Archive, Minia Jay describes learning Hatikvah and Zionist folk dances in her Bais Yaakov school in Warta (Minia Jay, Interview 23350, segment 7, Visual History Archive, USC Shoah Foundation, 1999 (accessed 12 May 2017)).

[59] Friedenson, who had Zionist sympathies and was associated with Po'alei Agudath Israel, the most socialist-oriented of the arms of the Agudah, founded a *hakhsharah* (training) programme in Łódź for Bnos members interested in living in Palestine, where the girls lived communally in preparation for immigration. See Weissman, 'Bais Ya'akov: A Women's Educational Movement', 78.

[60] 'How Should a Jew Educate His Child?' (Yid.) (Warsaw, 1930), cited in Kazdan, *The History of Jewish School Systems* (Yid.), 448.

ist children who are unfortunately raised to believe that 'our way is the way of the dog and cat; we have nothing to do with spiritual matters'. In the Bais Yaakov school, in contrast, he walks in during a lesson on the book of Esther, and hears one pupil ask how Queen Esther could have married a non-Jew. When the teacher responds that she had no choice, the student argues that she should have martyred herself rather than marry King Ahasuerus. The patient teacher explains to the clever, pious pupil that God had providentially arranged the marriage in order to save the Jewish people.[61]

But Tarbut was only part of a spectrum of school systems against which Bais Yaakov polemicized and competed for pupils. In a 1930 brochure detailing the question 'How Should a Jew Educate His Child?' the writer answers that 'if someone wants their child to remain a faithful Jew and an upright person, who doesn't wrench himself from his Jewish roots and wander far from the Jewish path, he must keep them away from the Tarbut and Cysho [Yiddishist] schools, which are nests of heresy, apostasy, and spiritual assimilation, and send their son only to *ḥeder* or other schools led by the Agudath Israel and their daughter—to the only religious school for girls—Bais Yaakov'. These other schools treat sports and gymnastics with 'the enthusiasm of Hellenistic *gymnasia* but consider the words of the prophets to be either 'politics or—in the most generous case—poetry'.[62] In at least three towns, Kazdan relates, full ceremonies of excommunication, 'complete with darkened lights and *shofar* blasts', were carried out against the Cysho schools.[63] Tarbut schools were also occasionally excommunicated, as happened in the town of Zambrów, where the Zionist youth responded to the excommunication, which resulted in the transfer of thirty girls from the Tarbut school to the new Bais Yaakov, by knocking out the window panes of the rival school.[64] Nor were stones thrown only by Zionist or leftist opponents of Bais Yaakov. The legend about Sarah Schenirer picking up the stones thrown at her in order to build schools may have some basis in fact: at a 1930 conference of Bais

[61] Ben-Rivkah, 'Two Kinds of Jewish School' (Yid.), 78–80.

[62] 'How Should a Jew Educate His Child?' (Yid.), cited in Kazdan, *The History of Jewish School Systems* (Yid.), 447–8. Kazdan writes that the Hebrew ideology behind the Tarbut schools was essentially secular, but 'the Bible was an essential foundation, not as the source of religious thought or religious life, but rather as the fount of national creativity, which must in the future also draw on the ethical teachings of this book' (*The History of Jewish School Systems* (Yid.), 414).

[63] Kazdan, *The History of Jewish School Systems* (Yid.), 448. Kazdan also cites a proclamation at the first World Congress of the Agudah in 1923, and another, from 1926, signed by 400 Warsaw rabbis, requesting that religious Jews not send children to Tarbut.

[64] Slowik, 'Cultural Struggle Infuses Life'.

Yaakov administrators, a principal protested the Agudah youth who threw stones at schools where plays were being rehearsed or performed.[65]

The very frequency of the calls to Orthodox parents to desist from sending their children to Tarbut (and even Cysho) schools suggests that some considered such places appropriate for their children. Despite the clear ideological boundaries between Tarbut and Bais Yaakov, the latter could not count on a natural constituency (as it could in the post-war period), and so was compelled to compete in the educational market by stressing its commitment to teaching Hebrew and, in full-day Bais Yaakov schools in the larger cities, insisting on the rigour of its secular studies.[66] But gaining students among secular families also meant risking losing their Orthodox base. At the 1930 conference where the stone-throwing Agudah youth were excoriated, one Bais Yaakov administrator claimed that the schools were full of pupils from non-Orthodox homes, which made it no surprise that some Orthodox families continued to resist sending their daughters there. In such an environment, it had to counter arguments from the right: while Agudath Israel characterized itself as the political voice of the Orthodox masses, many of these, including the hasidic groups of Aleksander and Belz, were either against the Agudah for various reasons, apolitical, had shifting allegiances, or split their vote among different parties.[67] The need for rabbinic endorsements that could counter such opposition continued throughout the interwar period.

Socialism, too, was an attractive option for Orthodox youth, though less dangerously so than Zionism. Agudah itself included a workers' party, Po'alei Agudath Israel, which attempted to meet the needs of the Orthodox working class, and, according to Bacon, 'added a tinge of socialism to its calls for "justice according to the Torah"'.[68] It may be no surprise that many of the leading figures in the Po'alei Agudah, including its chief ideologue Yehudah Leib Orlean, were also active in Bais Yaakov—the two movements could be described as the Agudah's

[65] For this legend, see Introduction, n. 7, above. On the conference, see 'A Conference of the Bais Yaakov Girls' Schools' (Yid.), 12. Although the report does not explain the violence, these youths probably objected to theatre as inappropriate for Orthodox girls. At the same conference, administrators discussed the relatively liberal standards in Bais Yaakov (as compared to the way that boys were treated) and resolved to produce a catalogue of permitted and forbidden reading material in the movement's libraries, some of which included books by such ostensibly off-limit Zionist writers as Hayim Nahman Bialik and Sha'ul Tchernichowsky. It is not clear that this resolution was ever carried out.

[66] Kazdan, *The History of Jewish School Systems* (Yid.), 489.

[67] For the relations between the Agudah and Aleksander hasidism, see Bacon, *The Politics of Tradition*, 193–4; on Belz, ibid.122, 303; on splitting the vote, ibid. 237–8.

[68] *Yidisher Arbeter Shtime* (2 July 1937), 4, 8, quoted in Bacon, *The Politics of Tradition*, 102.

left wing.[69] There is no doubt that socialism also had its attractions for young Orthodox women in interwar Poland; the lines between socialist youth movements and Bais Yaakov and Bnos were frequently crossed, in both directions. 'Esther' relates that her friend, whom she is forbidden to see by her Bnos 'sisters', left Bais Yaakov to join a socialist youth movement. She also describes herself as tormented by anger about the social conditions that keep her away from higher education (including the Bais Yaakov seminary) and interested in hearing about the new social forces, even as she remains an active Bnos member.[70] Gutta Sternbuch similarly describes 'the most idealistic and spiritual' of her Bais Yaakov pupils as going on to become 'leaders of radical movements'. One girl, who 'didn't know what political socialism was', was nevertheless 'lightheartedly called "the Socialist"', because 'she was filled with a fiery zeal', finding validation 'in God's laws' for 'her idealistic drive for truth and justice'.[71] The *Bais Yaakov Journal* clearly responded to the fascination among its readership for radical social movements, for instance by publishing a poem in 1933 about the arrest of three young female communists.[72]

But socialism was not only an ideological 'neighbour' of Bais Yaakov in the larger political and cultural landscape, it also affected it, at least to some extent. Bais Yaakov writers championed the principles of equality, democracy, collectivity, and social justice, and envisioned the Orthodox culture they were creating as a countercultural critique of materialism and capitalism. During the first years of the Bais Yaakov boarding school in 1 Katarzyna Street, there seems also to have been a voluntary embrace of poverty, what Judith Grunfeld-Rosenbaum called 'happy deprivation'. Such experiments continued in subsequent years: the Łódź Bnos established an urban kibbutz for young women preparing to emigrate to the Land of Israel, and other branches set up clothing cooperatives for their members. Such efforts were also part of seminary culture, despite its grand facilities: Deutschländer writes that the students in the Kraków Bais Yaakov seminary 'formed an independent Student Union, for purposes of self-government.

[69] On Orlean's activities in Po'alei Agudath Israel, see Seidman, *Personalities I Knew* (Heb.), 196–7. Orlean was the first president of Po'alei Agudah, wrote its major ideological treatise, worked to politically organize the movement from 1922 to 1932, and devoted himself completely to Bais Yaakov from 1933. His interest in the workers, like that of other intellectuals, owed more to his sense of social justice than to his own roots in the Orthodox proletariat.

[70] Shandler (ed.), *Awakening Lives*, 337–8.

[71] Sternbuch and Kranzler, *Gutta*, 50–1.

[72] Lipmanovitch, 'Three Arrested Women' (Yid.), 5. The poem expresses the curiosity of the witness to the arrest, asks 'were their sins political or moral?', and decides that the girls are communists and that, despite his initial sympathy for their plight, they represent bitter enemies.

The union established a special library for the students, as well as a cooperative for school supplies.'[73]

If the Po'alei Agudath Israel conceptualized social justice though the lens of the Torah, Bais Yaakov and Bnos sometimes also viewed the Torah through the lens of socialism, imbuing traditional Jewish practices with collectivist significance. This combination is evident in the Bnos movement's celebration of Tu Be'av (the fifteenth day of the Hebrew month of Av) as its special holiday, promoted throughout the Bais Yaakov world as 'the most beautiful Jewish holiday', and an 'old-new celebration for Jewish women'. Talmudic sources describe Tu Be'av as a harvest holiday, a day of joy associated with heterosexual romance, in which the unmarried girls of Jerusalem dressed in borrowed white garments and went out to dance in the vineyards, 'and whoever did not have a wife would go there to find a bride' (BT *Ta'an.* 31*a*). The *Bais Yaakov Journal* published many articles on this late-antique festival that was being revived in the Bnos movement. Reb Pinchas-Zelig Gliksman described the way the celebration turned 'the most important and weighty day of a person's life, when they choose a mate' into a religious celebration of the true values of family compatibility and shared spiritual commitment rather than physical beauty or wealth.[74] But descriptions of the celebration make it clear that in its new Polish context, Tu Be'av involved no matchmaking, but rather celebrated the summer colonies for girls in rural Poland. In one account of Tu Be'av 1932, the celebration began at sunset with a long hike through the thick woods 'which conceal everything', with 'our leader Frau Schenirer at the head, and 115 girls following, hand in hand behind our guide'. Deep in the pitch-dark woods, the girls lit a flaming bonfire, a Bnos leader gave a talk, and the dancing began.[75] Reflecting upon the holiday in her writings. Sarah Schenirer mined talmudic sources for material which could explain how the celebration taught girls the virtues of feminine modesty and class equality:

> Borrowed white dresses for each Jewish woman, without distinction between rich and poor—how beautiful that sounds! Today, when the young Jewish woman is drowning in a flood of different fashions, and often forgets the fashion of modesty, this factor must teach us a great deal. Jewish women assemble for their special holiday not only in plain white but even in borrowed dresses. No trace of luxury sparkles in their dress, there is nothing of the foolish pride that the rich feel towards the poor, and which draws the poor to imitate the desires and pleasures of the rich. Everyone must wear a borrowed

[73] Deutschländer, *Tätigkeitsbericht*, 2.

[74] Gliksman, 'The Most Beautiful Jewish Holiday' (Yid.), 3–4.

[75] 'Tu Be'av 1932 in Skawa' (Yid.), 27.

dress, which demonstrates clearly that nothing we possess is ours, but rather comes from God, and we need learn only what to do with what we have been given as a gift.

Sarah Schenirer discovers in the text the rationale for an egalitarian youth culture in which clothing is shared, economic differences militated against and overcome, and modern fashion rejected in favour of modest and simple dress. The focus on modesty as simplicity and the erasure of class differences is remarkable, given how commonly modesty is associated in Jewish culture with the distinctions not between classes, but between men and women, or with what Tova Hartman calls 'the religious male gaze'. Much of the traditional writing on *tseni'ut* that Hartman surveys justifies 'keeping women covered' to protect men from sexual arousal: 'The gaze-based ethos informs virtually every aspect of male/female relationships within Orthodox society', and conditions women's relationships to their own sexuality and bodies.[76] It would be hard to overstate the importance of modesty in Bais Yaakov; necklines and sleeve or skirt lengths were and still are monitored with the greatest stringency. The movement was often caught up in a discourse that saw women as both sexually vulnerable and sexually dangerous. Much of the international support it received derived from perceptions not of the value of women's Torah study, but rather of the importance of saving 'the daughters of poverty-strucken [*sic*] Eastern European Jewry' from the 'menace of moral destruction', as one fundraising publication put it, indirectly referring to the widely discussed Jewish overrepresentation among both prostitutes and traffickers in the international white slave trade.[77] It is striking that in at least one important reflection on the topic, Sarah Schenirer conveys the value of modest dress not by recourse to the language of the sexual dangers that await girls or of the men whose sexual control must be supported by female modesty (a familiar discourse in the Orthodox world today, as Hartman documents), but rather by reference to the envious gaze of a poorer woman at the elegant, fashionable, and more expensive dress of her richer friend.

This rhetoric of egalitarianism describes the aspirations of Bais Yaakov rather than the economic realities it was compelled to negotiate. Bais Yaakov was a relatively poor movement, working with a significantly smaller budget per stu-

[76] Hartman, *Feminism Encounters Traditional Judaism*, 52.

[77] Deutschländer, *History of the Beth Jacob Schools*, 6. See, for instance, the quoted testimony of Ernest Schiff (included in an appendix of testimonies at the end of that volume), that 'for the protection of girls and women . . . the Jewish religious education of girls and women is of the utmost importance to the whole of Jewry all over the world' (ibid. 29). Schiff is identified there as 'President of Jewish Shelter, London'.

dent than many of its competitors (including Horev, the Agudah's school system for boys).[78] Despite its stated commitment to meritocratic admissions standards and its regular attempts to raise funds for stipends, the seminary was financially out of reach for many students. 'Esther' bitterly laments that her less gifted and motivated but richer friend is admitted to the seminary, while she is unable to enrol despite her better preparation and her father's attempts to pull whatever strings he can to get her a reduction in tuition fees.[79] Bnos was directed, on the one hand, to the Orthodox working girl, with its focus on vocational training, social and economic justice, and collectivist culture. The seminary, on the other hand, had a distinctively middle-class feel, although it cultivated a more voluntary 'happy privation' that signalled the sympathies of Bais Yaakov with those struggling in the face of the pauperization of Polish Jewry in the 1930s.

The most fraught relationship Bais Yaakov had with the social ideologies of its time was with Jewish feminism. That it was a women's movement was clear to all, and those on the left who associated such movements with the battle for women's equality and rights celebrated it for that reason. The Jewish groups that arose elsewhere in Europe to support girls' education or to fight sex trafficking recognized Bais Yaakov as a partner in their shared struggle. This support apparently began after Dr Leo Deutschländer spoke at a conference in London of the Jewish Association for the Protection of Girls and Women in June 1927, and feminist activists associated with the anti-white-slavery cause were moved to lend Bais Yaakov publicity and financial support.[80] Reporting on her trip to Kraków in early 1936 to a group of Agudah activists in Frankfurt, Bertha Pappenheim spoke of Sarah Schenirer 'with deep respect', but suggested that she had focused too single-mindedly on training teachers in an environment in which nurses and

[78] Using numbers from the *Joint Distribution Committee Report on Jewish Schools in Poland* (Paris, 1938), Eisenstein provides a table for the budgets of the different schools systems in 1937: Tarbut, with 269 schools and 44,780 students, had a budget of 3,041,049 złoty; the Horev system, with 177 schools and 49,123 students, had a slightly larger budget of 3,347,712 złoty; Cysho had 169 schools and 16,486 students, on a budget of 1,911,308 złoty. Bais Yaakov, which claimed 248 schools and 35,586 students that year, operated on a budget of 1,264,522 złoty. In other words, Bais Yaakov had more than twice the number of students than Cysho, with a significantly smaller budget; and while it had roughly 70% of the students of Horev, it operated on about 35% of its budget. See Eisenstein, *Jewish Schools in Poland*, 96.

[79] Shandler (ed.), *Awakening Lives*, 329.

[80] See the endorsement of Hannah Karminski, secretary general of the Jüdische Frauenbund, in Deutschländer, *History of the Beth Jacob Girls Schools*, 30. Bertha Pappenheim, founder of the Jüdische Frauenbund, served on the Frankfurt Bais Yaakov committee, appears on a 1933 list of faculty members for the seminary in Vienna, and spent a week at the Kraków seminary in the autumn of 1935 (ibid. 69).

social workers were more urgently needed, given the thousands of poor children in the Orthodox community infected with tuberculosis.[81]

Despite these strong and mutually respectful connections, it was generally understood that Bais Yaakov was different in important ways from other Jewish women's organizations. In an article on the 1929 world congress at which the women's organization of the Agudah was founded, Dr Deutschländer declared it a great scandal that 'even so large an organization as the Bnos Agudath Israel was not invited to the World Conference of Jewish Women' that had been held in Hamburg two months earlier (and at which the Frauenbund was well represented). His complaint suggests that Bnos might have accepted an invitation if it had been offered, which is to say that it considered itself a Jewish women's organization among others. However, Deutschländer added, the Hamburg conference had 'treated religious approaches to such issues as the *agunah* with such dismissiveness that a religious person's heart shuddered'.[82] Bnos may have been a women's organization, but it was distinguished from its peers by a resistance to the fight for women's equality and an unwillingness to challenge rabbinic authority.

The question of whether Bais Yaakov was a feminist movement is thus a complex one, given its position as both inside and outside the international network of women's organizations of the period. This stance might be compared to what Gershon Bacon calls the 'insider-outsider' position of the Agudah within party politics, in which it 'would cooperate in the day-to-day work of the Jewish parliamentarians [in the Sejm] . . . while insisting on complete autonomy on issues it considered matters of conscience'.[83] Bais Yaakov strategically forged connections with women's organizations and activists far beyond Orthodox or even Jewish circles, taking advantage of the well-publicized struggle against the international white slave trade to raise funds in western Europe and the United States.[84] Bais Yaakov found support among women far beyond the Orthodox and even the Jewish community as an educational movement that protected Polish

[81] See H.K., 'Beth-Jacob-Schul-Werk', 27.

[82] Deutschländer, 'The Second World Congress' (Yid.), 2.

[83] Bacon, *Politics of Tradition*, 305.

[84] The seminary cost $60,000 to build. The Jewish community of Kraków contributed the land (valued at $8,000), and an additional $7,000 was raised in Poland. The Keren Hatorah contributed $5,000; committees in Germany, Holland, and Switzerland another $5,000; England, $10,000; and $25,000 came from the United States, much of it from the New York-based Joint Distribution Committee. See Eisenstein, *Jewish Schools in Poland*, 86–7, for these figures. Note that this fundraising occurred during a period in which the United States still lacked Bais Yaakov schools.

Jewish girls and women from becoming 'easy prey to the white slave traffic'.[85] Beginning in the 1930s, the stationery of first the Vienna and subsequently the London central office of Bais Yaakov reflects this understanding of where support might be found for its enterprise. A letter from Deutschländer to the American Jewish Joint Distribution Committee from that year includes a letterhead reading, 'Mädchenschulorganisation "Beth Jacob" fur Erziehung, Pflege und Schutz des jüdischen Mädchen' (Organization of Beth Jacob girls' schools for the education, cultivation and protection of Jewish girls), while a 1940 letter from the London office has the masthead, 'Beth Jacob Central Organization: Organization for the Education and Protection of Jewish Girls in Eastern Europe'.[86]

While Bais Yaakov sometimes made strategic connections with woman's organizations outside Poland, it never, to my knowledge, used the language of protection in its internal publications, which focus on the movement's educational mission. It avoided a topic that preoccupied many others in the Jewish world for many reasons, modesty no doubt paramount among them. But by avoiding talk of prostitution, Bais Yaakov was also able to skirt the sensationalism and patronizing attitudes toward east European Jewry that sometimes characterized this discourse. Those who fought sex traffickers inevitably (and ironically) also directed attention to women as sexual objects. In this regard, Bais Yaakov may have been *more* feminist than many apparently liberal women's organizations, by focusing on girls' and women's educational and religious experiences rather than their sexual vulnerability.

While Bais Yaakov was willing to collaborate with women's organizations outside Poland, strategic considerations worked to distance it from such organizations within Poland, and from the suspicion that it might also be impelled by feminist ideology. For detractors on the Orthodox right, Bais Yaakov was damning evidence of the infection wrought by modern ideologies. The movement

[85] See the report on a fundraising reception held at the American Women's Association Club House in 1933, and attended by Edith Zangwill (wife of Israel), Frieda Warburg (wife of Felix), Rabbi Leo Jung (president of the American Beth Jacob Committee), and Rebekah Kohut, who spoke of the work Bais Yaakov was doing to 'protect' girls from moral 'degradation and ruin'. The afternoon tea raised $1,000 for the school system, with Mrs Warburg contributing $500. See 'Mrs. Felix M. Warburg Appeals for Support of Beth Jacob'.

[86] Further evidence that this fundraising strategy worked beyond the Jewish community may be found in a signed endorsement at the bottom of the London stationery from Eleanor Roosevelt: 'Beth Jacob is the most poignant and most glorious work in modern Israel.' Letters with these mastheads appear in the archives of the Joint Distribution Committee, numbered respectively 2000143 and 618761.

was thus often compelled to state its position on women's rights: Orlean, in a memorial essay for Sarah Schenirer, pointedly asked whether she emancipated the Jewish woman: 'Didn't [she] raise the Jewish woman from her lowly status? Didn't she place her on an equal level with her learned husband, who had always prided himself on his knowledge?' But Orlean denies this characterization by stressing that she had no intention of upending the traditional order; she remained modest, and accepted that men deserved their higher status by virtue of their obligation to study Torah.[87]

The charge of feminism may not be entirely baseless, despite these denials.[88] It is true that Bais Yaakov mobilized a conservative discourse, its aim being to 'return the Jewish home to its former glory'. But it drew nearly as frequently from the language of progress, modernization, and awakening—particularly when it spoke of its character as a women's movement. The *Bais Yaakov Journal* often described Bais Yaakov students and Bnos members as 'warriors' and 'pioneers', even if they would soon enough—it was hoped—become wives and mothers. And the movement intended to maintain its connection to women after marriage, and indeed throughout their lives, as they moved up through Basya, Bnos, and Neshei Agudath Israel. Even if these regularly pledged their allegiance to Torah, rabbinic authority, and the Agudah (which was theoretically guided by Torah and rabbinic authority), Orthodox women did find occasions to fight for their rights, as for instance in 1934 around the hotly contested issue of immigration certificates to Palestine. After unsuccessfully requesting its own certificates from the High Commissioner in Palestine in 1933 the Agudah won the right from the Jewish Agency in 1934 to distribute a share of the available certificates among its members. Given that there were dozens if not hundreds of candidates for each certificate, the distribution was a source of extreme tension and frustration. The difficulties of deciding who might acquire such a precious document was further complicated by a controversy within the Agudah about whether it was proper or permitted for Orthodox adolescents to attend agricultural training camps to prepare themselves for immigration to Palestine, The matter was only resolved when the Gerer Rebbe outlined a compromise for male-only training farms, and ruled 'that only males would receive certificates for entry into Palestine'.[89] Later that year, a front-page article appeared in the *Bais*

[87] Orlean, 'A Woman of Valour' (Heb.), 46.

[88] Deborah Weissman writes that, despite its overt opposition to feminism, Bais Yaakov functioned through many of its activities to 'raise the feminist consciousness' of its students ('Bais Ya'akov: A Women's Educational Movement', 96).

[89] See Bacon, *The Politics of Tradition*, 89.

Yaakov Journal entitled 'GIVE US A HOLDING!', in which the pseudonymous Rachel Bas Tovim[90] sharply protested the exclusion of Bnos members from the certificate allotment. The title and the first paragraphs of the article recall the plea to Moses by the daughters of Zelophehad in Numbers 27: 4, asking for a share of the Land of Israel since their father had no sons: 'Give us a holding among our father's kinsmen!' Only after establishing a biblical precedent for her demands does Bas Tovim continue:

> We, the members of Bnos, remember well the courageous answer we gave at our Warsaw convention in March 1931, when we were asked to participate in the hypocritical farce that is the fight for women's rights. We who have been raised in the spirit of our Torah know that in Judaism there is no place for any fighting for women's rights, if only Jews remained steadfast in observing the Torah in all its details, and so the false, foolish slogans have no power to sway us to change God's holy commandments.
>
> But now the time has come when we must demand what we deserve, according to the rights the Torah has bestowed on us.
>
> Today, after the Agudah fought for and received rights for its members, a struggle in which we participated, we demand those same rights. We, too, deserve our rightful share in the Land of Israel from the Agudah leaders who make the decisions about who will go up to the land and who will not. The Agudah must rectify the injustice that has been done to Jewish women through the 'gentlemen's agreement' that makes it impossible for women to get their rightful share of certificates.[91]

In expressing her outrage at the exclusion of women from the distribution of certificates by 'a gentlemen's agreement' in which Bnos played no part, Bas Tovim also makes clear that she has no truck with what she considers a theatrical and foolish 'fight for women's rights'. It is the Torah that allows her to speak as forcefully as she does through the precedent of the daughters of Zelophehad, who similarly demanded the right to a portion of the Holy Land that was being distributed among the men of Israel. Her demands, heartfelt (and justified) as they are, astutely point to the perfect biblical warrant for women demanding their rightful share in the Land. Put in the correct (religious, textually learned) terms, and with the appropriate repudiation of any commonality with those who

[90] The pen name alludes to Sarah Bas Tovim (lit., daughter of 'good people'), who lived in the late seventeenth/early eighteenth century and authored a popular Yiddish *tkhine* collection; Bas Tovim became a pen name used by others writing in the genre, and was popular among writers in the *Bais Yaakov Journal*.

[91] Bas Tovim, 'Give Us a Holding!', 1. The 'gentleman's agreement' (the first word is transliterated from English) may refer to the compromise struck by the Gerer Rebbe, or perhaps to the Agudah agreement with the Jewish Agency that it would be responsible for distributing a share of the available certificates to its own members.

'fight for women's rights', even a woman objecting to unfair treatment from the Orthodox male leadership might be accorded a place on the front page of the *Bais Yaakov Journal*.[92]

Despite distancing itself from the 'foolish' struggle for women's suffrage and equal rights, the *Journal* was required to contend with these problems, publishing at least one article on the topic in virtually every issue. Writers often argued against modern feminist ideologies on the grounds that they focused on the woman as an individual, rather than recognizing the symbiosis that comes into play through marriage or the greater claims of community and religion. The challenges posed by feminist writers to Orthodoxy clearly registered powerfully in Bais Yaakov and other women's circles, but they were not lost on others. As Bacon has shown, once it found public visibility by winning seats in the Sejm (the Polish parliament), the Agudah was called upon to defend its opposition to female suffrage and women serving in public office (which applied principally to internal Jewish self-government). In 1922, after a Zionist group proposed granting women the right to vote in elections for the newly reconstituted *kehilah* (Jewish community council), the Agudah objected on the grounds that such innovations were unfaithful to traditional modes of communal leadership, a stance that prevailed through the interwar period.[93] Speaking more directly to the journal's readers, Rabbi Tuvye Yehudah Gutentag wrote that the stance against women's suffrage was not designed to keep them from expressing their opinions, but rather, because in Orthodox households husband and wife are so harmoniously united, a single vote could express the opinions of both.[94] Others argued that the prohibition against female involvement in public affairs was not about discrimination, but rather about the wise recognition that 'the woman-mother' has more important things to worry about'.[95] Nevertheless, there was an inherent, quite perceptible tension in this discourse: despite doubts about female suffrage, the Agudah was compelled to bow to political realities and run advertisements soliciting the vote of the readership of the *Bais Yaakov Journal* in the general elections (Oleszak suggests that the Agudah's support of Bais Yaakov

[92] That this battle was rewarded with success might be gleaned from the fact that Bnos sent its first group to Palestine later that year.

[93] For a discussion of these controversies, see Bacon, *The Politics of Tradition*, 91, and M. B. Shapiro, *Between the Yeshiva World and Modern Orthodoxy*, 218–19.

[94] Tavyomi (Gutentag), 'Women in Judaism' (Yid.), 100.

[95] Knablevitsh, 'Women's Emancipation' (Yid.), *Bais Yaakov Journal*, 89 (1932), cited in Lisek, 'Orthodox Yiddishism', 140.

owes something to similar political considerations).[96] So, too, did it celebrate the visible accomplishments of a famous woman while continuing to insist on the wisdom of keeping women from public service.

There were some contemporary observers who noticed the tensions inherent within Bais Yaakov. The secular Yiddish journalist and novelist Rachel Feygenberg praised the vibrancy of the movement, describing it as a fascinating combination of west European modernity and 'rigorously dogmatic' Orthodoxy. The appeal of Bais Yaakov surpassed its own constituency. Feygenberg describes how, in Kalisz, local women regularly gathered outside the local Bais Yaakov high school on Friday evenings to listen to the beautiful voices of young girls singing the sabbath service. As inspiring as this group prayer was, Feygenberg continued, it presented a cultural dilemma that Orthodoxy would have to face:

> As soon as you open the doors of tradition to girls and women, you have to stop relegating them to the women's section and begin to treat them as God's creatures, just as men are. The woman's voice too has to ring out in the synagogue. But according to tradition, a woman's voice is the symbol of all evil.[97]

As Feygenberg pointed out, Bais Yaakov's relationship to feminism is a complex or even contradictory one. On the one hand, writers, leaders, and ideologues absolutely rejected the language and many of the forms of 'the fight for women's rights' as a secular ideology that glorified rights rather than accepting obligations, that focused on the individual at the expense of religious community, and that encouraged women to abandon their 'natural' modesty and piety. Complaints against male authorities or an unfair system were made only gently, indirectly, and—if possible—garbed in biblical and rabbinic citations. On the other hand, Bais Yaakov literature echoed the language of 'women's awakening', and in its foundational story implicitly (and sometimes explicitly) criticized the organized Jewish world for neglecting its daughters. It could also be argued that the movement in its basic aim was feminist, freeing women to study Torah—an activity accorded the highest religious value in their world, but from which they had been previously excluded. As Joanna Lisek puts it, the journal's official 'position was

[96] According to Bacon, the Agudah was compelled to soften its position when challenged 'from sometimes unexpected directions'. When Eliyahu Kirschenbaum was approached by the Jewish Women's Association (YFA), he asserted that opposition to women's suffrage only referred to *kehilah* (community) elections, since these involved religious communal matters; the Agudah supported women's full equality in general political matters. See Bacon, *The Politics of Tradition*, 255–6. On the Agudah's electoral calculations, see Oleszak 'The Beit Ya'akov School in Kraków', 281.

[97] Feygenberg, 'The Agudah' (Yid.), 6.

hostile to the emancipation of women, but in practice [Bais Yaakov] was a consequence of it'. Lisek's reading of this unacknowledged feminism is that it served as a strategic incorporation of modern trends for the purposes of maintaining a threatened religious culture: 'The combination of ideological conservatism with modern strategies of action within the *Beys Yakov* movement and *Bnoys Agudas Yisroel* can be perceived in terms of so-called defensive modernisation.'[98] Whether its feminism represented a defensive strategy or a sincere embrace of women's rights, Bais Yaakov demonstrated its closeness to currents of modern life it claimed only to oppose. In combating feminism, the movement was required to construct for itself and for other interested parties an understanding of Orthodoxy that could refute those who characterized Orthodoxy as patriarchal and oppressive to women. This discourse found ways—some more persuasive than others—to demonstrate that Judaism, the Torah, and Orthodoxy evinced only the highest respect for the dignity, rights, and value of Jewish women. But even the necessity for constructing an Orthodox apologetics could itself be considered a feminist accomplishment, an acknowledgement that it was important to consider how women understood and experienced Judaism.

Yiddishism was the last of the broader cultural influences to make a mark on Bais Yaakov. It emerged only in 1929, when what could be called an Orthodox Yiddish revival began to manifest itself in Agudah periodicals. Nowhere did Orthodox Yiddishism have a greater impact than in Bais Yaakov and Bnos, where Yiddish was taken up as a central ideology, course of study, and cultural practice.[99] Curiously, this phenomenon had its origins not in eastern Europe, as one might expect, but rather in central Europe, with the powerful influence of the charismatic figure of Nathan Birnbaum (1864–1937) on the Agudah. Birnbaum was an activist and innovative thinker who "returned" to Orthodoxy after many years of 'exile' as a leader of both the secular Yiddish and Zionist camps. In one of his earliest publications after this return, *In Exile among Jews* (1920), he spoke about the need to revive Orthodoxy and raise the self-esteem of the Orthodox masses, who believed the secularists' claim that 'outside all is light, while inside [Judaism] reigns darkness'. Yiddish was an important tool in recovering the

[98] Lisek, 'Orthodox Yiddishism', 141.

[99] For a comprehensive analysis of Orthodox Yiddishism in the pages of the *Bais Yaakov Journal*, see Lisek, 'Orthodox Yiddishism'. Bais Yaakov Yiddishism seems to have been concentrated in Poland; in Lithuania, the *Bais Yaakov Ruf* was printed partly in Hebrew, and the paper rarely mentions Yiddish as an ideology or programme. The Orthodox Yiddish that was being revived and standardized was based on the Polish Yiddish rather than the Lithuanian Yiddish pronunciation.

honour and glory of tradition against all competitors, since 'among us, Yiddish is cherished as the language of our mothers and fathers, the language spoken by Jews in the east for hundreds of years, in which they have implanted their Jewish souls, filling it with *yiddishkeit*'.[100] Birnbaum had many fans among the editorial staff of the *Bais Yaakov Journal*, and his life story appealed to readers, who devoured accounts of young women who returned to Orthodoxy. The journal prominently featured his articles, accompanied by his photo (or a line portrait), and devoted an issue to his thought after his death in 1937, proclaiming his *shloshim* (the thirtieth day after his death) as a time for 'gatherings, eulogies, and memorials to the great personality, Nathan Birnbaum, of blessed memory'.[101]

Birnbaum's Yiddishism was bolstered by his son Solomon (Shloyme) Birnbaum, eminent professor of Yiddish at the University of Hamburg from 1922 to 1933, who standardized an Orthodox Yiddish orthography and Polish Yiddish pronunciation that was distinct from the YIVO, Lithuanian-influenced orthography.[102] He also wrote curricular material for use in Bais Yaakov, and edited a guest issue of the *Bais Yaakov Journal* on the subject of Yiddish.[103] The ideology of Orthodox Yiddishism expressed a commitment to the language spoken by traditional observant Jews, a language that was imbued with religious warmth and meaning, a 'language of the heart'. Loyalty to Yiddish was not for the sake of the language, as adherents argued was true for secular Yiddishists, but solely because of its long association with traditional Jewish life. While Orthodox Yiddishists were always careful to set themselves apart from those they called *Yidishistn apikorsim* ('Yiddishist heretics'), secular Yiddishists were often willing to overlook this hostility, so eager were they to encourage support for Yiddish among the Orthodox Jewish masses. Zalman Reisen, a Yiddish literary historian and journalist, praised the 'type of Orthodox Yiddishism embodied by the Bais Yaakov organization', acknowledging that Bais Yaakov distanced itself from secular

[100] N. Birnbaum, *In Exile among Jews* (Yid.), 3, 5.

[101] *Bais Yaakov Journal*, 142 (1937), is the Nathan Birnbaum special issue, entirely devoted to his life and work.

[102] Solomon's younger brother, Uriel Birnbaum, was a well-known graphic artist and illustrator who illustrated many Agudah and Bais Yaakov publications in his distinctive modernist style.

[103] As Lisek writes, the new orthography was discussed at the second national conference of the Agudah in Warsaw in 1930, supported by various publications beginning with Solomon Birnbaum's *Yidish und Yidishkeit* (Warsaw, 1925), and implemented in the *Bais Yaakov Journal* by 1930. This orthography, based on the Polish dialect, is marked by the frequent use of *yod* where YIVO would use *ayin* (so, *gigangin* rather than *gegangn*). See Lisek, 'Orthodox Yiddishism', 143. The special issue on Yiddish guest-edited by Solomon Birnbaum was *Bais Yaakov Journal*, 71/2 (1931).

Yiddishists, but nevertheless appreciating all that Bais Yaakov had done for the language.[104]

It was not entirely true that secular Yiddishists were uninterested in the historical connections between the language and traditional Jews, but these connections were certainly far more central to Orthodox Yiddishists, and in Bais Yaakov and Bnos the particular historical connection was made to early generations of Yiddish-speaking women. The *Bais Yaakov Journal* published articles about the *Tsene-rene* (the Yiddish-language 'women's Bible') and some writers dwelled on Yiddish as the *mameloshn*, the language of traditional mothers.[105] Eliezer Gershon Friedenson's cleverly entitled article, 'The Tongue in a Mother's Mouth', suggested that Yiddish was the natural language of Jewish mothers even as it felt the need to exhort readers with the bold proclamation: 'Jewish Mothers Speak Yiddish with Their Children!'[106] Writers fondly remembered the 'good old days' when 'on Friday night, when she was lighting the candles, the Jewish mother would pray the personal Yiddish prayers, warmly embracing the freshly bathed, sabbath-dressed daughter who stood by her side . . . and the grandmother would sit down with the *Tsene-rene* after the meal and her little granddaughter Rivkele would immediately come sit on her lap.' In these warm encounters, daughters found spiritual meaning and companionship that included both female ancestors and the language they spoke, 'our loyal companion Yiddish, the *mameloshn*'.[107] Birnbaum even suggested that traditional terms for Jewish women like *isha*, *yidene*, or *vayb* be restored, and the term *froy*, which was borrowed from modern German and increasingly displaced these old Yiddish terms, abandoned: 'The old terms signify *hineh baohel* ['she is in the tent', as befits a modest woman], while the new word has led the *froy* into public life.'[108] Because the newer term for 'woman' reflected a modern understanding of woman's place in society, this reversion to the old Yiddish terms could be mobilized to support a return to more

[104] Zalman Reisen, 'Ortodoksishe yidishizm', *Vilner Tog* (4 Oct. 1931), 269, cited in Lisek, 'Orthodox Yiddishism', 132. I have revised Lisek's translation to conform with my own spelling of Yiddish terms.

[105] The *Tsene-rene*, also known as the 'Women's Bible', was among the most popular and influential books of east European Jewry, a Yiddish adaptation of the Bible and compilation of midrashic sources by Yankev ben Yitskhok Ashkenazi of Janów; the earliest known edition is from 1622.

[106] E. G. Friedenson, 'The Tongue in a Mother's Mouth' (Yid.), 4.

[107] G. Gora, 'The Wellspring of Yiddish' (Yid.), 7.

[108] S. Birnbaum, 'Lady or Woman' (Yid.). These recommendations were never implemented, and the polite way to refer to Sarah Schenirer remained 'Froy Schenirer' (Mrs Schenirer).

traditional roles for Jewish women. Orthodox Yiddishists, in such writings, blended their ideology with a nostalgia for traditional gender roles, in opposition to what they saw as the nationalism, socialism, feminism, and secularism characteristic of their non-Orthodox counterparts. As Sarah Schenirer described the latter, for them 'Yiddish is an end in itself, they try to cut it off from its own roots, which give it its sap—the traditional religious Jewish spirit.'[109]

The revival of Yiddish in Bais Yaakov may be the best illustration of Katz's notion of Orthodoxy as 'traditionalism' rather than 'tradition'. Hence despite the rhetoric that cast Yiddish as the vernacular of hasidic and traditional Jewry and despite the continued use of Yiddish by a considerable number of religious Jews (this was less true in the urban centres of Bais Yaakov), the use of Yiddish in Bais Yaakov was not a natural outgrowth of the movement's connection to a Yiddish-speaking Orthodox society or the traditional past. Rather, it occurred primarily as an ideological effort to breathe new life into a language associated with tradition, but which many traditional Jews had already abandoned. In fact, Bais Yaakov was largely not a Yiddish-speaking environment (again, with the exception of the schools in many smaller towns). With German-speaking teachers and administrators working in all three of the seminaries, the language of instruction was frequently German. The curriculum of the Kraków seminary originally included formal instruction in the German language, which no doubt helped students understand teachers and read the canonical works of Hirsch and his followers that populated the library's shelves. Polish, too, was a language of instruction in those parts of the system that offered a secular programme (high schools and seminaries); it was also the language students spoke and read. The *Bais Yaakov Journal* had a Polish-language supplement from the third issue (1924) until 1930, when the new atmosphere of the Orthodox Yiddish revival made it ideologically incorrect.[110] Even then, many in the movement insisted that promoting it in Polish was crucial to attract parents and girls in the big cities. Speaking of the first years of Bais Yaakov, one student writes that 'the whole atmosphere around us was Polish'. Even in the summer colonies, 'we met Orthodox Jews who spoke only Polish', and in Kraków, 'hasidic men walked through the Jewish neighbourhood on sabbaths in their *shtreymls* [special fur hats], chatting in Polish'.[111] Even after the 1929 adoption of Orthodox Yiddishism as an ideology, as the American

[109] Schenirer, 'Yiddish and Yiddishkeit' (Yid.), in *Bais Yaakov Journal*, 71–2 (1931), cited in Lisek, 'Orthodox Yiddishism', 145.

[110] The journal did publish one Polish supplement in 1936, on the pressing issue of antisemitism.

[111] Y. Gora, 'The Early Days of the Bais Yaakov Movement' (Heb.), 173.

Chava Weinberg Pincus recalled, 'Some of the lectures were in German', and Hirsch's works were read in the original, 'a difficult, classical German'. Weinberg Pincus, who spent the 1932/3 school year in the Kraków seminary, also remembers that, despite Sarah Schenirer's frequent appeals, the girls 'were always chatting in Polish'.[112]

Sarah Schenirer herself, according to a memorial article by Yehudah Leib Orlean, took on the cause of Orthodox Yiddishism before she had fully mastered the language: 'Despite her complete mastery of Polish and German, she moved decisively towards the Jewish tongue, even if she did not yet have a full grasp of its grammar, made many mistakes, and felt at every step the absence of words and expressions for what she needed to say. But she did not give up.'[113] Birnbaum notes that her Yiddish was touched at first by German influence, both in writing and speech: 'But such a person could not remain so German or *daytshmerish* [Germanized Yiddish].'[114] The attempt to create a solely Yiddish-speaking environment was carried out with particular energy in Bnos, which, as a youth movement, was the best field for the battle against 'language-assimilation'. In many conferences, beginning with a regional conference in 1929, it announced it would henceforth require its members to speak Yiddish, in group meetings, if not elsewhere. At the 1937 Bnos conference, members were also encouraged to take on (or move back to) Yiddish or Hebrew names. But enormous efforts were required to cajole girls into speaking the language, even for special occasions or temporary periods. As the repeated exhortations testify, it was an uphill battle.

The proximity of Bais Yaakov to certain modern ideologies which it also saw as rivals is not just of heuristic interest, a way of understanding its character as an 'old-new' social phenomenon. It also had real sociological implications for the way its history played out in the larger landscape of interwar Polish Orthodoxy. While Bais Yaakov saw itself as combating these movements and took pains to differentiate itself from each of them, Orthodox girls and even their parents were less likely to see absolute distinctions between these different camps. Even activists could not always be counted on to toe the ideological line, as attested

112 Rubin (ed.), *Daughters of Destiny*, 195 and 203. Sara Seidman, who studied in Czernowitz in the late 1930s, similarly remembers that many teachers taught in German; occasional lectures by local rabbis, on the other hand, were generally in Yiddish.

113 Orlean, 'A Woman of Valour' (Heb.), 42. Nevertheless, Orlean continues, Schenirer was no 'language fanatic'. She recognized reality, and always showed a particular interest in the secular languages and subjects taught in Bais Yaakov schools. Moreover, she always recommended to her students that they study foreign languages, 'which are an important tool in life, enabling communication between people and nations'.

114 S. Birnbaum, 'Lady or Woman' (Yid.).

by Orlean's speech about Agudah discipline in Bais Yaakov or Sarah Schenirer's lament about 'Bais Yaakov teachers, who when they marry, manage to wriggle out of wearing *sheytlakh* [wigs]', and other complaints about Bnos girls who were Bnos 'in name only'.[115] Perhaps it is no surprise that, when Bais Yaakov teachers in Warsaw went on strike in 1934 to protest that they had not received paycheques in eight months, teachers in other schools in the community went on strike in solidarity.[116] Parents sent their daughters to Bais Yaakov supplemental schools for all sorts of reasons. Among the marketing ploys used by the movement's teachers was public performance, bringing theatre to small towns that had never experienced such pleasures. As Yaffa Gora writes about the Hanukah play she staged in Bychawa, 'The whole town was astir. It was the highlight of the year, and it was because of such plays that we succeeded in attracting to the Bais Yaakov school even pupils from the most distant families, since their girls felt that we were a source of joy, and longed to be part of our group.' After seeing her daughter act in a Bais Yaakov play, one mother said: 'I was angry at you, since our family is irreligious and our daughter wanted to go to your school only because of our neighbour. But today I felt that you gave meaning and substance to her Jewish education.'[117]

The young women's motives for attending Bais Yaakov seminaries, similarly, did not all conform with the movement's ideals. Sarah Schenirer's fears that a fancy new building could lead to diminished idealism were thus not entirely unfounded.[118] 'Esther', who never managed to attend the seminary, was eager to enrol not only because of her religious enthusiasm and intellectual ambitions but also because she desperately needed to find work, and teaching seemed to her an appealing profession. Gutta Sternbuch was sent by her parents. When characterizing her Bais Yaakov pupils, she described them as 'dreamers' who 'aspired to a spiritual life', an idealism that culminated for some of them, she writes, in their future leadership of political movements.[119] In other words,

115 Orlean, 'The Bais Yaakov Movement on Firm Foundations' (Yid.), 6, and Schenirer, 'The Last Night on Augustiańska 30' (Yid.), 4.

116 'The Strike in Bais Yaakov Schools' (Yid.), 5–6.

117 Y. Gora, 'The Early Days of the Bais Yaakov Movement' (Heb.), 171.

118 See Schenirer, 'The Last Night on Augustiańska 30' (Yid.), 4.

119 These 'dreamers' included two members of the Vitalzon family, who were descendants of Rabbi Haym Vital and followers of the Gerer Rebbe. Pessia and Dina Vitalzon were among the first graduates of Bais Yaakov in Warsaw. Dina became a communist and married Michael Greenberg, who earned the Hero of Stalingrad award for his wartime service in the Russian army and served after that as Minister of Commerce and Industry in Poland. Pessia taught at a Bais Yaakov

the idealism of Bais Yaakov, which was supposed to work as inoculation against other forms of idealism, sometimes acted as a bridge between the worlds of Orthodoxy and radical politics, as part of a single widespread yearning for something different that had overtaken Polish Jewish culture, and in which Bais Yaakov was only a single strand. 'Esther' devours the books she finds in the Bais Yaakov library by Marcus Lehmann and Selig Schachnowitz, but that does not stop her from also enjoying the historical novels of Sienkiewicz, Prus, and Orzeszkowa, all of them not Jewish, even reading, with guilty fascination, a book about 'the early Christian martyrs'. Despite the attempts to wall off Orthodox practices from all others, Bais Yaakov girls lived in an environment in which multiple affiliations and blurred boundaries between ideological circles allowed them to pick and choose from a range of offerings, even combining options that ostensibly stood in absolute contradiction.

This cultural field might also explain the mysterious case of Chana (or Chantshe) Baila Halshtok, described in an article by Aaron Zigelman in the memorial book of the town of Parysów. Zigelman recounts the remarkable story of a Bais Yaakov girl who arrived in town just in time to lead a new Bais Yaakov school, founded in the wake of a wave of Agudah enthusiasm that had caught up the local youth:

The young principal of the Bais Yaakov in Parysów, a charming and talented young woman, cleverly managed to attract all the girls who had joined Mizrahi and other movements back to the bosom of the Agudah. Chantshe Baila wanted to demonstrate that she had the power to bring back young people who had gone off the straight and narrow and distanced themselves from the world of Agudath Israel. For this mission she got in contact with a few members of the Tse'irei Agudah in town, telling them of her intentions. But these connections became just a little too tight. Suddenly it became clear that all of Chantshe Baila's work on behalf of Bais Yaakov and among the youth of Tse'irei Agudah was only an attempt to open the eyes of these young men and women and to seduce them away from the old-fashioned values and darkness in which they had been living up to that time.

With her excellent rhetorical skills, knowledge of general and Jewish literature, and unique abilities of persuasion, Chantshe Baila succeeded in luring the people she encountered to her revolutionary views. She also managed to solidify a loyal cadre of young followers who went wherever she went and agreed with every word she uttered.[120]

in Warsaw and was among the recipients of the certificate to Palestine in 1934 that Bnos lobbied for its members to receive, but once in Palestine, she became a Zionist activist in the Bnei Akiva and Hapoel Hamizrahi movements. (See <http://www.sztetl.org.pl/>.)

120 Zigelman, 'The Agudah and Bais Yaakov in Parysów' (Heb.), 64.

Chantshe Baila's clandestine activities in Parysów were exposed when a delivery of books she had ordered for the Bnos reading room were accidentally shipped to the wrong address; the books were from a communist publishing house. The gifted young woman left the town, and Bais Yaakov and Agudah activities in Parysów, according to the memoir, never recovered from the blow.

How are we to understand this curious episode? Zigelman seems certain that Chana Baila Holshtok was using Bais Yaakov as a cover for communist activity, in the same way that yeshiva students attracted to the Haskalah in the nineteenth century worked as tutors in small towns not only as a means of survival, but also to create a channel that could help them influence the town's youth. In this case, the young woman's radical politics would have created a further incentive for secrecy, since she would be hiding her views both from Orthodox authority figures and from the government.

But there is another intriguing possibility, which is that Holshtok was both a communist and a Bais Yaakov teacher, and that such hybrid identities were possible—though certainly not sanctioned. Bacon notes that Bais Yaakov and Bnos libraries and reading rooms were less carefully supervised than those of young Orthodox men: 'Alongside the new works of orthodox popular literature, the bookshelves might hold secular Polish novels—a far cry from the rabbinic tomes of the yeshiva students.'[121] Perhaps communist literature, too, was not entirely out of bounds for women's reading, as long as books were shipped to the right address. Holshtok's case recalls that of Shmuel Nadler, who dramatically renounced his affiliation with Agudath Israel in favour of the communist party at a public lecture at the Warsaw Jewish Literary Union in January 1934.[122] Beatrice Lang Caplan has shown that Nadler may have been drifting away from Orthodoxy much earlier than that, during the very years that he spent contributing to the *Bais Yaakov Journal*.[123] Perhaps in retrospect it is not surprising that Nadler gave such rousingly militant speeches to Bnos audiences as 'To the Barricades, Judith!' which begins by asking: 'Where are you, O proud, powerful, long-ago

[121] Bacon cites two other memorial books on this point: *Belchatow Yizkor Bukh*, 322, and *Wierushow—Sefer Yizkor*, 156. See *The Politics of Tradition*, 173.

[122] Nadler was reacting to the way the Warsaw Agudah shut down the Khinukh play discussed in Chapter 3, as well as what he considered the passivity and hypocrisy of Agudah in general. For more on this incident, see Portnoy, 'Politics and Poesy'.

[123] Caplan cites letters from Rabbi Shapiro to his young student in which he expresses his fear that Nadler is on the verge of abandoning Orthodoxy, published by Rabbi Eliezer Katzman in *Yeshurun*, 16 (2005), 270–5. See Caplan, 'Shmuel Nadler's *Besht-Simfonye*', 602.

Judith? Where are you today, heroine of Jewish strength, of strong Jewishness?'[124]

To put this more succinctly, the membership of the various Agudah and Bais Yaakov organizations was no doubt rarely as ideologically pure as the leadership may have wished or as the movements' publicity depicted them. Not only students like the socialist friend of 'Esther', but also Bais Yaakov teachers like Holshtok and even leading lights of Agudah literature like Nadler were groping their way to a consistent world-view, in which demands for social justice, dreams of rebuilding the Land of Israel, passion for the revival of traditional Jewish life, attraction to secular culture, and other strong pushes and pulls roiled within a single heart and mind. In the case of Chana Baila Holshtok, it may be impossible to judge with the information we have whether she was some kind of double agent or merely a complicated person (or both). But her case, like that of 'Esther', should alert us that the banner of Bais Yaakov flew over a more variegated landscape than its own literature was generally prepared to acknowledge.

Along with the modern movements from which Bais Yaakov drew, there was another model Bais Yaakov used in constructing its distinctive culture—the traditional family. It was the traditional family it was committed to restoring, in its beauty, piety, and harmony. This was the one influence it was proud to acknowledge and happy to embrace. Nevertheless, the family had a much larger role in the language of Bais Yaakov than it did in its cultural practices. More specifically, the movement read family and kinship metaphorically to include the exciting new social relationships it engendered between teacher, pupil, founder, students, and followers. Bais Yaakov often claimed to be rebuilding the traditional family devastated by modernity, but its more immediate effects in the high-status circles of the seminaries, working teachers, and Bnos leaders were to displace or replace the family, taking young women away from their home lives and into the 'total institution' of a seminary, summer camp, or youth group. Breindel Klepfish, describing her experience in the Bais Yaakov seminary in Kraków, writes that 'We live like one big family. We have a mother—Mrs Sarah Schenirer, we have teachers, but the relationship between teacher and student is so close that it is as if we were sisters,' adding that 'We do have a stern task-master and spiritual director, Mr Y. Orlean, but even his rebukes are so mild!' The seminary resembles a family, with a loving 'mother', a stern (but mild) 'father', and the teachers who are really older 'sisters'. Klepfish continues: 'Friday night. The candles are still burning when we return from the synagogue, singing the holy tune "Shalom

[124] Nadler, 'To the Barricades, Judith!' (Yid.), 7.

Aleichem". Mrs Schenirer makes the blessing over the wine, and then there are songs and the "Torah" that we say at the table. A feast of joy and satisfaction.'[125]

The 'big family' of the seminary mimics the Friday night practices of a traditional family, from candle-lighting to synagogue, returning home, and celebrating with a festive meal. But the girls, unusually, go to synagogue on Friday night. And as is evident from other descriptions of sabbath eves in the seminary, Orlean stays away or leaves before the (halakhically immodest) female singing can begin. Kiddush is not recited, as one would expect, by a father, but by the 'mother', and the 'family' at the table is composed entirely of women and girls.

While Bais Yaakov aimed to reproduce the warmth of a family in the supplemental schools, where the teacher was supposed to serve as both 'mother' and 'father' to the young pupils, this effect was greatest in the seminaries and summer colonies, where young women were completely removed from their families and plunged instead into an all-embracing world. Bais Yaakov also removed young teachers from their homes and placed them with unknown families in far-flung locations. 'Esther' describes how, traveling at the age of 17 to the small town where she was to found a Bais Yaakov (and where she boarded with the family of the chairman of the school board), she got lost somewhere on the banks of the Vistula. But suddenly, 'I felt a surge of independence within me. I had only one thought: to keep going! I could never give up. I had to accomplish what I had set out to do.'[126] Yaffa Gora, who was part of the first group of Lithuanian girls to study at the Kraków seminary in the 1920s, described her time in Bikhova, where she found herself directing a school at the age of 18: 'I was there for two years, and doubled enrolment from 70 to 150. I would work nine straight hours a day, from noon to 9:30. I was the only teacher, and also the director and the secretary.'[127] Gutta Sternbuch describes her arrival in the small town of Stopnitz (Stopnica), a *shtetl* 'in a cast-away corner that could be found in no atlas and where no train stopped', where she boarded with the family of the ritual slaughterer. Unlike 'Esther', Sternbuch describes her temporary home as 'a heavenly school of simplicity, sincerity, love for others, and for God', relating that she discovered in that house that 'even the most impoverished person possesses something that he can share with others: love and joy'.[128]

125 B. Klepfish, 'The Kraków Dream' (Yid.), 13–14. The word *tish* (table) in the passage may allude to the hasidic *tish*, at which the *rebbe* eats, sings, and discusses Torah with his followers.

126 Shandler (ed.), *Awakening Lives*, 335.

127 Y. Gora, 'The Early Days of the Bais Yaakov Movement', 169.

128 Sternbuch and Kranzler, *Gutta*, 47–8.

The removal of young women from their own family homes was not merely a collateral effect of the operations of a rapidly growing movement, though this was certainly part of the story. Basya Epstein (later, Rebbetzin Bender), who arrived at the Kraków seminary in 1929, describes the administrative stance on this issue:

After graduation, girls were not allowed to go home. Under the Mercaz [Central Bais Yaakov Office] system, directly after completion of their studies in Bais Yaakov, girls were sent to their teaching positions. Teachers were in great demand and time was precious. Letting girls go home would be a waste of that precious time.

Girls were never sent to teach in their hometown. The Mercaz felt that among family and friends girls would be distracted from the job they were trained for and their attention would turn to shidduchim and home life rather than their students. At this time the establishment of Bais Yaakov was crucial and preceded all else.[129]

As Epstein remarks, these rules were intended to maximize the workforce potential of Bais Yaakov graduates in a system in which they were sorely needed. But the rules undoubtedly had another function as well: securing the attachment of young women to the movement against any forces—even such traditional ones as matchmaking—that might pull their attention in other directions.

Bais Yaakov, as a female variation on what Menachem Friedman calls a 'cloistered community of learned youth', had a particularly complicated relationship with the family it was replacing. Traditionally, girls and young women were more tightly connected than boys to the family and the home, whether the home to which they would return, or the one which they would build as wives and mothers. This difference may account for the ubiquity and richness of family discourse in Bais Yaakov as opposed to yeshivas. By constructing kinship ties among unrelated individuals, the movement managed to obscure the extent to which these replaced, displaced, and postponed more traditional varieties of family relationships. In her moving last letter to her students, Sarah Schenirer explicitly compared the two forms of family—'spiritual' and biological:

Since this morning, I have not been able to stop crying. I, who always complained to you about how difficult it was for me to cry during prayer, suddenly feel for the first time the strength of the spiritual ties that bind me to my children. You undoubtedly remember how I always used to quote a Polish proverb, 'Blood is not water, a soul is not a body'. Yes, spiritual bonds are stronger, since they last forever!

The act of writing a will, a genre normally addressed to family heirs, may have

[129] Rubin (ed.), *Daughters of Destiny*, 178.

Figure 5.2 The training course in Rabka, 1928. Tsila Neugroschel (whose married names were first Orlean and then Sorotzkin), who was a student in that year, is leading a discussion at the left. Three teachers are in the front row among the students: in front of the chair, with a white collar, is Lotka Szczarańska; Judith Grunfeld-Rosenbaum is fourth from the right in the first row, also with a white collar; standing on the far right is Linke Schreiber from Vienna. This widely circulated photograph first appeared, with captions that allow the identification of these figures, in *Bais Yaakov Journal*, no. 46 (1929), p. 16. The accompanying story identifies the group as participants in the 1928 three-month-long summer training programme in Rabka, and describes Rabka as the most beautiful and popular spa and resort town in Poland, with healing mineral springs, fresh mountain breezes, magnificent vistas, thick woods with hiking trails, promenades, carriage rides, and a park in which a military band gave concerts twice a day. Jews were prominent in the town's tourism industry, and the town had a synagogue and mikvah. Bais Yaakov occupied two large buildings just outside the town, on a wooded mountaintop. See E. G. Friedenson, 'Pictures and Notes from My Visit to Rabka' (Yid.), 16–17. The photographer, identified as 'Janina', may be Janina Mierzecka, a well-known studio and art photographer who specialized in landscape photographs and portraits.

Courtesy of the Ghetto Fighters' House Museum Photo Archive, Israel

prompted this train of thought. There is also evidence that the final stages of her five-month long battle with cancer brought Sarah Schenirer's family of origin into her daily life, producing some tension (for her, at least) between her kin and her Bais Yaakov 'family'. 'Her relatives, who were trying to ease her pain and discomfort, would guard against anyone and everyone who wanted to see her. But she would always say: "Let them all in. They're my children."'[130] Her wish to see the bond with her students recognized as stronger than mere biological kinship was felt at least as passionately by her students. According to Joseph Friedenson, 'On the day they heard news of her death, tens of thousands of Jewish mothers and daughters rent their clothes and sat *shiva*', practices generally limited to blood relatives.[131] In this vein, Hanoch Teller writes that 'within the year [of Sarah Schenirer's passing] hundreds of Jewish mothers would name their new daughters Sarah'.[132] With practices such as these, Bais Yaakov did not merely appropriate the language of kinship to construct new forms of community, it also reshaped the forms (female) kinship could take within the world of Orthodoxy.

A certain tension already touched on in this study characterized the kinship discourse of Bais Yaakov. On the one hand, Sarah Schenirer's use of the language of sisterhood acknowledged the collaborative and egalitarian spirit of the Bnos and Basya youth movements: speakers addressed Bais Yaakov, Bnos, and Neshei Agudath Israel members as 'sisters' or 'sisters in spirit'; the *Bais Yaakov Journal* ran a column, discussed in Chapter 4, called 'From Sister to Sister'; even men like Friedenson sometimes addressed Bnos members as 'our religious sisters'.[133] Others in Agudah sometimes spoke of the organization as 'sisters and brothers'. Sarah Schenirer herself, however, was always described in anthems, poems, articles, and personal memoirs as 'the mother of Bais Yaakov, who despite being barren had thousands of daughters', or 'Mama Sarah', and in other maternal terms. The midrashic sensibilities of the movement helped bolster and expand this metaphor by linking her to the biblical matriarch who was long barren or, according to rabbinic sources, modestly kept to her tent. The parallel between the biblical Sarah (before she miraculously gives birth to Isaac at the age of 90) and Sarah Schenirer (who was unmarried during most of the period of Bais Yaakov's growth) obscures certain aspects of the latter's life story even while praising her by connection to the first Jewish matriarch. In calling Sarah Schenirer

130 Deutschländer, 'Sarah Schenirer and Bais Yaakov' (Yid.), 11.

131 J. Friedenson, 'The Bais Yaakov Girls' Schools' (Heb.), 62. These rituals are also sometimes performed by students upon the death of a revered teacher, as is certainly the case here.

132 Teller, *Builders*, 454.

133 See E. G. Friedenson, 'On the Hundredth Issue' (Yid.), 1.

a mother, the movement asserted the primal significance of Jewish family and descent while skirting the awkwardness of being led by a woman who spent most of her life outside traditional marriage and family.

Her status as a divorcée must have been plain for her colleagues and students to see, since she wore a wig (as married and divorced Orthodox women do) and was known as Frau (Mrs) Schenirer. Nevertheless, as Deborah Weissman points out, official publications make no mention of her marital status. Only after her death did vague references about her failed first marriage begin to circulate, ascribing its end to 'a family tragedy'.[134] Her Polish diary for the years (roughly) 1910–13, which recently surfaced, sheds light on her first marriage, and helps us see beyond the ubiquitous descriptions of her as a 'simple, pious seamstress'. In addition to running a high-class dressmaking studio, she attended lectures on health and hygiene (including sexual hygiene), children's education, philosophy (including a lecture comparing Leibniz's and Spinoza's conceptions of God), and writers such as Shakespeare, Goethe, and Molière. She was deeply immersed in contemporary Polish culture, mentioning and even quoting the writers Adam Mickiewicz, Juliusz Słowacki, Zygmunt Krasiński, and Stanisław Przybyszewski, and often alluding to her love of theatre. She struggled to reconcile these activities with her religious commitments, but felt that she had little choice but to seek intellectual stimulation outside Orthodox circles.

Marriage seems to have been the most difficult aspect of Sarah Schenirer's life. Unlike the more traditional matchmaking arrangements for her older brother Yehuda, Sarah's parents introduced her to a man she was expected to get to know before they sought her consent for the marriage. Even before she first met Samuel (Shmuel) Nussbaum (referred to as N. in the diary), she confessed to her diary that she was uncomfortable with these arrangements.

> Instead of being happy that they are letting me talk with the boy and get to know him before I get engaged, this meeting makes me strangely apprehensive. I always imagined that it would take place in such an ideally pious context that I wouldn't even be allowed to speak with him before the engagement. In my opinion, 'Torah is the best merchandise', and I've always been convinced that that is true. The best proof is my brother, who exchanged not a word with his wife before their engagement, and look how happy they

[134] *Beit Ya'akov*, 125 (1970), 22, records an obituary by a secular journalist describing Schenirer as having known 'great suffering' in her personal life: 'For many years she was alone, having been divorced from the husband of her youth following a family tragedy. In the later years of her life, she married Rabbi Landau and desired to live a bit for herself' (quoted in Weissman, 'Bais Ya'akov: A Women's Educational Movement', 46).

are. Why do I need this meeting? Would I really have the courage to say 'no, I don't like him'? With my beautiful face and huge bank account, who am I to dream so big?[135]

The more familiar narrative of Jewish modernization involves young women who dream of lovers who resemble the heroes of romance novels. Sarah Schenirer in some ways shared this narrative, objecting to her parents' matchmaking efforts and dreaming of something different than the man her parents found for her. But in her case, the man she dreamed of marrying was not a Polish hero but a 'penniless real Jew', a man like her beloved younger brother Shimon, whom she refers to as her 'ideal husband'. Despite this dream, the diary entry for 1 October 1910 records that she had agreed to become engaged to the far-from-penniless Nussbaum. 'I don't fancy the man in any way, but I didn't have the courage to say no', both because she dreaded disappointing her parents and had no confidence in her own worth. She confided to her diary that her friends and family considered her lucky to have found a man at all. The engagement brought teas with her prospective mother-in-law, assembling a trousseau, the exchange of gifts, misery, and doubt. As she wrote:

It's been a year since I first laid eyes on him and my feelings are just the same. Am I really such a cold-blooded creature, with no warmth in me? Or is the problem his personality? Or perhaps I'm just anxious about the future and making a living. But the future will take care of itself. Today, against my wishes and my will, we set a wedding date. Now the real misery begins. I'm too upset to gather my thoughts, my heart overflows with tears even while my eyes are dry.

Her diary records her hope for some grand event that would bring a halt to the wedding—the Messiah coming, the end of the world, even Halley's comet, which appeared in April 1910 (but failed to produce the hoped-for change).

She felt religious exaltation at the ritual immersion that preceded the ceremony, but her marriage itself was far less meaningful. The entry for 1 December 1910 reads:

At last, I'm alone, if only for a minute. It's all true. It's not a nightmare, like all those I had when I was still unmarried. The music is still ringing in my head. The dancing, the wedding, the visits, the congratulations everywhere I turned. It's been only two weeks since the wedding and, already, all my illusions about wedded bliss have vanished. Such happiness belongs only to women with prettier faces or more money. But am I really so ugly that I can't arouse warmer feelings? I ask for so little! All I want to do is work on both the material and spiritual plane, but he has no interest in that kind of work![136]

[135] *Sara Shenirer: Pisma Autobiograficzne.* The manuscript I was shown was still not typeset, and diary entries were still unclear in places.

[136] The Archiwum Narodowe w Krakowie (National Archive in Kraków), reference code

She was hurt that her husband showed her no love, concerned that she felt nothing for him, and upset that he took no interest in her spiritual aspirations, although he was happy enough with her financial contributions to the household. She wondered whether she was unique in these experiences, or whether her newly married friends were not as blissful as everyone assumed. On 17 November 1911, her first anniversary (according to the Hebrew date of the wedding), after resisting pressure from her husband and parents to give the marriage more time, she wrote, 'I have resolved that this is the absolute end. To show that I was serious, I removed my belongings from the apartment.' Despite the difficulty of this decision, the entry ends on a note of optimism and humour: 'But I want to end this chapter of my diary differently. With hope for a better future, with an intense desire to do something better for Jewry, perhaps within the Orthodox community. Oh, my dreams, my enthusiasm, my—shyness. It's almost funny.' Under pressure from parents and her husband, she reconciled with her husband a few times, but these efforts were futile and the marriage ended in 1913.

The diary sheds light on her first marriage, but questions remain. Was Nussbaum the first and only man her parents arranged for her to meet, as seems to be the case? Why was her marriage arranged along more modern lines than that of her older brother? Was his marriage arranged in hasidic circles to which she had no access? Were her parents less traditional or more modern than she was or wished to be? Were they trying to conform to their idea of what a young woman would prefer, perhaps based on their experience with their other daughters? Did the fact that she was marrying at the relatively late age of 27 limit her options? Whatever the case, the 'family tragedy' to which Bais Yaakov ascribes the failure of this marriage obscures the role that she herself played in this drama, in which she sought a divorce against strong pressure placed on her by both her parents and husband. It also obscures the degree to which she resisted the (Orthodox) marriage arranged for her because she felt it to be too bourgeois, too concerned with money and respectability, and not open enough to her own religious and intellectual aspirations. This kind of marriage seemed to be informed by new conceptions of romance, mutual love, and companionship that she shared, at least to some degree. She, too, hoped to find a true companion in her life's work, and dreamed that her marriage would be based on mutual love, attraction,

29/1472/0/2/538, no. 238, p. 35, records the marriage of Samuel Nussbaum, aged 28 years and 10 months, to Sarah Schenirer, aged 27 years and 4 months, on 28 Nov. 1910, with the further notation that the marriage was dissolved on 10 June 1913. If she was writing two weeks after her marriage, the diary entry of 1 December may be misdated.

and respect. But these same new conceptions of marriage could work against a woman of no beauty or wealth (as she saw herself), reducing her value in the new marriage market, where beauty and wealth had displaced the traditional emphasis on family pedigree and learning. From her perspective, expectations of wedded bliss only deepened the disappointment and self-doubt when this bliss failed to materialize.

Her unhappiness during this period was not limited to her marriage. As nearly every entry in the diary attests, she longed to work for her 'Jewish sisters', and felt empty and bored living a life that revolved around economic concerns and superficial social engagements. What this work would be was far from clear: The diary records a short-lived interest in public health, and the thought that she might join a cousin in Chicago, in the hope that a change of scene would open new opportunities. There were obstacles to fulfilling her ambitions beyond their amorphous character: her parents and husband had no interest in these dreams, and her friends considered her ambitions odd. Given this context, she was often shy about sharing her dreams. Of the people she spent time with, only her brother Shimon shared her religious passion. More generally, the society she lived in simply lacked outlets or structures for her religious aspirations. As she wrote in late 1912, 'Life drags on so monotonously. There is nothing in the Orthodox world for women to do.' Judith Grunfeld-Rosenbaum remembered that Sarah Schenirer spoke with envy of the spiritual experiences available in her society to hasidic men.[137] In his memorial speech after her death, Deutschländer touched on what he imagined (or perhaps knew) to be Sarah Schenirer's desires to participate in such pleasures: 'How strong must have been her desire to visit a Jewish *ḥeder*, to spend time in a yeshiva, sit at a hasidic *rebbe*'s table, participate in an important men's gathering. For those were certainly for her the brightest places, the most cherished ideals.'[138] Her diary records how envious she was of Shimon, who received a marriage gift of the complete Talmud from his friends and intellectual comrades, while her circle of friends and relatives exchanged jewellery and chatted about clothes. In this way, her hasidic brother provided Sarah Schenirer with a model not only of an ideal spouse but also of the kind of life she longed to lead.

The fuller image of Sarah Schenirer that emerges from this diary is of interest not only for purely biographical reasons. It also illuminates some aspects of the movement she founded. As discussed in Chapter 1, the rabbis who attempted to

[137] See n. 27 above.

[138] Deutschländer, 'Sarah Schenirer and Bais Yaakov' (Yid.), 10. See the discussion in Chapter 4.

respond to the crisis of girls' defections from Orthodoxy were dealing with an issue that lay far outside their experience or expertise. The pressing need, from the rabbinic perspective, was to secure the religious commitments of the next generation of Jewish wives and mothers, finding ways to meet 'the needs of the hour' within the constraints of Jewish law. Bais Yaakov literature portrays Sarah Schenirer as essentially sharing the concerns that drove these rabbis. Such Orthodox writers as Abraham Joseph Wolf stress her piety and respect for the Torah, emphasizing that 'she did not take a step to found a school until she received the consent of the Belzer Rebbe'. Wolf's defence of Bais Yaakov against the charge that it was innovative is bolstered by the regret he claims Sarah Schenirer felt in creating a youth culture that deviated from the ideal model of the traditional Jewish home. Any changes she made in girls' education were accompanied by 'nostalgia and longing for the way things had once been . . . If only Bais Yaakov could reach the level that earlier generations had reached with only mothers teaching daughters.'[139] But there is little evidence that she longed to turn back the clock to the times when girls could get all the religious education they needed within their own homes, or that she ever regretted the revolution she accomplished. Among the many obstacles to fulfilling her dreams that she writes about in the diary, she never mentions the halakhic limitations to girls' Torah study or worries about securing rabbinic permission. Her points of reference are not rabbinic or halakhic but rather social and cultural, reflecting her exclusion as a woman from Orthodox religious experiences, and her exclusion as an Orthodox Jew from the youth movements of her day. And while rabbis and activists hoped to bring Jewish girls and young women back to Orthodoxy to secure their function as wives and mothers, the religious experiences she hoped to share with these women had intrinsic religious value, connected girls and women with each other, and fulfilled her own most profound desires and dreams. In brief, what her diary makes clear is that she was looking not only to rescue other young women for Orthodoxy (although she certainly was hoping to do that), but also to find a way for *herself* to live a spiritual Jewish life. It may be key to its success that Bais Yaakov was led by a woman who was emotionally invested in constructing a culture in which women like herself might find work, intellectual engagement, companionship, and love.

Sarah Schenirer not only lent the movement much of its distinctive character, she also served as its living embodiment, its 'loving mother', as Bais Yaakov

[139] Wolf, 'Did Sarah Schenirer Innovate?' (Heb.), 38–9.

literature misses no chance to remind us. This discourse, however, could not entirely domesticate the ways her role as founder, pedagogue, publicist, and writer exceeded and displaced the maternal role. In an article entitled 'Sarah Schenirer: The Mother of Generations', Joseph Friedenson describes her piety and writes, 'No wonder she was called "the female version of the Chofetz Chaim".'[140] When Pearl Benisch was asked if Sarah Schenirer was a *chassidiste* (female hasid), she answered that she was rather a hasid 'in the full sense of the word'. Benisch added, 'In fact, there were Hasidic rebbes who used to stand up for her when she entered a room.'[141] These allusions to her stature in Orthodox society hint at the ways that her piety, saintliness, and religious activities were understood to take on traits previously associated only with the world of Orthodox men, and even to impinge on male prerogatives: leading a school, publishing books, running an organization, being venerated as a sage or a saint, giving public lectures, traveling widely without a man at her side. The tension between the male and female roles that she was to play in Bais Yaakov already appears in her diary, which moves between describing the penniless hasid she dreamed of marrying and the religious life she wished to experience herself. I would argue that, in this way, she vacillated between wishing to *marry* and wishing to *be* (a man like) her brother, in a cultural environment in which religious activism and enthusiasm were associated with men rather than educated young women. Bais Yaakov, more generally, was a place where girls and women could try on roles previously reserved for boys and men (literally, in the school plays in which girls donned beards and wore trousers). Yehudah Leib Orlean, describing Bais Yaakov as a substitute for the Jewish home that 'had become dull and dry', suggests that its teachers are required to 'fill the role of the father and mother'.[142] In this way and others, Bais Yaakov aimed to produce women who would become Orthodox wives and mothers like their own mothers, while also being women of a new

[140] Joseph Friedenson, 'Sarah Schenirer: The Mother of Generations'. See also the comparisons of Schenirer to other great sages, in Ginsparg Klein, 'A Traditional Revolutionary', 65.

[141] Benisch, *Carry Me in Your Heart*, 245. That Schenirer was not alone in being accorded these honours from the rabbinical establishment is also evident from the biography of her student Vichna Kaplan. According to Kaplan's son, the rabbi of Brisk (where she was serving as a young Bais Yaakov teacher) kept the great sage Rabbi Moshe Feinstein waiting while he spoke with her, explaining his actions by saying 'Yes, she is a young woman, but that young woman can compete with men—and not just any men, but great men.' Leibowitz with Gliksman, *Rebbetzin Vichna Kaplan*, 99.

[142] Yehudah Leib Orlean, 'Our Way', Jubilee Edition, Central Organization of World Agudath Israel (Autumn 1936), 65–7, quoted in Atkin, *The Beth Jacob Movement in Poland*, 84–5.

kind, female counterparts to the yeshiva students and young hasidim of Poland who resembled their fathers and brothers more closely than their mothers.

As I discussed in Chapter 2, the character of the Bais Yaakov 'family' has a generational as well as a gender component. Alongside the language describing Sarah Schenirer as the 'mother of Bais Yaakov', she frequently spoke of the seminarians, young teachers, and other female activists in the movement as her sisters. Given this gap between the metaphors of sisterhood and motherhood within the movement's discourse, how should we understand her relationship to Bais Yaakov? As a mother (even if she preferred to see herself as a sister)? As a sister (even if her sisters were inclined to see her as a mother)? Perhaps we should look elsewhere in the constellation of family connections for a model. One of the most interesting thinkers who deals with the metaphorical use of family relations to describe cultural transmission (particularly in the realm of literature) is the Russian formalist critic Victor Shklovsky, who revised an earlier model of dynamics that connected literary generations through fathers and sons and divided the possibilities into filial mimicry or rebellion. Shklovsky expands those options, positing that 'The legacy that is passed on from one literary generation to the next moves not from father to son but from uncle to nephew.'[143] That is, authors acquire techniques not (or not only) from their literary 'fathers', or canonized precursors, but also from their literary 'uncles', writers marginal to the literary mainstream in their own time and who had no immediate 'descendants', but who nevertheless belatedly supply new options for younger writers in search of alternatives to their 'parents'. In Shklovsky's model (also called 'the knight's move' for its oblique lines), writers are not limited to being pious followers or daring rebels; they may also be enterprising 'nephews' who seek to expand their options by discovering and borrowing from forgotten uncles.

Sarah Schenirer, I would argue, fulfils the role of a Shklovskian 'aunt', rather than either a 'mother' or a 'sister' in the Bais Yaakov movement. As an adult woman who functioned outside the framework of the traditional family, she was neither mother nor wife, but rather the unmarried aunt at the end of the family table who attracted the admiration of her nieces and became, for a time, their leader, replacing both mother and father. She made her own alternative status available for Bais Yaakov girls, demonstrating the possibility of religious public activism and communal living, in which they participated as individuals and part of a movement, rather than daughters, mothers, or wives. Bais Yaakov and Bnos opened a space between girlhood and womanhood for the experience of educa-

[143] Shklovsky, *Theory of Prose*, 190.

tion, activism, travelling and conferences, and 'sisterhood', and it was Sarah Schenirer who secured the value and legitimacy of this life-stage and all its potential. For many (but not all) Bais Yaakov students and Bnos leaders, this was a temporary status, and they went on, with the movement's blessing or active help, to enter traditional marriages. The *Bais Yaakov Journal* is full of announcements of engagements and marriages of beloved teachers or Bnos leaders. It is significant, however, that such announcements, by the journal's unwritten rules, nearly always listed the bride first, if it named the groom at all (the opposite was the case in announcements in other Agudah publications, where the bride's name was rarely mentioned). It is striking, as well, that Bais Yaakov publications in the post-war period so often mentioned important figures by their maiden names alongside their married names—the 1955 edition of Sarah Schenirer's collected writings, which lists the leading figures and teachers in interwar Bais Yaakov, refers to five teachers by their maiden as well as married names, including the best known of them, Judith Grunfeld-Rosenbaum, who combined an influential career as Bais Yaakov seminary instructor and director with marriage to an illustrious man. This is also the case with other compendiums of Bais Yaakov memoirs I have studied (the literature has not settled on whether hyphenated names should put maiden or married names first). In such unusual naming practices, Bais Yaakov makes evident its interest in women's activities before marriage, implicitly granting legitimacy to their youthful experiences and connections rather than reserving it for the illustrious rabbis they will marry. Given how rare it is within Orthodox circles for women to retain a maiden name, this practice is particularly striking.

Sarah Schenirer's own name is a similarly complex sign. She is typically called Frau Schenirer in Bais Yaakov literature of the interwar-period, signalling with the formal title that she was (once) married (but not to a rabbi, in which case she would have had the title 'Rebbetsin'), a status she also marked in the traditional Orthodox way by covering her hair with a wig. But she combined this title with her maiden name, and while she occasionally used the signature Sarah Landau (Schenirer) after she married Rabbi Yitzhak Landau in 1930 or 1931, the movement continued and continues to remember her by this maiden name.[144] Under

[144] For the signature Sarah Landau (Schenirer), see Dansky, *Rebbetzin Grunfeld*, 132, appended to the dedication of a book Schenirer gave as a wedding gift in 1932 to Judith Grunfeld-Rosenbaum. Rabbi Landau added a few words to his wife's dedication (Rubin (ed.), *Daughters of Destiny*, 176). Pearl Benisch quotes from a late 1930 letter signed 'Sarah Schenirer', and an April 1931 letter signed 'Landau Schenirer'. If she married in late 1930 or early 1931, that would have been shortly before the move from 30 Augustiańska, where according to Chana Wiselewsky Garfinkle she was

the piety of the wig and behind the formality and modernity of the title 'Frau', the persistence of her maiden name 'Schenirer' sends a more complicated signal, one that undercuts the ideal of harmonious Jewish family life so central to Bais Yaakov discourse, and just barely hints at the complicated and well-concealed story about her experience of marriage.[145] In her name and in her story, she provides an implicit alternative to the narrower role of wife and mother reserved for adult Orthodox women.

Sarah Schenirer's symbolic motherhood also serves to obscure her relationship with her actual family of origin. Beyond the pious ancestors and hasidic brother, her family only makes an occasional appearance in her writing or in other Bais Yaakov publications. Nevertheless it is clear from her memoir that, as with many families in the interwar period, hers included members with a wide range of religious affiliations. More details may be gleaned from a 2001 interview with her nephew Tulo Schenirer, who was born in 1927, survived the Kraków ghetto and subsequently the concentration camps of Płaszów and Mauthausen, emigrated from Poland in 1959, and settled in Tel Aviv. As he relates, his paternal grandmother (Sarah's mother) was 'very religious', but his own father Jakob (Sarah's brother), who worked in a bank, was 'traditional but not religious'. Asked about the other siblings, he answers:

There were many, with various convictions, ranging from very religious, to completely secular. The first brother, Abraham, we called him Romek, lived in Kraków—he's the one who was buried in Berlin. He was completely secular. Next was my father, Jakob; after him Aaron, who lived in Leipzig—semi-religious. Next came Szymon (Shimon), who was a judge in a rabbinic court in Kraków from 1935 to 1939. Next Juda (Yehudah), who lived in Tarnów, religious. After that were sisters. First of them: Hela, she married an academic teacher and she herself taught Hebrew . . . At times when she came to visit us, she would sit with me for an hour, and I would learn more from her than I could learn in school for a year—even though I attended a Hebrew school. That sister was moderately religious. Her husband owned a warehouse for iron on Mostowa Street. They lived there in the corner building, just beside the Wisła River. The next sister, Leah Mandel-

living in 1929, to the new seminary (see Rubin, *Daughters of Destiny*, 176). Oddly, it is more difficult to uncover information about her second than her first marriage, despite the interest it must have aroused. The marriage was not mentioned in the *Bais Yaakov Journal*, which regularly featured engagement and wedding announcements. The Kraków city archive yields further information: Sarah Schenirer applied for an identification card under her maiden name in 1933, but the city registry for 1933–4 for 1 Katarzyna (the site of the first seminary) lists 'Sara Landau' as living there. Might she have married that year?

145 On *froy* as a modern replacement for traditional Yiddish terms for woman, and as an emblem of women's entry into public life, see S. Birnbaum, 'Lady or Woman', 10.

baum, married Kalman Mandelbaum . . . They were also moderately religious. The next one was Sarah Schenirer. She got married very late, didn't have children. Moreover, she kept her maiden name. She is very well known. She established Bais Yaakov at Stanisława Street no. 10 or 9. It was near the Wisła River, perpendicular to Dietla Street, along the city's ramparts. My family used to say that the name was in honour of my father, Jakob.[146]

Of these many relatives, Tulo reports that 'they all died. They were in the Tarnów ghetto, and from there they were taken to Bełżec. I only managed to find the daughter of my uncle, my father's brother, who moved to Berlin in 1934 for surgery. He died there and the little girl lived in an orphanage in Berlin. I found her in 1967.' Tulo Schenirer, who died in 2012 in Tel Aviv, kept alive the memory of his aunt and took pride in her achievements.[147]

The accounts of Sarah Schenirer's illness, death, and funeral are among the most vivid and moving in the literature of Bais Yaakov, showing the power of metaphorical kinship while exposing the realities of her life in its final months, when she was drawn back into the world of her biological family.[148] In the most detailed description of those mournful days, an article in the *Bais Yaakov Journal* by 'Our special correspondent' describes the telephone ringing with a 'strange, hoarse tone, an uncanny tone', on a Saturday night at the editorial office in Łódź. Then, 'a stricken voice says, "Tomorrow at noon, the funeral. Our Sarah Schenirer . . ."' Friedenson arrives, hears the news, and 'instinctively everyone stands up. A few dozen Agudah activists . . . Our meeting is cancelled. For the first time—to honour a woman—our Mrs Schenirer.' After an arduous train journey from Łódź to Kraków, where they arrive early on the morning of the funeral, the Agudah activists join the throngs of men, women, and children streaming through a gloomy drizzle towards Sarah Schenirer's apartment on 8 Kordeckiego Street, before which Rabbi Wechsler delivers a brief eulogy. As the procession moves on towards the cemetery, the women and Bais Yaakov students remain in their places:

[146] Pordes and Grin (eds.), 'Tulo Schenirer', 270.

[147] Michal Schenirer Avni, email communication (22 Jan. 2016). According to Michael Goodman, his grandfather Abraham Schenirer had four children, two of whom died in Auschwitz and another who served in the Russian army during the war but whose fate is unknown. His mother Anni was sent from Berlin to England on a *Kindertransport* in 1939 (email communication 19 Dec. 2016). The closest known living descendants of Sarah Schenirer are her four great-nephews and nieces, Anni Goodman's two sons, and Tulo Schenirer's two daughters.

[148] As is common in traditional circles, Bais Yaakov refrained from naming the illness, but Tulo Schenirer, in his interview, describes it as stomach cancer.

In the window on the first floor, in her apartment, stands an old woman, wiping her eyes.

Tears stream down her face as she looks out at the street and wipes them away—

That is her mother. The old mother. The mother of Mrs Sarah Schenirer, of blessed memory. Her eyes follow her daughter through the window. An old rule of the Kraków sages: women do not attend funerals. Not even of close relatives. The mother stands by the window, the children stand on the street, and that is how they follow their mother. Her daughter.[149]

While Bais Yaakov literature devotes pages upon pages to testimony of the remarkably close 'family' that was the movement, Sarah Schenirer's family of origin is rarely mentioned. It is only when she is too weak to walk to the seminary on her own that we catch a rare glimpse of her second husband and her family, who try to stop her from getting out of bed (during her illness, she moved to a nearby apartment to make the walk shorter).[150] Deutschländer also mentions that she recruited her sisters to attend a Bais Yaakov seminary graduation in her place.[151] Tulo's interview gives us a glimpse of the relatives who claimed (or joked?) that Bais Yaakov was named after one of their own. These two families—biological and spiritual—both appear in a striking image, a vertical split screen, of the women left behind as her body is carried to the cemetery: the mother follows her daughter from the apartment window while the 'daughters' watch their 'mother' in the street below. This passage brings into powerful juxtaposition the two families who claimed her as their own; they are united in their shared exclusion as women, united in their shared mourning for Sarah Schenirer, but divided in their separate mourning for 'their mother. Her daughter.' Behind the near-obsessive focus on her role as mother of Bais Yaakov, it turned out, was a woman who was also someone's daughter (and who died too young). The face of a grieving mother thus intrudes, for a moment, on the symbolic motherhood of her daughter. At least for one person watching, the shock and profound grief of Sarah Schenirer's death was accompanied by another shock: the chasm that opened up in the family of Bais Yaakov.

149 'To Eternal Rest' (Yid.), 13.

150 The apartment at 1 Katarzyna Street that was the site of the first seminary remained in Schenirer's hands after the seminary moved to 10 Augustiańska Street, and records show that she was living there in 1933. She, her second husband (Rabbi Yitzchok Landau), and perhaps also her mother had moved to the apartment in 8 Kordeckiego Street a few months before her death. The report of the funeral places Sarah Schenirer's mother in the apartment from which the body was taken to the cemetery, and Pearl Benisch describes Rabbi Landau as comforting the weeping Bais Yaakov girls who were attending Schenirer's body on the sabbath after her death. See Benisch, *Carry Me in Your Heart*, 317.

151 Deutschländer, 'Sarah Schenirer and Bais Yaakov' (Yid.), 10.

EPILOGUE

'Bais Yaakov, Let Us Walk in the Light of the Lord' Destruction and Rebirth

In the days of Jael, caravans ceased
And wayfarers went
By roundabout paths.
Deliverance ceased,
Ceased in Israel,
Till you arose, O Deborah,
Arose, O mother, in Israel!'
(Judg. 5: 6–7)

THE EXPERIMENT that was Bais Yaakov was still expanding at a rapid rate and had hardly had a chance to come into its own when it fell victim to the destruction of European Jewry. Despite the disbanding of Bais Yaakov schools with the outbreak of the Second World War, numerous memoirs and histories of the movement attest to its continued clandestine activity during the war years. Stephen Howard Garrin writes that 'a major factor in the successful operation of the underground religious education network was the work of the *Beis Yaakov* graduates in Poland'.[1] Ella Shmuelevitz, author of the 1937 article on family purity discussed in Chapter 4, continued to teach and lead Bais Yaakov girls in the Kovno ghetto; Faiga Beigel, a 20-year-old activist and teacher, organized prayer services, study sessions, the recitation of psalms, and Torah lectures for Bais Yaakov girls in the Vilna ghetto in what was called a 'Women's House of Study'; and Yehudah Leib Orlean, who fled Kraków after a severe beating, continued to lead the movement in the desperate conditions of the Warsaw ghetto, corresponding with teachers and teaching students for as long as he could.[2] In 1941, there were six

[1] Garrin, 'But I Forsook Not Thy Precepts', 339. The clandestine and underground character of Bais Yaakov schools differed from place to place, and schools came out of hiding if they received permission to operate, as happened in Warsaw in 1941.

[2] See Sorasky, *The History of Torah Education* (Heb.), 439. On Orlean, see also Seidman, *The Warsaw Ghetto Diaries*, 363–9, and *Personalities I Knew*, 200–5. Seidman reports that, by the winter of 1939, Bais Yaakov had recommenced activities in Warsaw; in 1940 twelve Bais Yaakov teachers

Bais Yaakov schools still operating in some form in Warsaw, three of them under the aegis of Orlean while the other three were led by Eliezer Gershon Friedenson and Rivka Alter-Rappaport.[3] Other Bais Yaakov or Bnos groups existed in the ghettos of Kraków, Łódź, Będzin, Tarnów, and even in the camps of Auschwitz and Birkenau.[4]

The networks forged in the interwar movement aided in the rapid re-emergence of Bais Yaakov schools and Bnos groups in the immediate aftermath of the war, for example in the displaced persons camps of Eschwege, Feldafing, Föhrenwald, Frankfurt, Landsberg, and Zeilsheim. Bergen-Belsen had two Bais Yaakov schools and even a rudimentary teachers' seminary.[5] By 1951, there were 150 Bais Yaakov schools and Ohel Sarah kibbutzim in Germany, Austria, Italy, Sweden, France, and (until Soviet regimes shut them down), Czechoslovakia, Hungary, Romania, and Poland. A Bais Yaakov that had served the refugee community in Shanghai continued for a time after the war, and the British detention camp in Cyprus, which held Holocaust survivors attempting to immigrate illegally to Palestine, had both a Bais Yaakov school and a few Bnos chapters.[6] Bais Yaakov established itself more permanently after the Holocaust in the centres of Orthodox life throughout the world, particularly in North America and Israel. Bais Yaakov schools had already been founded in both countries during the interwar period, and the Beth Jacob High School established in 1938 by Sarah Schenirer's student Vichna Kaplan operated under the authority of the Central Office in Europe.

Bais Yaakov activists in both the Land of Israel and New York initially faced considerable difficulties. A brief memoir by Meir Sharansky, who founded the first 'new' Bais Yaakov in Tel Aviv in 1933, recounts the difficult beginnings of Bais Yaakov in a cultural context in which secular Zionism set the tone.[7] The first Bais

were teaching in the ghetto; by 1941 sixteen teachers were leading four Bais Yaakov schools. Orlean himself 'was teaching a group of his remaining students'. For more on the remarkable woman who inspired Bais Yaakov students in Vilna, see Foxman, 'Faigl fun vilner geto', 12.

[3] Garrin, 'But I Forsook Not Thy Precepts', 339.

[4] For this information, see 'Bais Yaakov during the Holocaust', 130–4. For the story of a group of ten Bais Yaakov girls who managed to remain together in Auschwitz and keep their faith, see Benisch, *To Vanquish the Dragon*.

[5] According to Sara Seidman (personal communication), Bergen-Belsen had a few Bais Yaakov seminary graduates; the two schools served pupils from Poland and Hungary respectively.

[6] Weissman, 'Bais Ya'akov: A Women's Educational Movement', 100.

[7] Orthodox girls' schools called Bais Yaakov, with no connection to the European system, with instruction in Yiddish, and with a more limited and traditional approach to curriculum, had

Yaakov class had only seven elementary-age pupils, and in the absence of funds to rent space, the school met on two benches on Rothschild Boulevard, with Rabbi Sharansky and Rivkah Yisraelit, a recent immigrant and graduate of the Kraków seminary, as teachers. Rabbi Sharansky ruefully recalled that in fact he served the struggling school for many years as director, teacher, fundraiser and janitor.[8] Nor was Jerusalem more welcoming, at least initially, despite the city's greater religiosity. In 1934, a public gathering for women at the Rosenberg Hotel in Jerusalem organized by Rabbi Sharansky to discuss the problem of girls' education was abruptly shut down at the last moment by the Chief Rabbi of the Orthodox Council of Jerusalem (the Edah Haharedit), Rabbi Yosef Zvi Dushinsky, who was objecting to the fact that the male speakers would be addressing a female audience; the organizers scrambled to find women speakers, and the meeting eventually went ahead. Despite this hiccup, the first Bais Yaakov in Jerusalem was soon established, with Rabbi Hillel Lieberman as director. An even more fateful turning point came with Eliezer Gershon Friedenson's visit to the country in 1935: he travelled around raising funds and appealing to communities to found schools, and by the end of that year, there were six Bais Yaakov schools in various cities, and Sharansky had established in Tel Aviv the first high school. In 1936, the enterprising Sharansky also founded in Tel Aviv the first Bais Yaakov teachers' seminary, to serve what was now a rapidly growing system.[9] By 1937, just a few years after Sharansky opened the first Bais Yaakov (known as Beit Ya'akov) in Tel Aviv, there were already seventeen schools in the Land of Israel, including five in Jerusalem, with 1,390 pupils in total, as well as an additional nine kindergartens.[10]

Nor was New York initially more hospitable to Bais Yaakov, despite the willingness of a diverse group of American Jewish philanthropists to support Bais Yaakov schools in Europe. In the 1920s and 1930s, a number of efforts to open Bais Yaakov schools ended in failure.[11] Here the problem was not secular

existed in the Land of Israel since the beginning of the twentieth century. After the 'new' Bais Yaakov schools were founded, where instruction was in modern Hebrew, these came to be known as the 'old' Bais Yaakov schools.

[8] Sharansky, 'The History of Bais Yaakov in the Land of Israel', (Heb.), 41.

[9] For this history, see ibid. 42–4.

[10] For a list of these schools and their enrolment, see Agudath Israel, *Programm und Leistung*, 373.

[11] Among the schools that failed were an afternoon Beth Jacob Hebrew School for Girls directed by Fruma Leah Mandel and inspired by but not associated with the European movement, and two other elementary schools for Orthodox girls. One of these, Bais Ruchel in

Zionism or ultra-Orthodox defences against innovation but rather the lax religious standards of an immigrant community intent on Americanization. The Orthodox community in New York showed little interest in sending girls to a private religious school that insulated them from the surrounding society when they could acquire what they considered a superior education at a public school at no cost. Many families considered it sufficient to send their daughters to Talmud Torahs or other after-school Jewish programmes, which were generally co-educational. The biography of Vichna Kaplan describes the difficulty she had recruiting students to the evening seminary she opened in 1938 in her apartment. As with Rabbi Sharansky's first elementary school, the first seminary class had only seven students. Within the next five years, even as Vichna and her husband Boruch Kaplan struggled to keep up with expenses and their growing family, a high school was established with its own building and, for a time, a dormitory, and a full-day intensive seminary programme was added to the evening courses. Other schools followed: in 1943, when there were eight schools in the United States, a National Council of Beth Jacob Schools was founded. By the mid-1950s, the central office was serving fifteen schools and a summer camp.[12]

The schools founded in the 1930s still considered themselves part of the larger Bais Yaakov movement, with its centre in Poland.[13] Rabbi Sharansky, whose sister was a charismatic teacher at the Kraków seminary, chose his first teachers from its graduates who had emigrated to the Land of Israel. Vichna Kaplan went further in emulating the model of the Polish Bais Yaakov movement, where she both studied and taught. It may be no coincidence that she commenced with a seminary programme in her own home, following Sarah Schenirer's practice of fifteen years earlier. At summer programmes in Connecticut and the Catskills, her adolescent students danced 'to the same tunes that Rebbetzin Kaplan and her friends had danced barely a decade before, with their beloved teacher Frau Schenirer: *Vetaher libeinu l'avdecha b'emes*'.[14] Other features of the interwar movement were also reinvented to meet the new conditions: a Hebrew-language

Williamsburg, Brooklyn, became a Bais Yaakov in 1941, under the directorship of Rabbi Avrohom Newhouse. A fourth school, Shulamith, was founded by Nacha Rivkin in 1929 and still exists.

[12] This office was still in operation in 1978, when it was headed by Rabbi Shimon Newhouse, but it seems to have dissolved sometime during the next decade.

[13] In his 1936 history of Bais Yaakov, Seidman lists schools in Jerusalem, Tel Aviv, Petah Tikva, Kfar Ata, Haifa, Herzliya, Benei Berak, and Tiberias. See Seidman, *Renesans Religijny*, 27.

[14] For an account of the early years of Bais Yaakov in America, see Leibowitz with Gliksman, *Rebbetzin Vichna Kaplan*, 286–97. On the girls dancing to the same tunes as were sung in Poland, see ibid. 326–7.

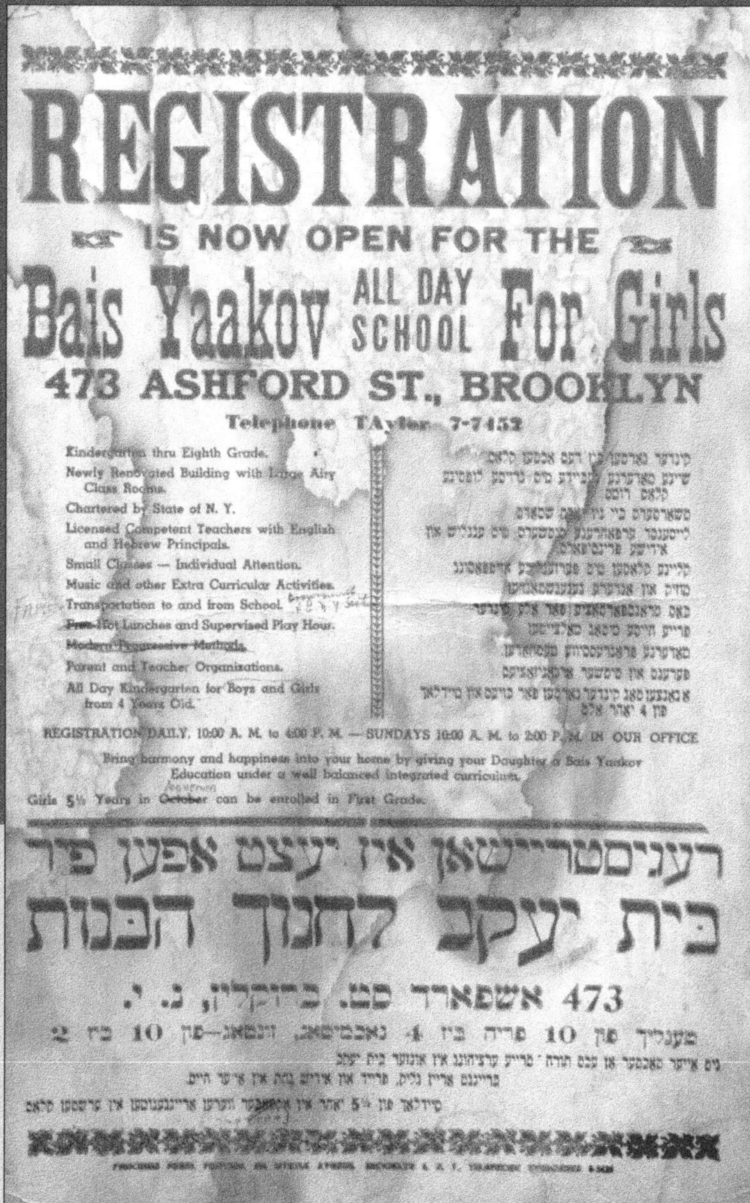

Figure 6.1 Poster (undated) announcing that registration is open for the Bais Yaakov all-day school for girls in the east New York neighbourhood of Brooklyn. While the English text declares 'Bring harmony and happiness into your home by giving your daughter a Bais Yaakov education under a well-balanced integrated curriculum', the Yiddish reads 'Give your daughter a real Torah-true education in our Bais Yaakov, bring happiness, joy, and Jewish *nakhes* into your home'.

Firschein Press, n.d. Letterpress on cardstock board, gift of Oscar and Theda Firschein, the Magnes Collection of Jewish Art and Life, UC Berkeley, 2017.8.84. Courtesy of the Magnes Collection of Jewish Art and Life

Figure 6.2 The Bais Yaakov of Williamsburg elementary school, at 415–425 Heyward Street in the Williamsburg neighbourhood of Brooklyn, in 1965. The Hebrew sign at the right of the door reads: *Beit yaakov leḥinukh habanot* ('Bais Yaakov Girls' School')

Brooklyn Public Library, Brooklyn Collection, Irving I. Herzberg Photograph Collection

journal for the Israeli movement was published from 1957/8 until 1980, and an English-language journal, the *Beth Jacob Monthly*, appeared in the United States for a few years beginning in 1954. Youth movements were also revived—Bnos (in the United States) and Bnot Batya (in Israel)—although with a narrower range of activities than had characterized the interwar movement. After the war these school systems grew quickly and continue to flourish today.

Bais Yaakov is by now a fait accompli, if not an absolutely essential part of the Orthodox landscape, although there are still elements of the Orthodox community that do not accept its legitimacy. Rabbi Samuel Judah Geshtetner, a follower of the Satmar Rebbe Joel Teitelbaum, argued in 1993 against 'a known educational institution'—refusing to call Bais Yaakov by its name—as having arisen only because of the crisis of conversion in that era.[15] If whatever legitimacy Bais Yaakov had in the interwar period derived from 'the needs of the hour', that hour has passed and this legitimacy should no longer be accepted. But even while resisting Bais Yaakov, hasidic movements such as Satmar have by now established their own school systems for girls (other hasidic groups that do not oppose Bais Yaakov have also founded schools, some even before the Holocaust). While the Satmar Bais Rochel distinguishes itself from Bais Yaakov by refraining from teaching Hebrew or the Bible and providing a bare minimum of secular subjects, it could be argued that these schools, too, owe their existence to the model, and indeed to the very logic that motivated Bais Yaakov's founding. When Joel Teitelbaum ruled in 1952 on the permissibility of opening girls' schools, he made the point that such an innovation was necessary because otherwise 'there would be no one for the boys to marry'.[16] Something like this very sentiment was expressed by the Gerer Rebbe in the interwar period.[17]

Despite the name and the conscious identification of these schools as more-or-less direct descendants of the interwar movement, Bais Yaakov in the post-Holocaust era is a rather different phenomenon. After a short-lived attempt to create a Central Office first in London (1937), then in Jerusalem (1939), and later in New York (1943), the Bais Yaakov schools around the world no longer have a central body or a periodical that unites them. They now operate in North America under the very loose affiliation of Torah Umesorah (better known as the educational

[15] In an anonymous volume entitled *Torat imekha* (On Women's Education) (New York, 1993), 64–5, cited in Fuchs, *Jewish Women's Torah Study*, 169.

[16] On the Satmar approach to girls' education, see Teitelbaum, *Vayo'el mosheh* (Brooklyn, NY, 1961), sections 41–2, and *Divrei yo'el* (New York, 1983), 45, cited in Loewenthal, 'Women and the Dialectic of Spirituality', 10 n. 11.

[17] See Ch. 1 n. 10 above.

arm of the Agudah, which also serves other Orthodox schools, coeducational or for boys only), and in Israel under the aegis of the Hinukh Atsma'i (the independent school system of the *haredi* sector, founded in 1953).[18] Despite the lack of a central coordinating body, Bais Yaakov quickly expanded in its two main centres. By 1960, Rabbi Sharansky proudly reported, Bais Yaakov was a burgeoning system with eighty elementary schools, ten high schools, five seminaries, nearly 1,000 teachers, and tens of thousands of pupils throughout the land.[19] In 1995, Shoshana Bechhofer estimated that there were 110 Orthodox Jewish all-girls high schools and 130 Orthodox Jewish all-girls elementary schools in North America, the majority of which would be considered part of the Bais Yaakov movement.[20] Without a central office issuing reports, more precise numbers are hard to come by, but there is no doubt that both centres continue to grow at a rapid rate.[21] Aside from the two main centres of North America and Israel, Bais Yaakov schools exist in at least eight other countries: Argentina, Belgium, Brazil, England, France, Russia, South Africa, and Switzerland.

By most accounts, Bais Yaakov has also evolved into a more staid and conservative system, although some traces of its interwar character remain, in smaller schools on the peripheries, in the summer camps, or in the travel to study in seminaries.[22] It no longer is the 'total institution' that it aspired to be in the interwar

[18] Torah Umesorah, more formally known as the Rabbinical Administrative Board of the National Society for Hebrew Day Schools, is the educational arm of the Agudath Israel; the Hinukh Atsmai schools in Israel receive some government support (estimated at 55% of the other tracks), and are given more freedom in setting curriculum, hiring teachers, and so on. In recent years, the government has exerted pressure on the system to increase its secular studies or lose financial support. [19] Sharansky, 'The History of Bais Yaakov in the Land of Israel' (Heb.), 45.

[20] Bechhofer, 'Ongoing Constitution of Identity', 9.

[21] In 2017 the Torah Umesorah website listed 53 all-girl Orthodox elementary schools with the name Bais Yaakov (or some variant) in North America, along with roughly twice that number of schools that are of the general Bais Yaakov type; there were also over 100 high schools that fall within this category (<www.torahumesorah.org/>, accessed 5 June 2017). Marvin Schick's rich analysis of Jewish day schools in 2013/14 shows an impressive growth of 'yeshiva-type' day schools (to which Bais Yaakov belongs) between 1998 and 2013, from 47,643 students to 75,681, but does not distinguish within that category between girls' and boys' schools (<avichai.org>, accessed 14 June 2016). Much of this growth can be traced to the burgeoning Orthodox community in Lakewood, NJ. For Israel, similar patterns of growth are evident: in 2017, one website of Orthodox schools in Israel listed 78 schools with some variation of the name Beit Ya'akov, including nine teachers' seminaries in Jerusalem alone (some seminaries by that title primarily served students from abroad). See <www.torahindex.com> and <www.cms.education.gov.il> (accessed 8 Feb. 2018).

[22] See the dissertations by Bechhofer, Ginsparg, and Rigler which discuss the growing conservatism of Bais Yaakov.

period for its elite seminarians and teachers, when it was called upon to provide a temporary substitute for families perceived to be in crisis. Schools are more likely now to serve a student body with fully observant parents, and from more homogeneous communities, than was the case either in interwar Poland or during the first decades of the movement in North America, when parents of varying levels of observance sent their daughters to the schools.[23] The Jewish family itself now stands on more solid foundations (thanks to some extent to Bais Yaakov). But the major factor that explains the changed character of Bais Yaakov is no doubt the broader 'slide to the right' (in Samuel Heilman's terminology) of post-war Orthodoxy, as younger generations have started taking on ever-greater halakhic stringencies and adopting stricter Orthodox practices.[24] Leslie Ginsparg Klein shows that, 'between the 1960s and the 1980s, the definitions of what constituted appropriate conduct and practice for Orthodox Jewish girls changed', with tightening restrictions on Bais Yaakov girls' dress as well as new rules about where they could go after school, exposure to popular culture, and other domains. As Ginsparg Klein is careful to remind her readers, these restrictions arose because of the very allure of American popular culture, and because 'Orthodox girls did not blindly follow the dictates of religious authority figures or categorically accept everything they were told' (nor did administrators always succeed in enforcing rules).[25] Assessing these differences, Stacy Eskovitz Rigler proposes that Bais Yaakov in the interwar period was 'interventionist' in its aim, taking radical measures to transform and revive a society in crisis and functioning in part as a 'missionary' movement. After the Holocaust, however, it evolved into a 'defensive' movement, attempting to cement and incrementally expand gains for North American Orthodoxy.[26] I argued in Chapter 4 that Bais Yaakov literature developed (at least) two types of discourse, one which celebrated the value inherent in girls' religious experience, and the other which emphasized the importance of educating them as future wives and mothers; in the post-war

[23] On the phenomenon of the 'winnowing' of non-observant Orthodox Jews from the Orthodox community over the past fifty years, see Eleff, 'The Vanishing Non-Observant Orthodox Jew'.

[24] Among the causes for this 'slide', according to Heilman, are educational systems that enforce a more stringent brand of Orthodoxy than practised in the family, as well as the increasingly prevalent practice of sending high-school graduates (both male and female) to study for a year at an Israeli institution, which introduced students to texts and practices that 'tended to be *frum*mer than the practices "back home"'; see Heilman, *Sliding to the Right*, 115.

[25] Ginsparg Klein, '"No Candy Store"', 140–1.

[26] Rigler, 'Girls' Education in Inter-Bellum Poland', 88–9.

period, the balance between these two ideologies shifted in favour of the discourse of female domesticity in both the American and Israeli centres.

This shift is practical as well as rhetorical. According to Menachem Friedman, who researches the Israeli scene, Bais Yaakov was instrumental in the post-Holocaust construction of a 'society of scholars', in which unprecedented numbers of men devote themselves to full-time Talmud study, with the family supported by their wives. This process began in the 1930s, when the Hazon Ish founded a *kolel* (institute for full-time Torah study) for young men who agreed to continue learning after marriage. But making such a way of life possible required the willing participation of women:

> In order to turn the vision of the Hazon Ish into reality, it was necessary to find graduates of the [Bais Yaakov] teachers' seminaries with the appropriate motivation, and in this regard, Rabbi Abraham Joseph Wolf came to the rescue . . . Wolf set a mission before the graduates of his [Benei Berak] seminary: to marry a yeshiva boy who intended to devote himself after marriage to studying in a *kolel*, and as surprising as it may seem, the girls enthusiastically accepted this idea.[27]

While in Europe only a small elite of men were supported by wives while they studied, 'in a relatively short time, by the end of the 1950s, the marriage of a yeshiva boy who was planning on continuing to learn in *kolel* and a Bais Yaakov teacher became the accepted and common pattern both in Israel and abroad. Any deviation from this model was testimony to a flaw either in the man, the woman, or both.'[28] With the new State of Israel partly funding the rapidly expanding Bais Yaakov school system, positions were available for large numbers of seminary graduates. In the United States, where they staffed many types of day schools, similar trends emerged. That the new 'society of scholars' owes much to Bais Yaakov is readily acknowledged: speaking of the thousands of men studying in the yeshivas and *kolelim* of Lakewood and Telz, one 1985 article in the now-defunct Orthodox *Jewish Observer* noted that such devotion would be impossible 'without wives who share their dedication and are willing to forego many of life's comforts to enable their husbands to learn Torah . . . These heroic young women are the products of the revolution begun by Sarah Schenirer.'[29]

It is this 'society of scholars' that points to what is, to my mind, the greatest

[27] Friedman, *The Haredi Woman* (Heb.), 10–11. Heilman describes this process as also having taken place in *ḥaredi* society in the United States, which, in addition to constructing a quasi-traditional division of marital labour, 'requires conformity to ever more conservative behavior'. See Heilman, *Sliding to the Right*, 83.

[28] Friedman, *The Haredi Woman* (Heb.), 10–11.

[29] Keller, 'Were It Not for Her . . .', *Jewish Observer*, 18/5 (1985), 32, cited in Bechhofer, 'Ongoing Constitution of Identity', 127.

distinction between Bais Yaakov culture in the interwar period and today. From the early support of fathers willing to send their daughters to Sarah Schenirer's school, to the adoption by the Agudah of Bais Yaakov and the devotion of some of the most creative and interesting Agudah activists to the movement, Bais Yaakov rallied men to the cause of Torah study for girls. Aaron Sorasky relates a tale about Gerer hasidim in the interwar period who, inspired by a speaker, relinquished money they had collected for the construction of a study hall for themselves in favour of establishing a Bais Yaakov school.[30] Of course the movement continues to attract male support and employ male administrators, but the enthusiastic stories about Bais Yaakov in more recent decades—as in the *Jewish Observer* article cited above—nowadays praise the devoted way in which the schools' graduates supported their husbands' Torah study, a rather different kind of gender interaction.[31]

Given that women's Torah study has ceded the spotlight to male Talmud study in Bais Yaakov discourse, it is not surprising that the old halakhic questions about the legitimacy of women's Torah study have surfaced anew. According to Ilan Fuchs, Rabbi Wolf limited the Jewish studies curriculum of the Benei Berak seminary, believing that a woman has 'no need for' Torah study on a high level; such study in fact 'denies her nature. Destined for disappointment she will ultimately harm the Jewish home.'[32] Bechhofer has analysed a debate around the value of a rigorous Jewish education for girls that arose in the *Jewish Observer* in the 1990s. According to one article, a Bais Yaakov girl spends her school years 'sharpening her intellect through a fascinating variety of subjects', but when she marries, she finds herself:

> bored, overwhelmed, and singularly unequipped to deal with the myriad demands of housekeeping . . . Add to this the shock she experiences upon discovering that she has had more exposure to Maharal [a philosophical/mystical commentary on the Bible] than her husband (and he's a top learner?!). In place of the soft, nurturing, domesticated homemaker, we have a new entity. She is more a carbon copy of her husband than a complementary help-mate.[33]

[30] Sorasky, *The History of Torah Education* (Heb.), 429.

[31] For an exploration of further changes in gender relations and family structure in the 'society of scholars', see Stadler, *Yeshiva Fundamentalism*, 132–4.

[32] Fuchs, *Jewish Women's Torah Study*, 66. Interestingly, Wolf sees *tiflut* as a danger for all who study Torah, though only women are in a position to avoid this danger, given their lack of an obligation.

[33] Uri Bergstein (pseudonym), 'Are Bais Yaakovs and Seminaries Doing Their Jobs?', *Jewish Observer*, 18/5 (1995), cited in Bechhofer, 'Ongoing Constitution of Identity', 240.

The pressures on Bais Yaakov to legitimate what continues to be its rigorous curriculum are complicated by the strength of Jewish feminism, not only in liberal but also in modern Orthodox circles, where such practices as women's Talmud study and prayer groups push continually against traditional boundaries. As in the interwar period, Bais Yaakov has to defend itself against the imputation of feminist aims (or origins), for instance, that it aims to produce 'carbon copies' of rather than 'help-mates' for Orthodox men. In this environment, claims that interwar Bais Yaakov constituted a feminist phenomenon must be repudiated.[34] In a chapter called 'Heresies of Memory', Bechhofer studies Orthodox responses to feminist appropriations of Sarah Schenirer, which the long-time editor of the *Jewish Observer*, Nisson Wolpin, calls 'Sarah Schenirer Revisionism'. Wolpin excoriates, in particular, Orthodox feminists who use Sarah Schenirer and Bais Yaakov as a 'role model' for 'women's prayer groups' and similar initiatives.[35] As Bechhofer shows, Wolpin combats depictions of Sarah Schenirer as a radical innovator on behalf of girls and women by emphasizing her piety and obedience to Jewish law and rabbinic authority, which are 'a far cry from the Orthodox Feminist agenda of . . . battle against the "male-dominated rabbinate"'. By contrast with these heretics, Sarah Schenirer was 'not a rebel by any stretch of the word'.[36] The stories of Sarah Schenirer that circulate in contemporary Bais Yaakov, in Bechhofer's view, serve the symbolic function of shoring up 'Orthodox defenses of traditional Jewish womanhood in the face of feminism'.[37] It is in this cultural context that the memory of Bais Yaakov's origins is curated, emphasizing Sarah Schenirer's piety over her revolutionary achievements, qualifying the experience of women's Torah study with the discourse of support for male Torah study, and insisting that innovation is acceptable only if it comes with rabbinical blessing. Such descriptions of Sarah Schenirer as 'knowledgeable in Jewish history and rabbinic literature', as well as 'fluent in a number of European languages and well-versed in the classics of European literature', as Rabbi Tuvia Yehuda Tavyomi (Gutentag) put it in a 1936 memorial address, have no place in the current atmosphere of Bais Yaakov memory.[38]

[34] Most prominent among such claims is I. Klepfisz, 'Di Mames, Dos Loshn/The Mothers, the Language'.

[35] Wolpin, 'The Sara Schenirer Revisionists', *Jewish Observer*, 18/5 (1997), 13–14, cited in Bechhofer, 'Ongoing Constitution of Identity', 143.

[36] Wolpin, (with L. Reisman), 'Orthodoxy and Feminism: How Promising a Shidduch?', *Jewish Observer*, 18/5 (1997), 13, cited in Bechhofer, 'Ongoing Constitution of Identity', 145.

[37] Bechhofer, 'Ongoing Constitution of Identity', 58.

[38] For this description, see Tavyomi (Gutentag), 'Eulogy for Mrs Sarah Schenirer' (Heb.), 27. As

In contrast with this domesticated image, the early post-Holocaust decades saw a resurgence of the more revolutionary image of a Bais Yaakov girl, as Bechhofer shows. Thus, in a 1975 article in *The Jewish Observer* commemorating the fortieth anniversary of Sarah Schenirer's passing, a writer described an argument he had with his cousin during the war about her risky behaviour:

'You dared to smuggle across the border?' I asked with anger. 'So did you!' came the reply. 'But I am different. I am a *Ben Torah*!' [male Torah scholar] 'So am I a *Bas Torah*!' [female Torah scholar]. She was a graduate of the Bais Yaakov Seminary in Kraków, and the flame of Sarah Schenirer was burning within her.[39]

The graduate of the Kraków seminary's equation of the *ben torah* and *bat torah*, repeated admiringly by the male cousin she bests in this argument, draws a parallel ('carbon copies') between the young man and young woman who are committed to Torah, more strikingly implying that the status of 'son' or 'daughter' of Torah signifies bravery and heroic devotion to an ideal, for young women as much as for men. According to Bechhofer, such rousing and egalitarian rhetoric has faded from Bais Yaakov in the years since this article appeared.[40] It is in accordance with this growing conservatism that the movement also avoids discussing the reasons it encountered opposition in its early years, in the service of a more pious narrative. But in obscuring the revolutionary elements of its own history, Bais Yaakov 'fails to provide credibility to Torah learning as a valued activity for girls'.[41]

The tension between innovation and tradition, piety and revolution, was of course already present in the interwar period, finding different balances at different times and for different constituencies. Other tensions that characterized the movement in Poland have also risen to the surface: Bais Yaakov always navigated between the push and pull of its ecumenical and missionary character, its interest in drawing new participants into its orbit, on the one hand, and the need to

Ginsparg Klein shows, Bais Yaakov documents from earlier periods have sometimes been doctored to make them conform with increasingly stringent contemporary norms (especially around issues of female modesty), a practice she calls 'Orthodox photoshopping' of the past; see Ginsparg Klein, 'The Troubling Trend of Photoshopping History'. Ginsparg Klein's primary example is the lengthening of sleeves in historical photographs of Bais Yaakov girls when these are reprinted in more recently published literature. On this general trend of Orthodox censorship of its own history, see M. B. Shapiro, *Changing the Immutable*.

[39] C. Shapiro, 'A Flame Called Sara Schenirer', 19, cited in Bechhofer, 'Ongoing Constitution of Identity', 126.

[40] See Bechhofer, 'Ongoing Constitution of Identity', 126 ff.

[41] Ibid. 137.

insulate its students from alien influences, on the other. When Sarah Schenirer and Grunfeld-Rosenbaum approached the Bobover Rebbe Ben Zion Halberstam in 1925 for a blessing for Bais Yaakov, he demurred on the grounds that 'by mixing girls from so many different backgrounds, they would tend to keep the easy customs and ways of some while abandoning the strictures of others . . . such a mixture of varied backgrounds was dangerous'.[42] By the post-war period, the Bobover community had fully embraced Bais Yaakov, and in that sense contributed to the movement's ecumenical character. It now served a broad swathe of the Orthodox world, with students from a variety of backgrounds. But other forces were moving much more forcefully in the opposite direction. While Bais Yaakov in Poland generally established only one school per town, and perhaps two or three in larger urban centres (where they were differentiated not by level of observance or community affiliation but rather by age and neighbourhood), the Bais Yaakov landscape in places like Brooklyn, Lakewood, or Jerusalem is significantly more ramified, with each school serving only a narrower and more defined segment of the Orthodox population. (Of course, the hasidic schools not affiliated with Bais Yaakov that arose in the 1930s and the post-war years further fractured this landscape.) It is a symptom of this fragmentation that, in both Israel and the United States, Gerer hasidim established their own branch of Bais Yaakov schools, called Bais Yaakov d'Gur (or d'Chasidei Gur); by contrast, girls from Gerer hasidic families in Poland had been integrated into the regular Bais Yaakov movement and thereby contributed to shaping the character of the movement as a whole. There is some variation in this picture: Bais Yaakov schools in large population centres compete in the same area for students, generally differentiating themselves by stricter observance or by catering to a slightly different Orthodox demographic; schools in smaller communities tend to serve the entire spectrum of Orthodox families in a given population centre, a diversity that may bring with it more tolerance. Bais Yaakov, especially in Israel, also began serving students from a range of non-east European backgrounds. One such school was Or Hayim, established in the 1950s to provide vocational training in a residential setting in Benei Berak for girls from Algeria, Egypt, India, Iraq, Kurdistan, Libya, Morocco, Tunisia, and Yemen, as well as eastern Europe and elsewhere.[43]

A startling expression of the ever-narrower segmentation of the commun-

42 Rubin (ed.), *Daughters of Destiny*, 135.

43 *Bet Yaakov*, 4 (1959), cited in Weissman, 'Bais Ya'akov: A Women's Educational Movement', 102.

ities served by Bais Yaakov schools came to public attention in 2007 in the still-controversial case of the Bais Yaakov in the West Bank settlement of Immanuel, in which, according to the *New York Times*, 'a group of Ashkenazi parents, who said they followed stricter religious practices than some of the Sephardim did, set up a separate educational track within the school, called the Hasidic track. A wall went up inside the building, and to prevent any social mixing the playground was split by a fabric-covered fence. About 75 girls moved over to the Hasidic side—a few of them Sephardim who agreed to the more stringent rules and dress code.'[44] In the aftermath of the division, a non-resident filed a suit against the school in the Supreme Court, accusing those who established the separate track of racism. The Supreme Court ruled against the school, leading some parents to resist the decision. When these were sent to prison, mass protests arose in their support. Whether this is seen—as on the Israeli left—as evidence of *ḥaredi* racism and discrimination, or—as on the right—as evidence of anti-*ḥaredi* prejudice and misunderstanding of Orthodox culture, the controversy generally plays itself out without reference to the interwar years, when the unity-in-diversity that characterized Bais Yaakov was understood to be an inherent feature of the beauty, power, and uniqueness of the movement.

The transformations of Bais Yaakov in recent decades are a sometimes paradoxical result of its own success. In interwar Poland, the Gerer Rebbe supported the movement because of the 'thousands of pious hasidic boys' who needed young women to marry. But once it had made some strides in the 1920s, he reported with evident satisfaction that 'the balance has shifted and now there are many more Orthodox women, Bais Yaakov graduates, than the number of young, Orthodox, male Torah scholars in the country'.[45] This gender or marital imbalance continues, manifesting itself on a number of discursive and practical levels. The appearance of Bais Yaakov girls on the Orthodox Polish scene during the interwar period was met with the ecstatic praise of young Agudah activists and old hasidic rabbis that the interwar literature records, of the 'valiant sisters' and 'brave pioneers'. Such odes have not entirely disappeared, but they have given way in Orthodox publications to laments about the 'shidduch crisis', the difficulties young women from Bais Yaakov circles face in finding the kind of mate their education has conditioned them to desire and anticipate. While the

44 Kershner, 'Israel's Ultra-Orthodox Protest Schools Ruling'.

45 For the quote, which he says he heard from the Gerer Rebbe's nephew, Rabbi Pinchas-Yaakov Levin, see Sorasky, *The History of Torah Education* (Heb.), 428, 438–9. Sorasky does not say precisely when the Gerer Rebbe made the later remark.

defection of so many Orthodox girls and women in the early twentieth century created 'economic' conditions that made the Orthodox young woman seeking a learned or hasidic mate a rare and therefore precious commodity, the success of Bais Yaakov helped create an over-supply of enthusiastic young women, in some sense driving down their (marital) value.[46] In this increasingly competitive market, new and somewhat contradictory stresses have been placed on young women and their families: on the one hand to be richer, more beautiful, and thinner; on the other, to be—and have the reputation for being—more stringently observant (and of course willing to work to support a husband who continues in learning for many years).[47]

For all these differences between the pre-Holocaust and post-Holocaust periods, Bais Yaakov continues to nourish a sense of its shared history. Bais Yaakov schools in the United States and Canada hold an annual convention bringing together girls from throughout the system, where this history is rehearsed and performed. But the most spectacular expressions of this collective identity are the much larger commemorations held on important *yahrzeits* (anniversaries) of Sarah Schenirer's death (smaller ones are held annually).These events have been held in enormous arenas (Madison Square Garden, New Jersey's Continental Arena, the Brooklyn Armory, and most recently the Barclays Center), with many thousands of mostly Bais Yaakov students bused in to attend and satellite hookups to Bais Yaakov schools across the country. This nostalgia for the movement's origins was already present during the interwar period, when the *Bais Yaakov Journal* reprinted its first masthead and other archival items, and regularly found reasons to recount the fascinating story of its beginnings. Some of Sarah Schenirer's charisma has attached itself to her first pupils, prize students, or close collaborators, who gain distinction by their degrees of closeness to the founding figure or the earliest Bais Yaakov schools. In Israel, one such figure was Chava Landsberg, who remained unmarried and devoted herself to leading the first Bais Yaakov in Jerusalem. In the United States, the torch was passed to Vichna Kaplan, who established and led the Bais Yaakov seminary in Williamsburg and then Boro Park. Pearl Benisch, who wrote the popular biography of Sarah Schenirer

[46] It is not entirely clear why the successes of Bais Yaakov have not been matched by equally great successes in the yeshiva movement; among the explanations I have seen for the imbalance between the numbers of men and women of marriageable age in this community is the tendency of young men to marry younger women (in 'yeshivish' rather than hasidic circles), an effect exacerbated by the high birth rate in the Orthodox community.

[47] See Ungar-Sargon, 'Ultra-Orthodox Jews Are Panicking'.

and Bais Yaakov, *Carry Me in Your Heart*, was her neighbour and Bnos 'sister', and also spoke of these experiences in many forums. Judith Rosenbaum, who married the prominent German-born scholar and translator of the writings of Samson Raphael Hirsch, Dayan Isidor Grunfeld, taught in Jewish day schools in London after the war and continued to write and lecture about her experiences for many decades.

Grunfeld-Rosenbaum describes what it meant to have a Bais Yaakov 'pedigree', for instance when she joined a relief mission, along with her husband, to a refugee camp in Cyprus in 1946. A group of young women she met on the island were cold to her until she asked them whether they had heard of Sarah Schenirer, adding, 'Well, I was a friend and colleague of hers.' A spirited conversation followed, which demonstrated how high she had risen in their esteem: 'An amazing thought hit me. The fact that I was married to a prominent dayan in London meant nothing to these girls. My university degree and experience as an educator was valueless in their eyes. It was only when they found out that I was associated with Sarah Schenirer that they warmed to me.'[48] Sarah Schenirer had established not only a new system for educating girls, but also what would become a new form of social status, kinship, and *yikhus* (lineage or pedigree) within the Orthodox world, one passed on from one woman to another, between teacher and student rather than parent and child. The line that began with Sarah Schenirer has even reached 'granddaughters': Carolyn Scharfer ends her essay on the movement by writing that 'I myself was a student of Judith Grunfeld-Rosenbaum.'[49] And Leslie Ginsparg Klein cites a 1992 speech by a Chicago principal on the occasion of a *yahrzeit* commemoration for Sarah Schenirer: 'I'm her grandchild (through Vichna Kaplan)—you my *talmidos* (students) are her great-grandchildren.'[50]

This lineage also symbolically unites the movement as a whole as kith and kin. Vichna Kaplan's daughter and successor, Rebbetsin Frumi Kirzner, a keynote speaker at Sarah Schenirer's seventieth *yahrzeit*, spoke of what bound together the 14,000 students in attendance, noting that with Sarah Schenirer as the mother of Bais Yaakov, 'We are all sisters.'[51] In the fictional 'last will and testament' of the 'Ninety-Three Bais Yaakov Girls' (who committed suicide rather than be taken as prostitutes by the German soldiers), Chaya Feldman's one request is that the New York-based Bais Yaakov leader and Agudah activist to whom she addresses the letter, Mr Meir Schenkalewsky, recite Kaddish for his ninety-three 'children';

[48] Rubin (ed.), *Daughters of Destiny*, 146.

[49] Scharfer, 'Sarah Schenirer', 74.

[50] Ginsparg Klein, '"Links in a Chain"', 9.

[51] Ibid. 11.

this request was reportedly fulfilled by at least one Jewish girl who, at her grandmother's request, lit a memorial candle and said Kaddish for the girls annually for over fifty years in honour of 'my hundred little sisters'.[52] In these and other practices, it is clear that the distinctive configurations of family in inter-war Bais Yaakov persisted in some form after the Holocaust, across a much less unified network of often competing schools, taking on the deeply cherished attachments that had previously accrued, for women, to the family understood more narrowly.

It is the figure of Schenirer, above all, that works to produce this Bais Yaakov 'family', even and perhaps especially after her death, eclipsing such previously central figures as Deutschländer, Friedenson, Orleans, and others. To the mass gatherings that serve as miraculous 'family reunions' we might add such acts as the 2001 placement of a plaque on the building that once housed the Kraków seminary by the Sarah Schenirer Dedication Committee of the Agudah Women of America commemorating the 'spark kindled in Kraków' that 'grew to a flame that radiated across Poland and across the oceans. This light of Torah continues to illuminate the hearts and minds of Jewish girls throughout the world.' Two years later, a tombstone was erected in the Jewish cemetery in the Podgórze suburb of Kraków where Sarah Schenirer was buried, which had been razed when the Płaszów concentration camp was built on the site.[53] In 2005, the world Agudath Yisrael and Bais Yaakov movements joined together for a pilgrimage to Kraków to commemorate the seventieth anniversary of Sarah Schenirer's death, with hundreds of graduates and others participating; this occasion was also marked by the establishment of a central Bais Yaakov archive in Jerusalem.

The memory of Bais Yaakov's origins is kept alive not only in the moment of

[52] These and other responses are documented by Baumel and Schacter, who cite a telephone interview in 1990 with Arlene Stempler, a woman who said Kaddish for five decades (Baumel and Schacter, 'The Ninety-Three Bais Yaakov Girls', 98). Baumel and Schacter suggest that the story of the Bais Yaakov martyrs could be true, but a much broader scholarly consensus deems it impossible for various reasons. Among the first historians who argued against the historical veracity of the story were Philip Friedman, in his 'Preliminary and Methodological Problems', 122 n. 14, and Eliav, *I Believe* (Heb.), 55. See also Garber, 'The 93 Beit Yaakov Martyrs', 69–92.

[53] The initiative and the text for the plaque and the tombstone came from Dr Shnayer Leiman, who had been leading tours of Poland and was troubled by the dearth of memorials to women; a Bais Yaakov graduate named Roni Cohen, who had been on a few of Dr Leiman's tours, led the fundraising effort. Dr Leiman's efforts to reconstruct the wording on the original tombstone included interviewing the Jew who had been forced to destroy it (email communication, 5 Apr. 2017).

placing or viewing the plaque or gravestone but also in the group travel that made this commemoration possible. The pilgrimage I witnessed in 2010 of a small number of Bais Yaakov girls to Sarah Schenirer's grave and the seminary building is part, as I learned, of a larger wave of pilgrimages. Since 1999 some of these have taken place within the framework of large tour groups aimed at Bais Yaakov students on break from their studies or returning from their seminary year in Israel. The website of one tour operator promises, 'You will *daven* at the *kevarim* of *tzaddikim* and see many other memorable sites including spectacular *shuls*, the original Beis Yaakov Building, Yeshivas Chachmei Lublin, the Rema Shul, the *kever* of the Noam Elimelech, to name a few.'[54] Whether on air-conditioned buses or as intrepid adventurers, the journeys of North American young women through Poland and Europe echo, in some belated and barely audible fashion, the travels of the young Bais Yaakov teachers of old throughout Poland on behalf of the new movement. Sarah Schenirer herself instituted many of these practices, hiking up mountains at dawn, riding trains and rickety carts to small towns, and walking through the streets of Kazimierz to visit the tombstones of Kraków's great Torah leaders. In revisiting these sacred walks and exhilarating journeys, the historian is privileged to be along for the ride.

[54] See the Nesivos website, <http://www.nesivos.com/> (accessed 11 July 2016).

PART TWO

COLLECTED WRITINGS

SARAH SCHENIRER

Translator's Note

IN 1933 the Central Secretariat of Bnos Agudath Israel in Poland issued Sarah Schenirer's *Collected Writings*, after advertising the upcoming publication in the pages of the *Bais Yaakov Journal*. The book included many articles that had previously appeared in the journal or elsewhere in Bais Yaakov publications; among them were reflections on Jewish themes, reports on events important to the world of Bais Yaakov and Bnos, and ethical instructions to young pupils. But it also included previously unpublished writings, including a brief but fascinating memoir that shed light on Sarah Schenirer's childhood and on the beginnings of the Bais Yaakov movement. As a frontispiece, the book included a drawing of Sarah Schenirer, one which circulated widely in the movement in the absence of a photograph (it was well known that she refused to have her photograph taken). Advertisements for the upcoming volume sometimes provided a table of contents, which promised that it would include excerpts from Schenirer's diary. In fact, those excerpts did not appear in the published work, although a few entries—whether the ones originally intended for publication or others is not clear—did appear in the 1950s in Hebrew translation. For more on this diary, see Appendix A.

In 1955, a number of Bais Yaakov administrators and former students of Sarah Schenirer undertook to have the volume reprinted in honour of the twentieth anniversary of her death. The volume they published is identical to the 1933 edition (although it does not include the drawing of Schenirer), with a number of additions: a foreword by Rabbi Shlomo Rotenberg commemorating the most prominent Bais Yaakov teachers and activists in interwar Poland, many of whom had been murdered in the Holocaust (a photograph of Yehudah Leib Orlean appeared on the first page of that foreword); and an introduction by Vichna Kaplan, a student of Sarah Schenirer and founder of the first Bais Yaakov high school in the United States. The volume similarly ended with material that had not appeared in the 1933 book: an essay by Sarah Schenirer sent to the seminary in the weeks before her death, and another essay by Rabbi Shlomo Rotenberg charting the beginnings of Bais Yaakov on American soil; a photograph of the Bais Yaakov seminary and high school is appended to this essay. These additional sections are of obvious significance, and I elected to translate the entire volume of the 1955 edition, with the exception of the list of subscribers who paid for the book in advance of publication, 200 of them graduates of the Bais Yaakov seminary, and another 236 students of the high school and seminary. A full scan of the 1955 edition is available in digital download from the National Yiddish Book Center website.

Foreword to the 1955 Edition

IN REPRINTING *The Collected Writings* of Sarah Schenirer, may she rest in peace, it is impossible to forget all Mrs Schenirer's close collaborators, who helped her create and develop the Bais Yaakov seminary in Kraków and the international Bais Yaakov movement in general. And while their deeds stand as a memorial to them, nevertheless let their names also be mentioned here, as a memory for all eternity.

RABBI YEHUDAH LEIB ORLEAN. Principal of the Bais Yaakov seminary in Kraków, Poland, gifted writer and orator. Among the most influential leaders in the ranks of the Polish Agudath Israel, especially among the youth and workers.[1] A long-time collaborator of Mrs Schenirer, director of the seminary; after her death he took on the key role of principal of the seminary, its leading educator and moral guide, teaching Jewish history and Judaism and giving lectures. He wrote the Judaic studies curriculum for the Bais Yaakov schools, and the textbook *Jewish Culture* for Bais Yaakov and Bnos, as well as *Jewish Life* and others. More generally, he presided over the flourishing of the Bais Yaakov seminary and put the Central Office of Bais Yaakov on a solid foundation, successfully managing the teachers in hundreds of Bais Yaakov schools throughout Poland.

During the last world war, Rabbi Yehudah Leib Orlean reached even more exalted heights. The whole bitter burden of the movement rested on the narrow shoulders of this quiet giant. Amidst the devastating troubles, his house became the Central Office for the whole Bais Yaakov movement. From there, the teachers drew solace and strength. At the risk of his own life, he issued a steady stream of writings, lesson plans, teaching materials, and encouraging letters to teachers and Bnos leaders everywhere in the country.

Rabbi Yehudah Leib Orlean died a martyr's death in one of the last transports

[1] The reference here is to the Tse'irei Agudath Israel and the Po'alei Agudath Israel, the youth and workers' arms of the Agudah party, in which Orlean was active. For more on Agudath Israel in the interwar period, see Bacon, *The Politics of Tradition*. For a brief biography and description of Orlean's activities in the Agudah and Bais Yaakov, especially during the Holocaust, see Seidman, *Personalities I Knew* (Heb.), 191–205. A photograph of Orlean appears on the second page of the appendix there.

to be organized by the Nazis, may their names be blotted out, shortly before the Liberation, on Simhat Torah 5705 (22 October 1944).

DR (LEO) SHMUEL DEUTSCHLÄNDER. Among the leaders of the World Organization of Agudath Israel. The founder and director of Keren Hatorah, the foundation for strengthening the Torah. It was thanks to the capable and energetic support of Dr Deutschländer that Mrs Schenirer's modest beginnings were developed and financially underwritten by Keren Hatorah. Hundreds of students were admitted to the seminary under the financial auspices of Keren Hatorah.

Dr Deutschländer founded and personally directed the Bais Yaakov seminary in Vienna, Austria. At the same time, this tireless activist was also running Keren Hatorah and travelling regularly to Kraków and to the summer colonies to study and speak with the students. With his knowledge and insights, drawn from the teachings of Rabbi Samson Raphael Hirsch, Dr Deutschländer always inspired the students, and his personality left a strong impression on them.

Dr Deutschländer, together with Mrs Schenirer, is the true founder of Bais Yaakov. Mrs Schenirer was the beginning, the soul, but Dr Deutschländer created the body, taking the tiny kernel and growing it into an international movement without parallel in Jewish history.[2]

DR JUDITH GRUNFELD-ROSENBAUM, may she be granted a long life, in London, England. Among Sarah Schenirer's collaborators.[3] A dynamic personality, oversaw the teaching of the Pentateuch, history, psychology. Enchanted students with the thoughts and writings of Rabbi Samson Raphael Hirsch. Had a powerful influence on the formation of the moral values of her students. Resides now and continues her educational work in London, England.

MISS CHAVA LANDSBERG. Among the first teachers in the seminary, and a chief co-worker alongside Sarah Schenirer. For many years a great spiritual influence in the seminary in Kraków. Educated many of the most important Bais Yaakov teachers and leaders in the world. Later founded the Bais Yaakov seminary in Jerusalem, directing it until her death in the year 5707 [1946/7].[4]

And now in alphabetical order:

[2] For a biographical sketch of Deutschländer, 'the Father of Bais Yaakov', see C. Shapiro, 'Dr. Leo Deutschländer', 14–17.

[3] For a biography of Grunfeld-Rosenbaum, see Dansky, *Rebbetzin Grunfeld*.

[4] Chava Landsberg was one of the first teachers brought by Deutschländer from Germany in 1925 to assist in teaching training.

MISS JUDITH BAUMINGER. Hebrew grammar instructor in the seminary and Bnos leader. Quiet, modest, never demanding anything for herself. Amazingly persistent in teaching moral behaviour.

RABBI MOSHE DEUTSCHER, RABBI ELAZAR SHAPIRO, and later RABBI MEIR HEITNER.[5] These were the silent partners who bore the financial responsibility for the seminary's boarding school and for the three-month-long summer colonies and professional development courses, which saw even greater successes than the boarding school. Honest, tireless workers. Laboured under the most difficult conditions without complaint, without publicity. Just keeping the seminary going was for them the highest reward.

RABBI ELIEZER GERSHON FRIEDENSON. Executive director of Bnos Agudath Israel. Editor of the unforgettable *Bais Yaakov Journal*, along with the children's supplements *New Saplings* and *Kindergarten*. Tireless activist and organizer. Founded Ohel Sarah, the trade school for girls.

RABBI ALEKSANDER ZYSHA FRIEDMAN. Among the main leaders of the Agudah in Poland. A learned and thoughtful man, a prolific writer and speaker. Along with Rabbi Orlean, among the authors of the Bais Yaakov curriculum. Wrote the curriculum for teaching Jewish prayer and served on the editorial board of the *Bais Yaakov Journal*. Among the founding fathers of Bais Yaakov.

MISS ESTHER GOLDSHTOFF. Among the first students of Sarah Schenirer, may she rest in peace. Among the best-trained pedagogues. Her exemplary lessons in *Ethics of the Fathers* were psychological and pedagogical models of learning and teaching. She gave lively and methodical lectures on Jewish history. She was the picture of Jewish modesty and goodness, always full of joy.

MRS ESTHER GROSS-HAMBURGER (in Israel). A teacher and spiritual leader in Kraków. Founded and directed the Bais Yaakov seminary in Czernowitz, Romania.[6] Even during the world war carried on the work of education with self-sacrificing devotion. Also performed rescue efforts. Later moved to the Land of Israel.

MRS BAILA GROSS-PASTOG. Bnos leader. Extraordinarily modest in her personal life. A government-certified teacher with advanced degrees, she directed the obligatory programme in secular studies. A model of pure goodness.

[5] Moshe Deutscher, Elazar Shapiro, and Meir Heitner were among the leaders of Agudath Israel in Kraków who took it upon themselves to support Bais Yaakov; Deutscher later served in the Polish Sejm (parliament).

[6] Now the west Ukrainian city of Chernivtsi. For more on the Bais Yaakov seminary in Czernowitz, see Sorasky, *The History of Torah Education* (Heb.), 434.

MRS CHANAH GROSSFELD-BIEGUN. A student of Mrs Schenirer, may she rest in peace, and of Dr Rosenbaum, long may she live, she was among the main educators in the seminary through her rich classes in the Bible and her moral lectures. And with the help of her husband Rabbi Yosef Biegun, the unforgettable editor and compiler of the *Yalkut yedi'ot ha'emet* of Rabbi Moses Hayim Luzzatto,[7] she became a beloved mother to the seminary. Also active in Bnos. She was a pure person, truly the archetype of a saintly woman. Thanks to her marvellous example, clarity, and warmth, she educated generations of dedicated, conscientious, and proud teachers.

MRS TSIPORAH SCHARANSKY (SZCZARAŃSKA-WASZASZ). Also among the earliest collaborators of Sarah Schenirer. She taught Jewish law and housekeeping, and was always practical, even bringing chickens into class when she taught the laws of *kashrut*. Travelled around founding new Bais Yaakov schools and talking to Bnos groups. Tireless. A model of competence and accomplishment.[8]

MRS GITTEL TEITELBAUM-PASS. Pedagogue and teacher of the writings of the Prophets. A person of calm strength. A Bnos leader. At home, a model Jewish mother. A paragon of patience.[9]

And these are the people, the creators and builders of the unforgettable Bais Yaakov seminary in Kraków, who made it possible for Bais Yaakov to become a glorious international movement to educate Jewish girls. They were the most prominent leaders that bore the burden, but with them and behind them also stood many other unknown people, the unsung heroes of the Bais Yaakov movement, the hundreds of teachers and quiet warriors who, with their holy sacrifice

[7] Moses Hayim Luzzatto (1707–47) was a philosopher, kabbalist, and ethicist, and his *Yalkut yedi'ot ha'emet* (Collection of Knowledge of the Truth) is a compilation of writings on which Biegun provided commentary. Biegun was not formally employed in the Bais Yaakov seminary, but he served as unofficial consultant both to Orlean and to various teachers. For more on Biegun, see Seidman, *Personalities I Knew* (Heb.), 220–31.

[8] Tsiporah Scharansky, or Lotka Szczarańska, is on the list of faculty in 1928, in the summer colony of Rabka, as well as on the platform at the founding conference of Neshei Agudath Israel, where she delivered a report on the Bnos activities in Poland. See Fig. 5.2 above and Fig. II.1 below. Schenirer mentions her by her married name in the essay 'Our Pioneers' (below, p. 275).

[9] For more on Gittel Teitelbaum, who was one of Schenirer's first students and among the first to be 'promoted' to teacher (and who continued to teach in the seminary for many years), see the letter from Grunfeld to Teitelbaum, and accompanying photograph, in Dansky, *Rebbetzin Grunfeld*, 11–13. See also Pass, 'A Human Life', 100–1, in which she describes the spiritual joy she experienced on strenuous hikes with Schenirer in the early years of Bais Yaakov.

and enormous dedication and stubbornness, created and developed the more than 300 Bais Yaakov schools in Poland, with their nearly 40,000 students. These were the people who carried the banner of Torah and *yiddishkeit* with pride and determination. And they, the unknown, unheralded Bais Yaakov teachers, the unsung everyday heroines, they were the ones who transmitted the heritage of our ancestors and strengthened generations, they were the ones who truly built the international network that is Bais Yaakov.

They fell at the hands of the evil ones, whose names should be blotted out. May God avenge their blood!

But their heroism was not in vain.

Their creation still lives! The building still stands! The inheritance is still cherished. In new lands and in different cities.

Bais Yaakov lives!

Rabbi Shlomo Rotenberg[10]

[10] Shlomo Rotenberg taught in the Bais Yaakov in Williamsburg in the 1950s.

Foreword to the 1933 Edition

Around fifteen years ago, when our leader Mrs Sarah Schenirer first approached the Jewish world with the idea of Bais Yaakov, she had almost no supporters, and only very few Jewish parents understood what she wanted and what she was talking about.

The Orthodox world was in despair over the problem of religious education for Jewish girls, and in any case could not believe that some humble, unknown woman would be able to overcome the obstacles and smooth the path.

Mrs Schenirer, who was full of faith and confidence in what she knew to be true, was not deterred by the dismissive and sceptical way she was treated. She took on the task of becoming a link in the long golden chain of Jewish heroines, who in every generation brought the Jewish people comfort, strength, and redemption.

This integrity, Jewish fire, work ethic, self-sacrifice, creativity, and deep faith in her ideal have already immortalized Mrs Schenirer in the history of the Jewish people as the great exemplar of a kosher and modest Jewish woman for many generations to come.

Much of the victory of the Bais Yaakov ideal and the collective return of thousands of Jewish girls to Israel of old should be credited to her fiery writings, which so profoundly express her spiritual feeling, warmth, and simplicity, and thus must strike a chord in the Jewish feminine soul.

We have collected in this book the most important essays, speeches on various occasions, and letters to young women and children that have been published over the past ten years in the *Bais Yaakov Journal* and *Kindergarten*, or other publications.

We are hoping in this way to produce something useful. The Jewish wife and mother, the Jewish girl and Jewish child, will find in this book ways of acquainting themselves with an authentically Jewish perspective on various life problems, learning the significance of Jewish holidays, becoming aware of many issues in Jewish life, and more deeply understanding the ideals of Jewish feminine life according to the Torah and of educating the younger generation according to the spirit of God's people.

Let this book become a handbook for Jewish girls, so that Jewish women read and pore over this book again and again. Let teachers and educators introduce the thoughts and ideas of Mrs Schenirer to all who are under their influence, which will be very helpful in strengthening and empowering the ideal of Bais Yaakov, so that it shall come to pass that 'the house of Jacob will be on fire'!!!

The Central Secretariat of Bnos Agudath Israel in Poland
Łódź, Sivan 5693 [May / June 1933]

A Letter from the Hafets Hayim The Holy Sage, Rabbi of All Children of Exile,[11] May His Saintly Memory Be for a Blessing

To the honoured leaders and those who cherish the Torah, those who tremble at the word of God who are in the town of Fristik, may God bless them and protect them.[12]

I have heard that God-fearing people, respectful of the word of God, have volunteered to found a Bais Yaakov school in this city for the study of Torah, the fear of God and the way of the land,[13] teaching Torah to Jewish girls. I said of their worthy endeavour, may God strengthen and establish the work of their hands, for this is a great and necessary matter in our day. When the stream of heresy, may the Merciful One spare us, reigns in all its power, and secular people of every variety prey on Jewish souls, everyone whose heart is touched by the fear of God must send his daughter to study in this school. And all those who have hesitations and concerns about the prohibition against teaching a daughter Torah have no reason or grounds for this in our times. But this is not the place to explain this at length.

Our generation is not like previous generations, when every Jewish home passed down the tradition from their grandfathers and grandmothers to walk in the way of the Torah and religion and to read the *Tsene-rene* every holy sabbath. But because of our many sins this is not the case in our own generation. And that

[11] Israel Meir (Hakohen) Kagan (1839–1933), known popularly as the Hafets Hayim after the title of his influential 1873 book, was perhaps the most respected and important rabbi in eastern Europe, a halakhist and codifier of Jewish law (including the question of Torah study for girls), and an ethicist whose works continue to be widely read in Jewish life.

[12] Fristik (Frysztak) is a small town in south-eastern Poland. For details on how the Agudah secured this letter of approbation after the rabbi in Fristik forbade the opening of a Bais Yaakov, see Benisch, *Carry Me in Your Heart*, 116.

[13] The Hafets Hayim uses the term *derekh erets* (literally, 'the way of the land'; see *Pirkei avot* 2: 2 and 3: 21), which has a number of meanings, including refined and polite behaviour, earning a living, and secular studies, or more specifically, the combination of Torah study with being at home in secular learning and the wider world encoded in the German neo-Orthodox slogan associated with Samson Raphael Hirsch, *torah im derekh erets*.

is why we must try with all our spiritual energy to increase the number of these schools and to rescue what is still in our power to rescue.

Writing for the sake of the honour of the Torah and religion,

With the help of God, Israel Meir Hacohen
23 Shevat 5693 [19 February 1933]

Introduction to the 1955 Edition

Sarah Schenirer established the great sanctification of the divine name in our generation—the Bais Yaakov movement. May her memory be blessed!

FOR MANY YEARS we dreamed of republishing the collected writings of Sarah Schenirer, of blessed memory, and circulating her published work to the Jewish masses. So our joy is very great, now that this dream is coming true.

This book is a treasure house of deep Torah thoughts, exalted insights, and marvellous ethical teachings. These are words that emerged from a pure heart, and thus make a deep impression in the heart of the reader.

We hope that this book will be an inspiration for the Jewish daughter in America, as it was in Europe.

A Word to All the Students of the Bais Yaakov Schools

Dear children,

It is difficult to express the emotions with which we, the students of Sarah Schenirer, may she rest in peace, pass along this book to you. Who among you has not heard the name Sarah Schenirer? A holy shudder runs through us just hearing the sound of her name. Her radiant countenance rises before our eyes now. She was the living embodiment of 'worship the Lord with gladness' [Ps. 100: 2]—to which she continually called us. In her eyes—a holy fire. On her face—a loving smile. She was a great woman. One breathed a holy spirit in her presence, and whoever stood by her side was incapable of concealing any evil thoughts in their mind. Something in oneself was elevated just by being in her presence.

With what love she spoke with each one of us! We did not feel that we were just one of thousands of Bais Yaakov girls, but rather as if each of us alone existed for her, that our mother was worrying 'only about me'.

Later, when we left the Bais Yaakov seminary in Kraków, she found time to write letters to each of us and to our students. Imagine our joy when we received a letter from her—like a letter from mama. Yes, she was our mother, our mama, a true mama for every child who had even the slightest connection with Bais Yaakov, as she often said. Unfortunately, she never had children of her own, but she would always say, 'I have thousands of children. Every Bais Yaakov girl is my child.' And truly only a mother, a real mother, could have felt such joy in her children's achievements.

And who could fail to see this joy when she was told that the children were studying hard, that they had improved in this or that ethical trait, that they were growing stronger in fulfilling the commandments of the Torah. A smile then brightened her face, and there was no limit to her happiness!

Oh, if only we were worthy of having her with us now, so that we could continue to receive her personal encouragement and courage for our holy work! But unfortunately we have not merited that.

Friday, at the time of candle lighting, on 26 Adar 5695 [1 March 1935], our mother left us. The news of her passing burst like a thunderclap on a sunny day! Even now, after nineteen years, we can hardly believe it is true. For she was always bursting with life, with activities—is she really no longer among the living?

Tears come over me as I relive these experiences in memory. Yes, a bitter loss, a terrible defeat the Jewish people suffered when she passed away!

Nevertheless, we know that 'the righteous in their death are called living [BT *Ber.* 18*a*]'!

Yes, our mother is truly gone, but she left us a valuable inheritance.

Some of her teachings and pearls of thought remain in her *Collected Writings*. Like a will, a holy will from a mother which must be read with attention to every word. This will was not written to you collectively, but rather directed at each one of you, every dear reader, each beloved daughter of Bais Yaakov.

You must understand what this book is and means. This is not a book meant only to grace a bookshelf. It is not a book to read but rather to study, to learn—every day.

Of course, not *only* to learn, but especially to fulfil! 'Not the study is the essence but rather the deed [*Avot* 1: 17]'! Yes, this book should be like a *Shulḥan arukh* for every Jewish daughter.

Our Sages say that when the living repeat something that a deceased person had said, his lips move in the grave [BT *Ber.* 31*b*]. When we study her writings, her lips will certainly move in the grave and they will whisper a motherly blessing for all of us, children of the Bais Yaakov movement!

With a feeling of the most fervent love and deepest admiration for the great departed one, our spiritual mother, we pass along this book to your hand! We hope that you will cherish it as a holy book! Let her words always remain for all of us a source of eternal encouragement for the Bais Yaakov idea!

Vichna Kaplan[14]

In the name of all the students of Sarah Schenirer in America,

26 Adar I, 5714 [1954], Brooklyn, New York

[14] On Vichna Kaplan see Ch. 5 n. 52 above.

1 Pages from My Life

I WAS BORN IN KRAKÓW, in Tamuz 5643 [July 1883]. My father, of blessed memory, was Rabbi Bezalel Hakohen of Turna [Tarnów], and he was a descendant of the Shakh, whose family were later among the first followers of the Sanzer Rebbe.[1] My father's mother, Sheina Feigl, of blessed memory, was truly a great saint. People still have many things to say about her piety, goodness, and modesty. On the frostiest days, she would carry warm tea to the yeshiva boys sitting in the study house. She would spare no expense to serve the holy Sanzer Rebbe, and all in all had the finest character. My mother, long may she live, is from Kraków, a granddaughter of Rabbi Abraham Lock of blessed memory, whose wife, my grandmother Chaya, came from the Carmel family and was a direct descendant of the Bach.[2]

People tell many admiring stories about my parents. They owned a large dry-goods store, and would distribute lots of goods among the poor. My grandmother would have new linen made every month, and she would give away the old linen to people who needed it. My father put all his energy into raising his children, educating them to be pious Jews. He was a fervent Belzer hasid, indeed a regular in the previous Belzer Rebbe's court.[3]

I went to public school for eight years, a school with non-Jewish pupils too. By the time I was 6 years old I had a nickname in school, 'Little Miss Hasid'. I also

[1] The Shakh, Rabbi Shabbatai Hakohen (1622–63) was born in Vilna and compiled a commentary entitled *Siftei kohen* on the 'Yoreh De'ah' and 'Ḥoshen mishpat' sections of the *Shulḥan arukh*, which is popularly known (like its author) by a Hebrew acronym pronounced 'Shakh'. The Sanz hasidic dynasty was founded by Rabbi Hayim Halberstam (1793–1876), the rabbi of the Polish town of Nowy Sącz (known in Yiddish as Sanz).

[2] The Bach, Rabbi Joel ben Samuel Sirkis (1561–1640), was the author of a commentary on the medieval legal code the *Arba'ah turim* entitled *Bayit ḥadash*, the initial letters of which form the name by which he is known.

[3] The founder of the Belz (Polish, Bełz) dynasty was Rabbi Shalom Rokeach (1781–1855), who became the rabbi of Bełz, a town now in western Ukraine, in 1817. He was succeeded by his youngest son, Yehoshua Rokeach (1855–94). The third Belzer Rebbe, his son Yissachar Dov Rokeach (1894–1926), was the one who gave his blessing to Schenirer's enterprise in Marienbad in 1917.

remember that in school I did especially well in the religion class. When the teacher called on students many of them couldn't answer, and the teacher would always praise me: 'Why does she know the answer?' 'Children,' she would add, 'you should be a little more industrious in religion, because religion is a holy thing.'

I had quite a talent for learning and, in addition, I worked hard. I passed every year with good grades, but I excelled at embroidery and sewing. Just as I was about to start seventh grade my family wanted to take me out of school so I could start working for a living, but I begged them to let me stay and finish seventh grade, and I graduated from elementary school successfully.

That year my eldest sister got married. I had to help in the kitchen, and wasn't so happy about that because I longed to continue my studies; but even though I was busy with housework, I did not give up learning and reading. I spent pleasant sabbaths reading the *Tsene-rene*. Every sabbath I read through the whole Torah portion, the prophetic reading for that week, and the *Naḥalat tsevi*.[4] Without that, it wouldn't have been a sabbath for me.

On sabbaths at our house, my sister's friends would gather to sing and dance, and I would sit by the side and read the Torah portion. They used to say that the whole house could be burgled in front of me and I wouldn't notice, so engrossed was I in the pleasures of reading Jewish texts. Even then it pained me to see my sisters acting in a barely Jewish way, without the slightest interest in a Jewish book. Sometimes I would reproach a Jewish girl, and she would just laugh and respond that I was a Little Miss Hasid. But that didn't bother me, and I would just go back to being the way I was.

And so I grew a little older, and when my parents' business began to take a downturn, my family needed me to find work as a shop assistant or something like that. I couldn't avoid trying to earn a living, but I was afraid of getting caught up in some situation with people I didn't know. I was afraid that finding work would get in the way of my obligations as a religious young woman and I looked for a way to make money by working from home, which is how I started doing piecework.

Once I sewed a dress for one of my sister's friends, and then I was asked to sew another dress, and a third, and that was how I became a seamstress, without ever having been formally trained in the craft. Customers were pleased with my

[4] The *Naḥalat tsevi* or *Taytsh-Zoyer* is a popular Yiddish adaptation of the ethical lessons and the narrative parts of the Zohar, compiled by Tsevi Hirsh ben Yerahmiel Chotsch and first published in Frankfurt in 1711.

work. Many of them would say to me that I put my heart and soul into it. I thought about that a lot. When I saw how concerned people were with the smallest detail when I was cutting and measuring their dresses, I would think to myself, 'And what do the "garments" of their souls look like?'

I would often work late into the night, and then after work I would spend time on my own interests. I remember my father once bought *Ḥok leyisra'el*, with a Yiddish translation, and I took it upon myself to read through the lessons on the Pentateuch, Prophets, Mishnah, and Talmud for each day, and I enjoyed it immensely.[5] But I was also very interested in all kinds of academic subjects, and from time to time I would attend lectures at a Christian women's club.

In truth, after every visit there I would regret it enormously, but in those days there was no other place to hear an intellectual discussion. I realize that someone might challenge me on this, because even then there were a variety of organizations for young women, but all it would take for me to defend myself is to relate one story that makes it clear that there really was no other place for me to go for such intellectual stimulation.

One Friday evening, my cousin, an active member of Ruth, came to visit and invited me to one of their gatherings.[6] I went along to make her happy, but was shocked to see with my own eyes a leader of the group turning on the light. I knew in advance that this club wasn't the most pious of organizations, but it never occurred to me that they would desecrate the sabbath in public. I was in a quandary about whether to stay or go, but I thought that somehow I was meant to be there. I remember that, sadly, the 'sermon' was full of sacrilege and heresy, and that daughters of hasidic parents sat listening to this. Their fathers were certainly busy at that moment with the Talmud and their mothers with the Yiddish Bible, and I remember that the thought was born in me that if our girls had an environment of their own and places to go to, things would certainly be very different.

On 9 Av [1 August] 1914 the Great War broke out, and not long after that we were forced to leave Kraków; it was this move that led to what is now called 'Bais Yaakov'.

[5] *Ḥok leyisra'el* is a compilation of readings from the Bible, Mishnah, Talmud, and Zohar, arranged in daily readings according to the portion of the week, a system deriving from one laid out by the kabbalist Hayim Vital but compiled by Yitzhak Baruch and Hayim Yosef David Azulai in its present form.

[6] Ruth was among the early Zionist women's clubs in Kraków.

5675 [late 1914]. Along with many other refugees from Kraków, we settled in the great city of Vienna. Ten weeks had gone by since we had arrived and we had experienced many difficulties For almost two weeks we wandered the streets, but it was almost impossible to find an apartment in the Jewish quarter. Vienna was like a pot on the boil, teeming with Jewish refugees from all over Galicia who had left their homes to flee from the storm of war.

Finally we managed to find a place to live in the sixth district, on Amperdämpfer Street. But then another worry set in: it wasn't a Jewish neighbourhood. It was an hour's walk from the Schiffschul, and I knew of no other synagogue in which to pray.[7] Where would we attend services? My landlady, seeing my anxiety, gave me the good news that there was an Orthodox synagogue on Stumpergasse. Yes, that synagogue was the cradle of the movement that is now so popular—Bais Yaakov!

On Friday afternoon I walked there with a prayer book and a Pentateuch, so that I would have them for the sabbath services. The synagogue sexton explained to me, though, that it hadn't been necessary to do so, since women who didn't carry on the sabbath were provided with prayer books there.

I was filled with joy. This meant that I was among Jews. Yes, even in Vienna there were Jews who didn't carry on the sabbath!

It was that same sabbath morning, I think, that I first went to the Stumpergasse synagogue to pray. Before the Torah reading I saw the *Rabbiner* appear at the pulpit.[8] That was new for me.

'What's going on?' I asked a woman sitting near me.

'It's the sabbath of Hanukah!' she responded. 'And the *Rabbiner* will speak about the significance of this day!'

Riveted to my seat, I listened with great fascination to the fiery, spirited words of the rabbi.

In his sermon, he depicted the greatness and sublimity of the historical figure of Judith, and through her, he eloquently and passionately called upon Jewish women and their daughters to act according to the model of this Jewish heroine.[9]

[7] The more centrally located and much larger Schiffschul (more formally known as Kehilat Adat Yisra'el), at 8 Grosser Schiffgasse, was an important Orthodox synagogue and study house serving staunchly traditional Hungarian Jews associated with the Hatam Sofer's followers. Bertha Pappenheim's father was a co-founder of the synagogue. The synagogue on Stumpergasse where Flesch served as rabbi was an offshoot of the Schiffschul at some distance from the Jewish neighbourhood, and was more formally known as the Tempel-und-Schulverein Stumpergasse.

[8] See Ch. 1 n. 82.

[9] On Judith, see Ch. 1 n. 2.

It's a shame that I have forgotten the beautiful thoughts and points of that sermon, and what I do remember I lack the eloquence to convey on paper.

There is one thing that I cannot forget. Even as I was caught up in the spiritual description of the character of Judith, it occurred to me: ah, if only all those women and girls in Kraków were here now to learn who we are and where we come from.

It struck me that our major problem is that our sisters know so little about our history, which alienates them from our people and its traditions. If only they knew of our holy martyrs, or had the slightest grasp of the heroism of our great men and women—things would be entirely different.

Later, however, I realized that when the whole world was engulfed in the flames of a horrific war, the fire of human hatred was roaring high, and the Jewish people were swimming in a sea of trouble and evil, it was unfortunately not the time to think about the future.

That moment, though, gave birth to a variety of schemes, with great, grandiose aims. Providence decreed, however, that these would have to wait. The bloody wounds of war were still open and painful.

Was this really to be my last night in Vienna? Would I really be in Kraków again tomorrow, ready to turn my schemes into reality? Perhaps I was already close to the goal?

After that first sermon by Rabbi Flesch, I became a regular visitor at the Stumpergasse synagogue. Nothing could stop me, neither terrible weather nor the frightful tumult of wartime. I unfailingly attended Rabbi Flesch's lectures on the Bible, Psalms, *Ethics of the Fathers*, and his profound meditations on various issues of the day. The more I learned, the more I was haunted by the question of how I could bring this knowledge to the Jewish girls of Poland, so they could hear and know the things that I was learning.

The clock was racing. My thoughts raced along with it, and my heart pounded feverishly. How would my plan to create an educational home, a religious spirit among Jewish daughters, be received in Kraków?

But I knew in advance. People would say: 'Really? In the twentieth century, you want to drag Jewish daughters back to piety and tradition?'

At the same time a secret voice murmured within me: 'You have to nurture the vision of a religious girls' school, to save this generation of Jewish women according to the spirit of Israel of old.'

So I decided to call a meeting of Jewish women as soon as I arrived home, to lay out my proposal before them. I was encouraged by the saying of our sages: 'Every gathering that is for the sake of Heaven will endure' [*Avot* 4: 14].

On the journey from Vienna to Kraków I was entirely absorbed in preparing a plan for the upcoming work.

The end of Av 5675 [August 1915]. It's been two weeks since I returned to my home town of Kraków, and in that period I've already managed to accomplish something. On my first day back I presented my proposal to a small circle of well-known religious women, naturally, the most religious in the city, who listened to me with evident joy. It was more difficult to find a place for a larger gathering. Only after great effort was I able to secure a room in the Kraków orphanage for a public meeting.

But soon new worries arose.

It's true that the older women were inspired by my plans, but what about the young ones, the future mothers of Israel: what would they have to say? Would they laugh me and my ideas out of the room?

Nevertheless, I persevered, and by that sabbath had prepared a lecture for a gathering of forty girls. The lecture was dedicated to *Ethics of the Fathers*, and the question I addressed was why one was supposed to study this text during the summer sabbaths in particular.[10] Expounding on the saying 'Make a fence around the Torah' [*Avot* 1: 1], I explained that the Torah is compared to a beautiful garden in which the most gorgeous flowers and delicious fruit grow. If there was no fence around the garden, evil people and wild beasts could destroy everything within it. So too did our holy sages make a fence around the Torah. We know, for instance, that desecrating the sabbath merits the death penalty ('whoever does work on the sabbath day shall be put to death' [Exod. 31: 15]) and so the sages came and built fences and moats to make it impossible to get anywhere near these prohibited actions. That is the reason for the prohibition against touching certain objects, such that it is forbidden to even put one's hand on anything that could be used to perform labour forbidden on the sabbath.

[10] Schenirer does not directly answer the question of why *Ethics of the Fathers* should be studied particularly in the summer, but this custom is sometimes explained as a response to the temptation to relax religious standards during the leisure of the summer months. The first verse of *Ethics of the Torah* ends with the rabbinic recommendation to build fences around the Torah, implicitly warning against relaxing standards under any circumstances, and this was the basis for her comments.

I could sense most of the girls looking at me with shock and wonder—really? This is what you brought us here to listen to? I could see the ironic smiles on many of their faces, and without a fare-thee-well, some of them just disappeared.

This was the cool, even dismissive, response my first lecture received. I understood then the enormous difficulty of the task I had set myself. But I girded my loins anew, strengthening my resolve not to abandon my ideals.

Months went by after that first lecture for the Kraków girls, with nothing to show for my efforts. But I was not disillusioned. The High Holy Days were upon us, and soon indeed the holiest of them all, Yom Kippur.

Somehow on that eve of Yom Kippur I felt more agitated and burdened than usual. Before my eyes swarmed images from the time when the Temple was still standing, with the high priest at the altar sending the sacrificial goat off to Azazel in the wilderness [Lev. 16], and when Jews had a sign in the crimson thread that turned white to indicate that God had forgiven their sins.[11] The high priest, the Temple service, the whole aura and ritual of Israel in those days—and today? The sublimity has vanished, the holiness gone, everything taken from us!

And what do we make do with today? Where are the hearts of the people of Israel, whose prayers and spiritual service are supposed to fulfil the same ends as the ancient worship in the Temple? Today's young Jews, especially young Jewish girls, have ceased to pray, and if they do set foot inside a synagogue, it is out of habit, and their heart and soul are not in it! Our daughters know nothing of their history, of the greatness of their people, have no understanding of the profound depths of Jewish liturgy, so how could I imagine that anything might change!

That whole day, until the start of the Kol Nidrei service in the synagogue, these thoughts gave me no rest. I kept coming back to the same idea: *We must open the eyes of our sisters, so they will see the great light of Israel!* Forget any doubts, ignore all the obstacles! What do I care if people smile at me and mock my plan? Once the ice begins to crack, they will look at me very differently! And anyway, what does my pride matter? If the intentions are true and the goal is noble, will they not bear fruit?

[11] This ritual is recorded in BT *Yoma 39b*. The usual practice of present-day Orthodox publications is to write 'G-d', but Schenirer and the Bais Yaakov movement only sometimes refrained from writing out the Yiddish word *Got* in the interwar period. I maintain academic usage here and spell out the name.

The cantor ended the evening prayer of Yom Kippur with the words 'Look to the Lord; be strong and of good courage' [Ps. 27: 14], and these words aroused a powerful faith in my heart. My resolve was strengthened as the choir burst forth in full voice with the end of *Adon olam*, 'The Lord is with me I will not fear!'

Today brought sad tidings to all of Austria: Kaiser Franz Joseph is dead.[12]

Yes, even an emperor, even the most powerful leader of an empire dies.

If kings and officers would keep that in mind, they would rule their lands and people very differently, with a little less cruelty, a little more human love.

This thought reminds me of a *midrash*. When King David would wake himself every night at midnight to study Torah, his evil inclination would argue with him: 'Every other king sleeps until noon, and you rouse yourself at midnight?' And King David would answer, 'But I'm going to the theatre!' And the evil inclination would think to itself, 'If that is the case, let him go the theatre.' When King David arrived at the house of study, he would say to himself, 'Isn't the whole of earthly existence just like a theatre? Every person plays his role: the king with his golden staff and the beggar with his poor stick. And the play ends the same way for everyone, with the curtain coming down. The same dirt covers the rich king and the poor beggar. Except that, for the one who carries his good deeds with him, a new eternal world opens up.'

That was what the King of Israel thought, the one about whom is said 'David, King of Israel, lives on!'[13]

Meanwhile days and weeks passed, and little by little my plan was beginning to develop. The girls' organization I was trying to form was starting to become a

[12] Franz Joseph I (1830–1916) was emperor of Austria and king of Hungary, Croatia, and Bohemia. He was generally well liked among Jews of the Austro-Hungarian empire for his liberal policies. In an 1880 visit to Kraków the emperor was greeted by a delegation of Orthodox Jews carrying a row of Torah scrolls and led by the chief rabbi of the city, Shimon Sofer (Schreiber), who was the son of the Hatam Sofer.

[13] These words, which form the lyrics of a familiar Jewish song, were the catchphrase for noting the appearance of a new moon, according to BT *Rosh hashanah 25a*. The well-known story of King David waking at midnight to study Torah is described in BT *Ber. 3b*, and a similar subterfuge is described in *Leviticus Rabbah* 26: 3 (on Lev. 35: 1), in *Midrash Rabbah Hamevuar*, ed. Steinberger. Neither source mentions the theatre, but David Zvi Katzberg relates that a story circulated among popular speakers and the general public in which King David pretended to be going to circuses and the theatre while actually going to synagogues and houses of study. See Katzberg, *Mevaser tsedek / Yalkut melitsot*, 257.

reality. I also founded a library with reading material sent from Frankfurt—the works of Samson Raphael Hirsch, Marcus Lehmann, and other similar authors.[14]

One thought was constantly on my mind. Would my efforts bear fruit? Was it possible to believe that I could accomplish anything with older girls, who had already formed their own individual perspectives on life?

Nevertheless, I continued working with all my heart. The members of the girls' organization showed an interest in my plans. And the new organization was also arousing interest in Kraków.

The truth is that I wasn't entirely happy with my newly founded Orthodox Girls' Union. Its activities were impressive enough, and the members listened to my lectures with enthusiasm and took an interest in the ideas I expressed. I had stopped working as a seamstress, putting aside my needle and storing away the sewing machine, and was dedicating my time entirely to the Union. But even though its success was considerable, I was still not satisfied.

What was missing was the main thing, the essential point with all its depth and strength, towards which my heart was striving. The main goal is to observe and do, so that learning leads to action!

Yes, the girls were inspired by a beautiful talk, charmed by an exalted thought, moved by a poetic passage in the Bible. But despite that, they still couldn't bring themselves to submit to the commandments of Jewish law and fulfil the obligations of Torah. And no wonder: most were young women already, and it wasn't easy to persuade them to take on a new, truly Jewish life, with all its customs and traditions.

So my mind was already moving along a different track. One had to begin with children, saplings that could still be bent. Only with young children would my ideal be perfectly realized. I would have to start schools for young girls, truly Jewish schools, where the educational spirit would be in accordance with the perspectives of Israel of old. For that purpose, no effort could be too great, no price too high. Thank God a religious Jewry still existed, who would have to be reminded of something essential that they had forgotten: their duty to the younger generation. They would have to be reminded constantly, given no rest, until the need for our young girls to also know something, and maybe even a lot, about our spiritual treasures deeply penetrated their consciousness. And when

[14] On Hirsch, see Ch. 1 n. 44. On Lehmann, see Ch. 2 n. 6.

these girls were no longer alienated from their own tradition, they would certainly become proud carriers of our eternal Jewish ideals.

'Throw away the machine, renounce the work of sewing clothes for the body, and take on instead the task of measuring and sewing garments for the soul, for the Jewish soul, so it may be protected from the arrows of heresy!' This thought pursued me and drove me to further my work. To gather small children and begin to introduce them to *Shema yisra'el*.

Since I couldn't get the plan of starting a girls' school out of my mind, I turned for advice to my brother, who was then living in Petschlau (Czechoslovakia).[15]

In his initial reply he just laughed at me: 'What's the point of getting mixed up with party politics?' When I told him that I was determined to go ahead with what I had decided to do and had no intention of giving up, he wrote back to me, 'So come to Marienbad, where the Belzer Rebbe (of blessed memory, the father of the present Belzer Rebbe) is currently staying . . . and we'll hear whether the leader of the generation approves of your plan!'[16]

My joy was boundless, and even though I was very short of money, I quickly prepared for the journey. As soon as I arrived in Marienbad, my brother and I went right away to see the rebbe. My brother, who was a regular visitor to the rebbe's court, wrote in his note 'she wants to lead Jewish girls along the Jewish path'. With my own ears I heard the rebbe speak the words 'Blessing and success', which were the most exquisite balm to my ears, and filled me with fresh courage. The blessing of this great and righteous man inspired the highest hopes in me that my efforts would find their fulfilment.

Heshvan 5678 [October/November 1917]. Finally, finally, the goal has been reached!

I'm sitting now in my very own schoolroom, and who could possibly appre-

[15] This may be the town of Petschau in Czechoslovakia, which had an Orthodox population. Heshl Klepfish, however, who retells the story, locates Schenirer's brother in Tshibin (Trzebinia), a small town to the west of Kraków: see Klepfish, 'Sarah Schenirer the Writer', 123.

[16] Marienbad is a spa town in Czechoslovakia that was frequented by the Belzer Rebbe and many other hasidic rabbis, as well as their hasidim and other ordinary Jews. The rebbe consulted by Schenirer was the third Belzer Rebbe, Yissachar Dov Rokeach (1851–1926). The one she refers to as alive at the time of her writing (early 1930s) was the fourth rebbe of Belz, the eldest son of the third rebbe, Aharon Rokeach (1877–1957).

ciate how I feel? Has anyone experienced anything like what I am going through now? Have they seen the radiant faces of my children? The way their eyes sparkle when I explain to them the meaning of a blessing. With joy they ask me, Are we going to meet again tomorrow so we can hear some more beautiful things?

There are twenty-five of them altogether, most of them children I sewed dresses for, and now I ask their mothers, Will you also allow me to provide them with spiritual clothing?

Twenty-five children, twenty-five souls that have been placed in my hands to bring to life. I have a little room, old benches, no blackboard yet. But even this poverty sends shivers of joy to my heart, for this is the place where my spiritual work is taking shape.

11 Kislev [26 November 1917]. The school is growing from day to day. My dreams are coming true. Thank God, I now have forty students. Somehow every difficulty seems to have vanished. Somehow, I've even passed the point of 'all beginnings are difficult' [*Mekhilta* on Exod. 19: 5].

The children really are good material. Innocent creatures who have never tasted sin. It's interesting to see how eagerly they arrive at school each day, how keen they are to hear fresh ideas. They already know that there's more to life than eating and drinking. They know that a person can only lead a happy life if they serve the Creator with true enthusiasm.

I'm so busy with all the work that nothing else exists for me. I barely notice the hours and days and weeks fly by. I never have a moment to rest.

And one more thing gives me joy: I'm not alone. Two people, whose names should be remembered for these deeds, have also recognized the great importance of this school and are helping me with it to the best of their ability.

The first is the young rabbi's wife, Mrs Halberstam, the granddaughter of the Divrei Hayim of Sanz, of blessed memory.[17] She has been working zealously to find children for my school, persuading parents and devoting to me every minute she can spare. The second is Mr M. Luksenberg, the father of one of the students, who as soon as he became aware of the mission of the school threw himself heart and soul into the project. It makes me very uncomfortable that he takes a few hours away from the time he had set aside for learning Torah to spend on us, but I comfort myself with the thought that girls' education is so important and

[17] Rabbi Hayim Yoel Halberstam (1793–1876), the founder of the hasidic dynasty of Sanz (Polish: Nowy Sącz) was known as the *Divrei ḥayim* for his work on Jewish law by that title.

burning a problem that it certainly constitutes an instance of 'It is time to act for the Lord, so one may violate the Torah' [Ps. 119: 126].[18]

I don't have the time or patience even to write these few sentences in my diary. I don't know when I'll have the opportunity again to take my pen in hand. The work has just begun, and until I've set it on the right course there can be no rest or peace of mind.

[18] On this verse, see Ch. 2 n. 34. The reason Schenirer is uncomfortable with Mr Luksenberg taking time away from his own Torah study to help her is that Torah study is an obligation for men, and he is sacrificing time that should be spent fulfilling this obligation for the sake of girls' religious education, which is not obligatory.

II Bais Yaakov and Bnos Agudath Israel

The Mission of the Bais Yaakov Schools

I

I think that by now everyone knows that the sole mission of the Bais Yaakov schools is to educate Jewish girls so that, with all their strength and with every breath, they will serve the Creator and fulfil the commandments of the Torah with seriousness and passion. They will learn that they are children of a people whose existence relies not on dwelling in their own land, in the way that other nations are closely connected to their land, but rather on their sole sacred ideal, the Torah, through which and only through which they became a nation. And it is because the sons and daughters of this nation abandoned the Torah and did not observe its commandments that they lost their holy land, the Land of Israel.

What constitutes the power of the Torah, for which we have sacrificed so much throughout the ages? Understand this well! Our Torah is not a religion like other religions, it's not an institution for worshipping God that brings together adherents on a few special holidays, or a guidebook for a few special worshippers. Our Torah is not a system of laws that derives from the human mind. It is a holy fire from the One God that gives sustenance to the Jewish soul, arouses the Jewish heart, and in each moment of life reminds each soul to remain faithful to God's law and to be totally bound up with it.

The Torah is binding on everyone, from the individual to the collective, whether one is a priest or an Israelite, a learned person or an ordinary Jew, a judge or a working man, a prophet or a villager. One must fulfil the commandments at home as in the field, in private or in the business world, in the Temple as in the street, in a store as in a workshop. It opens one's eyes to see the divine power in nature, to recognize Providence in the workings of history. It teaches us to understand our place among the nations. The Torah demands from us that we 'impress these words upon your very heart'—and that we should spread its ideals in the world, 'and teach them to your children—reciting them when you stay at home and when you are away', when one goes to sleep and awakes from sleep. It must be the one straight line that we walk as we lead our lives, the crown on our heads, the watchword of our domestic and public lives—'on the doorposts of your house and on your gates' [Deut. 11: 18–21].

Understand, Jewish women and girls! For thousands of years the Jewish people lived with the Torah. Millions of great men and women drew all their emotions, thoughts, and values about everything in life from its holy fire. The national treasure that we laboured for from time eternal has always been: the study of Torah.

The Bais Yaakov schools have as their mission to keep the Torah alive among women and to excite the passion for Torah among our daughters. The holy fire will burn high not when we build superb schools or assemble fine libraries. No! Only when the holy Torah is studied and disseminated will its flames burn high and hearts be warmed—only when the Torah becomes the very law of our life!

But that can be accomplished, I think, only through schools, authentically Jewish schools for girls.

I could go from city to city, from town to town, shouting at the top of my lungs: Jews! How long will you stand by, shrugging your shoulders, as your homes are destroyed? How can you just watch as your daughters sit at your holy sabbath tables in immodest dresses, their minds immersed in books that are alien to the spirit of Judaism?

And you, Jewish mothers! How can you be so cold-blooded that you just sit and watch as, from day to day, hour to hour, your daughters' hearts grow more and more distant and alienated from you? And are you then not torn away from them too? Only schools, real Jewish girls' schools, in which your daughters from their earliest years are filled with passion for our Jewish faith—that is the only solution! I know that creating these schools is very difficult under the present circumstances, especially when finding space for them is such a stubborn obstacle in our path, but with good and steadfast intentions all difficulties may be overcome.[1]

Take the Kraków Bais Yaakov, for example. In 1917 I founded this school, ridiculously enough, in one small room. By the time the Agudah officially took it over two years later there were already 280 children studying there. Today,

[1] I believe Schenirer's reference here is to the persistent problem of finding spaces in which to establish schools, which was difficult both because rooms were not always available and because government permits were required that could certify that these spaces were safe.

Tishrei 5664 [autumn 1923], we have a perfectly fine apartment with eight large and fully equipped rooms and a programme of vocational courses for up to a thousand students (may that number increase).

Any failures we experienced have always stemmed from the fact that there is a strong interest in boys' education, but people don't care about the education of girls. It's true that many chapters of the Agudah have followed the example of Kraków and founded Bais Yaakov schools. But in hundreds of towns nothing, unfortunately, has been done in this realm.

Wake up, my dear sisters, and show your sincere desire to fulfil the greatest task of our historical hour!

2

I have already mentioned the verse of the holy Torah 'and teach them to your children—reciting them'. Every Jewish father and mother who recites this verse twice daily must also feel compelled by it. The divine voice moves the heart of a Jewish father to the call: 'And this was my portion from all my labour' [Eccles. 2: 10]—this is the only thing that remains of all my toil. If my descendants remain Jewish, faithful to their Creator, then will my name be remembered and my life will have had a purpose.

This was the very same thought by which our parents and grandparents lived. They gave up their souls to God with joy, secure that the following generations would not besmirch their names by deviating, God forbid, from the right path.

I won't speak of those long-ago times, when Rabbi Akiva put away his shepherd's staff at the age of 40 to become the greatest spiritual leader of the Jews; nor will I speak of those later golden ages when there lived a great teacher, Rav Ashi, from whose yeshivas emerged the greatest Jewish spirits; nor about the still later periods in which other great men lived and worked: Alfasi, Rashi, Ibn Ezra, Maimonides, Nahmanides, Rashba, the Rosh, Abarbanel, and others whose names still shine brightly in history.[2] Let us just cast our eyes over the previous

[2] Rabbi Akiva, a leading *tana* who appears frequently in rabbinic literature; Rav Ashi, *amora* who led the Babylonian rabbinic academy at Sura; Rabbi Isaac ben Jacob Alfasi Hakohen (1013–1103), a Moroccan talmudist and legal scholar; Rashi, or Rabbi Solomon Yitzchaki (1040–1105), foremost medieval commentator on the Bible and Talmud; Ibn Ezra, or Rabbi Abraham ben Meir Ibn Ezra (1089–1167), philosopher, poet, and exegete; Maimonides, or Rabbi Moses ben Maimon (1135?–1204), physician, exegete, codifier of Jewish law, and the foremost Jewish philosopher of the medieval period; Nahmanides, or Rabbi Moses ben Nahman Girondi (1194–1270), leading medieval Jewish scholar, physician, kabbalist, and biblical commentator; Rashba, Rabbi Solomon ben Aderet (1235–1310), rabbinic authority in Barcelona; Rosh, Rabbi Asher ben Jehiel Ashkenazi

century: does not the heart of every pious Jew weep at the terrible injury that Torah study has suffered since the gates of the ghetto were flung open and Jewish youth was allowed to attend secular schools? Must we not lament for the great majority of Jewish homes along with the great prophet: 'Gone from the daughter of Zion are all that were her glory' [Lam. 1: 6]? For they, too, the Jewish daughters, were swept up with the tides of the time. The pure, poetic, exquisite Jewish life no longer appealed to them, everything Jewish seemed, in their eyes, ugly and fanatical. They were enchanted by whatever called itself 'Berlin' or 'Paris fashion'. They aspired to participate in this alien world, they wanted to see and be seen, to marvel and be marvelled at, and that is how Jewish homes were regularly destroyed!

The Torah sits and weeps. Yes, she weeps, to see these princesses, born in the image of God, gradually lose that divine spirit, turning into parrots or wax dolls. For what else is a Jewish girl who worships fashion but a loyal slave? When fashion orders her to, she wears a high collar in the heat of the summer, and when it tells her to, in the winter, she walks around with her neck bare. Yes, only fashion has the power to exert such authority over the morals of our daughters!

Jewish sisters! If you hold your dignity dear, pay heed to the call of your Torah! Beware of all that verges on immorality! Whatever fashion considers sacred, but which can rob you of your holiness and purity—keep away from it with all your energy, even if everyone laughs at you. 'It is better to be laughed at and mocked by fashion than for the Holy One to be angry at you for even a single moment' (*Horeb*).[3]

Every Jewish father must mourn, seeing the Jewishness of his environment diminished and weakened, his own child walking around with alien ideals and mocking him as a fanatic. But mothers are no less blameworthy in this matter. These Jewish mothers have apparently forgotten how their own mothers acted, how they themselves were raised. Our grandmothers certainly didn't sit before their mirrors in the mornings while their children were taken care of by a 'nanny' or 'governess'. They couldn't speak knowledgeably about what was playing at the theatre. The foundation of their lives was 'The beginning of wisdom is the fear of God' [Ps. 11: 10]. The first words a mother uttered to her child were in praise of God. At the age of 3 they brought the child to the Torah, and without

(1250 or 1259–1327), eminent talmudist; Abarbanel, Isaac ben Judah (1437–1508), Portuguese philosopher and exegete.

[3] The reference here, Schenirer's brief note, is to the 1838 work by Samson Raphael Hirsch, *Horeb: A Philosophy of Jewish Laws and Observances*.

any special pedagogical expertise they understood how to raise this child until he himself concluded that 'and you shall recite it day and night' [Josh. 1: 8] must be the ideal for his own life. And the principles that the *ḥeder* did not provide were provided as a matter of course in his parents' home. The child noticed the attention and respect with which his parents treated Torah scholars and yeshiva students, and that implanted in him the desire and will to devote himself to the study of Torah. It is therefore no surprise that with such an attitude towards Torah and its followers among the ordinary Jewish masses, there could rise up such world-renowned Torah authorities as Rabbi Jonathan Eybeschütz, the Penei Yehoshua, the Noda Biyehudah, Rabbi Mordecai Benet, the Hatam Sofer, and others of that calibre.[4] We can clearly see, then, that only a broad network of truly Jewish schools can correct this matter, and bring back the honour that was once accorded to the Torah.

I just want to remind parents, though, that in sending their children to religious schools they have not thereby absolved themselves of the responsibility of supervising them. The school must supplement the home. Parents are responsible for creating harmony between school and home, for seeing that the child is following school rules, for not allowing their child to maintain friendships with irreligious girls, and so on.

There is yet another duty incumbent on parents who want to raise their children in the spirit of Torah—to materially and morally support the Bais Yaakov schools, and with that support to fulfil the verse, 'But all the Israelites enjoyed light in their dwellings' [Exod. 10: 23], that the light of the Torah will penetrate every Jewish home.

3

Many times, in speech or writing, I have tried to remind our brothers and sisters about their holy duty to their children, and especially their daughters, who are being raised to be alienated from our spirit, culture, and Torah. This abnormal phenomenon is damaging and destroying the Jewish home, Jewish family life.

[4] Jonathan Eybeschütz (1690–1764), was a talmudist, kabbalist, and native of Kraków; Jacob Joshua Falk (1680–1756), wrote a commentary on the Talmud entitled *Penei yehoshua*, and was also born in Kraków; Ezekiel ben Judah Landau (1713–93) was an influential Polish-born legal scholar and author of the *Noda biyehudah*; Mordecai Benet (1753–1829) was the chief rabbi of Moravia and a close associate of the Hatam Sofer. The Hatam Sofer, Rabbi Moses Schreiber or Sofer (1762–1839), was a German-born leader of Hungarian (and, more generally, east European) Jewish militant Orthodoxy and a fierce opponent of Reform Judaism.

Children become enemies of their parents and of the Jewish people and all they hold sacred.

The father and mother believe that by sending their child to school, or hiring a teacher and paying his or her salary—they have fulfilled their obligations to the world and to themselves.

It's true that most parents these days have no choice but to turn their child over to a stranger to be educated. They themselves cannot manage this education alone. But why do they nevertheless not take the slightest interest in the person they are handing their children over to, or whether they are sending their child to an appropriate school or one that's entirely inappropriate? Why are they blind to the fact that the people to whom they have entrusted their child's soul are actually the secret enemies of this soul, and are waiting for just the right moment to desecrate the sacred shrine? Because these people aren't always free to act out their heresies openly they try to accomplish them through the children; they draw them into their schools and then shape them into enemies of all that should be nearest and dearest to them.

But these matters have all been sufficiently discussed and described. There are very few children that emerge from this danger unscathed, but even knowing this, our people have no desire to learn from these lessons. A child, especially a girl—they argue persuasively—must go to school these days. And what can we do if there are still no good Jewish schools that can shield them from the myriad evils of the outside world?

Of course this is a difficult issue, but we must know that the old safeguards that used to provide an impenetrable shield against the enemy are useless now. Today we come into daily contact with our most dangerous enemies. For that reason we need the most powerful devices that will allow us to pass through their hands unscathed.

It would certainly be ideal if we had the means of establishing entirely separate Jewish schools, where all the teachers were devoted to Jewish texts and tradition. Even if we have to accept that not every teacher in these schools would be entirely dedicated to our ideals, if the educational programme—including secular subjects—were basically in line with our tradition and the teachers strictly supervised, that would also be acceptable.

But the best armour against the dangers lurking around us is Bais Yaakov, where girls acquire an accurate conception of Jews and Judaism and an authentically Jewish education. Jewish pupils emerge from there armed with Jewish experiences and Jewish weapons.

We have spoken, but we can never be satisfied with mere speech. A network of Bais Yaakov schools stands as a living witness, calling out to and arousing our brothers and sisters: Create such schools in your own communities! Have mercy on your own daughters, and do not allow them to become alienated from you! A little effort, some more concern, and you will salvage your family life, your roots, from withering!

Bais Yaakov [O House of Jacob]! Come, let us walk by the light of the Lord [Isa. 2: 5]!

After the Second Teacher-Training Course [1926]

It's been a year since the teacher-training course in Robów, when I said goodbye to the group of student teachers who were leaving for a whole variety of provincial towns.[5] I can still see them, these educators of the young generation, sitting on the benches in the Robów woods. By the light of the moon I could see the sparkle in their eyes. In one eye trembles a tear at the thought that this exalted spiritual life in the lap of nature is coming to an end. In another, though, I catch a flash of joy for the spiritual treasures that have been acquired over the past six weeks.

I can read their thoughts: let us together raise ever higher our Torah banner, lead our lost sisters back to our people's truth, and together experience spiritual joy. And I wish that God may help them in their work for the Jewish people, in their desire to bring our lost sisters back to the flock!

A year has passed—now we are in Jordanów.

Again we are together, and some new faces have joined us. Aside from the fifty-five teachers that joined us again after Robów, there are forty new student teachers, who, God willing, will graduate around Passover and begin to work for the community.

We are no longer in the wild woods of Robów, with its Gypsy camps, where the natural landscape was a constant reminder of how much work was needed in order to cultivate our surroundings. Now we're in Jordanów. The geographical location is not so different from Robów—we are still surrounded by mountains, forests, and rivers—but here the slopes are carpeted with deckchairs, the road is paved, there are modern villas that house up to a hundred people, and all this teaches us what human enterprise can make out of the materials of Divine nature.

[5] The first teacher-training course took place in Robów in 1925, and the second in Jordanów in 1926.

Although only a year separates us from Robów, we can already see the fruits of that first step for the Bais Yaakov schools. Thanks to the spiritual assistance from the western lands—from Miss [Betty] Rothschild of Zurich, Switzerland, and of Miss [Judith] Rosenbaum from Frankfurt—and especially thanks to the indefatigable leadership and work of the esteemed Dr S. Deutschländer, our seminary studies have become professionalized and systematized, and our programme need feel no embarrassment in comparison with other similar programmes. On the contrary—we can serve as a model for them.

Truly magical is the image before my eyes of ninety-five girls, divided into five groups under the guidance of their leaders, sitting on the soft grass of the meadow, their eyes sparkling with interest in the deep thoughts they are hearing, right here in the lap of nature! How much hope that arouses! Each of them has, or will have, as many as 150 children under her care. She will slake their spiritual thirst from the effervescent springs of Torah. She will teach them how to revere the old ways of modesty. And so, with God's help, a generation of truly Jewish mothers will emerge, who will know well how to accomplish the task of raising children who can become true women of valour!

This joy is mixed for me with sorrowful thoughts, however. There are still so many Jewish daughters who long to partake in these treasures. We are deluged with applications to our seminary, but for lack of funds we cannot accept them all. We are so often short these days of what we need to feed our students! Even with the students we already have, we are so short of space that fifty girls sleep in one room!

We stand now on the threshold of a new year and with it comes new hope.

We know that when the month of Tishrei, so filled with spiritual treasures, has gone and quiet Heshvan arrives with its lengthening winter nights, then we will gather with some stalwart Jewish men and women and take the time to consider how we might strengthen the Jewish people and spread the light among them.

And, in the meantime, we await their collaboration!

The First Anniversary of Bnos [March 1927]

For a whole year I have stood at the side without daring to openly congratulate the newly formed movement of Bnos Agudath Israel. I was like someone who has finally arrived at a long-awaited goal and feels such powerful emotions that they cannot bring themselves to cross the threshold for a long, long time. I couldn't believe my eyes, even considering how many people showed up to the large public meeting in Łódź a year ago [March 1926]. I said to myself, this cannot be real!

But recently, after visiting a few Bnos groups, I came to the conclusion that this is not a dream but flesh-and-blood reality. My joy over this important development is inexpressible.

Remember, sisters! We are bound together by spiritual bonds, which everyone knows are much stronger than physical ones. A spiritual bond connects us, across the entire world. The Jewish daughter now takes open pride in her religious feelings. She knows that she is a member of an organization, whose mission statement dates back thousands of years, and which has taken upon itself to organize young Jewish girls under the banner of the old, ever new, holy Torah.

Do you know, dear sisters, what youth means? Youth means joy, courage in life, optimism, and a powerful belief in eternal ideals!

Every youth organization must have these principles embedded in its programme. Doubt, sadness, pessimism—these are the antithesis of youth!

And our Torah is the source of true joy, as King David says in Psalms, 'The precepts of the Lord are just, rejoicing the heart' [19: 9]! So how much joy, optimism, and faith in God must accompany the work of this organization, which works for the Torah?

Youth means enthusiasm, excitement, living and striving. Detachment, indifference—these are anti-youth. So that is what our youth organization must be, what our work for Torah and Judaism demands from us: inspiration, rejoicing in every breath and at every step.

The Bible says: 'By the pursuit of them a person shall live' [Lev. 18: 5]—we should experience God's commandments with *life* and excitement—which means that our youth movement must always be both lively and full of charm.

Our young girls must fulfil their Jewish duties. They must become a model for the service of God and our people.

The Kotzker Rebbe, of blessed memory, says that when our forefather Abraham saw how enthusiastically Isaac went to his own sacrifice even though God had not appeared to him, he came to the realization that his greatest obligation was to make fast friends with the younger generation.[6]

Young and old together, and only then will the prophecy be fulfilled that 'young people will put old ones to shame' [Mishnah *Sot.* 9: 15] with their glowing

[6] Menachem Mendel Morgensztern of Kotzk, better known as the Kotzker Rebbe (1787–1859), was a hasidic rabbi and leader famous for his insightful teachings.

dedication to the faith and to God, and then, only then, will the messianic age arrive.

Youth is loud, assertive, and that is truly its greatness; it is compared to 'ink written on new parchment' [*Avot* 4: 20]—it expresses loudly and clearly what youthfulness means.

Old age, in contrast, keeps its head down, makes no great outcry, but is nevertheless deeply imbued with its own ideas. Its learning is compared to ink written on old parchment. It may be difficult to read, but nevertheless it is absorbed and ingrained in the parchment, and that is what the young must learn from old people.[7]

In our youth movement, both must be strongly bound together. Young and old must stand together.

The most important tasks of Bnos Agudath Israel are these:

1. *Striving to advance, to lead.* Not beyond all boundaries, but rather with a strong connection to our sacred tradition, without which no Jew may take a step forward.

2. *To advance in the knowledge of Torah*, especially learning Jewish laws, in order to fulfil the duties incumbent on a Jew.

3. *To spread our ideals* with warmth and light in every corner: in every place where there is a member of Bnos, she must found a Bnos group and not rest until the Jewish spark that smoulders in the heart of every Jewish daughter flares up into a fiery blaze that encompasses all our sisters.

So. To work, sisters! To fight for everything holy to us, for our sacred Torah ideals.

And a final word:

Dear sisters! To be inspired is easy. A good talk can so inspire a person that she will seize her most precious possession and give it away, or promise to work forever for an ideal. But to *persist* in this ideal for years on end, for a whole life—that we unfortunately lack. And so, sisters, you have to strive for only one thing: To keep the fire of inspiration for God and his people burning within you, until your last breath!!

[7] *Avot* 4: 20 reads: 'Elisha the son of Abuya would say: One who learns as a child is compared to what? To ink written on new parchment. And one who learns as an elder is compared to what? To ink written on erased parchment.' Schenirer, perhaps quoting from memory, has 'old paper' (*neyar yashan*) rather than 'erased paper' (*neyar maḥuk*). The reference is to parchment that has been used and reused many times (as was the practice in eras when paper was scarce), rather than freshly inscribed.

Three Letters to Bnos Agudath Israel

I

Dear sisters!

First of all I call you to battle on behalf of the holy Torah, and although I am certain that you yourselves know what the Torah means for the Jewish people and for each individual Jewish person, I will try to outline this again briefly.

The first thing everyone must know is that the Torah is not just something to be studied in order to learn what is in it. The important thing is this: fulfilling what it teaches and commands us to do.

For those who study the Torah it is the most life-giving of waters and the brightest of lights, it is the most nourishing milk known to human beings, the wine that bestows the most joy. It is a hammer that shatters rocks, a sword to conquer worlds. It is a staff to guide one's feet, a light that illuminates the way, a companion in times of happiness, and an adviser in times of sorrow and need.

The Torah is, for all who understand it, a melody in the night, a tune that accompanies the traveller, a signpost at the crossroads, the source of all life and joy, power and courage.

Thus, even studying the Torah industriously is not enough. Every commandment, even if one understands its intent, must also be appreciated. Every word must emerge from the book to be lodged deep in the heart, until it is part of the very fibre of one's being.

It is just this way with the highest thoughts of faith. When a person believes that there is a Creator and sees this truth in every creature, but only understands all this with their mind and memory, the belief is of minor importance. *Raḥmana liba bai*, 'God desires the heart' [BT *San.* 106*b*]: we must feel this truth in our hearts, absorb it into every cell of our being.

Even if we recognize that the whole world is a temple and every creature is a worshipper of God, and we understand that we are not God's only servants—nevertheless, we have still not comprehended what it means to be true descendants of the Jewish people and its exalted calling.

And we see that calling in the fact that the first words spoken at Sinai were 'I am the Lord your God' [Exod. 20: 2], your God and lawgiver, the ruler of all your feelings and deeds.

'See, human being, everything you own is yours because I have given it to you. Everything emerges from my hand. You, your property, are holy to me, and your body, soul, emotions must fulfil my will. And then, only then, will you be a true person of Israel!'

So, dear sisters, this must be the first and most important aim of our Bnos Agudath Israel.

Striving to ascend to the mission of a 'Mensch Yisroel', a human being of Israel.[8] To lead a pure, holy, happy life as *a person in the spirit of Israel*!

2

Dear sisters!

The fear of heaven means that everything that the holy Torah teaches us about God's greatness, sovereignty, and justice should be so deeply rooted in us that we see those qualities everywhere, feeling them and wondering at them, and through the Holy One's greatness also feeling our own insignificance.

God's omnipotence. At the slightest hint from the Creator even the heavens and earth can vanish—and you? With your puny powers, your limited lifetime, you weak mortal, will you set yourself against the Almighty? Ah, in the blink of an eye God can annihilate and destroy you.

God's greatness. Everything that is and shall be, all creation that lives and acts, acts according to God's plan and wisdom. And you, a human with your brief lifespan, will you sin? Make your own way through life? Better fear God's punishment, which can cancel all your grand plans!

His presence fills all the earth [Isa. 6: 3]. God is everywhere, and who can hide from him? If one ascends to the heavens, one stands before him. If one falls into the grave, one finds him there too. Wherever one goes: east or west, north or south—everywhere you go, God stands before you!

Under you, over you, around you, and within you.

God's sovereignty. God is the sovereign of everyone and everything, heavens and earth, all of creation, whatever you see, the air you breathe and the blood that flows in your veins—everything belongs to him!

Life instructions. The Creator, who is encountered in every blade of grass, in every green twig and pebble you see rolling across the ground—all of these follow his command! The same God also gave humankind, and especially you, Jewish child, instructions for living. All the qualities of the One must be felt and, as it were, comprehended, and that will fill your heart with the fear of God, a pure

[8] Schenirer cites Samson Raphael Hirsch's notion of the 'Mensch Yisroel' but shifts the emphasis: for Hirsch the 'Mensch Yisroel' is an enlightened observant Jew, at home in Orthodoxy and the secular world; for Schenirer, the term seems to refer to a person who fuses knowledge of and obedience to the Torah with a mystical sense of connectedness to the (natural) world.

exalted wonder for him before whom the whole world, nature, and all of its treasures, shudder and tremble with the most sublime awe.

Dear sisters! In order to rise ever higher, and to absorb this awe with a more exalted consciousness, you should always think like the great and wise Jewish king, Solomon:

'The beginning of knowledge is the fear of the Lord', the source of pure wisdom is the deeply implanted fear of God.[9] Only that can lead to an exalted and joyful life.

'It is for her fear of the Lord that a woman is to be praised' [Prov. 31: 30]—a Jewish daughter, the future mother of Israel's children, will be praised and renowned only if the fear of the Lord accompanies her along all the days of her life.

3

Dear sisters!

The Love of God. Love, in general, means to feel oneself whole through and united with the separate existence and being of another. So to love God means to feel that we owe our entire being and activities in the world to God, the creator of the world. That is the reason we have a duty to love and fulfil the holy Torah, which is the first condition of loving God. In every step we take we must see the physical and spiritual good that God has bequeathed to us in every moment. 'You shall love the Lord your God with all your heart, and with all your soul, and with all your might' [Deut. 6: 5]. With all our heart, soul, and property must we love God.

With all your heart. We must use our spiritual aspirations and power in order to wholeheartedly fulfil God's will. We need to conquer the evil inclination and put the good inclination in its place. What God considers good and beautiful must find a place in the Jewish heart.

With all your soul and all your might. All of our power, both corporeal and spiritual, must be considered solely as a means for us to powerfully and fully devote ourselves to fulfilling the statutes of Judaism.

Once we understand that our hearts, the fibre of our being, and our material possessions are no more than means for actualizing our love for the creator of the universe, it becomes clear that we should love him, the Almighty, more than all of

[9] This verse appears both in Ps. 111: 10, and, in a slightly different form, in Prov. 1: 7; the book of Proverbs is traditionally attributed to King Solomon.

our worldly powers. Our faithfulness to God must be so strong that we would even die for the sanctification of God's name.

There are many ways to understand what it means to fill one's heart with love and fear of God. The main way is working on oneself, educating oneself to open one's heart and fill it with purity and holiness.

'Cut away, therefore, the fat from your hearts and stiffen your necks no more' [Deut. 10: 16].[10] The fat of the heart signifies lust and pride, which goes before every fall. Every Jewish son and every Jewish daughter must uproot everything that disturbs or places a stumbling block before our great mission.

Only in a pure heart can the tree of life, the holy Torah, take root, and only then can we give ourselves over to the worship of the Creator.

But how does one achieve the commandment of loving God?

The way to that goal is, first of all, knowing ourselves, our hearts and our minds.

We must not fool ourselves. We must scrutinize ourselves, exploring the deepest corners of the heart. After this moral stocktaking, we must gird ourselves with the strongest and most powerful will to free ourselves of every character flaw and overcome every resistance that keeps us from doing so. We must always remember that even if today does not go well, it can help us prepare for tomorrow. We can discern the difference between good and evil only through the Torah. From earliest childhood we must practise introspection and self-examination. We must uproot corrupt and evil ways, replacing them with the straight and true path, and then walk this path with a resolute step.

I know that this is not easy, and that it may even be very difficult. But one must know that 'A person is permitted to travel along the road he wishes to pursue' [BT *Mak.* 10*b*], and that heaven leads us along the ways we choose to go. 'Whoever comes to be purified is assisted in this aim' [BT *Shab.* 104*a*], so whoever seeks to be purified from sin, God helps him accomplish this. The main thing is to sincerely take on the inner task of becoming better and holier. 'You shall be holy to me, because I the Lord am holy' [Lev. 20: 26]!

You say that this is difficult. But only consider for a moment how hard people work for their bread and material sustenance, how one prepares from earliest

[10] While Schenirer typically cites a Hebrew source and then translates it into Yiddish, here she only produces a Yiddish translation of the verse in Deuteronomy, which reads *umaltem et orlat levavkhem* (literally, 'and you shall circumcise the foreskins of your hearts'), thus capturing the metaphorical meaning of the verse while avoiding (whether from modesty or because she is speaking to girls) the reference to literal circumcision.

youth to learn a trade so that one might be able to make a living later! All difficulties are ignored when it comes to taking care of our physical sustenance, so why do people worry so little about the soul? Why do we expect to spend no effort at all in taking care of the soul, the Jewish soul?

No, dear sisters! We must not forget that exalted hour when we all so enthusiastically proclaimed the Torah ideal, and saying 'We will do and we will hear' [Exod. 24: 7], took upon ourselves the holy duties at Mount Sinai!

Bnos Agudath Israel must fulfil these holy obligations with pride! We feel no such obligations towards the European gods of fashion, since their rites and ceremonies are anathema to the ethics and morals of our people. With the whole fire of our Torah, the whole fire of our heart must we remember our traditions of modesty, holiness, and humility, which are the rays that guide us to the lighthouse of fear and love of God.

A Word to my Jewish Sisters in Honour of the Jubilee Issue of the *Bais Yaakov Journal*

Before me lies a letter from the editor-in-chief of the *Bais Yaakov Journal*, Eliezer Gershon Friedenson, asking me to write something for the jubilee issue of the journal (no. 50) [1930]. A thought flashes up in me: do all the readers of the journal know what the word 'jubilee' means? I don't mean to embarrass anyone with that question. But the deeper one digs in our holy Torah, attempting to understand its spirit, the more one finds light and nourishment in it for our thirsty souls.

The biblical verse says: 'You shall count seven weeks of years—seven times seven years—so that the period of seven weeks of years gives you a total of forty-nine years' [Lev. 25: 8]. And it continues: 'Then you shall sound the *shofar* loud; in the seventh month, on the tenth day of the month—the Day of Atonement—you shall have the *shofar* sounded throughout the land and you shall hallow the fiftieth year. You shall proclaim release throughout the land for all its inhabitants. That fiftieth year shall be a jubilee for you, and each of you shall return to his family.'

'You shall count'. This means the Great Court, the Torah authorities. Only through them may be carried out the universal social liberation which every jubilee year brings.

'And you must count' [Lev. 23: 16], *count for yourselves*: this is the commandment of counting, *sefirah*, which is incumbent on each individual.[11] You shall count the days between the Exodus and the giving of the Torah. Every year you must remember, and because of the giving of the Torah, lead a renewed life, because God took you out of Egypt by freeing you internally.

These two ways of counting are closely bound together. The political freedom one acquires passively, as a gift from God, but the inner freedom is achieved only after intense combat with oneself.

We count days and weeks in order that we might, every day and every week, assess how much more capable we are of being the bearers of Torah. We count years and cycles of seven years until we are worthy of proclaiming God as master of our entire national land and of experiencing the jubilee: a year of freedom for all.

And how is this universal freedom proclaimed?

'And then you shall sound the *shofar*'—the first call comes by way of a *shofar*. The signal is proclaimed not by trumpets, but rather with the sound of a *shofar*, with which God also called us to our sacred mission at Mount Sinai. And we echo this doubly significant jubilee *shofar* when we blow the *shofar* on Rosh Hashanah. Both blasts are from a *shofar*, in the name of God. What the *shofar* signifies on Rosh Hashanah in terms of the connection between human beings and God is also what the blast of the jubilee *shofar* means for social relationships more universally.

These reflections on Rosh Hashanah and the jubilee also arouse thoughts in me about the *Bais Yaakov Journal* jubilee issue. Just as the *shofar* blast resounded everywhere on 10 Tishrei in the jubilee year, calling everyone in God's name in every Jewish settlement to return to him, to acquire again the lost moral purity that is our dearest possession, so too should the *Bais Yaakov Journal* jubilee awaken and arouse us to self-assessment not only as individuals but also together, so that we actively spread our ideals among all our sisters, to rally them until they rise up as one and join our sacred union under the motto: 'Worship God with joy' [Ps. 100: 2]. And when that happens, 'You will be holy in this jubilee year'!

[11] Schenirer is comparing the use of the Hebrew word 'to count' in the jubilee commandments in Lev. 25, which is in the singular and refers to the counting of years, and the commandment in Lev. 23, in which the verb 'to count' is rendered in the plural, and which refers to the commandment to count the days in the seven-week period between Passover and Shavuot, the time of *sefirat ha'omer* (the counting of the *omer*). This period begins from the day that the *omer* (a barley sacrifice) was offered in the Temple and continues until the day before Shavuot (the fiftieth day), when an offering of wheat was brought to the Temple. This is traditionally a period of semi-mourning and spiritual introspection.

Dear sisters! Holy must be this new era that begins with the appearance of the jubilee issue of the *Bais Yaakov Journal*. You must understand that the holy thought can be spread much more widely through the printed word. For that reason you should circulate the *Bais Yaakov Journal* in even the smallest town, in every corner in which a Jewish heart beats. It is the only thing that speaks so directly to our hearts about the holy mission we have taken on, and about the great confidence with which God entrusted to us the laws of *kashrut*, the laws of family purity, and our most precious task, the education of children.

But dear sisters! To be inspired is easy, but for this inspiration to last for years, for one's whole life—that is lacking among us Jewish daughters. I call to you, then, in this jubilee issue: remember that this ideal is not one among other ideals. It is our very life, and must accompany us until the end!

On the Occasion of our World Congress [1929]

The Eve of the Congress

And so the Orthodox woman has awakened from her long, lethargic sleep and has begun to organize. From day to day her work for society intensifies, with pride she carries the Torah banner of old, around which all the women of Israel will congregate.

This month all the delegates chosen by religious Jewish women will gather in Vienna to create a world organization of Orthodox Jewish women.[12] It has not been long since we first established the Bnos organization in Poland, and already from the dais of the World Congress the powerful voice of the religious Jewish woman rings out on the world stage. She is no longer isolated either in her thoughts or aspirations, the daughter of Israel who knows the Jewish sources. In every corner of the world she has close and intimate sisters in spirit.

I know full well that many of our pious Jews will view this with suspicion. We hold sacred the ideal of women's modesty: 'She is in the tent' [Gen. 18: 9], and 'all the glory of a princess is within' [Ps. 45: 14].[13] No doubt a portion of the com-

[12] The second World Congress of the Agudath Israel was held in Vienna in September 1929. and this is when the Neshei Agudath Israel was founded. *The Jewish Daily Bulletin* of 19 Sept. 1929, the day after the World Congress concluded, reported that more than 150 women delegates attended the women's meeting, which was held in the Bayerischer Hof hotel. There were two sessions at this meeting, both chaired by Mrs Franziska Goldschmidt of Zurich and featuring reports on the progress of Bais Yaakov by Judith Grunfeld-Rosenbaum.

[13] On the verse in Gen. 18, see Ch. 4 n. 44 above. The meaning of Ps. 45: 14 is uncertain (the 1917 JPS translation has 'All glorious is the king's daughter within the palace'), but the verse is

Figure II.1 The dais at the Neshei Agudath Israel Women's Conference at the 1929 World Congress of the Agudath Israel, held at the Bayerischer Hof hotel in Vienna during the same week that the Agudah met at the Sofiansaal Concert Hall. According to one report, the Neshei conference attracted 150 women. From left to right: Mrs Fanny Lunzer (London), Rebbetzin Leah Grodzinski (Vilna), Mrs Henny Schreiber (Vienna), Mrs Franziska Goldschmidt (Zurich), Mrs Ernestine Bondi (Vienna), Rebbetzin Feyge Mintshe Alter (Gur), Mrs Malka Meierovitsh (Riga), and Miss Lotka Szczarańska (Scharansky, a teacher at the seminary in Kraków). The speakers included two wives of distinguished leaders and Bais Yaakov supporters from eastern Europe, Abraham Mordecai Alter (the Gerer Rebbe) and Chaim Ozer Grodzinski (chief rabbi of Vilna), and two local women who served on the Bais Yaakov committee in Vienna: Mrs Bondi (who had family connections to Samson Raphael Hirsch) and Mrs Schreiber (who had connections to the Hatam Sofer and Akiva Eiger). Mrs Lunzer served on the Bais Yaakov committee in London. Mrs Meierovitz, a teacher at the Torah V'Derekh Eretz girls' school in Riga, reported on Bnos in Latvia, while Miss Szczarańska reported on Bnos in Poland. Judith Rosenbaum (not pictured) was the main speaker at this session, reporting on the progress of Bais Yaakov. Mrs Goldschmidt, who chaired the conference, was the daughter of the chief rabbi of Zurich, Tuvia Lewenstein, and headed the international committee that worked to link the women's initiatives of the Agudah. For more on this event, see 'Aus der Frauentagung', p. 5, and Deutschländer, 'The Second World Congress of Agudath Israel' (Yid.), pp. 1–2.

Courtesy of the Jewish Museum Vienna/Archive, number 003808_1

Figure II.2 A group of participants from the founding conference of the Neshei Agudath Israel (1929) in front of the Kunsthistorisches Museum in Vienna. Fourth from the right in the first row is Yachat 'Janke' Sofer, daughter of Yehuda Sofer, chief rabbi of Arad, Romania (1905–13). A cultured young woman, she was the manager of a millinery store in Vienna and was a guest at the conference. After her marriage she moved to Brașov, Romania, where she organized religious education for girls and women.

Courtesy of the Estate of Rabbi Joseph Sporn, son of Yachat (Sofer) Sporn

munity will regard our congress with suspicion and fear and see it as a deviation—God forbid—from Israel of old.

But these same pious Jews should know that this conference of Orthodox women is a necessary response to the dangers that prey on our sisters from various secularist directions. *Et la'asot lahashem*, 'It is time to act for the Lord'—from this perspective must our public efforts be understood.

We have recently been hearing about other women's congresses, which present themselves as if they were the sole representatives of the masses of Jewish women and put forth various resolutions that stand in absolute contradiction to the ideals and aspirations of religious women. Even though no one has appointed them to do so, they take upon themselves the right to proclaim various slogans against the spirit of our Torah and launch false accusations against our Torah sages.[14] Just recently we heard of a women's congress where certain things were said and written about the *agunah* question and about women's suffrage that we Orthodox women would never have dreamed of saying—although we know the meaning of 'women's rights' perfectly well, and no one feels more deeply than we do the plight of the unfortunate *agunah*.[15] But we also know that the Torah and Jewish law are supreme. And that is why we religious women, in just the same way as religious men, submit to the Torah and Jewish law, which always works for our benefit and happiness.

Our congress is necessary right now for just these reasons. *From our speakers' podium it must boldly be proclaimed that all those other women have no right to speak in the name of the religious Jewish woman.* The aims, approaches, and ideals of the great masses of religious Jewish women must be made clear before the whole world. The Jewish world must know that thousands and tens of thousands of Jewish women all over the globe cling to the Jewish religion and wish to continue to spin the golden thread of Jewish tradition.

But that does not mean that we do not have many problems requiring internal resolution. Family purity, luxury and fashion, the education of our children, and

traditionally understood as asserting that a woman's beauty is linked to her modesty, so that she is most beautiful (or only beautiful) when she remains 'within' and does not go out overmuch to public places. Both verses are used as shorthand for women's modesty.

[14] The year 1929 saw at least two other conferences, that of the German Jüdischer Frauenbund in Hamburg and WIZO, the Zionist women's organization, in Zurich. An article in the *Bais Yaakov Journal* placed the WIZO conference in Warsaw; perhaps this was a regional conference held in addition to the international one held in Zurich. See A.L., 'Łódź, Hamburg, Warsaw' (Yid.).

[15] On the *agunah*, see Ch. 1 n. 67.

so on.[16] The weightiest issue we are facing now is how to combat the Parisian way of raising children, which increasingly threatens the Jewish family.

Our task must also be to find ways and means to fight for the protection of the Jewish daughter and her moral improvement.[17]

It will be a great day when we come together to collectively consider how to improve Jewish family life and return the sanctity to Jacob's tent.

It will also be a great sanctification of God's name before the eyes of the world that our congress is taking place at the same time as the second World Congress of Agudath Israel. The honour and esteem of Orthodox Jews will be strengthened when, at the same moment as the sons of Israel declare in ringing tones their faithfulness to the God of Israel, the daughters of Israel proclaim to Orthodox Jewry: 'We are with you!'

During the great days of the month of Elul this year, we will fulfil 'We will go with our sons and our daughters, for we must observe the Lord's festival' [Exod. 10: 9], and this will be remembered for generations as the great holiday of the revival of the entire Jewish people.

After the Congress

We find ourselves in the splendid hall of the Bayerischer Hof, the same hall in which twenty-one years ago a conference in honour of the German writer Herder was held.[18] Oh, how happy it made me in those days to take an interest in German literature! Many Jewish girls and women sat in this room then, gazing in rapture at the lecturers.

Who could have dreamt in those days that all these years later Jewish women from every corner of the globe would gather in this very room to spread the ideal of Torah? From every corner of the world, from every country in which a Jewish

[16] The Neshei Agudath Israel indeed took on 'family purity' (strict adherence to Jewish menstrual laws) as its special mission, erecting or remodeling *mikvaot* (ritual baths) and sponsoring public lectures for women (including one delivered by the Hafets Hayim) on the topic.

[17] 'Protection' and 'moral improvement' are common euphemisms by which Bais Yaakov and other conservative organizations delicately discussed Jewish participation in the international white slave trade as traffickers and prostitutes. It was much more common for American and German supporters of Bais Yaakov to refer to this problem than for Schenirer and others in Poland, as I discuss in Chapter 1.

[18] Johann Gottfried von Herder (1744–1803) was a German philosopher, theologian, and poet. In her diary Schenirer mentions a 1908 visit to Vienna that made a great impression on her, during which she presumably attended the conference described here.

heart beats we have gathered. The writing on the banners, 'Not by might, nor by power' [Zech. 4: 6] and 'May all unite in a single fellowship' [*agudah aḥat*] bear witness to what is transpiring here.[19] The aim of this gathering, 'to organize the Jewish girls and women of the world under the banner of Agudath Israel', fills every heart with passion and exaltation.

Mrs Goldschmidt, the daughter of Dr Lewenstein of Zurich, calls on Jewish women to work together, to unite on behalf of the Torah and *yiddishkeit*. Her voice resounds powerfully, the voice of an authentically Jewish feminine heart, which penetrates deeply into the soul.

Soulful and moving are the words of the Gerer Rebbe's wife.[20] 'All beginnings are difficult' [*Mekhilta* on Exod. 19: 5], but as hard it is, a beginning must be made! The gathered women listen with bated breath to her emotional speech, which moves them to tears.

One after another the women ascend to the dais, delegates from the United States, England, Germany, Austria, Belgium, the Netherlands, Czechoslovakia, and elsewhere. Every speech is well considered, and each boils down to the same thing: let us unite, organize ourselves in order to help the suffering people of Israel! Let us devote our physical and spiritual energies to soothing and healing Jewish sorrows! Let us help build the House of Israel!

We find ourselves in an intimate circle in Mrs Bondi's home when suddenly the question of wigs comes up.[21] One of the delegates, a very intelligent woman and a teacher in the Riga girls' high school, found herself in an uncomfortable position when the resolution was put forward that all [married] women who wish to belong to the Women's Union of Agudath Israel must wear a wig. She acknowledges and confesses that she doesn't cover her hair because none of the young women in her city wear a wig. She is surprised, however, when the delegates from Germany report that all the young religious women in Germany wear a wig, 'even the most educated ones, with advanced degrees'. The delegate from

[19] The second quote appears in the High Holy Days liturgy: 'and they will all unite in a single fellowship to do your will with a perfect heart'. The verse contains the word *agudah* ('fellowship' or 'union') and is the source of the name of the Agudah organization.

[20] Mrs Feyge Mintshe Biderman Alter was the niece as well as second wife of the Gerer Rebbe, Abraham Mordecai Alter (1866–1948). The Gerer Rebbe was the primary hasidic leader in the Agudath Israel, and it was appropriate for his wife to be prominently featured on the platform at the newly founded women's organization.

[21] The Bondi family were grandchildren and great-grandchildren of Samson Raphael Hirsch.

Riga decides on the spot to start wearing a wig, and also to try to persuade all her female acquaintances to do likewise.[22]

Although we come from different countries and live among different ethnic groups, we feel united and mutually connected. Who unites us? What mutual language do we share? It is the ancient tongue of the prophets, the ideals of our forefathers and aspirations of our foremothers, the spirit of our holy Torah! We are the children of Israel. On us rests the responsibility of 'The wisest of women builds her house' [Prov. 14: 1]. 'Today you have become the people of the Lord' [Deut. 27: 9], from this day forward we all belong to the Jewish people, its Torah, its ancient culture. We must not allow ourselves to splinter into individual Jewish women in various cities and towns in different countries. We are no longer isolated and lonely individuals. We have become a world union, and every authentic and loyal Jewish woman should take pride in belonging to the Agudah's World Union of Jewish Women.

There is so, so much we got from the first international Women's Congress. Unfortunately, many of our Bnos leaders in Poland were unable to participate in this extraordinarily interesting gathering. But have no doubt, dear spiritual sisters. You were fondly remembered and everyone there was very pleased to hear about your work! Let us devote ourselves to it with renewed energy and sacrifice, since we are now, praise God, already an international organization!

Our Pioneers: Impressions of the Seminary Examinations in the Summer of 5691 [1931]

Once again, twenty-two teachers have completed the seminary course. It was truly a joy to see the great success these students had. Their ready answers to the questions they were asked were the beautiful fruit of two tireless years of hard work in the seminary.

22 The informal gathering described above took place after the second and last session of the Women's Conference of the Agudath Israel, on Saturday night, 21 September. The delegate who spoke about not covering her hair may have been Malka Meierovitsh, who appears in Fig. II.1. Ernestine Bondi (also in Fig. II.1) was a Bais Yaakov activist in Vienna, with her husband a supporter of the Schiffschul, and part of a larger circle of interrelated families that included many descendants of both Samson Raphael Hirsch and Marcus Lehmann.

But in the midst of this joy I was struck with a painful thought: do these young pioneers truly recognize the great faith and hope that I and many others are placing in them? Do they understand the enormous responsibility that they are taking on as educators of a new young generation? Will they be able to withstand, in times to come, the tests and trials that life will put before them? And a quiet prayer moved my lips: O, great Creator in heaven! Help your faithful children in their sacred work! Let them not be too sorely tested in their new path! Let the words of our Sages be fulfilled in them: 'If one comes in order to be purified, not only is he allowed to do so, but they, in heaven, assist him' [BT *Shab.* 104*a*]. Their hearts are in the right place, so please help them, Master of the universe, so that their good intentions will result in good and fine deeds!

The solemn atmosphere of the examination room did not dissipate for the entire day. The students said goodbye to each other in small groups, speaking quietly about the great responsibility that the people of Israel had placed on their shoulders.

I reminded them of a few thoughts that had been shared with the last group of graduates.[23]

'That you can learn and teach, we have seen in these exams. But whether you can truly educate young souls, that is the question that has troubled our hearts during these exams. We were reminded of the young priests in the Temple. Today, when it is unfortunately no longer standing, every Jewish home, every Jewish heart, is a Temple. The priests were in charge of safeguarding the purity of the Temple, and today this very duty is incumbent on you! You are going out into the world to build Temples!

Before the high priest commenced his sacred work, he was asked: "Perhaps there is something alien in your heart? Perhaps you have forgotten or perhaps you never learned everything you need to know? If you haven't, we don't blame you, but if there is something alien in your heart, it might render your sacred service ineffective" [BT *Yoma* 18*a*]. You are going out into the wider world, and will be entrusted with the pure souls of children. You have to raise these souls into true people of Israel. The future of the younger generation is dependent on

[23] This speech was first given by Rabbi Orlean in 1930, and quoted again with some minor differences in the letter to Bais Yaakov students that Sarah Schenirer wrote during her final illness. It is translated in Section VI below. See Chapter 4 for discussion.

you. How terrible will be your sin, if your heart—God forbid—is not entirely pure, entirely dedicated to our holy ideal.'

I didn't want to repeat the same things to the new group but I could feel the strong impression that my reminiscences had on them. I just ended with the hope that all these emotions that had overcome them in this moment would sink deeply into their hearts, and when the passing of time would try to sweep them away, they would remember this day and the voice of faithfulness would call to them: have you forgotten what you promised in your heart, there in Rabka, in the deep forest? For shame!

And again a hush, one could hear the heartbeat of each individual, without anyone speaking—and Mrs Waszasz began to talk fervently, in glowing terms, explaining to them their great mission as pioneers of a new movement to bring back the ancient riches of the Torah to Jewish life, and every word penetrated deep into the hearts of the young listeners.[24]

Again silence. Only the moon watched peacefully. And my dear students, as if they could feel what was transpiring in my own heart, took each other wordlessly by the hand and formed a big circle, singing with deep emotion: 'And purify our hearts to serve you in truth.'[25]

'And purify our hearts to serve you in truth'—my lips moved along, again a wave of thoughts overtook me. Is it only these children who know what they should be praying for? Is it not every Jewish mother that should be taking stock every day of her responsibility towards her children? Do so many of them not hold in their hearts an alien thought, that their child should be 'an ordinary human being', a modern, up-to-date person with only a little something Jewish added on as an afterthought?

And all you other Jewish girls, is it not high time that you should recognize that you hold your happiness in your own hands? How to achieve that? Everything that is foreign must be rooted out, and the commandments fulfilled with glowing passion.

Worship God with joy! [Ps. 100: 2]

And it seemed to me that the birds we had awakened echoed us in their wonder:

Worship God with joy!

[24] Mrs Waszasz is the married name of Lotka (Tsiporah) Szczarańska, the Bnos leader and seminary teacher who spoke at the women's conference of the World Congress in 1929.

[25] A phrase from the sabbath and festival liturgy.

Yiddishkeit and Yiddish [1931]

Issue 62 of the *Bais Yaakov Journal* lies in front of me. I read the resolutions of the [regional Bnos] Conference held in Pabianitz (Pabianice) on 9 Tevet [9 January 1930] and I see among other headings the topic of '*Yiddishkeit* and Yiddish'.[26] And reading these lines, I can see before my eyes the whole Pabianitz conference and hear the passionate words of Yehudah Leib Orlean on the subject of Yiddish and *yiddishkeit*, and the applause of the gathering at his proposal that all the delegates should for three months speak to all their friends, wherever they live, only in Yiddish.

But have they actually made good on this decision? Were their beautiful intentions well received? Let all the members—every one of them!—give an honest account. These days of counting the *omer* are indeed especially suited for just such soul-searching.[27]

I am certain that every member understood that Rabbi Orlean did not mean that they should speak Yiddish for three months and then go back to Polish, but that if they actually managed to speak only Yiddish for three months, they would become so accustomed to it that they could no longer speak another language.

But it pains me to say that I see very little success after the enthusiasm in Pabianitz.

Yes, my old cry, that it is easy to feel initial enthusiasm, but to hold onto that inspiration in connection with every commandment, every custom, for years on end, for an entire life, as long as God grants us the energy to serve him according to his will—this is exactly what is always lacking.

That is the reason, as everyone who knows me knows, that I am such an enemy of every kind of applause. Clapping is an externalized enthusiasm that heats up a conference hall, but as soon as one makes one's way into the fresh air outside, it cools right down.

And you, my dear teachers, Bnos members, Basya and Bais Yaakov children, you certainly know what I want, what I mean by the slogan, 'Worship God with joy'! Why then do you disappoint me so grievously?

You have become accustomed to many, many difficult things on account of

[26] Pabianitz (Polish: Pabianice) is a small city in central Poland. This article appeared in the *Bais Yaakov Journal*, 71/2 (1931), a special double issue on Yiddish guest-edited by Solomon Birnbaum, who laid out the new orthographical rules, which mirrored traditional Polish Galician pronunciation and spelling, in the same issue and in other publications. See Ch. 5 n. 103 above.

[27] On the *omer*, see n. 11 above.

our holy ideal—but somehow this issue of speaking Yiddish is too great a sacrifice for you?

I know, you'll respond: We want to, but . . .

But I say to you just what the Vilna Gaon, of blessed memory, would always say: 'If you will it, you too can become a Vilna Gaon.'[28]

A firm resolve will always succeed, but for this we have to truly want something.

This will not be painful for those who already speak Yiddish, of course, but only those who often speak Polish, to my great chagrin. Last week I rebuked a young student for speaking Polish with her friend. She responded: 'The teacher in the Polish school told me that Yiddish is the same as Polish for us, since Yiddish, after all, is only a dialect of German.' But this is exactly the kind of confused thinking that my older Jewish daughters should not consider using as an excuse.

I want to relate a few thoughts on the importance of Yiddish that my brother reminded me about.

The Duties of the Heart says that the tongue is the quill of the heart.[29] We know that the writer expresses the deepest emotions of his heart with this quill. So if he were to speak a foreign tongue, then the emotions would also be foreign, and we must know that Yiddish is dear to us only because our mothers, grandparents, and great-grandparents always spoke in that language. If only out of respect for our ancestors, we are obligated to speak Yiddish. But beyond that, Yiddish is also a sacred tongue for us, since so many great, righteous men, so many hasidim, so many Torah sages for hundreds of years and to this very day speak the language.

The tractate of *Sanhedrin* in the Talmud [92*b*] relates: 'Molten gold should be poured into the mouth of that wicked person [Nebuchadnezzar], for if an angel had not come and slapped him on his mouth to prevent him from continuing, he would have tried to overshadow the songs and praises that David recited in the book of Psalms.' The commentators ask: it is difficult to understand how one might think that Nebuchadnezzar could sing more beautiful songs than King David. One learned man explained: 'Nebuchadnezzar understood that in his mouth, these songs would lose some of their sanctity, which is why he wanted

[28] Elijah ben Solomon of Vilna (1720–97), the Vilna Gaon ('Genius'), was the foremost leader of mitnagdic (non-hasidic) east European Jewry. Schenirer is quoting here a popular Yiddish saying that parents would tell their children: *Vil nor goen* (punning on the Vilna Gaon's name), 'if you will it, you too can become a Vilna Gaon'.

[29] *Duties of the Heart* (*Ḥovot halevavot*) is a popular ethical work, originally written in Judaeo-Arabic by the Spanish Jewish eleventh-century philosopher Bahya Ibn Pakuda.

to recite them.' So too does *The Light of Life* say that when Balaam was about to bless the Jews, God ingeniously created a divide between his mouth and his speech, so that God's holy words would not pass through his corrupt mouth. That is what the passage means: 'And the Lord put something into Balaam's mouth' [Num. 23: 5] in order for there to be a gap between his impure lips and the prophetic and beneficent words he said to the Jews.[30]

The Talmud also says [*Sot.* 11*a*] that 'the measure of good is always greater [i.e. rewarded more] than the measure of punishment [for a bad deed]': a good quality in a person can always accomplish more than a bad one can damage.

It's obvious, then, that if so many great people speak Yiddish, it is clearly a holy tongue. A language is also the garment, the clothing of the soul. We have often discussed what this means. For us Jews the outside must closely mirror what is on the inside. Just as modest Jewish dress and behaviour are the most accurate signs of the true Jewish soul, the language that we speak works in exactly this way. I know that more than a few of my children will say, we can be Jewish through and through even if we speak Polish, there's no connection between the two things. But this is false. As I explained, for us outward appearance must match the inward truth.

And so I turn to all of you who still persist in speaking Polish among yourselves. Commit yourselves to speaking only Yiddish, everywhere! Whenever you're at home or in the street, and especially in a Bais Yaakov building! Show that you are true Jewish daughters. Don't ever be ashamed to speak your own Jewish tongue and God will certainly hasten the redemption.

One more thought:

More than one student must have asked herself why we have to bother with a new Yiddish orthography. I can only respond that there were two good reasons for this effort. First of all, the orthography that we have been using up to now is a product of the Haskalah [Jewish Enlightenment], as Dr Solomon Birnbaum has scientifically demonstrated in his book *Yiddishkeit and Language*. Secondly, variations in Yiddish spelling were particularly glaring in Bais Yaakov and the Bnos movement, since virtually every province has its own spelling, and our movement needs a unified orthography. As I already stated, the tongue is the quill of the heart, which means that we should all write according to a single model since

[30] *The Light of Life* (*Or haḥayim*), is a commentary on the Torah published in 1740 by the Moroccan rabbi and kabbalist Hayim Ibn Atar (1696–1743). In this passage he changes the usual translation of the verse by interpreting the Hebrew *davar* not as 'a word' but as 'a thing'.

our writings must be a visible expression of the unity of our thought. 'May all unite in a single fellowship to do your will with a perfect heart'!

And now, all of you, every one of my teachers, Bnos and Basya members, and especially Bais Yaakov students, whether you are from Kraków, Łódź, Warsaw, Jarosław, Tarnów, Lemberg [Lviv], Stryi, or anywhere we've seen the problem of speaking too often in Polish—firmly resolve that from this moment onward you will speak only Yiddish and be known by Jewish names! Devise methods to accomplish this. You might consider selecting monitors for each group who will remind the group what you've decided, or maybe you can put up large posters in prominent places that say: 'Speak only Yiddish!' Or however you choose to go about it. But let us already hear the good news that you've dedicated yourselves to this goal. You know very well that if your resolve is true, God will help.

In general, spread the word about Yiddish everywhere!

And just as one counts the *omer* every day, one should make a reckoning of the soul every day, asking if today saw any improvements in the matter of speaking Yiddish. And with God's help, we will certainly all gather next year in Jerusalem.

Fifteen Years of Bais Yaakov

Kraków, 1 Adar 5692 [8 February 1932]

Fifteen years have already passed since the founding of the first Bais Yaakov school.

I am sunk in memories of that long-ago time, and various facts and events rise before my eyes. Before I attempt to put them in any order, I want to relay the following letter I received from Romania, which begins like this:

My dear Mrs Schenirer!

In my imagination, I can see you turning over the envelope and trying to figure out who wrote this letter to you. My name certainly will not ring a bell. So I should begin by reminding you of my mother, Rachel Gross of Czernowitz [Chernivtsi], and then of myself. In 1914/15, during the Great War, we were in Vienna. We ran into each other almost every day at Rabbi Flesch's lectures in the Stumpergasse synagogue. I was then a young girl, and when anyone asked me if I found the lectures interesting, I always said that I did. You told me that you wanted to start a school for girls and once you asked my mother if you could borrow the book she happened to be holding at that moment, *Menorat hama'or*.[31]

[31] *Candelabrum of Light* (*Menorat hama'or*) is a popular ethical and exegetical work by the

When we left Vienna to return home, you and my mother continued to correspond. Years later I married someone from Kolomay (Kolomyia), and while I was at the home of my in-laws, I visited the Bais Yaakov school there and took a few issues of the *Bais Yaakov Journal* home with us. I was filled with joy to read your articles. I was also sorry that here in Romania nothing has been done in this regard.'

This letter brought back to me my oldest memories about our Bais Yaakov movement. This was the very first person to hear about my dreams, which in fact seemed to me at that time nothing more than dreams.

Heshvan 5677 [autumn 1916]

I am sewing dresses for Jewish girls, and I ask their mothers if they would be willing to lend me their daughters so that I might also work on their souls. The mothers agree. I rent a room from a nice Jewish woman and give my first lesson to twenty-five Jewish girls. I start by telling them what it means to make a blessing. I explain that every person must make a blessing when they're about to eat God's gift, otherwise they are considered to be stealing. The next morning a mother comes in to tell me with the greatest happiness that her 6-year-old daughter noticed her 5-year-old brother drinking water without making a blessing. She shrieked at him: 'Thief! When you drink God's water you have to make a blessing!'

Every day new students come forward to register. A hasidic man comes to enrol his daughter and asks me: 'What are you actually setting out to accomplish here?' I answer that I won't just be teaching them to pray, because that they could learn without me. My main intention is to awaken their desire to be Jewish. This man likes my answer and becomes the first helper I have in the school. But we only have a short respite in this little room. The landlady decides that she doesn't want a school in her building and we must find another place.

We find another location, and then a third one in the same building where I now live. I now have eighty students under my supervision, with new ones arriving every day. Things are out of control, so I hire as an assistant the girl who used to help with my sewing. I now have 280 students, and I can see that some of them will be neglected. What should I do? I don't want to hire teachers from another school. So I choose two of my most industrious students and hire them as teachers. They are barely 13, but they already grasp the great responsibility I have put on their shoulders.

fourteenth-century Spanish talmudist and rabbi Isaac Aboab which was translated into Yiddish in Vilna in 1880.

A branch of Agudah is founded in Kraków in 5679 [1919]. Rabbi Motl Luksenberg,[32] the father of the student I mentioned above, is the first to propose that they help develop my school. Rabbi Meir Rapoport, Rabbi Moshe Deutscher, and Rabbi Luksenberg step forward and decide to take the school under their supervision.[33] They will handle all the troublesome financial details. I consult with the Bobover Rebbe and he agrees to all this.[34] The Agudah takes over the leadership and has the apartment renovated. The student body grows. I appoint two new young teachers. Various community activists visit the school. Rabbi Asher Shapiro arrives, and is present for the oral examination of the students. It makes a strong impression when Rabbi Shapiro gives two Dutch guilders to a teacher and gives me another ten, saying, 'Let this money be the foundation of a Bais Yaakov building.' We all smile at these words. Outside the war is still raging, and we dream of buildings. But Rabbi Asher Shapiro is speaking with all sincerity. He travels to Antwerp with that goal in mind and when he returns in 5683 [1922/3] he works furiously to get the construction going. In the meantime, he is willing to settle for one storey, as long as it is at 30 Augustiańska. Eight large rooms, fully equipped. The dream is beginning to come true.

The Bais Yaakov in Kraków is in the meantime no longer an exception. There have been Bais Yaakov schools in Tarnów and Ostrowiec since 5681 [1920/1]. But we have no teachers. The organizers kept asking for teachers, and so I was compelled to send my young graduates to every corner of the world to spread our ideal. The Lubliner Rav, long may he live, visited the schools and, seeing the great need for teachers, sent us girls from his city to learn how to teach.[35] They studied with great devotion, stopping neither to eat nor to sleep. Their idealism and will conquered everything, and indeed, they later became a blessing for our movement.

Elul 5684 [September 1924]

The Central Committee of the International Agudath Israel meets in Kraków.[36] The committee members from abroad visit the school and decide to include

[32] In earlier references to him the title 'Rabbi' was not used.

[33] Rabbi Meir Rapoport (1848–1920) was the head of the rabbinical court of Kraków; Rabbi Moshe Deutscher was an Agudah activist and later served in the Polish Sejm.

[34] Ben-Zion Halberstam (1874–1941) was the second Bobover Rebbe.

[35] The Lubliner Rav, Meir Shapiro (1887–1933), was a prominent rabbi and Agudah activist and the head of the Yeshivat Hakhmei Lublin. In the early 1920s he was rabbi first in Sanok and, after 1924, in Piotrków, arriving in Lublin only in 1931.

[36] For a description of the organizational structure of the Agudah, see Bacon, *Politics of Tradition*, 70–99.

support for Bais Yaakov as part of the work of Keren Hatorah. Dr Deutschländer recognizes the significance of this undertaking and calls for a Bais Yaakov conference to be held in Warsaw.

4 Adar 5685 [28 February 1925]

The first Bais Yaakov Conference in Warsaw. I still remember the inspiring lecture by Rabbi Isaac Meir Levin. The speeches of Dr Deutschländer, Rabbi Levin, Friedman, and Friedenson who spoke with such fire about Bais Yaakov. Then came the report by Rabbi Asher Shapiro: in 5677 [1916/17] a Bais Yaakov school was founded with twenty-five pupils. In 5679 [1919] the school was taken over by the Agudah, at which point it had 280 students. In 5680 it already had 300 and in 5681 four new schools were founded in the province with ninety students. 5682—nine more schools; 5683—13; 5684—28, totalling fifty-four schools in all. The resolutions were put forward:

1. To temporarily turn the existing Kraków school into a teachers' seminary, bringing in instructors from outside the country to train students in pedagogical methods.
2. To organize a two-month professional development course for those teachers who are already employed.
3. To build a permanent seminary in Kraków that would serve as the pedagogical and operational centre of the movement.

Av/Elul 5685 [summer 1925], Robów

I already see the resolutions of the Warsaw conference bearing fruit. The professional development courses are mainly led by our German colleagues. At first I had doubts about whether Orthodox Jews from abroad were really suited for our hasidic way of life in Poland. But when I see Dr Deutschländer, Dr Ehrentreu, Miss Rosenheim, and Miss Mannes and hear their lectures—their authentic Jewish passion and dedication—I am filled with hope and joy.

The first professional development course ended successfully and now the new work begins. A group of thirty-six new students from all over Poland are now studying in the Kraków Bais Yaakov. They are taught by Miss Rothschild from Zurich, and later Miss Rosenbaum and Miss Landsberg. They work with dedication and fervour. They recognize their great role. A few years later, Shevat 5687 [January 1927] the first students to complete this systematic course of study take their exams. It is moving to see what great strides the students have made.

Their enthusiasm fills one with hope. Twenty-six schools are about to open and they will need teachers. There are also increasing numbers of candidates for our teachers' seminary, but there is no room to take them all. We don't know what to do, and the situation gets worse from day to day. It is this need for more space and teachers that leads to the ground-breaking ceremony of the new seminary building.

Adar 5686 [February 1926]

The first conference of Bnos Agudath Israel takes place in Łódź. I don't go to the conference, because I am sceptical about whether we can attract older girls, but the reports I received afterward persuaded me that it was more successful than I had anticipated.

16 Elul 5687 [13 September 1927]

There are thousands of people here, from Kraków and all the surrounding areas, led by the Krakówer Rav, the executive committee of the World Agudath Israel, Rabbi Levin, Rabbi Pinchas Kohn, Rabbi Jacob Rosenheim, Dr Deutschländer, and others.[37] Everyone is excited about the great occasion of laying a cornerstone for the educators among our generation of women. I tremble and send out a silent prayer to the Almighty, that he might guide this enterprise along the proper path.

The images of the work that followed pass before my eyes. The professional development courses in Jordanów (twice) and in Rabka (three times), and the Bnos conferences in Łódź, Ponevezh [Panevezys, Lithuania], and Warsaw. My visits to the new Bais Yaakov schools, where I clarify the goals and approaches of our educational system. And then the birth of the *Bais Yaakov Journal* and *Kindergarten*—these all are the truest signs that we might hope for success. And just this year we nearly completed the five-storey seminary building and 120 students from all over Poland are finally under one roof, with all their needs comfortably met.

Now, when fifteen years have raced by between those modest beginnings and the present situation, I can be happy—thank God. Nevertheless, I still occasionally worry about whether these new students are true idealists like the first ones

[37] Rabbi Yosef Nechemya Kornitzer was the chief rabbi of Kraków in the interwar period; Rabbi Pinchas Kohn (1847–1941) was the executive director of the World Agudath Israel; Rabbi Jacob Rosenheim (1870–1965) was a leader of the secessionist Orthodox Frankfurt Jewish community and founder and long-time president of the World Agudath Israel.

were or whether they are just out to make a living. But when I think of all the good experiences of the past fifteen years, I remember the saying of our sages: 'At fifteen to Talmud' [*Avot* 5: 25]. Once one turns 15 years old, one achieves the stage of learning and understanding the most difficult part of Torah—the Talmud—which means that one has reached the level of true maturity. Let us therefore hope that our own movement is by now sufficiently mature that the goals are clear to all, and may the Lord grant that the true love and fear of God of Bais Yaakov students will be the pride and glory of the entire Jewish people. Amen.

III The Jewish Year

Sabbath and the Woman

When the heavens and the earth and everything upon it were created through the divine word, all of creation set out to worship the Creator. The human being, crown of creation, was also called by the Creator to live and serve, but this service would have to emerge from deep conviction, of his own free will, unforced.

In order for human beings not to forget that the Creator is the true owner who bestowed the world on people to populate; so that human beings not consider themselves the creators of the universe and act according to their own laws; in order that they not stumble in conquering such a wide world, or—in brief—to remind human beings that their task is to be the servants of God, the entire creation was given God's gift of the seventh day, the holy sabbath. This day is dedicated, for human beings, to holiness and blessing. Holiness: the day would remind us that God created us for divine service. And blessing: the day would fashion our bodies and souls in preparation for fulfilling our sacred mission.

The sabbath is the day on which the Creator ceased his work and withdrew back into his invisible sovereignty, giving over the world to its stewards. The sabbath is a monument to God's sovereignty and to the human mission.

'Six days you shall labour, but the seventh day is a sabbath of the Lord your God, you shall not do any work' [Exod. 35: 2].

The human conquest of the world expresses itself as work that humans impose on other creatures that are used to fulfil the need for food, clothing, and so on. For that reason you must spend only six days working to master the world, and must rest on the seventh. In that way you show that the day is not yours, and those creatures you make such free use of all week long are also not yours. On that day, you return the world to its Creator and show that you have only borrowed it from him. It is for that reason that the smallest work you do on the sabbath is a deviation from all this, a denial—God forbid—of the mission of the 'Mensch Yisroel'.[1]

[1] See Section II, n. 8, above.

The sabbath is a sign, a mark for all times, that the Almighty is the creator and master of the universe, and that human beings, with all their powers, exist only to serve him. The sabbath is a special time, the day of the week sanctified by God as a holy day that can raise human beings up again to God if they lose focus in the course of the week and became distant from him. The sabbath is a 'covenant', a bond between God and human beings. Though people may persuade themselves that the world is their own and they can do with it as they wish, on the sabbath they understand that they share the earth with God.

Sabbath is also a blessing in that it brings light to our souls, warmth to our spirits, and strength to fulfil all the great and holy Jewish duties. Just as the sabbath receives from the rest of the week, as it says: 'whoever prepares for the sabbath will have plenty to eat on the sabbath', so too does sabbath generously bestow good things on us, as it says in the Zohar: 'All the blessings above and below depend on the seventh day' [Zohar on Exod. 20: 8].[2] Sabbath contains within itself the great blessing that gives us spiritual and physical energies for the rest of the week.

And so it is with the Jewish woman. Yes, it's true that she receives what her husband brings home for her to keep the house running, but just like the sabbath, she is also the blessing of the house. She and she alone is the one who can raise children who will serve God with all their might and all their consciousness. She and she alone can bring the glow of the Torah to her daughters and sons, so that no alien influence can lure them from the true Jewish path.

But she can acquire the strength for such inspiration only from proper sabbath observance, because sabbath is the heart of Israel.

Unfortunately, today we see many sad instances of Jewish mothers allowing their daughters to go to school on the sabbath. There are even some cases of daughters from strictly Jewish homes who work in offices on the sabbath.

Oh, Jewish mothers! Guardians and carriers of our divine mission expressed in the words: 'So shall you say to the House of Jacob' [Exod. 19: 3]![3] How can you desecrate the sabbath for the sake of the few pennies your daughters might earn, how can you lay hands on God's property and declare: 'It is mine'?!

And you, Jewish daughters! Have you explained to your sister that by working for a living on the sabbath she denies her identity as a daughter of Israel and

[2] This Zohar citation also appears in *Ḥok leyisra'el*, the Yiddish compilation Schenirer mentions studying. The translation here is from *The Zohar*, trans. Matt, iv. 497.

[3] See p. 138.

demonstrates that the human being has only material aims: ownership and profit? But perhaps you know nothing about what the name of Israel signifies!

Daughters of Israel, you who are meant to be the witnesses to the entire world that the calling of humanity is to serve God. Will you exchange the treasures of Zion, for which your ancestors were burned at the stake, for a few filthy coins? Do you believe that the money you earn on the sabbath can be a blessing? Can a blessing really come about through transgression? Yes, you will say that you have to earn a living, but do you not understand that a life lived with no ideals is not worth living? Do you not understand that the Creator who commands us to rest on the sabbath has more than enough for all to live on?

Now see how well God understands the frailty of human beings: the very first Friday, he rained down a double portion of manna [Exod. 16: 22], so that the weak need not worry that there would be nothing to eat on the sabbath.

Brothers and sisters, observe the sabbath properly, and the heart of Israel will remain strong.

'Let all of Israel observe one sabbath and the messiah will come' [BT *Shab.* 118*b*]!

Our Preparations for the Day of Judgement

From the beginning of the month of Elul the sound of the *shofar* calls to us each day: Awake! Wake up, you sleeping ones! The Day of Judgement is nearly upon us!

With trembling we ask: how have we prepared ourselves for the terrifying Day of Judgement?

The first prayer with which we begin the Amidah of Rosh Hashanah is: 'Remember us for life, O King who desires life, and write us into the Book of Life, for your sake, O living God.'

'Remember us for life'. May God, blessed be he, grant us the power to unite earthly life with the actions that humanity requires. 'For your sake'—because they are for you, for us to do your will, which results in a worthy life. O King who desires life, as the King of Kings wants for us.

But how does one arrive at such a life? How does one prepare to live such a life?

In the holy book *Tiferet shelomo* we find that the main preparation for Rosh Hashanah is to ensure that unity and friendship reign among the Jewish people, as our great poet says in Psalms 34: 'Who is the man who is eager for life, who desires years of good fortune. Guard your tongue from evil, your lips from deceitful speech. Shun evil and do good, seek peace and pursue it.'[4] We see that it does not say, 'who is eager to enjoy life' [*heḥafets baḥayim*], but rather 'who is eager for life' [*heḥafets ḥayim*], who desires the ultimate aim. 'Who desires years of good fortune': who loves the days, who sees good and happiness and the joy of life in every moment. We don't say, like people with a non-Jewish outlook, 'as opposed to fearing God', but rather exactly the opposite: the joy and love of life are the surest, quickest means of attaining the fear of God.

To understand this we should begin with 'Guard your tongue from evil'. One must see and master the word, and through it, the thought. Never to speak ill of another person. This demands constant vigilance from us, which begins with mastery of the tongue.

'And your lips from deceitful speech'. Truth must always be in our utterances; where we have nothing good to say, 'we must learn the difficult art of silence' (Samson Raphael Hirsch). The second way of achieving the fear of God is through 'shunning evil'. Keep your distance from evil, avoiding all things that might lead to it. Set boundaries even where things are in fact permitted, and do good. Do not miss any opportunity to do something worthy. 'Do': it isn't enough to have good intentions, but one must actually realize these intentions, and do good things.

First one must 'shun evil', and only then, 'do good'. One must not sweeten transgression by using it as a means for a good end, on the one hand sinning against the commandments of the Torah and on the other hand fulfilling them. Transgressions are forgiven only when the sinner has the opportunity to sin again and resists. They are not forgiven because of a good deed.

Only after we have fulfilled the obligations to the Creator do we say 'seek peace and pursue it'. We must seek peace among people—chase it, even to the point of self-sacrifice. But we must never sacrifice 'Shun evil and do good' for the sake of peace, in fact we must be prepared to live in a state of war with all of humanity if they disturb the peace we have made with the great and holy Creator.

Tiferet shelomo continues: 'With trumpet and the blast of the *shofar* raise a shout before the Lord' (Ps. 98: 6). To raise a shout, in Hebrew *hari'u*, is from the root *re'ut*, or 'friendship'. If you hear the *shofar* in a state of love and friendship,

[4] *Tiferet shelomo* (*Splendor of Solomon*, published 1867–9) is a classic work of hasidic literature by Rabbi Solomon Rabinowicz (1801–66), the founder of the Radomsk hasidic dynasty. Schenirer was married at the end of her life to his grandson, Rabbi Yitzhak Landau.

you will merit standing in the presence of the Lord, with no prosecutor able to damage your case.

'Trumpets' are instruments that call human beings together; with the *shofar* God calls to humans and it is with a trumpet that humans call to one another in God's name, one human being to their fellow human beings, to obey and serve him faithfully.

All nations must learn the Jewish truth, that trumpets—the call between human beings—must be combined with the *shofar*—the call from the Creator.

If we want God to heed our call and aid us in earthly matters, we must first heed God's call, to guide our interests according to his will, heeding the sound of the *shofar* on Mount Sinai. In order for him to help us, he must first be our king—'before the King, our Lord'.

As we make the correct preparations for the great Day of Judgement, we must not forget that it is also for us a Day of Remembrance, on which all of our thoughts, words, and deeds of the whole year are remembered on high.[5] It is also a Day of Remembrance insofar as one Jew remembers to pray for another, as our sages say: 'When one person prays for another, the one who prays receives help first' [BT *BK* 92*a*].

But what should we be praying for?

'One thing I ask of the Lord, only that do I seek, to sit in the House of the Lord all the days of my life' [Ps. 27: 4]: this verse we proclaim enthusiastically from the beginning of the month of Elul until the end of the service on the last day of Sukkot.

We understand that King David did not literally mean that he wished to sit in the House of the Lord all day, since even the priests do not spend the whole day in the Temple. He meant that everywhere, every place we sit, should be as holy as the House of God. As it says in Deuteronomy: 'Since the Lord your God moves about in the midst of your camp . . . let your camp be holy' [Deut. 23: 15]. Every part of our lives must be sacred, a reflection of the sanctity of the House of God.

On the Day of Remembrance we must also remember others. My Bnos, Basya, and Bais Yaakov daughters must demonstrate their love and friendship for their sisters by showing them the way to the fear of God, to true repentance, which can only be approached through confession, spiritual introspection, and remorse. But each of us must first do our own spiritual work, a true and complete repentance, and only then may we turn to work on behalf of others.

[5] Rosh Hashanah is known as the Day of Judgement (*yom hadin*) and the Day of Remembrance (*yom hazikaron*).

This work is with our estranged sisters, and we must never rest until we gather them all under the banner of our Torah.

In this regard we must not forget the printed word, which holds such great promise for us. This is why it is such a sacred obligation for every Bnos, Basya, and Bais Yaakov girl to circulate our very own publications, the *Bais Yaakov Journal* and *Kindergarten*, to every Jewish home.

And when we achieve that, we will surely achieve purity and forgiveness on Yom Kippur and with true joy will we build our sukkah, and we will fulfil the commandment of 'You shall rejoice' [Deut. 16: 14] with all of our heart.[6]

And our Bnos motto, 'Worship the Lord with joy!' [Ps. 100: 2], will become the motto of all the Jewish daughters of the entire Jewish world.

The month of Tishrei, during which the most significant Jewish holidays are observed, begins with Rosh Hashanah. This is the first day of the year, which reminds us of the obligations that Judaism imposes on us, and awakens us to the holiness and purity of the work we do for God during the whole year.

On this great day, the images of many women pass before our eyes: Sarah, Hannah, Rachel, who are all role models for us in our own life experiences.

Take the matriarch Sarah, who so longed to have a child from whom would come the people of Israel. When the angels came to her to relay their tidings that her wish was about to be granted, she, a 90-year-old woman who had already despaired of a child, could not contain her laughter. She just couldn't understand how it could happen to someone her age. Only after she actually gave birth to a son did she see that she had been wrong. 'God has brought me laughter; everyone who hears this will laugh at me' [Gen. 21: 6];[7] everyone will laugh, not believing that her longing was fulfilled in such an unnatural manner. She also saw that the world would have a hard time comprehending her child's descendants, who would always be bitterly mocked. But this did not bother her. On the contrary, she saw in this the great mission that her descendants, pursued and scorned, would nevertheless carry out among the family of nations. Precisely 'on Rosh Hashanah was Sarah visited' [see BT *RH* 10*b*], on Rosh Hashanah she heard the news that she would have a son, Isaac, whose name means laughter. On Rosh Hashanah she was shown how negligible and small human calculations are in the

[6] The verse 'You shall rejoice in your festival' is associated with Sukkot.

[7] Although the JPS 1985 has 'laugh with' instead of 'laugh at', it is clear that Schenirer, who felt the mockery of others so acutely, here intends 'laugh at'; my translation reflects this understanding.

face of God's will. The first day of the year must implant in every Jew this same conviction, which must guide every act, even if the whole world stands in mocking opposition.

With this episode, the matriarch Sarah plays an important role on Rosh Hashanah in the lives and thoughts of her children. Jewish girls have much to learn from her about how to implant these ideas in young hearts in order that later Isaacs may blossom.

And who Isaac truly was is something we also learn on Rosh Hashanah: 'After these things' [Gen. 22: 1]. After Isaac grew up and understood what his parents, Abraham and Sarah, learned from his birth, God showed himself to Abraham and commanded him to sacrifice his beloved son on the altar. Abraham did not hesitate for the slightest instant, taking Isaac, the son he loved so dearly, to Mount Moriah in order to sacrifice him to God. Isaac, who was still young and had hardly begun to drink from life's goblet, knew where he was being taken, but never doubted that he would fulfil God's command, even himself carrying the wood with which he would be burned.

In our awe at Isaac's extraordinary greatness and iron determination to fulfil God's will, we also get a glimpse of how strong and solid must have been the influence of his mother Sarah. How deeply her ideas must have been rooted in his heart, if he was ready at every instant to sacrifice himself and give up his young life to serve God.

On Rosh Hashanah we are clearly shown how we must act in educating our youth during the whole year, and what we must implant in their hearts so that they may be worthy of being children of our great ancestors.

Let us truly learn from this as much as we can.

In the Month of Heshvan

And so the solemn month of Tishrei is behind us and I am certain that the moving sounds of the *shofar* will accompany each of my sisters for the whole year, calling them continually to their holy work.

And do you know, my dear Bnos sisters, what the quiet month of Heshvan demands of you once again?

In the book of Malachi it is written: 'In this vein have those who revere the Lord been talking to one another. The Lord has heard and noted it, and a scroll of remembrance has been written at his behest concerning those who revere the Lord and esteem his name (Mal. 3: 16).' When those who fear God listen to one another, God has them inscribed in the Book of Remembrance, among those who esteem his name.

The month of Heshvan is already here, and with it the long winter nights. Let all the members of Bnos everywhere remember to spend an hour or two in these long nights considering how we might strengthen the Bnos organization and put it on a more solid footing.

Yes, talk is cheap, but accomplishments are very, very difficult, as more than one of you will protest. But let's look at the situation honestly.

In today's world, our holidays are only a weak echo of former times when we were in our own land, and in which the *simḥat beit hasho'evah* (the rejoicing at the place of the water-drawing) on Sukkot was beyond expression.[8] Nevertheless, I think you all felt on Simhat Torah a little taste of the religious enthusiasm that animates Jews, hasidim in particular.[9] Such collective celebrations always awaken our national feelings, allowing Jews to forget their personal cares and everyday worries. Just so should you bring all the girls you know into this circle of joyful communal life, with its celebratory gatherings.

At this point you yourselves can describe from your own personal experiences—thank God!—just how much happiness, how much joy there is in such collective living. Let's take, for example, the evidence found in the book of Samuel.

When 'the whole community of the Israelites assembled at Shiloh' [Josh. 22: 12], the individual played no role, but rather was swept up in the general enthusiasm and returned home full of inspiration. But when the roads to Shiloh turned to wilderness, when the people of Israel were unfortunately driven to find their happiness only in wealth, Elkanah went up to Shiloh alone with his wife and child [1 Sam. 1–3]. But he went with such solemn joy that his enthusiasm kindled a flame in the heart of every acquaintance and neighbour they met along the way, so that new people continually joined the procession. Yes, note well: Elkanah's solitary pilgrimage to Shiloh signified an entirely new epoch in Israel's history. This was also how Hannah became such a famous woman, and how

[8] Mishnah *Suk.* 5: 1 describes a water libation ceremony held in the Temple on the festival of Sukkot, in which tens of thousands of spectators would gather in the outer courtyard to watch the *simḥat beit hasho'evah*, dancing and singing songs of praise to God. According to the Mishnah, 'whoever has not seen the *simḥat beit hasho'evah* has never seen rejoicing in his life'.

[9] Simhat Torah is a festival following the seven days of Sukkot celebrating the conclusion of the annual cycle of Torah readings and the inauguration of a new cycle. Dancing with the Torah scrolls in the synagogue is a central component of the celebration.

they merited to have Samuel as their son, who restored Israel to its former glory.[10]

So do you know now what each of you can be? I have already said it: become a Hannah!

But how does one go about doing that?

The first thing is to learn. It is only ignorance that allows our daughters so easily to go astray, to blunder onto alien paths. First, learn! Learn the holy Torah, immerse yourselves in the words of our prophets. Contemplate the wisdom of our sages, learn the rules and the prayers, familiarize yourselves with the history of your people.

Learn, Jewish daughters, learn, so that the Jewish spirit will awaken within you and inspire you to become a Hannah. With every bit of Jewish knowledge with which you enrich your essence, you dig up a stone from the ruins of the Temple and forge a new brick to build a wall in the new Temple, the one that will stand forever.

Learn Jewish subjects! Wean yourselves from all the other so-called pleasures and recognize the value of Jewish learning! Remember, only Jewish learning can truly nourish our Jewish spirit.

Let the examples of previous generations of Jewish women stand before you, the enthusiasm with which they fulfilled their Jewish obligations to the point of sacrificing their lives. And where did they find their inspiration? Certainly not from alien books, which we can stomach only in small doses and only because we are in exile. Every minute they could spare was devoted to the *Tsene-rene*, the *Menorat hama'or*, the *Kav yashar*, the *Lev tov*, and the *Kitsur shulḥan arukh*.[11] You certainly must remember the episode in my diary when I first heard that sermon in Vienna, and thought: if I could only bring my Polish friends here so they would experience my joy.

And so it should be with you too, my Bnos sisters! Each of you should set out to win over one of your acquaintances, to persist in trying to show her how a life

[10] This *midrash* appears in *Tana deve eliyahu*, a tenth-century compilation that was also printed in Yiddish editions.

[11] The *Kav yashar* (*Just Measure*), by Tsevi Hirsh Koidanover (who produced both a Hebrew and a Yiddish version), is an immensely popular seventeenth-century ethical and kabbalistic collection of stories and moral guidance. *Sefer lev tov* (*Book of the Good Heart*), by Isaac ben Elyakim, is a 1620 Yiddish ethical compendium of proper religious behaviour in the synagogue and everyday life. The *Kitsur shulḥan arukh*, by the Hungarian rabbi Solomon Ganzfried, is a nineteenth-century abbreviation, updating and popularization of Joseph Karo's great legal compendium, the *Shulḥan arukh*; a Yiddish translation appeared in 1892.

lived according to the Torah is a life of joy, to explain to her how not a single secular person feels such joy even when she is saying to herself, 'Things are fine, things are going pretty well.' I can give you dozens of examples of secular people who confessed to me how deeply unhappy they are.

So now we can return to our character, to Elkanah. Do you think that an ordinary Elkanah could have had a Samuel, if his wife had not been a Hannah?

Can you have any more doubt about what a woman can accomplish after you really delve into the prayer of Hannah, which has been eternalized in our book of books?

But, my dears, you must not think that I am calling you only to study. What I am calling you to do is also fulfil your Jewish obligations without being ashamed of it.

This is your work for the month of Heshvan, my dear girls!

Heshvan is our month to recruit. That means we need to put all our energies into thinking about how to expand the circle of people who are aware of our movement. We must also carry out this month our collection of dues. Every group and every Jewish woman must take upon herself the one sign that they are members of Bnos Agudath Israel. Paying dues is also the mark of being connected to the international movement of Agudath Israel. Only these dues make it possible for us to count the number of individuals who are gathered under our historical banner.

Hanukah

The festival of Hanukah has been welcomed from time immemorial as a beloved guest in the Jewish family, since Hanukah is a holiday of conviviality and warmth. As soon as the Hanukah lights appear, the entire family gathers around them and together absorbs the spirit of the heroic Maccabees and the great miracles that our ancestors once experienced.

Of course we also know that every generation has its own heroes, even if they do not always demonstrate their heroism with sword in hand.

Hanukah is first of all a family celebration and only secondarily a national commemoration.

From the tiny village of Modi'in emerged the five heroic Hasmonean brothers, who rekindled the wick of Israel when it had been almost completely extinguished, since the oil of faith had ceased to flow. Even in this idolatrous environment, we can see with pride that a small number of individuals nevertheless managed to raise the banner of pure faith, 'Who is like you, O Lord, among the mighty?' [Exod. 15: 11] emblazoned in fiery letters on their battle flags.[12]

Who empowered these heroic children, who gave them the fiery will and deep beliefs that allowed them to enter this fearsome battle?

Old Mattathias kept the Jewish passion of his children alive, first of all in his heroic son Judah, just as his ancestor Judah, the son of Jacob, had assumed that role before him. And when one family took it upon themselves, in full consciousness and faith, to act as pioneers in the struggle for their people, many other families soon joined them, and in that way the entire nation was saved.

And today, too, our sages have emphasized above all the observance of a family celebration, 'a light for a man and his household'.[13] The Jewish light that burns in a family leads to the shining of Israel's light among the entire people.

It is only when we read the *haftarah* of the sabbath of Hanukah that we get an accurate understanding of the holiday itself.[14] The prophet Zechariah relates to us his remarkable dream about the *menorah* wrought of gold, and the seven pipes and the olive trees, and the meaning of the dream is, 'Not by might, nor by power, but by my spirit said the Lord of hosts' [Zech. 4: 6].[15] Not by military might or force but only by spirit does the Jewish people live.

The Jewish *menorah* sheds light on all the dark moments of human history. Israel's view on life has always been pure, full of sanctity. The Jew draws his wisdom not through complicated hydraulic systems but rather directly from the source. The Jewish perspective is unique and original and for that reason cannot be compared with that of other peoples, who base their existence on entirely different foundations.

[12] The traditional Jewish explanation of the name Maccabee is that it is an acronym for the Hebrew verse in Exod. 15:11, *Mi Kamokha Ba'elim YHWH*.

[13] BT *Shab.* 21*b* states that the basic commandment of lighting candles on Hanukah is *ner ish uveito*, 'a light [per night] for a man and his household'. Schenirer here emphasizes not the number of candles to be lit (about which the Talmud records different opinions) but rather the significance of the household, which she later also connects with the notion of the 'House of God'.

[14] The *haftarah* is the generic name for the reading from the Prophets that follows the reading of the weekly Torah portion in the synagogue on the sabbath and with which it is usually thematically linked.

[15] Zech. 4 relates a vision or dream in which the prophet says, 'I see a lampstand all of gold, with a bowl above it. The lamps on it are seven in number, and the lamps above it have seven pipes; and by it are two olive trees.'

Gazing into the Hanukah flames, we can see quite powerfully that our entire essence rests only on 'my [God's] spirit'. The most essential thing is to labour with all one's energies so that every Jewish home will become a House of God. 'A man and his household' also hints at the building of the Temple. By 'man' is meant God and by 'house' is meant the Temple. We must emerge from the eight days of Hanukah strengthened by hope and above all ready to work to rebuild Jewish life according to our ancient ideals.

During this period of Hanukah we must also strengthen our work in education, in the education of girls. Sisters! Let us undertake anew with deeper faith-consciousness our work for this exalted idea. Let us remember, 'Not by might, not by power, but by my spirit, said the Lord.'

Each year, when we light the Hanukah *menorah* and contemplate its meaning and significance, we feel ourselves somehow in an entirely different world, the world of the Hasmoneans. They remind us of the great battles on behalf of Judaism that our ancestors went through, and give us fresh spiritual energy to fight for the fulfilment of the Torah and its commandments.

In the flame of these lights that have already been burning for millennia flickers also the eternal flame that the Hasmoneans kindled in Jewish hearts and which will never be extinguished. The glowing rays that were first sent into the world by old Mattathias in order to warm and inspire the hearts of thousands of Jews to fight for their faith, their people, and their tradition will never lose their power.

We light eight candles. Eight bearers of the light of our people tremble before our eyes, and standing before us, they seem to be eight spiritual guides, with burning eyes and vibrant hearts, radiating the enormous enthusiasm and joy they represent.

Here now is the first of these, our great-grandfather the patriarch Abraham, a man alone among thousands of idol worshippers, who recognized the great Creator of the world and was not ashamed to preach the truth out loud to one and all.

And we see how the power of that eternal truth persuades everyone, and the light of the divine word reaches even the benighted masses, those who have spent a lifetime wallowing in idol worship. Abraham makes new disciples, spiritual followers, because he knows full well that there is no point in recognizing the truth if one does not share it with others.

And now the light starts to flicker, the light created for all of humanity and especially for the Jewish people, who find themselves in danger of disappearing for all eternity—God forbid!—in the idolatrous land of Egypt through the terrible material and spiritual conditions in which they find themselves. But then the heroic figure of Moses arises, who, despite having been raised in Pharaoh's royal court, has the courage to resist the atrocities visited on his people, even at the risk of his own life. He finally redeems them from the Egyptian yoke and gives them, to boot, the Torah, the laws of God, which will accompany and protect them throughout the generations.

And later, the figure of the prophet Samuel appears, to rescue the Jewish people from the evil influences of the surrounding lawless pagans. He is a man perfectly suited for that task, 'holy from his mother's womb' [Judges 13: 7]. His pious mother Hannah consecrates him to God. He travels throughout the Land of Israel 'from Dan to Beersheba' [1 Sam. 3: 20], strengthening Jewish faith, founding schools, and so on.

And this picture also fades quickly. The radiant era of the Temple shines for a moment before our eyes, but 'Jeshurun grew fat' [Deut. 32: 15]. The kingdom of David falls into bitter division, splits into two, and the wisdom of the ancestors is forgotten. The people worship at alien altars and the result is the Babylonian exile.

It does not take long before the Jews repent, turn back to their land, and then Ezra the Scribe appears. With the fire of his soul, he heals the damage that ignorance had made in Jewish life, giving back to the Jewish people the unique spiritual content of their life.

But this victory is also temporary. Because of their sins the Jewish people must walk the difficult path of exile yet again. The fear arises that—God forbid!—through the burden of exile the Jewish masses will forget the Torah. But then comes Rabbi Judah the Prince, who gathers and organizes the entire Oral Torah under the name Mishnah, and thus ensures that the Torah will never be forgotten by Jews.

Later, when the Jewish mind has been further clouded by the burden of exile, and the possibility emerges that Jews will no longer comprehend the profound laws of the Talmud, such bearers of light as Rashi and Maimonides arise to illuminate and clarify the difficult passages of the Talmud in accessible form.

We see too Rabbi Judah Halevi, who implants courage and love for the commandments in his Jewish brothers, and brings comfort to them with his heavenly poems.

We have these carriers of light to thank for our having remained faithful to our holy treasure, the Torah, despite the experiences of our long exile. Through them we have the fortune to light these Hanukah candles with the same enthusiasm and feeling with which they have been lit since the times of the Hasmoneans.

As we deepen our contemplation of the essence of Hanukah, a question arises: why did our sages command us to light candles in each home? And why, when the man of the house is absent, did they make it incumbent on women to light candles, rather than relying on candle-lighting in the synagogue?

There were deep considerations in this ruling. It is not enough that the father prays the Hallel service with great devotion, while his wife and daughter are occupied at home with other thoughts, or worse, thoughts that entirely contradict those of the father.

In each Jewish home, therefore, the Hanukah candles must be lit. These lights, which remind us of the self-sacrifice and dedication that our spiritual leaders, the Hasmoneans, demonstrated for the Torah, must be lit so that the wife and daughter may also be inspired by the Jewish tradition.

Everywhere, in every Jewish home, must Hanukah lights be lit!

Shabat Shekalim

Each year when we arrive at the sabbath on which we bless the New Moon of the month of Adar, or when that New Moon falls on this sabbath, we see on the calendar, alongside the Torah portion of the week, another brief notation: Shabat Shekalim. A few of our girls who may not be so familiar with the Jewish calendar will surely want to know the meaning of this phrase.

For that reason, we will pause and consider this. In order to prepare for the great sacred occasion of Passover, our sages ordained that additional Torah portions should be read on four preceding sabbaths, known collectively as 'the four portions', to make them special sabbaths: the portion of 'Shekalim' ['Coins'], the portion of 'Zakhor' ['Remember'], the portion of 'Parah' ['Red Heifer'], and the portion of 'Hahodesh' ['The New Month'].[16] The first of these is what we are talking about now, that of Shekalim. When we read the last part of the Torah portion in the synagogue, instead of repeating the last few verses of the regular portion as is normally done, we read that part of the Torah that speaks of the obligation of each Jew to give a half-shekel (a coin of that era) as a contribution to the maintenance of the Temple [Exod. 30: 11–16].

[16] The four sabbaths, two before Purim and two before Passover, are described in BT *Meg.* 29*a*.

If we look at the verses that speak of this commandment and delve deeply into them, we see that they teach us a great deal. First of all the verse says, 'This is what everyone who is entered in the records shall pay' [Exod. 30: 13]: all those counted must contribute a half-shekel to God, each without exception must participate in the collective work—no one may desist—but only contribute to the collective and for the collective. An individual can never carry out something complete and permanent, even if he uses every bit of his strength. But a collective can always build and complete the most solid of endeavours.

It only requires each individual participant to contribute to the limit of what he can, according to his capacities, and that effort will be reckoned as if he had built the entire enterprise on his own.

The portion 'Shekalim' also says, 'From the age of twenty years up' [Exod. 30: 14], each one is required to participate in this holy work. This is different from the way people tend to think, that the obligation of the commandments falls either on small children, who have not yet been beset by competing desires, or the old, who have left those behind. That is the reason that the Torah says 'from twenty years and up': at the prime of one's life is one obligated to work ceaselessly for *yiddishkeit*.

'The rich shall not pay more and the poor shall not pay less' [Exod. 30: 15]: we can see then why the Torah specifically designated a sum as small as a half-shekel as a contribution, in order to make it possible for everyone, rich and poor alike, to participate in the holy building and construction. That erased the boundaries between social classes in regard to the most sacred and greatest obligations of a human being. Everyone is equal when it comes to sacred work, and each has an equal part in both the obligation and the reward. Each must work according to their own abilities and means.

But what was actually done with these half-shekels? From the silver of these coins were fashioned the thresholds of the Tabernacle (*mishkan*), the foundation of this sacred edifice, and the funds were also used for the purchase of the sacrifices needed for a whole year.[17]

We can thus see that from such small sums great treasures can accumulate, as long as each person contributes what he can. And this is a lesson for us, that we too can achieve anything with a united effort and God's help, even with the smallest contributions.

[17] The half-*shekel* contributions were used for the construction of the Tabernacle (*mishkan*), the portable sanctuary that accompanied the Israelites in the desert and initially in the Land of Israel, until it was superseded by the Temple.

So let us take it upon ourselves to contribute as much as we are able to *yiddishkeit*—but really, each of us. No one must desist from this sacred work. And we must work not only in those moments of enthusiasm and heightened energies, but rather always, so that each small step we complete leads to another, even stronger action towards our Jewish goals. Just as the threshold of the Tabernacle was only the foundation for the holy ritual that was carried out each and every day.

Truly, we must work with all our energy for *yiddishkeit*—but this work must be tireless and without cease, and if it is, we can hope to succeed in reaching our goal.

Shabat Zakhor [The Sabbath of Remembrance]

The sabbath of Zakhor, which always falls on the last sabbath before Purim, is the second of the special sabbaths that help us prepare for the great festival of Passover.[18]

The Torah reading known as 'Zakhor' [Deut 25: 17–19] awakens in us, the Jewish collective, the consciousness that despite being dispersed throughout the world and differentiated from one another by abilities, property, and class, we are all, each and every one of us, obligated to carry out Israel's mission in the greater world. 'Remember what Amalek did to you.' 'Remember!' this portion calls to us, 'look back and remind yourself of what Amalek did to you when you were leaving the exile of Egypt, when you were taking your first steps to becoming the chosen people.'

On the issue of 'the war with Amalek', the Torah makes very clear the reasons for this difficult struggle. At precisely the point in the Torah when the outcry is recorded: 'Is the Lord present among us or not?', the next verse proclaims that 'Amalek came and fought with Israel.'

We also know that as long as Moses was able to keep his arms aloft, the Jews prevailed, but when Moses allowed his hands to fall, Amalek was victorious.

Amalek's sword only conquered those who asked the question, 'Is the Lord present among us or not?' But those who are steadfast in their faith and in their hearts are always redeemed.

The war with Amalek has remained a lesson for us for all times. In every moment when we allow doubt to overtake our faith, when our commitment to

[18] *Shabat zakhor* marks the reading of Deut. 25: 17–19. It is named for the passage that commands the Israelites to remember (*zakhor*) Amalek's evil deeds and blot out his memory; the Amalekites were a tribe that ambushed the Israelites in the wilderness.

the commandments of the Torah is weakened, it is then that the antisemitic Amalekites score a victory. We put weapons in the hands of Israel's enemies when we fail to respect our own sacred treasures. For how could they fail to despise our people when we ourselves, God forbid, reveal our own hatred for Torah and *yiddishkeit*? Indeed, every time new enemies arise against the Jewish people, we need to search our own souls to see whether the reason for the renewed anti-Jewish hatred is not our own indifference to our spiritual property.

Each year, when we read the portion 'Zakhor', the call resounds in our ears: *If you stand with hands lifted to the heavens, Amalek can have no power over you*!

'The Lord will battle for you.' The actual war with our enemies to prevent them from annihilating eternal Israel, God alone carries out. But we Jews must carry on an internal battle against our own evil inclination.

The path to victory over own base instincts, our corrupt habits, is through purity: to cleanse oneself of everything that corrupts the heart, poisons the soul, and as we see, to inscribe in one's memory the battle against the materialism of Amalek, and thus to achieve purity, as is taught in a later Torah portion, the portion of 'the red heifer' [Num. 19: 2–6].

Of course it is true that, as a divine ordinance, the matter of the red heifer does not require an explanation, but nevertheless we see that it too is a lesson to the Jewish people about how to master the baser physical desires through spiritual endeavour.

To fulfil the ceremonial requirements, the red heifer had to be a young female cow never used for any purpose; when it was first brought to the priest he put his hand on it; and after slaughtering it, he sprinkled its blood all around the altar. The red heifer ritual was introduced to represent the Temple for Jews in exile,[19] in order to show how the spiritual must reign over the material realm. The idea of purity means mastery over material things and corporeal nature. Even as we witness others directing their impulses only towards the material world, our obligation as Jews, as descendants of a 'kingdom of priests and holy nation', is to give our lives another significance.

And the first element of the work we do in order to control our material desires and not sink into the abyss of hedonistic idolatry is signalled by the

[19] While Schenirer's meaning is not entirely clear here, she focuses on the detail in the law of the red heifer that places its slaughter outside the Temple, perhaps to emphasize that this divine ordinance continues to have spiritual significance for post-Temple Judaism, when the ritual of the red heifer is no longer observed. As always, Schenirer understands impurity here as contamination by influences alien to Jewish ideals.

reference to 'the [new] month': we must renew, revive, and rejuvenate our ancient Jewish energies.

Only after we have learned to purify ourselves does the last sabbath before the month of Nisan come, and we proclaim: 'This month shall mark for you' [Exod. 12: 2]: the Creator of the world calls us to renew ourselves, so that just as the new moon shines at the beginning of the month, renewing and refreshing, so too should we renew our longing to live in holiness and sanctity, in order to merit the great Jewish redemption.[20]

Judith, Esther, and Mordecai

Two women in our history were especially noteworthy for having rescued the Jewish people: Judith and Esther. Judith, the great heroine of Hanukah, beheaded the terrible antisemite Holofernes with her sword, and Esther saved her people from the Jew-hater Haman.[21]

Interestingly, neither Esther nor Judith set out on their very dangerous rescue missions without first awakening the people to repentance and good deeds, that is, to distance themselves from alien ideas and fashions.

Let us consider our Esther. Despite being entirely immersed in the diaspora, very close to the permissive Persian culture where all the luxuries and pleasures of the world and the royal court were there for the taking, 'Esther obeyed Mordecai's bidding' [Esther 2: 20]; Mordecai's word and command were as holy for her as they had been when she was being raised by him.

There are unfortunately many parents who must let out a deep and heavy sigh as they read this verse. The festival of Purim is transformed for them into a sorrowful day of mourning. Here they hear the story of a Jewish woman who ascends to the royal throne, having achieved the highest status possible in human society and in the political realm, but who remains true to the one who reared her. His word is the holiest of holies and she cherishes his command as the apple of her eye.

But they, the parents of today's generation, cannot manage to maintain this discipline even in their own homes, while the children are still under their watch.

[20] The month of Nisan is considered, according to Exod. 12: 2, the first month of the year. Schenirer here also alludes to the etymology of the Hebrew word for 'month' (*ḥodesh*), which derives from a root meaning 'new'.

[21] See Ch. 1 n. 2 for explanations on the book of Judith. Perhaps Schenirer nevertheless does not elaborate on Judith in this essay because the story is less well known to traditional readers than that of Esther, since the book of Judith in non-canonical.

Even when their parents are around, the son and daughter act as if they know better than them, consider themselves finer people than their parents, those old-fashioned fanatics. The parents pay dearly just to maintain the barest modicum of proper behaviour from their children while they are still at home. And the very moment the children leave—the parents know full well—all this work goes out the window.

But it is for this reason that Jewish parents are required to assume the obligation of caring about their children's education, ensuring that their own efforts do not fail. They should take this sacred obligation with utmost seriousness.

For it was only for the sake of education that God chose Abraham as the bearer of his Torah. God knew that his children would receive an education in the Jewish spirit only through him, and that was why God so appreciated Abraham. The education that Abraham and Sarah gave Isaac is a shining example of the limitless power of childrearing.

When God wished to create a people that could withstand the greatest trials, survive the long and difficult exile, and emerge from martyrdom and suffering sanctified, beautified, and strengthened, he began with a poor old couple whose only child had just been born, a child for whom they had long prayed, and whom they brought up with such divine faith that this child allowed himself to be led to the sacrifice.

And because of the excellent education that Mordecai gave Esther, she remained faithful to his command even in the corrupt royal court, which shows Mordecai's greatness as a teacher.

But Mordecai, a highly cultured man who knew many languages, took no pride at all in his knowledge. No one knew a thing about these accomplishments. The royal officials who spoke in a foreign tongue were sure that Mordecai could not understand them [Esther 2: 21]. And that, too, led to the great redemption of the Jews.

Mordecai's spirit must rule today. We must follow his example in raising our own children.

Esther's obedience to Mordecai and his commands must demonstrate to our own daughters how to be faithful and obedient in following the rules and example of their Jewish elders.

Passover Thoughts

I

Passover, the festival of freedom, approaches!

Freedom! Who is not familiar with the sweet sound of that word, which signifies the most cherished gift of humanity?

But there is also its opposite, which sends a shudder through each of us. By which I mean: slavery.

A people groan under the heavy yoke of their oppressors. The strict taskmaster stands with whip in hand and drives them to their labour. One must not rest for a single moment, even a word must not escape one's lips. Babies are ripped from the breast and flung in the river.

But just at this very moment—can it be?

The call of liberation resounds in the breeze, the manacles crack and drop from the wrists. These very individuals who only yesterday were a herd of obedient slaves now stand before our eyes as a proud people with straight backs, united by a single ideal and led by a great leader. How did this happen? Is this not an unnatural occurrence?

Yes, you will undoubtedly respond, but was it really a miracle? Such things often happen among various nations, when in a very brief period they are liberated from oppression!

You Jewish daughters who ask this question, you—many of you who are even ashamed of the label 'Jew'—have you ever heard of people who have never lived as a nation, who have always been only slaves, for whom slavery was a deeply engrained habit, and who suddenly became an independent nation? And this happened not through a battle or revolution, but only through the power of God! Is this not visible evidence that we are a chosen people? That the miracles God performed before the eyes of the whole world freed us not only from physical shackles but, even more so, from spiritual ones.

And for this freedom that he bestowed on us we must be grateful, and follow his will.

'And you shall explain to your son on that day, "It is because of what the Lord did for me when I went free from Egypt"' [Exod. 13: 8].

You Jewish fathers! On the very night of your spiritual birth God commanded that you should fulfil your obligation with regard to your children. The night of the *seder* is indeed most appropriate for this task.

'And you shall explain to your son.' 'It could be from the beginning of the month [that we are required to tell the story of the Exodus]'—one might have thought that one should begin telling the child the story from the beginning of the month, which is why the verse states clearly, "On that day". Might one suppose that this means [that the story of the Exodus is told] during the day? And so it says further, "Because of this", which is to say, "when the matzah and bitter herbs are before you."'[22]

Here lies the key to Jewish education. Not through theory should one teach a child Torah, but rather with deeds. Only 'when the matzah and bitter herbs are before you'. When the child sees the father carry out all the commandments and receives a proper explanation, this teaching will remain with him forever.

We always try to explain the meaning of these commandments we fulfil on this night. There are three primary commandments: the Passover sacrifice, the matzah, and the bitter herbs. That is to say, the lamb that God commanded the Jews to prepare by the tenth day of Nisan. Since that day fell on the sabbath, everyone took their lamb into their own home and secured it to the bedpost.

The Egyptians looked on with gritted teeth as their Jewish slaves chained up these gods (the lamb was a great god for the Egyptians). This teaches us that people should always have courage to take the gods of their time and chain them before the eyes of those who worship them.[23] And then their victory will be assured.

O, you daughters of Israel! You, who follow the fashions of the time, both spiritual and material, intending to show in this way how progressive you are. You are mistaken! What you are showing, rather, is that you lack the courage of your ancestors, who put the idols of their time in chains!

All this is conveyed to us by the shank bone, the roasted piece of lamb on the *seder* table that commemorates the Passover sacrifice. And when the father shows the child the symbolic sacrifice, he must say to him: 'the Passover sacrifice to the Lord' [Exod. 12: 27]—that is a sacrifice to God, when he triumphed over

[22] Schenirer here quotes from and translates into Yiddish a passage in the *magid* section of the Passover Haggadah, which itself closely echoes a midrashic discussion on Exod. 13: 8 in the *Mekhilta*.

[23] The idea that the Passover paschal lamb was slaughtered to demonstrate to the Egyptians that their 'god' was helpless was advanced by a thirteenth-century exegete in France known as the Hizkuni (Rabbi Hezekiah ben Manoah), who asks why God commanded that the Israelites take a lamb on the tenth of the month but sacrifice it only on the fourteenth. The Hizkuni replies: 'until the fourteenth day' (Exod. 12: 6), 'so that the Egyptians would see their gods tied shamefully and disgracefully in the homes of the Israelites and would hear the sheep squealing with no one to save them'.

our tyrant and oppressor, and killed the Egyptian firstborns. And this should be said with such heartfelt love that it remains in the child's heart always.

And now the commandment of the bitter herbs. They remind us of the bread of poverty and the bitter herbs that we ate in those days, of the miserable state in which we found ourselves before we became free. We promised then that we would remember the hour of our liberation for all times, and do so with matzah and bitter herbs. And thus, as long as we live, we must serve God, and raise our children to fulfil today's sacred service.

We always try to make sure to feed our children, so why do we feel no need to quiet their spiritual hunger? We must not rely only on school to provide this nourishment on our behalf. No! We must implant in our children the principles of our faith from earliest childhood. We must never tire of answering every question a child asks. What we teach a child early on plants the seeds of radiant love for the Jewish people, providing inspiration that can last an entire lifetime.

And Passover teaches us yet another thing. We need not wait for a child to be able to ask: 'What is this?' But rather, 'And the one who does not know how to ask, you open his mouth.'[24] Take the child on your lap, and explain the Exodus from Egypt in words he can grasp. But tell him this story in such a way that later, he too will take his child on his lap and relate to him the story of the Exodus from Egypt. Tell the story with such enthusiasm that the child will feel that he is there, held in your arms, while the bundle of dough is on your shoulder, and the two of you are walking into the depths of the sea, and on either side of you rise the walls of water, and a single thought dominates your thinking: to fulfil God's will.

O, you, my Jewish sisters! If you think that by throwing the commandments overboard you are demonstrating the sharpness of your minds, try asking your fathers this question, just once at the *seder* table: 'What is this?' If you only considered each of these commandments, you would see how much spiritual significance, how much soul there is in this simple piece of matzah, this bitter herb, and I am sure that you would let go of all your alien ideas and become, right there at the *seder* table, true daughters of Israel.

2

But why did it come to pass? By whose merit were the Jews liberated from Egypt?

The *midrash* teaches us that it was by the merit of righteous women that we were all redeemed from the exile in Egypt. But what kind of merit could the

[24] 'What is this?' is the question asked by the simple child in the section of the Passover Haggadah on 'the four children'. The last child is the one who does not know how to ask.

women of those days have accrued, labouring morning and night under the most difficult conditions, without any opportunity to devote themselves to spiritual matters?

Three things, the *midrash* teaches us, brought the redemption: 'That they did not change their names, their language, or their dress.' These three things that they guarded so closely were what they had to thank for bringing their redemption.[25]

Jewish sisters! How are these three things faring among you now?

Unfortunately, things are not going so well in these three domains. I won't discuss the first two topics, which Jewish women today find so thoroughly distasteful. I will just touch on the third of these domains, the unique Jewish form of dress.

Now that nature is awakening from its long winter sleep to fresh life, and donning fresh green clothing, the desire to be seen in a new dress also stirs in the woman. And just at this point must the Jewish woman remember that clothing the body is of sublime significance for the Jewish people.

Already at the very beginning of human history people concealed their nakedness with clothing, in order for the sinning body not to lead the human being astray. And later our sages made sure that Jewish dress would accord with the highest standards of modesty and holiness. It was always women who understood this best, who recognized the evil effects that immodest dress have on the baser instincts, disturbing the harmony between body and soul—so they cultivated an unusual sensitivity that distinguished them from the women around them through the strict modesty of their clothing, which made them a model for their non-Jewish sisters.

So how does it look now, that modesty that once reigned among Jewish women? Have these women not mostly abandoned the ways of their mothers, who supported the Jewish people so strongly simply by the way they dressed?

Unfortunately we must state plainly that the Parisian fashion epidemic has overtaken the overwhelming majority of Jewish women today, infecting them

[25] Fischer, '"Name, Language, and Dress"', demonstrates that the three elements in the famous midrash cited by Schenirer never appear together in rabbinic literature, and the midrash is a composite of *Lev. Rabbah* 32: 5, *Tanna Devei Eliyahu* 23: 2, and other sources. As Fischer argues, 'The midrash-cum-myth that the Israelites in Egypt did not change their name, language, or dress was popularized throughout Hungary during the 1860s, and it remained part of specifically Hungarian Orthodox discourse until the destruction of Hungarian Jewry in World War II', spreading as well through other communities under the influence of Hungarian ultra-Orthodoxy.

with its ugliness. Only a very small portion have the courage to resist the kind of clothing that is in 'the latest style'. Only very few of these women recognize that worshipping at the altar of fashion, fulfilling the wildest demands of the fashion gods with the most outlandish enthusiasm, is the greatest absurdity of all.

But I have no desire to blame Jewish women or disparage them for casting off the dictates of this special Jewish concept of modesty. There are, naturally, other factors at work, including these women's ignorance of Jewish values and their lack of grounding in the eternal ethical and moral foundations of the Torah.

Be that as it may, these factors must be eliminated from the Jewish home. Which is the reason I am now turning to all my faithful Jewish sisters.

Remember that modesty and purity are among the most powerful foundations of the Jewish home! Where clothing is not in accordance with Jewish moral precepts, the divine spirit can find no rest! It is forbidden even to utter God's name in the presence of an immodestly clad woman![26] Let it not be said of you in generations to come: the Jewish daughters of that time did not understand the importance of maintaining their own modest style of dress, which was guarded through so many generations!

Thoughtful Jewish mothers! See to it that you implant in the hearts of your young children a reverence for moral dress and an abhorrence of immodest clothing! Remember that it was the Jewish women who proudly guarded the unique customs of Jewish appearance and kept away from the corruptions of immodesty who merited that the Jews were redeemed from Egypt! We too must follow their example and then we too may hope to be liberated from our exile today through the same divine hand.

The Time of the *Sefirah* [Counting of the *Omer*]

The beautiful and beloved Passover has taken its leave of us. The time when parents inspired the hearts of their children to our holy Torah with the commandments and customs of this holiday is now behind us. Every pedagogue in the world would have to agree that there is simply no better method for teaching than the holiday of Passover. Now we begin to count the weeks and days until we receive the Torah. In the same way that a smitten bridegroom longs for the day of his wedding, so too is Israel bursting with anticipation for the arrival of

[26] The prohibition against reciting a blessing or reading the Torah in the presence of a married woman with uncovered hair, or a naked person of either gender, is discussed in the *Shulḥan arukh*, 'Oraḥ ḥayim', 75: 6 and elsewhere.

the day that the Torah will be given to them. With every day that passes their desire mounts for the days still to come.

Rabbi Hiya teaches: '"You shall count off seven whole weeks [Lev. 23: 15]." When will they be whole?' (When will the curses and sorrows of our time pass away so that time will once again be whole?) And Rabbi Hiya answers: 'When Israel fulfils the will of the Holy One, blessed be he.'[27]

The preachers of modernity call upon our youth to throw off the burden of *yiddishkeit*. In this way, they think, we will be better off and happier.

Let those heretics call themselves 'liberated' and forget that there is no greater enslavement and oppression than submission to one's own ego.

The believer and the one who observes the Torah consider 'freedom' from an entirely different perspective, and counting the *omer* sheds light on this very issue.

The second night of Passover, when we began cutting the *omer* offering of the new barley crop and brought the first sheaves of barley to the priest, was also the first moment that the Jew was permitted to use the barley, although it may have already been ripe for some time.

When we were in our Holy Land, counting the *omer* was a way of proclaiming both to the people as a whole and to each individual Jew: this land that you possess, the plough with which you work this land, and the fruit that you obtain from it, all this is nevertheless not the essence of your Jewish life. Only if you fulfil the Torah will all this indeed be yours, and if—God forbid—you do not, you will lose this verdant land and its sweet fruit.

And what happened?

As long as Israel indeed understood the essence and significance of counting the *omer*, Israel inhabited the land and reaped its own wheat in joy and song. But as soon as the Jewish people forgot their mission, this land, along with their freedom and all their national possessions, were taken away.

The Jew has been wandering through exile for two thousand years now and has no fields he can call his own. His home has been taken from him, all his national

[27] See *Zohar*, iii. 97*a*–*b* (trans. Matt, viii. 126–7), for a more elaborate version of this commentary on Lev. 23: 15, in which Rabbi Hiya compares the impurity of Egypt to menstrual impurity, and the counting of seven weeks between the cessation of impurity with the Exodus and the purification ritual on Mount Sinai to the seven days between the cessation of the menstrual flow to the purification.

treasures lie in ruins, and under these conditions the counting of the *omer* has become very problematic. Especially since we no longer have a high priest, or the Holy Land, and we cannot see the Temple before our eyes, it is difficult for a Jewish heart to really feel this longing for repentance, now that even the remnants of those national cultural treasures that we took with us into exile are also in such grievous decline.

The history of this exile, with its many tragic chapters, tells us that the period of the counting of the *omer* was set apart for the bloodiest and most terrifying suffering and destruction.[28] But we emerged from these devastating experiences strengthened in our faith.

The Jewish soul remained awake, and its longing and life were not stifled. Our own hearts, it is true, have grown a little drowsy, and indeed it is our most sacred obligation to awaken the Jewish soul from its lethargic sleep.

All the sacred martyrs who died for God's name in fire and flame with 'Hear! O Israel!' on their lips, all of them are alive before our eyes during these days of counting the *omer*.

Let us read the tragic pages of their lives and deaths, and this alone will lead us to stronger faith. Let us spend these days on which we count the *omer* also counting our qualities and flaws. For us, the girls of Bnos Agudath Israel, counting the days, weeks, and years ahead of us has long been a sign of our ideals, of our longing to ascend to the Land of Israel, 'Teach us to count our days rightly' [Ps. 90: 12]!

And while we gather in the post-Passover summer evenings in synagogues and study houses to count the days until we receive the Torah, let us also remember the conditions in which our ancestors in their various different exiles counted the *omer*. which will also remind us of the troubles that Jews had to live through to survive in the face of their enemies.

They gave their lives to God in the ultimate self-sacrifice rather than allow these enemies to desecrate their sacred possessions. Year in, year out, under the most horrific conditions, they counted the days of the *omer* until the holiday of the giving of the Torah. They sacrificed their own little sheaf of barley for the

[28] BT *Yev.* 92*b* recounts the death of 24,000 of Rabbi Akiva's students in the weeks between Passover and Shavuot. While this is the primary reason for the mourning observances of this period, Jewish memory also dates other devastations to this time of year, including attacks during the Crusades and the Khmelnytzky uprising of 1648–9.

Torah,[29] and lived in the hope of better times when they could observe the commandments of the Torah undisturbed.

These terrible times are now, thank God, behind us. Our own circumstances are now certainly much easier. Shouldn't we then dedicate ourselves with even greater fervour to sacrificing our own sheaves of barley, the first fruits of our own labour, to the Torah?

Unfortunately things are not going well in that regard. We may count the *omer* but we also value our little bundles of grain more highly than the Torah. We want to make sure that our children will be rich in material things, but neglect to worry about making their connection to the Torah equally rich. And always, above all, we worry mainly about maintaining appearances.

We are in desperate need of schools where our children can learn what it means to sacrifice their first sheaves of grain for God and the Torah, what it means to count down the days until the day comes that we receive the Torah.

We need the sort of homes from which a generation can emerge that is prepared to follow the model of our ancestors, to sacrifice themselves even under the most horrific conditions.

Do we have enough such schools? And can those that exist take in the many poor children who beg for the opportunity, for the great joy, of being accepted into the school so that they, too, might fulfil their hunger for *yiddishkeit*?

As we count the days of the *omer* sacrifice until the giving of the Torah we must awaken in ourselves the enormous power of our ancestors in the various eras of the exile, who so magnificently understood what it meant to sacrifice their sheaves of grain for the Torah, and who rebuilt on the ruins of their lost sacred places 'the House of Jacob', the Jewish home. We must with greatest determination put this building that our ancestors established on stronger foundations, for the pride and glory of the entire Jewish people.

Shavuot and Ruth

The lightning flashes of Sinai have long since died down. But Mount Horeb has still not entirely gone quiet. Each and every day a heavenly call goes out from there, saying: 'Woe to humanity for insulting the Torah' [*Avot* 6: 2]. Humanity is shamed when the Torah is shamed!

[29] The term *omer* here refers to the sheaf of barley that is brought as a sacrifice on the second day of Passover, inaugurating the period named after this sheaf (Lev. 23: 15). Schenirer is clearly speaking metaphorically here.

The holiday of the Torah will soon be upon us, the day on which we accepted the holy Torah on Mount Sinai. A remarkable holiday, this time of accepting the Torah.

Every Jewish holiday has its symbol, Rosh Hashanah—the *shofar*; Yom Kippur—fasting; Sukkot—the sukkah and *etrog*; Passover—its matzah. But Shavuot has no symbol—why?

Because this holiday is itself a symbol for all generations, signifying that on this day, the Holy One, blessed be he, gave us his Torah amid thunder and lightning. And because God is unique and his Torah is unique, this significance cannot be expressed in any symbol.

When we unroll the Torah scrolls in synagogue on this holiday and encounter the words of the Ten Commandments, a shudder passes through us. We feel exalted by the atmosphere of Sinai. Each of us feels as if we were standing at Sinai alongside our millions of brothers and sisters, listening to the words of the Creator!

'And God spoke all these words, saying' [Exod. 20: 1]: the Creator of the world spoke! Any doubt about what was said, any question about the divinity of every word of the Torah was eliminated. And what was also eliminated was the possibility that we might change the word of the one true God to align it with our own personal opinions.

But there is something else we read on this holiday free of symbols, the book of Ruth. Is it not somewhat curious that the sages decided that this book, which seems to be just a little tale of days gone by, must be read on Shavuot, this holiday of holidays?

But when we look more closely at this little book, we recognize how much we—Jewish women in particular—can learn from its few pages.

Elimelekh, a wealthy Jewish aristocrat from Bethlehem, cannot bear to witness his brothers' suffering in a time of famine, and rather than helping them, he escapes to a foreign land, to Moab. His punishment follows quickly: he and his two sons, Mahlon and Chilion, die young, and his wife Naomi is left a poor and broken widow with her two daughters-in-law, Ruth and Orpah.

And when Naomi learns that the famine has ended in the land of Judah, she cannot remain in Moab any longer and decides to return home.

And so the three impoverished widows set out on the road to the Holy Land, facing an entirely unknown future. Naomi knows only one thing about what she will encounter. She knows that no palaces full of riches await her return, but rather that people will look upon her as a fallen aristocrat, proof that God has punished her for abandoning them in a time of need. She knows this well, but nevertheless, her longing for home proves more powerful.

At the border of the land of Judah, a dramatic scene takes place: Naomi takes leave of her daughters-in-law, thanking them for accompanying her this far and begging them to return to their royal parents, who are no doubt awaiting their return with open arms.

Naomi doesn't want their pity for her to sway them into following her into the Holy Land or into acting as if they were Jewish women. She tells them to turn back and bestows on them her wish that they find their lost happiness with other men.

They kiss, and together the two daughters-in-law cry in a single voice: 'No, we want to go with you, to your people!' They know full well the difficulties of Jewish faith, they understand that an alien environment awaits them in the Land of Israel, but even so, they wish to remain with her.

Naomi explains to them that she cherishes their love for her and is grateful to them, but that is the precise reason she has no desire for them to sacrifice themselves on her behalf. With her, they have no chance of happiness. A woman, after all, can only find true happiness in her husband's house. And with me, she says, you will certainly see no children!

Three times she urges them to turn back, exactly as one does with someone who is considering Jewish conversion. She wants to make sure that they are not acting on impulse, that they have really thought through their decision. Despite how deeply moved she is by the tears of her daughters-in-law, she tests their characters with cool calculation.

Orpah has a very weak character. She is drawn to her own home. And so she allows herself to be persuaded. Even in the midst of her tears it becomes clear that the obligations demanded by Judaism are too much for her, and she would not last long with her mother-in-law. And so she says goodbye to Naomi, covering her with warm and tender kisses. She is not a heartless woman, she can cry and kiss.

The *midrash* recognizes these tears as true, heartfelt, and sincere, not a masquerade. It is because of these tears that she merits having as a descendant the heroic Goliath the Philistine, who later did battle with Ruth's great-grandson David.

'But Ruth clung to her' [Ruth 1: 16]. Ruth did not weep copious tears, or bestow kisses, she just 'clung to her', holding Naomi tight, which is clear evidence of her steadfast character, her greater spirituality and morality in comparison with her sister-in-law Orpah. The latter tried to express her compassion and admiration for Naomi through her tears and kisses. She knows she is too weak and small to take on such exalted qualities on her own. But Ruth shows that she does not wish to attach herself to Naomi only through sympathy, kisses, and tears. Rather, she takes it on herself to accompany her to the very source of the sublimity she sees in her. She understands that Israel's mission does not satisfy itself with the admiration and sympathy of other nations, but only when the spirit of Jewry will reign over the entire world and sink deep into every heart. This is the significance of the exalted kiss of Orpah and the silent clinging of Ruth.

Naomi still has her doubts about the steadfastness of Ruth's decision and tries to dissuade her further: 'See, your sister-in-law has returned to her people and her gods. Go follow your sister-in-law' [Ruth 1: 15]!

But Ruth has already fully grasped the great mission of the Jewish daughter. She knows that Judaism demands spiritual morality from each person and that the commandments have only one aim: to ennoble human beings with good qualities so that they will fulfil both the commandments understood by all and those our weak minds cannot comprehend. At the border of Judah Ruth takes upon herself the holy Torah exactly as the Jews did at Mount Sinai. An interesting dialogue takes place between her and her mother-in-law. Naomi says to her, 'Every step a Jew takes is measured. On the seventh day, therefore, he may not walk further than a sabbath distance!' To that, Ruth answers, 'I will walk in your footsteps. As far as you walk, so too shall I walk!' Naomi continues: 'Our family life is like a fortress [to keep the marriage strong and pure]. The barrier separating man and wife [when she is ritually impure because she is menstruating] must be strong!' Ruth answers, 'I will readily be walled in that fortress. Where you spend the night—there will my own bed be!' Naomi goes on to explain that our God is different from the other gods, just as we are different from all other nations, and we possess 613 commandments that no other nation has, and thus, 'God, Torah, and Israel are one!' To that Ruth responds with passion: 'With all my heart am I part of your people. Your God, the Creator of everything, is also mine, and thus I too belong to your people. We will die and be buried in one place. I swear to you: only death can part us!'[30]

[30] This midrashic expansion of and supplement to the biblical conversation between Ruth and Naomi appears in *Ruth Rabbah* 2: 22 and 2: 24, and BT *Yoma* 47*b*. *Ruth Rabbah* 4: 6 also stresses Ruth's modesty and punctiliousness in observing Jewish law, as described later in this essay; see *Lamentations Rabbah*, ed. Steinberger, 88–9, 90–1, 126.

Naomi cannot and must not dissuade her further. And she herself is awestruck at the royal princess who leaves behind a carefree life, a life of pleasure, to choose the difficult life of an impoverished Jewish daughter.

When Naomi finally falls silent, allowing Ruth to walk along with her, only then does Ruth feel truly happy and free. She has had enough of passion and the earthly pleasures that she had experienced so fully with her royal parents. It is the one who throws off such pleasures and takes on the yoke of the commandments who is truly free, since only they produce true spiritual pleasure and free us from those other passions.

Is it any wonder, then, that the sages ordained that this little story be read on Shavuot, from all the stories in the Bible? What beautiful harmony is lent to the story of the giving of the Torah by the tale of the amazing foreign woman who took this same Torah upon herself with such devotion!

And we read in the chapters that follow how punctilious Ruth is in following the commandments. The first one she encounters is the commandment of gleaning, a commandment we are not very familiar with now that we no longer live in the Holy Land. In those days, when the grain was harvested, poor people would follow the reapers through the fields and collect the stalk or two that were left behind on the ground [Lev. 19: 9–10; Deut. 24: 19–21]. This is the commandment of gleaning.

Ruth asks her mother-in-law for permission to glean along with the other poor people. She joins them, and none of them recognizes that they have a Moabite princess in their midst.

But within the very first days, Boaz, who owns many of the fields, grows curious about her. It is not her beauty that draws him, but rather her gentility, her caution, her modesty as she bends and stands up straight again, the way she makes sure to follow the commandment of gleaning and never takes more than two of the stalks that have been left behind. He takes an interest in her, approaches her, and so the story continues until she becomes his wife, and from this couple emerges King David, the whole House of David up to the Messiah, who will redeem humanity and who himself is also a descendant of Ruth.

This must be a great lesson for all those Jewish daughters who, God forbid, abandon the holy Torah for foreign cults. Let them take a look at Ruth, the Moabite, who came to us from a pagan culture, and see how richly she was rewarded for observing all the commandments.

'Don't go to glean in another field' [Ruth 2: 8]. Why should you pick in foreign fields? What will you find there?

In the Month of Tamuz

It's hot outside, the sun burns brightly and the fields laugh with us in joyful expectation of a plentiful harvest. Unfortunately, the most beautiful natural landscapes, the most confident tidings of a bountiful year, cannot bring Jews joy. As soon as the month of Tamuz arrives, every true Jewish heart turns to the past and immediately images of destruction, pillage, and annihilation rise in our mind's eye.

Many pages of our history are stained with tears. But the pages that are truly soaked in tears are those that relate to these 'three weeks'. The greatest Jewish catastrophes—Nebuchadnezzar (Babylonia), Titus (Rome), and Ferdinand (Spain)—took place during this period.[31] It is as if all these disasters were designed to tell Jews that these different punishments were only extensions of the same primal disaster, so that the exile that began with Nebuchadnezzar would not end until all the failings that brought that first exile upon us disappeared entirely. It is for that reason that these days should be devoted not only to mourning, but also to repentance and strengthening our will to recognize these failings and uproot them from our Jewish circles.

The two horrific destructions of the Temple are the clearest reminders that the reason we must wander through foreign lands is that we have not fulfilled our obligations to God and to the holy Torah. We must gather before the Creator and closely sift through our deeds in order to determine whether even now we are failing to act in accordance with his will.

Let us imagine that first 17th of Tamuz in our history. The same sun that saw the savage Romans break through the walls of Jerusalem also witnessed this scene, 1,500 years earlier: forty days had barely passed since the Jewish people called out so enthusiastically, 'We will do and we will hear' [Exod. 24: 7], and already it had come to this.[32] On that beautiful early morning, right from day-

[31] The three weeks between the seventeenth day of the month of Tamuz and the ninth day of Av are a period of mourning for the destruction of the first and second Temples, destroyed respectively by the Babylonian general Nebuchadnezzar in 586 BCE and by the Roman general Titus in 70 CE. The third catastrophe dated to this period is the expulsion of the Jews from Spain by Ferdinand II of Aragon (and Isabella I of Castile), in which Jews were ordered to leave by 31 July 1492 (27 Tamuz 5252).

[32] The JPS rendering of *na'aseh venishmah* is 'we will faithfully do'. This does not capture the

break, a great outcry was heard in the Jewish camp. Not a war cry, not a victory song, but rather cries of joy, 'A sound of song' [Exod. 32: 18] that cuts deep into the heart: a song of jubilation celebrating . . . a golden calf!

And the Creator then said to Moses: 'Hurry down! Your people have quickly abandoned the ways of my Torah. They have made themselves a molten calf and bowed low to it and sacrificed to it, saying, "This is your god, O Israel, who brought you out of the land of Egypt"' [Exod. 32: 8]! Moses, our divinely appointed leader, descends from Mount Sinai with the tablets in his arms, approaches the camp, and sees the people dancing around the calf. His blood boils, he throws the tablets to the ground and they shatter at the base of the mountain. On the 17th of Tamuz these tablets were broken; can we ever really forget the sin that caused this? Must we not reassemble the fragments of the shattered tablets and take from them a lesson and a warning? Should we not consider why the tablets were broken? And how we ourselves appear, in the light of their destruction?

And the verse there states: 'When he finished speaking with him on Mount Sinai, he gave Moses the two tablets of the covenant' [Exod. 31: 18], the tablets that will bear witness that he, the Creator, spoke with him, so that they may teach us how to fulfil his words. As it says there, 'stone tablets inscribed with the finger of God'. The stone, the material world, was thus granted its redemption when God inscribed his laws on it. This teaches us that the body first receives its true worth when it is subjected to the spirit and words that God wills.

And the tablets were 'inscribed on both their surfaces' [Exod. 32: 15]. They were inscribed through and through, whichever way one turned them. Not superficially or partially must we comprehend the word of Sinai. It must penetrate us deeply, filling all our senses; on all sides must the divine scripture radiate within us, clear and thoroughly comprehended.

But what do we see? After just forty days those wholehearted promises were entirely forgotten. And so the tablets lie shattered, but only the stone is broken; the writing, the divine writing is not destroyed, it has flown back up to the heavens. It cannot abide within a people that dances around a calf.

And the consequences of this? Those we can see from that day to our own: we were driven from our own land, suffering agony upon agony, and we were forced to wander in exile. But not forever. The time will come when repentance will

traditional understanding of the Hebrew as signalling 'we will do [even before] we hear', a more complete submission to God's will. This episode also appears in Deut. 9.

take hold, the sin of the calf will be forgiven, and then will come the true redemption!

The Destruction of the Temple

Jerusalem has fallen, twice it has fallen. This is the darkest, most horrifying moment of our history.

For three weeks now, since the 17th of Tamuz, the day that the walls of Jerusalem were first breached, we have already begun to mourn and lament the destruction of the Holy Temple. This liminal time is the 'dusk', the very border between sadness and hope. We do not yet know what the future will bring. It is true that the enemy is at the gates, but we still live with the faintest hope: perhaps a miracle will occur.

But finally the destruction commences. The decree has been signed, our fate sealed. Nothing can help us now. Everything is burning, all is destroyed. Countless Jews are slaughtered and the rest must take up their walking staffs and set out into the darkness of exile.

We fast on both these days: at the beginning and at the end. The 17th of Tamuz and the 9th of Av. If our fasting is to mean for us what it should mean, a day of true repentance, then we must be inspired to delve more deeply into the essence of *yiddishkeit*.

Is today not the most appropriate time to proclaim to one and all:

Jews! Do not lose yourselves in the pursuit of new pleasures! Come back to yourselves, if you truly crave that for which the Jewish soul has longed for nearly 2,000 years!

Putting this question to ourselves brings us back to the question that was raised at the very moment of the destruction:

'Why is the land in ruins?' And no answer could be found until 'the Lord replied: Because they forsook the Torah I had set before them.' If only they had deserted me and kept my Torah![33]

[33] *Lamentations Rabbah, Petikhta* 2, 'Rabbi Huna and Rabbi Jeremiah in the name of Rabbi Hiya bar Abba said: It is written, "They deserted me and did not keep my Torah" [Jer. 16: 11, JPS trans. revised] . . . If only they had deserted me and kept my Torah, for if they would observe it, its light would bring them back to goodness.'

We have abandoned God's Torah. The calendric notation for the three weeks is not just a notation: it leads us into the time of our catastrophe and we hear the prophet Jeremiah proclaim, 'Hear the word of the Lord, O House of Jacob!' [Jer. 2: 4] and call heaven and earth to serve as witnesses against Jews.

We hear these words and feel that even though Jerusalem and the Holy Temple were destroyed, they are still the sacred ruins of our exile. We hear the thunderous words of God through the lips of the prophets and whether we want to or not we ask ourselves:

'What would Jeremiah or the prophet Isaiah say if they were to come here today?'—'Hear the word of the Lord, O House of Jacob!' [Jer. 2: 3]. These were the very words that Jeremiah spoke in those last days of Jerusalem. Rabbi Levi explains these words thus: 'Hear, since at some point it will enter your heart! Hear it as the teaching of Torah, so that you will not have to hear it as words of reproach! Hear it as words of reproach, so that you will not be forced to hear it as words of punishment! Hear it as words of punishment, so that you will not have to hear it as enemy trumpets! Hear it in your own land, so you won't have to hear it in a foreign land! Hear it while you are alive, so you won't have to hear it after your death! Let your ears hear these words, so that your dry bones will not have to hear them—because at *some* point you will have to hear them! Hear God's word, O House of Jacob [*beit ya'akov*], all you Jewish families!'[34]

We Jewish women must also consider the word of the prophet that opens our eyes to the true cause of our decline. How many of the sins that led to the destruction of the Temple might we already have atoned for through our good deeds?

We must consider deeply, my dear sisters, not look through those rose-coloured glasses that make us think that everything we do should be in accordance with the spirit of the times, whether in the way that we dress or our culture and so on. Let us once and for all rip the blinders off our eyes so that we can see that what is foreign is not always good and beautiful, but rather, that which the Holy Torah teaches us—that is good, that is life.

Only then will we truly know how close or how far we are from that moment when the call will come:

'Awake, arise, O Jerusalem!' [Isa. 52: 2].

[34] *Yalkut Shimoni on the Prophets*, ed. Hyman, *remez* 264, on Jer. 2: 3.

Shabat Nahamu (The Sabbath of Consolation)

Only a few days have gone by since we sat on the ground as mourners and lamented. All of us, without exception, mourned our spiritual mother, Zion and Jerusalem, the Holy Temple that supported us, raised us, and nourished us in the divine spirit. She is no longer with us, that attentive mother; motherless and lonesome they remain, her children. Helpless and poor orphans, without a mother, but not without a father, an immortal Father, who never abandons them even for the briefest minute in their difficult exile, even if they cannot see him.

The echo of these mournful lamentations still rings in the ears, but even so it does not lie heavily on our hearts; our moods are freer, lighter. How can that be? How can people so quickly transform their emotions? After three weeks of sadness, Shabat Nahamu has come to us, the sabbath of consolation.[35] Gone is the painful awareness of our deep loneliness, we gaze up at the heavens with the most beautiful hope. But how can such sad feelings disappear so quickly?

When we delve into this matter, something becomes clear. Imagine a man who has lost his beloved child. His pain is enormous. He aches with the most profound sorrow. He sits dejectedly on the ground, and it seems to him that nothing in the world can quell his grief. Even his friends' words of comfort cannot lighten his agony in the slightest. But after a while, he manages to stand up, gradually grows a little calmer, even though the child he lost will never return to him. Time is simply stronger than his agony, it washes over him until it finally conquers him. The greatest joy, the deepest agony, both give way with time, only rarely leaving a trace.

That is the way emotions operate within a Jew even when, God forbid, he loses a child, knowing that 'For dust you are, and to dust shall you return' [Gen. 3: 19]. But the sorrows of parents are different when their child dies a spiritual death to them. Then their pain is much greater, then their sorrow is more terrible, and never to be forgotten.

Why?

Because as long as that child is still alive, the pain he is causing them cannot cease. Great, great is this pain, but great as well is the hope that this child will make good the damage he has caused.

Jerusalem is destroyed, its holy places desecrated, the Jewish people driven

[35] The sabbath immediately following Tishah Be'av is called Shabat Nahamu, 'the sabbath of consolation', which takes its name from the first verse of the *haftarah* portion (Isa. 40: 1–26) read on that day.

from their home, but still alive. And while it is alive, time cannot diminish the sorrow. Every 9th of Av brings the Jew precisely the same mournful anguish.

Yes, only the memory of the dead can be forgotten, because that which is buried in the earth must slowly fade. That which still lives and exists can and will never be forgotten. Jerusalem lives and will live. And the comfort that washes over us on the sabbath of consolation is the clearest sign that our mother Zion will finally take us back again onto her lap.

'Comfort, O comfort my people, says your God' [Isa. 40: 1]!

We have arisen from the ground on which we sat, grief-stricken and tear-stained. We have wiped the ash from our foreheads and shed our mourning clothes. The comfort we receive from above breathes fresh hope into our hearts. The best guarantee that our hopes will be answered is the pure joy of this sabbath of consolation.

The Fifteenth of Av

Sorrow and sadness are the major motifs of the first half of the month of Av, but now we have arrived at the second half—and everything has changed. The sabbath of consolation is the first ray of this comfort and ease, and on the 15th of Av, Tu Be'av, we have a holiday of absolute joy. In this dramatic transformation lies the power of the eternal Jew, who is so immersed in the past, so at one with the suffering and joys of this heroic history that simply his awareness of that past is capable of leading him from deepest mourning to the purest joy.

But what happy circumstances occurred on the 15th of Av?

There were five such events:

1. The plague that engulfed the Israelites in the wilderness after the sin of the spies finally subsided.[36]
2. The collection of wood to be burned on the altar for the entire year was completed.
3. The prohibition against marrying into the tribe of Benjamin was lifted.[37]
4. The Jews finally received permission to bury the dead of the city of Beitar, after the slain bodies had lain unburied for eighteen months.[38]
5. Jewish maidens gathered in the gardens to dance.[39]

[36] See Num. 13: 1–33. The explanations for the festival are found in BT *Ta'an.* 26*b* and 30*b*.

[37] See Judg. 19–21.

[38] Beitar was the last stronghold of the failed Bar Kokhba revolt, which took place in 132–6 CE.

[39] Mishnah *Ta'an.* 4: 8: 'There were no happier days for the people of Israel than 15 Av and Yom

This last observance has special relevance to Jewish women, and we should take note of its instructive features for us today. Borrowed white dresses for each Jewish woman, without distinction between rich and poor: how beautiful that sounds! Today, when the young Jewish woman is drowning in a flood of different fashions, and often forgets the fashion of modesty, this factor must teach us a great deal. Jewish women assemble for their special holiday not only in plain white but even in borrowed dresses. No trace of luxury sparkles in their dress, there is nothing of the foolish pride that the rich feel towards the poor, and which draws the poor to imitate the desires and pleasures of the rich. Everyone must wear a borrowed dress, which demonstrates clearly that nothing we possess is ours, but rather comes from God, and we need learn only what to do with what we have been given as a gift. Such holidays were the truest sign of the spiritual and moral level of Jewish daughters of yore.

And today?

It's hardly necessary to point out how low we have sunk in comparison with what we once were. The only hope and guarantee that we can reach the exalted level of the Jewish daughter of yore is and must be Bnos Agudath Israel, the youth organization of observant Jewish girls. Bnos Agudath Israel thus plays a historical role, and must carry it out faithfully; if it succeeds in its mission, we will once again merit to celebrate the ancient holiday of the 15th of Av in the Land of Israel.

The Practice of Blessing God

We can only marvel at our sages, who understood how to transplant the seeds of Jewish festivals, solemn and joyous feelings that sabbaths and holidays bring us, into everyday life, so that they might continuously arouse us to sanctity and introspection.

The practice of blessing God contains many such kernels.

They are the best way for rich and poor, the tired and well-rested, to carry with them the concept of Temple sacrifice in every moment of their everyday life.

Whoever wants to be truly pious should take every opportunity to recite the praises of God through the ordained blessings, the sages tell us. The primary thing that differentiates a Jew from a non-Jew is blessing God.

The blessings are short, extremely pithy. As plain and laconic as truth itself. All they do is express the gratitude that is in our heart.

Kippur, since on these days the daughters of Jerusalem went out dressed in white and danced in the vineyards, saying: "Young men, consider whom you choose [to be your wife]".'

Just as our poet, King David, heard God's voice in every powerful and beautiful thing, 'The voice of the Lord is power, the voice of the Lord is majesty' [Ps. 29: 4], the blessings for us are the voice of the most beautiful natural phenomena, which must arouse us to praise God in our hearts.

When the terrifying power of nature lets itself be heard in thunder or in an earthquake, the Jew does not fall to the ground like an idol-worshipper, but rather recognizes it as the power of the Creator, and with great awe blesses God 'whose strength and power fill the world' [BT *Ber.* 59*a*].

When the Jew sees a lightning bolt split the heavens and remembers the first day of Creation, when God said 'Let there be light!', or when the sun, once in twenty-eight years, returns to the very same position as it was when God created it during the six days of Creation, he does not consider this an interesting new natural phenomenon, but rather a further action of God, and he expresses this recognition by blessing God 'who has created the world'.[40]

Should he see something beautiful, a natural wonder of the world, he calls out with delight to bless God, 'who has such [beauty] in his world'.

And should he happen to glimpse some unusual creature, a dwarf or a Negro or some such, he recognizes it as part of the incomprehensible multifariousness of all that is created and says: 'who varies the creatures' [BT *Ber.* 58*b*].

And the man who excites admiration with his exalted spirit and mind is recognized by the Jew as a gift of God and therefore greeted by blessing God 'who has bestowed of his wisdom to human beings', or a powerful man or king by the blessing 'who has bestowed of his honour on human beings' [BT *Ber.* 58*a*]. Man on his own does not possess great abilities or power. He must first be blessed as such by God.

And so it is with each of the other blessings. Our father in the heavens not only provides us with nourishment, he also brings forth beautiful flowers to give our eyes joy. And so when we see the first trees in bloom, we bless God for them: 'whose world is lacking in nothing, and who created in it fine creatures and fine trees for the enjoyment of human beings' [BT *Ber.* 43*b*].

The rainbow in heaven reminds us of the sign of God's covenant that he would never again punish human beings with a flood as long as they continued to heed the seven commandments of the descendants of Noah, so in seeing a rainbow we bless God 'who remembers the covenant and who is faithful to his covenant and

[40] The alignment of the sun with its position on the fourth day of creation described in BT *Ber.* 59*b* occurs once every twenty-eight years, and the blessing recited on this occasion is called *birkat haḥamah*, 'the blessing of the sun'.

true to his word!' God does well not only to humanity as a whole, he also protects each individual human being separately. Every moment is a gift from him.

And we can see the great wisdom with which the sages composed the blessings: 'Who has given us life', 'Who is good and does good', 'Blessed is the true Judge'. All of these teach us that the good and the bad derive from our true Judge, and everything he does is in our best interests.

It is not only in extraordinary moments that we must praise God. Every day we must recognize his help in everything we do. We express this in the morning blessings: 'Who straightens the bent', 'stretches out the land', 'gives the weary strength', etc. Even the most ordinary physical acts are accompanied with a blessing, when we quiet our hunger and thirst and attend to our physiological needs. In each of these we see the power and love of the Creator.

With the institution of blessings the sages primarily wanted to point to the sovereignty of God. We have a 'Ruler of the World' and everything that happens comes from him, and without him the smallest thing cannot transpire, and each of us is obligated to fulfil our debt to him with all the strength we possess.

The Hebrew word for 'world', *olam*, means what we see around us, the heavens and earth with all their many splendours. But *olam* also means 'eternity'. We must strive not to see the visible world as all that there is, God forbid, forgetting the eternal future. The word 'world' reminds us of both these things.

But on the other hand, the word 'world' also reminds us not to take the world before us for granted, since just as every drop is a part of the ocean, and without it there would be no ocean, so too can we not comprehend this other eternal world without the one that rises before our eyes. For that reason, every moment is an inescapable part of eternity. Must we seek eternity only in some other world? Does it not already begin right here?

The 'Ruler of the World' is our God.

All the odes to God's sovereignty in nature are worthless. Worthless if we do not recognize his omnipotence, his greatness, his wisdom, his justice, goodness, as his worshippers, if we do not see that the Jew must play a special role that has been appointed to him as a Jew and as a human being. We are reminded of that in the words of the blessings, 'Our God'. Even the phrase 'Ruler of the World' or the bare word 'God' does not express this.

God is that greatness that our senses cannot comprehend. He is the one who provides life to his creatures to live eternally, and so each of them belongs to him at every minute of their lives, with every fresh breath, not only with regard to the past but also in their future.

But he is not just the invisible, not only he who is concealed, who can only be thought or discussed but never encountered. No! The human being who recognizes him everywhere in the natural world that surrounds us, in every power, in every sweet pleasure—he is very near to this person, who gazes at him and speaks to him as *atah*, 'thou' [*du*]. This intimate word is the clearest sign that our relationship with God is different than that of other nations.

All other nations pray to their gods and beg them: 'Bless me, please bless me!' Whether it is primitive people praying to their gods or an educated man speaking with his God, they demonstrate their dependence and weakness with these words. It is different, however, for the Jew. The Jew does not call out 'Bless me!' The Jew already knows that he is blessed with everything he naturally has, both spiritual and physical blessings, joys and sorrows. For that reason a blessing is not a petition but rather a bestowal. The words that bring us closer to God are not 'bless me' but rather 'blessed are you', may you be blessed. And it is from this word that the sages named this practice 'blessing'.

To bless someone means to express the hope that all their desires will be fulfilled. And this is exactly what our God requires of us!

'Blessed are you, God' is the Jewish battle cry of our life struggle. With every blessing we must consider how we might be blessed with the will to fulfil all our obligations before God. And then will we feel truly gratified and fulfilled!

IV Jewish Women's Lives
The Sacred Obligations of the Jewish Woman

IN THE MISHNAH we read: 'Rabbi Eliezer ben Hisma said: *The laws of kinin* [bird offerings] *and the beginnings of a woman's ritually unclean period are the body of the laws; astronomy and geometry are condiments to wisdom'* [*Avot* 3: 18].[1]

This same Rabbi Eliezer was one of the greatest astronomers of his time.[2] The Talmud relates that Rabban Gamliel the Prince and Rabbi Joshua were once on a sea voyage, and Rabban Gamliel ran out of food and had to rely on Rabbi Joshua's provisions. Rabban Gamliel asked his friend: 'How did you know how long our voyage would last, so that you could take along sufficient supplies?' The latter answered, 'a certain star rises once in seventy years and leads the sailors astray, and I knew it would rise and lead us astray'. Marvelling at his friend's scientific erudition, Rabban Gamliel the Prince proclaimed: 'My knowledge is nothing compared to the astronomic teachings of Rabbi Eliezer ben Hisma' [BT *Hor.* 10*a*].

Thus, as we can see, Rabbi Eliezer was considered a major authority on astronomy in his own time. It is particularly notable, then, that he constructed a parallel between astronomic knowledge and the laws of the Oral Torah.

Geometry, like mathematics in general, is one of the greatest of sciences, with its solid grounding in pure truth. That two and two equals four, or that the area of a rectangle may be determined by the measurement of one side in relation to another, these things can hardly be disputed. All other sciences, the so-called 'higher sciences' like physics, medicine, or even law, rely essentially on hypotheses. We can see this regularly in life, when one philosopher devotes his whole life to building an entire system, and then along comes a second philosopher and demolishes his work, demonstrating that the hypotheses that underlie it are outdated and false.

[1] The Mishnah terms these sciences *parpraot* (perhaps from the Greek word meaning 'peripheral')—side dishes or condiments.

[2] The *tana'im* are the rabbis whose opinions are recorded in the Mishnah, compiled around 220 CE.

Mathematics and geometry have an entirely different status for humanity. They belong to the essential building blocks of every human civilization or world culture. Without them it would be impossible to imagine a world with economy and trade, or with art and science. The plough we use in our fields would be an entirely abstract concept without the principles of geometry it relies on. And astronomy, although it is not built on as solid a foundation as mathematics, is even now considered the oldest and most glorious of the sciences, moving the human spirit to wonder and amazement at the great Creator.

And precisely these two crucial universal sciences are those that are called by Rabbi Eliezer Hisma 'condiments to wisdom'!

The *mishnah* I cited above about the laws of bird sacrifice and *nidah* refers, incidentally, to some of the most difficult sections in the Talmud. The *mishnah* of *kinin* deals with the problem of the bird sacrifices that a woman who has just given birth or other individuals who have experienced impurity are obligated to bring after they recover. That is how it is connected with the issue of the beginning of a woman's ritually unclean period, as part of the statutes of women's purity.

As we Jewish women know, our obligations during the seven-day-long period of purification are bound up with a variety of other regulations. How picayune must these micro-obligations seem to today's ostensibly intelligent woman, as compared to astronomy or geometry?

If we were to try to compare mathematics and astronomy, on which entire worlds are constructed, to the regulations governing 'nests, from which doves fly to and fro', or the minutest regulations of women's purification, would this woman not just burst into laughter?

We must however take into consideration that this comparison was made not by a man of limited education, but rather by someone who was considered one of the finest mathematicians and astronomers of his time, while also being one of the greatest and most well-rounded Talmud scholars. That this educated man should deem the laws of bird offerings and menstruation the most important in the many volumes of the Talmud certainly could not have happened without great consideration.

Even the fact that he expressed their significance through a comparison is a sign that we must learn these laws, which he considered the most essential in Jewish law, from a variety of perspectives.

But the most meaningful expression of the importance of these laws is the way he dismisses, by contrast, the two sciences of astronomy and geometry that made him so famous: 'Astronomy and geometry are only condiments to wisdom.'

Our Culture of Modesty

The first Jewish principle is to fear God. That must be the most constant Jewish pursuit. A person cannot be empty, always sunk into a void.

We acquire a basic knowledge of the teachings that lead a person to fear God in books of ethics [*musar*]. Because *yiddishkeit* and piety are so weak among women, studying Jewish law and ethics must take pride of place in Bnos activities.

This literature describes the steps and levels of ethical work. *Mesilat yesharim* teaches people how to approach *yiddishkeit*.[3]

Improving the way one fulfils an obligation also improves one's attitude towards the obligation. And this method will lead every Jewish daughter to recognize the destructive ugliness of frivolous fashions.

Indeed, if each Jewish woman were to give an honest accounting, she would come to the conclusion on her own that luxuries lead Jewish women off the true way and send them down alien, twisted, and false paths.

The battle against immodest dress is at the very centre of our culture of modesty! The modesty of Jewish women saved the Jews from exile. Jewish women can and must hold fast to the culture of modesty.

By following fashion Jewish women become its victims!

Modesty was always the pride and glory of the Jewish people. We must continue to carry this pride and glory!

I do not mean to say that if, for example, cloche hats came back into style, people would be required to refrain from wearing them. No, on the contrary! Whatever is not against Jewish law and *yiddishkeit* is permitted!

But women have recently become slaves to fashion and we must see to it that they are freed from this slavery!

This work must be carried out systematically: first among Bais Yaakov teachers, then among Bais Yaakov students, and then among members of Bnos.

One must work towards this goal with foresight and in gradual steps. Modesty must be among the primary and most significant values of Bnos Agudath Israel.

[3] *Mesilat yesharim* (1738) is a highly influential ethical text composed by Rabbi Moses Hayim Luzzatto (1707–46), which is structured to lead the reader through stages of ethical achievement, for example, from carefulness to alacrity, cleanliness, abstention, purity, piety, and so on.

But modesty must not be considered a sacrifice an individual makes on behalf of an ideal, but rather be felt as a sacred internal necessity. Our teachers must be the first to step onto this stage to serve as role models for the whole movement.

We who aim to build the Jewish future on our spiritual principles must remember that the Torah nourishes the Jewish soul. It is not enough to refrain from desecrating the sabbath, one must also continually strengthen the thought of sabbath observance; just as Nahshon ben Aminadav was the first to jump into the sea [at the Exodus, see *Exodus Rabbah* 13 and elsewhere], so must we be the first today to free ourselves from the destructive zeitgeist.

The time will come when Jewish history will dwell deeply on our Bnos movement. We must therefore see that we fulfil our obligations and hold fast to the Torah laws.

If you really want to be Bnos Agudath Israel you must understand how to accomplish our ideals with your whole heart.

Bnos Agudath Israel, which wishes to educate girls to be truly Jewish, must join the battle against wanton fashion and create its own simple style of dress, in conformity with Jewish aesthetics and ethics. We have no reason to be ashamed of the Torah and Jewish sanctity. On the contrary, we should take pride in these before the eyes of the world. I would be happy to see this accomplished in reality, and I hope that just as a long time ago the Jewish redemption came through righteous women [BT *Sot.* 11*b*], so too will the redemption be hastened in our own times.

The Jewish Woman and *Kashrut*

> 'You shall be holy people to me, you must not eat flesh torn by beasts in the field'
> (Exod. 22: 30)
>
> 'For I am the Lord your God: you shall be holy for I am holy'
> (Lev. 11: 45)

The Bible does not say 'holy people' (*anashim kedoshim*) but rather 'people of holiness' (*anshei kodesh*): people who are committed to their holy mission. The one who turns away in disgust from non-kosher food is not in himself holy, but it is much easier for him to achieve the spiritual-moral greatness for which we all strive. Without *kashrut*, it is impossible to reach this.

The first laws of the Torah concerning consumption teach us that it is wrong to assume that the rules about eating kosher are merely a part of a system of rules about physical hygiene and health; rather, they are intricately connected to our spiritual sanctity and purity. We must always find some positive lessons in this area, just as in other divine laws of the Torah for which a reason or significance is stated clearly (as Rabbi Samson Raphael Hirsch says in his commentary on 'Shemini').[4]

It is understandable, in this regard, that God, Creator of the holy soul and of the body, is the best judge of the influence of various foods on the operations of the soul.

There is an interesting story that is told in the *Degel maḥaneh efrayim* in relation to the issue of forbidden foods.[5]

On the verse, 'Circumcise the foreskin of your heart and stiffen your neck no longer', the writer relates something he heard from his grandfather, the holy Ba'al Shem Tov, may his memory be for a blessing:

'Already in the times of Maimonides, may his memory be a blessing, a sect of men, great philosophers, corrupted with many false ideas, wrote a letter to Maimonides asking him to show explicitly where the notion of the resurrection of the dead is stated in the Torah, since the passages in the Midrash and Talmud on this topic are not direct citations of the Torah.

'On receiving this letter, Maimonides—who did not wish to deal directly with such people—called his student Rabbi Samuel Ibn Tibbon to respond in his name with the following words:

'Surely you know that the life force of a human being comes from what he eats and drinks. Nourished by these various foods, the blood circulates in all the limbs and organs of a human body. The richest of this blood is that which nourishes the heart and mind. That is why, when one eats those foods that are considered kosher in the Torah, one's blood and life force are purely Jewish; that makes the mind more receptive to such delicate matters as divine faith. Even those things that are beyond our mental comprehension are subject to thoughtful consideration by our sages, who have received these matters through transmission, one man to another, teacher to student, since the time that the Torah was given to Moses on Sinai, because each of them is entirely bound up in the Torah and its

[4] Hirsch does not comment on this topic in 'Shemini' (Lev. 9: 1–11; *Pentateuch*, 47), but in his commentary on Exod. 22: 30, he argues against 'those who wish to explain the laws of kosher through principles of health, climate, and other contingent circumstances that would make them irrelevant to our own time. The Torah specified the meaning of these rules and said that they are related not to health but rather to spiritual purity and moral protection' (*Pentateuch*, 275).

[5] *Degel maḥaneh efrayim* (1810), by Rabbi Moses Hayim Ephraim of Sudilkov, presents the teachings of his grandfather the Ba'al Shem Tov, among others, on the weekly Torah portion.

wise interpreters. By contrast, those who eat forbidden food build up impure blood, which results in corrupt consequences for the life force of the heart, and along with that the mind is also dulled with false and evil thoughts, and so cannot make sense of matters that are beyond logic. That is also the reason they cannot reach any harmonious agreement even with those whose beliefs they share.

'So when you ask this question, which judges the sages without understanding or properly calculating what makes them who they are, you are undoubtedly hampered by the unfortunate effects of eating forbidden food, and no holy concept can make the slightest impression on you. One can only hope that you will soon meet a bitter end.'

'And indeed these philosophers were very quickly lost to history.' With these words did the Ba'al Shem Tov end his tale.

And now the *Degel maḥaneh efrayim* picks up the tale and explains that the meaning of the verse 'circumcise the foreskin of your heart' is that you must root out the stupidity from your heart, so that your heart might be purified through kosher food, and that will certainly result in 'And your neck shall no longer be stiff.' And then will you understand the importance of overcoming all the obstacles that stand in the way of your fulfilling the commandments of the Torah.

This interesting and characteristic tale clearly demonstrates how food operates on the spirit.

My own observations support the conclusions cited above. During the Great War, I noticed a horrifying breakdown of family relations within some Jewish homes. Analysing the reasons for the tear in the social fabric, I came to the conclusion that it was caused by the great economic crisis that led some people to use Christian butter and milk, made without proper rabbinic supervision or Jewish oversight. All this I could discern clearly in the extraordinarily immoral appearance of a few of my acquaintances.

These family relations, it is true, were quickly repaired in our own circles in Galicia, but unfortunately in other places the rift became a festering wound which remains to the present day.

The war had scarcely made itself felt before I was able to observe with astonishment, while I was still in Poland, the phenomenon that became natural and ordinary in nearly every Jewish home, that people permitted themselves to use butter made by Christians, defending themselves with the excuse that it was hard to find butter made by Jews.

Even if we were to agree that butter can be made only from cow's milk (which is not the case, since butter sometimes also contains margarine), it is wrong to conclude that it is only milk from a non-Jew that is forbidden while butter from a Christian is kosher, especially for children.

It is no great wonder that Jewish commandments are treated so dismissively. It certainly would make matters easier for Jewish families if there were employment bureaus to help people achieve what they need so they can be punctilious in leading an ethical life.[6]

Even though this touches on issues that should be taken up by more competent and authoritative Jewish organizations, I do not want to ignore the phenomena that make it difficult to observe the most important commandments in the Torah.

And since we are considering *kashrut* in Jewish society, let us also deal with other neglected matters. While in Germany no religious Jew would consider eating chocolate or a tea biscuit that was not certified as kosher, here we take such matters lightly. There are many notable cases where hasidim themselves do not eat such things, but permit their wives and children, even if just by looking the other way, to eat such chocolate or tea biscuits. A non-Jewish confectioner once explained to me very clearly that lard is sometimes used in the making of chocolate, and that bakers use an ingredient made from pigs' brains to soften the tea biscuits. It's no surprise, then, that a woman or child who treat themselves to such forbidden food can later no longer fully carry out a truly Jewish life.

Moreover, we should note that many Jews allow themselves to drink tea at a train station, justifying this by saying that this entails no real risk of eating something non-kosher, particularly if they avoid the lemon and the spoon; and here I should mention that I was once mocked as simpleminded and childish when I spent an entire night sitting in a train station without agreeing to drink a glass of tea.

And once in a similar situation I happened to witness the following incident: I noticed that the owner of the station buffet put a few sausages in a teapot to warm them up, and then poured out the hot water, rinsed the pot and made fresh tea in it. But when I didn't want to drink tea at a train station for just this reason, I was dismissed as a fanatic.

And how do things stand with our own kitchens? This holy work that was exclusively assigned to our domain—how many times have I been shocked to see

[6] Employment bureaus that could find positions for Orthodox Jews who wished to observe the sabbath were part of the Bnos agenda from the start, as well as for Po'alei Agudath Israel, which organized Orthodox workers with similar goals in mind.

how carelessly this work has been treated by entrusting it to a Christian woman? By rights, every Jewish woman should guard her kitchen as the apple of her eye and not entrust it to even a Jewish maidservant, not to speak of the fact that a rabbi should make the decision over even the smallest questionable case; yet this kitchen slips right out of the control of Jewish hands and is entrusted to alien ones.

And even with regard to a Jewish maid one must not relinquish control as long as there is the slightest doubt about her trustworthiness in keeping kosher.

Some women seem to think that they don't need to understand the economic aspects of their household as long as they have a Jewish maid. There is surely no need to point out the disastrous consequences of putting a maid in charge of the household budget. The woman of the house is naturally not kept informed about what is spent on food, and ends up suffering real financial losses. After all, storekeepers have employees with their own special talents for making a sale. The whole enterprise makes a pretty picture!

So can we really be so indifferent to letting a stranger run a household when in addition to financial harm, there is also a casual approach to keeping kosher? Can we really permit ourselves to eat something in a home where the woman of the house is not fully in charge of running things, even if there is a Jewish maid?

A well-known woman told me the following story: she met a Jewish maid carrying a big bird. 'What's that you have there?' she asked. 'It's a goose', the maid answered cheerfully, 'I got a nice deal on it.' The woman looked at the goose and started. She asked, 'Are you aware that your goose is not kosher?' The maid just stood there, dumbstruck, as if she couldn't understand what she was hearing. And really, how should a Jewish maid know the difference between kosher and non-kosher when the lady of the house sits in the salon by the mirror, or absorbed in a book, trusting the maid with everything?

Dear sisters! If you were to open the book of Jewish history, you would immediately ask yourselves: what has become of us, the Jewish people? And you would have much cause for wonder. What is the great national force of the Jewish people, which steadies us even in the most powerful storms?

Is it our wealth, which helps us through danger? No! Our wealth has in fact often been the cause of our persecution, even when the hatred is concealed under the cloak of religion.

Have we been helped by our love of foreign people? Certainly not. Exactly the opposite: our love for other peoples only brings us greater humiliation.

The great secret of Jewish national survival is authentic clinging to divine responsibilities, when the words, 'A people of holiness shall you be to me', become our guide. For these words were Jews brought to the auto-da-fé, burned at the stake for their holy faith. Can we, great-grandchildren of these martyrs, really treat with such indifference the appalling spectacle of the transgression, each and every day, of the fundamental principle of 'people of holiness', the laws of *kashrut*?

We appeal to you, sisters, Jewish women and girls: back to *yiddishkeit*! You must faithfully preserve the commandments of *kashrut* that God gave you, in each and every one of its details. Spend the extra money on really kosher butter, cheese, chocolate, etc. In general, do not allow a Jewish maid to have the final say, not to speak of letting a Christian servant run the kitchen on her own.

And in order to achieve a truly kosher home, it is necessary to learn the rules in the *Kitsur shulḥan arukh* regarding types of kosher food, immersing dishes, and so on. I was once in a certain city and discovered that not a single Jewish woman there knew that it was necessary to carefully inspect a carp, not only the head and scales but also the entire body.

'A people of holiness shall you be to me.' We do not need to be angels, just people; people, however, who are also 'holy'! 'For I am holy, the Lord your God.' For God cannot abide any impurity, anything unclean.

V Ten Letters to Jewish Children

The Quiet Month of Heshvan

Dear children! The month of Tishrei, with its solemn days and the celebration of Sukkot, is already gone. Now the quiet month of Heshvan has arrived. You have certainly heard that the life of a person is compared to a tree. Let us be a tree, which brings forth beautiful sweet fruit. The month of Heshvan can help with that. How? Listen, I will tell you! Rosh Hashanah awakened us all to repent. And the same way that the roots are the foundations of a tree, repentance is the foundation of *yiddishkeit*. On Yom Kippur God forgives our sins. And our trunk becomes stronger in the face of the strong winds, so these winds cannot, God forbid, harm us.

Then the celebration of Sukkot comes, and Jewish children enjoy true happiness. The joy of the Torah, which we Jewish people began to read from the previous year, starting with Genesis, and which we finish on Simhat Torah, these things are the delicious fruit of the Jewish tree.

In the month of Heshvan we have to take care that these fruit should not be neglected.

Each of us has to take it upon herself to be a fully committed Jewish girl. We also have to make others good and pious, as God has told us to do. For that, the *Bais Yaakov Journal* can be very helpful, and for smaller children, our beloved, beautiful *Kindergarten* magazine. Both these magazines are your best friends, and you should make sure that every Jewish house has them.

I am asking you, then, dearest children, to use the month of Heshvan to circulate these magazines among everyone you know and gather subscriptions for them.

I think that you will be successful in this work, because whenever we take it upon ourselves to do something good, we have faith that God will help us.

My Purim Gift to You

The clock strikes midnight. The future teachers of Bais Yaakov are already asleep. It is very quiet. And I dream about you, my faraway children, spread out among all the Bais Yaakov schools in Poland. It occurs to me that you must all be learning now about the three commandments that accompany the cheerful and joyous festival of Purim: reading the book of Esther, eating a festive meal, and sending gifts.

I think: what gift should I send my children? And then I realize that the best and most beautiful Purim gift I can send is a little letter to you, dear children.

For you surely know that everything passes but a word abides, especially if it is a word spoken from the depths of a heart, in sincere friendship and love.

For you surely know that my only wish is that you will grow into true Jewish daughters with true Jewish pride and with the passion to serve the holy Creator.

And who can serve as a better model than our sister Queen Esther?

This is what the Bible tells us: 'Esther was taken into the royal palace' [Esther 2: 16]. Another girl would have been ecstatic to start her life in the glorious palace of a king, to live in luxury, amid riches and beauty and the comforts of life. Esther, though, had to be compelled to go into the palace; she would much rather have stayed in the simple home of her dear uncle Mordecai than to live in a palace. And when they clothed her in expensive royal gowns and fabrics, gold-encrusted veils with costly pearls, and shod her in diamond-covered slippers, the Bible tells us, Esther 'did not ask for anything' [Esther 2: 15]. She was not impressed with the luxury and glory, and in fact it was her reserve and Jewish modesty that charmed all who saw her, and that was the reason she was chosen from among the girls of 127 provinces.

But even afterwards, when she had power over the lives and livelihoods of millions of people, she still took no pride in that. She continued to obey her uncle Mordecai's commands, just as she had when she was still a child being raised in his house.

It was because of her modesty that she merited to be the saviour of her unfortunate people.

That was our sister Queen Esther, and that is how each Jewish girl must also be.

These words are what I wanted to send you as a Purim gift!

Flee from Falsehood!

You know that the holy Creator gave us the sabbath and the holidays to bring us pleasure and for us to worship him with sincere prayers and make a special effort to learn Torah.

But that is not the only aim of those holy days. Their most important aim is to help us to carry into everyday life the same desire to serve God with true joy. 'And purify our hearts to serve you in truth', we pray in every Amidah on every sabbath and holiday.

You probably already know that we have 613 commandments, which are divided into those that connect us with God and those that connect us with other people.

We often try with all our might to fulfil those commandments that are between us and God, but pay very little attention to our responsibilities to other people. That is the reason I decided to start by discussing the great and holy responsibilities that a person has in relation to a friend.

But where to begin? I think that, since I already mentioned 'And purify our hearts to serve you in truth', we should begin by talking about the great commandment to always tell the truth, and the sin of telling lies.

As we know, the words of our great Creator can never be doubted, and we are instructed to follow him in all his ways. That alone is enough to teach us to tell the truth always and never utter a false word. But aside from that we find in many books that no transgression is as serious as a lie, and no commandment is greater than upholding the truth. The whole world rests on truth. We learn this in the *Ethics of the Fathers*: 'On three things the world stands: on truth, on justice, and on peace' [*Avot* 1: 18]. But truth is the root of peace and justice, and it alone holds up the world. 'The seal of the holy one, blessed be he, is truth' [BT *Yoma* 69*b*]! The city of Jerusalem was destroyed because its inhabitants had stopped telling the truth.

What does it mean to tell the truth, and what does it mean to lie?

To tell the truth means: never saying something that isn't the case, or that one doesn't actually believe.

Lying means: saying something other than what one knows to be true, or that one truly thinks.

And why is lying such a terrible sin?

None of us can know everything on our own. That is why each of us has to depend so heavily on what other people tell us.

Just think about it, dear children: if we tell someone something that isn't true, and this person acts according to information we supplied, what disastrous consequences might ensue! And imagine if this person were to repeat what you said to yet other people, and other people would do the same thing that the first person did, or perhaps instead figure out that it is a lie and then mock the person for repeating what you said as a fool or a liar. And this person is not at fault, since all she did was believe you! So one mustn't tell a lie even in jest, or because one believes that something good will come out of the lie.

The Talmud has something to say on exactly this matter. A great *tana* had a bad wife, who never wanted to cook the dish that he liked to eat. When their son grew up a little and noticed this, he always told his mother to cook the opposite of what his father had asked him to say. And in this way, the father got exactly what he wanted. Once, the father shared his joy with the son that his wife had started to treat him better, and the son admitted that he had been asking his mother to cook the opposite of what the father wanted. But the father did not praise him for this, rather ordering him to stop his deception, since the tongue must not be compelled to tell a lie. Our mouths must hold only truth, and then God who is truth will lead us along the ways of truth [BT *Yev. 63a–b*].

We must also avoid a lie that can hurt no one. The Talmud tells another story along these lines. A very pious man named Tobias would say, 'Even if I were to be tempted with all the treasures in the world, I still would not tell a lie!' He lived in the city of Kushta (which means 'truth'), and in this city no one died before their time because no one ever told a lie. It once happened in this city that a man lost two of his children. Terrified, the inhabitants of the city came to him to ask if he had told a lie, which would account for his children dying before their time. At first he denied this, but then he remembered a story about a woman neighbour who had knocked on his door and asked to see his wife. Since his wife had just awoken, he responded that she was not at home. The people of the town said to him: 'Please leave our town and not let the Angel of Death loose among us' [BT *San. 97a*].

And so we see that a person should never tell a lie; even just considering telling a lie, without actually expressing this lie in words, must also be resisted. For even without speaking it is possible to transgress the prohibition against lying. For instance, if we hear someone tell a lie and say nothing, and so allow another person to believe the lie since we were there and kept silent, we are just as guilty of lying as the actual liar.

And deception is also considered a lie. That is, when we lavish praise on our friend that we do not actually believe. Or when we proffer a warm invitation to someone because we know that she cannot accept. Such deception must be avoided.

Flattery is also a form of lying. And there is another terrible kind of lie: hypocrisy, which means that one acts pious when people are looking, and then sins when no one is there to see. This transgression is so terrible because through it, one, as it were, denies God, the God who sees everything.

Truth demands that everything we express must be something we actually feel, and it is truly a great sin not to keep a promise that we have made. For that reason, if we absolutely cannot keep a promise we made to someone, we must beg their forgiveness.

I hope that you, my dear ones, will take all this to heart and always remember what our Torah teaches us: 'Flee from falsehood!'

One Must Not Swear!

This time we will discuss the great sin of swearing. In many cases, people swear because they haven't been careful enough to avoid lying. But since I discussed the ugliness of telling lies in my previous letter, I'll focus this time on the sin of swearing.

The most terrible form of swearing is swearing in God's name. That is, when you call upon God as witness that you are telling the truth, since God is the true Creator, and the Creator of truth. And if you then tell a lie and swear in God's name that it is the truth, this is a both a false oath and a denial, God forbid, of the Creator.

In olden times, when someone swore on the king's life and it later emerged that they had sworn falsely, this person would be given the death penalty, just as if they had committed treason. If that is how an oath is treated in relation to a king of flesh and blood, how much more must we guard against misusing the name of the King of all Kings!

People swear in God's name unintentionally, without understanding how great a sin they are committing. I hear a child blurt *Jak Boga kocham*—'honest to God' in Polish—and I just have to shudder. This is in fact an actual oath, since it makes no difference in what language one swears. But when I scold the girl she starts to explain that she meant nothing by it, it's just a habitual expression. But the oath has already been uttered.

I am sure you all remember the third of the Ten Commandments: 'You shall not swear falsely by the name of the Lord your God' [Exod. 20: 7; Deut. 5: 11]. Do not swear in God's name, for the one who commits such a sin will not go unpunished. The sin of swearing is so grave that not only the swearer suffers the consequences, but also the person's entire family.

Nor may we encourage others to swear. This is why our sages decreed that money should never be borrowed without a written note, and that an investment should never be made without a witness.

The Talmud relates: Rabbi Ashi once sent a request to Ravina to borrow five *zuzim*, since he had the opportunity to purchase part of a field. Ravina answered: 'Show me a promissory note signed by witnesses and I will loan you the money'! And Rabbi Ashi was surprised: 'Do you really require such a thing from me?' Ravina answered: 'I require a note especially from you, since you are always immersed in your learning and therefore likely to forget that you borrowed some money' [BT *BM* 75*b*].

How great the punishment is for swearing may be seen in the book of Joshua, in which Achan and his entire family are punished because Achan broke Joshua's oath by taking booty from Jericho [Josh. 7].

And I want to lay out all the various forms that an oath might take. Even if one says only the words 'I swear', this is in fact an actual oath, as if one had sworn in God's name. And the same holds true for saying 'Swear to me!' And it doesn't matter if one says this to a child or to an adult, to a Jew or to a non-Jew. It also makes no difference in which language one says it.

There's also a meaningless oath, in which one swears that something is true about which there can be no doubt that it is in fact the case. Or when one swears that one will do something that is clearly impossible to do.

And then there are unnecessary oaths. For instance, someone swears about something when no one asks him to; this is common among merchants.

And the same holds true of promises. A promise is just like an oath, and constitutes the same transgression.

Even when something is true, it is forbidden to swear that it is. The exception is in a court, and if an oath is required by law one is permitted to swear. But even in that case, if there is any possibility of avoiding the oath, for instance by paying a fine, one is obligated to do so.

The heaviest divine punishments are reserved for false oaths. But pointless oaths, even true ones, also bring poverty, hunger, and need.

Therefore, my dear children, keep your distance from every kind of oath. If your friend asks you to swear, say to her: 'I suspect that you must be used to people telling lies, otherwise it would not have occurred to you that I might not be telling the truth and you wouldn't be trying to get me to swear!'

But since you are studying in a Bais Yaakov school, growing up to be true Jewish daughters, and since you are all together in spirit in your Basya groups and aware of what it means to be a Jewish child, you must also dedicate yourselves to being models of honesty and serenity, good children with the shining qualities that befit you.

Stay Away from Evil Speech [*leshon hara*]

The Torah states: 'Do not bear tales among your people' [Lev. 19: 16]. By circulating gossip from one person to another, you disturb the loving relationships among people. There cannot be peace in places that are full of gossip.

For the great sin of speaking ill the Temple was destroyed [BT *Yoma 9b*]. We say this in our prayers: 'Because of our many sins we were exiled from our land'![1]

The transgressions of speaking ill and of gossip include many terrible sins, among which are:

1. Repeating something you noticed or heard about someone without their permission, even when it isn't something bad, is considered gossip.
2. Saying something bad about another person, even if it is true, is considered speaking ill.
3. Making something up about another person by saying that they did something bad, when the entire story is untrue, is certainly speaking ill.

It is a great sin even to occasionally transgress in one of these ways. And if one makes no attempt to guard oneself against them, then the punishment is great, and the person who neglects to be careful of committing these sins may be lost forever.

Nor can we speak ill in concealed form. For example, it is forbidden to say that so-and-so is *now* a good person, from which it can be inferred that they used to be a bad person. One must also not praise a person in the presence of his enemy.

[1] From the *Vayevarekh david* ('and David blessed') section of the morning prayers, taken from 1 Chr. 29: 10–13.

That leads to the person who hears the praise speaking ill of the one you praised, and the one who did the over-praising is also guilty of that sin.

Someone who listens to and welcomes evil speech is committing an even greater sin than one who merely passes on gossip. And this is because gossip is only passed on if there are people interested in hearing it.

Our sages indeed say that 'evil speech kills three people': the one who says it, the one about whom it is said, and the one who listens. And the last commits a greater sin than the first [BT *Arakh.* 15*b*].

The Torah gives us the best example of the punishment suffered by Miriam and the spies for evil speech. Miriam only uttered one critical word about her brother Moses, and aside from God no one even heard it, and nevertheless she was immediately punished [Num. 12]. And the spies merely spoke harshly about the land, about trees and stones, and for that sin a plague descended and all those who had spoken ill died off [Num. 13].

In contrast to these incidents, the *midrash* includes among the four merits that redeemed the Jews from the land of Egypt that they refrained from speaking ill.[2]

Speaking ill also includes telling a secret that has been confided to you. Whoever cannot be trusted to control their tongue cannot be trusted with anything. And so the story is told of a wise man who was asked what he had done with a secret that had been confided to him, and he said: 'I have dug a grave in my heart and buried the secret in it.' A second wise man answered the same question with the words: 'I have already forgotten what you asked me.'

Dear children! A person must give a full account of every word he utters. Now I will tell you a nice story about this.

A great hasidic *rebbe* once heard his hasidim marvelling at the telephone, the telegraph, and the train. The *rebbe* stood up and said:

'Telephone, telegraph, train—these are all fine things, very useful things. But maybe the greatest use of these things is that the telephone shows us clearly that what one says in one place is heard somewhere else, so that if one speaks in Kraków they hear it in Warsaw, London, and even New York; so certainly what is spoken on earth is heard in heaven! The telegraph is the best proof that a price must be paid for every word. When one sends a telegram one pays fifteen *groschen*, for example, for every word. It stands to reason, then, that if God gave a person the power of speech, must every word not also be precious? And the train also teaches us an interesting lesson. Just notice how much trouble we run into if we miss a train by even a single minute. We have to wait a long time for the

[2] See Fischer, '"Name, Language, and Dress"', for the variations on this midrash.

next train, and we arrive where we need to be much later than we should have. And if we are late for a sabbath or holiday by one minute, how much greater is the damage!'

Remember, dear children, guard every word, your tongue, your ears, your time! And if Jewish children act according to the commandments of the Torah, the messiah will come and rescue us from the dark exile swiftly and in our days!

Honour Your Father and Mother

An important matter that all children must be very careful about is the commandment of honouring your father and mother.

Many of you will no doubt say that you already know this from your teacher, but, as we have already stated, matters that connect one person and another are easily forgotten, and there is no human relationship closer than with one's parents!

We learn in the holy Torah: 'Honour your father and mother so that you may live long in the land that God has given you.' This commandment is repeated twice [Exod. 20: 12; Deut. 5: 16].

As Jews, we fulfil this commandment not only because our parents support us from the moment of our birth by giving us food to eat, clothing to wear, and sending us to school, but also because they are our connection with the Jewish people.

It is through our parents that we are children of a people that God chose from among seventy nations and made into a holy people, a sacred nation, which alone stood at Mount Sinai and heard the Ten Commandments.

On the tablets that God gave his people, along with the commandment to fear the one Creator, was also inscribed in fiery letters the commandment to honour one's parents.

And do you know why? Because parents are God's messengers. He commanded them to feed and clothe us. By honouring our parents we also honour God himself.

Our sages expound in the Talmud that when a man honours his father and his mother, God says: 'I ascribe merit to them as though I were dwelling among them and they were honouring me' [BT *Kid.* 30*b*].

And we can indeed see that God immediately added the reward for this commandment: through it will we live in happiness and joy in our own land.

But how do we fulfil the commandment to honour one's father and mother?

We must do it in two ways: with awe and with respect. We must relate to our parents as exalted persons and honour them in word and deed.

So one must obey one's father and mother. When parents ask one to go somewhere, one must not say: 'I'm tired! I don't feel like doing that now!' No, one must always obey the parent's command.

One must not argue with what they say. And so the Talmud teaches: 'Even if one's father or mother were to toss a purse filled with golden coins into the sea, one may not be angry with them.' Or 'If a person is hosting a gathering and his father or mother walks in and spits in his face, he must not talk back to them, but rather accept it as if it were a punishment from God.'

The Talmud even recounts the story of a non-Jew, Dama ben Netinah, who was very punctilious about this commandment: 'One time two Jews came to him to buy some precious diamonds for the Temple, and he could have earned 600,000 dinars. But his father happened to be asleep just then and the keys to the cabinet were under the father's pillow. He gave no thought to the enormous sum, but rather only thought that he must not awaken his father' [BT *Kid.* 31*a*].

This same non-Jew Dama was once at a ball attended by the greatest people of Rome, and he was wearing the finest silk clothing. Suddenly his mother walked in, tore off his cloak, smacked him on the head, and spat in his face. But he just stood in silence, not speaking a single word against his mother.

If that was how a non-Jew honoured his parents, how must we, who possess the holy Torah, honour our parents?

First of all one must obey one's father and mother. One must never refuse to do what they ask or to run errands for them, one must refrain from sitting in their regular seats, and speak only when they give permission. Even at synagogue or a gathering one must refrain from sitting in the seats that are reserved for them. One must always try to appreciate what they are saying, to stand up when they walk into a room, and never to walk ahead of them. When they are asleep, one must speak softly, keep calm, and in general refrain from disturbing them.

Good children give away their dearest possessions for the sake of honouring their parents. One must serve one's parents with love and provide them with the most beautiful and best things. The commandment to honour one's parents must be kept, even at great cost. Impoverished parents must be supported, even taking the last piece of bread from one's own lips.

Supporting and providing for one's parents must always be done with a smiling face, with love and a generous spirit.

The Talmud tells us how someone gave his father a roasted fowl to eat and thereby lost his share in the World to Come. You will ask, why? Because when the father asked his son, 'Where did you get this?' his son answered, 'What does it matter, old man? Eat up and be still!'

Another son managed to win back his share in the World to Come, even though he allowed his father to work in a mill. That was because he took his father's place in a worse situation while his father took his job in the mill, and the son even consoled his father with kind words [BT *Kid.* 31*b*, expanded in JT *Kid.* 31*b*].

There is, however, an occasion when one should not obey the will of one's father or mother. That is when they order their child, God forbid, to transgress the Torah. Therefore it says in the Torah, just after the commandment of honouring one's father and mother, 'and my sabbaths shall you observe'. For both parents and children are required to observe God's Torah. In the event that parents tell their child to do something that is against the Torah, the child is not allowed to scream at them or revile them, but must rather say evenly and calmly, 'In the Torah it says thus and thus!'

And even when one's parents are unfortunately no longer alive, one must mention them only with the greatest respect, and always add the words, 'May their memory be a blessing.'

And you certainly know that one must also respect an older brother or sister, and of course a teacher as well as every other individual, even one's own friend.

Love your Neighbour as Yourself!

Dear children! Now we will speak of our responsibilities to the people who live near us in God's world. All children should indeed know these things.

When we say that one must love other people, it makes no difference who those people are, whether they are one of our people or from another nation. A person is a person.

The Torah teaches us: God is good to all. His compassion encompasses all his actions. The Creator nourishes everyone and everything, the strongest animal and the weakest bird.

We also know from the Torah that the human being was created in God's image. Humans resemble their Creator. Already from that fact it is clear that we must make no distinction between one individual and another. When we humiliate another person it means that we are also—God forbid—shaming God, whom that person resembles.

Every human being descends from Adam and Eve and is therefore a child of the same father and mother. Is it not difficult for parents, does it not cause them great grief, when brothers and sisters cannot get along? In the same way, God is very sad when his children, human beings, great and small, do not live together in peace.

The holy Torah teaches 'Love your neighbour as yourself', ending this commandment with the words, 'I am God', which is to say, 'I am the God who created you all equally, and because of me you must all love one another.'

You must love every human being, both those who are close to you and those who are entirely foreign to you. 'Love the stranger, for you were strangers in Egypt' [Deut. 10: 19]. It is forbidden to hate even those who do not share your beliefs.

Only with love and friendship can one bring other people closer to Jewish beliefs. Many passages in the Torah relate how the Jewish people treated other nations, showing them love.

We can see this in our father Abraham, with what hospitality he greeted guests, how he interceded with God on behalf of Sodom and Gomorrah [Gen. 18]. Our teacher Moses came to the rescue of foreign shepherds, and protected them [Exod. 2]. Joshua kept his promise to the idol-worshipping Gibeonites [Josh. 9]. King Solomon prayed at the dedication of the Temple that the prayers of anyone who came there would be answered [1 Kgs. 8: 41–3]. There is much more evidence from many different eras that teaches us that love for one's fellow human being must be very strong. The commandment of 'Love your neighbour as yourself' commands us also to feel happiness when the other person is happy and sympathize with the other's pain and sadness, exactly as if it were our own experience.

And because each human being was created in the image of God it makes no difference whether the person is beautiful or ugly, clever or foolish. The greatest sin is therefore to shame another person. It is exactly the same transgression as killing someone and spilling their blood since the shamed person first turns red, and then as white as a corpse.

Rabbi Haninah says: 'All who go down to Gehinnom [eventually] ascend, except for the one who shames his fellow in public and the one who calls him names' [BT *BM* 58*b*]. One must never call someone a name, even if the person is already accustomed to the name and is no longer bothered by it. Anyone who shames someone or hurts their feelings is unworthy of belonging to the Jewish people.

Did you know, my dear children, about this terrible sin? Have you ever considered how terrible it is to shame a friend?

Once, I heard some children cursing at each other and calling each other various names and it grieved me greatly. But I cannot imagine that Bais Yaakov girls would ever do such a thing!

And if it is the case that a student may have once embarrassed her friend or called her a name, let her immediately go apologize and take it upon herself never to do such a thing again.

What does it mean to shame someone? If one speaks ill of someone, even without mentioning her name, but everyone can guess the person that was meant—that counts as embarrassing them. When one mentions someone's flaws, things they used to do but no longer do, or when one brings up to someone that they don't come from the best family, or says something critical about her parents, that counts as shaming, too.

And do you know, my dear children, how one comes to make such mistakes? It happens when someone speaks too much, and without thinking first. This is what King Solomon meant when he said, 'When one speaks too much, one speaks without rhyme or reason' [Prov. 10: 19].

So take it upon yourselves, my children, to strengthen the friendship among you and fulfil with all your heart the commandment to 'Love your neighbour as yourself.'

Do Not Seek Vengeance!

Our holy Torah commands us to love all people, even those who do not love us. One must not hate even an enemy. Our sages tell us that if a friend needs help and an enemy needs help, the obligation is to [first] help our enemy, in order to subjugate our desire for revenge [BT *BM* 32*b*].[3]

Revenge means that when someone treats me badly the desire to treat him badly flares up in me, but a Jew must never give in to that feeling. If someone doesn't want to lend her friend a book or pencil or some such thing, and then wants to borrow something from that same person, who says: 'Don't you remember when I wanted to borrow something from you and you wouldn't

[3] The passage in the Talmud ends with 'our evil inclination' rather than 'our desire for revenge'.

lend it? Now you want to borrow something from me, and I don't want to lend it to you.' This constitutes revenge, my dear children, and it is strictly forbidden!

When someone embarrasses you or treats you badly, you must quickly forget and forgive this wrong, even if they don't apologize. In your own heart you have to defend this person and give them the benefit of the doubt. And even if it seems pretty clear to you that someone really meant to harm you, even then you must not be angry with them. Everything, after all, comes from God and is determined in advance.

Nothing happens unless God wills it, although it is also true that God chooses good messengers to deliver good things, and bad messengers to deliver—God forbid—misfortune. Revenge therefore means going against the will of the Holy One, blessed be he.

The clearest example of this is the story of Joseph, who did not take revenge on his brothers who sold him into slavery. On the contrary, he said to his brothers: 'Do not be distressed, my dear brothers, for God only sent me here to save you from hunger' [Gen. 45: 5].

Aside from seeking vengeance, it is also forbidden to hold a grudge. A grudge is when someone lends you something that you had refused to lend on a prior occasion and then says, 'You see, despite the fact that you weren't willing to lend me that item, I'm still lending you something.' These words show that the person hasn't entirely forgotten their grievance, and that in itself is wrong.

Another terrible transgression is cursing someone. One must not curse someone even if they aren't present. An even greater sin is cursing in God's name. And one must never remain silent when someone curses someone else, listening to the curses without objecting.

Yes, my dear children, I know full well that you won't understand how it is possible to do all this. How can you lend something to someone who isn't willing to lend anything herself? How can you resist even reproaching someone for their unwillingness? How can you refrain from wanting to embarrass someone like that, or even feeling a little resentful of them?

But this is the reason, my dear ones, that you are children of Bais Yaakov! You must be a model of truly Jewish behaviour, with your beautiful and noble characters. And rest assured that gradually these things will become second nature to you.

Avoid Arrogance!

And now we will discuss a very unattractive character trait that many children have, even those in Bais Yaakov, of taking too much pride in themselves.

But how do you avoid this, you will certainly ask me. What can we do to avoid making too much of ourselves?

The first tool in this struggle is not to consider what you have or are to be truly your own. Not your possessions, not your physical powers or beauty, not your intellectual gifts or your talents. You must know that you acquired none of these things of your own accord. The Creator, who gives us everything that we have, bestowed these on us, and he is truly the one who controls them. Everything comes from God: strength, riches, health, wisdom, beauty, and all the other things that give human beings so much satisfaction.

There is only one thing that is entirely in our hands, and that is the fear of God. So why should we take pride in things that are not truly our own? Can we really take credit for things that we have not ourselves accomplished?

You should recognize, then, that what you have received from God just makes it all the clearer how great he is and how insignificant we are. And the greater our reason and intelligence, the greater should be our obligations.

But you yourselves know this well. A teacher demands more from a gifted student than from one who is less gifted, and the smallest flaws in the work of a gifted student count more than the worst mistakes in a less talented one.

Certainly some of you will be thinking: I'm a dedicated student, I work hard at my assignments and know the lessons well, so can I really not take a little pride in my own work as compared to my lazy friend, who hardly studies at all?

But my dear ones! Who is it that gives you the strength and insight to absorb what you are taught, if not God? So how can you take pride in something that isn't your own doing?

The great Jewish thinker Nahmanides, Rabbi Moses ben Nahman, left a letter for his son and instructed him to read it every day. In that letter he speaks of the unattractive character trait of pride:

> You should know, my son, that whoever is proud commits treason against God, since he boasts of clothing that belongs to the Creator. And what is it really that a person should feel proud of? His wealth? God, after all, decides who will be rich and who poor. His status, then? How can a person boast of his status when it says clearly in the morning prayers, 'wealth and honour are yours to dispense'. Or your intelligence, which God can

take away at any moment? Everything is in his hands. He lays low the haughty and raises up the lowly, and for that reason you should always be modest and not seek status, so that God may exalt you.[4]

I have spoken to you of the Hatam Sofer, who lived in Pressburg, where we established a Bais Yaakov in which his granddaughter, herself a graduate of the seminary in Kraków, now teaches. This great Jewish man, who in his own generation was considered not only the greatest in his country but indeed in the entire world, wrote in his will:

> My dear children! If God blesses you with prestige and happiness, which indeed I hope for and trust him to do, do not hold your head up higher than others! You must always remember that we are children of Abraham, students of our teacher Moses, servants of King David, of blessed memory. Our father Abraham said, 'I am but dust and ashes' [Gen. 18: 27]. Our great leader Moses said, 'Who are we?' [Exod. 16: 7]. King David said, 'I am a worm, less than human' [Ps. 22: 7]. The messiah himself will reveal himself to us as a 'humble man riding on an ass' [Zech. 9: 9]. If this is so, from where is our 'arrogance and haughtiness' [Isa. 9: 8]?[5]

And some of you, my dear children, will no doubt ask: is it really so wrong of me to feel proud of having done something good for another person, either through my own actions or with my property?

But just think, dear children, of all the good things that God does for us every day, and of course every good thing and everything that makes us happy comes from the Creator, so really, how could we feel proud for merely being God's messengers and passing along a little part of those good things to someone else?

And so the human being, the Jew, the Jewish child, who considers himself a servant of God must never be haughty and always know that pride is the gateway to transgression, since arrogance leads to sin. As soon as a person is absorbed with his own self and feels satisfaction in his own capacities and deeds, he begins to gradually idolize himself and this leads to a deep morass from which he cannot easily extricate himself.

Already at the very beginning of human history we can see that pride led to a great fall, how wishing to be like God and to know good and evil led to the sin of eating from the Tree of Knowledge.

[4] On Nahmanides, see Section II, n. 2, above. This letter, which he recommended that his son read once a week and which is still read regularly by many Jews, was sent from Jerusalem, where he sought refuge from Christian persecution, to Spain, where his son held a position in the Castilian court.

[5] For an English translation of this famous ethical will, see Mendes-Flohr and Reinharz (eds.), *The Jew in the Modern World*, 196–9. The passage cited is on p. 196.

It was striving to have more than someone else that led Cain to murder his brother Abel, and the generation that built the Tower of Babel did so in order to assert its greatness and glory. And we can see that all through Jewish history false pride led to many sad circumstances.

'Every haughty person is an abomination to the Lord' [Prov. 16: 5]. God has no use for those who take pride in themselves! When someone insults us and we are angry with them for it, it is only because we haven't been sufficiently humble.

To be unassuming, to be mild in our relations with others, will always make us happy and instil in us the good and noble qualities of true Jewish children.

But we also have to be wary of false modesty. For instance, when someone asks you to do them a favour, never hesitate and say to yourself, why did they think of asking me? No, you must use every means at your disposal to help your brother or sister to whatever extent you are able. There is no finer character trait than always coming to the aid of someone who is suffering or in need, as the holy Torah teaches us.

My dear children, by weaning yourselves from empty vanity you will very quickly attain the highest ideal of being true children of your people, whom God calls 'Israel, in whom I glory' [Isa. 49: 3].

Our Holiday

No doubt you are asking yourselves now, my dear children, what holiday I could be thinking of here? And my answer to you is the fifteenth anniversary of the founding of our Bais Yaakov schools. Fifteen years have passed since you and I first got to know one another, and since I first started to tell you about the greatness of our holy Torah, and by now we have had fifteen years of our beloved Bais Yaakov schools.

And so, I ask you, can we really let such a cherished and important anniversary go by without a celebration?

And I think you all will very rightly agree that we must give a full account of everything we have accomplished during these fifteen years, in order to know how to carry on into the future.

And you will undoubtedly answer straight away: with all the Bais Yaakov schools and Bnos and Basya groups, have we not really accomplished a great deal?

But I must make it very clear, despite this, that we should not be talking about the number of students or members of Bnos, but rather about the quality of the *yiddishkeit* that we have acquired during these years, which is what we should try to measure.

Of course you know that we now have our own magazines, *Bais Yaakov*, *Kindergarten*, and *New Saplings*, and besides these the textbooks *Yiddish Language* and *Jewish Life*. But I ask you, have you yourself bought copies of these books?[6]

But maybe you will answer that these are hard times, and that you don't have the money for such things. But I can tell you that this is wrong, for surely you have no problem asking your loving parents for food when you are hungry, even in these difficult times, no? And if so, you must surely know that these books are like bread for your soul. And surely your dear parents would listen to you and agree that this is the right thing to do.

If you consider how much money you spend on Polish books for reading or for school, why are authentically Jewish books any less worthy? On the contrary, they must take priority in your budget, over what you read for pleasure and over your school books.

And you must be very careful, dear children, to never—God forbid—stop studying in a Bais Yaakov school. You must encourage each other and point out to each other that it is forbidden to stop one's studies of *yiddishkeit* in the middle. But I think you know that yourselves, no? After reading through all my letters to you, you have no doubt taken it upon yourselves to improve your characters, to stop speaking ill of people, or being proud, greedy, hateful, and so on.

But you should know that it's important not only to improve your character, but also to actually meet these commitments and do the right thing, since good intentions are never enough.

So today I'd like to give you a few ideas about how to accomplish this.

When someone decides to try to become a better person, the first thing they have to do is clear out all the bad things from their heart. If a field is overgrown

[6] In total, 160 issues of the *Bais Yaakov Journal* appeared between 1924 and 1939, and 120 issues of *Kindergarten*, the latter first as a supplement and then as a separate publication. *New Saplings* was a magazine intended for school use in the earliest grades, and appeared much less frequently. The first volume of *Yiddish Language*, by Nuta Berliner and Eliezer Schindler, appeared in 1932, while the second and third volumes appeared in 1933. Schenirer here is referring to the first volume of *Jewish Life*, by Orlean, which appeared in 1932; a second was published in 1938. In all, the Bais Yaakov press run by Eliezer Gershon Friedenson published over twenty textbooks, along with *Collected Writings*, six plays and other texts by Sarah Schenirer, a songbook for the movement, publicity brochures, a biography of Schenirer in Polish by Hillel Seidman, a children's biography of Schenirer in Yiddish by Friedenson, and other reading material for Bais Yaakov students. On this, see Atkins, *The Beth Jacob Movement in Poland*, 106–11.

with weeds, it's difficult for the good fruit to grow, and it's the same thing for a heart that is overgrown with so many bad traits that no good deeds can emerge. If someone recognizes in themselves that they're a little arrogant, or jealous, or angry, they shouldn't try to defend these feelings, but rather deal with them exactly as one would treat such flaws in a stranger, strictly judging them and rooting them out by force.

Every night you should make an internal reckoning of the day that just passed, asking whether you have improved your character at all in the course of that day. If so, you must keep going along that path, and if—God forbid—not, you should try again the next day to improve your character flaws.

You must keep trying, just in this way. And you must welcome criticism gladly. Let me tell you a beautiful story about criticism. Once, the great Rabbi Bunim went to his own rabbi and said:

'Today, someone embarrassed me.'

'And what did you do?' asked the rabbi.

'I gave him a kiss', Rabbi Bunim answered.

'If so', said the rabbi, 'you must certainly now tell me who it was!'

'It was', answered Rabbi Bunim, 'the *Shevet musar*, a book of morals. I was reading that book today and I found a passage that made clear that I had not been behaving correctly and showed me how to improve my ways. And for that welcome reproof I gave it a kiss.'[7]

You see, dear children, how we must treasure criticism, in order to know how to follow the correct path.

Take all these things to heart, then, that I have written to you on the occasion of the anniversary of our schools. And try to fulfil all these things, and God will send us the redeemer, amen!

[7] Elijah Hakohen of Izmir's *Shevet musar* (first published in Ladino in 1748) was among the most popular works of *musar* (ethical) literature produced in Ottoman society (despite the fact that Elijah Hakohen was suspected in some circles of Shabateanism). The Rabbi Bunim in Schenirer's tale may be the hasidic rebbe, Simha Bunim Bonhart of Peshischa (Przysucha) (1765–1827), a key leader of Polish hasidism, who is associated with *Shevet musar* in other stories. Rabbi Simha Bunim also seems to be the oral source of a saying frequently attributed to Sarah Schenirer: 'Everyone must have two pockets, with a note in each pocket, so that he or she can reach into one or the other, depending on the need. When feeling lowly and depressed, discouraged or disconsolate, one should reach into the right pocket, and, there, find the words: "For my sake was the world created". But when feeling high and mighty one should reach into the left pocket, and find the words: "I am but dust and ashes".' In some versions, Schenirer's recommendation for the right pocket is that it contain the saying 'It is the time to act for the Lord', a slogan of rabbinic Judaism in general and of the Bais Yaakov movement in particular.

VI A Letter from Mrs Schenirer, May She Rest in Peace

SENT during her illness on the occasion of the last *siyum* in the Bais Yaakov Seminary [1935].[1]

My beloved and dear children, long may you live

'What can we say, how can we speak, and how can we justify ourselves?' [Gen. 44: 16]. Since 'many are the thoughts in the heart of a human being, but God's plan will prevail' [Prov. 19: 21].

Yes, human thoughts are weak, very weak, but whatever God decides, 'this, too, is for the best' [BT *Ta'an.* 21*a*].

Praised be God for his abundant kindness.

Since this morning, I have not been able to stop crying. I, who always complained to you about how difficult it was for me to cry during prayer, suddenly feel for the first time the strength of the spiritual ties that bind me to my children.

[1] Along with the historical description of Bais Yaakov in the United States that follows, this letter was added to the second edition of Schenirer's *Collected Writings*. A *siyum* is a festive celebration of the completion of a tractate of the Talmud or (in this case) another major unit of learning, or simply a graduation. This 'Letter from Sarah Schenirer' is sometimes referred to as her 'Last Will and Testament', and is dated in late December or early January (*parshat* 'Shemot' was the Torah reading for 29 Dec. 1934). According to Pearl Benisch, it was written shortly before Schenirer travelled to Vienna for medical treatment (*Carry Me in Your Heart*, 308). In his article on Schenirer's final illness, Deutschländer describes her last visit to the seminary for this graduation: 'She enters the building in the afternoon, when most of the students are out for a walk. A messenger races into the dining room, where a few teachers are lingering over lunch, to say, "Frau Schenirer is on her way." Hearts begin to pound. A few students appear and the news travels like wildfire that she's here, in the entrance hall. Frau S. sits down in the ground-floor dining hall. People stand frozen in shock, their eyes welling with tears, their shoulders quivering. Frau S.'s face is all the evidence they need that the illness has not passed. This is no lucky return to work. The breath catches in the throat. Please, let this not be the last visit' (Deutschländer, 'Sarah Schenirer and Bais Yaakov' (Yid.), 10). He cites two letters sent from Vienna, dated 24 Jan. and 6 Feb. 1935, which both end with a plea that her students pray and recite psalms for her full recovery (ibid. 10–11).

You undoubtedly remember how I always used to quote a Polish proverb, 'Blood is not water, a soul is not a body.' Yes, spiritual bonds are stronger, since they last forever!

And that is why I am so sure that just as I am weeping as I write these words to you, so too will you weep as you read them. May God help these mutual tears rise before his glorious throne and bring a full redemption, and in the meantime a complete healing.

And now, I turn to you, my dear children, who are leaving our home and going out in the world to become leaders and educators of Jewish daughters.

I am certain that, praise God, you understand your sacred mission. We have a good Creator, blessed be he, who helps a person along the way that he chooses, just as he always helped me during these years that have passed by sending me people who were loyal and honest helpers in my work.

I just want to point out that there are two dangers that await my children. And in our case they are more dangerous and more powerful than for others.

The first one is that receiving praise and adulation from people after a successful lecture can make someone proud, so that they start to believe that they are really something special, earning fame and glory by their own efforts.

The other danger is exactly the opposite. Some people worry too much about whether they are really fulfilling their responsibilities, and God forbid, they fall into a depression. In the first case, you should remember what I told you about Rabbi Shmelke, of blessed memory, who before the first sermon he gave withdrew into his room to spend an hour alone. There he recited to himself all the words of praise he had received and all the titles that he had ever been awarded and those he believed he would get in the future.

Someone was hiding in the room and heard all this, and amazed at the rabbi's behaviour, asked him about it. And the rabbi answered:

'Since I was afraid that the praise I would hear from my people would infect me with a sense of pride, I inoculated myself against that by saying all those words of praise myself, so that later they might make not the slightest impression on me, since words of praise that a person utters to himself mean nothing if no one else hears them.'[2]

And in the opposite case, when someone worries about whether they have properly fulfilled their obligations, they must carry out an honest reckoning about whether they indeed have fulfilled them, and if they have, they should

[2] This story is told of Rabbi Samuel Horowitz, also known as Shmelke of Nikolsburg (1726–78), one of the early hasidic leaders.

remind themselves of what I told you to say every day after prayers—the passage about fear of God, which states:

'And now, O Israel, what does the Lord your God demand of you? Only this: to revere the Lord your God, to walk only in his paths, to love him, and to serve the Lord your God with all your heart and soul' [Deut. 10: 12].

Although I know that you understand the meaning of this passage very well, I want to review it with you again.

'And now, O Israel', you know that in the prior passages it is stated that your future depends on your faithfully fulfilling the commandments, that is to say, 'to revere', 'to walk', and 'to love'. The first obligation is to revere, and to walk and love are the consequences of that true reverence, as we studied together in [Samson Raphael Hirsch's] *Horeb*, and that reverence is acquired through the consciousness, with every step, of God's greatness and our own inconsequentiality.

'To walk only in his paths'—this thought alone can lead us to fulfil all his commandments and to feel the joy that this fulfilment brings, as we say every day in the morning prayers: 'Happy is the man who listens to your commandments and Torah and places your word on his heart.'

Yes, 'Her ways [the ways of the Torah] are pleasant' [Prov. 3: 17], and this feeling of soul-pleasure brings us to the love of God, which is the highest and greatest happiness, giving oneself over to God, feeling close to him, 'serving God', and with these feelings of love mobilizing all our energies, thoughts, and emotions, all our spiritual and physical capacities, for the sake of fulfilling God's will on this earth.

But you know, since the reverence of God is such a great thing, God left it entirely in our hands, as our sages explain: 'Everything is in the hands of heaven except for the fear of heaven' [BT *Ber.* 33*b*]. This is the sole thing that is '*of you*', that is to say: that God asks of you, the one thing that God expects from us, as opposed to everything else that we receive from him. God requires nothing for his house of treasures except for the reverence of God; and the key to the metaphysical knowledge and true behaviour that leads to revering God is the fulfilment of *all the commandments*. Yes, my dear children, *all the commandments*! As King David says, 'God's Torah is *perfect*, renewing the soul' [Ps. 19: 8]! One cannot accept 80 or even 99 per cent of it. Because it is *perfect*, and only when one embraces the whole of it does it renew the soul and bring happiness.

And so, my dear children, you have already passed, thank God, all the oral and written tests and done well, but now comes the true, the most difficult, test of all: life.

Life is unfortunately often very difficult, but you are armed with the strongest weapons of all, which are, indeed, *revering, loving, and serving* God.

Yet, despite myself I am overtaken by a distressing thought. Do these children of mine, these young pioneers, truly comprehend what I and a great portion of the Jewish people are entrusting to them? Do they understand the great responsibility they are taking upon themselves, of educating a new generation? Will they be able to withstand all the temptations that they will encounter along this new path on which they are embarking, with which *life* will test them?

And a quiet prayer escapes my heart, as always in such times: 'O, great Creator, help my faithful children in their holy work!'

Let them not be too sorely tested on their new path, and let them also fulfil the words of our Sages, which have accompanied me, thank God, since my very first steps: 'Whoever comes to be purified is assisted in this aim' [BT *Shab.* 104*a*], 'A person is permitted to travel along the road he wishes to pursue' [BT *Mak.* 10*b*], and that heaven leads us along the ways we choose to go. I know that this is not easy, and that it may even be very difficult.

They certainly have the best intentions, so please, dear Father in heaven, help them so that from these shining intentions will emerge the best and most beautiful deeds.

I am reminded of the words of our distinguished Mr Orlean, when he witnessed an exam in Rabka. They still echo in my ears:

> That you can learn and teach, of that we have seen in these exams. But whether you can truly educate young souls, this is the question that has troubled our hearts, as we watched you take your exams.
>
> We were reminded of the young priests in the Temple. These priests were charged with the sacred duty of safeguarding its purity. Today, when it is unfortunately no longer standing, every Jewish home, every Jewish heart, is a temple. And today this very duty is incumbent on you! *You are going out into the world to build temples.*
>
> Before the high priest commenced his sacred work, he was asked, 'Perhaps there is something alien in your heart? Perhaps you have forgotten or perhaps you never learned everything you need to know' [BT *Yoma* 18*a*]. If you haven't, we don't blame you, but if there is something alien in your heart, it might render your sacred service ineffective.
>
> You, dear children, are going out into the wider world and will be entrusted with the pure souls of children. You have to raise these souls as true people of Israel!

> Remember, the fate of the younger generation, and thus of the entire people, is dependent on you. How terrible will be your sin if your heart, God forbid, is not entirely pure, entirely dedicated to our holy ideal.[3]

Yes, I still feel the deep impression that those words made on me.

I am sure that all you, all my children, made the strongest resolution at that moment to remain true to our ideals, but we have to remember that life is often hard.

So be strong, be steadfast in your holy work! Remember the words that we studied together from the writings of Rabbi Samson Raphael Hirsch, of blessed memory: 'Inspiration is easy, very easy—but to remain inspired for years on end, for an entire lifetime, that is the crucial thing.' Let our powers never slacken, let us never tire of dedicating ourselves to the work of the Creator. Yes, that is the main quality we lack.

And so this is what I ask of my children, most of all!

Never tire or weaken, whether because of material troubles, which are unfortunately so common, or because things do not go well with the children. Every occupation has its difficulties. So why should our holy work be any different? Be strong in the face of everything!

I should stop now, but it has been so long since we studied together and today you are celebrating the conclusion of a phase of learning—nearly the whole Torah—and I am reminded of a hasidic tale about a student who came to his rabbi and said, with great happiness: 'Rabbi, I just got through the entire Talmud.' And his rabbi asked him, 'And did the Talmud also get through to you?'

Yes, my beloved children. Just consider what great treasures of Torah-learning you now possess. But you know full well that 'It is not the study that is important, but rather the deed' [*Avot* 1: 17].

That, for us, is the entire point.

Since I have already demonstrated that reverence for God and humility are the most important and most difficult character traits to acquire, and that you must continually work on them, I just want to add a final thought from this week's Torah portion, the beginning of the book of Exodus.

It is written: 'An angel of the Lord appeared to him in a blazing fire out of a bush . . . yet the bush was not consumed' [Exod. 3: 2].

[3] This section of the letter recalls Yehudah Leib Orlean's 1930 speech in Rabka, which Schenirer cited in abbreviated form in her remarks on the 1931 graduation, translated in Section II above, and discussed in Chapter. 4.

The two letters that comprise the word 'fire' are *alef* and *shin*. When the names of these letters are spelled out, the middle letters are *lamed* and *yod*—the letters of the word *li*, which means 'to me'. The *lamed* is the tallest letter in the Hebrew alphabet and the *yod* is the shortest, and that shows us that 'Wherever one finds a reference to the greatness of the Holy One, blessed be he, one also finds a reference to his humility' [*Meg.* 31*a*]. So the letters *lamed* and *yod* teach us that God is both the greatest and at the same time the most humble. As the holy Rashi comments on that passage, God appeared 'not from a tree but only in the bush, for "I am with him in distress" [Ps. 91: 14]'. This shows us modesty, divine providence, and faith in God.

The holy Torah ends with the words, 'and for all the great might and awesome power that Moses displayed before all Israel' [Deut. 34: 10]. This teaches us that the righteous man has the same power as God to perform miracles, since at the time of Creation God told the world to obey the words of the righteous, as our holy books state, and so the end of the Torah is linked with the beginning, 'In the beginning when God began to create the world', to teach us to have faith in God and in our sages.

And the prophetic books in the Torah end with Habakkuk, who ends his book: 'Lo, I will send the prophet Elijah to you' [Mal. 3: 23], and the first words of that chapter are 'O Lord! I have learned of your renown; I am awed' [Hab. 3: 2].[4]

As we know, Habakkuk was the son of the Shunamite whom Elisha the prophet revived after his death, so one can clearly see the power of the righteous.[5]

Respect for the righteous leads to the fear of God, as the sages say, 'And you shall fear God', also means 'including Torah scholars'. And we say this, too, every day, 'And they had faith in the Lord and his servant Moses' [Exod. 14: 31].[6]

[4] Schenirer, who was extremely ill at the time of writing of this letter and apparently working from memory, seems to have confused the two (similar) sources here; later publications often correct the error.

[5] In a comment on the verse 'I am awed' cited by Schenirer, *Zohar* i. 7*b* associates Habakkuk with the child brought back to life by Elisha: 'This verse was spoken when he saw his death and was restored to life by Elisha. Why was he named Habakkuk? Because it is written: "At this time next year, you will be *ḥoveket* (embracing) a son" (2 Kgs. 4: 16). He was the son of the Shunamite! Furthermore, there were two embracings—one by his mother, one by Elisha—as is written: He placed his mouth on his mouth (2 Kgs. 4: 34)' (trans. Matt, i. 47). Schenirer's citation of this teaching thus alludes not only to the power of the righteous but also, less directly, to death and the hope for resurrection.

[6] The teaching is attributed to Rabbi Akiva in BT *Pes.* 22*b*, where he teaches that the word *et* before God in the verse indicates that it includes the sages. The first section of the morning service (*Pesukei dezimrah*) includes a reading from Exod. 14: 30–15: 18; Schenirer quotes 14: 31.

And so Habakkuk ends with the words 'Lo, I will send the prophet Elijah to you', to show that redemption can come only through faith.

So, I end with the verses I always cite—not mine, but rather King David's—which should always accompany you:

Worship the Lord with gladness [Ps. 100: 2]! *I am ever mindful of the Lord's presence* [Ps. 16: 8]! *The beginning of wisdom is the fear of the Lord* [Prov. 9: 10]! *God's Torah is perfect, renewing the soul* [Ps. 19: 8]!

May the Lord guard your going and coming now and forever [Ps. 121: 8]. So may God hear our prayers, and send us soon the complete redemption, amen.

Your Sarah Schenirer,

Kraków, [in the week of] the Torah portion 'Shemot'

[Exod. 1: 1–6: 1], 5695 [Jan. 1935]

VII With Perseverance and Faith From Kraków to New York

SMALL AND INSIGNIFICANT were the beginnings, sixteen years ago, after Sukkot 5699 [1938]. The conditions were difficult, our raw material—the students—were young and these ideas were foreign to them. Our chances of success were slim indeed. But fervour and idealism raised the flag of Bais Yaakov on American soil, leading to the full realization of a dream.

The seminary began quietly exactly as had happened in Kraków— without pomp, in a small private room at 156 South Ninth Street in Williamsburg. Just one evening class, with seven students.

But the words of instruction were like a revelation. With great thirst the innocent American girls swallowed the light of the Torah. And from these meagre beginnings the number of students grew, and a few months later it was already necessary to move the seminary to a larger location with two rooms, on 240 Keap Street, and within a short time we had a staff of three of the best graduates of the Kraków seminary.

And very quickly the seminary also outgrew Keap Street. The young institution was blossoming. The reverberations could hardly have been anticipated. Jewish New York was recognizing a new world, the new-old idea of giving their daughters a Jewish education. Girls found their way to the seminary from near and far. And again, our overcrowding had, by the end of 5701 [1941], led us to the old yeshiva building on 505 Bedford Avenue.

In 5704 [1943/4] the seminary took the enormous step of moving into the present large school building at 143 South Eighth Street. Into 'a palace', as people then said. A vessel that held within it great potential and true blessing. And it was there on South Eighth Street that the glorious pages of the history of the Bais Yaakov Teachers' Seminary in America began to be written.

A Bais Yaakov high school was also established on South Eighth Street. It grew ceaselessly, both in numbers and in quality. Students streamed from the most distant cities in America. From Canada and Mexico. From Brazil, from Uruguay, from Argentina. Word spread all over America. Until the present day, when it has become an enormous educational institution with more than 500 students, a staff of forty teachers, a five-semester full-time seminary of the most exemplary rigour, an evening seminary, and the high school, in which the students acquire not only a clear and rigorous Torah education along with a first-class programme of government-sanctioned secular studies, but also preparation for life, instruction for future mothers in how to run a Jewish household.

But not only are studies, not only is knowledge the greatness of the seminary. The Bais Yaakov education is about living *yiddishkeit*, the whole package and entirety of Jewish life. This is something that leaves its mark on all who pass through it. And this something is really everything! It is the secret of its success! It forges the students in the seminary. It spreads its charm over and uplifts the external and material facilities of the school. It gives it the special Bais Yaakov character. And this is the reason that the students of the Bais Yaakov seminary are so immediately recognizable and unique.

We have come a long way since those beginnings in 5699 [1938/9]. The small seed has grown into an enormous tree. The seminary has become a major factor in Jewish community life in America. The students acquire there the riches of the living Torah, methodically and with pedagogical insight. There they absorb the fervour and the professional knowledge they need to be true teachers of a younger generation. And indeed we now have hundreds of graduates working as dedicated teachers in the Bais Yaakov schools and in various educational institutions throughout this country.

And Bais Yaakov continues to grow.

Again it is growing crowded within the walls of our seminary building. Everyone calls for expansion! The way forward is wide open. With decisiveness and faith we continue to build. Always growing, for Torah and *yiddishkeit*.

The responsibility is great. The burden heavy.

But the seminary proudly carries the banner of girls' education.

This book was reprinted by the
Bais Yaakov Teachers' Seminary in America with
the collaboration of the Committee for the Publication of the
Collected Writings of Sarah Schenirer,
of blessed memory.

The committee comprised the following former students of
Sarah Schenirer, of blessed memory, and
other graduates of the Kraków seminary:

Basya Bender
Vichna Kaplan
Chava Pincus
Chana Rottenberg
Batsheva Soloveitchik
Chava Wachtfogel
Rochel Zissner

As well as the following teachers who
presently serve in today's Bais Yaakov seminary and high school:
Chana Weisel Sarah Zeilberger

APPENDICES

APPENDIX A

From the Diary

Translator's Note

In 1932 the *Bais Yaakov Journal* began advertising Sarah Schenirer's upcoming *Collected Writings*, which promised to provide an autobiography of her childhood by 'the founder of the movement herself'. Along with this autobiography, the book would also feature a chapter called 'Pages from My Diary' with 'five chapters of interesting descriptions'. When the book was published the following year, however, it contained only the autobiography, now called 'Pages from My Life'; there was no mention of a diary. But 1955 saw the publication of the first volume of what would eventually be a four-volume Hebrew collection devoted to Sarah Schenirer and Bais Yaakov, *A Mother in Israel: The Writings of Sarah Schenirer, the Story of Her Life, Essays, Stories and Plays*. The inaugural volume was essentially a Hebrew translation of the *Collected Writings*, with seven additional essays by such Bais Yaakov leaders as Eliezer Gershon Friedenson, Dr Leo Deutschländer, Yehudah Leib Orlean, and others. Interestingly, this volume also included a section titled 'From the Diary', with eleven entries. The preface to the volume relates that the diary was translated from Polish by the Bais Yaakov teacher Bluma Vaytman.

But the story of the diary does not end there. In 2014 a shorter excerpt from Sarah Schenirer's Polish diary was published in *Cwiszn*, a quarterly magazine on Jewish literature and art.[1] The entries in the published Polish diary largely overlapped with those in the Hebrew translation, with the exception of the last entry, from 12 September (probably 1913). In the last stages of finishing this book, I was also given access to scans of roughly eighty handwritten pages of a Polish diary for the years 1910–13, which were being edited and assembled for publication (some of the pages had become loose, and their order was unclear). I was generously allowed to quote from these pages but was asked not to translate the document until after it had seen Polish publication. The diary, which strikes me for many reasons as authentic, sheds light not only on a difficult period of Sarah

[1] 'Sarah Schenirer: Diary (excerpts)', *Cwiszn*, 3–4, pp. 68–70.

Schenirer's life—her failed first marriage—but also on her motivations and character, as I discuss in Chapter 5. The published diary should also help explain why the diary may have been withdrawn from the manuscript before its 1933 publication: to take one example, Sarah Schenirer confides to her Polish diary that she went to see a play by the bohemian playwright Stanisław Przybyszewski, appending to that description a meditation on a midrash regarding King David. The Hebrew rendering of that entry omits any reference to her visiting a theatre, a secular practice that was criticized in Bais Yaakov. Despite this and other examples of censorship (or self-censorship), the Hebrew translation of the diary is still of interest, and I have translated the entire document in what follows. I also included a final entry, from 12 September, that appeared in the Polish version in *Cwiszn*. While the Hebrew translation ends with Sarah Schenirer expressing her desire to visit the Holy Land (a dream she was never to fulfil), the mood expressed in the 12 September entry is emblematic of the last entries of the fuller Polish diary, reflecting the writer's relief to be free of a marriage that brought her no joy.

Kraków, 5671 [1910/11]

With this entry I begin a sort of record of my life. Time is short, and so, with God's blessing, I will begin.[2]

I was born in the city of Kraków. By the time I was 7 years old I was already known as 'Little Miss Hasid', but I was talented at schoolwork. (Curious, where have those talents gone today?) And it is true that even though I never paid much attention at school or spent much time on my schoolwork at home, I still always got the first prize in every class. In first grade, *Children's Tales*, in second grade, another book of short stories, and likewise in other grades I received various books as prizes.

How sweet those moments were of school life! They are inscribed in my memory forever.

Once my teacher caught me unprepared for a class in nature, and she responded to the situation with these words: 'The best students in the class are Freilich, Probstein, Rubinstein, and Schenirer, but of all the students, Schenirer is

[2] This diary is translated from a Hebrew translation of excerpts from Schenirer's Polish diary, by Bluma Vaytman, which appeared, to my knowledge for the first time, in Rottenberg (ed.), *A Mother in Israel*, i. 31–46. The only exception is the last entry (pp. 379–80), which is translated from Polish.

also the best at slacking off—and that is really quite an accomplishment.' So there you have it, both the best and the laziest—two opposites!

And another incident from my school days that I will never forget. In second grade, the principal once visited us during a religion class and saw how no one could answer the question of why we fast on 10 Tevet—I was the only one who stood up and gave the correct answer, and the principal was astonished: how did you remember that? And she added 'Children, you should know that religion is a very important subject.' I was often praised in that way.

On holiday I would often go to Kalwaria, and the beautiful landscape and views would fill me with awe and wonder.

When I was in seventh grade my elder sister got married. My mind was preoccupied with finishing school and going on with my education, but these dreams all came to nothing.

Three years ago I was at the spa resort with a group of friends and family. How glorious that was, how splendid the surroundings! There was no limit to my happiness and wonder at the fact of God's glory at every step, in every vista, during this period when I finally had some time to reflect.

Whoever wishes to know the greatness of the Creator should go out to the fields, to the breadth of nature, and there, before the mighty mountains that stand strong against the storms, it will be evident how small and pitiful is a human being who can die at any moment, whenever God calls him back to him.

The time passed pleasantly. There was only one thing that bothered me: many people there allowed themselves to eat religiously problematic food, which might have mixed meat and milk, and when I didn't eat with them, they mocked me, laughing and calling me 'Little Miss Hasid'. But I am no longer ashamed of this nickname. And within me arose certain thoughts. Do! Act! Prove to everyone that in order to be a Jew one has to fulfil every positive commandment of the Torah, as many as the days of the year, whether one is in a glorious palace or a miserable hut, whether in the city or a village, in every place one must remember that it is no simple matter to live a Jewish life.

God took us out of the House of Bondage, where we were enslaved to the will of other humans, and instead made us his servants. If only I could explain to them that every one of the 613 commandments, even something as trivial as combing one's hair on the sabbath, is as significant as the prohibition against writing or smoking on the sabbath!

I saw them sitting around a table without having washed their hands before eating bread, without making a blessing on the food, without considering at all that despite their having paid for the food before them—they were sinning against God and the Jewish people.

Oh! If only I could have explained all this to them!

But they made me a butt of their mockery. No! I will gather my strength, and maybe, at some point, I will have the courage to speak these thoughts aloud. But can this really happen? I, who am shy to let out a word—but nevertheless, who knows?

Summer 5668 [1908]

That same summer I was with my friend in Krynica,[3] and again I was struck with wonder at the beauty of creation, the glory of nature, and the immensity of the Creator. I was especially taken with the mineral waters. I reflected again on the power of the Creator and his immense wisdom with which he also graced human beings, in order to learn how to make use of nature.

The previous winter I had occasion to visit Vienna for a festive trip, celebrating the sixtieth year of the emperor's reign. I saw amazing sights there. Pomp and splendour beyond comprehension, and such throngs of people I was worried I would be trampled. How much honour was granted to a mere human being, flesh and blood that was destined to rot in a grave along with every mortal beggar. It is true that the Creator commanded us to pay respect to human rulers, and even designated a blessing for a king, no doubt in order to help us realize that if one must honour a mortal king, how much more must we honour the King of Kings, who sees all our deeds, who knows all our thoughts, and from whom nothing is concealed. How much honour and respect must we pay to him for every breath, every step!

But just look and see how our Jewish girls pray, how listlessly, and with what boredom they mouth the words. Of course some of them are doing it just for the sake of their parents. As if God needed our prayers!

Sisters! When will you finally understand that the sole task of human beings is to serve the Lord with all their heart, with all their soul, and with all their might? A person must observe the Torah and the commandments not for the sake of their parents, and not for fear of Hell's flames, and not in order to reap any reward in the World to Come, but only out of deepest love of God, who chose us from among the nations and sanctified us with his commandments.[4]

[3] The largest resort town and spa in Poland, near the southern border.

[4] In the Polish diary, this entry ends: 'Enough for today though, the hour has struck two. Have

5675 [late 1914], 1.30 a.m.[5]

Despite my intention to write in this diary every day, I am so busy that I don't have even a few minutes for myself. Nevertheless, so many things have happened since I began writing it. The High Holy Days are already behind us. How many prayers and how many hot tears have been shed before his glorious throne. How awesome is this month of Tishrei! How well designed it is to inspire exaltation in us.

Consider! The *shofar* calls out: 'Awake, you sleepers! See! Our eternal Shepherd neither slumbers nor sleeps! He calls us to account! Beware! Better yourselves, as long as you are still able to!' Whether one knows it or not, something deep within every one of us shudders in awe at the sound of the *shofar*. We see before our eyes the fateful judgement, and some inner core is moved to better our ways.

And now Yom Kippur is upon us, the day in which we resemble angels on high, who do not eat or drink. We devote the entire day to serving God through our prayers, and he in turn gives us the full confidence that our sins have been forgiven.

What a fool is the person who sins all through the year, knowing that when Yom Kippur comes he will fast and pray all day—and expects that God will forgive his sins, so that the following day he can pick up where he left off.

But God cannot be so easily fooled! He sees into the secret places of our hearts, looks out through his 'telescope' from above, and laughs at the person who imagines that he can trick him.

And now comes Sukkot. How many elevated concepts are interwoven with this holiday! The person, recently cleansed of sin and transgression after the holy Yom Kippur, arrives at this festival of joy. For seven days of the holiday we praise God for sanctifying us with his commandments. Every time we enter the sukkah we are reminded of how the Creator protected us as we wandered through the wilderness, shielding us from beasts of prey, from snakes and scorpions, with a pillar of fire, like this very sukkah.

But this festival also arouses solemn thoughts in us. It reminds us that just as we now leave behind the solid walls of our strong houses and go out to live, as we have been commanded, in a temporary structure, so too will we be compelled at some point to leave our houses forever and enter another four walled structure,

I lost my mind! If my mother knew, but enough, to bed! And I solemnly promise myself to write something here every day.'

[5] This diary entry seems to be out of order, if the date given is correct.

in the grave, and be buried in the ground as a feast for worms. And so all who have foresight are already preparing for this spiritual journey, so that they will not arrive above with empty hands, for there is no status on high, no difference between rich and poor, between the wise man and the fool, between those with an illustrious pedigree and those without. Only fulfilling the 613 commandments can avert the terrible decree.

Yesterday there was a lecture at the university on the topic of 'The Masterworks of Polish Literature'.[6] A few Jewish girls were drawn to the lecture. But the ones who are truly to blame for attracting these girls are the secular organizations, where the sabbath is regularly desecrated. Brothers! Do you not recite every morning in the Shema the verse, 'lest your hearts be drawn and you go astray, and the heavens will cease their bounty and you will be lost from the good land'? These words paint an entirely accurate picture of our situation today. If we do not walk in the ways of God, he will scatter us among the nations and they will rule us. Do you not know that it is only because we have neglected the holy Torah that we are in exile now? Do you not know that without proper observance of Torah and the commandments, Judaism cannot survive!

5671 [1910/11], 1.00 a.m.

I am engaged to be married, may the timing be propitious.

They tried to persuade me to go to the theatre to celebrate the engagement.[7]

[6] The Polish diary describes this as a lecture at the People's (or Folk) University. Schenirer adds: 'Even though the talk was good, the topic was good, well organized, I felt odd, not in my element, but what can I do? Where can I go? There just aren't any organizations for Jewish girls.' The term 'People's University' refers to the early twentieth-century project of providing the masses with free or low-cost public lectures, courses, and other educational activities, based on earlier models in German and Scandinavia. The first People's University in Polish lands opened in 1900 near Warsaw, but Kraków soon became a centre of such activities. The diary also mentions a lecture on education by Wilhelm Feldman, a writer and socialist leader in the Kraków People's University who had been raised as an Orthodox Jew.

[7] The Hebrew translation of Schenirer's diary was edited not only to omit any mention of her unhappiness during her engagement, but also to leave the impression that she did not actually go to the theatre with her friends. The Polish diary reads, for this passage: 'In honour of my engagement, my girlfriends took me today to the theatre to see Przybyszewski's *Festivities of Life*. It was quite good, but I nevertheless felt a sort of distaste for Przybyszewski, a discomfort I must have expressed involuntarily.' Stanisław Przybyszewski (1868–1927) was a Polish playwright associated with decadent naturalism and Symbolism, who was well known among the bohemians in Kraków. His play *Festivities of Life* debuted there in 1910.

I remembered then the words of the *midrash* I read on the sabbath. King David, may peace be upon him, decided to get up each night at midnight to sing God's praises. The evil inclination came and said: 'Are you out of your mind? Other kings lie abed until noon, while you want to get up at midnight?' David answered him cunningly: 'You are right, I will get up and go to the theatre each night.' The evil inclination answered: 'Well, that satisfies me.' And David, once his most dangerous foe left him alone, would get up each night at midnight and write his eternal psalms, about people who left the ways of the Torah and made no effort to conquer their enemy, but this enemy conquered them and had them entirely in his power.[8]

And is it not true that our lives are like a theatre, with one person wearing a crown on his head and the second carrying the staff of a beggar? And when the curtain falls on the play of our life, don't the king and beggar go down to the same grave?

Rather than wasting time in a theatre, is it not better, then, to use our time for study and delving into the holy books? To know our role and mission on the face of this earth, recognizing that each day brings us closer to the end, when we will be called to account for each of our deeds, whether we are beggars or kings.

---

4 Nisan, 12.30 a.m.

Passover is already approaching. How great is this holiday, in which both rich and poor so carefully inspect each crack and corner! How eagerly we await this holiday!

Before my mind's eye stands Moses, the most modest man and the greatest, redeeming his brothers from Egyptian captivity, dividing the Red Sea so that the people might walk through it; and I see the trees that sprouted up in the seabed to quiet the hunger of their children, and Pharaoh chasing them, and the sea covering him and all his soldiers, and the nation, seeing the Egyptians drowning from the seashore, sang the Song of the Sea along with Moses. And Miriam did not want to hang back: she too took her tambourine in hand (so that the men would not hear a woman's voice!) and led the women in singing psalms. And after that, when they had camped in the wilderness, Moses spoke his first words to the people: 'You saw what I did to the Egyptians and I how carried you on the wings of eagles and brought you to me [God]. And now if you will heed my voice and

[8] The well-known story of King David waking at midnight to study Torah is described in BT *Ber.* 3*b*; for further details, see Ch. 8 n. 13 above.

keep my covenant you will be my chosen people, above all other nations [Exod. 19: 5].' And all the people shouted in unison: 'We will do and we will obey!'

But I can also envision the impatience of the people of Israel at having to wait ninety-four days before they heard the word of God again. And then—fire, thunder, and lightning, and the world was all atremble, and the voice of God was heard in the fire, speaking the Ten Commandments. And then Moses ascended Mount Sinai for forty days, and it was there that he acquired from the hand of God the Ten Commandments inscribed on the two tablets of stone, a sign of the eternal covenant with us, and he learned the entire Torah and all the commandments from the mouth of the Glorious One. Can any other nation boast of such an honour?!

5671 [1910]

Rosh Hashanah has come and gone. My God! How many tears, prayers, supplications, and songs of praise passed before you on that Day of Judgement. So, please, heed our prayers and lead us along the paths of truth! Accept the prayers of your children and bring us to Zion your city, so we may serve you truly and faithfully.

5671 [1910]

The holy day, Yom Kippur, is now behind us.

Oh, how effectively this day purifies us from sin, turning us into spiritual giants truly capable of mending our ways, proving to us that when a person is exalted he may rise even above the angels, as long as he triumphs over his evil inclinations. Oh! What a deep impression this day makes on the human soul!

And again the same thoughts. When will I be able to act on behalf of my sisters? If only I could achieve this, I would be the happiest person, seven times happier than any millionaire. Oh, what will it take for me to merit this great happiness, to see with my own eyes our daughters studying the essential teachings of Judaism, in the same way that they study the frivolous poetry of the gentiles? But have I lost my mind? How people would mock me then! They would point at me and say: 'Look at Little Miss Hasid, that backward, pathetic woman.'

2 p.m. on the eve of the sabbath

The sabbath is rapidly approaching. This is the wondrous day that takes us out of our backbreaking daily labour and grants us the highest spiritual pleasures that life offers. Sometimes I wonder whether other people are as deeply affected by this day as I am. When I open my books on the sabbath and discover there the words of Torah and Midrash and so on—I forget everything else in this world and float above it in a higher realm of pure delight.

12.30 a.m., following the sabbath

The winds of Enlightenment are blowing through the Jewish street. The hearts of young girls are captivated by propagandistic lectures on secular subjects.

If I only had the courage, I would lift my voice and cry bloody murder against this scandal. I would explain to them that secular subjects will never extinguish the flame that burns in the Jewish soul, which is fuelled and satiated only by the study of Torah. Secular subjects are to the soul as gold is to the body. Can gold satisfy physical hunger? Never! A parable that illustrates this tells of the king who wandered in the wilderness. His stores of food had run out. The desperate king was on the verge of dying of starvation. And suddenly he saw from afar a small hut and he hurried towards it and presented himself to the inhabitant as a king, asking for bread and promising the man in the hut that he would be richly compensated. When the man saw the king before him he was stunned, and he arose and brought the king a loaf of bread fashioned from gold. The king was enraged: 'Man, have you taken leave of your senses? Can gold satisfy a hungry belly?' Only then did the man understand that even a king cannot make a meal of golden food—just as the hungry Jewish souls get no nourishment from worldly subjects, since only its Creator knows what can nourish it. I doubt very much that any girl in the *gymnasium* could possibly be as happy as I am during those hours when I immerse myself in sacred books.

5671 [1910/11]

Does each of our Jewish women take honest stock of herself, with regard to what it means to educate a child? To educate an impressionable creature entrusted to us by the Creator and to make it into a person, a true Jew? Are parents aware that it is their own behaviour that makes the first and deepest impression on their child, for whom they serve as role models and exemplars?

And so it is of primary importance that parents ensure that they should act properly and nobly in their own lives, suffused by the spirit of Torah and tradition, in order to imprint the love of Torah and Judaism on their impressionable child. If only the mother would dedicate herself to educating her children while they are still very young and, instead of corrupting their souls with fairy tales about witches with red caps and other such nonsense, would teach them from their very first words the Shema and explain the true meaning of these words in simple and inspiring language, and tell their young children about all the wonders and miracles that God has done for us and what he requires from us—that would help the child truly grow up to achieve great things!

If one accustoms children to Torah commandments from infancy, it will not be difficult for them later to wash their hands before every meal, and such tasks will not be onerous or burdensome. And if one raises them on stories about great sages, like Rabbi Akiva and others who dedicated their lives and souls to Torah and sanctity, children will certainly understand the greatness of their nation, which lives for all eternity whether in its own land or in exile, since what it requires for its existence is not land but only the Torah.

5672 [1911]

When I look at my mother, her face ashen and her hair grey, it seems to me as if ten years have passed overnight.

My God! Can it be that I have lost my father? Yes, that seems to be the bitter truth.

On Friday I was left an orphan, bereft of my father.

Girls! You girls who still have a father and mother, remember well to obey them in everything they ask of you, since one day it will be too late for that, much too late. And even more so, to listen to our Father in heaven.

O you happy ones! Do you know that soon enough your joy will give way to sorrow? Just a moment ago you were happy and joyful, and here comes grief and pain. What, then, is the value of a human being, crown of creation, before that terrible master—Death?!

5672 [1911]

And now another Rosh Hashanah and Yom Kippur have passed. My God! Who knows what awaits us this year? As for me, I have only a single request: the redemption of Israel and the coming of the messiah, and nothing else beyond that.

5672 [1912]

Passover is approaching, the great festival of liberation. Liberation can only be appreciated by someone who was enslaved and is now free.

Unfortunately, we did not and still do not know how to properly appreciate this freedom. We do not understand how to truly serve the One who brought us to freedom.

Ah, if only we lived a life of Torah and tradition, where would we be now? There in our beautiful land, in rebuilt Jerusalem and in our Holy Temple! Unfortunately we have stopped our ears from hearing. For is it not practically within our reach, to be the masters of that land! No great achievement is necessary to get there, neither large sums of money nor the approval of other nations, but only a few words: 'We have sinned! Bring us back to you and we will return!' For if we observed just one sabbath fully, we would immediately be redeemed! So let us try it! Ah! Why am I talking to this paper? If I were at least able to persuade those Jews who call themselves 'nationalists' that not the affiliation as Jew but *only our Torah and its observance can bring us back to our Holy Land and to rebuilt Jerusalem* I would be the happiest woman on earth—but why do I keep talking to the wall?

I am taking it upon myself (without promising) to visit our Holy Land at any cost.

12 September

I'm in our familiar old Kraków again and again the tram's bells clang in my head. I can hardly believe that only yesterday I was in Zakopane.[9] I don't want to think about it anymore, so why did I have to rush home? Why didn't I fly away from there to somewhere far away? To forget about everything and just work only for my ideas. But what then? I have the courage to escape into my writing, but not into the world. Why am I so afraid? No one will ever read this. So to write briefly about my four days in that beautiful town. Four weeks after this great misfortune,[10] I knew that without a few days of rest I wouldn't be able to go on living, so I said to myself: 'To the mountains, my dear brother, freedom awaits you there.'[11] A long time ago, when I didn't expect this misfortune, I bought a

9 A Polish resort town.

10 An allusion to her divorce.

11 Schenirer quotes here from a well-known poem, later turned into a song, by the Polish poet and geographer Wincenty Pol (1807–72): 'To the mountains, my dear brother, adventure awaits you there.' Schenirer changes the word 'adventure' to 'freedom'.

discount ticket to Zakopane, since I've always dreamed of visiting that town. I left [Kraków] on 30 August and got to Sucha, where my younger sisters had spent an enjoyable four weeks, and then, with my youngest sister and two of her friends, we left for Zakopane. The impression the view of the Tatra Mountains made on me is inexpressible. Once again I've begun to admire the might of God, and to experience these thoughts. What am I, compared with these mighty mountains, that the Eternal should so constantly remember me? Oh! If all Jews would live exactly according to his holy will, we would be sitting in our holy Jerusalem now. Oh! But Mr Evil Inclination has won. Well then, if I were to write down all of my thoughts the ink would run out, so I shall be brief: we made the trip to Dolina Kościeliska, where I admired the huge caverns of Krakus and Smocza Jama and Racławicka etc. The next day we headed towards the goal of this whole journey, Lake Morskie Oko,[12] travelling by local cart for six hours. Along the way we admired a beautiful lake, and my admiration had no end. Try to imagine yourself by a huge lake with nearly green water, surrounded by towering mountains. We rested for a while there, I said the afternoon prayers, and then we went on to the mountains after an eleven-and-a-half-hour hike to Czarny Staw, which left an even more powerful impression because this beautiful lake was located so much higher and the mountains all around seemed to climb, as it were, all the way to heaven. At 10 p.m. we were back in Zakopane. We also visited the Strążyska valley, saw the Siklawa River and some waterfalls, and on Thursday to H. And then those few days on my own, in which I immersed myself so fully in God's miracles, came to an end. But enough for today.[13]

[12] The largest lake in the Tatra Mountains.

[13] This entry, which describes Schenirer's recovery after the dissolution of her marriage, was not published in Hebrew translation, but appeared in *Cwiszn*, 3–4, p. 70.

APPENDIX B

Sarah Schenirer's Family Tree

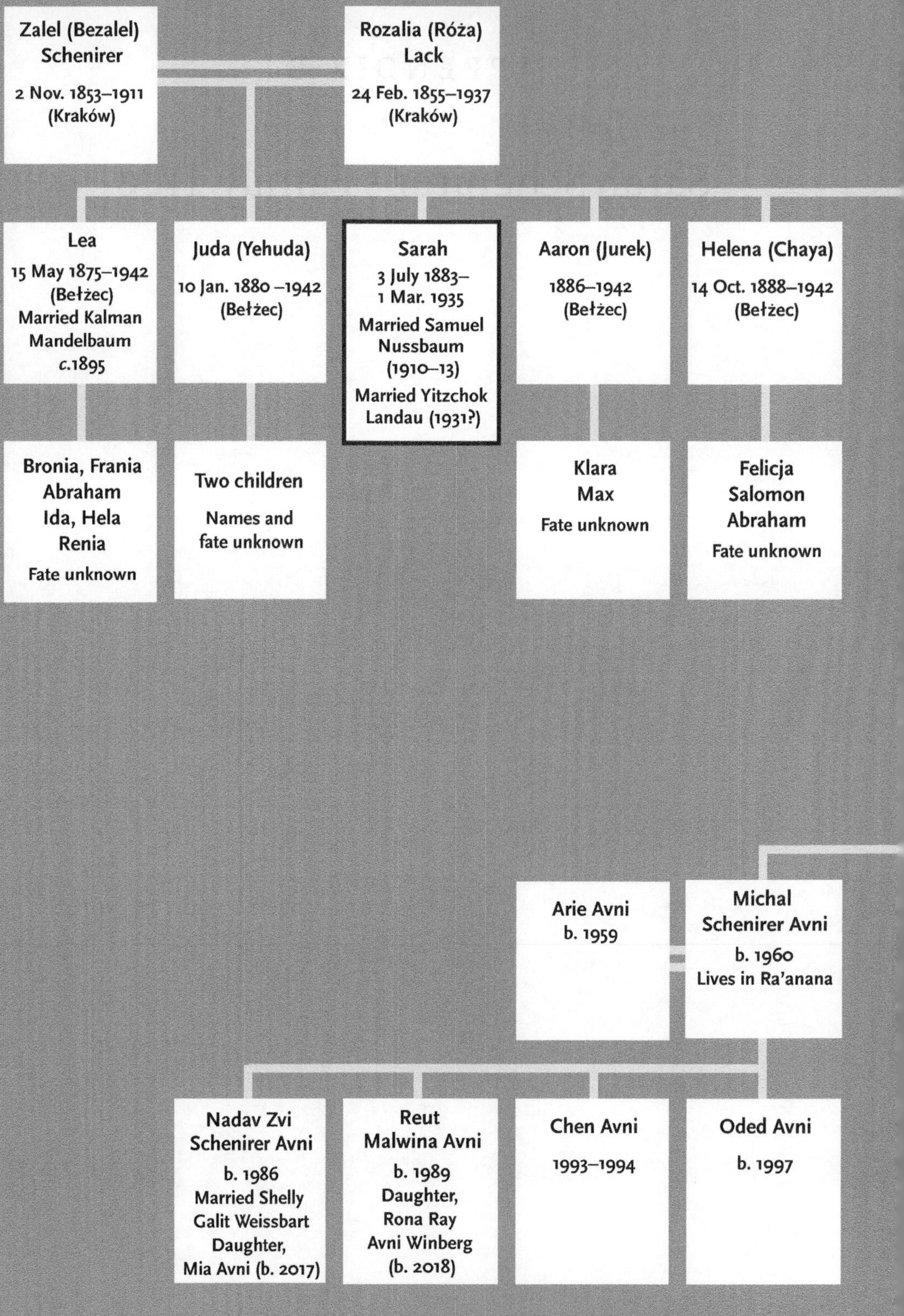
Zalel (Bezalel) Schenirer
2 Nov. 1853–1911 (Kraków)
Rozalia (Róża) Lack
24 Feb. 1855–1937 (Kraków)
Lea
15 May 1875–1942 (Bełżec)
Married Kalman Mandelbaum c.1895
Juda (Yehuda)
10 Jan. 1880 –1942 (Bełżec)
Sarah
3 July 1883– 1 Mar. 1935
Married Samuel Nussbaum (1910–13)
Married Yitzchok Landau (1931?)
Aaron (Jurek)
1886–1942 (Bełżec)
Helena (Chaya)
14 Oct. 1888–1942 (Bełżec)
Bronia, Frania
Abraham
Ida, Hela
Renia
Fate unknown
Two children
Names and fate unknown
Klara
Max
Fate unknown
Felicja
Salomon
Abraham
Fate unknown
Arie Avni
b. 1959
Michal Schenirer Avni
b. 1960
Lives in Ra'anana
Nadav Zvi Schenirer Avni
b. 1986
Married Shelly Galit Weissbart
Daughter, Mia Avni (b. 2017)
Reut Malwina Avni
b. 1989
Daughter, Rona Ray Avni Winberg (b. 2018)
Chen Avni
1993–1994
Oded Avni
b. 1997

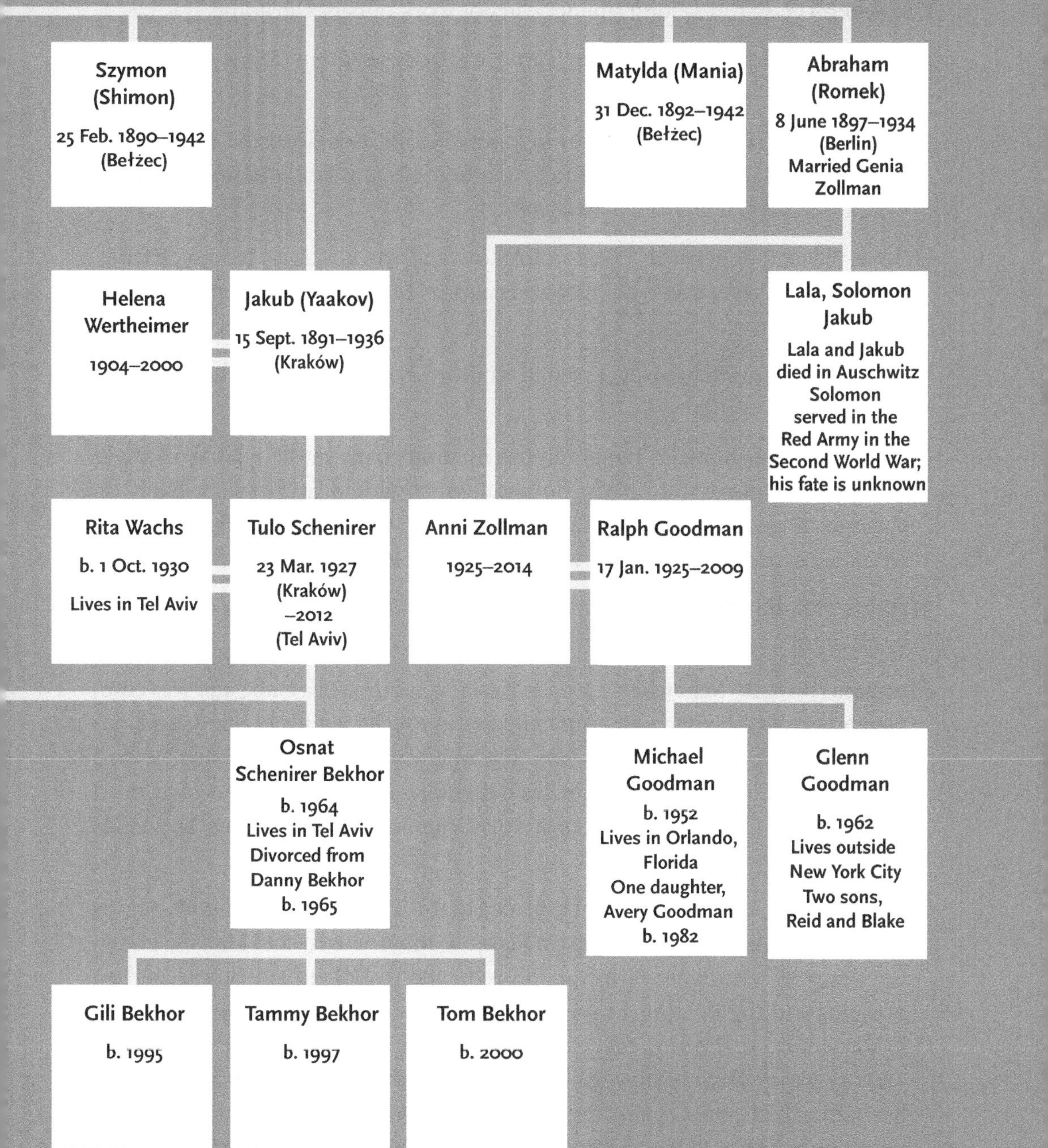
Szymon (Shimon)
25 Feb. 1890–1942 (Bełżec)
Matylda (Mania)
31 Dec. 1892–1942 (Bełżec)
Abraham (Romek)
8 June 1897–1934 (Berlin)
Married Genia Zollman
Helena Wertheimer
1904–2000
Jakub (Yaakov)
15 Sept. 1891–1936 (Kraków)
Lala, Solomon Jakub
Lala and Jakub died in Auschwitz
Solomon served in the Red Army in the Second World War; his fate is unknown
Rita Wachs
b. 1 Oct. 1930
Lives in Tel Aviv
Tulo Schenirer
23 Mar. 1927 (Kraków) –2012 (Tel Aviv)
Anni Zollman
1925–2014
Ralph Goodman
17 Jan. 1925–2009
Osnat Schenirer Bekhor
b. 1964
Lives in Tel Aviv
Divorced from Danny Bekhor
b. 1965
Michael Goodman
b. 1952
Lives in Orlando, Florida
One daughter, Avery Goodman
b. 1982
Glenn Goodman
b. 1962
Lives outside New York City
Two sons, Reid and Blake
Gili Bekhor
b. 1995
Tammy Bekhor
b. 1997
Tom Bekhor
b. 2000

Zalel (Bezalel) Schenirer Born in Tarnów. Worked in a shop owned by his wife.

Rozalia (Róża) Lack Born in Kraków, where her family had lived for a few generations; a shopkeeper.

Lea Schenirer Sarah's eldest sibling. Did not work outside the home.

Juda (Yehuda) Schenirer Lived in Tarnów, strictly religious. Made a living as a merchant.

Aaron (Jurek) Schenirer Lived in Leipzig until he was deported by the Germans in 1938 and returned to Kraków, where his family found him work in a bakelite factory. Traditionally religious.

Helena (Chaya) Schenirer Lived in Kraków and worked as a Hebrew teacher. Her husband had a metal goods warehouse on Mostowa Street. Orthodox but rather modern.

Szymon (Shimon) Schenirer Lived in Kraków. From 1935 to 1939 he served on the rabbinical court.

Jakub (Yaakov) Schenirer Fought in the Austrian army in the First World War and later in the Polish army. Subsequently worked at Holzer's Bank on Getrudy Street in Kraków. Married in 1925. Died suddenly of meningitis. Attended synagogue only on Jewish festivals but kept a kosher home.

Matylda (Mania) Schenirer Lived in Kraków and worked as a secretary in a brick factory in Bonarka.

Abraham (Romek) Schenirer Lived in Kraków, worked in a bank, and was completely secular. Married with four children, in 1934 he left for Berlin to undergo surgery, taking his family with him. The operation was unsuccessful; he died and was buried in Berlin. One of his daughters, Anni, survived the war in an orphanage in Germany. Her cousin Tulo Schenirer discovered this, and made contact with her in 1967.

Tulo Schenirer Born in Kraków. Displaced to the Kraków ghetto in 1941, he was later held in concentration camps in Płaszów, Mauthausen, and Linz III, a satellite camp of Mauthausen. In 1945 he returned to Poland and studied urban planning and engineering. In 1959 he emigrated to Israel, marrying Rita Wachs in December of that year. Rita was born in Lwów, but survived the war on false identity papers in Skierniewice in central Poland, together with her mother; her father had managed to flee to Hungary. After the war the family was reunited, and in 1949 they emigrated to Israel. Tulo and Rita had two children.

Sources

Indeks do ksiag spisu ludności Krakowa z r. 1890 (Index of the Population Census of Kraków from 1890), Litery M–Z (Obcy), p. 364.

Indeks do ksiag spisu ludności miasta Krakowa z r. 1910 (Index of the Population Census of Kraków from 1910), Litera S, p. 67.

Aleksander B. Skotnicki, *Polsko-izraelskie losy Tulo Schenirera i jego rodziny* (The Polish and Israeli Fate of Tulo Schenirer and His Family) (Kraków, 2009).

Spis ludności miasta Krakowa z r. 1890 (The Population Census of Kraków from 1890), Dz. VIII, vol. 35, nos. 69–88, pp. 298–9.

Spis ludności miasta Krakowa z r. 1910 (The Population Census of Kraków from 1910), Dz. VIII, vol. 16, no. 18, pp. 4–5.

APPENDIX C

Map of Sarah Schenirer's Kraków

1. 9 Krakowska Street, the probable birthplace of Sarah Schenirer. In 1890 the Schenirer family lived here together with a Catholic wet nurse, Mariana Kleńczyk, who was born in 1865 in a village near Myślenice, not far from Kraków.

   Source: *Spis ludności miasta Krakowa z r. 1890* (Population Census of Kraków), Dz. VIII, nos. 69–88, vol. 35, pp. 298–9.

2. 5 Krakowska Street, the next home of the Schenirer family.

   Source: *Spis ludności miasta Krakowa z r. 1910* (Population Census of Kraków), Dz. VIII, vol. 16, no. 18, pp. 4–5.

3. 1 Św. Katarzyny Street. Sarah Schenirer lived in Apartment 7 and held classes of the first Bais Yaakov school here. She is listed as 'Landau Sara, private tutor' in the index of Kraków residents.

   Source: *Spis mieszkanców Krakowa* (Index of Kraków Residents) 1933/4, Dz. VIII, vol. 66. p. 512.

4. 30 Augustiańska Street: the second location of the Bais Yaakov school.

   Source: Aleksander B. Skotnicki. *Polsko-izraelskie losy Tulo Schenirera i jego rodziny* (The Polish and Israeli Fate of Tulo Schenirer and His Family) (Kraków, 2009), 21.

5. 10 Św. Stanisława Street: the Bais Yaakov Seminary.

6. 8 Kordeckiego Street, Sarah Schenirer's home from 1935. She moved here to be near the seminary, despite the deterioration in her health.

   Source: *Bais Yaakov Journal*, 125 (1935), 13.

7. 40 Szeroka Street: the Rema Synagogue.

8. 23 Św. Gertrudy Street, the home of Sarah Schenirer's brother Jakub (Jacob) Schenirer; his son Tulo was also born here

   Source: *Spis mieszkanców Krakowa* (Index of Kraków Residents), Dz. VIII, vol. 105, p. 551.

9. 4 Smoleńsk Street: the Felicjanek Convent, to which Michalina Araten fled after leaving her hasidic home.

From Kraków Street Plan 1935, drawn by Stanisław Wyrobek and published in Kraków by Wydawnictwo Polonia / Zakład Graficzny Franciszek Zieliłski & Co. Reproduced with permission from Cartographia Cracoviana (Jakub Wojkowski).

0M 100 200 300 400 500 600 700 800 900 1KM

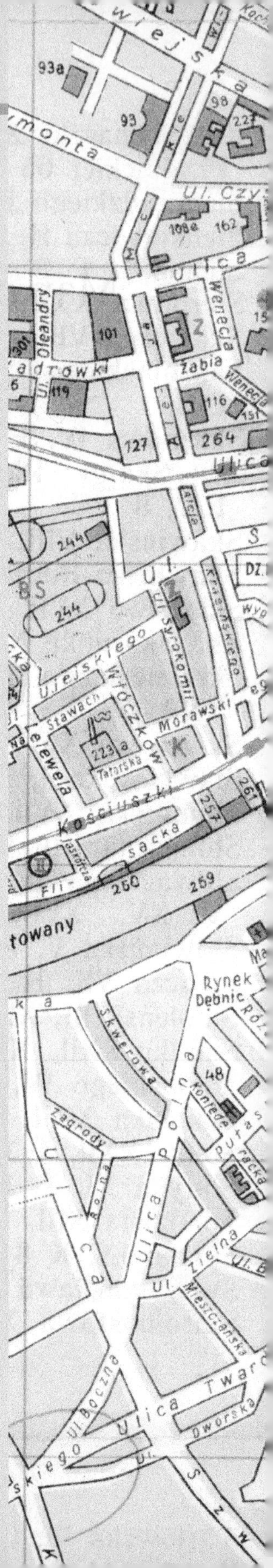

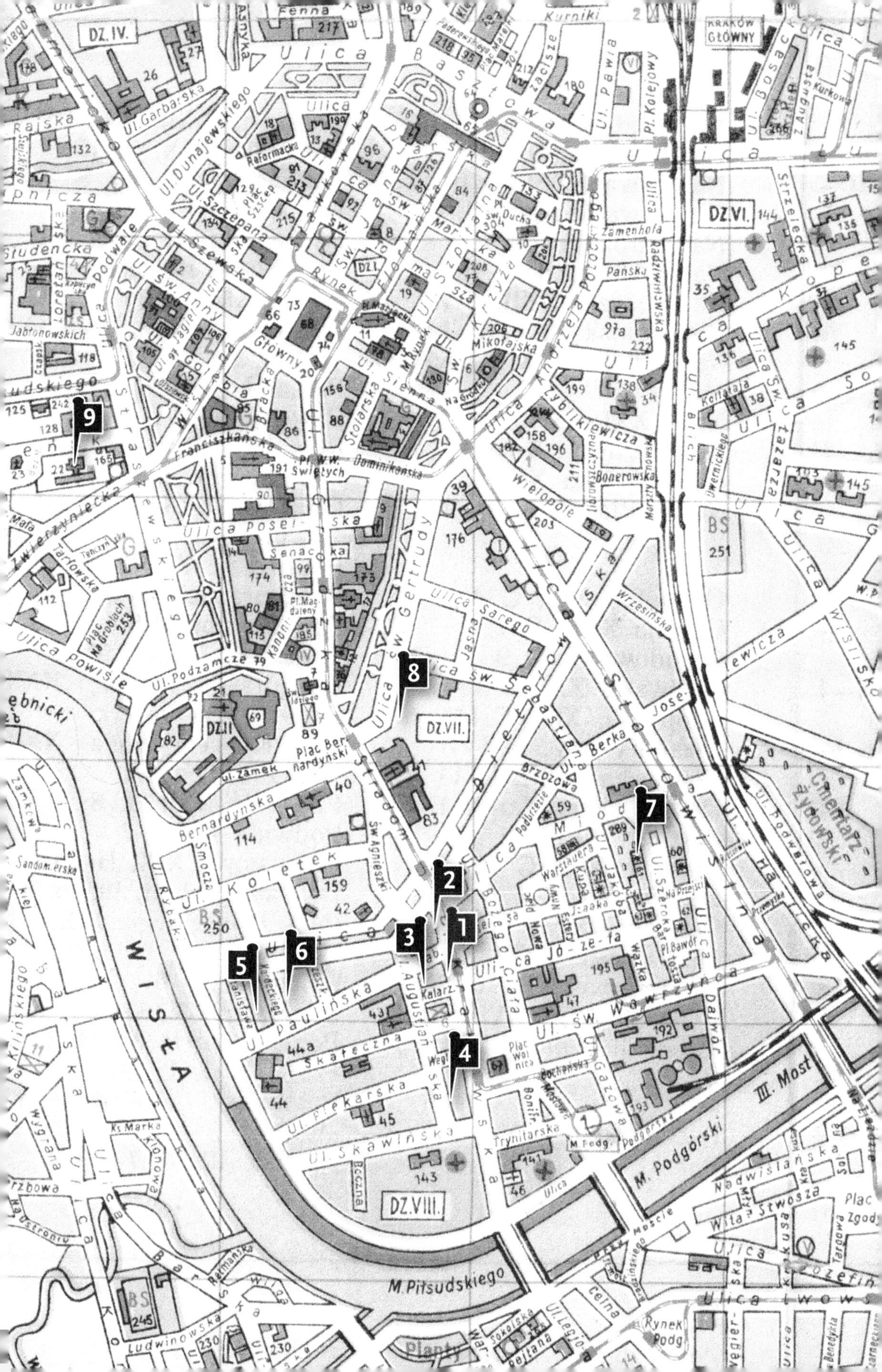

DZ. IV.
DZ.VI.
DZ.I.
DZ.II
DZ.VII.
DZ.VIII.
KRAKÓW GŁÓWNY
Ulica Basztowa
Ul. Garbarska
Ul. Dunajewskiego
Ul. Szczepańska
Ul. Szewska
Ul. św. Anny
Ul. Jagiellońska
Ul. Sławkowska
Ul. Floriańska
Ul. św. Jana
Ul. św. Marka
Ul. Szpitalna
Ul. św. Tomasza
Ul. św. Krzyża
Ul. Mikołajska
Ul. Sienna
Stolarska
Rynek Główny
Pl. Mariacki
Plac Szczepański
Reformacka
Studencka
Podwale
Jabłonowskich
Franciszkańska
Pl. W.W. Świętych
Dominikańska
Ulica Poselska
Senacka
Pl. Magdaleny
Kanonicza
Ul. Podzamcze
Ulica Powiśle
Zwierzyniecka
Plac Na Groblach
Ulica św. Gertrudy
Ulica Sarego
Ulica św. Sebastiana
Ul. Zamek
Plac Bernardyński
Bernardyńska
Stradom
Ul. Koletek
Smocza
Ul. Paulińska
Skałeczna
Ul. Piekarska
Ul. Skawińska
Ul. Augustiańska
Katarzyny
Bożego Ciała
Ul. św. Wawrzyńca
Plac Wolnica
Trynitarska
Ulica Józefa
Miodowa
Ul. Szeroka
Pl. Bawół
Ul. Berka Joselewicza
Brzozowa
Wielopole
Bonerowska
Ulica Zyblikiewicza
Ulica Andrzeja Potockiego
Ulica Starowiślna
Ul. Dietla
Wrzesińska
Zamenhofa
Pańska
Radziwiłłowska
Ul. Pawia
Pl. Kolejowy
Ulica Lubicz
Ulica Kopernika
Ul. Bosacka
Strzelecka
Ul. Blich
Kołłątaja
Ul. Podwale
Cmentarz Żydowski
III. Most
M. Podgórski
M. Piłsudskiego
WISŁA
Plac Zgody
Ulica Józefińska
Ulica Lwowska
Rynek Podg.
Celna
Nadwiślańska
Wita Stwosza
Ludwinowska
Barska
Zamkowa
Sandomierska
Ks. Marka
Powstańców
Nadwiślańska
1
2
3
4
5
6
7
8
9

APPENDIX D

Maps of Bais Yaakov Schools, 1935

The following two maps appeared in Leo Deutschländer, *Tätigkeitsbericht der Beth Jacob Zentrale* (Vienna, 1935), and are reprinted courtesy of the Leo Baeck Institute.

BETH JAKOB-SCHULEN IN POLEN

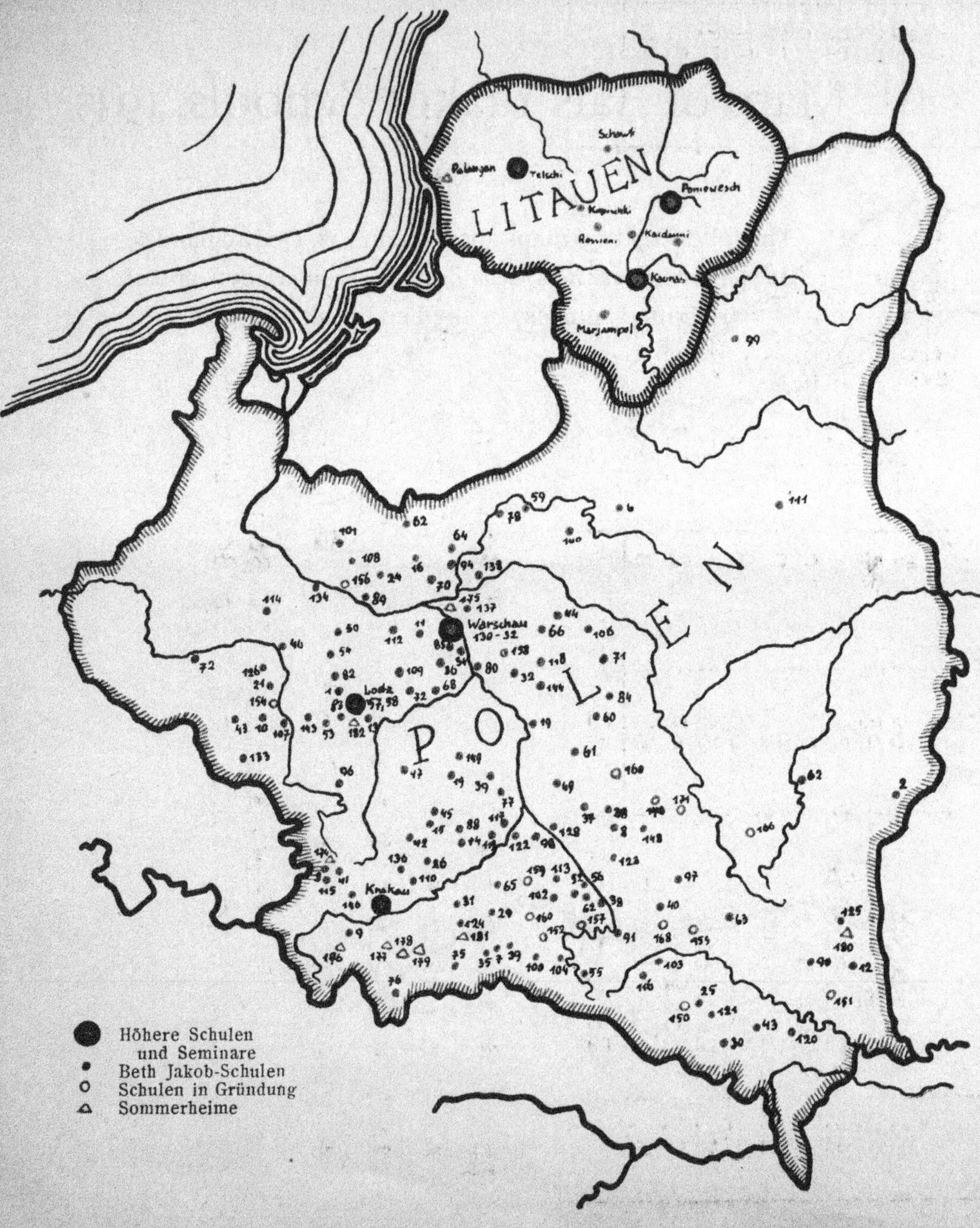

UND LITAUEN

1 Aleksandrow
2 Annopol
3 Bendzin
4 Biala Podlaska
5 Biala Rawska
6 Bialystok
7 Biecz
8 Bilgoraj
9 Bielitz
10 Blaszki
11 Blonie
12 Bodzanow
13 Brzeziny
14 Busk
15 Chenciny
16 Ciechanow
17 Ciechocinek
18 Czyzew
19 Demblin
20 Dlugoschodlo
21 Dobra
22 Dobrzyn
23 Dombrowa
24 Dobrin
25 Drohobycz
26 Dzialoszyce
27 Falenica
28 Frampol
29 Dembica
30 Dolina
31 Dombrowa
32 Garwolin
33 Gombin
34 Gora Kalwarja
35 Gorlice
36 Grojec
37 Janow b. Lublin
38 Jaroslaw
39 Jaslo
40 Jaworow
41 Jaworzno
42 Jendrzejow
43 Kalusz
44 Kaluszyn
45 Kielce
46 Kolo
47 Konskie
48 Krakau
49 Krakau
50 Krakau
51 Krasnik
52 Kutno
53 Lagow
54 Lancut
55 Lask
56 Lenczyce
57 Lesko
58 Lezajsk
59 Lodz
60 Lodz
61 Lodz
62 Lodz
63 Lodz
64 Lomza
65 Lubartow
66 Lublin
67 Luck
68 Lwow
69 Mekow
70 Mielec
71 Minsk
72 Mlawa
73 Mogelnice
74 Mosciska
75 Nasielsk
76 Miendzyrsec
77 Nowe-Miasto
78 Nowy-Dwor
79 Nowykorczyn
80 Nowy-Soncz
81 Nowytarg
82 Opatow
83 Ostrolenka
84 Ostrowiec
85 Otwock
86 Ozarow
87 Ozorkow
88 Pabianice
89 Parczew
90 Piaseczno
91 Pilica
92 Piaski
93 Pinczow
94 Plock
95 Plodhajce
96 Przemysl
97 Przeworsk
98 Prytyk
99 Pultusk
100 Racionz
101 Radomsk
102 Rawa-Ruska
103 Rozwadow
104 Rudniki
105 Rymanow
106 Rypin
107 Rzeszow
108 Sambor
109 Sanok
110 Serock
111 Siedlce
112 Sieradz
113 Sirpc
114 Skiernjewice
115 Slominiki
116 Slonim
117 Sochaczew
118 Sokolow
119 Sompolno
120 Sosnowiec
121 Stary-Sambor
122 Staszow
123 Stoczek
124 Stopnica
125 Stanislawow
126 Stryj
127 Taronbrzeg
128 Tarnogrod
129 Tarnow
130 Tarnopol
131 Turek
132 Tlustle
133 Ulanow
134 Warka
135 Warschau
136 Warschau
137 Warschau
138 Wieruszow
139 Wloclawek
140 Wlodzislaw
141 Wolbrom
142 Wolomin
143 Wiszkow
144 Wiszogrod
145 Wysokie
146 Zaklikow
147 Zawichost
148 Zdunska-Wola
149 Zelichow
150 Zychlin
151 Chrzanow
152 Suchedniow
153 Szczebrzeszyn
154 Sziedlowiec
155 Boryslaw
156 Buczacz
157 Brzezow
158 Chorzele
159 Warta
160 Grodek-Jag.
161 Dobryzin
162 Dubiecko
163 Kolbiel
164 Kolbuszowa
165 Krasnystaw
166 Krynica
167 Laskarcew
168 Modliborzyce
169 Nowemiasto
170 Przasnysz
171 Radziechow
172 Skarzysko
173 Sadowawisnia
174 Strzyzow
175 Turobin
176 Tyszowce
177 Wlodowa
178 Zamosc
179 Bendin
180 Dluga Siedła
181 Jeksma
182 Jordanow
183 Rabka
184 Skawa
185 Tarnopol
186 Tarnow
187 Theodory

Neueröffnet wurden 38 Schulen

Map 1. Poland and Lithuania.
The largest circles mark high schools, trade schools, and teachers' seminaries (with three each in Lithuania and Poland, including the seminary in Kraków). The small dots indicate Bais Yaakov schools of other varieties (generally afternoon schools, with a few all-day elementary schools in larger cities). The hollow circles indicate schools still being formed. The triangles are summer homes and colonies, most of them in the resort area south of Kraków, but one near Warsaw and the other near Łódź. The note at the bottom of the list of locations indicates that thirty-eight schools were in the process of opening.

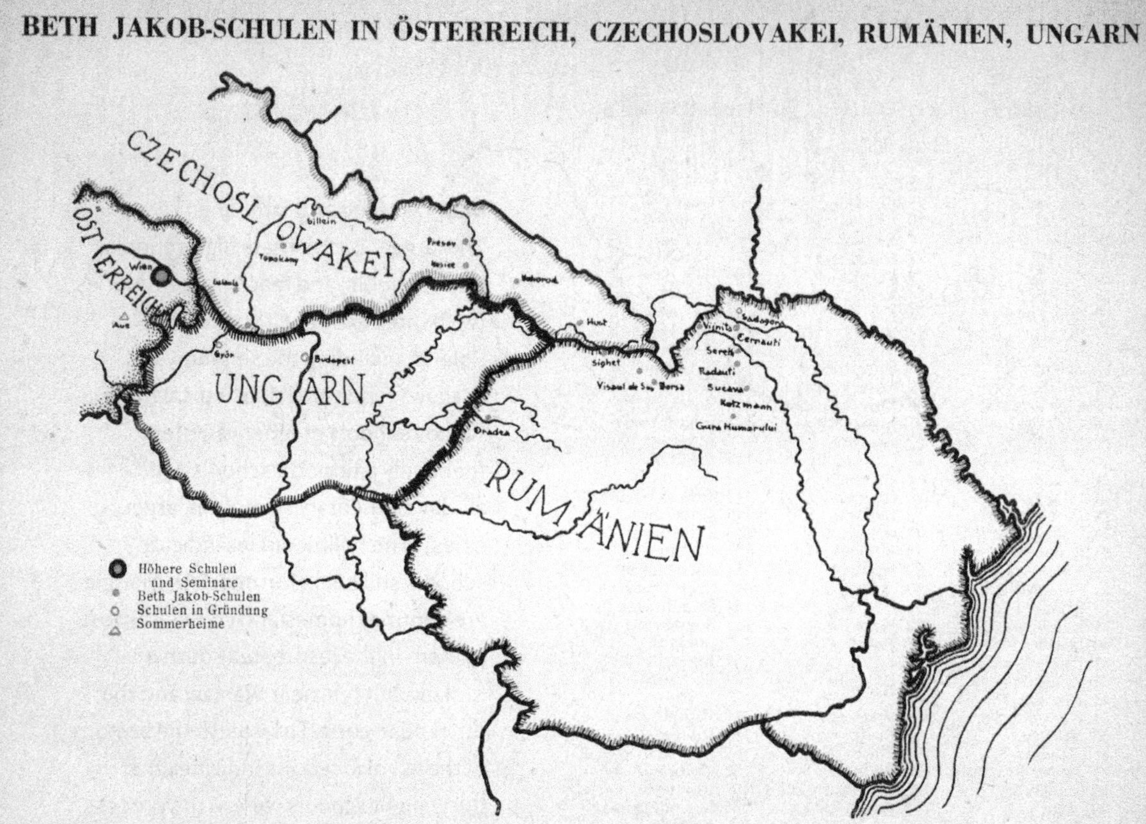

Map 2. Austria, Czechoslovakia, Romania, and Hungary. This map, which uses the same symbols as Map 1, shows the Bais Yaakov schools in Austria, Czechoslovakia, Romania, and Hungary. It shows only one seminary, in Vienna (with a summer home nearby), but in 1935, the year the map was published, another seminary opened in the Romanian city of Cernauti (better known to Jewish historians as Czernowitz, and presently a Ukrainian city named Chernivtsi).

APPENDIX E

The Bnos Agudath Israel Anthem

The Bnos Agudath Israel anthem first appeared in *Bais Yaakov Journal*, 46 (1929), 6, and was reprinted, with music, *in Bais Yaakov Journal*, 67–68 (1931), 7. It also appeared that year in a songbook entitled *Undzer gizang: lider far bais yaakov shuln, basya farbandn un bnos agudas yisrael organizatsies* (Our Melodies: Songs for Bais Yaakov Schools, Basya Associations, and Bnos Agudath Israel Organizations), published by the Bais Yaakov Press (Łódź, 1931), 4–5. The songbook also included an anthem for Bais Yaakov and one for Basya, both written by Eliezer Schindler, along with a poem by Miriam Ulinover set to music, entitled 'Antikelekh' (Precious Objects). From the Library of the YIVO Institute for Jewish Research, New York

Moderato
Mir di ojs der wajtte techter fi num ojs der wajlten folk, be ten dich Jsru els wech ter
p
in zer ar bet gib er folg hit uns up fin freinde knechsoff nemfu Ju les uns a rojs mir'n
mf
flum een dich in kinds hoze in dojn gaist in ja nuno hojs
piu mosso
stark in mech tig, grojs in lech tig
f
un zer stru bin ojt er folg zajn ye tuf je di alt nu je toj re got in i dier folk
5

– הימן –

פון בנות-אגודת-ישראל

א.

מיר די אויסדערוויילטע טעכטער
פונים אויסדערווייילטן פאלק,
בעטן דיך ישראלס וועכטער,
אונדזער אַרבעט גיב ערפאלג;
היט אונדז אָפּ פון פרעמדער קנעכטשאפט,
נעם פון גלות אונדז ארויס,
מיר-ן פלאַנצן דיך אין קינד-הארץ
און דיין גייסט אין יעקב-ס הויז.
שטאַרק און מעכטיק גרויס און ליכטיק
אונדזער שטרעבן, ציל, ערפאלג:
זיין געטרייע די אַלט-נייע:
תורה, ג–ט און יידיש פאלק!

ב.

קום צו אונדז, א. וויטע שוועסטער,
האסט געבלאנדזשעט שוין גענוג,
וואַרף די אַלטע עבודה זרה-ס,
קום אין אַלטער היים צוריק;
זיי אַ גוטע און פרומע טאכטער,
גיב דיין שטים אין אונדזער כאר,
זיי אַ גוטע, פרומע מוטער,
פאַר-ן צוקונפטיקן דור.
שטאַרק און מעכטיק, גרויס און ליכטיק
אונדזער שטרעבן, ציל, ערפאלג:
זיין געטרייע די אַלט-נייע:
תורה, ג–ט און יידיש פאלק!

ג.

צניעות פון דער מוטער שרה
און דער מוטער רבקה-ס גייסט,
טרערן פון דער מוטער לאה
און דער מוטער רחל-ס טרייסט;
און דער מוטער חנה-ס תפילה
און דער שוועסטער יהודית שווערד –
היט דאָס אַלעס, היט אין לעבן
און אין האַרצן זיי עס ווערט!
שטאַרק און מעכטיק, גרויס און ליכטיק
אונדזער שטרעבן, ציל, ערפאלג;
זיין געטרייע די אַלט-נייע:
תורה, ג–ט און יידיש פאלק!

שמואל נאדלער

We the chosen daughters
Of a chosen folk,
Implore you, Israel's Guardian,
Grant success to our work.
Save us from an alien bondage,
Release us from our exile's yoke,
In children's hearts we will implant you,
Let your spirit fill Jacob's home.
Fierce and mighty, great and bright
Are our efforts, aims, and goal
To be faithful to the old-new
Torah, God, and Jewish folk!

Come to us, you distant sisters
You have wandered too long
Throw away your tired idols
Come back to the ancient home;
Be a good and pious daughter,
To our chorus lend your tone.
Be a good and pious mother,
For the generation yet to come.
Fierce and mighty, great and bright
Are our efforts, aims, and goal
To be faithful to the old-new
Torah, God, and Jewish folk!

Modesty from Mother Sarah,
Mother Rebecca's spirit, too,
The tears of Mother Leah,
Mother Rachel's comforting word;
And Mother Hannah's fervent prayer,
And Sister Judith's sword—
Protect these with your actions,
And be worthy of them in your heart.
Fierce and mighty, great and bright
Are our efforts, aims, and goal
To be faithful to the old-new
Torah, God, and Jewish folk!

Bibliography

ADLER, ELIYANA R., *In Her Hands: The Education of Jewish Girls in Tsarist Russia* (Detroit, 2011).

AGUDAS JISROEL (Provisional Committee), *Agudas Jisroel: Berichte und Materialien* (Frankfurt am Main, 1912).

AGUDATH ISRAEL, *Programm und Leistung: Keren Hathora und Beth Jakob 1929–37: Bericht an die dritte Kenessio Gedaulo*, conference publication (London and Vienna: Keren Hathora-Zentrale, 1937).

A.L., 'Łódź, Hamburg, Warsaw' (Yid.), *Bais Yaakov Journal*, 43 (1929), 1.

ALIZA, B., 'Awake!' (Yid.), *Bais Yaakov Journal*, 1 (1923), 7.

'After the Second World Congress' (German), *Der Israelit*, 39 (26 Sept. 1929), 1–3.

ANDERSON, BENEDICT, *Imagined Communities: Reflections on the Origin and Spread of Nationalism* (London, 1991).

'Answers to Our First Survey' (Yid.), *Bais Yaakov Journal*, 83 (1932), 13.

ATKIN, ABRAHAM, 'The Beth Jacob Movement in Poland (1917–1939)' (Ph.D. diss., Yeshiva University, 1959).

'Aus der Frauentagung', *Der Israelit*, 39 (26 Sept. 1929), 5.

BACH, ARI, 'Why Beth Jacob?', *Beth Jacob Monthly*, 1 (1954), 14–15.

BACON, GERSHON C., *The Politics of Tradition: Agudat Yisrael in Poland, 1916–39* (Jerusalem, 1996).

—— 'The Rabbinical Conference in Kraków (1903) and the Beginnings of Organized Orthodox Jewry', in David Assaf and Ada Rapoport-Albert (eds.), *'Let the Old Make Way for the New': Studies in the Social and Cultural History of Eastern European Jewry Presented to Immanuel Etkes*, vol. ii: *Haskalah, Orthodoxy, and the Opposition to Hasidism* (Jerusalem, 2009), 199–225.

'Bais Yaakov, Sign Up to Be an Advance Subscriber' (Yid.), *Bais Yaakov Journal*, 89 (1932), 5–6.

BAKST, BAILA, 'In a Place Where There Are No Men' (Heb.), in Aryeh Bauminger (ed.), *A Mother in Israel: Memorial Book for Sarah Schenirer* [Em beyisra'el: sefer zikaron lesarah shenirer] (Benei Berak, 1983), 143–4.

BAS TOVIM, RACHEL, 'Give Us a Holding!' (Yid.), *Bais Yaakov Journal*, 120 (1934), 1.

BAUMEL, JUDITH TYDOR, and JACOB J. SCHACTER, 'The Ninety-Three Bais Yaakov Girls of Cracow: History or Typology?', in Jacob J. Schacter (ed.), *Reverence, Righteousness, and Rahamanut: Essays in Memory of Rabbi Dr. Leo Jung* (Northvale, NJ, 1992), 93–130.

BAUMINGER, ARYEH (ed.), *A Mother in Israel: Memorial Book for Sarah Schenirer* [Em beyisra'el: sefer zikaron lesarah shenirer] (Benei Berak, 1983).

BECHHOFER, SHOSHANA M., 'Ongoing Constitution of Identity and Educational Mission of Bais Yaakov Schools: The Structuration of an Organizational Field as the Unfolding of Discursive Logics' (Ph.D. diss., Northwestern University, 2004).

BENISCH, PEARL, *Carry Me in Your Heart: The Life and Legacy of Sarah Schenirer, Founder and Visionary of the Bais Yaakov Movement* (Jerusalem, 1991).

—— *To Vanquish the Dragon*, 2nd edn. (Jerusalem, 1991).

BEN-RIVKAH, 'Two Kinds of Jewish School' (Yid.), *Bais Yaakov Journal*, 3/3 (1926), 78–80.

BERGER, BENJAMIN, *On the Education of Girls* [Amirah levat ya'akov: devarim aḥadim le'avot ve'imahot al ḥinukh habanot] (Budapest, 1924).

BERGNER, HINDE, *On Long Winter Nights: Memoirs of a Jewish Family in a Galician Township, 1870–1900*, trans. and ed. Justin Daniel Cammy (Cambridge, Mass., 2005).

BIALE, RACHEL, *Women and Jewish Law* (New York, 1984).

BIRNBAUM, NATHAN, *In Exile among Jews* [In goles bay yidn] (Zurich, 1920).

BIRNBAUM, SOLOMON, 'Lady or Woman' (Yid.), *Bais Yaakov Journal*, 128 (1935), 10.

—— 'A Problem' (Yid.) [on textbooks for Orthodox boys], *Bais Yaakov Journal*, 94–5 (1932), 32.

BOYARIN, DANIEL, *Unheroic Conduct: The Rise of Heterosexuality and the Invention of the Jewish Man* (Berkeley, Calif., 1997).

BRISTOW, EDWARD J., *Prostitution and Prejudice: The Jewish Fight against White Slavery, 1870–1939* (New York, 1983), 234–6.

BROWN, BENJAMIN, 'On the Value of Torah Study for Women in the Hafets Hayim's Writings' (Heb.), *Diné Israel: Studies in Halakhah and Jewish Law*, 24 (2007), 79–118.

'By-Laws of the Beth Jacob Schools', RG 49.18.1, YIVO Digital Archives, 1–2.

CAPLAN, BEATRICE LANG, 'Shmuel Nadler's *Besht-Simfonye*: At the Limits of Orthodox Literature', in Justin Cammy, Dara Horn, Alyssa Quint, and Rachel Rubinstein (eds.), *Arguing the Modern Jewish Canon: Essays on Literature and Culture in Honor of Ruth R. Wisse* (Cambridge, Mass., 2008), 599–612.

CHEVRONI, M. 'The Unacknowledged Heritage: The Contribution of German Chareidim to the New Yishuv', *De'ah vedibur* (2 Jan. 2005); <http://chareidi.org/archives5765/voero/VRH65features2.htm>.

COHEN, NAOMI G., 'Women and the Study of Talmud', in Joel B. Wolowelsky (ed.), *Women and the Study of Torah: Essays from the Pages of Tradition* (Hoboken, NJ, 2001), 1–17.

'Communiqué from the Bais Yaakov Central Office in Kraków' (Yid.), *Di Yidishe shtime* (27 Jan. 1928), 4.

'A Conference of the Bais Yaakov Girls' Schools' (Yid.), *Haynt* (18 Feb. 1930), 12.

'Curious News from across the Country' (Yid.), *Heyntige nayes*, 123 (31 May 1934), 3.

DANSKY, MIRIAM, *Rebbetzin Grunfeld: The Life of Judith Grunfeld, Courageous Pioneer of the Bais Yaakov Movement and Jewish Rebirth* (New York, 1994).

'A Debate Evening Concerning the Content of the *Bais Yaakov Journal* (Report on a Gathering in the Seminary)' (Yid.), *Bais Yaakov Journal*, 82 (1932), 4.

DEUTSCHLÄNDER, LEO (ed.), *Bajs Jakob: Sein Wesen und Werden* (Vienna, 1928).

—— (ed,), *The History of the Beth Jacob Schools* (Vienna, 1933).

—— 'Sarah Schenirer and Bais Yaakov' (Yid.), *Bais Yaakov Journal*, 125 (1935), 9–11.

—— 'The Second World Congress of Agudath Israel and the World Congress of Orthodox Women' (Yid.), *Bais Yaakov Journal*, 46 (1929), 1–2.

—— *Tätigkeitsbericht der Beth Jacob Zentrale* (Vienna, 1935).

EISENSTEIN, MIRIAM, *Jewish Schools in Poland, 1919–39: Their Philosophy and Development* (New York, 1950).

ELEFF, ZEV, 'The Vanishing Non-Observant Orthodox Jew', *The Lehrhaus*; <http://www.thelehrhaus.com/scholarship/2017/6/7/the-vanishing-non-observant-orthodox-jew>.

ELIAV, MORDECHAI, *I Believe* [Ani ma'amin] (Jerusalem, 1965).

ELLINSON, ELYAKIM (GETZEL), *Women and the Commandments* [Ha'ishah vehamitsvot] (Jerusalem, 1977).

ENGEL, YOSEF, *Sefer otserot yosef* (Vienna, 1921).

ETZION, ISAAC RAPHAEL HALEVI, 'Yavneh Schools in Lithuania' (Heb.), in Natan Goren (ed.), *The Jews of Lithuania* [Yahadut lita], vol. ii (Tel Aviv, 1972), 351–70.

'The Examinations in the Bais Yaakov Seminary' (Yid.), *Bais Yaakov Journal*, 81 (1931), 13.

Exodus Rabbah: Midrash Rabbah Mevuar, ed. Abraham Zvi Steinberger (Jerusalem, 1991).

FEYGENBERG, RACHEL, 'The Agudah and the Difficult Problem of Educating Girls' (Yid.), *Der Moment* (26 May 1929), 6.

FISCHER, ELLI, '"Name, Language, and Dress": The Life Cycle of a Well-Known but Nonexistent Midrash'. Unpublished paper presented at the conference 'Always Hungarian: The Jews of Hungary through the Vicissitudes of the Modern Era', Bar-Ilan University, 31 May 2016.

FOXMAN, JOSEPH, 'Faigl fun vilner geto', *Der Amerikaner* (9 Aug. 1957), 12. Published in English as 'From the Pages of Tradition: Faigel dem Rov's', trans. and ed. Shnayer Z. Leiman, *Tradition*, 45/3 (2012), 89–94.

FREUD, SIGMUND, 'The Uncanny', in *The Uncanny*, trans. David McClintock (London, 2003), 123–62.

FRIEDENSON, ELIEZER GERSHON, 'Agudath Israel and "Bais Yaakov"' (Yid.), *Bais Yaakov Journal*, 19–21 (1925), 127.

—— 'Letter from the Editor' (Yid.), *Bais Yaakov Journal*, 1 (1923), 2.

—— *Mama's Will: A Collection for Children and Youth* [Di mames tsavo'e: zamlbukh far kinder un yugnt] (Łódź, 1936).

FRIEDENSON, ELIEZER GERSHON, 'On the Hundredth Issue of the Journal' (Yid.), *Bais Yaakov Journal*, 98–99 (1933), 1.

—— 'Pictures and Notes from My Visit to Rabka' (Yid.), *Bais Yaakov Journal*, 46 (1929), 16–17.

—— 'Sarah Schenirer and the Pioneering Spirit' (Yid.), *Bais Yaakov Journal*, 148 (1938), 1.

—— 'The Tongue in a Mother's Mouth' (Yid.), *Bais Yaakov Journal*, 74 (1931), 4.

FRIEDENSON, JOSEPH, 'The Bais Yaakov Girls' Schools in Poland' (Heb.), in Zevi Scharfstein (ed.), *Jewish Education and Culture in Europe Between the Two World Wars* [Haḥinukh vehatarbut ha'ivrit be'eiropah bein shetei milḥamot ha'olam] (New York, 1957), 51–82.

—— 'The Movement from Its Beginnings until after the Holocaust' (Heb.), in Aryeh Bauminger (ed.), *A Mother in Israel: Memorial Book for Sarah Schenirer* [Em beyisra'el: sefer zikaron lesarah shenirer] (Benei Berak, 1983), 125–34.

—— 'Sarah Schenirer: The Mother of Generations'; <https://web.archive.org/web/20120204224811/http://www.tzemachdovid.org/gedolim/jo/tworld/schenirer.html>.

FRIEDMAN, MENACHEM, *The Haredi Woman* [Ha'ishah haḥaredit] (Jerusalem, 1988).

—— 'Haredim Confront the Modern City', in P. V. Medding (ed.), *Studies in Contemporary Jewry*, 2 (Bloomington, Ind., 1976), 74–96.

FRIEDMAN, PHILIP, 'Preliminary and Methodological Problems of the Research on the Jewish Catastrophe in the Nazi Period', *Yad Vashem Studies*, 2 (Jerusalem, 1958), 95–131.

FRIEMAN, SHULAMIS, 'Facing Adversity', in *Seamstress of Souls: Legacy of Bais Yaakov*, supplement to *Binah: The Weekly Magazine for the Jewish Woman* (Nov. 2010), 10–15.

'From Sister to Sister' ('Hannah') (Yid.), *Bais Yaakov Journal*, 78 (1932), 13.

'From Sister to Sister' ('Sarah') (Yid.), *Bais Yaakov Journal*, 79 (1932), 14.

FUCHS, ILAN, *Jewish Women's Torah Study: Orthodox Religious Education and Modernity* (London, 2014).

GARBER, ZEV, 'The 93 Beit Yaakov Martyrs: Towards the Making of Historiosophy', *Shofar*, 12/1 (1993), 69–92.

GARRIN, STEPHEN HOWARD, 'But I Forsook Not Thy Precepts (Ps. 119: 87): Spiritual Resistance to the Holocaust', in Jonathan C. Friedman (ed.), *Routledge History of the Holocaust* (London, 2011), 337–47.

GEFEN, A., 'Organizing Orthodox Young Women' (Yid.), *Bais Yaakov Journal*, 5–6 (1924), 57.

GINSPARG KLEIN, LESLIE, '"Links in a Chain": How American Bais Yaakov Schools Have Adapted the Legacy of Sarah Schenirer' (unpublished paper).

—— '"No Candy Store, No Pizza Shops, No Maxi-Skirts, No Makeup": Socializing Orthodox Jewish Girls through Schooling', *Journal of the History of Childhood and Youth*, 9/1 (2016), 140–58.

—— 'A Traditional Revolutionary: Sarah Schenirer's Legacy Revisited', *Jewish Action*, 76/4 (Summer 2016), 62–5.

—— 'The Troubling Trend of Photoshopping History'; <http://www.thelehrhaus.com/scholarship/2016/11/16/the-troubling-trend-of-photoshopping-history>.

GINSPARG, LESLIE, 'Defining Bais Yaakov: A Historical Study of Yeshivish Orthodox Girls High School Education in America, 1963–84' (Ph.D. diss., New York University, 2009).

GLIKSMAN, PINCHAS-ZELIG, 'The Most Beautiful Jewish Holiday: Thoughts on Tu Be'av' (Yid.), *Bais Yaakov Journal*, 45 (1929), 3–4.

GORA, GERSHON, 'The Wellspring of Yiddish' (Yid.), *Bais Yaakov Journal*, 96 (1932), 7.

GORA, YAFFA, 'The Early Days of the Bais Yaakov Movement: Chapters of a Memoir' (Heb.), in Aryeh Bauminger (ed.), *A Mother in Israel: Memorial Book for Sarah Schenirer* [Em beyisra'el: sefer zikaron lesarah shenirer] (Benei Berak, 1983), 165–75.

'The Grand Celebration of Laying the Cornerstone of the Bais Yaakov Seminary' (Yid.), *Bais Yaakov Journal*, 4/8 (1927), 2–3.

'A Great Uprising in the "Fortress" of the Agudah' (Yid.), *Haynt* (28 Dec. 1933), 6.

GREENBAUM, ABRAHAM, 'Traditional Education of East European Jewish Women: The Generations before the First World War'; <http://aapjstudies.org/manager/external/ckfinder/userfiles/files/Greenbaum.pdf>.

GREENBERG, BLU, *On Women and Judaism: A View from Tradition* (1981; Philadelphia, 1998).

GREENFELD, CHAVA, 'The Day We Were Orphaned' (Heb.), in Aryeh Bauminger (ed.), *A Mother in Israel: Memorial Book for Sarah Schenirer* [Em beyisra'el: sefer zikaron lesarah shenirer] (Benei Berak, 1983), 162–5.

GRILL, TOBIAS, *Der Westen im Osten: Deutsches Judentum und jüdische Bildungsreform in Osteuropa (1783–1939)* (Göttingen, 2013).

GRUNFELD-ROSENBAUM, JUDITH, 'Sara Schenierer', in Leo Jung (ed.), *Jewish Leaders*, 2nd edn. (Jerusalem, 1964), 405–32.

GUTENTAG, TUVYE YEHUDAH, *see* TAVYOMI

HALPER, SHAUN JACOB, 'Coming Out of the Hasidic Closet: Jiří Mordechai Langer (1894–1943) and the Fashioning of Homosexual-Jewish Identity', *Jewish Quarterly Review*, 101/2 (2011), 189–231.

HARTMAN, TOVA, *Feminism Encounters Traditional Judaism: Resistance and Accommodation* (Waltham, Mass., 2007).

'A Hasidic Revolt in Błonie' (Yid.), *Hayntige nayes* (11 Mar. 1934).

HEILMAN, SAMUEL C., *Sliding to the Right: The Contest for the Future of American Jewish Orthodoxy* (Berkeley, Calif., 2006).

HIRSCH, SAMSON RAPHAEL, *The Collected Writings*, vol. vii, ed. Elliot Bondi and David Bechhofer (New York, 1992).

HIRSCH, SAMSON RAPHAEL, *The Hirsch Siddur* (Jerusalem, 1978).

——*Horeb: A Philosophy of Jewish Laws and Observances*, trans. I. Grunfeld (New York, 1962).

——*Neunzehn Briefe über Judenthum* (Frankfurt, 1836); 1st pub. in English as *The Nineteen Letters of Ben Uziel: Being a Spiritual Presentation of the Principles of Judaism*, trans. Bernard Dranchman (New York, 1899), repr. as *The Nineteen Letters on Judaism* (Jerusalem, 1969).

——*Pentateuch* [Hirsch's commentary], vol. iii, trans. Isaac Levy (London, 1962).

——'Women and Family According to the Talmud' (Yid.), *Bais Yaakov Journal*, 36 (1929), 7–8.

H.K. [Hannah Karminski?], 'Beth-Jacob-Schul-Werk', *Blätter des Jüdischen Frauenbundes für Frauenarbeit und Frauenbewegung*, 12/ 2 (Feb. 1936), 27.

HYMAN, PAULA E., *Gender and Assimilation in Modern Jewish History: The Roles and Representations of Women* (Seattle, Wash., 1995).

——'Yiddishe Froyen Asotsiatsiye-YFA (Jewish Women's Association)', in Jewish Women's Archive, *Encyclopedia*; <http://jwa.org/encyclopedia/article/yiddishe-froyen-asosiatsiye-yfa-jewish-womens-association>.

ITSIK, ZELIG, 'Bais Yaakov, Come Let Us Walk to Trial' (Yid.), *Moment* (16 Nov. 1927), 4.

Jewish Association for the Protection of Girls and Women, *Official Report of the Jewish International Conference on the Suppression of the Traffic in Girls and Women* (London, 1910).

KAHANA-SHAPIRO, AVRAHAM DOV-BER, *Lecture on Family Purity* [Fortrag iber taharas hamishpokhe], 2nd edn. (Frankfurt, 1936).

K-K, 'Pedagogical Signposts' (Yid.), *Bais Yaakov Journal*, 3/3 (1926), 81–3.

KAPLAN, MARION, 'Bertha Pappenheim: Founder of German–Jewish Feminism', in Elizabeth Koltun (ed.), *The Jewish Woman: New Perspectives* (New York, 1976), 149–63.

——*The Jewish Feminist Movement in Poland: The Campaigns of the Jüdischer Frauenbund, 1904–38* (Westport, Conn., 1979), 117.

KARO, JOSEPH. *Shulḥan arukh: Yoreh de'ah*, with glosses of R. Moses Isserles, trans. Chaim N. Denburg, vol. ii (Montreal, 1955).

KATZ, JACOB, 'Orthodoxy in Historical Perspective', in P. V. Medding (ed.), *Studies in Contemporary Jewry*, 2 (Bloomington, Ind., 1986), 3–17.

KATZBERG, DAVID TZVI, *Mevaser tsedek/Yalkut melitsot*, commentary on Leviticus (Budapest, 1930).

KAZDAN, CHAIM SZLOMA, *The History of Jewish School Systems in Independent Poland* [Di geshikhte fun yidishn shulvesn in umophengikn poyln] (Mexico City, 1947).

KERSHNER, ISABEL, 'Israel's Ultra-Orthodox Protest Schools Ruling', *New York Times* (17 June 2010), A4.

KIEVAL, HILLEL, *Languages of Community: The Jewish Experience in the Czech Lands* (Berkeley, Calif., 2000).

KLEPFISH, BREINDL, 'The Kraków Dream' (Yid.), *Bais Yaakov Journal*, 116 (1934), 13–14.

KLEPFISH, HESHL, 'Sarah Schenirer the Writer', in Aryeh Bauminger (ed.), *A Mother in Israel: Memorial Book for Sarah Schenirer* [Em beyisra'el: sefer zikaron lesarah shenirer] (Benei Berak, 1983), 113–24.

—— 'Women, To the Pen!' (Yid.), *Bais Yaakov Journal*, 108 (1932), 10.

KLEPFISZ, IRENA, 'Di Mames, Dos Loshn/The Mothers, the Language: Feminism, Yidishkayt, and the Politics of Memory', *Bridges*, 4 (1994), 12–47.

KUPER, G., 'Letter from Warsaw' (Yid.), *Forverts* (10 Mar. 1928), 2.

LANDAU, MENDEL, *Mekits nirdamim* [Report on the 1903 Kraków Congress] (Piotrków, 1904).

LEIBOWITZ, DANIELLE S., with DEVORA GLIKSMAN, *Rebbetzin Vichna Kaplan: The Founder of the Bais Yaakov Movement in America* (Jerusalem, 2016).

Lamentations Rabbah (Midrash Rabbah Mevuar), ed. Abraham Zvi Steinberger (Jerusalem, 1989).

Leviticus Rabbah (Midrash Rabbah Hamevuar), ed. Abraham Zvi Steinberger (Jerusalem, 1993).

LICHTENSTEIN, RUTH (ed.), *Seamstress of Souls: Legacy of Bais Yaakov*, supplement to *Binah: The Weekly Magazine for the Jewish Woman* (Nov. 2010).

LIPMANOVITCH, A. Y., 'Three Arrested Women' (Yid.), *Bais Yaakov Journal*, 98–9 (1933), 5.

LISEK, JOANNA, 'Orthodox Yiddishism in *Beys Yakov* Magazine', in *Sprach- und Kulturkontakte in Europas Mitte*, vol. ii: *Ashkenazim and Sephardim: A European Perspective* (Frankfurt, 2013), 113–26.

LOENTZ, ELIZABETH, *Let Me Continue to Speak the Truth: Bertha Pappenheim as Author and Activist* (Cincinnati, 2007).

LOEWENTHAL, NAFTALI, 'Spiritual Experience for Hasidic Youths and Girls in Pre-Holocaust Europe—A Confluence of Tradition and Modernity', in Adam Mintz and Lawrence Schiffman (eds.), *Jewish Spirituality and Divine Law* (Garden City, NJ, 2005), 407–54.

—— 'Women and the Dialectic of Spirituality in Hasidism', in Immanuel Etkes (ed.), *Within Hasidic Circles: Studies in Hasidism in Memory of Mordecai Wilensky* [Bema'agelei ḥasidim: kovets meḥkarim mukdash lezikhro shel mordekhai vilenski] (Jerusalem, 1999), 7–65.

MANEKIN, RACHEL, 'The Lost Generation: Education and Female Conversion in *Fin-de-Siècle* Kraków', in ChaeRan Freeze, Paula E. Hyman, and Antony Polonsky (eds.), *Jewish Women in Eastern Europe*, Polin 18 (2005), 189–219.

—— 'Orthodox Jewry in Kraków at the Turn of the Twentieth Century', in Michał Galas and Antony Polonsky (eds.), *Jews in Kraków*, Polin 23 (2011), 165–98.

—— '"Something Entirely New": The Development of the Idea of Orthodox Education for Girls in the Modern Period' (Heb.), *Masekhet*, 2 (2004), 63–85.

MENDES-FLOHR, PAUL, and JEHUDA REINHARZ (eds.), *The Jew in the Modern World: A Documentary History*, 3rd edn. (Oxford, 2010).

Midrash Rabbah Mevuar, ed. Abraham Zvi Steinberger (Jerusalem, 1986).

'Mrs. Felix M. Warburg Appeals for Support of Beth Jacob Schools; Gives $500', *Jewish Daily Bulletin* (24 Feb. 1933), 2.

NADLER, SHMUEL, 'Hymn of the Bnos Agudas Israel' (Yid.), *Bais Yaakov Journal*, 46 (1929), 6; repr., with music, in *Bais Yaakov Journal*, 67–8 (1931), 7.

—— 'To the Barricades, Judith!' (Yid.), *Bais Yaakov Journal*, 42 (1929), 7–8.

Obituary [Z kroniki żałobnej], *Nowy Dziennik* (4 Mar. 1935), 11.

OLESZAK, AGNIESZKA M., 'The Beit Ya'akov School in Kraków as an Encounter between East and West', in Michał Galas and Antony Polonsky (eds.), *Jews in Kraków*, Polin 23 (2011), 277–90.

ORLEAN, YEHUDAH LEIB, 'The Bais Yaakov Movement on Firm Foundations' (Yid.), *Bais Yaakov Journal*, 108 (1933), 6.

—— 'Our First Survey of the Readers of the *Bais Yaakov Journal*' (Yid.), *Bais Yaakov Journal*, 77 (1931), 1.

—— 'A Woman of Valour' (Heb.), in Yehezkel Rottenberg (ed.), *A Mother in Israel: The Writings of Sarah Schenirer, the Story of Her Life, Essays, Stories, and Plays* [Em beyisra'el: kitvei sarah shenirer, toledot ḥayeiha, ma'amarim, sipurim umaḥazot], 4 vols. (Tel Aviv, 1955–60), i. 16.

—— 'The Woman Question' (Yid.), *Bais Yaakov Journal*, 1 (1923), 6–7.

PAPPENHEIM, BERTHA, 'Kleine Reise-Notiz', *Blätter des Jüdischen Frauenbundes für Frauenarbeit und Frauenbewegung*, 12/1 (Jan. 1936), 1–2.

—— *Leben und Schriften*, ed. Dora Edinger (Frankfurt, 1963).

—— 'Zur Sittlichkeitsfrage', in *Referate gehalten auf dem 2. Delegiertentage des Jüdischen Frauenbundes, Frankfurt a. M. 2. und 3. Oktober 1907* (Hamburg, 1907), 21–2.

PARUSH, IRIS, *Reading Jewish Women: Marginality and Modernization in Nineteenth-Century Eastern European Jewish Society* (Waltham, Mass., 2004).

PASS, GITTEL, 'A Human Life', in Yehezkel Rottenberg (ed.), *A Mother in Israel: The Writings of Sarah Schenirer, the Story of Her Life, Essays, Stories, and Plays* [Em beyisra'el: kitvei sarah shenirer, toledot ḥayeiha, ma'amarim, sipurim umaḥazot], 4 vols. (Tel Aviv, 1955–60), iv. 100–2.

PLASKOW, JUDITH, *Standing Again at Sinai: Judaism from a Feminist Perspective* (San Francisco, 1991).

PORDES, ANIS D., and IREK GRIN (eds.), 'Tulo Schenirer', in *Ich miasto: Wspomnienia Izraelczyków, przedwojennych mieszkańców Krakówa* (Warsaw, 2004), 270–80.

PORTNOY, EDDY, 'Politics and Poesy', *Tablet* (18 Mar. 2010); <http://www.tabletmag.com/jewish-life-and-religion/28568/politics-and-poesy>.

PRESSLER, BENTSION, 'Hymn to the Jewish Daughter' (Yid.), *Bais Yaakov Journal*, 74 (1931), 58.

PROSHANSKY, LEAH, 'On Abandoned Women: The Cry of Pain of the *Agunah*' (Yid.), *Froyen Shtim*, 2 (1925), 10–14.

'Provincial Mirror' (Yid.), *Haynt* (16 Jan. 1930), 4.

'The Resolutions of the First Bais Yaakov Conference' (Yid.), *Bais Yaakov Journal*, 15 (1925), 74.

RIGLER, STACY ESKOVITZ, 'Girls' Education in Inter-Bellum Poland: The Bais Yaakov Schools' (MA thesis, Hebrew Union College—Jewish Institute of Religion, 2003).

'The Rise of the Bais Yaakov Movement in Poland (1923–33)' (Yid.), *Bais Yaakov Journal*, 100–2 (1933), 183–4.

ROSENHEIM, JACOB, 'At the Third Summer Course in Jordanów, Elul 5687' (Yid.), in Leo Deutschländer (ed.), *Bajs Jakob: Sein Wesen und Werden* (Vienna, 1926), 25–6.

—— 'New Tasks for Bais Yaakov and Bnos' (Yid.), *Bais Yaakov Journal*, 143 (1937), 38.

ROTTENBERG, YEHEZKEL, (ed.), *A Mother in Israel: The Writings of Sarah Schenirer, the Story of Her Life, Essays, Stories, and Plays* [Em beyisra'el: kitvei sarah shenirer, toledot ḥayeiha, ma'amarim, sipurim umaḥazot], 4 vols. (Tel Aviv, 1955–60).

ROTTENBERG-GORA, YAFFA, 'In Those Beautiful Days' (Heb.), *Beit Yaakov*, 182 (1975), 27.

RUBIN, DEVORA (ed.), *Daughters of Destiny: Women who Revolutionized Jewish Life and Torah Education* (Brooklyn, NY, 1988).

Ruth Rabbah (*Midrash Rabbah Hamevuar*), ed. Abraham Zvi Steinberger (Jerusalem, 1986).

SCHARFER, CAROLINE, 'Sarah Schenirer: Founder of the Beit Ya'akov Movement: Her Vision and Her Legacy', in Michał Galas and Antony Polonsky (eds.), *Jews in Kraków*, Polin 23 (2011), 269–75.

SCHARFSTEIN, ZEVI, 'On Our Brothers' Lives in Galicia: Girls' Education' (Heb.), *Ha'olam*, 37 (1910), 11–12.

SCHENIRER, SARAH, *Collected Writings* [Gezamelte shriftn] (Łódź, 1933; repr. Brooklyn, 1955).

—— 'From the Diary', trans. Bluma Vaytman, in Yehezkel Rottenberg (ed.), *A Mother in Israel: The Writings of Sarah Schenirer, the Story of Her Life, Essays, Stories and Plays* [Em beyisra'el: kitvei sarah shenirer, toledot ḥayeiha, ma'amarim, sipurim umaḥazot], 4 vols. (Tel Aviv, 1955–60), i. 31–42.

—— 'The Goal of the Bais Yaakov Schools' (Yid.), *Bais Yaakov Journal*, 1 (1923), 5.

—— 'Important Guests at the Kraków Seminary' (Yid.), *Bais Yaakov Journal*, 74 (1931), 16.

—— 'In Frankfurt am Main: Notes on a Journey' (Yid.), *Bais Yaakov Journal*, 15 (1925), 60–1.

—— *Judith*, in Yehezkel Rottenberg (ed.), *A Mother in Israel: The Writings of Sarah Schenirer, the Story of Her Life, Essays, Stories and Plays* [Em beyisra'el: kitvei sarah shenirer, toledot ḥayeiha, ma'amarim, sipurim umaḥazot], 4 vols. (Tel Aviv, 1955–60), iii. 32–65.

SCHENIRER, SARAH, 'The Last Night on Augustiańska 30' (Yid.), *Bais Yaakov Journal*, 73 (1931), 4.

—— *Sara Shenirer: Pisma Autobiograficzne*, ed. Dariusz Dekert and Joanna Lisek (Warsaw, 2018).

—— 'Sarah Schenirer: Diary (excerpts)', *Cwiszn: Pomiędzy. Żydowski kwartalnik o literaturze i sztuce*, 3–4 (Winter 2014), 68–70.

SCHNUR, ABRAHAM, 'Jewish Women and Torah Study' (Yid.), *Bais Yaakov Journal*, 149 (1938), 5.

SCHOLEM, GERSHOM, *Major Trends in Jewish Mysticism* (New York, 1946).

SCHWARTZMAN, MEIR, 'Leah Halpern: The Young Artist' (Yid.), *Bais Yaakov Journal*, 94–5 (1932), 23.

SEIDMAN, HILLEL, *The Jewish Religious School Systems in the Framework of Polish Legislation* [Dos yidishe religyeze shul-vesn in di ramen fun der poylisher gezetzgebung] (Warsaw, 1937).

—— *Personalities I Knew* [Ishim shehikarti] (Jerusalem, 1970).

—— *Renesans Religijny Kobiety Żydowskiej: Sara Szenirer—Człowiek i Dzieło* (Łódź, 1936).

—— *The Warsaw Ghetto Diaries*, trans. Yosef Israel (Southfield, Mich., 1997).

'The Sensational Press about Bais Yaakov' (Yid.), *Central Bais Yaakov Bulletin*, 3/1 (1933), 5.

SHAFRAN, YITZHOK, 'The Bais Yaakov School' (Yid.), in Aviezer Burstein and Dov Kosovsky (eds.), *Gorowo: Memorial Book* (Heb. and Yid.) (Tel Aviv, 1966), 110–13.

SHANDLER, JEFFREY (ed.), *Awakening Lives: Autobiographies of Jewish Youth in Poland before the Holocaust* (New York, 2002).

SHAPIRO, CHAIM, 'Dr. Leo Deutschländer: Father of the Bais Yaakov Movement', *Jewish Observer* (Summer 1975), 14–17.

SHAPIRO, MARC B., *Between the Yeshiva World and Modern Orthodoxy: The Life and Works of Rabbi Jehiel Jacob Weinberg, 1884–1966* (London, 1999).

—— *Changing the Immutable: How Orthodox Judaism Rewrites Its History* (Oxford, 2015).

SHARANSKY, MEIR, 'The History of Bais Yaakov in the Land of Israel', in *The Twenty-Fifth Anniversary of the Bais Yaakov High School and Seminary in Tel Aviv, 1935–1960* [Sefer hayovel ha-25 shel beit hasefer hatikhon vehaseminar leganenot ulemorot beit ya'akov be tel-aviv, 5696–5621] (Tel Aviv, 1960), 41–53.

SHKLOVSKY, VICTOR, *Theory of Prose*, trans. Benjamin Sher (Normal, Ill., 1990).

SHMUELEVITZ, ELLA, 'Family Purity' (Yid.), *Bais Yaakov Ruf*, 6 (1935), 7–8.

SLOWIK, NOAH, 'Cultural Struggle Infuses Life', in Yom-Tov Levinsky (ed.), *Zambrów Memorial Book*, English online version, <http://www.museumoffamilyhistory.com/z/yb.htm>.

SORASKY, AARON, *The History of Torah Education in the Modern Period* [Toledot haḥinukh hatorati betekufah haḥadashah] (Benei Berak, 1967).

STADLER, NURIT, *Yeshiva Fundamentalism: Piety, Gender, and Resistance in the Ultra-Orthodox World* (New York, 2009).

STAMPFER, SHAUL, *Families, Rabbis, and Education: Traditional Jewish Society in Nineteenth-Century Eastern Europe* (Oxford, 2010).

STEINBERG, JONAH, 'From a "Pot of Filth" to a "Hedge of Roses" (and Back): Changing Theorizations of Menstruation in Judaism', *Journal of Feminist Studies in Religion*, 13/2 (1997), 5–26.

STERNBUCH, GUTTA, and DAVID KRANZLER, *Gutta: Memories of a Vanished World* (New York, 2005).

STEYER, ELIMELEKH, 'A Letter to a Sister' (Yid.), *Bais Yaakov Journal*, 99 (1932), 10.

—— 'Sarah Schenirer—the Legend' (Heb.), in Yehezkel Rottenberg (ed.), *A Mother in Israel: The Writings of Sarah Schenirer, the Story of Her Life, Essays, Stories, and Plays* [Em beyisra'el: kitvei sarah shenirer, toledot ḥayeiha, ma'amarim, sipurim umaḥazot], 4 vols. (Tel Aviv, 1960), iv. 60–5.

—— 'Then, When They Appeared. . .' (Yid.), *Bais Yaakov Journal*, 142 (1937), 12.

'The Strike in Bais Yaakov Schools' (Yid.), *Haynt* (18 Feb. 1934), 5–6.

'Survey' (Yid.), *Bais Yaakov Journal*, 10–11 (1924), 43.

SZARANSKI, BENJAMIN (ed.), *Remember: Memorial Project for the Bais Yaakov Movement in Europe* [Zekhor: mifal hantsaḥah litenu'at 'beit ya'akov' be'eiropah] (Tel Aviv, 2004).

TAVYOMI (GUTENTAG), TUVYE YEHUDAH, 'Eulogy for Mrs Sarah Schenirer, of Blessed Memory, on the First Anniversary of Her Death' (Heb.), in *The Twenty-Fifth Anniversary of the Bais Yaakov High School and Seminary in Tel Aviv, 1935–1960* (Tel Aviv, 1960), 26–32.

—— 'On Textbooks for Bais Yaakov Schools' (Yid.), *Bais Yaakov Journal*, 5/1 (1928), 7.

—— 'The Wisdom of Women' (Heb.), in Yehezkel Rottenberg (ed.), *A Mother in Israel: The Writings of Sarah Schenirer, the Story of Her Life, Essays, Stories, and Plays* [Em beyisra'el: kitvei sarah shenirer, toledot ḥayeiha, ma'amarim, sipurim umaḥazot], 4 vols. (Tel Aviv, 1960), iv. 17–28.

—— 'Women in Judaism' (Yid.), *Bais Yaakov Journal*, 4–6 (1927), 100–1.

TELLER, HANOCH, *Builders: Stories and Insights into the Lives of Three Paramount Figures of the Torah Renaissance* (New York, 2000).

'To Eternal Rest' (Yid.), *Bais Yaakov Journal*, 125 (1935), 12–13.

'Tu Be'av 1932 in Skawa' (Yid.), *Bais Yaakov Journal*,110 (1932), 27.

UNGAR-SARGON, BATYA, 'Ultra-Orthodox Jews Are Panicking over Their Matchmaking Crisis: Are There Too Many Unmarried Women in the Community?' (3 Feb. 2015); <https://newrepublic.com/article/120918/ultra-orthodox-jews-panicked-over-shidduch-matchmaking-crisis>.

WATT, IAN, *The Rise of the Novel: Studies in Defoe, Richardson, and Fielding* (London, 1957).

WEBER, MAX, *On Charisma and Institution Building: Selected Papers* (Chicago, 1968).

WEISSLER, CHAVA, *Voices of the Matriarchs: Listening to the Prayers of Early Modern Jewish Women* (Boston, 1998).

WEISSMAN, DEBORAH, 'Bais Ya'akov: A Historical Model for Jewish Feminists', in Elizabeth Koltun (ed.), *The Jewish Woman: New Perspectives* (New York, 1976), 139–48.

—— 'Bais Ya'akov: A Women's Educational Movement in the Polish Jewish Community: A Case Study in Tradition and Modernity' (MA thesis, New York University, 1977).

—— 'Sarah Schenirer', in Jewish Women's Archive; <http://jwa.org/encyclopedia/article/schenirer-sarah>.

'What Does Our Survey Teach Us?' (Yid.), *Bais Yaakov Journal*, 83 (1932), 13.

'What Is Bnos?' (Yid.), *Bais Yaakov Journal*, 129 (1935), 12.

WODZIŃSKI, MARCIN, 'Women and Hasidism: A "Non-Sectarian" Perspective', *Jewish History*, 27 (2013), 399–434.

WOLF, ABRAHAM JOSEPH, 'Did Sarah Schenirer Innovate in Any Way?' (Heb.), in Aryeh Bauminger (ed.), *A Mother in Israel: Memorial Book for Sarah Schenirer* [Em beyisra'el: sefer zikaron lesarah shenirer] (Benei Berak, 1983), 37–41.

Yalkut Shimoni on the Prophets, ed. Dov Hyman (Jerusalem, 2009).

'"Yehudis" Summer Camp Acquires Its Own Torah Scroll' (Yid.), *Bais Yaakov Journal*, 104 (1933), 15–16.

'*Yiddishkeit* and Yiddish' (Yid.), *Bais Yaakov Journal*, 71–2 (1931), 8.

'Z kroniki żałobnej', *Nowy Dziennik* (4 Mar. 1935), 11.

ZALKIN, MORDECHAI, 'Heder', in *The YIVO Encyclopedia of Jews in Eastern Europe*; <http://www.yivoencyclopedia.org/article.aspx/Heder>.

—— 'Let It Be Entirely Hebrew' (Heb.), in Shmuel Glick (ed.), *Remember Your Word to Your Servant: Festschrift for Dov Rappel* [Zekhor davar le'avdekha: asufat ma'amarim lezekher dov rapel] (Ramat Gan, 2007).

ZEITLIN, HILLEL, 'Bais Yaakov, on the First Conference of Bais Yaakov Activists in Warsaw' (Yid.), *Moment* (10 Feb. 1930), 3.

ZIGELMAN, AHARON, 'The Agudah and Bais Yaakov in Parysów' (Heb.), in Yehiel Granatstein (ed.), *Parysów Memorial Book* [Sefer parisov] (Tel Aviv, 1971), 62–5.

The Zohar: Pritzker Edition, trans. Daniel C. Matt, Nathan Wolski, and Joel Hecker, 12 vols. (Stanford, Calif., 2003–2017).

ZOLTY, SHOSHANA PANTEL, *'And All Your Children Shall Be Learned': Women and the Study of Torah in Jewish Law and History* (Northdale, NJ, 1997).

Index of Citations

Index of Subjects

Page numbers in *italics* refer to illustrations.
BY: Bais Yaakov; SS: Sarah Schenirer

Printed and bound by CPI Group (UK) Ltd, Croydon, CR0 4YY
09/06/2025
14685829-0001